Sales Force Management

Planning,
Implementation,
and Control

The Irwin Series in Marketing
Consulting Editor   Gilbert A. Churchill, Jr.,   *University of Wisconsin, Madison*

Gilbert A. Churchill, Jr.
Graduate School of Business
University of Wisconsin

Neil M. Ford
Graduate School of Business
University of Wisconsin

Orville C. Walker, Jr.
School of Management
University of Minnesota

Sales Force Management

Planning, Implementation, and Control

1985   Second Edition

Homewood, Illinois   60430

ISBN 0-256-03184-3

Library of Congress Catalog Card No. 84–81122

Printed in the United States of America

7 8 9 0   K   2 1 0 9

Preface

Historically, the practice of sales management has resembled the practice of medicine by tribal witch doctors. Sales managers have often had to rely on large doses of folklore, tradition, intuition, and personal experience in deciding how to motivate and direct the performance of their sales forces. While many firms spend thousands to discover why their customers behave the way they do, too few expend much money or effort on studies of the motivation and behavior of their own salespeople.

Until very recently, sales managers received little information or guidance from marketing academicians. Over the years there was little published theory and even less empirical research concerning the variables influencing one salesperson to perform better than another.

From the 1930s until the early 1970s marketing scholars relegated the study of sales management to "second-class" status. Much of the work that did find its way into the literature during this period was experiential and unsophisticated. Sales motivation and performance were typically viewed as a function of one or a few independent variables—such as aptitude, financial compensation, or recognition—taken separately. Few attempts were made to identify a reasonably exhaustive set of factors influencing sales motivation and performance or to specify their interrelationships.[*]

Fortunately, the situation that existed for 40 years began to change about 15 years ago, and since the early 1970s there has been a fair amount of research focusing on salespeople. Much of this research has been aimed at understanding why salespeople behave as they do. What factors are critical to their performance? Although there are still many unanswered questions, much has been learned.

One of the main purposes of this book is to organize what has been learned and to integrate that knowledge in a management perspective. More particularly, evidence suggests that at least five factors influence a salesperson's job behavior and performance, namely:

1. Environmental variables.
2. Role perceptions.
3. Aptitude.
4. Skill levels.
5. Motivation level.

---

[*]Orville C. Walker, Jr., Gilbert A. Churchill, Jr., and Neil M. Ford, "Where Do We Go From Here? Selected Conceptual and Empirical Issues Concerning Motivation and Performance of the Industrial Salesforce," in *Critical Issues in Sales Management: State-of-the-Art and Future Research Needs*, eds. Gerald Albaum and Gilbert A. Churchill, Jr. (Eugene: University of Oregon, College of Business Administration, 1979), p. 11.

The sales manager who understands how these factors affect a salesperson's behavior has an advantage in planning and directing that behavior toward desired ends and in evaluating the results that are produced. This book should assist that understanding on several counts. In the first place, it summarizes the evidence with respect to the impact of these factors on a salesperson's behavior and performance; more important, it does so via an integrated model. The student in sales management no longer needs to grapple with isolated studies and findings to understand salesperson behavior but can do so from the integrated perspective provided. Although environmental influences often must be taken as given, the sales manager can follow a number of policies and procedures to affect the aptitude, skill levels, role perceptions, and motivation of the members of the sales force. For example, recruiting techniques and selection criteria can be developed to ensure that salespeople with the required abilities are hired. A second major way that the book should facilitate understanding is to emphasize the link between the determinants of salesperson performance and the job of the sales manager. In fact, the research evidence is summarized from a sales management perspective—via the normal activities in which sales managers engage.

A second major purpose in writing the book is to integrate the total discipline of sales management for the beginning student. This purpose was fostered by our dissatisfaction with most of the existing texts on sales management. They seem to lack structures that organize the discipline for the student in that one ends up discussing planning issues at several different points within the text, discussing evaluation issues before implementation issues, or discussing implementation questions before questions on strategy. This is unfortunate in our opinion because it causes unnecessary confusion and frustration for beginning students. The subject can be approached from a logical perspective.

This book adopts the view that the entire spectrum of activities in which sales managers engage involves three interrelated processes or programs.

1. The formulation of a strategic sales program, which involves organizing and planning the company's overall personal selling efforts and integrating these efforts with the other elements of the firm's marketing strategy.

2. The implementation of the sales program, which involves selecting appropriate sales personnel and designing and implementing policies and procedures that will direct their efforts toward the desired objectives.

3. The evaluation and control of sales force performance, which involves the development of methods for monitoring and evaluating sales force performance so that necessary adjustments can be made to either the sales program or the way it is implemented when performance is unsatisfactory.

The structure of the book reflects this view. The first chapter introduces the subject with an overview of the duties and responsibilities of the sales manager and how these activities relate to these three processes. Chapter 1 also outlines in detail the structure of the remainder of the book, which is divided into three parts corresponding to the three processes. More particularly, Part 1, which includes

Chapters 2–7, looks at the major decisions involved in the design of a strategic sales program.

Part 2, which includes Chapters 8–14, looks at the questions surrounding implementation. Part 3, consisting of Chapters 15–17, discusses the techniques by which sales force behavior and performance can be monitored and controlled.

The book is designed to be used for an introductory course in sales management and with a variety of teaching perspectives. Instructors who primarily emphasize the lecture-discussion mode should find ample material for either a one-quarter or a one-semester course in the chapters and the discussion questions at the end of each chapter. Those who prefer case-oriented instruction should find sufficient cases at the end of each part to challenge the decision-making skills of even the best students.

Users of the first edition of this book will quickly note that the above comments are very similar to those made in the first edition. Indeed, the basic philosophy and structure of the book have not changed, although a number of important changes have been made with respect to the material. Some of the major ones include:

● Much greater emphasis on financial considerations and a much better balance between financial and behavioral considerations. The greater emphasis on financial considerations is brought about both through new text material and new problems at the end of the chapters that emphasize financial and other ratio analyses.

● Incorporation of the latest technologies affecting management of the sales force including the role telemarketing can play as part of the personal selling strategy, the use of computer modeling techniques for sales territory design, and the use of microcomputers and electronic spreadsheet analysis for directing and evaluating the efforts of salespeople.

● A thoroughly revised discussion of the issues involved in demand estimation including better clarification of the distinctions between market potential, sales potential, sales forecast, and sales quota, and more precise discussion regarding the various sales forecasting or demand estimation techniques. The material is now handled in one chapter whereas it was handled in two chapters in the first edition.

● A completely revised discussion of the material on sales training. The new discussion has more of a managerial and less of a descriptive orientation than it did previously, and sales training is now covered in a single chapter.

● More examples throughout of successful and unsuccessful sales management practices.

● More cases; almost 40 percent of the cases are new. Further, a number of those cases that have been carried over from the first edition have been revised and expanded.

While each of the chapters has been revised and updated, some of the major chapter by chapter changes include:

Chapter 1—*An Overview of Personal Selling and Sales Management.* New discussion of how and why selling expenses vary from industry to industry as a function of the complexity of the product, the number and location of potential customers, and the size of the average sale. Also, revision of the material on sales compensation and selling costs to reflect the most recent information.

Chapter 2—*The Environment, Marketing Planning, and the Sales Program.* New discussion of the ethical issues faced by sales managers including what sales managers might do to improve the ethical performance of their subordinates.

Chapter 3—*Selling Activities and Account Management Policies.* A new section on account management policies and sales program planning. The new section includes a flowchart of the steps involved in the sales program planning process and provides an explicit rationale for the subsequent sections on organizational buyer behavior and sales activities. There is also a new section on the new technologies and their organizational implications.

Chapter 4—*Organizing the Sales Effort.* A new section that discusses the relative advantages and limitations of using a company sales force versus external agents, and the criteria to consider when deciding which organizational alternative to use. There is also a new section that discusses the new trend of organizing by selling function.

Chapter 5—*Demand Estimation.* Thorough reorganization of the old chapters on "Market Opportunity Analysis" and "Sales Forecasting" into one new chapter on "Demand Estimation." The new discussion allows much better integration of the methods for estimating aggregate demand and breaking down the aggregate estimates by territory. There is also an expanded discussion on choosing a sales forecasting method that emphasizes which method should be used under what circumstances.

Chapter 6—*Sales Territories.* Greater emphasis on determining how often individual accounts should be called upon that includes a strategic planning perspective for determining account call frequencies and an emphasis on computer sales effort allocation models.

Chapter 9—*The Salesperson's Role Perceptions.* A completely rewritten chapter to reduce the incidence of unfamiliar jargon and to place greater emphasis on the managerial implications of salespeople's role perceptions.

Chapter 10—*Personal Characteristics and Sales Aptitude: Criteria for Selecting Salespeople.* Incorporation of the latest information regarding the relationship between various aptitude variables and salesperson performance.

Chapter 12—*Sales Training: Objectives, Techniques, and Evaluation.* Condensation of the two prior chapters on sales training into one new chapter that has much more of a behavioral orientation.

Chapter 13—*Motivating the Sales Force.* Simplification of the motivation model and elimination of the mathematical description of the model and the inclusion of a new section of supervisory leadership that emphasizes how a sales manager's supervisory style can impact the motivation levels of the salespeople he or she supervises.

Chapter 14—*Designing Compensation and Incentive Programs.* A thorough up-dating of the material on sales compensation to reflect the latest available information and the incorporation of a new section of selling expenses and the role they play in a company's sales force compensation scheme.

Chapter 15—*Sales Analysis.* Inclusion of a new section of Decision Support Systems and how they can help sales managers more effectively evaluate the salespeople under them. The section includes a discussion of the use of micro-computers and electronic spreadsheets for managing the sales force.

Chapter 16—*Cost Analysis.* An expanded discussion of the return-on-assets model (ROAM) and how it can be used to increase the return on those assets devoted to the personal selling effort.

Chapter 17—*Behavior and Other Performance Analyses.* A greatly expanded dis-cussion on the use of other objective measures of performance other than sales, cost, and ROAM analysis. The discussion particularly emphasizes the use of ratio analysis and how it can aid managerial thinking.

A book like this is never the work of a single author or even a small group of authors; rather there are many people and institutions whose contributions need to be acknowledged. In the first place, we wish to thank the many scholars and sales managers who have labored so diligently over the last 50 years and particu-larly over the last 15 to move the study of sales management out of the dark ages and into the mainstream of marketing thought. We would also like to acknowl-edge the special contributions of the Marketing Science Institute, which sup-ported much of the recent research, and especially Steve Greyser and Alden Clay-ton for their willingness to commit MSI's energies and resources to the study of sales management before it became a fashionable topic. Their visionary interest certainly helped produce the critical mass of effort necessary to move the study of the topic forward.

There were also a number of visionary sales managers who have lent their support to our research effort over the years. They have our undying gratitude. We wish to acknowledge especially the contributions to this book of James Bushong, Automated Machine Division; E. Wyatt Cannady, formerly with Ohio Medical Products; John Luke, Eastman Kodak; and Lou Tedesco, Diamond Power Specialty. Several other industry associates provided support in the form of case materials and text examples. Their cooperation is greatly appreciated. They are: Larry Hagerty, Dynasty Computer; Marlene Futterman, Direct Selling Education Foundation; Jack Kaltenberg, Kaltenberg Seed Farms; Robert Benson, American Breeders Service; David A. Scott, S. C. Johnson, Inc.; and H. Doug Plunkett, Wormald U.S., Inc.

There are a number of unexciting, but nevertheless critical, tasks associated with the production of a book such as this. The following students all made signif-icant contributions to the competent completion of these tasks: Karen Backes,

Cathy Brink, Regina Downey, Greg Ford, Peggy Friedman, Larry Hogue, Yong Jin Hyun, Russ Jamison, Karen Kolb, Larry LaMarche, David Malley, Andrew Marein, Nancy Rodenberg, James Trautschold and Jackie Vanderberg. We gratefully acknowledge these contributions and the contributions of the students who classroom-tested the first edition of the manuscript. The book is better because of their insightful input.

Janet Christopher typed the major part of the manuscript and the instructor's manual, and her willingness to operate under tight deadlines and the quality of her output are sincerely appreciated.

We appreciate the intellectual stimulation provided by our academic colleagues over the years. We wish to acknowledge especially the following people who read or formally reviewed the manuscript: Julius Grossman, Mohawk Valley Community College; E. Laird Landon, University of Houston; Pete Lyon, University of Houston; Peter Riesz, University of Iowa; and Rosann L. Spiro, Indiana University. Robert E. Collins, Oregon State University, provided assistance for the development of software applications for several cases. While we did not heed all their comments, we did use many of them. All errors and omissions remain the responsibility of the authors.

Finally, we wish to thank our families, and each of their many members, for their encouragement and support while this book was being written. It is with love we dedicate it to them.

Gilbert A. Churchill, Jr.
Neil M. Ford
Orville C. Walker, Jr.

Contents

1. **An Overview of Personal Selling and Sales Management**   **2**
Are Stereotypes Accurate? The Diversity of Sales Jobs: *Retail Selling versus Industrial Selling. Types of Industrial Sales Jobs.* Some Attractive Characteristics of Sales Jobs: The Saleperson's Viewpoint: *Freedom of Action. Variety and Challenge. Opportunities for Advancement. Compensation. Working Conditions. Selling Costs as a Major Part of Marketing Budgets.* The Role of Personal Selling in a Successful Marketing Strategy: The Case of Lanier Business Products, Inc.: *A Customer-Oriented Product Policy. Advertising to Generate Brand Awareness. The Role of Sales Force. A Changing Environment Causes Problems. The Current Situation.* What Is Involved in Sales Management: *Formulation of a Strategic Sales Program. Implementation of the Sales Program. Evaluation and Control of the Sales Program.*

Part 1
Formulation of a Strategic Sales Program   32

2. **The Environment, Marketing Planning, and the Sales Program**   **34**
Evan-Picone: The History of a Successful Sportswear Marketer: *Aquisition and a New Strategy. Another New Strategy Leads to a Comeback.* Relationships among Environmental Factors, Marketing Plans, and the Sales Program. Marketing Planning: *The Importance of Planning. The Planning Process.* Impact of the Environment on Marketing and Sales Planning: *The External Environment. The Organizational Environment.* Environmental Constraints on Sales Force Performance: *The Effects of Organizational Factors on Sales Productivity. Effects of the External Environment on Sales Productivity. Implications for Sales Managers.*

3. **Selling Activities and Account Management Policies**   **64**
The Role of Personal Selling in the Marketing Mix. Promotional Tools: *Advantages of Personal Selling as a Promotional Tool. Determinants of the Proper Role of Personal Selling in a Firm's Overall Marketing Strategy.* Account Management Policies and Sales Program Planning. The Organizational Buying Process: *Who Makes Organizational Buying Decisions? The Organizational Buying Center. Stages in the Organizational*

Buying Process. Selling Activities: *Sales Jobs Involve a Wide Variety of Activities. Steps in the Selling Process. Major Account Management Approach.* Appendix A: *Alternative Selling Techniques.*

4. **Organizing the Selling Effort   100**
Ansul Company's Flexible Sales Organization: *A Rapidly Changing Sales Organization.* Ansul's Attention to Sales Organization Is Not Typical. Purposes of Sales Organization: *Division and Specialization of Labor. Stability and Continuity of Organizational Performance. Coordination and Integration.* Horizontal Structure of the Sales Force: *A Company Sales Force or Independent Agents? Geographic Organization. Product Organization. Organization by Customers or Markets. Organization by Selling Function. Telemarketing and the Organization of "Inside" and "Outside" Sales Forces.* Organizing to Service National and Key Accounts: *Alternative Organizational Approaches for Dealing with Key Accounts. Team Selling. Multilevel Selling.* Vertical Structure of the Sales Organization: *Number of Management Levels and Span of Control. Management Roles and Staff Support.* Some Additional Questions.

5. **Demand Estimation   132**
Clarification of Terms. Estimation of Demand. Importance of Sales Forecast. Users' Expectations: *Advantages. Disadvantages.* Sales Force Composite: *Advantages. Disadvantages.* Jury of Executive Opinion: *Advantages. Disadvantages. Delphi Technique.* Market Test: *Advantages. Disadvantages.* Time Series Analysis: *Moving Averages. Exponential Smoothing. Decomposition. Advantages. Disadvantages.* Statistical Demand Analysis: *Advantages. Disadvantages.* Choosing a Forecasting Method. Developing Territory Estimates: *Industrial Goods. Consumer Goods.*

6. **Sales Territories   174**
The Need for Sales Territories: *Sales Force Morale. Market Coverage. Evaluation and Control.* Sales Force Size: *Breakdown Method. Workload Method. Incremental Method.* Sales Territory Design: *Select Basic Control Unit. Estimate Market Potential. Form Tentative Territories. Perform Workload Analysis. Adjust Tentative Territories. Assign Salespeople to Territories.*

7. **Sales Quotas   208**
Purposes of Quotas: *Provide Incentives for Salespeople. Evaluate Sales Performance. Control Sales Efforts. Problems with Quotas.* Characteristics of a Good Quota Plan. The Quota-Setting Process: *Select Types of Quotas. Determine Relative Importance of Each Type. Determine Level of Each Type.*

Cases for Part 1

Case 1-1: Gildersleeve Furniture Enterprises   **231**
Case 1-2: Sidex Corporation: The Dynasty Proposal   **234**
Case 1-3: Omega Medical Products, Incorporated   **253**
Case 1-4: Olsen Seed Farms   **261**
Case 1-5: HOMAP, Inc.   **268**
Case 1-6: Delaware Paint and Plate Glass Industries, Inc.   **270**
Case 1-7: National Manufacturing Company (A)   **275**
Case 1-8: Midwest Medical Equipment Corporation   **283**
Case 1-9: The Goldman Chemical Company   **286**

Part 2
Implementation of the Sales Program   294

8. **Model of Salesperson Performance   296**

The Model. The Role Perceptions Component. The Motivation Component. The Aptitude Component. The Skill Level Component. The Personal, Organizational, and Environmental Variable Component. Rewards. Satisfaction. Importance for Sales Management.

9. **The Salesperson's Role Perceptions   308**

The Salesperson's Role. Susceptibility of the Salesperson's Role: *Boundary Position. Large Role Set. Innovative Role.* Role Conflict and Ambiguity: *Common Expectations and Key Areas of Conflict and Ambiguity. Consequences of Conflict and Ambiguity. Causes of Conflict and Ambiguity.* Role Accuracy: *Nature of Role Accuracy. Causes, Consequences, and Management Implications of Perceived Linkages.* The Role Component and the Sales Manager.

10. **Personal Characteristics and Sales Aptitude: Criteria for Selecting Salespeople   334**

What Is Sales Aptitude? The Characteristics that Sales Managers Look for. The Relationship between General Personal Characteristics and Sales Performance: *Personal Characteristics. Skill Levels. Aptitude—Mental Abilities. Aptitude—Personality Characteristics. Specific Research Evidence. A Comprehensive Overview of Past Research. Possible Reasons for Inconsistent Research Findings. Race, Sex, and Sales Aptitude.* Personal Characteristics of the Salesperson, Customer Characteristics, and Sales Performance: *Research Evidence. Implications and Problems.* Task-Specific Determinants of Sales Aptitude: *Trade Selling. Missionary Selling. Technical Selling. New Business Selling.* Implications for Sales Management.

11. Sales Force Recruitment and Selection   360

Who Has the Responsibility for Recruiting and Selecting Salespeople? Recruitment and Selection Procedures. Job Analysis and Determination of Selection Criteria: *Job Analysis and Description. Determining Job Qualifications and Selection Criteria.* Recruiting Applicants: *People within the Company. People in Other Firms. Educational Institutions. Advertisements. Employment Agencies.* Selection Procedures: *Application Blanks. Personal Interviews. Reference Checks. Physical Examinations. Tests.* Equal Employment Opportunity Requirements in Selecting Salespeople: *Requirements for Tests. Requirements for Interviews and Application Forms.*

12. Sales Training: Objectives, Techniques, and Evaluation   390

What's Wrong with Sales Training Programs? Improving Sales Training. Objectives of Sales Training: *Increase Productivity. Improve Morale. Lower Turnover. Improve Customer Relations. Manage Time and Territory Better.* The Timing of Sales Training. Training the New Sales Recruit. Content of Training Programs for New Recruits: *Product Knowledge. Market/Industry Orientation. Company Orientation. Time and Territory Management. Other Subjects.* Location of Training Programs: *Centralized Training versus Decentralized Training: Pros and Cons.* Relative Importance of Methods. Descriptions of Methods: *On-the-Job Training. Classroom Training. Home Study.* Training Experienced Sales Personnel. Training Sales Managers. Recent Developments in Sales Training. Measuring the Costs and Benefits of Sales Training: *Sales Training Costs. Measurement Criteria. Measuring Broad Benefits. Measuring Specific Benefits.*

13. Motivating the Sales Force   432

Fitwell's Fashion Shop: *What Went Wrong?* The Psychological Process of Motivation: *Expectancies—Perceived Links between Effort and Performance. Instrumentalities—Perceived Links between Performance and Rewards. Valence for Rewards.* Can the Motivation Model Predict Salesperson Effort and Performance. The Impact of a Salesperson's Personal Characteristics on Motivation: *Satisfaction. Demographic Characteristics. Job Experience. Psychological Traits. Management Implications.* The Impact of Environmental Conditions on Motivation. The Impact of Organizational Variables on Motivation: *Supervisory Variables and Leadership. Incentive and Compensation Policies.*

14. Designing Compensation and Incentive Programs   454

Procedures for Designing a Compensation and Incentive Program. Assessing Company Objectives and Determining What Dimensions of Sales Performance to Encourage. Assessing Salespeople's Valences and Choosing an Attractive Mix of Rewards. Determining the Appropriate

Level of Total Compensation: *Dangers of Paying Too Much. Dangers of Paying Too Little.* Choosing the Most Effective Form of Financial Compensation: *Straight Salary. Straight Commission. Combination Plans. Other Issues in Designing Combination Plans.* A Summary Overview of Financial Compensation Methods. The Reimbursement of Selling Expenses: *Direct Reimbursement Plans. Limited Reimbursement Plans. No Reimbursement Plans.* Sales Contests: *Contest Objectives. Contest Themes. Probability of Winning. Type of Rewards. Promotion and Follow-through. Criticisms of Sales Contests.* Nonfinancial Rewards: *Promotion and Career Paths. Recognition Programs.*

Cases for Part 2

Case 2-1: Crosby Flour Mills, Ltd. **487**
Case 2-2: Agrisystem Farm Machines, Inc. (A) **491**
Case 2-3: Reliable Meter Company **497**
Case 2-4: Golden Bear Distributors **503**
Case 2-5: General Typewriter Company **510**
Case 2-6: Mid-State Coat Company **512**
Case 2-7: Chips-to-Dip, Inc. **516**
Case 2-8: Denver Illini Genetics **523**
Case 2-9: Western Business Forms, Inc. **533**
Case 2-10: Genner Security Systems, Inc. **537**
Case 2-11: Heathcoate Pharmaceuticals **542**
Case 2-12: Acme Machine Corporation **547**
Case 2-13: Agrisystem Farm Machines, Inc. (B) **550**

Part 3
Evaluation and Control of the Sales Program 558

15. Sales Analysis 560

Nature of Control. Marketing Audit: *Objectives. Policies. Organization. Methods and Procedures. Personnel.* Sales Analysis. Key Decisions: *Type of Evaluation System. Sources and Processing of Information. Desired Breakdowns.* A Hierarchical Sales Analysis: *Iceberg Principle. Simple versus Comparative Analysis. Isolate and Explode.* Decision Support System (DSS).

16. Cost Analysis 590

Cost Analysis Development. Accounting versus Marketing Costs. Full Cost or Contribution Margin: *Direct versus Indirect Costs. Specific versus General Expense. Which to Use.* Procedure: *Purpose. Natural Accounts versus Functional Accounts. Allocate Functional Costs. Sum Allocated Costs.* The Process Illustrated: *Apportion Natural Account Costs to Functional Accounts. Allocate Functional Costs to Segments. Profitability of*

Stan Tucker by Customer. Prospects and Problems. Return on Assets Managed.

17. Behavior and Other Performance Analysis   622
Performance versus Effectiveness. Objective Measures: *Output Measures. Input Measures. Ratios. Caution Is in Order.* Subjective Measures: *Problems in Use. Behaviorally Anchored Rating Scales.* Decision Support Systems and Use of Microcomputers. Corrective Action.

Cases for Part 3

Case 3-1: Susan Kay Greenhouses   **651**
Case 3-2: Pure Drug Company   **656**
Case 3-3: Sierra Chemical Company (A)   **679**
Case 3-4: Supersonic Stereo, Inc.   **689**
Case 3-5: Christopher Industries   **695**
Case 3-6: Anderson Distributors, Inc.   **708**
Case 3-7: Wentworth Industrial Cleaning Supplies   **717**
Case 3-8: Twin City Electric Motor Company   **735**

Index   739

An Overview of Personal Selling and Sales Management

*Nobody dast blame this man. You don't understand: Willy was
a salesman. And for a salesman, there is no rock bottom to his
life. He don't put a bolt to a nut, he don't tell you the law or
give you medicine. He's a man way out there in the blue, riding
on a smile and a shoeshine. And then you get a couple of spots on
your hat, and you're finished. Nobody dast blame this man. A
salesman is got to dream, boy. It comes with the territory.*

Arthur Miller,
Death of a Salesman

Many people have unflattering attitudes toward selling jobs and the people who
do them for a living. The words *selling* and *salesperson* tend to conjure up images
of lonely losers who spend most of their lives on the road, like Willy Loman in
Death of a Salesman; or of fast-talking smoothies who will tell anybody anything to
close a sale, like Professor Harold Hill, the "bang beat bell-ringin' big haul, neck or
nothin' rip-roarin', every-time-a-bull's-eye salesman" of *The Music Man.* The
selling profession's image has made it a convenient target for derogatory jokes,
which, in turn, have helped to reinforce the unsavory stereotypes.

Several studies have surveyed students' perceptions of sales jobs and their
attitudes toward sales careers. The results of three such studies conducted over a
20-year period are summarized in Table 1–1. These studies suggest that, while
students' perceptions of sales jobs have become more favorable over the years, a
majority still hold negative views concerning the attractiveness of sales careers.[1]

On the positive side, in the most recent survey in 1980, over 80 percent of the
students felt that sales jobs are challenging and require creativity, and more than
60 percent perceived them to offer good financial rewards and opportunities for
advancement. As you can see from Table 1–1, these responses represent a substantial change in perceptions from those of students in earlier studies.

But it is still not a bed of roses for sales recruiters on college campuses. Students continue to see sales jobs as low in status and prestige, lacking job security,
involving large amounts of travel which interferes with leisure time and home
life, and making little contribution to society. To make matters worse, a majority
of students in the 1980 study indicated that they considered prestige, job security
and "contributions to society" important factors to look for in selecting a job.
Consequently, companies continue to face the problem that negative stereotypes
may make some talented college graduates reluctant to consider selling—and
even sales management—as possible careers.

---

[1] In 1962, a study involving 919 undergraduates and graduate students was reported in "Selling Is a Dirty Word,"
Sales Management, October 5, 1962, pp. 44–47. Professors Paul and Worthing interviewed 200 undergraduates at a
southern university and reported the results in Gordon W. Paul and Parker Worthing, "A Student Assessment of Selling,"
Southern Journal of Business 5 (July 1970), pp. 57–65. Finally, a survey of 219 undergraduates at a midwestern university
in a major metropolitan area was discussed by Alan J. Dubinsky in "Recruiting College Students for the Salesforce,"
Industrial Marketing Management 9 (February 1980), pp. 37–45.

Table 1–1
Summary of the findings of three surveys of college students' perceptions and attitudes toward sales jobs

	Findings of Surveys Conducted by		
Perceptions and Attitudes*	Sales Management (1962)	Paul and Worthing (1970)	Dubinsky (1980)
1. Students associate personal selling with:			
a. Frustration	Agree	DNI	DNI
b. Insincerity and deceit	Agree	Disagree	DNI
c. Low status/low prestige	Agree	Agree	Agree
d. Much traveling	Agree	Agree	Agree
e. Salespeople are "money hungry"	Agree	DNI	DNI
f. High pressure/forces people to buy unwanted goods/little contribution to society	Agree	DNI	Agree
g. Low job security	Agree	DNI	Agree
h. Just a "job," not a "career"/little professionalism	Agree	DNI	Disagree
i. Uninteresting/no challenge	Agree	DNI	Disagree
j. No need for creativity	Agree	Disagree	Disagree
k. Personality is crucial	DNI	Agree	DNI
l. Too little monetary reward	Agree	Agree	Disagree
m. Interferes with home life/little leisure time	Agree	DNI	Agree
2. Students prefer nonsales positions much more than sales positions	Agree	Agree	DNI
3. Students' contact with sales-people largely limited to door-to-door and retail store personnel	Agree	Agree	DNI

*The table shows whether a majority of the respondents in each study "agree" with each perception/attitude item, "disagree" with the item, or whether the study did not investigate (DNI) the item.
Source: Adapted from Alan J. Dubinsky, *A Call for Action: Students' Assessments of Personal Selling*, paper presented at the Midwest Business Administration Association Conference, Chicago, 1978; and Alan J. Dubinsky, "Recruiting College Students for the Salesforce," *Industrial Marketing Management* 9 (February 1980), pp. 37–45.

Are the Stereotypes Accurate?

It is not the purpose of this book to promote selling or sales management as desirable careers. However, to discuss the effective management of salespeople, it is necessary to have a reasonably accurate and objective understanding of what sales jobs and salespeople are like. Unfortunately, the existing stereotypes are neither very accurate nor objective. They tend to be based on a limited exposure to salespeople and the kinds of work they do. They also ignore—or underestimate—some positive characteristics of selling careers that make them attractive to thousands of workers. Indeed, a recent study comparing the perceptions of students with those of salespeople from a variety of types and sizes of firms found that the salespeople rated sales jobs significantly more positive than the students on such dimensions as status and prestige, security, contributions to society, financial rewards, professionalism, and feelings of accomplishment.[2] Finally, and most serious of all, the negative stereotypes ignore the crucial role that personal selling and the effective management of the sales force plays in determining the success of a firm's overall marketing program.

The Diversity of Sales Jobs

Any stereotype oversimplifies reality; thus, people tend to think of all sales jobs and salespeople as being the same. Actually, there are many different types of selling jobs requiring widely different training and skills and offering varying levels of compensation and opportunities for personal satisfaction and advancement.

Retail Selling versus Industrial Selling

Many people have a narrow view of selling because they are not familiar with the different types of selling jobs. The surveys summarized in Table 1–1, for example, found that college students' knowledge of selling and salespeople is largely based on their experiences with people in *retail selling.* These jobs involve selling goods and services to ultimate consumers for their own personal use, such as door-to-door salespeople, insurance agents, real estate brokers, and retail store clerks. A much larger volume of sales, however, is accounted for by *industrial selling*—the sale of goods and services at the wholesale level. Industrial selling involves three types of customers:

1. *Sales to resellers*—as when a clothing manufacturer's sales representative sells merchandise to a retail store, which, in turn, resells the goods to its customers.
2. *Sales to business users*—as when manufacturer X sells materials or parts to manufacturer Y who uses them in producing another product or when a Xerox salesperson sells a law firm a copier to be used in conducting the firm's business.
3. *Sales to institutions*—as when an IBM salesperson sells a computer or typewriters to a hospital or a government agency.

---

[2] Alan J. Dubinsky, "Perceptions of the Sales Job: How Students Compare with Industrial Salespeople," *Journal of the Academy of Marketing Science* 9 (Fall 1981), pp. 352–367.

In many ways, the activities involved in both retail and industrial selling, and in managing the two types of sales forces, are very similar. Success in either type of selling requires interpersonal and communications skills, solid knowledge of the products being sold, an ability to discover the customer's needs and problems, and the creativity necessary to show the customer how a particular product or service can help satisfy those needs and problems.[3] Similarly, managers must recruit and train appropriate people for both types of sales jobs, provide them with objectives that are consistent with the firm's overall marketing or merchandising program, supervise them, motivate them, and evaluate their performance.

However, retail and industrial selling also differ in some important ways. Many of the goods and services sold by industrial salespersons are more expensive and technically complex than those in retailing. Similarly, industrial customers tend to be larger and to engage in extensive decision-making processes involving many people within their organizations. Consequently, the activities involved in selling to industrial buyers, as well as the qualifications and training required of the people who perform them, are often quite different from those in retail selling. Furthermore, the decisions made in effectively managing an industrial sales force are broader than those required for a retail sales force. Consequently, although many topics in this book apply to the management of both types of salespersons (selection and training), others apply only to the management of industrial salespeople (sales territory design).

Types of Industrial Sales Jobs

Even within the broad area of industrial selling, there are different kinds of jobs requiring different skills. Various authors have described more than 100 different ways in which sales jobs might be classified.[4] One of the most commonly used—and useful—classification schemes identifies four types of industrial selling found across a wide variety of industries.[5]

1. *Trade selling*—where the sales force's primary responsibility is to increase business from presently identified customers and potential customers by providing them with *merchandising and promotional assistance.* A Procter & Gamble salesperson selling soap and laundry products to chain-store personnel is an example of trade selling.
2. *Missionary selling*—where the sales force's primary job is to increase business from current and potential customers by providing them with *product information* and other personal selling assistance. Missionary salespeople

---

[3] The activities involved in personal selling as well as some alternative approaches for selling to both retail and industrial customers, are discussed in more detail in Appendix A, pp. 000-00.

[4] For a brief summary of some of these classification schemes, see Alan J. Dubinsky and P. J. O'Connor, "A Multidimensional Analysis of Preferences for Sales Positions," *Journal of Personal Selling and Sales Management* 3 (November 1983), pp. 31–41.

[5] Derek A. Newton, *Sales Force Performance and Turnover* (Cambridge, Mass.: Marketing Science Institute, 1973), p. 5.

often do not take orders from customers directly but persuade customers to buy their firm's product from distributors or other wholesale suppliers. Examples include representatives of brewers, who call on bar owners and encourage them to order a particular brand of beer from the local distributor, and medical "detailers," who call on doctors as representatives of pharmaceutical manufacturers.

3. *Technical selling*—where the sales force's primary responsibility is to increase business from presently identified customers and potential customers by providing them with technical and engineering information and assistance. Sales engineers for machine-tool and computer manufacturers are examples of people engaged in technical selling.

4. *New business selling*—where the salesperson's primary responsibility is to identify and obtain business from *new customers* that the company has not dealt with before.

Each type of sales job involves somewhat different activities and requires different skills and training. Therefore, although most of this book focuses on managing industrial selling in general, from time to time special attention will be paid to some unique problems encountered in managing people in these different types of jobs.

Some Attractive Characteristics of Sales Jobs: The Salesperson's Viewpoint

Even though many people view selling as a low-status, uninteresting, and unattractive job, most industrial salespeople find their jobs rewarding and satisfying. Several recent surveys have found some dissatisfaction among salespeople in a broad cross-section of industrial goods firms. Those people tended to be unhappy with the policies and actions of their companies and/or their sales managers, however, not with the general nature of the sales job itself. In other words, most salespeople like what they do. Nevertheless, they are not always pleased with their firm's training programs, promotion policies, compensation methods, or the supervisory styles of their sales managers.[6]

Why do so many people like their sales jobs in spite of the negative image of selling in the eyes of the public? Many analysts have reached a variety of answers to this question. Some attractive aspects of selling careers most commonly mentioned by these authors—as well as by salespeople themselves—include: (1) free-

---

[6] Neil M. Ford, Orville C. Walker, Jr., and Gilbert A. Churchill, Jr., "Job Satisfaction and Discontent among Industrial Salespeople," Working Paper 8–75–35 (Madison: Graduate School of Business, University of Wisconsin, 1975); and Gilbert A. Churchill, Jr., Neil M. Ford, and Orville C. Walker, Jr., "Organizational Climate and Job Satisfaction in the Salesforce," *Journal of Marketing Research* 13 (November 1976), pp. 323–32. It is interesting to note that these findings seem to be equally true for both male and female sales representatives. See John E. Swan, Charles M. Futrell, and John T. Todd, "Same Job—Different Views: Women and Men in Industrial Sales," *Journal of Marketing* (January 1978), pp. 92–98.

dom of action and opportunities for personal initiative, (2) a variety of challenging activities, (3) opportunities for career development and advancement, (4) financial rewards, and (5) working conditions that are often much better than perceived by the general public.[7]

Freedom of Action

A common complaint among workers in many professions is that they are too closely supervised. They complain about superiors "breathing down their necks" and about bureaucratic rules and standard operating procedures that constrain their freedom to do their jobs as they see fit. Salespeople, on the other hand, spend most of their time in the field calling on customers where there is no one to supervise their every move. They are relatively free to organize their own time and to get the job done in their own way as long as they show satisfactory results.

The freedom of a selling career appeals to people who value their independence, who are confident that they can cope with most situations they will encounter, and who like to show some personal initiative in deciding how to get their job done. However, there are also responsibilities and pressures that go along with this freedom. The salesperson is responsible for his or her territory. Although no one closely supervises the salesperson's behavior, management usually does keep close tabs on the results of that behavior-sales volume, quota attainment, expenses, and the like. To be successful, then, the salesperson must be willing and able to manage himself or herself, to organize time wisely, and to make the right decisions about how to do the job. Unfortunately, not everyone wants such responsibilities. For example, one survey found that some sales representatives were dissatisfied with their supervisors, not because they were being supervised too closely but because they felt they were not being supervised enough.[8] These people were uncomfortable about having to take so much responsibility for determining their own job behavior and performance.

Variety and Challenge

People soon become bored doing routine tasks. Consequently, many companies have instituted "job enrichment" programs to expand the variety of activities in, and increase the challenge of, their employees' jobs. Boredom is seldom a problem among industrial salespeople, however. Each potential customer has different needs and problems for the salesperson to solve. Those problems are often anything but trivial, and a salesperson must display a great deal of insight, creativity, and analytical skill to close a sale. For example, a six-person selling team from IBM spent four years studying patient care and handling procedures in a

---

[7] For example, see Frederic A. Russell, Frank H. Beach, and Richard H. Buskirk, *Textbook of Salesmanship*, 10th ed. (New York: McGraw-Hill, 1978), chap. 2; or Ben Enis, *Personal Selling: Foundations, Process and Management*, (Santa Monica, Calif.: Goodyear, 1979).

[8] Churchill, Ford, and Walker, "Organizational Climate."

large hospital before they were able to design and sell a data processing system that fit the hospital's needs. Many analysts expect this kind of creative problem solving to become an even more common part of selling in the future. New technologies—like telemarketing and electronic reordering systems—are making what was a primary function of the salesperson, order taking, almost obsolete. As a result, the salesperson of the future will be "more of a trainer, a technical adviser, and consultant as opposed to an order-taker."[9]

To make the job even more interesting, conditions in the marketplace are constantly changing. Salespeople must frequently adjust their sales presentations and other activities to changing economic and competitive conditions.

For many people in the selling profession, variety and challenge are the most rewarding aspects of their jobs. In one study, industrial salespeople rated the "sense of accomplishment" and the "opportunities for personal growth" provided by their jobs second only to financial compensation as the most attractive rewards they received.[10]

Opportunities for Advancement

Many business people feel that, before an executive can do an effective job of managing, he or she must "know the territory." What better way is there to learn about a company's customers, products, and competitive strengths and weaknesses than to spend time in the field calling on customers and meeting the competition face to face? It is not surprising, then, that studies that trace the routes of corporation presidents through the ranks find that the sales department furnishes basic experience more often than any other functional area. Of course, there are many managerial opportunities at lower levels of the corporate hierarchy—most obviously in sales management and marketing management.

On the other hand, promoting top salespeople into the ranks of management can sometimes cause problems. Successful selling often requires different personal attributes and skills than successful management. There is no guarantee that a good salesperson will also be a good sales manager. Also, successful salespeople have been known to refuse promotion to managerial positions. Sometimes this is because they simply enjoy selling, but in many cases, it is because they can earn more money selling than they can in a middle-management position.

Compensation

As the preceding suggests, selling can be a very lucrative profession. As Table 1–2 indicates, starting salaries for sales trainees are quite high. They are comparable to those paid in other functional areas of business.

---

[9] "Rebirth of a Salesman: Willy Loman Goes Electronic," *Business Week* February 27, 1984, p. 104.
[10] Gilbert A. Churchill, Jr., Neil M. Ford, and Orville C. Walker, Jr., "Motivating Different Salespeople: Personal Characteristics and the Attractiveness of Alternative Rewards," *Journal of Business Research* 7 (1979), pp. 25–50.

Table 1–2
Starting salaries of sales trainees
with college degrees

	Average Annual Salary, 1983
Trainees with bachelor's degrees	
Nontechnical degree	$17,568
Technical degree	22,560
Trainees with MBA degrees	
With a nontechnical undergraduate degree	$26,580
With a technical undergraduate degree	30,288

Source: "Compensation," *Sales and Marketing Management*, February 20, 1984, p. 68.

More important, the rate of growth of a salesperson's earnings is determined largely by his or her performance. A salesperson's compensation can grow more rapidly and reach higher levels than that of personnel in other departments at comparable levels in an organization. There are often no arbitrary limits placed on the maximum earnings a salesperson can make. Figure 1–1 shows the average compensation for industrial salespeople with various amounts of experience and selling responsibilities. These averages fail to show, however, that the most successful salespeople commonly have much higher earnings. For example, a recent study of 319 sales forces found that top performers earned about 33 percent more than average performers in their companies, and over 10 percent of these top salespeople had total earnings of more than $80,000 per year.[11]

Although salespeople are sometimes reluctant to give up their high-paying jobs to move into managerial positions, one should not assume that sales managers are candidates for public assistance. Most firms recognize the importance of good managerial talent and reward it appropriately, particularly as a person reaches the top executive levels of the sales organization. Total compensation of over $250,000 a year is not unheard of for national sales managers or vice presidents of sales in large firms.

Working Conditions

According to the stereotype, salespeople travel extensively, live on big expense accounts, spend much of their time entertaining potential clients, and consequently have little time for home and family life. Again, this is not a very accurate description of the working conditions encountered by most salespeople.

Some selling jobs do require a substantial amount of travel, but most salespeople can sleep at home nearly every night. As we shall see, a major determinant of the size of sales territories is the density of potential customers. In many lines of trade, customers are sufficiently concentrated that firms must define relatively

---

[11] Charles A. Peck, *Compensating Field Sales Representatives* (New York: The Conference Board, 1982), pp. 25–27.

Figure 1–1
Average compensation for different
types of sales positions, 1971–1983

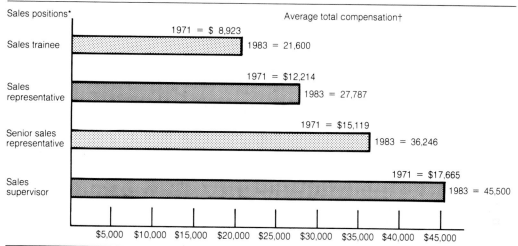

Sales positions*   Average total compensation†

Sales trainee
1971 = $ 8,923
1983 = 21,600

Sales representative
1971 = $12,214
1983 = 27,787

Senior sales representative
1971 = $15,119
1983 = 36,246

Sales supervisor
1971 = $17,665
1983 = 45,500

$5,000 $10,000 $15,000 $20,000 $25,000 $30,000 $35,000 $40,000 $45,000

*A "senior sales representative" is at the highest level of selling responsibility in his or her firm, usually has years of experience, and is assigned to major accounts and territories. A "sales supervisor" is a veteran salesperson whose primary function is to train and direct the activities of other salespeople, although he or she may also sell to selected key accounts.
†Includes salaries plus commission incentives. Figures are based on consumer goods and industrial goods firms as well as insurance companies, services, transportation companies, and utilities.
Source: Adapted from "Compensation," *Sales and Marketing Management,* February 20, 1984, p. 62.

small sales territories to gain adequate customer contact. Also, there has been a gradual trend toward smaller territories in many industries as the number of customers has grown and as firms attempt to provide better customer service to each sales area. Consequently, people who sell things like office equipment, cleaning supplies, or grocery products commonly have territories limited to a single city or a fraction of a single state.

Although some sales jobs still require extensive traveling, modern sales managers are usually aware of the problems such travel can cause for both the salesperson and the firm. Many companies attempt to design their larger territories and schedule the salesperson's calls in such a way that he or she regularly reaches home every couple of days. Where necessary, some firms fly their salespeople home every weekend regardless of the distance.

Selling Costs as a Major Part of Marketing Budgets

One obvious indication of the importance marketers attach to personal selling is the amount of money they spend building and maintaining effective sales organizations. Substantial amounts of time and money are spent just in training new

Table 1–3
Average cost of sales training
per salesperson

Type of Company	Training Cost Including Salary, 1983*	Median Training Period (weeks), 1983
Industrial products	$24,600	20
Consumer products	16,600	18
Services†	16,000	20

*In addition to salary, this category covers such items as instructional materials prepared, purchased, and rented for training program; transportation and living expenses incurred during training course; instructional staff; outside seminars and courses; and management time spent with a salesperson when it is part of the training budget.
†Includes insurance, financial, utilities, transportation, retail stores, etc.
Source: *Sales and Marketing Management*, February 20, 1984, p. 72.

salespeople to do their jobs effectively, as shown in Table 1–3. Notice that training time and expense both vary with the type of sales job. Companies with sales forces that must sell more technically complex industrial goods typically have the most extensive training programs. In some high-technology fields like computers, the formal sales training program may last up to two years. Companies may spend

Figure 1–2
Industrial marketing costs by size
of company

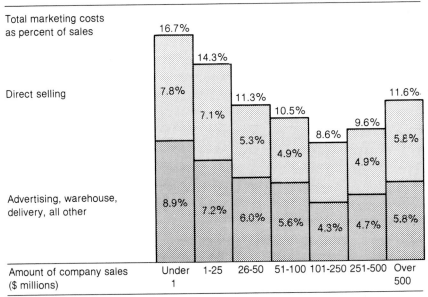

Source: *Sales and Marketing Management*, February 26, 1979, pp. 55 and 66.

more than $50,000 before a salesperson becomes a productive part of the firm's marketing program.

Even after the sales force has been trained, their compensation, travel, and entertainment expenses—together with the costs of administering their activities—usually account for a substantial portion of a firm's total marketing budget. Figure 1–2 shows average direct selling costs and other total marketing costs for industrial goods and services companies in various sales volume categories. Overall, selling costs account for about half of these firm's total marketing costs—a strong indication of the importance they attach to personal selling.

Of course, selling costs vary from industry to industry depending on the complexity of the product, the number and location of potential customers, and the size of the average sale. Sales force expenses as a percentage of sales across a variety of consumer and industrial goods industries are shown in Table 1–4.

Table 1–4
Sales force selling expenses as a percentage of sales in major industries

Industry	1983
Consumer goods:	
Durable goods	9.0%
Ethical pharmaceuticals, surgical supplies, and equipment	16.9
Food	3.5
Major household items	4.4
Proprietary drugs and toiletries	7.9
Industrial goods:	
Automotive parts and accessories	5.5
Building materials	5.4
Chemicals and petroleum	1.4
Computers, office and educational supplies, and equipment	10.7
Containers, packaging materials, and paper	1.6
Electrical materials	3.9
Electronics and instruments	5.2
Fabricated metals (heavy)	3.8
Fabricated metals (light)	4.9
Fabrics and apparel	5.3
Iron and steel	2.4
Machinery (heavy)	5.4
Machinery (light)	9.2
Printing and publishing	9.7
Rubber, plastics, and leather	4.4

Note: includes only salespeople's total compensation plus their expenses: that is, travel, lodging, meals, and entertainment.
Source: *Sales and Marketing Management*, February 20, 1984, p. 60.

As marketers are fond of saying, however, the impact of a particular activity should be judged not only by how much it costs, but also by the results it produces in sales and profits. The contribution of a highly motivated well-managed sales force to the success of a marketing program can best be illustrated with an example. Consider the marketing success—as well as the recent problems—of Lanier Business Products, Inc.

The Role of Personal Selling in a Successful Marketing Strategy: The Case of Lanier Business Products, Inc.[12]

In the mid-1960s, Lanier Business Products, Inc., was a regional distributor of dictating machines in the South with annual sales of about $12 million. By 1982, the Atlanta-based company had become a nationwide manufacturer and marketer of both dictating and word processing equipment with earnings of about $13 million on sales of $350 million. Lanier dominated the dictating equipment market, accounting for one third of total sales in an industry that included such formidable competitors as Sony, Dictaphone, and Norelco. More surprisingly, Lanier startled the information-processing industry in 1980 when it grabbed the lead in standalone word processor sales with a 12.7 percent share of the market. The firm accomplished the feat just three years after entering a market that had been dominated by such strong competitors as IBM and Wang. For reasons discussed later, however, Lanier then encountered some problems in its word processing and office systems business, and by 1983, its market share had sagged to only 7.6 percent of the industry's $1.5 billion in sales.

Lanier's experiences provided a useful case for illustrating the importance and impact of sound sales management for two reasons. First, the firm's success in the dictating equipment market—as well as its early accomplishments in selling word processors—is largely due to a customer-oriented market approach and an aggressive, well-managed sales force. On the other hand, its recent problems show what can happen when a firm fails to adjust its marketing and sales programs to meet changing customer needs and environmental conditions.

A Customer-Oriented Product Policy

Gene W. Milner started with Lanier as a salesman in 1953. When he became Lanier's chairman and chief executive officer in 1967, he saw the dictating machine industry as a marketing nightmare. The products that Lanier distributed often were not evaluated very favorably by customers, but the company's pleas to manufacturers for changes were often ignored. Some manufacturers introduced

---

[12] This example is based on material found in Rush Loving, Jr., "At Lanier a Better Mousetrap Isn't Quite Enough," *Fortune*, February 26, 1979, pp. 70–78; "Lanier Aims to Win Back Its Office Leadership," *Business Week*, May 16, 1983, pp. 133–36; and "Harris Makes a Marriage of Convenience," *Business Week*, August 8, 1983, pp. 31–32.

new models or improved old ones only every five or six years. Consequently, Milner decided to turn Lanier into a manufacturer. He set up a research department, bought patents and production rights to some of the machines the company had been distributing, leased a factory, and began making dictating machines and accessories.

One thing that made Lanier different—and successful—was its orientation toward customers and their needs. Management paid close attention to what the market wanted and kept in touch with both customers and company salespeople. Indeed, Milner still requires all 20 of his top executives, including himself, to go on sales calls at least once a month. More important, the company was willing to quickly initiate product modifications that customers wanted. The research staff in Atlanta took ideas generated by customers or salespeople, devised ways to make them work using available technology, and built production models. Some product innovations that Lanier has introduced as a result of this approach include dictating machines with two tapes to allow a secretary to type letters while the boss goes on dictating, machines that use standard tape cassettes like those in home tape recorders, minicassettes, pocket-sized dictation machines, and tiny vest-pocket recorders.

This customer-oriented approach also characterized Lanier's entry into the word processing market in 1976. Since the firm did not have the technical expertise to design and build its own machines, it purchased a 37 percent stake in AES Data Ltd., a Montreal-based manufacturer. As a result of this partnership, AES made—and Lanier marketed—the "No Problem" word processor. It was a stand-alone unit that was relatively inexpensive, easy to operate, and very well-suited to the needs of the majority of Lanier's existing customers—smaller, independent business firms and professional offices.

Advertising to Generate Brand Awareness

Since Lanier had been a regional distributor operating only in the South, one of Milner's first tasks after turning the firm into a manufacturer was to make Lanier a familiar name in offices throughout the country. It had to be known to secretaries and other users of office equipment as well as office managers and purchasing agents. To accomplish this, the firm launched a national advertising campaign. It used the comedy team of Stiller and Meara, and subsequently golfer Arnold Palmer (see Figure 1–3), to praise the company's equipment in radio commercials and on Monday night football telecasts.

The Role of Sales Force

According to Chairman Milner and other observers, one of Lanier's greatest marketing assets during its drive to success was its aggressive, well-managed sales force.

Figure 1–3

One for the road. One for the office.

Arnold Palmer gets more done when he travels with Lanier's Vest Pocket Secretary. And now, back at the office, he's got Lanier's new OMNI microcassette desktop.

Talking is so much faster than writing that when you dictate, you cut way down on the time you spend on paperwork. And that leaves you more time for the things that are really important to your career.

Now Lanier, the company that makes the remarkable little Vest Pocket Secretary portable dictating unit, introduces OMNI, a small and simple-to-use microcassette desktop.

OMNI was designed to take full advantage of today's little microcassettes (the same 60-minute microcassettes the Vest Pocket Secretary uses). So it's a lot smaller than standard-cassette desktops. In fact, OMNI takes up less room on your desk than a standard piece of typing paper. And like the Vest Pocket Secretary, OMNI is a snap to use.

Lanier's OMNI and Vest Pocket Secretary. Together they'll help you get more accomplished both at the office and on the road.

LANIER BUSINESS PRODUCTS, INC.

Organization. One reason the Lanier sales force put a great deal of selling effort behind the company's products was that they sold only those products. Some of Lanier's competitors made extensive use of distributors who sold other product lines. Lanier covered 60 percent of the country with its own company salespeople, however, and the remaining 40 percent was covered by distributors who sold Lanier products exclusively. Thus, one reason Lanier outsold Sony, whose recorders were considered the best-engineered products on the market, was because Sony's dictation equipment was sold by distributors who were also busy selling television sets, stereos, and other products.

Compensation and Incentives. Another reason Lanier's salespeople were highly motivated was the company's compensation system. Whereas other business products companies paid salespeople straight salaries and small commissions, Lanier generally paid only commissions—large ones that ranged from 5 to

15 percent. Salespeople were also offered extra bonuses of 1 to 4 percent for exceeding their annual sales quotas. They earned an extra commission of 1 percent for the sale of accessory equipment and 5 percent for persuading a customer to sign a service contract. This system of commissions and incentives enabled the most successful of Lanier's 2,000 salespeople to earn more than $100,000 per year during the early 1980s.

Training.   When Lanier salespeople went into the field to call on customers, they were well prepared. Many competitors trained their sales personnel to understand the technical details and engineering features of the equipment they sold. Lanier's executives felt that their customers were not very interested in such details, however, and that technical talk often confused potential clients or worried them into backing away from a purchase. Consequently, much of Lanier's sales training focused on the ways in which specific Lanier machines could be used. Salespeople were encouraged to stress the product's simplicity, practicality, and impact on office productivity.

When a Lanier salesperson went into a potential customer's office, he or she asked to see how the paperwork was handled. The salesperson then became an overnight expert about the business involved and prepared a plan for increasing its productivity through the use of a specific Lanier machine. When the salesperson gave a prospect a demonstration, he or she programmed the machine to do that prospect's actual paperwork.

Once a salesperson demonstrated a product to a prospective customer, he or she was expected to move quickly to close the sale. Says one saleswoman, "Other companies expect you to take four months. But Lanier expects a sale in three weeks."

A Changing Environment Causes Problems

In 1980, the same year that Lanier reached the number one position in the word processing market, both customer needs and the competitive environment started to change. Customers began moving from standalone word processors to clustered systems that could integrate many word processors or to office computer systems that could perform a variety of tasks in addition to work processing, such as data analysis and electronic mail. Several of Lanier's major competitors—including IBM and Wang—introduced new clustered office computer systems during 1980, while Lanier continued to concentrate on its popular standalone models.

Product and Marketing Problems.   In response to these environmental changes, Lanier decided to develop and manufacture its own office computer systems. The company increased its spending on research and development (to $8 million in 1982) and began to manufacture an office computer that was marketed as the EZ-1 word processor and the Computereze business system. Unfortunately, these new products were not ready for the market until 1981, an entire year behind the competition.

To make matters worse, in the rush to develop new products for the changing market, Lanier lost track of its customer-oriented philosophy. The new EZ-1 system was more expensive than competitive models, and its design and operation was not very compatible with customer needs. "The EZ-1 software was cumbersome," notes one data processing manager. For example, it made it difficult to insert or delete words. As a result, Lanier started out as an also-ran in the office systems market, capturing a paltry 4.3 percent share of a business that accounted for nearly half of all word processor sales in 1982.

Sales Management Problems. Lanier's problems in capturing customers for its new office computer systems were made worse by the fact that the firm was slow to change its sales plans and programs. The company's training and compensation programs, as we discussed earlier, were effective for producing aggressive salespeople who were skilled at selling relatively nontechnical devices to small accounts. Those programs, however, were not entirely consistent with the company's new objective of marketing complex computer systems to large corporations. As one analyst pointed out, "by and large, they have an unskilled set of salespeople working on commission who are not used to selling big systems with extended selling cycles."

In a move to correct such problems, Lanier reorganized its sales force. It was split into two separate groups, with each group concentrating on different products and customer types. Seven hundred salespeople were assigned exclusively to sell office computer systems to large accounts, while the remaining 1,300 were directed to sell the full range of company products—including dictating and copying equipment—to a broader range of buyers. Lanier also instituted an extensive retraining program for its "major account" salespeople. Nevertheless, many analysts wondered if these moves weren't too little and too late for Lanier to be able to recapture its lead in the office automation industry.

The Current Situation

On July 22, 1983, Harris Corp. announced a planned takeover of Lanier Business Products, Inc., in a stock transfer valued at about $375 million. This marriage of convenience was seen as a way to bolster both companies' sagging efforts in the office market.

Harris, a Florida-based electronics giant with sales of $1.7 billion in 1982, was best known for selling large computer systems to corporations and the federal government. Its $236 million in annual research and development spending and its expertise in communications and semiconductors was seen as a way to close Lanier's technology and product development gap in the office automation industry. On the other hand, Lanier's marketing experience and aggressive sales force were seen as a way for Harris to strengthen its selling efforts in the office market, a market where the firm had little experience of its own. As Harris' Chairman Joseph Boyd pointed out, "We've got to quickly put together a plan effectively linking Harris' product development and networking ability with Lanier's sales force if we expect this to succeed." However, a number of industry analysts remain skeptical. In their view, Lanier's failure to adjust its marketing and sales management policies to changes in the customer and competitive environment at the time those changes first started to occur has put the firm in a competitive hole that may be difficult to climb out of, regardless of how much money its new parent company is willing to spend on new technology.

What Is Involved in Sales Management

The Lanier example provides some clues to managing an effectiveness sales force. However, several policies formulated and activities performed by Lanier's sales managers were not explicitly discussed. The following is a more detailed look, then, at what sales management is all about.

1. *The formulation of a strategic sales program.* The strategic sales program should take into account the environmental factors faced by the firm. It should organize and plan the company's overall personal selling efforts and integrate these with the other elements of the firm's marketing strategy.
2. *The implementation of the sales program.* The implementation phase involves selecting appropriate sales personnel and designing and implementing policies and procedures that will direct their efforts toward the desired objectives.
3. *The evaluation and control of sales force performance.* The evaluation phase involves the development of methods for monitoring and evaluating sales force performance. This enables necessary adjustments to be made either to the sales program or to the way it is implemented when performance is unsatisfactory.

The specific activities involved in these three processes, along with the variables that influence those activities, are summarized in an overall model of sales management in Figure 1–4. Although the basic thrust of this book is to explore the components of this model in detail, it might be useful to briefly discuss the variables and sales management activities involved in each of the three processes.

Formulation of a Strategic Sales Program

The activities and influences that are explicitly involved in formulating a company's strategic sales program are shown in Figure 1–5. The design of a sales program requires five major sets of decisions.

Figure 1–4
An overview of sales management

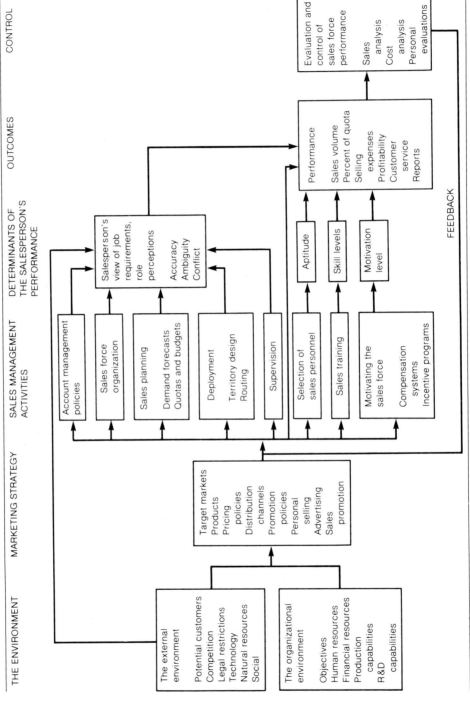

Figure 1–5
**Activities and influences involved in
formulating a strategic
sales program**

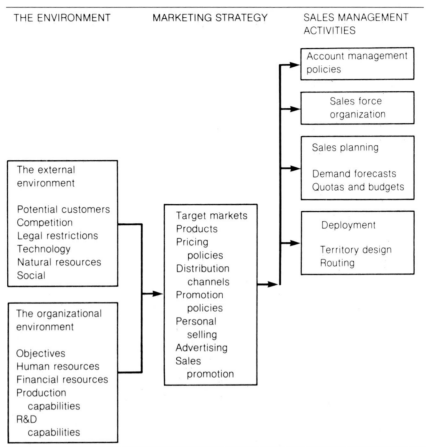

THE ENVIRONMENT   MARKETING STRATEGY   SALES MANAGEMENT
                                                    ACTIVITIES

1. How can the personal selling effort best be adapted to the company's environment and integrated with the other elements of the firm's marketing strategy? In sum, what should be the firm's personal selling strategy?
2. How can various types of potential customers best be approached, persuaded, and serviced? In other words, what account management policies should be adopted?
3. How should the sales force be organized to call on and manage various types of customers as efficiently and effectively as possible?
4. What level of performance can each member of the sales force be expected to attain during the next planning period? This involves forecasting demand and setting quotas and budgets.

5. In view of the firm's account management policies and demand forecasts, how should the sales force be deployed? How should sales territories be defined? What is the best way for each salesperson's time to be allocated within his or her territory?

A company's sales program is not designed in a vacuum. The policies and plans involved in such a program must take into account the influences and constraints imposed by the external environment. The demands of potential customers and the actions of competitors are two obvious environmental factors that affect a firm's sales program. For example, Lanier's early policy of urging its salespeople to stress the simplicity of the company's products and their contribution to productivity, rather than their technical characteristics, was based on management's perceptions of customer interests. Another reason for the policy was that several of the firm's competitors offered equipment that was technically as good or better than Lanier's.

In addition to customers and competitors, other environmental factors, such as energy shortages, technical advances, government regulations, and social concerns, can affect a company's sales policies and plans. A few years ago, for instance, a large paper products manufacturer was forced to tell its salespeople not to exceed their quotas because a shortage of pulpwood supplies prevented the company from filling an increased volume of orders.

A firm's internal environment also helps to determine the kinds of sales program it can implement. The availability of human and financial resources, the firm's production capacity, and its expertise in research and development can limit the company's ability to pursue particular types of customers or to expand its sales volume and market share. In Lanier's case, the firm's inadequate research and development efforts and its unskilled sales force made it difficult to attract and satisfy large customers in the market for complex office systems.

The most important consideration in formulating a sales program is to ensure that it is carefully integrated with the rest of the firm's marketing strategy. Again, Lanier's experience illustrates this. The firm's early sales program was successful, in part, because it was backed by customer-oriented, innovative product policy, a unique exclusive distribution strategy, and a media advertising program that helped to generate brand awareness among potential customers. On the other hand, its recent problems are due largely to its failure to produce new products that are responsive to changing customer needs, to noncompetitive pricing, and to a failure to adjust sales management policies to fit changes in the company's customers and product line.

Personal selling is only one promotional tool, and promotion is only one element of a marketing strategy. Management must decide what promotional objectives need to be accomplished in view of the firm's product line, price policies, and distribution network. Decisions must then be made concerning what combination of promotional tools—personal selling, media advertising, and sales promotion—can accomplish those objectives most efficiently and effectively. Finally, account management policies and sales plans must be devised that spell out the firm's personal selling objectives, and appropriate organizational and deployment policies must be developed for accomplishing those objectives.

Part 1 of this book, which consists of Chapters 2 through 7, examines the decisions and activities involved in formulating a strategic sales program. Chapter 2 explores the relationships among a firm's environment, the elements of its overall marketing strategy, and its sales program. Chapter 3 focuses on the needs of various types of customers and the design of appropriate account management policies for serving those needs. Chapter 4 looks at alternative ways of organizing the sales force to provide the desired level of customer contact and service. As pointed out in Chapter 2, two of the key ingredients in a marketing plan are an opportunity analysis and a demand forecast. Chapter 5 consequently discusses the conduct of a marketing opportunity analysis and reviews the main demand forecasting methods. Finally, Chapters 6 and 7 examine deployment decisions, including the design of sales territories, the determination of how many salespeople are needed to provide adequate market coverage, methods of allocating a salesperson's effort within his or her territory, and the establishment of sales quotas.

Implementation of the Sales Program

As with any kind of management, implementing a sales program involves motivating and directing the behavior of other people—the members of the sales force. To be effective, the sales manager must understand why the people in his or her sales force behave the way they do. Then policies and procedures can be designed to direct that behavior toward the desired objectives.

The model of the activities involved in implementing a sales program, shown in Figure 1–6, suggests that five factors influence a salesperson's job behavior and performance.

1. *Environmental variables.* Regardless of how highly motivated or competent a salesperson is, his or her ability to achieve a particular level of job performance is influenced—and sometimes constrained—by factors in the environment. The ability to reach a given sales volume, for instance, can be affected by such things as the market demand for the product being sold, the number and aggressiveness of competitors, and the health of the economy. Similarly, other elements of a firm's marketing mix, such as the quality of its products and the effectiveness of its advertising, can affect a salesperson's ability to reach a high level of sales performance.

2. *Role perceptions.* Before a salesperson can perform his or her job adequately, he or she must understand what the job entails and how it is supposed to be performed. The activities and behaviors associated with a particular job are defined largely by the expectations and demands of other people, both inside and outside the organization. Thus, a salesperson's job (or *role*) is defined by the expectations and desires of his or her customers, sales manager, other

Figure 1–6
Activities involved in implementing
a sales program

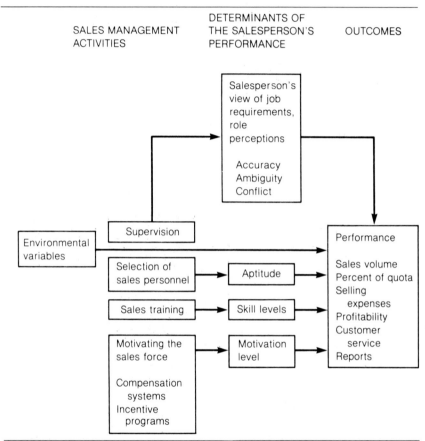

SALES MANAGEMENT
ACTIVITIES

DETERMINANTS OF
THE SALESPERSON'S
PERFORMANCE

OUTCOMES

company executives, and family members. The salesperson's ability to do the job well, then, is partly determined by how clearly he or she understands those role expectations. Also, the salesperson may sometimes face conflicting demands, as when a customer wants a lower price but company management refuses to negotiate. The salesperson's ability to resolve such conflicts helps determine his or her success or failure on the job.

3. *Aptitude.* A salesperson's ability to perform the activities of his or her job is also influenced by the individual's personal characteristics, such as personality traits, intelligence, and analytical ability. No matter how hard they try, some people are never successful at selling because they do not have the aptitude for the job. Of course, different kinds of sales jobs involve different tasks and activities, so a person with certain characteristics may be unsuited for one selling job but tremendously successful at another one.

4. *Skill levels.* Even when salespeople have the aptitude to do their jobs and an understanding of what they are expected to do, they must have the skills necessary to carry out the required tasks effectively. For instance, a salesperson must have a thorough knowledge of the product and how it works, how to make an effective sales presentation, and other sales skills.

5. *Motivation level.* A salesperson cannot achieve a high level of job performance unless he or she is motivated to expend the necessary amount of effort. A person's motivation, in turn, is determined by the kind of rewards he or she expects to receive for achieving a given level of performance—such as more pay or a promotion—and by the perceived attractiveness of those anticipated rewards.

A sales manager can use several policies and procedures to influence the aptitude, skill levels, role perceptions, and motivation of the members of a sales force. Implementing a sales program involves designing those policies and procedures so that the job behavior and performance of each salesperson are shaped and directed toward the specified objectives and performance levels.

The sales manager must decide what kinds of aptitude are required for the firm's salespeople to do the kind of selling involved and to reach the program's objectives. *Recruiting techniques and selection criteria* can then be developed to ensure that salespeople with the required abilities are hired.

A person's selling skills improve with practice and experience. In most cases, though, it is inefficient to let the salesperson simply gain the necessary skills through on-the-job experience. Good customers might be lost as the result of mistakes by unskilled sales personnel. Consequently, most firms have some kind of *formal training program* to give new recruits some of the necessary knowledge and skills before they are expected to pull their own weight in the field. The sales manager must determine what kinds of selling skills are required by his or her salespeople. He or she can then design training programs that develop those skills as effectively as possible.

Even after completing a training program, salespeople may run into unusual situations where they face conflicting demands or are uncertain about what to do. *Supervisory policies and procedures* are needed so salespeople in the field can obtain advice and assistance from management with no undue restriction on their freedom to develop innovative approaches to customers' problems.

Finally, a salesperson's motivation to expend effort on the job is largely a function of the amount and desirability of the rewards he or she expects to receive for a given job performance. The sales manager, then, should determine what rewards are most attractive to the sales force and design *compensation and incentive programs* that will generate a high level of motivation. Such compensation programs involve monetary rewards, as when Lanier motivated its sales force to aggressively pursue new customers by offering large commissions for each new sale. Incentive programs can also include a variety of nonfinancial rewards, however, such as recognition programs, promotions to better territories or to management positions, or opportunities for personal development.

Part 2 of this book explores the policies and procedures involved in implementing a firm's sales program. Chapter 8 discusses the determinants of a salesperson's performance and job behavior in more detail. Chapter 9 describes the kinds of role expectations and demands salespeople receive from their customers, managers, and families. It also discusses how supervisory policies can be designed to help them deal with ambiguous and conflicting demands. Chapters 10 and 11 then examine the personal characteristics that are related to selling aptitude and the ways in which recruiting and selection procedures can be designed to build a sales force with the abilities needed to carry out the required selling tasks and activities. The objectives of sales training and a variety of training techniques are examined in Chapter 12. Finally, Chapters 13 and 14 discuss the kinds of rewards that motivate people to expend effort on various aspects of their jobs and how those rewards can be incorporated into effective sales compensation and incentive programs.

Evaluation and Control of the Sales Program

For a salesperson to be appropriately rewarded for his or her job performance, that performance must first be measured and evaluated. Lanier's compensation plan, for example, provides salespeople with commissions and bonuses based on their total sales volume and the attainment of their sales quotas. At a minimum, then, the firm must monitor and record each salesperson's sales in relation to the quota to know how much bonus and commission the person deserves.

From a sales manager's point of view, it is equally important to monitor the aggregate performance of the sales force as a means of evaluating and controlling the firm's strategic sales program and the way it is implemented. Although this is particularly true when new programs or policies are put into effect, even a successful program should be carefully monitored over time. Changes in economic conditions, customer needs, competitors' actions, or other parts of the firm's marketing mix can cause successful programs and policies to suddenly become inappropriate and ineffective, as Lanier has recently discovered to its dismay. Thus, overall performance should be measured frequently and compared with the planned performance levels specified in the sales program so that any deviations can be quickly identified. Then timely changes in the strategic program or in specific implementation policies and procedures can be made.

As the model of sales evaluation and control activities outlined in Figure 1–7 shows, several different performance dimensions can be measured and evaluated. Data can be collected not only on sales volume and attainment of quotas, but also on selling expenses, the profitability of sales, the quality of services provided to customers, and the timeliness and completeness of call reports and other kinds of information requested from the firm's sales personnel.

Figure 1–7
**Evaluation and control of sales
force performance**

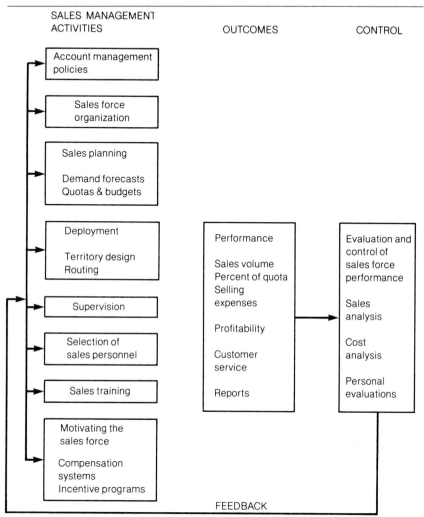

There are three major approaches that a company might utilize in evaluating and controlling the sales force to monitor sales program performance.

1. *Sales analysis.* Sales volume can be monitored for each salesperson. In addition, sales figures are often broken down by geographic district, by each product in the line, and by different types of customers. Sales results can then be compared with the quotas and forecasts specified in the firm's sales plans.

2. *Cost analysis.* The costs of various selling functions can be monitored. These might also be examined across individual salespeople, districts, products, and customer types. When put together with the data from sales analysis, this procedure allows a firm to judge the profitability of various products and customer types. However, cost analysis presents some difficult technical questions concerning how certain costs—such as administrative salaries and overhead—should be allocated among salespeople or products.

3. *Behavioral analysis.* A salesperson's ability to achieve a certain sales volume is sometimes constrained by factors beyond his or her control, such as competition or economic conditions. Therefore, some managers feel that it is necessary to evaluate the actual behavior of salespeople as well as their ultimate performance in terms of sales volume. A number of techniques attempt to measure and evaluate various aspects of a salesperson's job behavior, including self-rating scales, supervisor ratings, and field observations.

Although sales analysis is the most common method of control, a growing number of firms use a combination of all three methods for identifying shortcomings in the design or implementation of their sales programs and for helping to decide on appropriate changes.

Part 3 of this book is devoted to a discussion of control procedures. Chapter 15 examines the techniques of sales analysis, and Chapter 16 focuses on cost analysis. Finally, Chapter 17 discusses behavioral analysis and explores some corrective measures that a sales manager can take when performance falls short of planned levels.

Summary

This introductory chapter sought to do three things: (1) provide some appreciation for personal selling and the nature of sales jobs, (2) highlight the critical role that personal selling can and often does play in a firm's overall marketing strategy, and (3) preview the activities involved in managing a firm's personal selling effort.

The mention of personal selling typically conjures up a negative image, but many stereotypes are inaccurate because they fail to reflect the different types of sales jobs. Therefore, they fail to portray accurately what the life of a salesperson is truly like. The broadest distinction among sales jobs is between retail selling and industrial selling. Retail selling is concerned with the sale of goods and services to ultimate consumers for their own personal use. Industrial selling involves the sale of goods and services to customers for the production of other goods and services. It includes sales to resellers, business users, and institutions. Some advantages associated with industrial selling as a career are: (1) freedom of action and opportunities for personal initiative, (2) a variety of challenging activities, (3) attractive opportunities for career development and advancement, (4) substantial financial rewards, and (5) working conditions that are often much better than those perceived by the general public.

Personal selling is a basic component of the marketing program of almost every firm and a critical component in many of them. It is not unusual for a firm's expenditures on the personal selling component of the marketing mix to be greater than the expenditures on all other elements combined, particularly for firms that produce industrial goods. Even when the expenditure is not this great, however, it is imperative that the personal selling program be integrated with the other elements of the marketing mix if the marketing effort is to produce its maximum possible impact.

Sales management involves three interrelated processes: (1) the formulation of a strategic sales program, (2) the implementation of the sales program, and (3) the evaluation and control of sales force performance. It is the purpose of this book to describe the variables and sales management activities involved in each of these processes. More particularly, each major section of the book elaborates one process: Part 1, the formulation of the sales program; Part 2, its implementation; and Part 3, the task of evaluation and control.

Discussion Questions

1. The text describes the negative image associated with sales careers. What impact has this image had on sales management? What can managers do to improve the image of selling?

2. "At the present time it is apparent that the popular perception of sales personnel and sales-type jobs is a bit negative." Is this statement accurate for a large part of society? What evidence would you cite to support it? What possible factors could have contributed to the development of such a perception?

3. The Kimberly Clark Corporation of Neenah, Wisconsin requires newly hired product managers to spend six months in the field working as sales representatives before returning to Neenah for assignment to a product line. An occasional objection is: "I didn't go to college for four years and then go on for an MBA to end up selling." Why would a company require six months of field selling experience as part of its training program? How would you handle the objection?

4. What are the major differences between industrial sales and retail sales?

5. How do you account for the finding that, despite the negative image of a sales career, most salespeople like their jobs?

6. The personal selling effort was shown to be only part of the total marketing effort. How does the personal selling force fit in? How important is it?

7. A common practice in some companies is to assign sales responsibilities to district and regional managers. In some companies, district and regional managers are responsible only for sales management activities. How can you explain this situation.

8. How does the job of selling differ for the following situations? What are the most important activities for each job?
   a. A Procter & Gamble sales representative selling soap and laundry products to grocery stores.
   b. An Eastman Kodak sales representative selling cameras to retail camera stores.
   c. A Scott Paper Company sales representative selling paper towels to manufacturers.
   d. A Phillips Petroleum sales representative selling lubricating greases to manufacturers.
   e. An Abbott Laboratories pharmaceutical representative calling on the medical profession.
   f. An Ohio Medical Products sales representative selling respiratory equipment to hospitals.

9. What type of sales training would be needed for the selling situations described in question 8?

10. Is the sales management task different for those selling situations listed in question 8?

11. The marketing manager of the Enterprise Corporation faced the problem of conflict between the sales manager and the advertising manager over the issue of budget allocation. The sales manager wanted to cut the advertising budget by $100,000 so that he could hire two more sales reps. The advertising manager objected claiming that advertising, rather than hiring more sales reps, was the most effective way to increase sales. As marketing manager how would you resolve this conflict?

12. What is involved in formulating the strategic program?

13. Marketing is being introduced into organizations that at one time paid little attention to the subject. Most medical organizations have become marketing oriented. Most public accounting firms now advertise, and some have hired marketing directors. How do you account for this delay? What selling activities do these organizations have to consider?

14. Recently, more and more women have entered the field of industrial selling. What unique problems might an industrial saleswoman face as opposed to a woman accountant? What problems might a woman accountant face that the industrial saleswoman would not encounter?

15. When asked in class if she would give expensive gifts to customers to keep their business, Karen said she would not, explaining, "I would try to persuade the customer that our products are better than others on the market and that they are fairly priced." Yet, five years later, Karen admits to giving

expensive gifts and vacation trips to customers, claiming: "Everybody else in this industry does it, so I have to do it to survive." How do you account for this change?

16. In the 1970s, worldwide shortages of gasoline prompted most companies to change their methods of marketing. What changes occurred in the field of selling?

Part 1

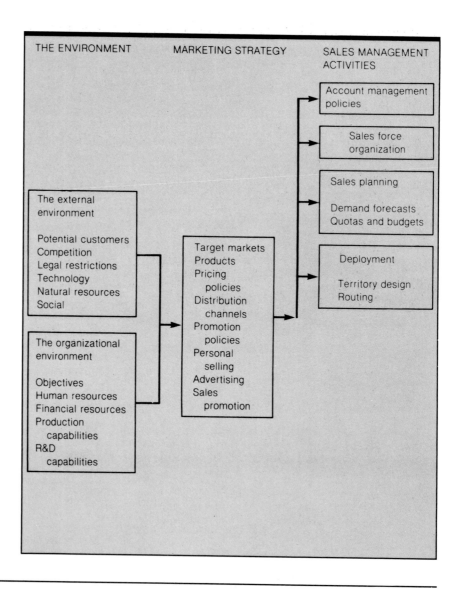

THE ENVIRONMENT MARKETING STRATEGY SALES MANAGEMENT ACTIVITIES

The external environment

Potential customers
Competition
Legal restrictions
Technology
Natural resources
Social

The organizational environment

Objectives
Human resources
Financial resources
Production
　capabilities
R&D
　capabilities

Target markets
Products
Pricing
　policies
Distribution
　channels
Promotion
　policies
Personal
　selling
Advertising
Sales
　promotion

Account management policies

Sales force organization

Sales planning

Demand forecasts
Quotas and budgets

Deployment

Territory design
Routing

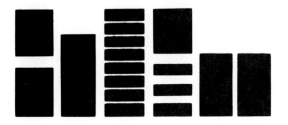

Formulation of a Strategic Sales Program

Part 1 examines the decisions and activities involved in formulating a strategic sales program. Chapter 2 explores the relationships among a firm's environment, the elements of its overall marketing strategy, and its personal selling program. Chapter 3 focuses on the needs of various types of customers and the design of appropriate account management policies for servicing those needs. Chapter 4 focuses on alternative ways of organizing the sales force to provide the desired level of customer contact and service. Chapter 5 discusses the conduct of a market opportunity analysis and forecasting methods: two key ingredients in a marketing and sales plan. Chapters 6 and 7 examine deployment decisions, including the design of sales territories, the determination of how many people are needed to provide adequate market coverage, methods of allocating a salesperson's effort within his or her territory, and the establishment of sales quotas.

Chapter **2**

The Environment, Marketing Planning, and the Sales Program

Developing a strategic sales plan involves understanding the impact of the environment on the firm's marketing plan and how the sales program fits into the firm's strategy. This chapter explores these questions and discusses the process by which marketing plans can be developed.

Evan-Picone: The History of a Successful Sportswear Marketer[1]

In the world of women's fashion, the term *sportswear* has nothing to do with athletics. Instead, it refers to a category of clothing in which each item—blazers, skirts, slacks, vests, etc.—is carefully coordinated and displayed with other items in the same line. Since each item is sold separately, women of all proportions can find a comfortable fit. More important, one purchase often leads to another because these clothes do not go out of style quickly, and customers often add to their outfits over time.

The market for women's sportswear is sizable, adding up to about $34 billion a year in wholesale sales. It is also highly competitive, however, with about 7,000 domestic sportswear manufacturers plus thousands of foreign competitors. Most manufacturers concentrate on one of two customer segments. One is a large group of price-conscious consumers who buy sportswear from J. C. Penney and other large chains that offer reasonable quality clothing at low prices. Another consumer segment consists of a growing number of more affluent shoppers who want high-quality clothes with labels bearing the names of well-known designers. In recent years, clothing from designers like Calvin Klein, Ralph Lauren, and Diane von Furstenberg have become a key weapon of department stores in their fight against the price competition of the discount chains.

One sportswear manufacturer has gained great success by focusing on a more narrowly defined group of consumers. Evan-Picone makes high-quality, tailored sportswear with classic styling primarily for career women. One indication of the company's success is that Evan-Picone was the most frequently mentioned label in a recent survey of the purchase preferences of career women conducted by the Associated Merchandising Corporation. Another is the company's sales record—about $200 million in wholesale sales in 1982.

Behind the success of Evan-Picone are two men who learned the clothing business not in *haute couture* salons but in the rough-and-tumble New York garment trade. Chairman Joseph Picone is a native of Sicily and a master tailor who oversees the manufacturing side of the business. Irving Spitalnick, a salesman from Brooklyn, served as president and ran the firm's marketing program until he

---

[1] This example is based on material found in Louis Kraar, "Palm Beach Inc.'s Lucrative Labels," *Fortune*, January 15, 1979, pp. 104–7; "Apparel's Last Stand," *Business Week*, May 14, 1979, pp. 60–70; and "A Frayed Palm Beach Tries to Patch Itself Up," *Business Week*, May 24, 1982, pp. 161–64.

resigned in 1981. The Evan in the company name is from Picone's first partner, Charles Evans, now a real estate developer in New Jersey.

The "Evan-Picone look" in tailored women's wear was first invented in 1949. Then Picone figured out how to produce skirts in volume while still making them look custom-made by applying the section-shop method, which had been used for decades in making men's suits. He broke the production job down into 40 simple steps so that fairly unskilled sewing machine operators could make the garments on an assembly line. Picone supervised the work carefully, however, and had certain finishing touches done by hand, such as making the buttonholes and doing the final stitching.

Acquisition and a New Strategy

By 1962, Evan-Picone had a sales volume of about $12 million. Then the firm caught the eye of Revlon, which acquired it as a means of diversifying outside the cosmetics business. As acquiring companies often do, Revlon imposed a new and different set of objectives on Evan-Picone's management—objectives that required major changes in the firm's marketing strategy. As Spitalnick said, "Without trying to interfere, Revlon was a giant interference."

Although Evan-Picone had gained its initial success by focusing on an exclusive clientele, Revlon's objective was to expand the firm's sales volume by broadening its customer base. To do this, Revlon urged it to manufacture a broader variety of clothes, including items in the lower price ranges, such as jeans. Reaching a broader target market also required more extensive retail distribution. To convince a broader range of retailers to carry the firm's clothes, Evan-Picone's sales force was expanded to 28 people who made frequent calls on buyers in department stores and specialty shops. Finally, to service its expanded retailer network, the firm was forced to maintain a large warehouse of inventory.

The new marketing strategy was successful in expanding Evan-Picone's sales volume. The firm's sales doubled to about $25 million in five years. However, the increased distribution expenses and overhead caused the company's profits to fall from about 10 percent of sales to a barely marginal level. And even worse, the firm's foray into the production of a wider variety of mass-appeal clothing items severely damaged its image of quality in consumers' minds.

Another New Strategy Leads to a Comeback

Picone bought back the shell of his company from Revlon in 1967 and set out to restore the quality of the garments. A new marketing strategy to aid the firm's recovery was devised by Spitalnick. It was based on his belief that "a giant wave of women would go to work not only as sales clerks and secretaries but as managers. And the oncoming executive women would not want to wear flimsy clothes."

To appeal to this new target market, the firm's product line was reduced and redesigned. A line of well-tailored, easy-to-care-for garments was made from the sturdy suiting fabrics that had been traditionally reserved for men.

Since the company's target market and product line were now more narrowly defined, it had to be more selective in choosing retail outlets to distribute its product. The total number of retailers carrying Evan-Picone clothes was reduced from 5,000 to fewer than 900. Today most of the firm's sales come from only 80 of the nation's largest and best-known department store chains.

To motivate the big-name department stores to gamble on Evan-Picone's comeback, Spitalnick promised to supply clothes of designer quality at prices at least 30 percent lower than those with other distinguished labels. He also pledged to give the store active help in merchandising Evan-Picone clothes to consumers. To accomplish this, Spitalnick devised an entirely new sales program. All of the firm's 28 salespeople were fired and replaced with five "merchandising representatives." Instead of concentrating solely on executives and department buyers, as the old sales force had, the new representatives devoted most of their efforts to a group closer to the final customer—the sales clerks. The representatives staged fashion clinics for the clerks in each store or chain carrying Evan-Picone clothes. These clinics were designed to provide the clerks with general information about fashion trends, specific information about new items in the Evan-Picone line, and advice on how to coordinate and sell the firm's clothes. The sales clerks and supervisors attending each clinic were also provided with useful sales promotion items such as gold-colored notebooks for listing the names and sizes of regular customers. These were designed to help the selling efforts of both the store and Evan-Picone.

The new sales program was so successful that it was rapidly expanded. Today, the firm has 16 representatives who conduct more than 300 fashion clinics each year.

As the firm's new marketing strategy began to produce successful results, a new crisis developed. By 1972, the growing demand for Evan-Picone clothing had overwhelmed both the firm's financial resources and its production capacity. Joseph Picone felt it was time to take on a partner, but he was wary of being smothered by another domineering parent company after his experience with Revlon. The problem was solved when Picone and Spitalnick were introduced to Elmer Ward, Jr., president of Palm Beach, the men's clothing manufacturer. As Spitalnick says, "We had good chemistry from the first day."

Both firms benefited when Palm Beach purchased Evan-Picone for about $4.7 million. Two of Palm Beach's seven plants were not fully utilized, so Picone solved his capacity problem by quickly converting them to the production of women's sportswear. Thus, the acquisition not only provided Evan-Picone with the additional capacity and resources needed for further growth, but also helped improve Palm Beach's return on investment. Return on equity rose from slightly over 6 percent in 1972, when Palm Beach acquired Evan-Picone, to over 25 percent in 1978. This growth is even more impressive when it is compared to total apparel industry performance, which showed a return on equity decline from approximately 11 percent to 8 percent for the same period.

Starting in 1978, the wisdom of Evan-Picone's unique marketing strategy and sales plan and the benefits of its merger with Palm Beach became even more apparent to both firms. Evan-Picone's sales shot up from $70 million in 1978 to nearly $200 million in 1981. Stimulated by its subsidiary's fantastic performance, Palm Beach's total sales volume more than doubled during the same three-year period to $497 million, while operating profits jumped 40 percent to $42.9 million. Nearly two thirds of those profits—an estimated $30 million—were generated by Evan-Picone.

Evan-Picone's performance sagged a bit in early 1982 because of changes in the market environment. Consumers began to tire of the kind of conservative suits and blazers that were the foundation of the company's line. As a result, orders started to fall, and Palm Beach reported a 29 percent drop in earnings for the first quarter. Without changing its basic marketing strategy or sales approach, Evan-Picone did adjust some of its tactics in response to new customer desires. For one thing, the firm began to change its product mix. More than a third of its fall line for 1982 consisted of lighter-weight, more casual clothes. To communicate these changes to customers, about $4.5 million was budgeted for the firm's first-ever national advertising campaign. While it may prove impossible for Evan-Picone to recapture and maintain the meteoric rates of growth it experienced in the late 1970s, its basic strategy—together with its tactical adjustments to changing consumer tastes—has worked to preserve its premier position in the women's sportswear business. Evan-Picone continues to anchor the better women's sportswear departments in most major department and specialty stores. As the chairman of Lord and Taylor recently pointed out, "Evan-Picone is still very important to most stores."

Relationships among Environmental Factors, Marketing Plans, and the Sales Program

The history of Evan-Picone illustrates three important points concerning how factors in the environment influence marketing and sales management decisions and programs.

1. To be successful, a firm's marketing plans must be adapted to the influences and constraints imposed by both the external and internal corporate environments. As these environments change, appropriate adjustments should be made in the firm's marketing strategy.

When Evan-Picone was purchased by Revlon, for instance, new market share and sales volume objectives were imposed by the parent company. In response, Evan-Picone's managers had to revise their marketing strategy to include a broader target market, a wider product line, lower price lines, and more extensive retail distribution. On the other hand, the company's successful comeback strategy in the early 1970s was keyed to the rapidly growing trend of women working in managerial jobs. To adjust to this trend, the company narrowed its product line and concentrated on only high quality, easy-to-care-for clothes. It focused its distribution on well-known department stores in major urban areas. The increased production capacity and financial resources that resulted from the firm's acquisition by Palm Beach enabled this new marketing strategy to be implemented more effectively.

2. A firm's sales program is only one part of an integrated marketing strategy. As changes are made in other elements of the marketing strategy, the sales program must be adjusted if it is to remain effective.

When Evan-Picone was owned by Revlon, its marketing strategy called for extensive retail distribution; consequently, the sales program involved a large sales force with each salesperson covering a relatively small territory. To maximize the number of retail stores carrying the company's line, salespeople were instructed to call on store executives and department buyers and "push" the firm's products into as many stores as possible. The change to a new marketing strategy in the early 1970s resulted in a drastic reduction in the size of the sales force due to a more selective retail distribution policy. Also, the new strategy attempted to build a strong brand image so that consumer preferences would help "pull" the company's clothes into the desired department stores. Finally, account management policies were changed and sales representatives began to focus on providing retailers with merchandising assistance in the form of fashion clinics for store sales clerks and sales promotion items.

3. Regardless of how well conceived a sales program is or how well it is integrated into a firm's overall marketing strategy, its implementation depends on the willingness and ability of individual members of the sales force to carry out its policies and procedures. Factors in the external and corporate environments can directly influence a salesperson's actions in the field and his or her ability to achieve the desired level of performance.

Evan-Picone's marketing strategy in the Revlon era resulted in a loss of the brand's quality image and identity. The company's attempt to sell lower priced clothes in the mass market put it in direct competition with many other firms. As a result, a sales force of 28 people produced only about $25 million in sales and marginal profits. The firm's more recent strategy, however, has resulted in strong brand identity and consumer preference. Few competitors offer designer-quality clothes at less than designer prices, and demand for such clothes has grown rapidly with the increased participation of women in the labor force. Consequently, a smaller sales force of only 16 people produces nearly $200 million in sales and very satisfactory profits.

Each of these relationships may seem self-evident, but they must be carefully considered when planning a firm's marketing strategy and sales program. The remainder of this chapter therefore examines the marketing planning process in more detail. Particular attention is given to: (1) how marketing and sales plans are adapted to environmental conditions and (2) how environmental factors impose constraints on the ability of individual salespeople to implement a sales program successfully. In Chapter 3, we turn our attention to the design of strategic sales programs that are both integrated into other elements of the firm's marketing mix and adapted to the needs of potential customers.

Marketing Planning

The Importance of Planning

Planning is deciding what to do in the present to achieve what is desired in the future. In other words, planning requires decisions concerning the firm's goals and objectives for the future and the actions that should be taken to accomplish them.

Planning involves an analysis of where the organization is and how it got there, and a projection of where the organization will end up if it continues to move in the same direction. Given such an analysis, the company can compare where it wants to be with where it is likely to be. Management can then formulate a strategy for moving closer to what is desired. Thus, a *strategy* is a statement of the methods and procedures that will be used to reach certain objectives.[2]

A strategy provides a broad blueprint to guide the firm's future efforts; however, more detailed programs or *tactics* must be developed to spell out how resources are to be allocated and what actions are to be taken, by whom, and when. To use a football analogy, the overall game plan formulated by the coaching staff is a strategy. It is a broad statement of what the team should do to win the game, given its strengths and weaknesses and those of the opponent. One such strategy might be to keep the ball on the ground and run at the tackles. The specific plays designed and practiced by the team are their tactics. Although the quarterback's selection of plays should be guided by the game plan, the tactics used must be adapted to the specific situations encountered during the game, such as an occasional pass to keep the defense honest.

In today's changing environment, planning is crucial to the success of the enterprise. Yet, because things change so rapidly, some managers argue that planning is a waste of time. They point out that changing conditions may force management to revise its plan or scrap it entirely in favor of a new one. Although this is true, it is still essential that management have a plan to guide the organization. Without a clearly stated plan, the firm may overreact to short-lived disruptions in the environment, and erratic changes in direction can cause confusion among both employees and customers. As one author suggests, a plan is like the rudder on a ship. The plan may be completely disrupted because of changing conditions just as a ship's rudder may not be very useful during heavy seas. Yet the rudder is essential for providing direction to the ship and holding it on course after the storm is over. So, too, the plan helps to guide the firm safely past rocks and shoals to reach long-term goals.[3]

Evan-Picone is a good example of a firm that adjusted its tactics in response to

---

[2] From Mark E. Stern, *Marketing Planning: A Systems Approach* (New York: McGraw-Hill, 1966), p. XII. Copyright 1966, McGraw-Hill, Inc. Used with the permission of McGraw-Hill Book Company.

[3] Thomas F. Stroh, *Managing the Sales Function* (New York: McGraw-Hill, 1978), p. 59.

changing environmental circumstances without abandoning its basic strategy. The firm added more light-weight, casual clothes to its product mix in order to satisfy changing consumer desires, and it initiated an advertising campaign to communicate those product changes to potential customers. But the firm's actions continued to be guided by its basic strategy of producing high-quality clothes for working women and using a small sales force to distribute them through a selected group of department and specialty stores.

The Planning Process

A sales program constitutes only one part of a marketing plan, and the marketing plan is only one element of the total strategic planning process in most firms. This is particularly true for companies with multiple divisions and those that have divided their operations into "strategic business units" in order to improve the coordination of planning and the allocation of company resources across related groups of products or markets. Since such firms involve multiple "businesses," their overall strategic planning process typically occurs in several stages and involves a series of different plans to guide activities at different levels of the organization. This hierarchy of plans commonly includes:

The Corporate Strategic Plan. This plan specifies the range of activities to be included in the firm's mission, spells out corporate objectives—such as targets for revenue growth and return on investment—and establishes broad strategies for new business development, acquisitions and divestitures. Financial analyses and projections are also an important part of the corporate strategic plan since they typically spell out how corporate resources are to be allocated across the firm's various divisions or business units.

Strategic Business Unit Plans. Included here are the specific mission and objectives of each business unit, as well as the coordination of the various functional plans—usually including financial operations and marketing plans—that spell out how the unit will achieve its objectives.

Marketing Plans. These plans outline specific marketing objectives for each product or product line, analyze marketing opportunities, identify target markets, and integrate the various elements of the marketing mix into a consistent marketing strategy.

Programs for Individual Marketing Functions. These include the strategies, policies, and activities to be followed by each functional area in the process of implementing a marketing plan. This is where a strategic sales program—such as Evan-Picone's program of focusing sales effort on the retail salespeople in carefully selected major department stores—fits into a firm's overall strategic planning process.

The ways in which firms assign responsibilities for developing the above types of plans vary considerably according to company size, the complexity of formal planning procedures, and management's preferences. While the specifics of the total, corporate planning process are beyond the scope of this book,[4] it is important to remember that marketing plans and sales programs are only component parts of a larger whole. Corporate and business unit strategic plans are an important part of the organizational environment that must be considered when developing marketing and sales programs. They help define the mission and objectives to be accomplished and determine the amount and kinds of resources allocated to the marketing of specific products. With those constraints in mind, the essential steps involved in the marketing planning process are outlined in Figure 2–1 and discussed in the following sections.

Company Mission and Goals. A statement of an organization's mission attempts to answer the most basic questions about its reason for being. What is our business? What should it be? These seem like simple questions, but they are often difficult for management to answer. In fact, many organizations never bother to define or communicate their mission clearly. Others state their missions too broadly. For example, some managers say that their purpose is simply to make a profit. As a statement of mission, however, this says nothing about how that profit is to be earned, so it provides no guidance for selecting among various marketing opportunities and alternative strategies.

On the other hand, many organizations define their missions too narrowly by focusing on the production of a particular product or service. As technology and customer needs change, specific products and services become obsolete, and firms that define their mission in such narrow terms can become obsolete as well. There are few streetcar companies today, for instance, but many organizations are attempting to satisfy the need for urban mass transit through a variety of other means.

The most appropriate way for a firm to define its mission is in terms of the broad human needs it will try to satisfy. Volkswagen might define its mission as providing economical private transportation, while Walt Disney Productions describes its mission as providing family entertainment.

When an organization's mission is defined in terms of satisfying a need, it becomes easier to identify attractive marketing opportunities. When an oil company defines its mission as satisfying people's energy needs, for instance, it is then clear that the company should be exploring a variety of energy sources—such as solar power—in addition to locating new sources of petroleum. Similarly, a clearly defined mission helps management evaluate available opportunities and avoid those that are inconsistent with the firm's purpose.

Although a clear sense of mission is a necessary first step in planning, this mission must be translated into more specific objectives for each business unit and each functional area of the firm, including marketing. To achieve its mission of satisfying the need for economical private transportation, Volkswagen's mar-

---

[4] There are a number of excellent sources that the interested reader might turn to for more information about the strategic planning process. These include: Charles W. Hofer and Dan Schendel, *Strategy Formulation: Analytical Concepts* (St. Paul, Minn.: West Publishing, 1978); David W. Cravens, *Strategic Marketing* (Homewood, Ill.: Richard D. Irwin, 1982); and George A. Steiner, *Strategic Planning* (New York: The Free Press, 1979).

Figure 2–1
The marketing planning process

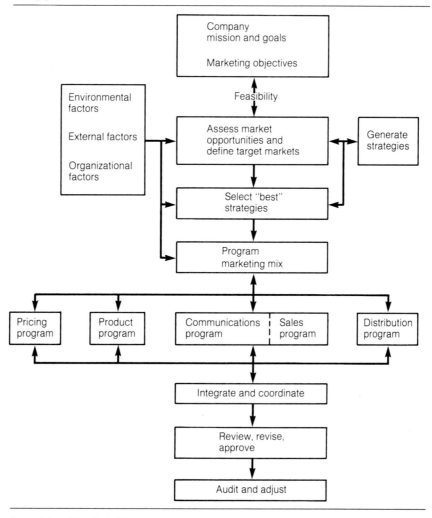

Source: Adapted from Mark E. Stern, *Marketing Planning: A Systems Approach* (New York: McGraw-Hill Book, 1966), p. 13. Copyright © 1966, McGraw-Hill, Inc. Used with the permission of McGraw-Hill Book Company

keting department might be assigned the objective of securing 1 percent more share of the American market over the next year. Such detailed functional objectives guide the planning of each department within the organization, ensure that the plans of each functional area will be reasonably consistent, and motivate the personnel in each functional area by providing them with specific goals. Specifying marketing objectives is one thing, however; determining whether they are feasible is another. The latter consideration involves an assessment of the market opportunity available to the firm.

Market Opportunity Analysis. In the broadest sense, a market opportunity exists whenever some human need is unsatisfied. However, an unsatisfied need represents a viable and attractive opportunity for a firm only if:

1. The opportunity is consistent with the mission and objectives of the firm.
2. There are enough potential customers for the needed product or service so that the total potential sales volume is, or will be, substantial.
3. The firm has the necessary resources and expertise to capture an adequate share of the total market.

Thus, Evan-Picone's decision to make high-quality clothes for career women was based on a judgment that such women represented a large and rapidly growing potential market and that Evan-Picone's production methods would enable it to capture a substantial share.

Evaluating market opportunities, then, involves first evaluating the various environmental factors affecting the market and estimating the total market potential for a particular good or service. Next, the firm must evaluate its capabilities and strengths compared with those of competitors to estimate the share of the total market potential it can reasonably hope to secure. Later, after a specific marketing strategy has been determined, the firm can develop sales forecasts of the actual sales volume it expects to attain over a specified time.

These estimates of total market potential, company sales potential, and sales forecasts are critical to the firm's sales plans. They provide the basis for defining sales territories, deploying salespeople, and setting sales quotas. Methods for analyzing market opportunities and generating sales forecasts are examined in more detail later in this book.

One other point to keep in mind concerning market opportunities is that they usually do not involve every consumer or organizational buyer in the marketplace. This reflects the fact that people—and organizations—differ. They have different needs, attitudes, and amounts of money to spend. As a result, they tend to buy different kinds of products and services for different reasons. Therefore, market opportunities must be defined—and marketing strategies developed—for specific target markets. These target markets consist of only one or a few market segments with relatively homogeneous potential customers.

Generate Strategies. Strategy generation is a creative task. There are typically several strategies that will achieve the same objective. For example, a firm interested in increasing its share of the market might attempt to acquire new customers by either (1) positioning itself head-to-head against major competitors and attempting to establish a sustainable competitive advantage on some dimension-like product quality or low price, or (2) differentiating itself from competitors by focusing on a unique market niche where the competition does not have a strong position. Table 2–1 outlines a number of possible strategies. It also summarizes a number of functional programs—including variations in the amount and emphasis of personal selling efforts—that would be appropriate for implementing each strategy.

The key at this stage is to be as creative as possible. The idea is not to evaluate

Table 2–1
Some appropriate marketing strategies and functional programs for achieving various marketing objectives

Marketing Objective	Potential Marketing Strategies	Functional Programs for Implementing Strategies
Achieve viable level of sales volume (for new product type; introductory stage of life cycle)	Stimulate primary demand—increase number of potential users by: (1) increasing willingness to buy	a. Increase awareness through heavy advertising of product benefits b. Focus sales efforts on potential new accounts; demonstrate superior benefits of new product c. Expand variety of offerings through development of product-line extensions
	(2) Increasing customer's ability to buy	a. Penetration pricing b. Attractive credit terms c. Introductory sales promotions d. Use sales efforts and trade promotion to attain more extensive distribution e. Use sales engineering and installation services to increase compatibility of new product with customers' existing operations
Market share growth (for products with low shares in growing markets)	Stimulate selective demand—acquisition of new customers by: (1) Head-to-head positioning	a. Develop superior product features b. Reduce price (if costs are lower than competitors') c. Spend more than competitors on advertising sales force, sales promotion d. Use sales effort and trade promotion to attain broader/better distribution than competitors
	(2) Differentiated positioning	a. Identify market segment with unique needs not being satisfied by competitors b. Design unique product benefits/services to satisfy target segment c. Develop unique distribution channels d. Focus sales effort on target customers and stress unique benefits/comparisons in presentations

Table 2–1 *(concluded)*

Marketing Objective	Potential Marketing Strategies	Functional Programs for Implementing Strategies
Market share maintenance (for products with a high current share of growing markets)	Stimulate selective demand— acquisition of customers new to the market (e.g. late adopters) by: (1) Head-to-head positioning (2) Differentiated positioning	(See above) (See above)
	Retention of current customers by: (1) Maintaining satisfaction	*a.* Product improvement/ quality control *b.* Reminder advertising to maintain familiarity *c.* Sales efforts focused on service and maintenance of current accounts
	(2) Simplifying the purchase process	*a.* Improve logistics/ delivery time *b.* Develop complete product lines *c.* Price protection contracts *d.* "Sole-source" selling *e.* "Systems" selling
	(3) Reduce attractiveness of switching	*a.* Develop brand extensions; multiple brands *b.* Competitive prices and promotions *c.* "Key" account or national account services *d.* Automated re-order system
Cash flow maximization (for products with a high share of mature markets)	Retention of current customers by: (1) Maintaining satisfaction (2) Simplifying purchase (3) Reduce attractiveness of switching	(See above) (See above) (See above)
	Increase rate of purchase by current users	*a.* Identify and promote alternative uses *b.* Reduce price; quantity discounts *c.* "Sole-source" selling *d.* Increase frequency of sales calls on major accounts
Harvesting (for products in mature or declining markets)	Retention of customers with minimum effort	*a.* Maintain quality of existing products *b.* Minimizing product improve- ment/line extension efforts *c.* Competitive pricing *d.* Reduce advertising and sales promotion to maintenance levels *e.* Concentrate sales force efforts on maintenance of profitable accounts

Source: Parts of this table were adapted from material found in Joseph P. Guiltinan and Gordon W. Paul, *Marketing Management: Strategies and Programs* (New York: McGraw-Hill, 1982), chap. 6.

strategies but to generate them. Listing some far-out strategies is not only acceptable but also desirable. Later stages in the process will reduce this original list to a more reasonable set; however, the generation of as many ideas as possible to begin with will ensure that the better strategies are entertained when evaluating alternatives. The most sophisticated evaluation procedure "can do no better than to select the best strategy that has been proposed."[5]

Select Strategies. "The basis for selecting the more promising strategies should be related directly to the marketing objectives. For example, if the major marketing objective of a company is to increase market share, then the strategies yielding high market share increases should be retained for more detailed analysis during the integration phase of the planning effort."[6] Typically, a company will have several marketing objectives, and the strategy that is best for one might be detrimental in achieving another. Consequently, the best overall strategy may not be the best for any single objective.

Program Marketing Mix. As mentioned, a marketing program reflects a particular allocation of financial and human resources. The decision involves three questions: (1) How much is going to be spent on the total marketing effort? (2) How is that expenditure going to be allocated among the elements of the marketing mix? (3) How are the dollars and effort allocated to an element going to be divided among the possible activities associated with that element? This is where the formation of the firm's strategic sales program enters the planning picture; it is one part of the firm's communications program. As suggested by Table 2–1, both the amount of resources that should be devoted to the sales function and the activities to be emphasized by the sales force are shaped by the overall marketing strategy to be pursued and the kinds of communication tasks necessary to implement that strategy.

Review and Revision. Those in charge of the functional areas of the business are typically charged with generating plans for the functions they supervise. This raises the possibility that the marketing plan prepared by a product manager may be incompatible with the business unit's financial or production plans. For example, the cash flows generated by projected product sales might be insufficient or provide too low a return on capital invested to produce the product. The various functional plans, therefore, must be reviewed and integrated into a cohesive whole at the business unit and corporate level.

Audit and Adjust. Today's volatile environment makes planning crucial and also necessitates periodic evaluations of those plans. As competitors adjust their strategies and other environmental conditions change, it may be necessary to revise the firm's plans and programs to adapt to the new conditions. When goals and objectives have been spelled out in specific and measurable terms during the planning process, controlling the marketing plan is rather straightforward. It involves periodic comparisons of actual results with the sales volume, market share, and expense and other objectives specified in the plan. When the results deviate

---

[5] Stern, *Marketing Planning*, p. 15.
[6] Ibid.

from planned levels, management can attempt to find out why and, if necessary, take corrective action. This could involve adjusting specific elements of the marketing mix, adopting a new marketing strategy, or possibly reevaluating the market opportunities pursued by the firm. The sales manager, as we have seen, plays a major role in this evaluation and control process since he or she is responsible for evaluating the results of the sales program. Part 3 of this book is devoted to a discussion of this control and adjustment process.

Impact of the Environment on Marketing and Sales Planning

Throughout the planning process, the marketing manager must carefully consider the influences and constraints imposed by environmental factors that are beyond his or her control. Factors both external to the firm and within the organization affect the feasibility of various marketing strategies and programs. Environmental factors influence marketing strategies and programs in four basic ways.

1. Environmental forces can constrain the organization's ability to pursue certain marketing strategies or activities. An example is when the government declares the sale of a product to be illegal or when a well-entrenched competitor makes it unattractive for the firm to enter a new market.
2. Environmental variables, and changes in those variables over time, help determine the ultimate success or failure of marketing strategies. The rapid growth in the number of women joining the labor force in recent years, for instance, has made Evan-Picone's strategy of appealing to working women increasingly successful.
3. Changes in the environment can create new marketing opportunities for an organization, as when the discovery of a new technology allows the development of new products.
4. Environmental variables themselves are affected and changed by marketing activities, as when new products and promotional programs help to change lifestyles and social values. In view of the increased activity by consumer groups, environmentalists, and other public-interest groups and agencies, marketers today must consider how proposed programs will affect the environment as well as how the environment will affect the programs.

Consequently, one of the most important—but increasingly difficult—parts of a marketing manager's job is to monitor the environment, predict how it might change, and develop marketing strategies and plans well suited to environmental conditions. Because it is one part of the overall marketing plan, the strategic sales program must be adapted to the environmental circumstances faced by the firm as a whole. Some specific environmental factors to be considered when developing marketing plans in general, and strategic sales programs in particular, are examined below.

The External Environment

Factors in the external environment are beyond the control of the individual manager; however, companies do try to influence external conditions over the long run through political lobbying, public relations campaigns, and the like. For the most part, the marketer—and the sales manager—must take the environment as it exists and adapt strategies to fit it. The variables in the external environment that have an impact on marketing programs can be grouped into five broad categories: (1) economic, (2) social, (3) legal/political, (4) natural, and (5) technical.

The Economic Environment.   People and organizations cannot buy goods and services unless they have the money. The total potential demand for a firm's product, depends on the country's economic conditions—the amount of growth in the economy, the unemployment rate, and the level of inflation. These factors must be considered when analyzing market opportunities.

Another critical economic variable is the amount of competition in the firm's industry—both the number of competing firms and their relative strengths in the marketplace. Ideally, a company's marketing and sales programs should be designed to gain a differential advantage over competitors.[7] For example, Lanier Business Products, rather than matching the claims of technical superiority made by its larger competitors, instead instructed its sales force to stress the simplicity of its products and the increases in productivity resulting from their use.

A third aspect of the economic environment is the existing structure of distribution in an industry. This includes the number, types, and availability of wholesalers, retailers, and other middlemen that a firm might use to distribute its product. Much of a firm's personal selling effort may be directed at trying to persuade such middlemen to stock and provide marketing support for the company's products. The firm may thereby gain an adequate level of distribution to ultimate consumers or business users.

The Social Environment.   Markets consist of people. As the number and demographic, educational, and other characteristics of the population change over time, market opportunities change. This also affects opportunities in industrial markets, since an organization's demand for goods and services is derived from the demand for its own products.

The way potential customers think is an even more important determinant of whether a marketing strategy or sales program will succeed or fail. Changes in social values and lifestyles influence what people buy and their reactions to various marketing activities and promotional appeals.

Social and Ethical Dilemmas.   The social environment affects salespeople in a number of ways. Some recent concerns that have received public attention are discrimination in hiring and promotion practices, high-pressure selling tac-

---

[7] Alan J. Dubinsky, Eric N. Berkowitz, and William Rudelius, "Ethical Problems of Field Sales Personnel," *MSU Business Topics*, Summer 1980, p. 12.

tics, and lavish entertaining and other expense account abuses. These issues are discussed throughout the text. They all reflect the fact that sometimes inconsistencies between social values and common business practices raise thorny ethical questions for salespeople and their managers. An *ethical question* arises when an individual feels pressure to take actions that are inconsistent with what he or she feels to be right; either in terms of personal values or the welfare of his or her customers.[8] The dilemma is that such pressures often arise because management—or salespeople themselves—believe that a questionable action is necessary to close a sale or maintain parity with competition. This point was illustrated by a survey of 59 top sales executives concerning commercial bribery—attempts to influence a potential customer by giving gifts or kickbacks. While nearly two thirds of the executives considered bribes unethical and did not want to pay them, 88 percent also felt that *not* paying bribes might put their firms at a competitive disadvantage. Uncertainty about what to do in such situations—often due in part to a lack of direction from management—may lead to job stress, poor sales performance, and unhappy customers.

The broad range of ethical questions faced by salespeople, and some indications about what managers might do to help their subordinates deal with such questions, are illustrated by the results of a recent survey of 160 sales representatives from 30 different companies.[9] Respondents were presented with 12 selling situations and asked (1) whether they thought the situation posed an ethical question, (2) whether their company had an existing policy about how to deal with such situations, and (3) whether they would like a stated company policy concerning the issue. The percentage of respondents who answered "definitely yes" or "probably yes" to the three questions are shown in Table 2–2.

The survey's results suggest that the more subjective the situation, the greater the proportion of salespeople who thought it posed an ethical problem. For example, the two cases where a majority of respondents agreed that an ethical question existed involved the issue of whether to let personalities affect the terms of sale and whether to offer less competitive prices or terms when the salesperson's firm is the customer's sole source of supply. On the other hand, respondents were least likely to see ethical dilemmas in those situations involving practices that could be justified as merely "good ways of doing business;" such as circumventing the purchasing department to increase the chances of a sale (backdoor selling) or asking purchasers for information about competitors.

The findings in Table 2–2 also suggest that many situations salespeople see as involving ethical questions are not addressed by management directives and that many sales personnel want more explicit guidelines to help them resolve such issues. One way that management can help salespeople avoid the stress and inconsistent performance associated with ethical dilemmas, then, is to develop written policies that address problem situations. The important thing, however, is not just to have a written policy, but to have one that is *helpful* to the sales force. Such policies should provide clear guidelines for decision making and action so

---

[8] *Sales and Marketing Management,* May 10, 1976, p. 36.
[9] Dubinsky et al., "Ethical Problems," pp. 11–16.

Table 2–2
Evaluation of twelve sales situations or practices

Situation or Practice	Respondents Replying "Definitely Yes" or "Probably Yes"					
	An Ethical Question?		Have Stated Policy Now?		Want a Stated Policy?	
	Rank	Percent	Rank	Percent	Rank	Percent
1. Allowing personalities—liking for one purchaser and disliking for another—to affect price, delivery, and other decisions regarding the terms of sale.	1	52	3	47	3	57
2. Having less competitive prices or other terms for buyers who use your firm as the sole source of supply than for firms for which you are one of two or more suppliers.	2	50	2	52	1	61
3. Making statements to an existing purchaser that exaggerate the seriousness of his problem in order to obtain a bigger order or other concessions.	3	49	7	31	6	44
4. Soliciting low priority or low volume business that the salesperson's firm will not deliver or service in an economic slowdown or periods of resource shortages.	4	42	6	34	5	46
5. Giving preferential treatment to purchasers who higher levels of the firm's own management prefer or recommend.	5	41	10	28	8	40
6. Giving physical gifts, such as free sales promotion prizes or "purchase-volume incentive bonuses," to a purchaser.	6	39	1	56	2	60
7. Using the firm's economic power to obtain premium prices or other concessions from buyers.	7	37	5	37	7	42
8. Giving preferential treatment to customers who are also good suppliers.	8	36	8	30	10	33
9. Seeking information from purchasers on competitors' quotations for the purpose of submitting another quotation.	9	34	9	29	9	39
10. Providing free trips, free luncheons or dinners, or other free entertainment to a purchaser.	9	34	3	47	4	55
11. Attempting to reach and influence other departments (such as engineering) directly rather than go through the purchasing department when such avoidance increases the likelihood of a sale.	11	29	12	22	11	30
12. Gaining information about competitors by asking purchasers.	12	27	11	29	11	30

Source: Alan J. Dubinsky, Eric N. Berkowitz and William Rudelius, "Ethical Problems of Field Sales Personnel," *MSU Business Topics,* Summer 1980, p. 14.

that employees facing similar situations will handle them in a way consistent with the organization's goals. To further reduce uncertainty, policies must also be clearly communicated to both sales personnel and customers. Periodic review sessions—perhaps involving the company's legal staff—can help salespeople remember what the policies are as well as provide an opportunity to discuss any new or unusual situations that might arise. Perhaps the most effective way for management to influence the ethical performance of their salespeople, however, is to lead by example. Formal policies do not have much impact when ambiguous signals are sent because top management gives lip service to one set of standards while practicing another. This problem was evidenced by the comments of a purchasing manager in another study of business ethics: "Our management doesn't want my buyers influenced by the very things they're telling our sales force to do to make sales."[10]

The Legal/Political Environment. Many of the changes in society's values are eventually reflected in new laws and government regulations. Throughout this century, the number of laws regulating the conduct of business—including personal selling activities—has increased dramatically at all levels of government. Two broad categories of laws are particularly relevant to the formulation of sales programs: (1) antitrust laws and (2) consumer *protection* legislation.

The antitrust laws are aimed primarily at preserving and enhancing competition among firms in an industry. They restrict marketing practices that would tend to reduce competition and give one firm a monopoly through unfair competition. Some antitrust law provisions that are of great relevance to sales management are outlined in Table 2–3.

The restrictions on anticompetitive behavior spelled out in the antitrust laws apply to firms selling goods or services to middlemen, business users, or ultimate consumers. When a firm sells to consumer markets, however, it faces additional restrictions imposed by federal, state, and local consumer protection laws. These laws are aimed more directly at protecting consumer welfare by setting standards of quality and safety for specific products. They also require that consumers be provided with accurate information to use in making purchase decisions. Since personal selling is one means of providing consumers with information, many laws requiring full disclosure and prohibiting deceptive or misleading information have a direct impact on selling activities.

One other type of legislation has a direct effect on sales managers as they attempt to implement their sales programs: the equal employment opportunity laws. It is unlawful to discriminate against a person in either hiring or promotion because of race, religion, nationality, sex, or age. For this reason, certain types of aptitude tests are illegal if they are culturally or sexually biased or if they are not valid predictors of a person's job performance. The legal aspects of recruiting and selecting sales representatives are examined in Chapter 11.

The Natural Environment. The natural environment is an important consideration in the development of marketing and sales plans. It is the source of all the raw materials and energy resources needed to make, package, promote, and distribute a product. Over the past decade, firms in many industries—such as steel, aluminum, plastics, and synthetic fibers—have encountered resource or energy shortages that forced them to limit the sales of their products to custom-

---

[10] William Rudelius and Rogene A. Buchholz, "Ethical Problems of Purchasing Managers," *Harvard Business Review*, March-April 1979, p. 8.

Table 2–3
Selected antitrust and consumer protection laws of particular relevance when formulating sales programs and policies

Antitrust provisions

Conspiracies among competing firms to *control their prices*, or to *allocate markets* among themselves, are *per se* illegal under the Sherman Act.

The Robinson-Patman Act prohibits a firm and its representatives from *discriminating in the prices or services* offered to competing customers. The major purpose of this law is to protect smaller customers from being placed at a competitive disadvantage by "key account" programs or price promotions which offer special incentives to larger buyers. However, the law does allow a marketer to grant discounts to larger buyers based on savings in the costs of manufacturing or distributing the product. Thus, some quantity discounts are legal.

Tying agreements, where a seller forces a buyer to purchase one product in order to gain the right to purchase another, are illegal under the Clayton and Sherman Acts. A computer manufacturer, for example, cannot force a customer to agree to buy cards, paper, and other supplies needed to run a computer as a precondition for buying the computer itself.

Reciprocal dealing arrangements, the "I'll buy from you if you buy from me" type of agreements, are illegal where the effect is to injure competition. Such arrangements do tend to be anticompetitive because large companies—which are large buyers as well as large suppliers—tend to have an advantage over smaller firms.

The Federal Trade Commission Act prohibits "unfair methods of competition" in general. Thus, deceptive product claims, interfering with the actions of a competitor's sales representative, and other unfair acts are all illegal.

Consumer protection provisions

The Fair Packaging and Labeling Act makes *unfair or deceptive packaging* or labeling of certain consumer commodities illegal.

The Truth-in-Lending Act requires *full disclosure of all finance charges* on consumer credit agreements.

State "cooling-off" laws allow consumers to cancel contracts signed with door-to-door sellers within a limited number of days after agreeing to such contracts.

The Federal Trade Commission requires that door-to-door salespeople who work for companies engaged in interstate commerce clearly announce their purpose when making calls on potential customers.

Many cities and towns have so-called Green River Ordinances, which require all door-to-door salespeople to obtain a license.

ers. One might assume that sales representatives could take life easy under such circumstances, letting customers come to them for badly needed goods. In fact, however, the sales force often has to work harder during product shortages, and well-formulated account management policies become even more crucial for the firm's success. During such periods the sales force is often required to help administer rationing programs, which allocate scarce supplies according to each customer's purchase history. Since shortages are usually temporary, though, sellers have to be sensitive to their customers' problems so they will not lose customers when the shortage is over. Consequently, account management policies must be formulated to treat all customers fairly, minimize conflict, and maintain the firm's competitive position for the future.[11]

The Technical Environment. The most obvious impact of the technical environment on marketing is in providing opportunities for new product development. Technical advances have been occurring at a rapidly increasing rate, and new products are accounting for an increasing percentage of total sales in many industries. In some divisions of the 3M Company, for example, more than half of current sales volume is generated by products that were not in existence five years ago. There are indications that the importance of new products to the marketing success of many firms will continue to accelerate. In one study involving more than 700 companies, managers expected new products to increase their companies' sales growth by an average of one third during the five year period 1982–87, while the portion of total company profits generated by new products during the same period was expected to be 40 percent.[12]

Rapid development of new products requires some adjustments in a firm's sales programs. New sales plans must be formulated, the sales representatives must be retained and, in some cases, new representatives must be hired.

Advancing technology is also affecting sales management in more direct ways. Improvements in transportation, communications, and data processing are changing the way sales territories are defined, sales representatives are deployed, and sales performance is evaluated and controlled in many companies. Indeed, new communications technologies—together with the escalating costs of a traditional field sales call—are changing the ways in which the personal selling function is carried out. The sample case is giving way to the video cassette, and telemarketing, teleconferencing, and computerized reordering systems are replacing the face-to-face sales call in a growing number of situations.[13] The impact of these new technologies in the sales force, and the conditions under which they are most likely to improve sales efficiency and effectiveness, are examined in more detail in Chapter 4.

Problems in Environmental Scanning and Forecasting. While it is clear that marketing and sales managers "should" keep a close watch on—and attempt to forecast changes in—the external environment as a basis for formulating marketing and sales plans, this is often easier said than done. Unfortunately, there are many examples of well-executed marketing and sales programs that came to grief because one or more elements of the environment changed unexpectedly. One example is Evan-Picone's problems as the result of a shift in preferences among working women toward more informal clothes. Another case is provided by the experiences of the video game division of the Parker Brothers toy company. In 1982, the division began marketing cartridges of popular video games, like "Frogger" and "Q-Bert," for use in Atari, Mattel and Texas Instruments home video machines. In its first year, the division racked up spectacular earnings of $20 million on sales of $74 million, and its management—like most in

---

[11] Michael B. Rothfeld, "A New Kind of Challenge for Salesmen," *Fortune*, April 1974, pp. 156–60.

[12] *New Products Management for the 1980's* (New York: Booz, Allen & Hamilton, 1982).

[13] "Rebirth of a Salesman: Willy Loman Goes Electronic," *Business Week*, February 27, 1984, pp. 103–4.

the industry—assumed the good times would roll on. Consequently, the game company geared up to produce $225 million of cartridges in fiscal 1983. Unfortunately, the home video market became saturated, hardware companies closed up shop, and game companies flooded the market, driving prices down. Instead of selling $225 million, Parker Brothers had to settle for revenues of $117 million, took a large loss, and did not expect the division to become profitable again until at least 1986.[14]

Part of the reason for such failures to predict changes in the environment is that many corporations are not sophisticated in the techniques they employ for environmental scanning and forecasting. In a recent study involving 48 organizations, it was found that business corporations tend to be less sophisticated in their approach to environmental analysis than either consulting firms or government agencies. Partly because of the pressures of day-to-day operating activities, environmental scanning and forecasting within business firms occurs primarily in response to current crises rather than in an attempt to identify future threats and opportunities. Responsibility for environmental analysis usually rests with line managers or the corporate planning staff rather than involving people with special training in long-range forecasting. Efforts rely primarily on quantitative analysis of past trends and the extrapolation of those trends into the future, rather than the use of more qualitative methods to help identify "discontinuities" or major changes that may occur in the future.[15]

There is some indication that the quality of environmental analysis and forecasting efforts is improving in some companies. A number of firms have established specialized "environmental forecasting units" within their planning staffs, and others have appointed teams of line managers and staff planners to conduct ongoing evaluations of the corporate environment. In most cases, though, the responsibility for identifying and reacting to environmental changes still rests primarily with line marketing and sales managers as part of the process of developing effective marketing plans and sales programs.

The Organizational Environment

The policies, resources, and talents of the organization also make up a very important part of the marketer's environment. Marketing and sales managers may have some influence over organizational factors due to their participation in making policy and planning decisions; however, in the short run, marketing and sales programs must be designed to fit within organizational limitations. Once again, the variables in the organizational environment can be grouped into five broad categories: (1) goals, objectives, and culture, (2) personnel, (3) financial resources, (4) production capabilities, and (5) research and development capabilities.

---

[14] Bill Saporito, "When Business Got So Good It Got Dangerous," *Fortune*, April 2, 1984, p. 61–64.

[15] Liam Fahey, William R. King, and Vadake K. Narayanan, "Environmental Scanning and Forecasting in Strategic Planning—The State of the Art," *Long Range Planning* 14 (February 1981), pp. 32–39.

Organizational Goals, Objectives and Culture.   As we have seen, the process of formulating marketing plans—and the sales programs that are part of those plans—begins with the specification by top management of a company mission and objectives for each functional area within the firm. As the company mission and objectives change over time, marketing and sales programs must be adjusted. The changes in Evan-Picone's marketing strategy and sales program when the firm was purchased by Revlon, and again when Picone regained control, illustrate the impact of changing company objectives.

In some firms, a well-defined mission together with a successful corporate history and top management's values and beliefs lead to the development of a strong *corporate culture*. Such cultures shape the attitudes and actions of employees and help determine the kinds of plans, policies, and procedures that managers can implement.[16]

IBM provides a good example of how a company's culture can shape its sales programs and policies.[17] The firm's culture is summarized by the following statement by Thomas J. Watson, Jr., who was IBM's chairman for many years.

We want to give the best customer service of any company in the world. . . IBM's contracts have always offered, not machines for rent, but machine services, that is the equipment itself and the continuing advice and counsel of IBM's staff.

While IBM has usually *not* been the technological leader in its industry, its strong culture, with its unquestioning commitment to customer service, has always made it a formidable competitor. Its culture is also clearly reflected in many of its sales management policies. For example, new salespeople receive 15 months of training in order to fully understand applications of the equipment they sell, and advanced training continues throughout their careers. More than 1,000 salespeople per year go through the "President's Class," where the purpose is to teach them how customer presidents think. Account representatives also have "full liability" for the equipment in place in all of their accounts. They are docked, out of bonus and salary, for commissions paid on earlier sales if any of that equipment has to be replaced. Such a reward system keeps the account representatives highly concerned with the customer's satisfaction even after a sale has been made.

Personnel.   The number of people in the organization, together with their skills and abilities, constrains the kinds of marketing strategies and sales programs that can be undertaken. In view of the special difficulties involved in recruiting highly qualified people for sales positions and the often lengthy training programs needed to teach new sales representatives necessary skills, it is often difficult to expand a sales force rapidly to take advantage of new products or growing markets. In some cases, however, it may be possible for a firm to compensate for a lack of knowledgeable employees by utilizing outside agencies or specialists on a fee-for-service or commission basis, such as agent middlemen.

Financial Resources.   An organization's financial strength influences many

---

[16] Terrence E. Deal and Allan A. Kennedy, *Corporate Cultures* (Reading, Mass.: Addison-Wesley, 1982).

[17] Much of the following discussion is based on material found in Thomas J. Peters and Robert H. Waterman, Jr., *In Search of Excellence: Lessons from America's Best-Run Companies* (New York: Harper & Row, 1982), pp. 159–62.

aspects of its marketing programs. It can constrain the firm's ability to develop new products as well as the size of its promotional budget and sales force. Like Evan-Picone, companies sometimes must take drastic measures, such as selling out to larger firms, to obtain the financial resources needed to realize their full potential in the marketplace.

Production Capabilities. The organization's production capacity, the technology and equipment available in its plants, and even the location of its production facilities can influence its marketing and sales programs. A company may be prevented from expanding its product line or moving into new geographic areas because it does not have the capacity to serve the increased demand that would result. Coors Brewing Company, for example, produces a beer that is in demand throughout the country. As a result of limited production capacity, however, Coors beer was sold for many years in only about 25 to 30 percent of the U.S. market. The company was reluctant to expand its production facilities because of the difficulty of finding water of the same quality as that at their plant in Colorado. However, such expansion ultimately became necessary for Coors to remain competitive with other major brewers.

Research and Development Capabilities. An organization's technical and engineering expertise is a major factor in determining whether it will be an industry leader or follower in new product development. Excellence in engineering and design can also serve as a major promotional appeal in the firm's sales program, as it is for BMW and Mercedes Benz. As the experience of IBM shows, however, a firm can often find ways to satisfy customer needs and compete effectively even when it is not always the technological leader in its industry.

Environmental Constraints on Sales Force Performance

A firm's marketing plan and sales program should be adapted to the general environmental conditions throughout the market. The problem is that some environmental factors vary from one geographic region to another. Consequently, even when two salespeople work for the same company, sell the same products, and have similar aptitude, skill, and motivation, one may outperform the other because the environment in his or her territory is more favorable.

Researchers have identified factors in both the organizational and the external environments that account for at least part of the variation in productivity within a firm's sales force.[18] Organizational variables that can cause differences in per-

---

[18] For example, see David W. Cravens, Robert B. Woodruff, and Joe C. Stamper, "An Analytical Approach for Evaluating Sales Territory Performance," *Journal of Marketing* 36 (January 1972), pp. 31–37; David W. Cravens and Robert B. Woodruff, "An Approach for Determining Criteria of Sales Performance," *Journal of Applied Psychology* 57 (June 1973), pp. 242–47; Henry C. Lucas, Charles B. Weinberg, and Kenneth W. Clowes, "Sales Response as a Function of Territorial Potential and Sales Representative Workload," *Journal of Marketing Research* 12 (August 1975), pp 198–305; Charles A. Beswick and David W. Cravens, "A Multistage Decision Model for Sales Force Management," *Journal of Marketing Research* 14 (May 1977); and Adrian B. Ryans and Charles B. Weinberg, "Sales Productivity: A Multiple Company Study," *Sales Management: New Developments from Behavioral and Decision Model Research,* ed. Richard P. Bagozzi (Cambridge, Mass.: Marketing Science Institute, 1979), pp. 92–129.

formance include: (1) regional variations in the expenditure of money and effort on other elements of the firm's marketing and promotional mix, (2) variations in the firm's past experience in different territories, and (3) regional variations in sales management practices—particularly in the number of sales personnel supervised by different field sales managers. External factors that may vary from one region to another include: (1) intensity of competition, (2) total market potential, (3) concentration of potential sales—the proportion of customers who are relatively large purchasers, and (4) geographic dispersion of customers. The impact of variations in each factor on a sales representative's productivity is summarized in Table 2–4.

The Effects of Organizational Factors on Sales Productivity

Variations in Company Marketing Efforts. Since personal selling is only one element of a firm's marketing mix, the success of personal selling efforts is strongly influenced by the intensity of the company's other marketing and promotional activities. When the firm's marketing efforts are more intensive in one region than in others, salespeople in that region have an advantage over those in other areas. Consider a firm that concentrates a large portion of its advertising expenditures in local media on the West Coast, for example. It should be easier for sales representatives in those territories to gain access to purchasing agents and to close sales successfully than for representatives in territories in the East or Midwest. Similarly, a salesperson in a territory located near a company warehouse may be able to offer customers quicker delivery and better service than one in a more distant territory.

Variations in Past Experience. Many firms enjoy a stronger market position in certain geographic regions. This is particularly true for smaller firms that often start out producing for a local or regional market and then attempt to expand into new geographic markets as they become successful. Sales representatives in territories where their company is well established—where the firm has enjoyed a large and/or steadily growing market share in recent years—should have an easier job. They can more readily maintain old customers and gain access to new ones than salespeople who must work to establish an awareness of their company and its products.

Variations in Sales Managers' Span of Control. Ideally, sales management policies and practices should be consistent throughout the company and affect all members of the sales force similarly. In practice, however, this is not always the case. One policy that often varies from one sales region to another is span of control—the number of sales personnel directly supervised by a field sales manager. For reasons such as variations in the density of potential customers and the quality of transportation networks, some sales managers are responsible for more salespeople than others. Obviously, the more subordinates a manager must

Table 2–4
The impact of variations in environmental factors on the productivity of individual salespeople

Environmental Factors	Impact on Salesperson's Productivity
Organizational variables	
1. Relatively high expenditures on marketing and promotional efforts	Positive
2. A positive sales history within a territory	
a. A relatively high market share in recent years	Positive
b. An increasing market share in recent years	Positive
3. A large span of control—field sales manager supervises a relatively large number of salespeople	Negative
External environmental variables	
1. Relatively intense competitive activity	Negative
2. Relatively high total market potential within the territory	Positive
3. Concentration of potential—relatively large proportion of big customers	Positive
4. Geographic dispersion of accounts—relatively large distances between customers	Negative

Source: Based on a summary of research findings presented in Adrian B. Ryans and Charles B. Weinberg, "Sales Productivity: A Multiple Company Study," in *Sales Management: New Developments from Behavioral and Decision Model Research*, ed. Richard P. Bagozzi (Cambridge, Mass.: Marketing Science Institute, 1979), pp. 92–129.

supervise, the less time he or she can spend training, advising, and monitoring the performance of each salesperson. As discussed in a later section of this book, a large span of control can cause salespeople to feel uncertain about how to do their jobs. This, in turn, can lead to lower levels of job satisfaction and productivity in the sales force.

Effects of the External Environment on Sales Productivity

Variations in the Intensity of Competition. A firm may be more firmly established and have a larger market share in some regions than in others, and the intensity of its marketing efforts also may vary across geographic areas. Obviously, the same may be true for some or all of the firm's competitors. Consequently, salespeople in different territories often face competitive efforts of varying intensity. Those who face well-entrenched and aggressive competitors are likely to have a more difficult time attaining a given sales volume than those with weaker competition.

Variations in Territory Characteristics. Since population density varies among geographic regions, the *total sales potential* for some consumer goods and services is greater in some areas than in others. This is even more true for industrial goods and services because the manufacturers in an industry often tend to locate close to one another. This is true of automobile manufacturers in Detroit and aerospace firms on the West Coast. Consequently, some of a firm's sales territories may contain more potential customers and total sales volume than others.

Even when the total market potential of two territories is about the same, however, differences in the characteristics of customers can cause variations in sales productivity. In a territory where potential demand is *concentrated* among a small number of large customers, a representative should produce a given dollar volume of sales with less traveling, fewer presentations, and fewer orders than in a territory where there are many small customers. On the other hand, potential customers may be widely *dispersed* geographically and the sales representative may have to cover a large area. Then travel time increases and the number of accounts that a single representative can call on will be smaller than in a territory with many potential customers clustered close together.

Implications for Sales Managers

Regional variations in the preceding factors can lead to substantial differences in sales productivity among a firm's sales representatives. Indeed, existing research indicates that such factors account for between 30 and 80 percent of the variation in the dollar sales volumes produced by a firm's sales force.[19] Therefore, it is important for sales managers to take these differences into account when developing sales plans and when evaluating the performance of sales representatives.

Regional variations in the firm's promotional expenditures, its past market share, the intensity of competition, market potential, and the concentration and dispersion of potential customers should be carefully considered when deciding how to divide up the market into sales territories and when determining sales forecasts and quotas for each territory. Also, environmental differences make the sales representatives' job more difficult and less productive in some regions than in others. It is not sufficient to evaluate a salesperson's performance solely on the basis of his or her sales volume or selling expenses. Such evaluations can lead to

---

[19] See the summary of results of empirical sales force productivity studies in Ryans and Weinberg, "Sales Productivity."

unfair and invalid comparisons of performance among representatives. Consequently, many firms supplement sales volume and cost analyses with more qualitative behavioral evaluations of selling performance—items to be discussed in more detail later.

Summary

A firm's marketing plan must reflect the environment in which the firm operates. This chapter provided an overview of the elements of a marketing plan and the way the environment influences these elements.

Planning is deciding what to do in the present to achieve what is desired in the future. The planning process begins with a statement of the company's mission and goals. Marketing goals that result from these corporate goals are best achieved through a marketing plan. The marketing plan logically includes: (1) the assessment of market opportunities available to the firm and an estimation of the resources necessary to capture an adequate share of the market, (2) the generation of possible strategies, (3) the selection of a strategy that best achieves the stated objectives, and (4) the programming of the marketing mix or allocation of resources to the marketing effort, including the sales function. The plans prepared by each functional area need to be reviewed and integrated at the corporate level. This may entail some revision to make them compatible. Once adopted, the plans must be continually monitored and adjusted as conditions warrant.

The environmental factors that can severely affect a marketing plan can be grouped into the two broad categories of external and organizational environments. The external environment includes the (1) economic, (2) social and cultural, (3) legal/political, (4) natural, and (5) technological environments. The organizational environment includes the firm's (1) goals and objectives, (2) personnel, (3) financial resources, (4) production capabilities, and (5) research and development capabilities.

As part of the firm's marketing program, the company's personal selling program must also be adapted to the external and organizational environments. Some important organizational variables that can cause differences in performance among salespeople are: (1) regional variations in the expenditure of money and effort on other elements of the firm's marketing and promotion mix, (2) variations in the firm's experience in different territories, and (3) regional variations in sales management practices—particularly in the number of sales personnel supervised by field sales managers. External factors that can vary from one region to another include (1) intensity of competition, (2) total market potential, (3) concentration of potential sales—the proportion of customers who are relatively large purchasers—and (4) geographic dispersion of customers.

Discussion Questions

1. The Evan-Picone example illustrates how environmental changes can alter a firm's marketing program. The chapter cites three important points. Using these points, what changes have occured in how AT&T competes in the market today? What changes have occured in the public accounting industry?

2. List three important ways that factors in the environment influence marketing and sales management decisions and programs. Of the three, which do you feel is the most important for a sales manager to remember?

3. Sometimes firms acquire other firms that are not related to their line of business. For example, Ralston-Purina acquired the St. Louis Blues, a professional hockey team, and the arena where the Blues play. What justification exists for this acquisition?

4. As a new employee of an organization, you have become aware of an obvious need for more planning on the organization's part. However, your superiors feel that planning is a waste because of the rapidly changing environment of the organization. Present a persuasive argument advocating more extensive planning.

5. If you were in top management in the following organizations, how would you most appropriately define your organization's mission?
   a. McDonald's restaurants.
   b. Pittsburgh Pirates baseball club.
   c. A local parent-teacher association.
   d. Allstate Insurance Company.

6. As a result of changes in their code of ethics, public accounting firms are now able to publicly advertise and to engage in other marketing activities. According to some authorities, public accounting firms must first engage in "internal marketing" before they engage in "external marketing." What do these terms mean?

7. After initiating a new marketing mix for a product line, your company's sales have jumped dramatically. Sales have been so good that your suggestion to audit continually and possibly adjust the marketing plans have been viewed by your superiors as unnecessary and a waste of time and money. What do you think about this line of reasoning?

8. During the late 1970s, the United States was confronted with a paper shortage that led to consumer hoarding of paper towels, toilet paper, and paper napkins. What impact would this shortage have on sales representatives who sell both industrial and consumer paper products?

9. Deregulation has been the term of the 1980s. For example, the Motor Carrier Act of 1980 eliminated the controls on who could carry what freight at what rates over the nation's highways. The 1980 law contributed to an orgy

of rate-cutting and discounting. Estimates are that more than 100,000 over-the-road truck drivers lost their jobs as a result of deregulation. A few companies have prospered, including CRST, a Cedar Rapids, Iowa, trucking company. What strategies did CRST adopt in order to survive? If you were in CRST's position, what would you have adopted?

10. In an attempt to increase the number of sales calls that salespeople can make per day, a firm is planning to install Fuzz-Busters in company cars. What implications does this have?

11. What implications for sales and marketing programs do the following pieces of legislation have?
    a. The Robinson-Patman Act.
    b. The FTC Act.
    c. "Cooling-off" laws.

12. The Justice Department is seeking to eliminate the accounting profession's last major barrier to competition: namely, the prohibition against one accountant soliciting another's client without the client's invitation. The controversy does not involve advertising, which is allowed. It deals with direct solicitation. What are the pros and cons of the Justice Department's action?

13. Karen Coenen, sales representative for Midway Corporation, manufacturers of electronic instruments, has been told to pad her expense account since this is a common practice. She has been told that everyone else does it so she should too. She feels that since everyone else is doing it she might as well go along with the group. Do you approve, somewhat approve, somewhat disapprove, or disapprove? If you were confronted with this situation, would you pad your account?

14. Dave Nevin was in a quandary. One of his better customers had asked Dave for a contribution to a political campaign for a candidate who had a rather shady reputation. The request was for $50, which represented a small sum compared with the commissions that Dave had earned last year. Dave made out a personal check for $50, thinking that if he did not, he might lose the account. Dave relayed his experience to his wife, Barbara. She disagreed with her husband's action and even called him spineless. What would you have done in such a situation? Do you approve or disapprove?

15. "There's a limit to honesty," said the district sales manager. "I want all questions answered honestly, but don't volunteer information that will have a negative effect on sales. If the customer doesn't ask, don't talk about it." Comment.

Chapter 3

Selling Activities and Account Management Policies

Chapter 2 stressed that a firm's personal selling program should be integrated with the other elements of the marketing mix. When deciding on the proper role of personal selling in an overall marketing strategy a firm's marketing and sales managers must answer two sets of questions.

1. What proportion of the firm's total promotional budget should be devoted to the sales force? How much emphasis should be given to personal selling relative to other promotional tools, such as media advertising and sales promotion?

2. How should each customer and prospective customer be managed? What specific activities should the firm's salespeople carry out to accomplish the company's communications and marketing objectives? What account management policies should be adopted to guide the selling activities of the sales force?

The Role of Personal Selling in the Marketing Mix

Personal selling is only one of the promotional tools that marketing managers might use to communicate with potential customers. Each promotional method has certain advantages for communicating certain kinds of information to certain customers under specific conditions. The decision concerning how much emphasis to give personal selling relative to the other tools in the promotional mix, then, depends on the communications tasks that must be accomplished. As Figure 3–1 indicates, these communications tasks are determined by the firm's marketing objectives and strategy, resources, the kinds of customers in its target market, and the nature of the other three elements of its marketing mix. This chapter will briefly explore the relative strengths and weaknesses of personal selling as a promotional tool, the kinds of communications tasks for which it is particularly well suited, and the circumstances under which such tasks are likely to arise. In other words, we will examine the factors that a marketing manager must consider in deciding whether or not personal selling should play a major role in the firm's overall marketing strategy.

But simply budgeting the funds necessary to hire a large sales force is no guarantee that the force will effectively perform its role in the firm's marketing program. Selling success depends on how the sales force members do their jobs— the kinds of selling activities they engage in and the manner in which those activities are carried out. Each salesperson must know the basics of salesmanship—gained through training, experience, or both—before he or she can make an effective sales call. Such knowledge alone is not sufficient for outstanding selling performance, however. As one authority points out, the salesperson "must have guidelines to help decide such things as which specific activities are the key to selling success, . . . what selling strategy to use with various customers, . . .

Figure 3–1
Factors influencing the role of personal selling in a firm's marketing strategy

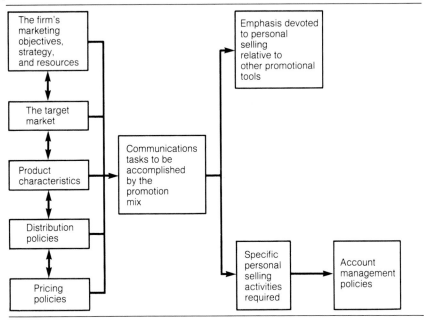

and how to divide his or her time between servicing existing accounts and prospecting for new ones. . . ."[1]

Therefore, as a first step in designing a strategic sales program, the sales manager should develop clearly defined account management policies to guide the efforts of his or her sales representatives. The second part of this chapter examines the activities that salespeople perform in doing their jobs and some of the account management policies adopted by today's more successful marketing organizations.

Promotional Tools

The promotion element of a firm's marketing mix incorporates activities aimed at communicating information about, and stimulating demand for, the firm's products or services among potential customers in the target market. Most textbooks

---

[1] B. Charles Ames, "Build Marketing Strength into Industrial Selling," *Harvard Business Review*, January-February 1982, p. 52.

Table 3–1
Types of promotional activities

Personal selling	Oral communication with a potential customer on a person-to-person basis.
Advertising	Nonpersonal communication that the organization pays to have transmitted to a target audience through a mass medium, such as television, radio, newspapers, magazines, direct mail, transit cards, billboards, catalogs, or directories.
Sales promotion	Activities and materials that induce potential customers to take action and purchase the firm's product or service, usually by drawing the customer's attention to the product or by offering an added incentive for purchase. Sales promotion methods are usually classified into two types based on the audience they are directed toward. *Consumer sales promotion* activities are designed to produce short-run sales increases among ultimate consumers by offering such things as "cents-off" coupons, free samples, and contests. *Trade sales promotion* activities encourage wholesalers or retailers to stock and aggressively market the firm's products by offering such things as quantity discounts, free goods, display materials, and sales contests.
Publicity	Nonpersonal communication of information about a firm or its products is transmitted through a mass medium at no charge to the firm. Examples include magazine, newspaper, radio, or television news stories about new products, new stores or personnel, or policy changes in an organization.

categorize promotional activities into four basic types: (1) personal selling, (2) advertising, (3) sales promotion, and (4) publicity. These types are briefly defined in Table 3–1.

Advantages of Personal Selling as a Promotional Tool

The advantages of personal selling as a promotional tool stem largely from the fact that it involves face-to-face communication with a potential customer. Personal sales messages are often more persuasive than advertising or publicity in the mass media. For one thing, in a face-to-face setting, the potential buyer is more likely to feel obliged to pay attention to the sales representative's message. Also, since the salesperson communicates with only one potential customer at a time, he or she can tailor the message to fit the needs and interests of that specific customer. In addition, communication flows in both directions during a sales call. The sales representative receives immediate feedback from the customer in the form of questions, objections, and nonverbal communication such as yawns and shrugs. Thus, the representative often knows immediately when a particular sales approach is not working, and then he or she can try a different tack.

Another advantage of face-to-face contact in personal selling is that the sales representative can communicate a larger amount of complex information than can be transmitted with other promotional tools. The salesperson can demonstrate the product or use visual aids to help get the message across. And since the salesperson is likely to call on the same client many times, he or she can devote a great deal of time to educating that client about the advantages of a particular product. The long-term contact in personal selling is particularly important when the product can be customized to fit the needs of an individual customer—as in the case of computer systems and insurance policies—or when the terms of the sale are open to negotiation.

The primary disadvantage of personal selling is that a sales representative can communicate with only a small number of potential customers. Consequently, personal selling is much more costly per person reached than the other promotional tools. Whereas an advertisement in *Reader's Digest* costs about 0.3 cents per reader, for example, the cost of an average industrial sales call is estimated to be between $80 and $150.[2]

Determinants of the Proper Role of Personal Selling in a Firm's Overall Marketing Strategy

Economists argue that a firm should budget additional financial resources for personal selling activities only if two conditions are met:

1. The firm receives a greater profit return from the last (marginal) dollar invested in personal selling than it would by spending that dollar on any other part of the marketing program or on any other company activity.
2. Each dollar spent on personal selling produces at least one dollar of marginal income.

Of course, lack of information and uncertainties in costs and revenues make it impossible for a marketing manager to apply this kind of marginal analysis explicitly in deciding how much emphasis to give personal selling in the overall marketing mix. Nevertheless, the concept is valid, and it suggests an important point. Since the costs of communicating with a potential customer through personal selling are high relative to other promotional tools, major emphasis should be given to the sales force only in those marketing situations where the advantages of personal selling as a promotional method outweigh its high costs.

In other words, personal selling should play a substantial role in the firm's marketing mix only when the communications tasks involved in its marketing strategy are performed better by face-to-face selling than any other method. Such communications tasks include:

---

[2] Thayer C. Taylor, "Sales Call Costs in a Holding Pattern," *Sales and Marketing Management,* February 21, 1983, p. 36.

1. Transmitting large amounts of complex information about the firm's products or policies.
2. Adapting product offerings and/or promotional appeals to the unique needs and interest of specific customers.
3. Persuading customers that the firm's products or services are better on at least some dimensions than the similar offerings of competitors.

As we saw in Figure 3–1, the nature of the communications tasks actually faced by a firm—and therefore the appropriate amount of personal selling effort to be used in that firm's marketing strategy—depends on the company's objectives, marketing strategy and resources, the number and kind of customers in its target market, and the nature of the other elements of its marketing mix.

Company Resources, Objectives and Marketing Strategy. Although the costs per person reached are high for personal selling, a firm can often implement a successful personal selling effort for a smaller total financial outlay than for either an advertising or a sales promotion campaign. Indeed, one major advertising agency refuses to represent consumer goods manufacturers unless they are willing to spend at least $5 million annually on their advertising campaigns. One reason for this policy is that the agency believes an effective national advertising campaign cannot be undertaken for less. Obviously, the high costs involved in extensive advertising and sales promotion efforts constrain the ability of smaller firms with limited promotional budgets to use such methods. Instead, such firms must often rely on personal selling—perhaps supplemented with less expensive local, regional, or cooperative advertising—as their primary promotional tool.

As we saw in Chapter 2, formulating a marketing plan involves setting specific objectives for a particular product in a chosen target market and then developing a marketing strategy to accomplish those objectives. Those objectives and strategies help determine the kinds of communications tasks that must be accomplished and the most appropriate promotional tools to use, as suggested by the relationships outlined in Table 2–1 in the previous chapter. For example, if a firm is introducing a new product to the market or entering an existing product into new markets, marketing objectives might be to stimulate primary demand and to generate awareness of the product among potential customers. Media advertising and sales promotion are the best tools to accomplish such an objective because they can communicate basic information about the product to many potential buyers with great efficiency. If the firm's objective is to expand distribution by convincing more wholesalers or retailers to carry the product, then a strong personal selling effort and perhaps a trade promotion program are indicated. The highly persuasive nature of personal selling also makes it an appropriate tool when the objective is to take market share away from established competitors, especially if the product is a relatively complex industrial or consumer durable good. Finally, if the objective is simply to maintain the market share of a product that is already well established in the marketplace, "reminder" advertising should play the primary role in the promotional mix.

Characteristics of the Target Market. Because various promotional tools differ greatly in their costs per person reached, the number of potential customers in the firm's target market, their size, and their geographic distribution influence the ingredients of the promotional mix. Since the costs per sales call are relatively high, personal selling is most often emphasized when the target market contains relatively few customers, the average customer is likely to place a relatively large order, and customers are clustered close together. Thus, firms that sell to industrial markets with few potential customers, and those that distribute their products through a small number of wholesale middlemen, commonly rely on personal selling as their primary promotional tool. On the other hand, firms that sell to large, geographically dispersed, consumer markets must place primary emphasis on the more cost-efficient advertising and sales promotion methods.

Product Characteristics. Most marketing textbooks suggest that the promotional mixes for industrial products concentrate heavily on personal selling; those for consumer durable goods utilize a combination of personal selling and advertising; and producers of consumer nondurable goods rely most heavily on advertising and sales promotion. The reason for this is that industrial goods and consumer durables tend to be more complex than nondurables, so potential buyers need more information to make a purchase decision. Also, industrial goods can often be designed or modified to meet the needs of individual customers, and consumer durables often present the buyer with a range of optional features from which to choose.

Although the preceding statements are true in most cases, they are generalizations and, as such, should be viewed with caution. Industrial goods producers usually stress personal selling, but they might also do extensive advertising to build awareness of the company and its products so that the sales force can gain access to potential customers more easily. For example, Lanier Business Products, Inc., uses both print and broadcast advertising to back up its personal selling efforts. Similarly, whereas a manufacturer of toothpaste or laundry detergent might spend large sums on consumer advertising, it might also maintain a large sales force to call on retail stores and build reseller support in its distribution channel. These points are supported by the findings of a survey in which top executives of 336 industrial, 52 consumer durable, and 88 consumer nondurable goods producers were asked to rate the relative importance of various promotional tools in their companies' marketing strategies. As the results in Table 3–2 indicate, personal selling was considered more important and media advertising less important in industrial goods firms than in consumer nondurable companies. However, all the promotional tools were seen to play at least some part in the promotional mixes of all manufacturers. More interesting, personal selling was viewed as the *single most important* promotional tool in *all three kinds* of firms.

A similar study in which questionnaires were mailed to 985 companies representing a cross section of U.S. industry allowed a comparison of the results in Table 3–2 with the situation 10 years later. The conclusion was somewhat surprising.

These findings suggest that marketing strategy remained remarkably stable, considering the environmental changes which have occurred (rising influence of consumerism, increasing legal pressures, marketing costs, a vigorous emphasis

Table 3–2
Ratings of the relative importance of the elements of the promotional mix for different product types*

| | Producers of | | |
| | Industrial Goods | Consumer Durables | Consumer Nondurables |
Promotional Tool			
Sales management and personal selling..............	69.2	47.6	38.1
Broadcast media advertising	0.9	10.7	20.9
Print media advertising	12.5	16.1	14.8
Sales promotion activities	9.6	15.5	15.5
Branding and promotional packaging.......	4.5	9.5	9.8
Other	3.3	0.6	0.9
Total	100.0	100.0	100.0

*Executives were asked to rate the relative importance of each tool using a scale of 100 points.
Source: Jon G. Udell, *Successful Marketing Strategies in American Marketing* (Madison, Wis.: Mimir Publishers, 1972), p. 47.

by company top management on improving profits in marketing operations, "stagflation," and a general leveling off in the influence of U.S. business internationally). Even the activities or tactics used to implement the facets of marketing strategy remained generally stable.[3]

Distribution Policies. As mentioned, personal selling is often necessary to build reseller support and develop adequate distribution for a product, regardless of whether it is a consumer or an industrial good. Of course, the importance of the sales force's role in building a distribution channel is influenced by the firm's strategy for inducing resellers to buy its product. When a firm follows a "pull" strategy, it attempts to build strong customer demand for its brand. This in turn encourages wholesalers and retailers to carry the product to satisfy their customers and reap the resulting sales and profits. A strong advertising program is a key to such a strategy.

When a firm uses a "push" strategy to build reseller support, on the other hand, it offers direct inducements to potential wholesalers and retailers to encourage them to stock the product. It is hoped that, when consumers see the product in the store, they will like it and buy it. A wide range of inducements can be offered to resellers as part of such a strategy, including larger-than-average margins, various trade sales promotion offerings, contests for the reseller's salespeople, cooperative advertising programs, sales aids, and point-of-purchase promotion materials. The manufacturer's sales force plays a principal role in imple-

---

[3] Clyde E. Harris, Jr., Richard R. Still, and Melvin R. Crask, "Stability or Change in Marketing Methods," *Business Horizons* 21 (October 1978), p. 35.

menting a push strategy. It is up to them to explain the advantages of carrying the firm's products to potential channel members and to persuade them to stock and aggressively merchandise those products.[4]

Pricing Policies. A firm's pricing policies can also influence the composition of its promotion mix. "Big-ticket" items, both industrial goods and consumer durables, typically require substantial amounts of personal selling. Such expensive products are often technically or aesthetically sophisticated, and customers perceive a substantial amount of risk in purchasing them. Therefore, potential buyers usually want the kind of detailed information and advice they can only get from a salesperson before making their decisions.

Also, personal selling is essential in marketing products or services where the ultimate selling price is open to negotiation. Negotiations over price can take place only when there is face-to-face contact between a salesperson and a potential buyer. Although negotiated pricing policies are most commonly found among marketers of industrial goods and services, they are also followed in the sale of some consumer durables such as automobiles.

Account Management Policies and Sales Program Planning

After a firm's marketing or business unit managers have decided how large a role personal selling is to play in their overall marketing strategy, it is up to the sales manager to formulate sales plans and account management policies to shape that role. As we saw in Chapter 1, *Sales Program Planning* is concerned with allocating the firm's sales efforts across different types of potential customers. *Account Management Policies* then specify what individuals within each type of customer organization the salesperson should attempt to contact, what kinds of selling and service activities should be engaged in, and how those activities should be carried out. For example, many companies have explicit policies concerning such things as (1) whether salespeople should work through customers' purchasing departments or attempt to call directly on higher level management decision makers, (2) the amount of effort and detail to be included in preparing sales proposals for different types of accounts, and (3) the kinds of information to be reported back to the home office after a sales call is made.

The major steps in formulating sales programs and account management policies are outlined in Figure 3–2. The process should begin with a careful consideration of the objectives and target markets specified in the marketing plan and an analysis of the sales potential represented by various customers and potential customers within the targeted market segments. The tools and techniques for estimating sales potential are discussed in Chapter 5. Next, the sales manager

---

[4] For a more detailed discussion of the role of personal selling and other promotional tools in gaining reseller support, see Benson P. Shapiro, "Improve Distribution With Your Promotional Mix," *Harvard Business Review*, March-April 1977, p. 115–23.

Figure 3–2
The sales program and account management planning process

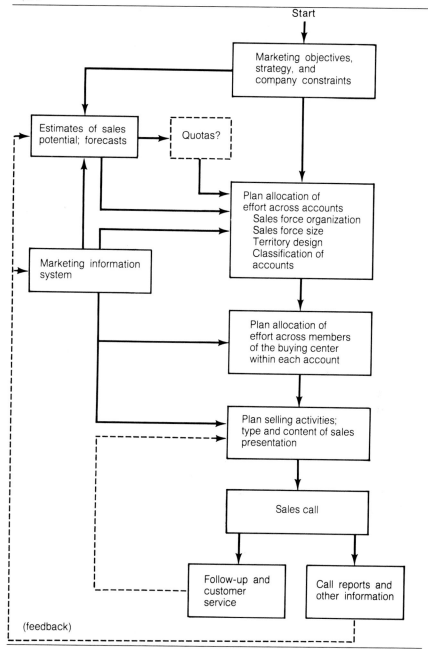

Source: Adapted from John M. Gwin and William D. Perreault, Jr., "Industrial Sales Call Planning," *Industrial Marketing Management* 10 (1981), p. 229.

must plan a basic sales program—involving a determination of the number of salespeople needed, how they are to be organized within the firm, and the design of their sales territories—as a first step toward directing appropriate amounts of effort toward target customers.

In some firms, sales planning stops here. Once salespeople are assigned to territories, it is up to them to decide how frequently to call on specific customers. While this has the advantage of giving the salesperson maximum flexibility to adjust his or her efforts to the unique situations that might arise in a specific territory and minimizing the time and expense involved in formal planning, the problem is that individual salespeople do not always match their selling efforts to the sales or profit potential of the accounts in their territory. Some salespeople are "cherry pickers" who spend inordinate amounts of time with current customers where there is a high probability of getting an order, rather than working to develop new customers—even though they may offer much greater long-run potential. Other salespeople are simply reluctant to call on certain companies or types of accounts because of negative past experiences, personality conflicts, or a dislike for the procedures involved. In the fashion industry, for example, some salespeople are said to be "plate glass shy" because they are reluctant to call on large department stores where they have to deal with sophisticated buyers and compete with many other sellers. The point is that salespeople often concentrate on those accounts where there is a high probability of attaining reasonable sales volume with reasonable effort, without regard to long-run potential or profitability.

To overcome such problems, some firms carry sales planning one step further by classifying the accounts in each territory—or the various products handled by their sales force—into several categories according to their relative sales potential, profitability, or importance to the accomplishment of the objectives specified in the marketing plan. Policies can then be formulated concerning the amount of effort each salesperson should devote to each class of customers or products. For example, salespeople might be instructed to call on all high potential Type A accounts at least once a month, while less important B accounts are visited only once every two months. Such policies are often further formalized through the development of separate volume or activity quotas for each category of customers or products and reinforced by tying incentive bonuses or other rewards to the accomplishment of those quotas. These approaches for detailed planning of the allocation of sales efforts according to the relative potential or profitability of different types of customers or products are explored in more detail in Chapters 6 and 7.

The next step in sales planning is to decide how individual sales calls will be carried out. As Figure 3–2 indicates, this involves two sets of decisions: (1) what individuals within the customer's organization should be contacted, and (2) what selling activities should be engaged in and how should they be carried out? While this kind of "sales call planning" is primarily the responsibility of the individual salesperson, this stage in the planning process is often the manager's last real opportunity to actively and constructively affect what the salesperson does in the field. Consequently, the manager should take the initiative to ensure that responsibility for this aspect of planning is assumed by the sales rep and provide appropriate account management policies to guide his or her activities before, during, and after the sales call.[5] The formulation of useful and effective account management policies, however, requires an understanding of (1) how the buying process works and what members of a customer organization are likely to influence that process of various stages and (2) the kinds of activities that salesperson engage in when carrying out their jobs. Consequently, the next two sections of this chapter examine these issues and some of their implications for the development of account management policies.

The Organizational Buying Process

Many topics in this book are appropriate to managing all kinds of selling; however, the primary emphasis is on commercial or industrial selling. Consequently, let us focus on the buying process engaged in by organizations—both industrial users and middlemen.[6]

The organizational buying process is illustrated by the following description of the activities engaged in by a purchasing agent who buys integrated circuits for a computer manufacturer.

My job starts when I get a requisition from Manufacturing or Engineering. I look at the specifications for the item and the quantity requested. I also look at the item's cost, the frequency with which the same item has been purchased in the past, the number in inventory and its effect on inventory costs. We also try to forecast whether larger quantities of the same item will be needed in the future. Finally, if several requisitions are made for similar but slightly different items, I contact Engineering or Production Control to determine whether minor modifications can be made. All of these things are done so we can place the largest possible order to increase our leverage with the supplier and gain the lowest possible price.

The most important factors to be considered in buying integrated circuits are quality, price, and delivery time. There are at least six different quality levels. My biggest problem is finding the right quality level to fit the specifications at the lowest price. I also have to consult with Manufacturing to work out delivery requirements so we can gain the lead times necessary to build our computers on schedule.

We usually consider at least two alternative suppliers. I check with Materials Engineering to put together a list of potential suppliers and we review each of them on the basis of their past performance with regard to quality and meeting delivery schedules. Finally, we make a decision and place the order.[7]

---

[5] John M. Gwin and William D. Perreault, Jr., "Industrial Sales Call Planning," *Industrial Marketing Management* 10 (1981), pp. 225–34.

[6] For more comprehensive reviews of the literature surrounding organizational buying behavior, see Wesley J. Johnston, "Industrial Buying Behavior: A State of the Art Review," in *Review of Marketing*, ed. B. Enis and K. Roering (Chicago: American Marketing Association, 1981), pp. 75–88; and Rowland Moriarity, *Industrial Buying Behavior* (Lexington, Mass.: D. C. Heath, 1983).

[7] From an interview conducted as part of the research for Joanne M. Klebba, *The Structure of the Purchasing Function as Determined by Environmental Uncertainty*, unpublished Ph.D. dissertation, Graduate School of Business Administration, University of Minnesota, 1978.

Who Makes Organizational Buying Decisions?

As the preceding statements illustrate, organizational purchasing often involves people from different departments within the firm. These participants in the buying process can be grouped into five categories: users, influencers, gatekeepers, buyers, and deciders.[8]

Users. The people in the organization who must use or work with the product or service often influence the purchase decision. For example, drillpress operators might request that the purchasing agent buy drills from a particular supplier because they stay sharp longer and reduce downtime in the plant.

Influencers. Influencers provide information for evaluating alternative products and suppliers, and they often play a major role in determining the specifications and criteria to use in making the purchase decision. They are usually technical experts from various departments whose knowledge is useful for making wise decisions. In the integrated circuits example, the buyer relied on people in the engineering and manufacturing departments to help determine the specifications of the circuits to be purchased, and the materials engineering department helped identify and evaluate potential suppliers.

Gatekeepers. Gatekeepers control the flow of information to other people involved in the purchasing process. They include the organization's purchasing agent and suppliers' salespeople. Gatekeepers influence a purchase by controlling the kind and amount of information that reaches the other decision makers.

Buyers. The buyer is usually referred to as a purchasing agent or purchasing manager. In most organizations, buyers have the authority to contact suppliers and negotiate purchases. In some cases, they are given wide discretion in carrying out their jobs. In other instances, though, they are tightly constrained by technical specifications and other contract requirements determined by technical experts and top administrators.

Deciders. The decider is the person with the final authority to make a purchase decision. Sometimes buyers have this authority, but often it is retained by higher executives in the organization. When a company buys a large computer installation, for instance, the final decision is likely to be made by the chief executive or a top management committee.

The Organizational Buying Center

All the people who participate in buying a particular product or service can be referred to as a buying center. Estimates of the number of people in the buying center for a typical purchase range from 3 to 12. Of course, different members of

---

[8] Frederick E. Webster and Yoram Wind, *Organizational Buying Behavior* (Englewood Cliffs, N.J.: Prentice-Hall, 1972).

the buying center may participate at different stages in the decision process. One study of 2,400 respondents from firms in a wide variety of industries found that engineering and other technical personnel were active throughout the purchasing process. They helped to initiate the purchase, establish specifications, and choose the supplier.[9] Administrative personnel were found to be most active in initiating purchases, whereas purchasing agents were most involved in the final choice of product and supplier. This participation by people from different departments at different stages in the buying process is illustrated in Figure 3–3.

Figure 3–3
Participation by various company departments at different stages of the purchasing process in the radio, television, and communications equipment industry

	Who is most likely to initiate a project leading toward the purchase of new equipment to:	Overall corporate policy and planning	Operations and administration	Design and development engineering	Production engineering	Research	Finance	Sales	Purchasing	Others in company	Others outside of company
MOTIVE	Replace existing equipment?	14.2	39.6	37.7	53.8	12.3	.9	.9	7.5	14.2	1.9
	Expand capacity?	44.2	43.3	24.0	42.3	3.8		2.9	1.0	4.8	2.9
	Change production processes?	12.7	18.6	30.4	84.3	5.9			1.0	3.9	1.0
	Take advantage of new materials?	5.0	9.9	63.4	53.5	23.8			3.0	3.0	1.0
	Manufacture new products?	38.2	32.4	48.0	32.4	14.7	1.0	3.9	2.0	2.9	3.9
KIND OF EQUIPMENT	Who surveys alternatives and determines kind (not make) of equipment?	5.7	16.2	56.2	50.5	17.1	1.0		12.4	8.6	1.0
	Who determines specifications and characteristics to be met by the equipment?	1.9	11.3	62.3	52.8	18.9	.9		5.7	12.3	1.9
MAKE OR SUPPLIER	Who surveys available makes of the specified equipment and chooses suppliers from whom to invite bids?	1.9	10.5	42.9	36.2	8.6			62.9	11.4	1.9
	Who evaluates offered equipment for accord with specifications?	1.0	8.7	57.3	52.4	16.5			9.7	19.4	1.0
	Who decides which supplier gets the order?	11.3	21.7	42.5	33.0	10.4	1.9		58.5	10.4	.9

Note: Percentages indicate the frequency with which the various management functions were reported to participate in the successive steps of the purchasing process. Shading highlights the three most-mentioned functions for each purchasing step.
Source: From *How Industry Buys/1970.* Copyright © 1969 by *Scientific American, Inc.* All rights reserved.

[9] "How Industry Buys—1970," *Scientific American* (New York: Scientific American, 1969), p. 54.

Sales Planning Implications. Since different employees of a customer's organization may be active at different stages of the purchase process, an important part of sales planning involves trying to determine who the salesperson should contact, when each contact should be made, and what kinds of information and appeals each participant is likely to find most useful and persuasive. Unfortunately, the answers to such questions are likely to be different for each potential customer, making information gained from past experience with an organization—and from customer surveys or other forms of market research—useful ingredients for planning individual sales calls.

In many cases, however, the roles played by various members of the buying center are sufficiently consistent across similar types of firms that it is possible for a company to establish policies to guide its salespeople's efforts. For example, a recent study of 140 commercial construction companies found that in smaller firms (defined as those with annual sales volumes under $25 million), presidents and vice presidents exert significantly more influence at all stages in the decision process than purchasing agents or construction engineers, while the situation is reversed in large firms—reflecting increased job specialization and decentralization of purchasing in bigger companies.[10] A firm selling to this industry might adopt a policy of encouraging its salespeople to seek appointments with the top executives when calling on smaller customers, but to initiate contacts through the purchasing department in larger organizations. Similarly, customers' buying centers are likely to involve a wider variety of participants when they are considering the purchase of a technically complex, expensive product—such as a computer system—than when the purchase involves a simpler or less costly product. Consequently, firms who sell technically complex capital equipment sometimes organize their salespeople into "sales teams," or utilize "multilevel" selling, with different salespeople calling on different members of the customer's buying center in order to reach as many decision participants as possible and to give each participant the kinds of information he or she will find most relevant. These team approaches to selling are examined in more detail in the next chapter.

When a firm develops policies or organization structures to guide its salespeople's efforts in dealing with customers' buying centers, however, managers must periodically review their assumptions about the roles and influence of the various decision participants. For example, for years, Kodak's strategy for selling X-ray film to hospitals was to sell through lab technicians. The company did not notice that this purchase was becoming increasingly centralized in many hospitals, with professional administrators exerting the major influence on the decision. As its sales declined, Kodak finally grasped the change in buying practices and hurriedly changed its sales strategy.[11]

---

[10] Joseph A. Bellizzi, "Organizational Size and Buying Influences," *Industrial Marketing Management* 10 (1981), pp. 17–21.

[11] Philip Kotler, *Marketing Management: Analysis, Planning and Control* (Englewood Cliffs, N.J.: Prentice-Hall, 1984), p. 167.

Stages in the Organizational Buying Process

We have seen that different members of a customer's buying center may exert influence at different stages in the decision process. This raises the question of what "stages" are involved. One widely recognized framework identifies seven steps that organizational buyers go through in making purchase decisions: (1) anticipation or recognition of a problem or need, (2) determination and description of the characteristics and the quantity of the needed item, (3) search for and qualification of potential suppliers, (4) acquisition and analysis of proposals or bids, (5) evaluation of proposals and selection of supplies, (6) selection of an order routine, and (7) performance evaluation and feedback.[12]

Anticipation or Recognition of a Problem or Need. Most organizational purchases are motivated by the requirements of the firm's production processes, merchandise inventory, or day-to-day operations. Consequently, a firm's demand for goods and services is derived demand. Its needs are derived from its customers' demand for the goods or services it produces or markets. This characteristic of derived demand makes organizational markets quite volatile. Fluctuations in economic conditions can produce changes in a firm's sales, which can result in rapid changes in production schedules and in accumulations or depletions of inventories. As a result, the organization's requirements for goods and services can change dramatically in a short time.

Many different situations can lead someone within an organization to recognize a need for a particular product or service. In some cases, need recognition may be almost automatic, as when a computerized inventory control system reports that the stock of an item has fallen below the reorder level. In other cases, a need may arise when someone identifies a better way of carrying out the organization's operations. New needs might also evolve when there are changes in the focus of the firm's operations, as when top management decides to make a new product line. In all these situations, needs may be recognized—and the purchasing process may be initiated—by a variety of different people in the organization, including users, technical personnel, top management, or purchasing managers.

Determination and Description of the Characteristics and Quantity of the Needed Item. The kinds and quantities of goods and services to be purchased are usually dictated by the demand for the firm's outputs and by the requirements of its production process and operations. Consequently, the criteria used in specifying the needed materials and equipment must usually be technically precise. Similarly, the quantities needed must be carefully considered to avoid excessive inventories or downtime caused by lack of needed materials. For these reasons, a variety of technical experts, as well as the people who will ulti-

---

[12] Patrick J. Robinson, Charles W. Faris, and Yoram Wind, *Industrial Buying and Creative Marketing* (Boston: Allyn Bacon, 1967).

mately use the materials or equipment, are commonly involved in this stage of the decision process.

It is not enough for the using department and the technical experts to develop a detailed set of specifications for the needed item, however. They must also communicate a clear and precise description of what is needed, how much is needed, and when it is needed to other members of the buying center and to potential suppliers.

Since organizational buyers tend to use precise and explicit technical and economic criteria when deciding what to buy, organizational buying is often described as being more "rational" than consumer purchasing. Consumers, after all, sometimes buy things for social or emotional reasons. Although this generalization may be largely true, we will see that organizational buyers can also be influenced to some extent by social and emotional considerations.

Search for and Qualification of Potential Suppliers. Once the organization has clearly defined the kind of item that is needed, a search for potential suppliers begins. If the item has been purchased before, this search may be limited to one or a few suppliers who have performed satisfactorily in the past. Organizational buyers, like consumers, often develop loyalties to their old and trusted suppliers.[13] In such circumstances, it can be difficult for new suppliers to "get a piece of the action" unless they have something unique to offer. On the other hand, if the purchase involves a new item, or if the item is complex and expensive, organizational buyers often search for several potential suppliers to ensure that they can select the one with the best product and most favorable terms.[14]

Acquisition of Proposals or Bids. After a set of potential suppliers is identified, the buyer may request specific proposals or bids from each. When the item is a frequently purchased, standardized, or technically simple product—like nails or typewriter ribbon—this process may not be very extensive. The buyer might simply consult several suppliers' catalogs or make a few phone calls. For more complicated and expensive goods and services, however, lengthy and detailed sales presentations and written proposals may be requested from each potential vendor.

Evaluation of Offerings and Selection of Suppliers. During this stage of the purchasing process, various members of the buying center examine the acceptability of the various proposals and potential suppliers. There may also be some negotiation between the buying organization and one or more potential vendors over the content of their proposals, including prices, credit terms, and delivery schedules. Ultimately, one or more suppliers are selected, and purchase agreements are signed.

The people in the buying organization's purchasing department are usually responsible for carrying out this phase of the process. Technical and administrative personnel may also play a role in supplier selection, however, especially when the purchase is complex and costly.

---

[13] Yoram Wind, "Industrial Source Loyalty," *Journal of Marketing Research* 7 (1970), pp. 450–57.

[14] Anita M. Kennedy, "The Complex Decision to Select a Supplier: A Case Study," *Industrial Marketing Management* 2 (1983), pp. 45–56.

What criteria do members of the buying center use in selecting a supplier? Since organizational buying is largely a "rational" decision-making process, we would expect "rational" criteria to be considered most important—such as the quality of the product, the price, and the service offered by the supplier. However, social and emotional factors can also influence this decision. For example, Table 3–3 shows the relative importance attached to various supplier selection criteria by people who buy materials and equipment for building contractors and construction firms. As you can see, service, product quality, and price are considered most important, but social and emotional factors were also mentioned—such as the reputation and prestige of the supplier, friendship with the supplier, and the personality of the supplier's sales representative.

Table 3–3
Relative importance to building contractors of criteria used in choosing suppliers

Importance Ranking	Factor Influencing the Choice of Supplier
1	Service
2	Quality of product
3	Supplier stands behind product
4	Low price
5	Supplier's reputation for fair dealing
6	Nearness of supplier
7	Friendship with supplier
8	Salesperson's personality
9	Availability of credit
10	Prestige of supplier
11	Reciprocity

Source: Guy R. Banville and Ronald J. Dornoff, "Industrial Source Selection Behavior—An Industry Study," *Industrial Marketing Management*, June 1973.

In the study reported in Table 3–3, Professors Banville and Dornoff also found that the relative importance of different supplier selection criteria varies with the nature of the organization making the purchase and the kind of product being purchased. Larger contractors attached more importance to attaining the lowest price, whereas smaller contractors were more concerned with selecting a supplier who would stand behind the product. Also, service and price were more important to contractors choosing a supplier for standardized, nontechnical items like concrete. On the other hand, product quality was more important in buying technically complex items like kitchen appliances.[15]

---

[15] Guy R. Banville and Ronald J. Dornoff, "Industrial Source Selection Behavior—An Industry Study," *Industrial Marketing Management*, June 1973. In a study of 19 major U.S. corporations and 26 British companies, Lehman and O'Shaughnessy also found that the relative importance of the various criteria used to make purchase decisions varied with the type of products being purchased. See Donald R. Lehman and John O'Shaughnessy, "Difference in Attribute Importance for Different Industrial Products," *Journal of Marketing* 38 (April 1974), pp. 36–42.

Selection of an Order Routine. Until the purchased item is delivered, it is of no use to the organization. Consequently, after an order has been placed with a supplier, the purchasing department is often involved in expediting the delivery of the goods. Other internal activities also must occur when the order is delivered. The goods must be received, inspected, paid for, and entered in the firm's inventory records.

Performance Evaluation and Feedback. When a purchase has been made and the goods delivered, an evaluation process begins. This evaluation focuses on both the product and the supplier. The goods are inspected to determine whether they meet the specifications described in the purchase agreement. Later, the using department can judge whether the purchased item performs according to expectations. Similarly, the supplier's performance can be evaluated on such criteria as promptness of delivery, quality of the product, and service after the sale. In many organizations, this evaluation is a formal process, with written reports submitted by the user department and by other persons involved in the purchase. The information is kept by the purchasing department for use in evaluating proposals and selecting suppliers the next time a similar purchase is made.

Repeat Purchase Behavior. The steps described above apply only to what Robinson and his colleagues have labeled "new task" purchases, where a customer is buying a relatively complex and expensive product or service for the first time (e.g., a custom-built office building or a new computer system).[16] At the other extreme is the "straight rebuy" where a customer is reordering an item it has purchased many times before (e.g., office supplies, bulk chemicals). Such repeat purchases tend to be much more routine than the new task situation. Straight rebuys are often carried out by members of the purchasing department with little influence from other employees of the firm, and many of the steps described above (involved with searching for and evaluating alternative suppliers) are dispensed with. Instead, the buyer chooses from those suppliers on an "approved" list, giving weight to the company's past satisfaction with those suppliers and their products.

From the seller's viewpoint, being an "in" or approved supplier can provide a significant competitive advantage, and policies and procedures should be developed to help maintain and enhance such favored positions with current customers. As we shall see later in this chapter, many firms have developed "major account management" policies to help preserve the long-term satisfaction of their largest customers. Also, suppliers are offering new technologies—such as computerized reordering systems—to their customers to help them make their reordering process more efficient while simultaneously increasing the likelihood that they will continue to reorder from the same supplier. For example, customers of American Hospital Supply Corp. can enter purchase orders into their computers, have them contact American Hospital's mainframe, find out instantly what is available and when it can be shipped, and place the order automatically. This system increases the probability that existing customers will reorder from Ameri-

---

[16] Robinson, Faris, and Wind, *Industrial Buying.*

can Hospital while at the same time freeing the firm's 3,100 sales representatives to spend more time contacting potential new accounts and informing existing customers about new products.[17]

For potential suppliers who are not currently on a buyers approved list, the strategic selling problem is more difficult. An "out" supplier's objective must be to move the customer away from the automatic reordering procedures of a straight rebuy toward the more extensive evaluation processes of a "modified rebuy" purchase decision—a situation where the buyer is interested in modifying the product specifications, prices or other terms it has been receiving from existing suppliers and is willing to consider dealing with new suppliers in order to obtain them. Since the need to consider a change in suppliers can be identified by a variety of different members of a firm's buying center, an out supplier might urge its salespeople to attempt to bypass the customer's purchasing department and call directly on users or technical personnel in an attempt to persuade them that the firm's products offer advantages on some important dimension—such as technical design, quality, performance or financial criteria—over the products they are currently using.

Selling Activities

Sales Jobs Involve a Wide Variety of Activities

Given the preceding examination of purchase decisions from the customer's point of view, the perspective now turns to the activities engaged in by sales representatives when attempting to influence those decisions. Unfortunately, very few studies have investigated the job activities engaged in by salespeople or have attempted to uncover the underlying dimensions of the sales job. In the only such study appearing in the sales management literature, Professors Lamont and Lundstrom conducted extensive exploratory interviews with sales managers, product managers, and sales representatives employed by a leading manufacturer of building materials.[18] Sixty separate job activities were identified on the basis of those interviews. The company's 156 sales representatives were then asked to rate the relative importance of each of the 60 activities on a seven-point scale. These responses were examined with the statistical technique of factor analysis to identify the underlying dimensions or categories of salesperson behavior represented by the 60 job activities.

---

[17] "Rebirth of a Salesman: Willy Loman Goes Electronic," *Business Week*, February 27, 1984, p. 104.

[18] Lawrence M. Lamont and William J. Lundstrom, "Defining Industrial Sales Behavior: A Factor Analytic Study," *1974 Combined Proceedings* (Chicago: American Marketing Association, 1974), pp. 493–98.

Table 3–4
Job factors and selected activities associated with each factor in a study of building materials sales representatives

Job Factor	Activities
1. Assisting and working with district management	Assisting district sales management in market surveys, new product evaluations, etc. Preparing reports on territorial sales expenses. Managing a sales territory within the sales expense budget. Using district management to make joint sales calls on customers.
2. Customer service	Arranging credit adjustments on incorrect invoicing, shipping, and order shortages. Informing customers of supply conditions on company products. Assisting customers and prospects in providing credit information to the company.
3. Personal integrity and selling ethics	Representing company products at their true value. Working within the merchandising plans and policies established by the company. Investigating and reporting customer complaints.
4. Direct selling	Knowing correct applications and installations of company products. Making sales presentations that communicate product benefits. Handling sales presentations.
5. Developing relationships with customers	Maintaining a friendly, personal relationship with customers. Using equipment to strengthen the business relationship with customers. Providing customers with technical information on company products.
6. Keeping abreast of market conditions	Keeping customers informed of market conditions that affect their businesses. Keeping the company informed of market conditions.
7. Meeting sales objectives	Identifying the person with authority to make the purchasing decision. Closing the sale and obtaining the order. Selling company products at a volume which meets or exceeds expectations.
8. Maintaining complete customer records	Maintaining customer records that are complete and up to date. Checking customers inventory and recommending orders.

Source: Lawrence M. Lamont and William J. Lundstrom, "Defining Industrial Sales Behavior: A Factor Analytic Study," *1974 Combined Proceedings* (Chicago: American Marketing Association, 1974), pp. 493–98.

Eight separate job dimensions were identified. These are shown in Table 3–4, along with some of the specific activities included in each dimension.

One major conclusion of the Lamont and Lundstrom study is that the salesperson's job is more complex than many people think. The job factors or dimensions identified suggest that a salesperson's job can involve a much wider variety of activities than simply calling on customers, making sales presentations, and taking orders. As indicated in Table 3–4, factor 1 (assisting and working with district management) shows that one important aspect of the sales job is aiding management with various analysis and control activities. Factor 6 (keeping abreast of market conditions) indicates that salespeople are an important source of market information for both company management and customers.

Factors 4, 5, 7, and 8 describe activities directly related to the selling process. Factor 4 (direct selling) represents the selling skills and product knowledge required to perform a sales job. Factor 5 (developing relationships with customers) indicates that the salesperson must use a combination of product knowledge and entertainment to build strong personal relationships with customers. Factor 7 (meeting sales objectives) covers the objective aspects of selling, including identifying the buying authority, closing the sale, and meeting quotas. Factor 8 (maintaining complete customer records) suggests the importance of analyzing customer sales and inventory data to recommend purchases and influence the purchasing process. In addition to these salesmanship activities, factor 2 (customer service) indicates that many routine servicing activities—such as settling complaints and credit transactions—are important for maintaining satisfied customers over time. Finally, factor 3 suggests the importance of high personal integrity and ethics in the salesperson's dealings with both company management and customers.

Although Lamont and Lundstrom's findings provide interesting insights into the complexities of personal selling, their study examined sales jobs in only one company in a single industry. Some sales jobs in other firms or other industries are even more complex, while others are simpler. Many more studies are needed before a reasonably complete taxonomy of the behavioral dimensions of various types of selling jobs can be developed.

Steps in the Selling Process

A variety of analytical and administrative duties are important components of the job of the sales representative in a firm's marketing effort. However, the account management policies formulated as part of a firm's strategic sales plan typically concentrate on guiding those activities involving direct interaction with customers and potential customers—that is, the activities involved in the selling process itself. There have been no detailed empirical investigations of the selling process, but some observers have suggested conceptual schemes that outline various stages in the process and indicate the kinds of activities engaged in at each stage.[19] The essence of most of these conceptual schemes can be captured by viewing the selling process as consisting of six stages: (1) prospecting for customers, (2) opening the relationship, (3) qualifying the prospect, (4) presenting the sales message, (5) closing the sale, and (6) servicing the account.

Although the selling process involves only a few distinct steps, the specific activities engaged in at each step—and the way those activities are carried out—can vary greatly from one salesperson to the next. Consequently, as we have seen, a firm's strategic sales plan should incorporate account management policies to guide each salesperson in the field and ensure that all the firm's selling efforts are consistent with its overall marketing strategy. In view of this, each stage in the selling process will be examined together with some of the more common account management policies that firms use to direct the behavior of their sales representatives at each stage.

Prospecting for Customers.   In many types of selling, prospecting for new customers is critical. It can also be one of the most disheartening aspects of selling, however, especially for beginning salespeople. Prospecting efforts are often met with rejection, and immediate payoffs are usually minimal. Nevertheless, the ability to uncover potential new customers often separates the successful from the unsuccessful salesperson. A story is often told in selling circles about a recent graduate who became an insurance salesman. In the first year, he received several sales awards for bringing new business to his company. Two years later he quit his job and switched to a career outside of the sales field. What happened? He simply exhausted his list of friends and relatives. In other words, he was successful as long as he was selling to a select list of prospects, but when that list dwindled, he was unable to generate any new customers. A more successful salesperson would have been searching out new prospects continuously.

In some consumer goods businesses, prospecting for new customers simply involves cold canvassing—going from house to house knocking on doors. In most cases, though, the target market is more narrowly defined, and the salesperson must identify prospects within that target segment. Salespeople use a wide variety of information sources to identify relevant prospects, including trade association and industry directories, telephone directories, other salespeople, other customers, suppliers, nonsales employees of the firm, and social and professional contacts.

New technologies—particularly the use of various forms of telemarketing systems—can also help salespeople identify and qualify potential new accounts. Many firms set up incoming Wide-Area Telecommunication Service (WATS) phone lines and publicize toll-free 800 numbers in their media advertising and other promotional material. When prospects call for more information about a product or service, an operator attempts to determine the extent of interest and whether the prospect meets the company's qualification standards for new cus-

---

[19] For examples, see Frederick A. Russell, Frank H. Beach, and Richard H. Buskirk, *Textbook of Salesmanship*, 10th ed. (New York: McGraw-Hill, 1978), pp. 119–377; and W. J. E. Crissy, William H. Cunningham, and Isabelle C. M. Cunningham, *Selling: The Personal Force in Marketing* (New York: John Wiley & Sons, 1977), pp. 140–326.

tomers. If so, information about the caller is passed on to the appropriate salesperson or regional office.

One question that should be addressed by a firm's account management policies is how much emphasis salespeople should give to prospecting for new customers versus servicing existing accounts. The appropriate policy for a firm depends on the nature of both its product and its customers. If the firm's product is in the introductory stage of its life cycle, if it is an infrequently purchased durable good, or if the typical customer does not require much service after the sale, the firm's sales representatives should devote a substantial amount of time to prospecting for new customers. This is the case in industries such as insurance and residential construction. Indeed, such firms may design their compensation systems to reward their salespeople more heavily for making sales to new customers than for servicing old ones, as we shall see in Chapter 14.

On the other hand, firms with large market shares, or those that sell frequently purchased nondurable products or products that require substantial service after the sale to guarantee customer satisfaction should adopt a policy that encourages sales representatives to devote most of their efforts to servicing existing customers. Food manufacturers that sell their products to retail supermarkets and firms that produce component parts and supplies for other manufacturers fall into this category. As discussed later in this chapter, some very large customers may require so much servicing that a sales representative is assigned to do nothing but cater to that customer's needs. In such circumstances, firms have specialized their sales positions so that some representatives only service existing accounts, while others spend all their time prospecting for and opening relationships with new customers.

Opening the Relationship. In the initial approach to a prospective customer, the sales representative should try to accomplish two things: (1) determine who within the organization is likely to have the greatest influence and/or authority to purchase the product he or she is trying to sell, and (2) generate enough interest within the firm to obtain the information needed to qualify the prospect as a worthwhile potential customer.[20] We have seen that an organizational buying center often consists of individuals who play different roles in making the purchase decision. Thus, it is important for the salesperson to identify the key decision makers, their desires, and their relative influence. We have also seen that selling organizations can formulate policies to guide sales representatives in approaching prospective customers. When the firm's product is inexpensive and routinely purchased, salespeople might be instructed to deal entirely with the purchasing department. For more technically complex and expensive products, the sales representative might be urged to identify and seek appointments with influencers and decision makers in various functional departments and at several managerial levels in the prospect's organization. Indeed, when the purchase deci-

---

[20] Benson P. Shapiro, *Sales Program Management: Formulation and Implementation* (New York: McGraw-Hill, 1977), p. 159.

sion is likely to be very complex, involving many people within the customer's organization, the seller might adopt a policy of multilevel or team selling.

Qualifying the Prospect.   Before the salesperson attempts to set up an appointment for a major sales presentation, he or she should determine whether the prospect qualifies as a worthwhile potential customer. Obviously, if the prospect does not qualify, the sales representative can spend the time better elsewhere. Qualification is difficult for many salespeople, however, because it requires them to put aside their eternal optimism and make an objective, realistic judgment about the probability of making a profitable sale.

As one authority points out, the qualification process involves finding the answers to three big questions:

1.   Does the prospect have a need for my product or service?
2.   Can I make the people responsible for buying so aware of that need that I can make a sale?
3.   Will the sale be profitable to my company?[21]

To answer such questions, the sales representatives must collect information about the prospect. Knowledge must be gained about the prospect's operations, the kinds of products it makes, its customers, its competitors, and the likely future demand for its products. Information also must be obtained concerning who the customer's present suppliers are and whether there are any special relationships with those firms that would make it difficult for the prospect to change suppliers. Finally, the financial health and the credit rating of the prospect should be checked.

Because so many different kinds of information are needed, nonselling departments within the company—such as the credit and collections department—often are involved in the qualification process. Also, company policies should be formulated to guide the salesperson's judgment concerning whether or not a specific prospect qualifies as a customer. These policies might spell out minimum acceptable standards for such things as the prospect's annual dollar value of purchases in the product category or the credit rating that must be met before he can be accepted as a customer. Similarly, some firms specify a minimum order size to avoid dealing with very small customers and to improve the efficiency of their order-processing and shipping operations.

Presenting the Sales Message.   The presentation is the core of the selling process. The salesperson actually transmits the information and attempts to persuade the prospect to become a customer. Making good presentations is obviously a critically important aspect of the sales job. Unfortunately, many salespeople do not perform this activity very well. In one survey of organizational buyers, for example, 40 percent of the respondents classified the presentations they generally witness as less than good.[22]

One decision that must be made in preparing for an effective sales presenta-

---

[21] Ibid., p. 160.
[22] "How Buyers Rate Salesmen," *Sales Management*, January 15, 1971, pp. 21, 23.

tion concerns how many members of the buying company should attend. Since more than one person is typically involved in making a purchase decision, should a sales presentation be given to all of them as a group? The answer depends on whether or not the members of the buying center have widely divergent attitudes and concerns, and whether those concerns can all be addressed effectively in a single presentation. If not, scheduling a series of one-to-one presentations with different members of the buying group might be more effective.

In many cases, the best way to convince prospects of a product's advantage is to demonstrate it. This is particularly true if it is technically complex. Two rules should be followed in preparing an effective product demonstration. First, the demonstration should be carefully rehearsed to reduce the possibility of even a minor malfunction. Second, the demonstration should be designed to give members of the buying center hands-on experience with the product. For example, Lanier's salespeople are careful to learn about their clients' office operations so they can demonstrate their products actually doing the tasks they would be expected to do after they are purchased.

Different firms have widely different policies concerning how sales presentations should be organized, what selling points should be stressed, and how forcefully the presentation should be made. Encyclopedia companies commonly train their door-to-door salespeople to deliver the same memorized, forceful presentation to every prospect. A person selling computer systems, on the other hand, may be trained in very low-key selling where he or she primarily acts as a source of technical information and advice and does little "pushing" of the company's particular computers. The policy that a firm embraces with respect to sales presentations should be consistent with its other policies for managing accounts. In order to formulate intelligent sales presentation policies, of course, a sales manager must have some knowledge of the alternative presentation methods that might be employed and their relative advantages and limitations. Unfortunately, the space limitations of this chapter make it difficult to present a lengthy discussion of such issues. However, the interested student is urged to examine Appendix A at the end of the chapter, where a variety of sales presentation methods are discussed and evaluated in more detail.

Closing the Sale. *Closing* refers to obtaining a final agreement to purchase. All the salesperson's efforts are wasted unless he or she can get the client to "sign on the dotted line;" yet this is where many salespeople fail. It is natural, even within organizations, to delay making purchase decisions. But as the time it takes the salesperson to close the sale increases, the profit to be made from the sale goes down, and the risk of losing the sale entirely increases. Consequently, the salesperson's task is to speed up the final decision. Often, this can best be done by simply asking for an order. "May I write that order up for you?" and "When do you want it delivered?" are common closings. Another closing tactic is to ask the client to choose among two alternative decisions, such as, "Will that be cash or charge," or, "Did you want the blue one or the red one?"

Servicing the Account. The salesperson's job is not finished when the sale is made. Many kinds of service and assistance must be provided to customers after a sale to ensure their satisfaction and repeat business. Unfortunately, this is another area where many salespeople do not perform very well. Sixty-one percent of the respondents in a survey of organizational buyers were dissatisfied with services after the sale. As one buyer said, "Service is the first thing that gets sold and the last thing delivered."[23]

The salesperson should follow up each sale to make sure that there are no problems with delivery schedules, quality of the goods, or customer billing. In addition, the salesperson often plays a role in supervising the installation of the equipment, training the customer's employees in its use, and ensuring proper maintenance. In most cases, the salesperson must work closely with other departments in his or her firm to make sure that the customer's interests are represented and that no problems lead to customer dissatisfaction.

This kind of service can pay great dividends for both the salesperson and his or her firm. For one thing, satisfied customers are more likely to be repeat purchasers in the future. Also, good service can lead to the sale of other related products and services. In many capital equipment lines, for instance, service contracts—along with supplies and replacement parts—account for greater dollar sales revenue and higher profit margins than the original equipment itself.

A firm's account management policies should provide its sales representatives with clear guidelines concerning the kinds and extensiveness of customer service they should provide. When service after the sale is critical in determining the future of a firm's relationship with its major customer, the firm might organize its sales force to include "major account managers" who specialize in providing continuing service to the company's largest customers.

Major Account Management Approach

One account management policy that is becoming increasingly critical to effective sales management is the firm's posture with respect to winning and keeping "major accounts"—those very large customers who represent a disproportionate share of the firm's total sales volume. Environmental changes are forcing firms in many industries to place greater emphasis on such accounts. This is true for both industrial goods producers and consumer goods firms that sell to wholesalers or retailers in the distribution channel.

The major account is becoming more important to many firms for several reasons. For one thing, industrial concentration and growth have produced some extremely large organizations with equally large purchasing requirements. The 195-unit Jeans West chain, for instance, makes much larger purchases, demands a more sophisticated selling approach, and expects better service than a single-unit, neighborhood sportswear store. There has also been a trend toward centralized purchasing within large organizations as a means of gaining greater buying

---

[23] Ibid., p. 23.

efficiency. Consequently, it is no longer easy for several suppliers to split up a prospect's business by making separate sales to different divisions. Another trend has been the increasing complexity—and price—of many products. The sale of a single computer system to one large customer can represent millions of dollars in revenue.

In response to the growing importance of major accounts, some firms are adopting a "major account management" selling philosophy. This philosophy stresses the dual goals of making sales and developing long-term relationships with large customers.[24] Selling is part of a major account management, but this approach also stresses that the salesperson can perform other functions for the customer that make him or her a valuable adjunct to the customer's organization. The salesperson can provide expert advice and counsel to the customer, including advice on the engineering, design, and installation of complete product systems.

The practice of purchasing total systems originated with the government's practices in buying major weapons and communications systems. Instead of making all of the individual decisions involved in purchasing and putting together the various components of such systems, the government solicits bids from price contractors, who are then responsible for assembling the entire package or system—either by making the components or buying them from subcontractors. Recently, many nongovernment organizations have also turned to the purchase of integrated systems as a means of reducing the costs and uncertainties associated with buying technically complicated and interrelated products. Consequently, sellers are engaging in *systems selling* more frequently as one way of trying to provide better service and satisfaction to their major customers. Systems selling involves two components: (1) the design of well-integrated groups of interlocking products (which is likely to involve negotiations with other subcontractors or original equipment manufacturers) and (2) the implementation of a system of production, inventory control, distribution, and other services to meet a major customer's needs for a smooth-running operation.[25]

Major account management policies also often place a great deal of emphasis on activities to be performed by the salesperson *after* a sale is made. These activities typically include routine servicing like expediting credit approval and delivery. They can also include more extensive service where the salesperson acts as the *customer's representative* to the selling company and attempts to ensure that his or her company is adequately meeting the needs of the buyer.

Because major account management requires that a salesperson devote almost constant attention to the needs of a single customer, firms that use this approach typically have two separate sales forces. One calls on smaller customers, and one is a force of "account managers" who devote all their time to one or a few major

---

[24] Benson P. Shapiro, "Account Management and Sales Organization: New Developments in Practice," in *Sales Management: New Developments From Behavioral and Decision Model Research*, ed. Richard P. Bagozzi (Cambridge, Mass.: Marketing Science Institute, 1979), pp. 265–94. Also see Arthur J. Bragg, "National Account Managers to the Rescue," *Sales and Marketing Management*, August 16, 1982, pp. 30–34.

[25] Philip Kotler, *Marketing Management*, pp. 165–66.

accounts. Indeed, some national accounts are so large and important that a firm may assign an entire team of representatives (consisting of people from various functional departments of the company) to a single customer. The sales team may include representatives from different levels in the company's management hierarchy, too. Each has the responsibility of dealing with purchase influencers and decision makers at corresponding levels in the customer's organization. In other words, implementing a major account management program can have important implications for the way a firm organizes its sales force. These and other organizational considerations involved in strategic sales planning are examined in Chapter 4.

Summary

If a firm is going to maximize the effectiveness of its marketing program, the personal selling effort must be effectively integrated with the other elements of the marketing mix. More particularly, the chapter sought to highlight: (1) the factors affecting the role personal selling should play, (2) the organizational buying process, and (3) how that process affects the activities assigned to the personal selling effort and the kinds of account management policies that managers might formulate to help guide that effort.

The advantages of personal selling as a promotional tool stem largely from the fact that it involves face-to-face communication with a potential customer. For many products and in many industries, advertising is viewed as more effective than personal selling in creating awareness and in reinforcing already held opinions. Personal selling, on the other hand, is viewed as more effective in changing opinions and behaviors. The role personal selling should play in the firm's marketing strategy is logically a function of: (1) the company's resources and objectives, (2) characteristics of the target market (3) product characteristics, (4) distribution policies, and (5) pricing policies.

Many people can be involved in an organizational buying decision, and their roles include those of user, influencer, gatekeeper, buyer, and decider. The stages in the buying process can include:

1. Anticipation or recognition of a problem or need.
2. Determination and description of the characteristics and quantity of the needed item.
3. Search for and qualification of potential buyers.
4. Acquisition of proposals or bids.
5. Evaluation of offerings and selection of suppliers.
6. Selection of an order routine.
7. Performance evaluation and feedback.

The exact structure and time spent at each stage in the process depend on what is being bought and the firm's experience with it.

Effective sales management requires the recognition of the various roles and how they operate at different stages of the process. These considerations help the sales manager determine the mix of activities in which salespeople should engage. The mix of activities can be diverse and can include such things as assisting and working with district management, customer servicing, direct selling, developing relationships with customers, keeping abreast of market conditions, and maintaining records. The company's view of the purchasing process and the roles played by those in the prospect's firm affect the account management policies it adopts. Many firms have explicit policies on what salespeople are to do at each stage of the buying process.

In response to the growing importance of major accounts—those very large customers who represent a disproportionate share of the firm's total sales volume—many firms are also developing explicit policies regarding how such customers should be handled. Often these policies dictate that a salesperson should perform functions for the customer's organization that make him or her more valuable to the customer. These functions might involve designing complete systems, which include components not manufactured by the representative's employer, or assisting in the installation of such systems. Sometimes the salesperson is told to act as the customer's representative to make sure that the customer's needs are satisfied.

Discussion Questions

1. To what extent do the nature of the product, the target market, distribution policies, and company resources influence the types of promotional activities to be used?

2. How can a company determine whether it is spending too much money on personal selling relative to advertising?

3. The organizational buying center varies as a function of size of company and product or service being purchased. How does size of the company influence the composition of the buying center? How would the composition of the buying center differ for each of the following products?
   a. Purchase of a new computer.
   b. Purchase of a new copying machine.
   c. Selecting a different public accounting firm.
   d. Selecting a new textbook for an industrial marketing course.
   e. Choosing a different source for industrial oils and lubricants.
   f. Purchase of a new cardiology machine.
   g. Choosing a marketing research firm.

4. A sales representative for the Business Systems Markets Division of Eastman Kodak is planning her sales call activities. The products produced by BSMD range from microfilm supplies to copiers. What should the sales representative be aware of in approaching a customer? How might the organizational buying process differ for microfilm supplies versus copiers?

5. What does the term *derived demand* mean?

6. Many of the activities sales representatives are expected to perform as described in the Lamont and Lundstrom study (see Table 3–4) are not directly related to sales. As a result, sales representatives are hesitant to perform these activities. What can be done by sales managers to ensure that these activities are performed?

7. What is the most critical issue in the mental-states selling approach?

8. Sales transactions, especially those made to industrial customers, have been known to last as long as several years. In one situation, a sales rep called on one customer for eight years just to get on the approved supplier list. Two years later, the sales rep received the first order. What implications does this situation have on compensation, motivation, and maintaining morale?

9. The Germaine Corporation, located in Atlanta, Georgia, has a centralized purchasing function that orders parts and materials for all of its plants located throughout the southeast. The Specialty Chemicals Corporation, located in Galveston, Texas, classifies Germaine as a key or national account. A key account team from Galveston handles all of the negotiations. Specialty's sales reps are expected to call on the plant managers and other personnel to maintain good account relationships. The sales reps do not receive any commission on sales to Germaine and are beginning to complain. One sales rep stated: "We go out and develop an account, and when it gets large enough, we lose it to the home office. And we lose all the commissions too." What can be done to solve this problem?

10. What is meant by team selling? What are the advantages and disadvantages of this approach?

11. According to one authority in the field of sales management, "more emphasis on serving the buyer and less attention to motivating salespeople would generate greater sales and more profits." How can you justify this statement when most sales managers claim that motivation is their primary problem.

12. How has telemarketing affected account management policies?

13. In 1975, the Allied Bridge Construction Company of New York purchased its first mainframe computer. Ten years later, Allied replaced their original computer with a new system. Would this purchase be classified as a straight rebuy, modified rebuy, or new task purchase situation? How can you explain that two companies buying the same computer would treat the process differently?

Appendix A

Alternative Selling Techniques

Many of the issue that sales managers must deal with in performing their jobs—including the development of account management policies, the choice of selection criteria for hiring new salespeople, and the design of effective training programs—require an understanding of alternative selling techniques and their advantages and limitations. Of course, there are probably as many variations in the way sales presentations are made as there are salespeople. But most selling techniques conform to one of four broad philosophical orientations or approaches toward dealing with customers. These are (1) the stimulus-response approach, (2) the mental-states approach, (3) the need-satisfaction approach, and (4) the problem-solution approach.[1]

Stimulus-Response Approach. The stimulus-response approach to selling is based on the notion that every sensory stimulus produces a response. Sales recruits thus learn what to say (the stimulus) and what buyers are likely to say in most circumstances (the response). In a well-planned stimulus-response model, most of the unfavorable buying responses are known. This allows the company the opportunity to train representatives to respond appropriately. If the prospect responds, "I can't afford to buy this product now," the sales representative has memorized not one but several responses to overcome this objection. One answer might be, "Well, we have an excellent financing program that you should be able to afford. Let me explain it to you." The emphasis in training is thus on the standardized sales presentation, the likely responses by customers, and the possible rejoinders to overcome their objections.

There are some advantages to this approach. A well-developed "canned" sales presentation ensures that the salesperson will give a smooth, complete talk that covers all the important selling points in a logical order. The stimulus-response approach also enables a firm to hire inexperienced salespeople and get them ready for the field with only minimal training. On the other hand, the stimulus-response approach has some major disadvantages that limit its appropriateness for many types of personal selling. The most obvious disadvantage is that it ignores differences in the needs and interests of different customers. Since customers differ, they will not all respond in the same way to a canned sales talk. Also, when salespeople memorize their presentations, they cannot adjust them to the feedback provided by the customer, particularly when the customer's response is not one for which the representative has been trained. One story about such problems involves a pot-and-pan salesperson who insisted on going through the

---

[1] R. Gwinner, "Base Theories in the Formulation of Sales Strategy," *MSU Business Topics*, Autumn 1968, p. 37–44.

entire memorized presentation even though the couple had already decided to buy the product.

Of course, salespeople can be allowed some degree of freedom to adjust their canned presentation to the specific demands of a given selling situation. One way of accomplishing this is to provide the salesperson with a standardized presentation printed on flipcharts or slides but then instruct the individual to add individual comments where necessary. The results of a survey of sales executives—shown in Table A–1—show that such "semiautomated" presentations are thought to be more effective than a completely memorized sales pitch.[2]

Table A–1
Sales executive rankings of sales presentation effectiveness

Objective	Fully Automated	Semi-automated	Memorized	Organized	Unstructured
Conserves the prospect's time	3	2	5	1	4
Tells the complete story	2	3	4	1	5
Delivers an accurate, authoritative, and ethical message	1	2	4	3	5
Persuades the prospect	4	3	5	1	2
Anticipates objections	3	2	5	1	4
Facilitates training of salespeople	3	2	5	1	4
Increases salesperson's self-confidence	4	2	5	1	3
Facilitates supervision of salespeople	3	2	4	1	5

Notes:
Fully automated: Sound movies, slides, or filmstrips dominate the presentation. The salesperson's participation consists of setting up the projector, answering simple questions, and writing up the order. Many audiovisuals are available.
Semiautomated: The salesperson reads the presentation from copy printed on flip charts, readoff binders, promotional broadsides, or brochures. The salesperson adds his own comments when necessary.
Memorized: The salesperson delivers a company-prepared message that he has memorized. Supplementary visual aids may or may not be used.
Organized: The salesperson is allowed complete flexibility in wording; however, he does follow a company pattern, checklist, or outline. Visual aids are optional.
Unstructured: The salesperson is on his own to describe the product any way he sees fit. Generally, the presentation varies from prospect to prospect.
Source: From Marvin A. Jolson, "Should the Sales Presentation Be 'Fresh' or 'Canned'?" *Business Horizons*, October 1973, p. 85.

Due to its rigidity, the stimulus-response approach is seldom employed in the sale of complex industrial goods where buyers' needs and product applications are likely to vary from one customer to the next. Its primary application today is in situations where a relatively simple, standardized product is being sold to large numbers of potential customers who are likely to respond favorably to a standardized appeal, as in selling encyclopedias and other consumer goods door-to-door.

---

[2] Marvin A. Jolson, "Should the Sales Presentation Be 'Fresh' or 'Canned'?" *Business Horizons*, October 1973, pp. 80–86.

The survey results in Table A–1 do suggest, however, that sales presentations are much more effective when management provides salespeople with guidelines to help organize their approach to the customer than when presentations are entirely unstructured. The mental-states approach is one means for providing such organization.

Mental-States Approach. This approach to selling is based on the idea that a buyer's mind passes through several successive stages before he or she ultimately decides to make a purchase. It is based on the AIDA theory of persuasion, which stresses that promotional messages must attract the prospect's attention, gain interest, create desire, and stimulate action to complete a sale successfully.

Firms that use the mental-states approach emphasize the use of a selling "formula" in designing a presentation that organizes selling points to coincide with the buyer's movement through the stages of attention, interest, desire, and action. One major advantage of this approach over a strictly memorized presentation is that the salesperson can tailor the sales pitch to each individual prospect. Most companies that use the mental-states approach have found that salespeople can be trained to control the direction of a sales interview by carefully observing the responses of the prospect. They then modify the presentation to stress those points most relevant to the prospect's current state of mind.

This type of selling strategy is used most commonly by firms with products or services that are complicated and difficult for prospective customers to understand. It is particularly appropriate when repeat calls on a long-run basis are likely to be required to close a sale. Consequently, this kind of selling approach is more common in industrial markets than in retail or consumer goods markets.[3]

As with the stimulus-response approach, one disadvantage of a selling formula aimed at moving a prospect through successive mental states is that it is a salesperson-oriented rather than a customer-oriented method. In an effort to move the prospect from one mental state to the next, the salesperson has a tendency to dominate the interview and the customer may have little chance to participate. Little attention is paid to variations in needs or circumstances among customers. Companies that use this approach tend to emphasize the sales presentation itself at the expense of those steps in the selling process that precede and follow the presentation. Perhaps the most serious difficulty with the mental-states approach, however, is that there is no general agreement among psychologists that mental states do, in fact, exist in the minds of potential buyers or that all buyers proceed through the same states in the same sequence. Even if such states do exist, however, it can be difficult to train the salesperson to figure out which state a prospect is in at the moment. It is also hard to know when to leave the selling points related to one mental state and move on to the next.

Need-Satisfaction Approach. Compared with the previous two selling strategies, the need-satisfaction approach is much more compatible with the modern marketing philosophy that emphasizes the customers to be served rather than the product to be sold. Under this approach, the customer's needs are the

---

[3] R. Gwinner, "Base Theories," p. 40.

starting point in making a sale. The salesperson's task is to identify the prospect's needs, making the prospect aware of that need, and then persuading the prospect that his or her product or service will satisfy that need better than any other alternative.

Firms that utilize this approach emphasize the importance of the early stages in the selling process, such as opening the relationship and qualifying the prospects. The salesperson must become familiar with the prospect's business, industry, and even customers and competitors to tailor a sales presentation to the prospect's unique needs and concerns.

One major advantage of the need-satisfaction approach is that it is customer-oriented and flexible. Proponents of this approach contend that it provides the basis for a friendly buyer-seller relationship with two-way communication. Because the salesperson concentrates on discovering each prospect's needs and developing presentations that demonstrate how the product can satisfy those needs, this approach helps to minimize sales resistance. Over time, the salesperson may become a trusted source of information, and his or her advice and counsel may be sought and accepted by the customer.

The advantages of the need-satisfaction approach outweigh the disadvantages in most selling situations. Nevertheless, the approach does have some practical limitations that make it inappropriate under some conditions. For one thing, it demands highly qualified sales personnel who have an excellent understanding of their potential customers. They must have the training and experience to adjust their selling methods to the needs and concerns of each individual prospect. Also, this approach requires a great deal of time for the salesperson to become familiar with the prospect. Consequently, it is an expensive method, and it should be used only when the value of the potential sales justifies the expense. Finally, firms are likely to adopt this philosophy of selling only when their overall business philosophy is customer-oriented rather than product-oriented. Thus, the need-satisfaction approach is more common in the sale of consumer durables than in the sale of industrial goods. This is gradually changing, however, as more industrial goods producers embrace a customer-oriented philosophy of marketing.

Problem-Solution Approach.   The problem-solution theory of selling is a logical extension of the need-satisfaction approach. Both are customer-oriented approaches where the sales representative focuses on the prospect's individual needs. Under the problem-solution method, however, the salesperson goes one step further to help the prospect identify several alternative solutions, analyze their advantages and disadvantages, and select the one best solution. The salesperson completely deemphasizes the product offering and concentrates on providing expert advice to the prospect much like a true business consultant. The problem-solving approach may lead a sales representative to suggest that a prospect buy a competitor's product, for example. The primary objective is to form long-term relationships with customers in which the sales representative is seen as a trusted source of technical information and advice.

As with the need-satisfaction approach, the problem-solution method requires extremely competent, well-trained, and experienced sales representatives. It also requires that the salesperson spend a great deal of time with each prospect. Consequently, it is a very expensive selling method.[4] In view of these limitations, this approach is seldom used in consumer goods markets. Instead, it is used primarily in selling technically complex and expensive industrial goods, such as computer systems and production machinery.

---

[4] Dan T. Dunn, Claude A. Thomas, and James L. Lubawski, "Pitfalls of Consultative Selling," *Business Horizons*, September-October 1981, pp. 59–65.

Chapter **4**

Organizing the
Selling Effort

A very important ingredient in any effective sales management program is the organizational arrangement used to structure the personal selling effort. This chapter examines some issues involved in deciding how to organize a sales force, and it outlines some different organizational designs, together with their advantages and limitations.

Ansul Company's Flexible Sales Organization

Ansul Company of Marinette, Wisconsin, started to produce high-quality fire extinguishers and other fire protection equipment as the result of an acquisition in 1939. By the mid-1970s, the firm's Fire Protection Group accounted for 51 percent of its $120-million annual sales volume and 73 percent of its pretax profits.[1]

In the early years, Ansul's sales force sold directly to customers. Indeed, its primary task was to educate customers because Ansul pioneered the use of dry chemical fire extinguishers. Such extinguishers use a mixture of dry chemical powders, rather than water, to put out flames. At the time, many people were skeptical about whether dry chemicals were more effective in extinguishing certain types of fires. To help its salespeople get the word across, Ansul established a school in 1940 to train customers in fire-fighting techniques. The school, now the largest of its kind in the world, was a first step in Ansul's policy of meticulous attention to customer service. A second was its switch from direct selling to the use of distributors.

As dry chemicals gained acceptance, Ansul had to assure customers that the firm's equipment would be serviced. The switch to using a select group of local wholesale distributors, each of whom maintained an inventory of Ansul products and a service department, accomplished that. The primary job of Ansul's own sales force, then, was building the distributor organization and working with distributor sales and service people to help sell and train end users.

During the 1970s, Ansul adopted more sophisticated account management policies, and the primary role of its sales force became helping the firm's distributors develop their business and marketing skills. As one 22-year sales veteran says, "We're managers of our own territories." He spends most of his time making joint calls with distributor salesmen, training them and distributor servicemen on new products, riding service trucks to see how Ansul customers and equipment are being cared for, and training end users in the proper use of fire-fighting equipment. In addition, Ansul conducts a 10-month, self-study Profitable Distribution Management program to help its distributors upgrade their skills in finance, growth planning, management of operations, and leadership.

---

[1] This example is based on material found in S. Scanlon, "Ansul Blazes New Sales Patterns," *Sales Management*, December 9, 1974, pp. 25–28, reprinted with the permission of the Ansul Company, and on conversations with Mr. H. Doug Plunkett of the Ansul Company in April 1984.

A Rapidly Changing Sales Organization

In the latter half of the 1970s, Ansul was acquired by Wormald International, Ltd., of Sydney, Australia, a leading manufacturer of fire-protection products outside the U.S.

In the 1980s, Ansul continues to maintain a flexible sales force to meet changing market needs and to enter new markets. Although the basic sales force organization of the 1970s remains unchanged, the ability to plan and execute a flexible sales force structure was formalized in 1982 with the establishment of a Market Development Department. This department is responsible for the identification of new market segments and the development of the associated marketing and sales plans. When a new segment is identified, Ansul shifts specific salespeople into a task team designated to work directly with end users and influencers to develop the market and establish brand loyalty. In addition, these task teams work with Ansul's field salespeople and distributors to train them in specific selling techniques for the target market.

Following the acquisition by Wormald, the North American operation integrated forward into the direct selling and installation portion of the fire-protection market to target large projects that were beyond the technical and financial resources of its independent distributors.

The result of maintaining sales force flexibility and forward integration has been a rise in U.S. fire protection sales from $61 million in 1975 to $120 million in 1984.

Ansul's Attention to Sales Organization Is Not Typical

Organizing the activities and management of the sales force is a major part of strategic sales planning. Also, as discussed in Chapter 3, certain organizational issues must be resolved to implement specific account management policies effectively, such as using separate account managers to handle major national customers. Certainly, Ansul Company's experience illustrates the value of an innovative and well conceived sales organization in helping a firm implement its account management policies and pursue new markets.

Unfortunately, Ansul's strategic use of organizational restructuring is not common among either industrial or consumer goods marketers. One authority states that "sales organization is perhaps the most neglected part of sales force management. It certainly requires less attention than motivation programs or compensation but often has more impact."[2] This chapter begins with a discussion of the

---

[2] From Benson P. Shapiro, *Sales Program Management: Formulation and Implementation* (New York: McGraw-Hill, 1977), p. 377. Copyright © 1977, McGraw-Hill, Inc. Used with the permission of McGraw-Hill Book Company.

purposes of organization—the things that a good organizational plan should accomplish. Next, issues related to the horizontal organization of the sales effort are explored. Horizontal organization is concerned with how specific selling activities are divided among various members of the sales force. Questions related to horizontal organization include the following:

1. Should the company employ its own salespeople, or should some or all of its selling efforts be contracted to outside agents—such as manufacturer's representatives?
2. How many different sales forces should the company have, and how should they be arranged? Should separate sales representatives be assigned to different products, types of customers, or sales functions?
3. Who should be responsible for selling to major national accounts?

Finally, the *vertical* structuring of the sales organization is discussed. Vertical structuring refers to organizing a firm's sales managers and their activities rather than the personnel in the sales force. Vertical organization issues include:

1. How many levels of sales management are appropriate? What span of control is best?
2. Should sales-related functions—such as order entry, credit, or repair and maintenance—be integrated into the sales organization? If so, at what level?
3. What management functions should each sales manager perform? Should staff specialists be hired to perform certain functions? To what level of management should such specialists report?
4. How can the activities of specialized sales forces, staff specialists, and related departments be integrated and coordinated?

An understanding of these issues should provide greater appreciation for the crucial role organizational decisions play in the development of an effective strategic sales program.

Purposes of Sales Organization

An organizational structure is simply an arrangement of activities involving a group of people. The goal in designing an organization is to divide and coordinate activities in such a way that the group can accomplish its common objectives better by acting as a group than they could by acting as individuals. The starting point in organizing a sales force, then, is determining the goals or objectives to be accomplished; these are specified in the firm's overall marketing plan. The selling activities necessary to accomplish the firm's marketing objectives must then be divided up and allocated to members of the sales force in such a way that the objectives can be achieved with as little duplication of effort as possible. More specifically, an organizational structure should serve the following purposes:

1. Activities should be divided up and arranged in such a way that the firm can benefit from the *specialization of labor.*
2. The organizational structure should provide for *stability and continuity* in the firm's selling efforts.
3. The structure should provide for the *coordination* of the various activities assigned to different persons in the sales force and different departments in the firm.

Division and Specialization of Labor

Two centuries ago, Adam Smith pointed out that the efficiency with which almost any function is performed can be increased by dividing it up into its component activities and assigning each activity to a specialist. Division and specialization of labor increase productivity because each specialist can concentrate his or her efforts and become more proficient at the assigned task. Also, management can assign individuals only to those activities for which they have aptitude.

In some cases, the personal selling function is so simple and straightforward that a firm could gain few, if any, benefits by applying the principles of division and specialization of labor to its sales force. Salespeople in such companies are expected to carry out all the activities necessary to sell all the products in the company's line to all types of customers within their territories. On the other hand, in many firms the selling function is sufficiently complicated that increased efficiency and effectiveness can be gained by dividing up the necessary selling activities. Different activities are assigned to various specialists, creating two or more specialized sales forces.

The question with which management must wrestle is: What is the best way to divide the required selling activities to gain the maximum benefits of specialization within the sales force? Should independent agent middlemen be used to perform some or all of the firm's selling efforts? Should selling activities be organized by product, by customer type, or by selling function (for example, prospecting for new accounts versus servicing old customers)? As discussed in a later section of this chapter, each basis for horizontally structuring the sales organization has its own advantages and disadvantages. Which one is best depends on the firm's objectives, target market, product line, and other internal and external factors.

The benefits of division and specialization of labor can be gained with managerial functions as well as selling functions. Some firms use a simple "line" form of vertical organization in which the chain of command runs from the chief sales executive down through levels of subordinates. Each subordinate is responsible to only one person on the next higher level, and each is expected to perform all the necessary sales management activities relevant to his or her own level. The most common form of vertical organization structure—especially in medium- and large-sized firms—is the "line and staff" organization. In this form, several sales management activities—such as personnel selection, training, and distributor relations—are assigned to separate staff specialists. This kind of specialization, however, raises some questions concerning organizational design, such as what specific functions should be assigned to staff executives, how can staff activities be integrated with those of line sales managers, and to what level of sales management should staff executives report? These questions are examined further in a later section of this chapter.

Stability and Continuity of Organizational Performance

Although many companies use the principles of division and specialization of labor in designing their sales organizations, they sometimes ignore a related caveat concerning good organizational design: organize activities, not people. In other words, activities should be assigned to positions within the sales organization without regard to the talents or preferences of current employees. Once an ideal organizational structure has been designed, people can be trained or, if need be, recruited to fill positions within the structure. Over time, occupants of lower positions in the organization should be given the experience and training necessary to enable them to move into higher positions. In athletic terms, the organization should build "depth" at all positions. This provides a measure of stability and continuity of performance for the organization. The same activities are carried out at the same positions within the firm even if specific individuals are promoted or leave.

It can be difficult to avoid building an organization around specific individuals. Sometimes the vitality and effectiveness of an organization can be increased by adapting the structure of activities to take advantage of the particular strengths and talents of individuals. For example, a district sales manager may be given a disproportionate share of sales training duties because he or she is recognized as a particularly effective and inspiring developer of young talent. As a rule, however, such "people adaptations" should be kept to a minimum. This avoids having the organization become so dependent on the abilities of specific people that it is impossible to find replacements when those individuals leave the organization.

Coordination and Integration

The advantages of the division and specialization of labor are clear, but specialization also causes a problem for managers. When activities are divided and performed by different individuals, ways must be found to coordinate and integrate those activities so that all efforts are directed at accomplishing the same objective. As two well-known organization theorists point out, the more an organization's tasks are divided up among specialists, the more difficult the problem of integrating those tasks becomes.[3] The problem is even worse when outside agents—like manufacturers' representatives—are used, because the manager has no formal authority over them and cannot always control their actions.

Sales managers must be concerned about the coordination and integration of the efforts of their salespeople in three different ways. First, the activities of the sales force must be integrated with the needs and concerns of customers. Second, the firm's selling activities must be coordinated with those of other departments, such as production, product development, logistics, and finance. Finally, if the firm divides its selling tasks among specialized units within the sales force, all those tasks must be integrated. Consequently, the primary function of the vertical structure of a firm's sales organization is to ensure these three kinds of integration. Questions of vertical organization—such as how many levels of sales management the firm should have, the appropriate span of control for each sales executive, and the most effective use of staff specialists—should be examined with an eye toward effective integration of the firm's overall selling efforts.

Horizontal Structure of the Sales Force

There is no best way to divide selling activities among members of the sales force. The best sales organization varies with the objectives, strategies, and tasks of the firm. Furthermore, as the firm's environment, objectives, or marketing strategy change, its sales force may have to be reorganized. In other words, there are several common bases used for structuring the sales effort, and each has unique advantages that make it appropriate for a firm under certain circumstances. The first issue to be decided is whether the firm should hire its own salespeople or use outside agents. When a company sales force is used, alternative approaches include: (1) geographic organization, (2) organization by type of product, (3) organization by type of customer, and (4) organization by selling function.

A Company Sales Force or Independent Agents?

This book focuses primarily on issues associated with the management of an internal company sales force, where all of the salespeople and their managers are employees of the firm. In many cases, though, one organizational option that is important to consider is the use of independent agents instead of company salespeople. While only about 10 percent of total industrial sales volume is accounted

---

[3] Paul R. Lawrence and Jay W. Lorsch, *Organization and Environment: Managing Distribution and Integration* (Boston: Division of Research, Graduate School of Business Aministration, Harvard University, 1967).

for by independent agents, this percentage varies considerably across industries. For example, while the percentage of sales made through independent manufacturers' representatives is 4 percent for grocery products and only 2 percent for alcoholic beverages, it jumps to 43 percent for electrical goods, 32 percent for furniture and home furnishings, and 19 percent for apparel. Also, the use of outside agents as an alternative approach to organizing the sales effort seems to have increased somewhat in recent years. During the period from 1972 to 1977, there was a 107 percent increase in sales volume by manufacturers' representatives compared to a more modest 77 percent increase by company-owned sales branches.[4]

Of the various types of agent middlemen a manufacturer might use to perform the selling function, the two most common are manufacturers' representatives and selling (or sales) agents.[5] *Manufacturers' representatives* are agent middlemen who sell part of the output of their principals—the manufacturers they represent—on an extended contract basis. They neither take ownership nor physical possession of the goods they sell, but concentrate instead on performing only the selling function; they are compensated solely by commissions. Reps are agents in the legal sense of the word in that they have no authority to modify their principals' instructions concerning the prices, terms of sale, etc., to be offered to potential buyers. Manufacturers' reps cover a specific and limited territory and specialize in a limited range of products, although they commonly represent several related but noncompeting product lines from different manufacturers. These characteristics give reps the advantages of having (1) many established contacts with potential customers in their territories, (2) familiarity with the technical nature and applications of the types of products they specialize in, (3) the ability to keep expenses low by being able to spread fixed costs over the products of several different manufacturers, and (4) the appearance as a totally variable cost item on their principals' income statements, since the reps' commissions vary directly with the amount of goods sold.

Selling agents are also agent middlemen who do not take title or possession of the goods they sell but are compensated solely by commissions from their principals. They differ from reps, however, in that they usually handle the entire output of a principal (thus, operating as the entire sales force for the manufacturer rather than as a representative in a single, specified territory). In order to accomplish their purpose, selling agents are usually granted broader authority by their principals to modify prices and terms of sale, and they play an active role in shaping the manufacturer's promotional and sales programs.

Deciding When Outside Agents Are Appropriate. The decision about whether to use independent agents or a company sales force to cover a particular product/market is difficult to make because it involves a variety of considerations and trade-offs. In general, though, the two most important sets of factors for

---

[4] Thayer C. Taylor, "A Raging "Rep" Idemic," *Sales and Marketing Management*, June 8, 1981, pp. 33–35.

[5] Louis W. Stern and Adel I. El-Ansary, *Marketing Channels*, 2d ed. (Englewood Cliffs, N.J.: Prentice-Hall, 1982), Chap. 3 and pp. 150–51.

a manager to consider are: (1) economic criteria and (2) control and strategic criteria.[6]

Economic Criteria. In a given selling situation a company sales force and independent agents are likely to produce different levels of costs and sales volume. A first step in deciding which form of sales organization to use, then, is to estimate and compare the costs of the two alternatives. A simplified example of such a cost comparison is illustrated in Figure 4–1. The fixed costs of using external agents are lower than those of using a company sales force because there is usually less administrative overhead involved and agents do not receive a salary or reimbursement for field selling expenses. But costs of using agents tend to rise faster as sales volume increases because agents usually receive larger commissions than company salespeople. Consequently, there is a break-even level of sales volume (Vb in Figure 4–1) below which the costs of external agents are lower but above which a company sales force becomes more efficient. This helps explain why agents tend to be used by smaller firms or by larger firms in their smaller territories where sales volume is too low to warrant a company sales force.

Figure 4–1
Illustrative cost comparison for the choice between a company sales force and independent agents

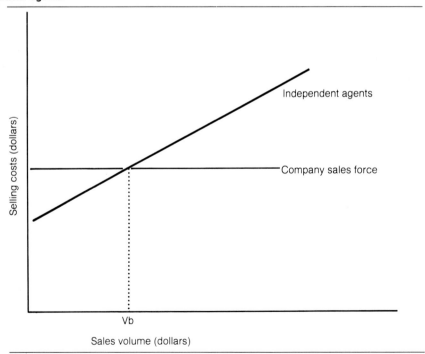

----

[6] Ibid., chap. 5.

Low fixed costs also make agents an attractive alternative when a firm is moving into new territories or product lines where success is uncertain. Since the agent does not get paid unless sales are made, the costs of failure are minimized.

The other side of the economic equation, of course, is sales volume. The critical question is whether company salespeople are likely to produce a higher volume of total sales than agents in a given situation. Most sales and marketing managers believe that they will. This belief is based on the fact that company salespeople concentrate entirely on the firm's products, they may be better trained, they may be more aggressive since their future depends more on the company's success, and customers often prefer to deal directly with a supplier. On the other hand, an agent's contacts and experience in an industry can make him or her more effective than a company salesperson—particularly in situations where the company is new or is moving into a new geographic area or product line.

Control and Strategic Criteria.   Regardless of which organizational form produces the greatest sales in the short run, many managers still argue that an internal sales force is preferable to agents in the long run due to the difficulty of controlling agents and getting them to conform to their principals' strategic objectives. Agents are seen as independent actors who can be expected to opportunistically pursue their own short-run objectives. This makes them reluctant to engage in activities with a long-run strategic payoff to their principal, such as cultivating new accounts or small customers with growth potential, performing service and support activities, or promoting new products.[7] Some evidence in support of this argument is provided by a recent study which found that manufacturers' representatives are more dissatisfied with close supervision and attempts to control their behavior than are company salespeople.[8]

In general, then, most marketing executives argue that it is best to use agents to represent a small company or for territories with low sales potential where the benefits from scale economies outweigh the difficulties of motivating and controlling the agent's behavior. It is usually considered preferable to switch to direct salespeople as soon as a company or territory can support the higher fixed costs.

Geographic Organization

The simplest and most common method of organizing a company's sales force is to assign individual salespeople to separate geographic territories. In this kind of organization, each salesperson is responsible for performing all the activities necessary to sell all the products in the company's line to all potential customers

---

[7] For a more extensive discussion of opportunism and other determinants of "transaction costs" in dealing with external agents, see Oliver E. Williamson, *Markets and Hierarchies: Analysis and Antitrust Implications* (New York: The Free Press, 1975); and Erin M. Anderson and Barton A. Weitz, "A Framework for Analyzing Vertical Integration Issues in Marketing," Report #3-110, (Cambridge, Mass.: Marketing Science Institute, 1983).

[8] Jayashree Mahajan, Gilbert A. Churchill, Jr., Neil M. Ford, and Orville C. Walker, Jr., "A Comparison of the Impact of Organizational Climate on the Job Satisfaction of Manufacturers' Agents and Company Salespeople: An Exploratory Study," working paper #7-83-10, Graduate School of Business, University of Wisconsin, 1983.

Figure 4–2
Geographic sales organization

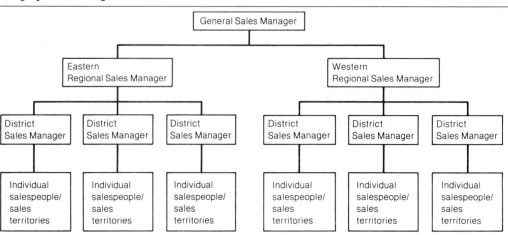

in his or her territory. A geographic sales organization is illustrated in Figure 4–2.

The geographic sales organization has several strengths. Most important, it tends to have the lowest cost. Because there is only one salesperson in each territory and territories tend to be smaller than they are under other forms of organization, travel time and expenses are minimized. Also, the simplicity of this organization usually means that fewer managerial levels are required for coordination. Thus, sales administration and overhead expenses are kept relatively low.

The simplicity of a geographic organizational structure leads to another advantage involving the firm's relationships with its customers. Since only one salesperson calls on each customer, there is seldom any confusion about who is responsible for what or about who the customer should talk to when problems arise.

The major disadvantage of a geographic sales organization is that it does not provide any benefits of the division and specialization of labor. Each salesperson is expected to be a jack-of-all-trades. Each must sell all the firm's products to all types of customers and perform all the selling functions. Also, this organizational structure provides the individual salesperson with a good deal of freedom to make decisions concerning which selling functions to perform, what products to emphasize, and which customers to concentrate on. Unfortunately, salespeople are likely to expend most of this effort on the functions they perform best and on the products and customers they perceive to be most rewarding, whether or not such effort is consistent with management's objectives and account management policies. For instance, many salespeople concentrate on obtaining routine orders from long-standing customers rather than pursuing new prospects where the likelihood of obtaining a sale and commission is lower. Management can try to direct the efforts of salespeople through close supervision, well-designed compensation and evaluation plans, and clearly defined statements of policy, but the basic problem remains. Since each salesperson is expected to perform a full range of selling functions, he or she—rather than management—can control the way that selling effort is allocated across products, customers, and selling tasks.

Although a geographic approach to sales organization has its limitations, its basic simplicity and low cost make it very popular among smaller firms, particularly those with limited, uncomplicated product lines. Also, while it is unusual for larger organizations to rely exclusively on geographic organization, they do commonly use it in conjunction with other organizational forms. For example, a firm may have two separate sales forces for different products in its line, but each sales force is likely to be organized geographically.

Product Organization

Some companies have separate sales forces for each product—or related groups of products—in their product line, as shown in Figure 4–3. International Business Machines, for example, has one sales force for office equipment such as typewriters and dictaphones, and another for computers.

Figure 4–3
Sales force organized by product type

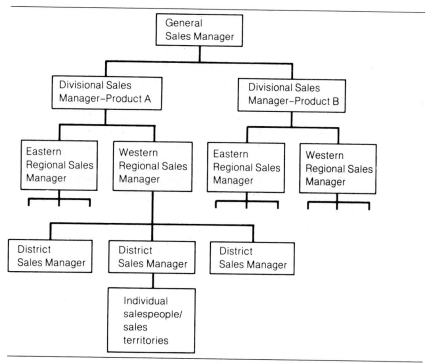

The primary advantage of specializing the sales organization by product is that individual salespeople can develop familiarity with the technical attributes, applications, and the most effective selling methods associated with a single product or related products. Also, when the firm's manufacturing facilities are organized by product type—as when separate factories produce each product—a product-oriented organization can lead to closer cooperation between sales and production. This can be very beneficial when the product is custom-tailored to fit the specifications of different customers or when production and delivery schedules are critical in gaining and keeping a customer. Finally, a product-oriented sales organization can enable sales management to control the allocation of selling effort across the various products in the company's line. If management decides that more effort should be devoted to a particular product, it can simply assign more salespeople to that product.

The major disadvantage of a sales force organized by product type is duplication of effort. Salespeople from different product divisions are assigned to the same geographic areas and may call on the same customers. This leads to higher selling expenses than would be the case with a simple geographic organization. It also leads to a need for greater coordination of the efforts across the various product divisions, which, in turn, requires more sales management personnel and higher administrative costs. Finally, this duplication of effort can cause some confusion and frustration among the firm's customers, who must deal with two or more sales representatives from the same supplier.

Since the major advantage of a product-oriented organization is that it allows salespeople to develop specialized knowledge of one or a few products, this form of organization is most commonly used by firms with product lines that are large and diverse. It is also used by manufacturers of highly technical products that require different kinds of technical expertise or different selling methods. A product-oriented sales organization is often the result of a firm growing through merger. When one firm acquires another, it may be expedient to treat the acquired firm as a separate division and allow it to maintain its own sales organization for selling its own products. This was the case, for example, when Pillsbury acquired Green Giant in 1978. Green Giant continues to manage its own marketing and sales operations.

Organization by Customers or Markets

In recent years, it has become increasingly popular for firms to organize their sales forces by customer type. Ansul Company, with separate sales forces for end users, governments, and original equipment manufacturers, uses this kind of sales organization. Other examples of customer-oriented sales organizations are shown in Figure 4–4.

Organizing a firm's sales force by customer type is a natural extension of the

Figure 4–4
Sales forces organized by
customer type

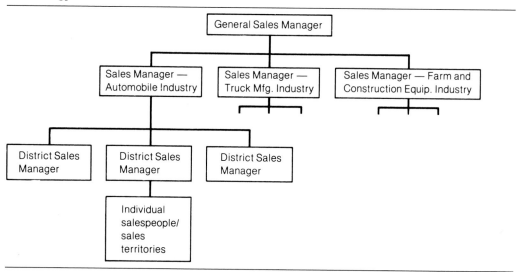

"marketing concept" and a strategy of marketing segmentation.[9] When sales-people specialize in calling on a particular type of customer, they gain a better understanding of such customers' needs and requirements. They can also be trained to use different selling approaches for different markets and to implement specialized marketing and promotional programs. A related advantage of customer specialization is that, as salespeople become familiar with their customers' specific businesses and needs, they are more likely to discover ideas for new products and marketing approaches that will appeal to those customers. This can be a definite advantage in rapidly changing, highly competitive markets. Finally, this organizational structure allows marketing managers to control the allocation of selling effort to different markets by varying the sizes of the specialized sales forces.

The disadvantages of a customer-oriented sales organization are much the same as those of a product-oriented structure. The duplication of effort that results from having different salespeople calling on different types of customers in the same territory can lead to higher selling expenses and administrative costs. Also, when customer firms have different departments or divisions operating in different industries, two or more salespeople may end up calling on the same customer. This can cause confusion and frustration among customers.

---

[9] For a more detailed discussion of the merits of this approach, see Mack Hannan, "Reorganize Your Company around Its Markets," *Harvard Business Review*, November-December 1974, pp. 63–76.

Many firms must feel that the advantages of a customer-oriented sales organization outweigh its limitations because it is growing in popularity as an organizational approach. This is particularly true for firms with products that have widely different applications in different markets or firms that must use different approaches when selling to different types of customers, as when a company sells to the government as well as to private industry. Also, specialization by customer type is a useful form of organization when a firm's marketing objectives include the penetration of previously untapped markets, as was the case with Ansul Company.

Organization by Selling Function

Different kinds of selling tasks often require different abilities and skills on the part of the salesperson. Thus, it may be logical under some circumstances to organize the sales force so that different salespeople specialize in performing different selling functions. One such functional organization recommended by some authorities is to have one sales force specializing in prospecting for and developing new accounts, while a second force maintains and services old customers.[10] Such functional specialization can be difficult to implement, however. Since a firm is likely to assign its most competent, experienced, and "flashiest" salespeople to the new accounts sales force, new customers might object to being turned over from the salesperson who won their patronage to a maintenance salesperson with a personality better suited to mundane tasks. It also can be difficult for management to coordinate the development and maintenance functions because there is likely to be some feelings of rivalry and jealousy between the two sales forces.

Another form of functional specialization, however, is commonly and successfully used by many industrial product firms: "developmental salespeople" who are responsible for assisting in the development and early sales of new products. The functions assigned to developmental specialists usually include conducting market research, assisting the firm's research and development and engineering departments, and selling new products as they are developed. Indeed, these specialists are often part of a firm's research and development department rather than in the regular sales force. Such specialists can serve a very useful role in ensuring the development of successful new products, particularly when they are experienced and have a great deal of knowledge about customers' operations and needs as well as about their own firm's technical and production capabilities.

---

[10] George N. Kahn and Abraham Shuchman, "Specialize Your Salesmen!", *Harvard Business Review*, January-February 1961, pp. 90–98.

Telemarketing and the Organization of "Inside" and "Outside" Sales Forces

One unique form of specialization by selling function that is rapidly gaining in popularity is the use of inside telephone salespeople and outside field salespeople to accomplish separate selling objectives. Obviously, not all selling functions can be performed over the phone, but telemarketing has proven very useful for carrying out selected activities, including:

Prospecting for and qualifying potential new accounts, which can then be turned over to field salespeople for personal contact. This function can often be facilitated by including a toll-free 800 phone number in all of the firm's promotional materials so that interested potential customers can call to obtain more information about advertised products or services.

Servicing existing accounts quickly when unexpected problems arise, such as through the use of technical-assistance "hotlines."

Seeking repeat purchases from existing accounts that cannot be covered efficiently in person, such as small or marginal customers and those in remote geographic locations.

Gaining quicker communication of newsworthy developments, like the introduction of new or improved products or special sales programs.[11]

The popularity of telemarketing as a means of supplementing the activities of the field sales force is growing for two reasons: (1) customers like it, and (2) it can increase the productivity of a firm's sales efforts. From the customers' point of view, the increased centralization of purchasing, together with growing numbers of product alternatives and potential suppliers in many industries, have placed increased demands on the time of purchasing agents and other members of organizations' buying centers. Consequently, they like sales contacts over the phone—particularly for more routine purposes, such as soliciting reorders or relaying information about special sales programs and price promotions—because they take less time than personal sales calls. Indeed, according to a study of trends in the wholesale-distribution industry conducted by Arthur Andersen & Co., customers say personal contact with a salesperson is becoming less important to them than contact with a capable inside sales force. The study predicts that by 1990, half of the average wholesale distributor's sales force will be inside and that the role of the outside salesperson will shift toward greater emphasis on promotion and customer instruction and service.[12]

From the seller's viewpoint, a combination of inside and outside salespeople offers a way of improving the overall efficiency of the sales effort. Since some

---

[11] Jeffrey Pope, "Ringing Up Industrial Sales by Phone," *Sales and Marketing Management*, October 12, 1981, pp. 50–51.

[12] "Rebirth of a Salesman: Willy Loman Goes Electronic," *Business Week*, February 27, 1984, p. 104.

estimates suggest that average field travel expenses (e.g., car rental or mileage, hotels and meals) are now higher than the average salesperson's wages and commissions,[13] moving some salespeople inside allows the firm to lower the costs of routine sales activities substantially. At the same time, it enables the more expensive outside sales force to concentrate on activities with the highest potential long-term payout, such as new account generation and servicing major accounts. The efficiency of telemarketing makes it a particularly useful tool for implementing an account management policy that directs different amounts of effort toward classifications of customers based on differences in size or potential. In the past, some firms prohibited their sales forces from calling on very small customers—or told them to visit such accounts only infrequently—because their purchase volume was simply not large enough to cover the cost of a sales call and still contribute to profit. But an inside sales force can call on such customers on a regular basis with much lower costs.

The A. B. Dick Co. is a good example of a firm that uses telemarketing to service its smaller accounts. With more than 100,000 of its customers buying less than $200 of office supplies per year, the company realized it was not economically sound to have its field salespeople visiting those accounts regularly. By adopting a telephone direct marketing effort to service low volume customers, the firm was able to focus its field selling efforts on the larger institutional market. Coordinated with special mail promotions to maximize response, the telephone was used to sell and record orders directly. A first call to each small customer sought permission for later, regular phone contact. The initial results of the program were impressive. Ten percent of the companies contacted by phone placed an order at the time of the initial call. Another 8 percent of these "small" customers were discovered to have the potential for larger equipment and supply purchases. These accounts were qualified over the phone and passed along to the field sales force for future follow-up. Finally, 60 percent of all the customers contacted asked to become part of the continuing telephone sales program.[14]

As we will discuss in several later sections of this book, however, implementing two or more specialized sales force—as in the case of inside and outside salespeople—can cause additional problems for sales managers. Since each specialized sales force focuses on different types of selling activities, separate policies and procedures are often required. For example, many authorities suggest that an effective telemarketing program requires the development of standardized "scripts" for the salesperson to follow (i.e., a modified stimulus-response type of sales presentation, as described in Appendix A), even though their counterparts in the field might have much more flexibility to tailor their presentations to the needs of individual customers. Such differences in policies and procedures, in

---

[13] Ibid.

[14] Murray Roman, "Reach Out and Sell Someone with Business Telemarketing," *Industrial Marketing*, August 1982, pp. 78–79.

turn, may require the recruitment of different types of salespeople for the two sales forces and the development of different training and compensation programs.

Organizing to Service National and Key Accounts

Regardless of how their sales forces are organized, many firms are being forced to develop new organizational approaches to deliver the customer service necessary to attract and maintain large and important customers—their national or key accounts. As discussed in Chapter 3, the increasing technical complexity of products, industrial concentration, and the trend toward centralized purchasing make a few major accounts critical to the marketing success of many firms in both industrial and consumer goods industries. In an attempt to provide the kind of service demanded by those key customers, many firms adopt a selling philosophy of major account management. This stresses the goal of making sales and developing long-term relationships with a firm's key customers. Firms adopt national account management policies in the belief that they will lead to improved coordination of selling activities and improved communications with major customers. This, in turn, should enable the seller to capture a larger share of purchases made by those customers and to improve profitability. As Table 4–1 indicates, respondents from 23 large industrial firms largely agree that such expectations were actually achieved as a result of implementing national account programs.[15]

Table 4–1
Perceived advantages to the selling company in using national account marketing (N = 23)

Advantage Mentioned	Percent of Respondents
1. Increased sales to customers designated as national accounts	91
2. Increased profits from customers designated as national accounts	83
3. Increased market share	74
4. Improved customer communication	74
5. Improved customer coordination	30
6. Improved new product acceptance	30
7. Improved forecasting	17

Source: Adapted from Thomas H. Stevenson, "Payoffs From National Account Management," *Industrial Marketing Management* 10 (1981), p. 120.

---

[15] Thomas H. Stevenson, "Payoffs From National Account Management," *Industrial Marketing Management* 10 (1981), pp. 119–24.

Alternative Organizational Approaches
for Dealing with Key Accounts

When a firm decides to implement a national account program, a major question to be resolved is: Who in the organization should be responsible for carrying out the functions of national account management? Some firms have no special organizational arrangements for handling their major customers but instead rely on members of their regular sales force to sell to national and key accounts. This has the advantage of requiring no additional administrative or selling expense. The disadvantage is that major accounts often require more detailed and sophisticated treatment than smaller customers. Consequently, servicing major accounts may require more experience, expertise, and organizational authority than the average salesperson possesses. Also, if the sales force is compensated largely by commission, there can be difficult questions about which salesperson should get the commissions for sales to national accounts when one person calls on customer's headquarters while others service its stores or plants in other territories.

In view of these difficulties, many firms have adopted special organizational arrangements for the major account management functions. These arrangements include: (1) assigning key accounts to top sales executives, (2) creating a separate corporate division, and (3) creating a separate major accounts sales force.[16]

Assigning Key Accounts to Sales Executives. The use of sales or marketing executives to call on the firm's national or key accounts is a common practice, especially among smaller firms that do not have the resources to support a separate division or sales force. It is also common when the firm has relatively few major accounts to be serviced. In addition to the relatively low cost of the approach, it has the advantage of having important customers serviced by people who are high enough in the organizational hierarchy to have the authority to make—or at least to influence—decisions concerning the allocation of production capacity, inventory levels, and prices. Consequently, they can provide flexible and responsive service to their accounts.

On the other hand, one problem with this approach is that the managers who are given key account responsibilities sometimes develop a warped view of their firm's marketing objectives. They sometimes allocate too much of the firm's resources to their own accounts to the detriment of smaller, but still profitable, customers. In other words, such managers sometimes become obsessed with getting all the business they can from their large customers without paying sufficient attention to the sales, operating, or profit impact. Another problem is that

---

[16] Much of the following discussion of these approaches is based on material in Benson P. Shapiro, "Account Management and Sales Organization: New Developments in Practice," in *Sales Management: New Developments from Behavioral and Decision Model Research,* ed. Richard P. Bagozzi (Cambridge, Mass.: Marketing Science Institute, 1979), pp. 265–94, and in Benson P. Shapiro and Rowland T. Moriarity, Jr., "Organizing the National Account Force," working paper #83-52 (Cambridge, Mass.: Graduate School of Business, Harvard University, 1983). For some specific examples of the implementation of various national account programs, see Arthur Bragg, "National Account Managers to the Rescue," *Sales and Marketing Management,* August 16, 1982, pp. 30–34.

assigning important selling tasks to managers obviously takes time away from their management activities. This can lead to a deterioration of the coordination and effectiveness of the firm's overall selling and marketing efforts.

A Separate Key Account Division. Some firms have created an entirely separate corporate division for dealing with their major accounts. For example, some apparel companies have separate divisions for making and selling private-label clothing to large general-merchandise chains, such as Sears, Wards, and J. C. Penney. The primary advantage of this approach is that it allows for close integration of manufacturing, logistics, marketing, and sales activities. This can be important in cases where one or a few major customers account for such a large proportion of the firm's total sales volume that variations in their purchases have a major impact on the firm's production schedules, inventories, and allocation of resources.

The major disadvantages of this approach are the duplication of effort and the tremendous additional expense involved in creating an entire manufacturing and marketing organization for only one or a few customers. It is also risky in the sense that the success or failure of the entire division is dependent on the whims of one or a few customers.

A Separate Sales Force for Major Accounts. Rather than creating an entire separate division to deal with major customers, it is more common for companies to create a separate national or key account sales force. There are several ways in which such sales forces are commonly organized. Sometimes major account managers report to field sales managers in the firm's regular sales organization, whereas in other companies, they report through a separate management hierarchy. In some companies, the account managers perform all necessary selling activities themselves, including in-store or in-plant servicing of the account. In others, the account managers coordinate an entire selling team of assistants who work on the account. In still other situations, the national account manager calls on the customer's headquarters, while field salespeople from the regular sales force service the customer's facilities in their territories. Under this arrangement, if the field salespeople are compensated by commission, they are usually given some portion—perhaps half—of their normal commission for sales made to a national account's local stores or plants. However, this kind of arrangement can cause some bookkeeping problems. When an order is shipped to a central distribution point and then distributed by the customer to its plants or stores in several different sales territories, it can be difficult to determine how much of the sale should be credited to each field salesperson.

Regardless of how it is organized, a separate sales force has several advantages in dealing with key accounts. By concentrating on only one or a few major customers, the account manager can become very familiar with each customer's problems and needs, and he or she can devote the time necessary to provide a high level of service to each customer. Also, the firm can select only its most competent and experienced salespeople to become members of the national account sales force, thus ensuring that important customers receive expert sales attention. Finally, a separate national account sales force provides an internal benefit to the selling company. Because only the most competent salespeople are typically assigned to national accounts, such an assignment is often looked on by members of the sales organization as a desirable promotion. Thus, promotion to the national accounts sales force can be a useful way for the firm to motivate and reward top salespeople who are either not suited for or not interested in moving into sales management.[17]

In addition to the problem of allocating national account sales to individual members of the field sales force, using a separate sales force for major accounts suffers from many of the other disadvantages associated with organizing sales efforts by customer type. The most troubling problems concern the duplication of effort within the sales organization and the resulting higher selling and administrative expenses.

Team Selling

As mentioned, in some firms the account manager is responsible for working with an entire team of people in selling to and servicing major customers. The customer's buying center is likely to consist of people from different functional areas with different viewpoints and concerns. Thus, it is reasonable that those concerns can best be understood and met by people from equivalent functional areas of the selling firm. For instance, if the customer's treasurer is concerned about financing and credit arrangements, someone from the seller's finance department is probably best able to address those concerns.

One major disadvantage of a team selling approach is its high cost in time and personnel. It also presents a major problem of coordination. Unless the selling efforts of all team members are carefully integrated, conflicting impressions may be given to various members of the customer's organization.

Team selling is most appropriate for the very largest customers, where the potential purchase represents enough dollars and involves enough functions to justify the high costs. Although team selling is usually used to win new accounts, it is sometimes also used with lower-level personnel for maintenance selling. Production schedulers, expeditors, and shipping personnel may join the sales team to keep an existing account satisfied.[18]

Multilevel Selling

Multilevel selling is a variation of team selling. In multilevel selling, the sales team consists of personnel from various managerial levels who call on their counterparts in the buying organization. Thus, the account manager might call

---

[17] Andrall E. Pearson, "Sales Power Through Planned Careers," *Harvard Business Review*, January-February 1966, pp. 105–16.

[18] For examples of successful team selling, see "Specialist Selling Makes New Converts," *Business Week*, July 28, 1973, pp. 44–45.

on the customer's purchasing department while the selling firm's vice president of finance calls on the buyer's financial vice president. One advantage of this approach is that it represents proper organizational etiquette—each member of the selling team calls on a person with corresponding status and authority, rather than going above or below his or her own level. Also, it is useful for higher-level executives to participate in opening a relationship with a major new prospect, since they have the authority to make concessions and establish policies necessary to win and maintain that prospect as a customer.

Vertical Structure of the Sales Organization

At the beginning of this chapter, it was stressed that the sales organization must be structured vertically as well as horizontally. The primary purpose of the vertical organizational structure is to define clearly what managerial positions have the authority for carrying out specific sales management activities. It also provides for the effective integration and coordination of selling efforts throughout the firm.

Number of Management Levels and Span of Control

Two questions that must be answered in designing an effective vertical structure for a sales organization are (1) how many levels of sales managers should there be, and (2) how many people should each manager supervise (span of control)? These questions are related. For a given number of sales people, the greater the span of control, the fewer the levels of management and the fewer the managers needed.

There are major differences of opinion about what is the best policy concerning span of control and the number of vertical levels for a sales organization. Some managers think they have greater control and attain greater responsiveness when the sales force has a "flat" organization with few management levels. Their argument is that, if there are few levels between the top sales executive and the field salespeople, he or she can be close to them, thus facilitating communication and more direct control. On the other hand, some managers argue that such flat organizations actually limit communication and control because they necessitate large spans of control.

The flat organization with large spans of control has lower administrative costs because of the relatively small number of managers involved. Others argue, however, that such cost savings are an illusion since the lower quantity and quality of management in such organizations can lead to less effectiveness and productivity.

In view of these disagreements, it is difficult to generalize about the most appropriate number of management levels and span of control for a specific organization. However, there are a few guidelines for managers to follow. The span of control should be smaller and the number of levels of management should be larger when (1) the sales task is complex, (2) the profit impact of each salesperson's performance is high, and (3) the salespeople in the organization are well paid and professional. In other words, the more difficult and important the sales job, the greater the management support and supervision that should be provided to the members of the sales force. The findings of two empirical studies appear to support this generalization. One study examined the relationship between the span of control and sales force performance and morale across different types of selling. It found that the optimal span of control was smaller for more complex and difficult types of sales jobs.[19] The findings of this study are summarized in Table 4–2.

Table 4–2
Optimal spans of control for field sales managers for different types of selling

Type of Sales Job	Optimal Span of Control for Field Sales Managers
Trade selling	12–16
New business selling....................	10
Missionary selling......................	10
Technical selling.......................	7

Source: Reprinted by permission of the *Harvard Business Review*. Adapted from "Get the Most Out of Your Sales Force" by Derek A. Newton (September–October 1969), pp. 130–43. Copyright © 1969 by the President and Fellows of Harvard College; all rights reserved.

Another survey of the organizational practices of firms in different industries found that the median span of control of field sales managers is generally smaller in firms that sell relatively complex and expensive industrial goods than it is in firms that sell consumer products or services. The results of this survey are shown in Table 4–3.

Another general rule of thumb is that the span of control should usually be smaller at higher levels in the sales organization. This is because top level managers should have more time for analysis and decision making. Also, the people who report to them typically have more complicated jobs and require more organiza-

---

[19] Derek A. Newton, "Get the Most Out of Your Sales Force," *Harvard Business Review*, September-October 1969, pp. 130–43.

Table 4–3
**Median spans of control for field
sales managers in different types
of industries**

Industry	Median Reported Span of Control for Field Sales Managers
Services	10
Consumer products	8
Industrial products	6

Source: Morgan B. MacDonald, Jr., and Earl L. Bailey, "The Field Sales Supervisor,"
Conference Board Record 5 (July 1968), p. 34.

Table 4–4
**Spans of control at various levels in
a typical sales organization**

Number of People	Position	Span of Control
1	Marketing vice president	
1	National sales manager	4
4	Regional sales manager	5
20	Zone sales manager	8
160	District sales manager	10
1,600	Salesperson	—

Source: Benson P. Shapiro, *Sales Program Management: Formulation and Implementation* (New York: McGraw-Hill, 1977), p. 385.

tional support and communication than persons in lower-level jobs. Consequently, the spans of control at various levels in a "typical" sales organization look like those depicted in Table 4–4.

Management Roles and Staff Support

In addition to deciding how many subordinate sales managers should supervise at various levels in the organization, another question that must be addressed is how much authority each manager should be given in managing his or her subordinates. Specifically, where should the authority to hire, fire, and evaluate field salespeople be located within the organization? In some sales organizations, first-level field or district sales managers have the authority to hire their own salespeople, whereas in other organizations, the authority to hire and fire is located at higher management levels. As a general rule of organization, the more important a decision is for the success of a firm, the higher the level of management that should make that decision. Therefore, in firms that hire many low-paid salespeople who perform relatively routine selling tasks and have only a small impact on the firm's overall profit performance, hiring and evaluation authority is usually given to first-level sales managers. On the other hand, firms that have professional salespeople who perform complex selling tasks and have a major profit impact usually place the authority to hire and fire at higher levels. This is particularly true when the sales force is viewed as a training ground for future sales or marketing managers.

Selling Responsibilities. In addition to their supervisory and policy-making roles, many sales managers—particularly those at the field or district level—continue to be actively involved in selling activities. Since many sales managers are promoted to their positions only after proving to be competent and effective salespeople, their employers are often reluctant to lose the benefit of their selling skills. Consequently, sales managers are often allowed to continue servicing at least a few of their largest customers after they join the ranks of management. Indeed, some firms rely on their sales managers for selling and servicing key accounts. Sales managers themselves often prefer this kind of arrangement. They are reluctant to give up the opportunities for commissions and direct contact with the marketplace that they gain by being actively involved in selling.

The danger is that sales managers sometimes spend too much time selling and not enough time managing their subordinates. Consequently, some firms place tight limits on the amount of actual selling in which managers can engage. This is particularly true in larger firms where coordinating and supervising a vast sales force require greater attention by management personnel.

The results of a survey displayed in Table 4–5 show the large proportion of time devoted to selling by field sales managers. The results also show that managers in larger sales forces typically spend more time managing and less time selling than their counterparts in smaller firms.

Table 4–5
Size of the sales force and the median percentage of time spent on selling by sales managers

Size of Sales Force	Median Percentage of Time Spent on Selling
500 or more	20%
200–499	25
100–199	30
50–99	30
25–49	30
Less than 25	50

Source: David A. Weeks, "The Sales Manager as an Organizational Orphan," *Conference Board Record* 7 (May 1970), pp. 31–37.

Sales-Related Functions. Many firms face markets that demand high levels of service. Firms that sell capital equipment, for instance, must provide their customers with installation and maintenance service; fashion manufacturers must provide rapid order processing and delivery; and firms that sell electronic components must offer special product design and engineering services. These services must be integrated with the rest of the firm's marketing and selling activities for the company to compete effectively. The question from an organizational viewpoint, though, is whether sales managers should be given the authority to control such sales-related functions. The answer depends on the specific function and on the characteristics and needs of the firm's customers. Order processing and expediting are the least visible but most important sales-related functions. In some firms, persons responsible for order processing report to top-level sales management, whereas in other firms, they report to operations management, perhaps as part of an inventory control or data processing department. Usually, the more important rapid order processing and delivery are for keeping customers satisfied, the more appropriate it is for sales management to have authority over this function.

Repair and engineering services tend to be responsible to the sales organization in some firms and to the manufacturing or operations department in others. Again, such functions are most likely to be attached to the sales organization when they play a critical role in winning and maintaining customers. This is particularly true when the product must be designed or modified to meet customer specifications before a sale can be made.

The credit function, on the other hand, is almost always the responsibility of the firm's controller or treasurer, and it seldom reports to the sales organization. This is because salespeople and their managers may be tempted to be too generous with credit terms to close a sale.

In firms where sales-related functions do not report directly to the sales organizations, team selling is often a useful means of coordinating such functions—at least when dealing with major customers where the cost of such an approach is justified. Although the account manager has no formal authority to control the actions of team members from other departments, he or she can coordinate the team's activities at the field level.

Staff Support. Most larger sales organizations utilize some staff personnel in addition to their line sales managers. Staff executives are responsible for a limited range of specific activities, but they do not have the broad operating responsibility or authority of line managers. Staff executives commonly perform tasks that require specialized knowledge or abilities that the average sales manager does not have the time to develop. They must also collect and analyze information that line managers need for decision making. Thus, the most common functions performed by staff specialists in a sales organization are recruitment, training, and sales analysis. A typical line and staff sales organization is diagrammed in Figure 4–5.

The creative use of staff specialists can enable a sales force to function with fewer managers because of the benefits of specialization and division of labor. It

Figure 4–5
Line and staff sales organization

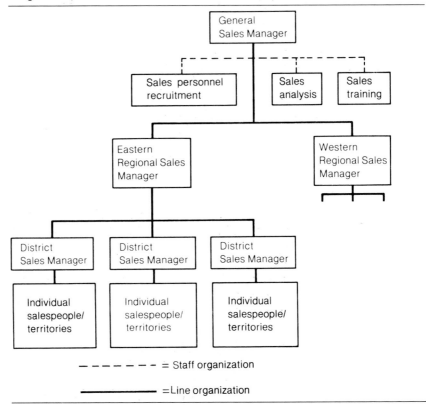

can also improve the effectivenesses of the sales organization while cutting costs. In addition, staff positions can be used as a training ground for future top-level sales managers.

On the other hand, staff positions are justified only when the sales organization is large enough so that staff specialists have enough work to keep them busy. A staff specialist in sales training, for instance, would not be justified if the firm hires only three or four trainees each year.

Some Additional Questions

Although a large number of issues concerning the strategic organization of the sales force have been examined, there are some related questions yet to be explored. How many salespeople should a firm hire? How should those people be deployed? How should sales territories be defined? What quota, if any, should be assigned to each sales territory?

The answers to these questions depend on the markets to be served, the potential sales volume in those markets, and the selling effort necessary to capture a desired share of that potential volume. In the next chapter, then, methods of market analysis and sales forecasting are discussed before the questions of sales force size, deployment, and quotas are brought up again in Chapters 6 and 7.

Summary

This chapter examined some important issues regarding the organization of the sales force. More specifically, it looked at the benefits a good organizational plan can provide and at the major issues involved in deciding on the horizontal and vertical organization of the sales effort.

A good organizational plan should satisfy three criteria. First, it should allow the firm to realize the benefits that can be derived from the division and specialization of labor. Second, it should provide for stability and continuity in the firm's selling efforts. This can best be accomplished by organizing *activities* and not people. Third, it should produce effective coordination of the various activities assigned to different persons in the sales force and different departments in the firm.

Questions of horizontal organization revolve around how specific selling activities are to be divided among members of the sales force. The first issue to be resolved is whether to use company employees to perform the sales function or to rely on outside manufacturers' representatives or sales agents. The cost of using outside agents is usually lower than those of a company sales force at relatively low sales volumes. However, most executives believe that company employees will generate greater levels of sales and that they are easier to control than agents.

When a firm does employ its own sales force, four types of horizontal organization are commonly found, structured according to: (1) geography, (2) type of product, (3) type of customer, and (4) selling function. Geographic organization is the simplest and most common. It possesses the advantages of low cost and clear identification of which salesperson is responsible for each customer. Its primary disadvantage is that it does not provide the firm with any benefits from division and specialization of labor.

Specializing the sales force along product lines allows salespeople to develop great familiarity with the technical attributes, applications, and most effective methods of selling those products. This can be advantageous when products are technically complex or when the firm's manufacturing facilities are also organized by product type. The major disadvantage associated with organization by product type is duplication of effort.

Organizing the sales force by type of customer or market serviced allows salespeople to understand the needs and requirements of the various types of customers better. Salespeople are more likely to discover ideas for new products and marketing approaches that will appeal to those customers. However, this scheme also produces duplication of effort, which tends to increase selling and administrative expenses.

A selling function organizational philosophy holds that people should be allowed to do what they do best. Thus, it makes sense to have, say, one sales force specializing in prospecting for and developing new accounts while another maintains and services old customers. These arrangements are often difficult to implement because of coordination problems. A variation, which is much less difficult to implement, is to have developmental salespeople who assist the regular sales force in selling new products that the specialists also had a hand in researching and developing. A newer form of this organizational approach that is rapidly growing in popularity is the use of inside telephone salespeople to handle reorders from smaller customers and other routine selling tasks, while outside field salespeople concentrate on new accounts and customer service.

In addition to deciding on a basic structure, a firm needs to specify how it intends to service national and key accounts in its horizontal organizational plans. Three arrangements are most commonly found: (1) assigning key accounts to top sales executives, (2) creating a separate corporate division, and (3) creating a separate major accounts sales force.

Two key questions must be addressed in deciding on an effective vertical structure of the sales organization: (1) how many levels of sales managers should there be, and (2) how many people should each manager supervise? The answers are related; for a given number of salespeople, greater spans of control produce fewer levels of management. Although it is difficult to unequivocally state the optimal span of control for a firm, it is true generally that the span of control should be smaller in those firms where (1) the sales task is complex, (2) the profit impact of each salesperson's performance is high, and (3) the salespeople in the organization are well paid and professional. In sum, the more difficult and important the sales job, the smaller the span of control should be to allow for greater management support and supervision. The span of control should also be smaller at higher levels in the sales organization than at lower levels to allow increased time for analysis and decision making required by the higher-level sales positions.

Another question that must be addressed in designing the vertical structure of the sales organization is how much authority should be given each manager in the sales management hierarchy, particularly with respect to hiring, firing, and evaluating subordinates. As a general rule, the more important such decisions are to the firm, the higher the level of management that should make such decisions.

Discussion Questions

1. The BMC Company, unlike other firms manufacturing similar products, uses the services of 22 manufacturer's agents. The other firms in the industry have their own company sales forces, although a few use both systems. What conditions would lead to a company using manufacturer's agents?

What are the advantages and disadvantages of using manufacturer's agents?

2. In order to increase market penetration, the Flexible Packaging Division of Crown Zellerback reorganized its sales force into separate film and flexible forces. How would such a move help to increase market penetration? What costs are likely to be incurred in this reorganization?

3. In your opinion, which type of horizontal selling structure is most compatible with the basic idea underlying the marketing concept? Which is least compatible? Explain.

4. "The complexity of our products ranges from pipe, valves, and other related products to heat exchanges and other complex process products. The technical support demands vary significantly." In what way can product complexity affect sales force organization?

5. The Xerox Corporation finds that its market penetration in small towns for low-end copiers is very weak. Xerox decided to hire 1,300 part-time sales reps to invade this market. The reps will work as independents and be paid a straight commission. Is this approach logical?

6. Sales development and sales maintenance may be considered as two separate dimensions of the salesperson's job. In what ways may personnel requirements for these two dimensions of the job differ?

7. Flexible was the word used to describe Ansul Company's organization. Briefly discuss what flexible means in terms of sales force organization and management.

8. What kind of vertical structuring should the following sales forces have? Why?
   a. A sales force for an advanced computer equipment firm.
   b. A sales force selling encyclopedias door to door.
   c. A sales force trying to get retailers to stock a new consumer product.

9. What kind of relationship exists between the hierarchical levels of a sales organization and the spans of control of members occupying the levels? What is the reasoning behind this?

10. The Prestolite Division of the Allied Corporation reorganized its electronics, motor, and wire divisions into a single unit, located in Toledo, Ohio. Previously, Prestolite had three sales forces handling these products. What conditions prompted Prestolite to make this change?

11. "Our product line now numbers 75 different products. Moreover, the recently added products are more technical than those that have been around for some time. We need to split up our sales force to allow product line specialization." These views were stated by Don Berceau, product manager for Arcade Electric. Arcade's sales manager, Kevin Hunt, felt otherwise and stated: "That's the last thing we need—having a customer called on by two Arcade sales representatives instead of only one. What we need to do is to expand our sales force and cut back on the number of customers assigned to each representative." What would you suggest?

12. LaMarche's Enterprise manufactures both technical and nontechnical products. Its sales force is organized in the same manner; the technical sales force has 175 people, and the nontechnical group numbers 128. To what extent would such a division affect the following?
    a. Recruiting.
    b. Sales training.
    c. Compensation.
    d. Supervision.
    e. Span of control.

13. Negotiation is commonly used in industrial marketing when buyers and sellers interact. Often, negotiation teams from the selling organization meet with negotiation teams from the buying organization. If you are to develop a negotiation team, who would you want to have as members? What should this team know?

14. The advent of telemarketing has resulted in the development of inside sales forces. Some companies assign sales trainees to the inside or telephone sales force as part of the training program. Other companies view the two positions as being separate. What functions would an inside (telephone) sales force perform? How would these functions differ from those performed by the external sales force? How would compensation plans differ if at all?

Chapter 5

Demand Estimation

Chapter 5

Demand Estimation

As pointed out in Chapter 2, a pivotal element in the marketing and sales plans of any firm is a market opportunity analysis. This analysis involves the study and assessment of the various environments that affect the business. It also requires determining the market potential for the goods or services that the firm currently produces or is considering producing. The magnitude of this total potential in conjunction with the firm's unique capabilities and strengths determines the portion of the market it may be able to secure. The strategies it plans to use then lead to the sales forecast of the amount it can reasonably expect to capture.

There seems to be a good deal of semantic confusion surrounding the terms used to describe a firm's marketing opportunities. Consequently, the first section of this chapter reviews the main terms that are used and discusses the interrelationships among these concepts. The remainder of the chapter discusses the various methods by which demand estimates can be developed and the advantages and disadvantages of each method.

Clarification of Terms

Market opportunity analysis requires an understanding of the differences in the notions of market potential, sales potential, sales forecast, and sales quota.

Market potential is an estimate of the maximum possible sales of a commodity, a group of commodities, or a service for an entire industry in a market during a stated period. There are several things to note with respect to this definition. First, market potential is defined for a particular market during a specified time period. The market, in turn, refers to a specific customer group in a specific geographic area. Thus, the statement, "the market potential for portable air compressors (commodity) to the construction industry (specific consumer group) in the Chicago metropolitan area (specific geographic area) in 1985 (specific time period) is 10,000 units or $10 million (maximum sales)," is a complete specification of market potential. Further, the omission of any of the items would make the statement incomplete.[1]

Sales potential refers to the portion of the market potential that a *particular firm* can reasonably expect to achieve. Whereas market potential represents the maximum possible sales for all sellers of the good or service under ideal conditions, sales potential reflects the maximum possible sales for an individual firm.

The *sales forecast* is an estimate of the dollar or unit sales for a specified future period under a proposed marketing plan or program. The forecast may be for a specified item of merchandise or for an entire line; it may be for a market as a whole or for any portion of it. Note that not only does a sales forecast include specifications of the commodity, customer group, geographic area, and time period, but it also includes a specific marketing plan as an essential element. If the proposed plan is changed, predicted sales are also expected to change. Further-

[1] Philip Kotler, *Marketing Management: Analysis, Planning, and Control*, 5th ed. (Englewood Cliffs, N.J.: Prentice-Hall, 1984), pp. 224–33.

more, forecasted sales are typically less than the company's sales potential. The firm may not have sufficient production capacity to realize its full potential, or its distribution network may not be sufficiently developed, or its financial resources may be limited. For similar reasons, forecast sales for an industry are typically less than the industry's market potential.[2]

The distinction among the notions market potential, sales potential, and sales forecast is captured in Figure 5–1. Historical sales are shown because they often play a key role in determining the sales forecast. Note that one can speak of a company forecast or an industry forecast; in fact, the latter is often developed before the former is generated. Just as the company forecast presumes a specific marketing plan, the industry forecast presumes a specific level of marketing effort by all the firms that serve the industry. As the company's marketing plan becomes

Figure 5–1
Relation among market and sales potentials and sales forecast

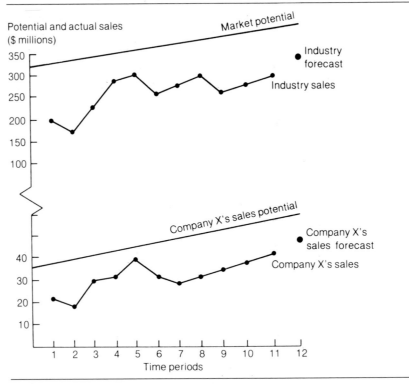

Source: Adapted from Douglas J. Dalyrmple and Leonard J. Parsons, *Marketing Management: Text and Cases*, 3d ed. (New York: John Wiley & Sons, 1983), p. 106. Used by permission.

---

[2] Richard R. Still, Edward W. Cundiff, and Norman A P. Govoni, *Sales Management: Decisions, Policies, and Cases*, 4th ed. (Englewood Cliffs, N.J.: Prentice Hall, 1981), pp. 48–49.

Figure 5–2
Market potential, sales potential,
and sales forecasting process

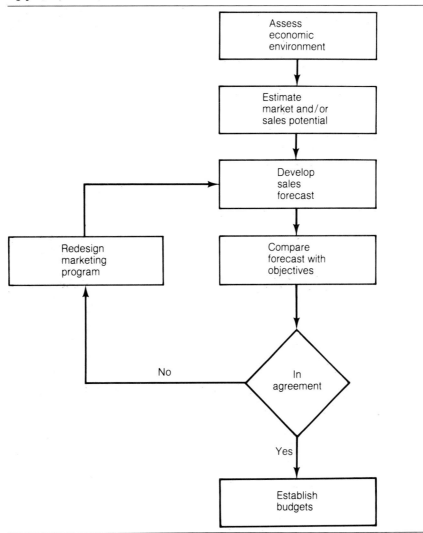

more effective, realized sales and then forecasted sales should come closer to sales potential. The same occurs for industry sales and market potential as the marketing efforts of the competitors serving the market become more effective.

Figure 5–2, which shows the relationship between potentials and forecasts, should provide some understanding of the process involved in developing a sales forecast. Typically the process begins with a forecast of the economic environment. Sometimes this is simply an implicit assessment of the immediate future. Is the outlook bright or gloomy? Then, given an initial estimate of industry potential and an assessment of the company's competitive position, an assessment of the firm's sales potential can be derived. This, in turn, leads to an initial sales forecast, often based on the presumption that the marketing effort will be similar to what it was last year. The initial forecast is then compared with objectives established for the marketing effort when allowances for the level and structure of the effort are made. If the marketing program is expected to achieve the objectives, both the program and the sales forecast are adopted. That is rare, however. Rather, it is typically necessary to redesign the marketing program and then revise the sales forecast, often several times.

Although a revision of objectives may also be necessary, eventually the iterative process should produce agreement between the forecasted or expected sales and the objectives. The sales forecast then becomes a basic input in establishing budgets for the various functional areas. Note that the sales forecast presumes a particular marketing program. This is the key to understanding some of the advantages and disadvantages of the various sales forecasting methods discussed later in the chapter.

Note, finally, the idea of a sales quota. A *sales quota* is a sales goal or objective that is assigned to a marketing unit. Sales quotas are typically one of the key measurements used to evaluate the personal selling effort. They apply to specific periods and can be specified in great detail—for example, sales of a particular item to a specified customer by salesman John Jones in June.

Estimation of Demand

While the notions of potential and forecast are distinct conceptually, they become blurred when estimates of demand are actually developed. This occurs because the various techniques available for estimating demand place differing amounts of emphasis on the proposed marketing effort. Some neglect the contemplated level of marketing effort for all practical purposes and concentrate on the maximum amount of the commodity that might be demanded by an industry or particular customer group. Estimates produced with such an emphasis are, of course, closer to being market or sales potential estimates than they are sales forecasts. Other techniques give great weight to the marketing effort planned for the period in question and are sales forecasts in the true sense of the word. Still other techniques use historic sales as a basis for future demand estimates. They rely on the implicit assumption that marketing effort in the future period will be similar to what it was in the past. The key thing to note from a user's perspective is where on the spectrum one is operating. Is the projection based on near ideal conditions and thus represents *potential* in the true sense of the term? Is it based on historic marketing effort? Or does it reflect a level of marketing effort and a particular program for that effort? As a matter of fact, we will find it useful when comparing the sales forecasting techniques later in the chapter to focus on what they presume about the level of marketing and the marketing program.

The starting point for any analysis of demand is to determine who uses or will use the product by specifying the important characteristics of users. The market for figure salons like Elaine Powers, for example, is limited to women. They are not equally attractive to all women, however; those between the ages of 18 and 40 patronize them more. Working women are more likely to patronize them than are nonworking women, and among nonworking women, those without young children are more likely than those with young children.

For established products, specification of important user characteristics or factors that affect use is relatively easy because of the company's experience and research. For new products, this specification may rely on an analogy with similar products. Alternatively, it might require a survey of potential users or even a small market test.

It is necessary to determine not only who uses the product but also the rate at which the product is likely to be consumed. A manufacturer of riding lawnmowers might specify that its potential market consists of all households with more than one-third acre of yard and an income of at least $15,000. The firm could not expect to sell every such household a new riding lawnmower every year, however. In estimating market potential, the firm would probably want to estimate new demand and replacement demand, taking into account the expected life of lawnmowers. This technique is used in estimating the market potential for major appliances and other consumer durables.

The usage estimate is much different for a frequently consumed product like toothpaste, of which a household uses several tubes each month, than for soft drinks, of which a household might be expected to use a six-pack each week. Both users and rates of usage must be determined to derive the estimates of demand. Furthermore, the manager must understand the basis on which the demand estimate rests.

One manufacturer considered making stoves for use on boats. A brief analysis clearly indicated that these stoves would be used only on boats with enclosed cabins. The market analyst assigned the job of determining the market potential for these stoves came up with a rather substantial figure for the total number of boats in the United States. With such a sizable market potential, the manufacturer went into production. When sales results were disappointing, an investigation showed that the figure for the number of boats included everything from an eight-foot, flat-bottom rowboat to sea-going yachts.[3]

The analysis of demand might also take into account who buys the product. This is particularly important when the purchaser is different from the user. While the number of users and their likely rate of use will determine the total potential for the product, buyers and their motivations for buying will affect how much of that potential is likely to be realized. Thus, while an individual firm

---

[3] William J. Stanton and Richard H. Buskirk, *Management of the Sales Force*, 6th ed. (Homewood, Ill.: Richard D. Irwin, 1983), p. 412.

might choose to direct a major portion of its promotional efforts to buyers, it might also channel a portion of that effort to users.

A final factor to consider when analyzing demand are market motivations. Why do customers buy the product? What might influence prospective customers to buy it? Some products have naturally-induced causes of sales. For example, when people marry and set up a household, they typically buy major appliances and furniture, and some manufacturers of these products use the marriage rate as a basis for estimating the size of their markets. Thus, "a manufacturer of baby furniture may base its entire market analysis on birth rates, for births are the events that cause the demand for these products."[4] For a similar reason, a manufacturer of office furniture might base its estimate of demand on the number of new businesses formed in the firm's market area. Alternatively, the firm might use the number of new businesses as an indicator of new demand while using other indicators to estimate replacement demand. For example, a manufacturer of pumps for the pulp and paper industry breaks the demand for pumps into three components—(1) exchange demand, (2) demand for minor investments, and (3) demand for major investments—and develops separate prediction equations for each of the components using different factors as input.[5]

Importance of Sales Forecast

An accurate estimate of demand, typically in the form of a sales forecast, is critical to the successful functioning of most businesses. The following are testimonies regarding its value.

There are few, if any, functions of the business which are more fundamental and far-reaching in their effect on the health of the enterprise than the forecasting or prediction of future sales. An estimate of future prospects, whether based on the most elegant and sophisticated studies, or on plain intuition, hunch, judgment, or a combination of all these, should be the basis for financial planning, production setting, inventory levels, employment levels, directing sales promotion, expanding or contracting production and allied facilities, calculating profit or loss, and many other phases of business activity. In the final analysis, the success of a business depends to a very great extent upon the skill of management in predicting and preparing for tomorrow's business conditions.[6]

The sales forecast, in the opinion of one senior marketing executive, is "the most important piece of data which is presented to management." Another describes his company's sales forecast as "the basic core of our planning effort."[7]

---

[4] Ibid., p. 391.

[5] Clas Wahlbin, "Analyzing Variations in Demand for an Industrial Good," *Industrial Marketing Management*, 6 (1977), pp. 223–36.

[6] Robert G. Murdick and Arthur E. Schaefer, *Sales Forecasting for Lower Costs and Higher Profits* (Englewood Cliffs, N.J.: Prentice-Hall, 1967), p. 8.

[7] Stanley J. PoKempner and Earl L. Bailey, *Sales Forecasting Practices: An Appraisal* (New York: The Conference Board, 1970), p. 1.

The sales forecast is a primary planning tool. It is used by companies to:

1. Plan marketing and sales programs.
2. Allocate resources.
3. Project cash flows.
4. Decide on capital appropriations.
5. Establish production schedules.
6. Time purchase of materials and supplies.
7. Control inventories.
8. Plan manpower requirements.
9. Establish operating budgets.
10. Provide benchmarks for gauging the performance of various individuals and units in the company.[8]

The sales forecast is also of fundamental importance in planning and evaluating the sales effort. Consequently, the sales manager should be familiar with the techniques by which sales forecasts are developed. The methods discussed in this chapter are listed in Figure 5–3.[9]

Figure 5–3
Classification of sales forecasting methods

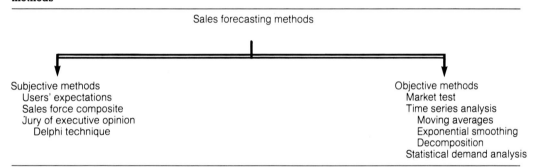

Sales forecasting methods

Subjective methods
  Users' expectations
  Sales force composite
  Jury of executive opinion
    Delphi technique

Objective methods
  Market test
  Time series analysis
    Moving averages
    Exponential smoothing
    Decomposition
  Statistical demand analysis

Users' Expectations

The *users' expectations method* of forecasting sales is also known as the buyers' intentions method because it relies on answers from customers regarding their expected consumption or purchases of the product. The customers may be sur-

---

[8] Ibid.

[9] For a discussion of some other, less common forecasting techniques, see one of the many excellent books on the subject, such as: Frank H. Eby, Jr., and William J. O'Neill, *The Management of Sales Forecasting* (Lexington, Mass.: D. C. Heath, 1977); Spyros Makridakis and Steven C. Wheelwright, *Forecasting: Methods and Applications* (New York: John Wiley & Sons, 1978); and Douglas Wood and Robert Fildes, *Forecasting for Business: Methods and Applications* (New York: Longment Group Limited, 1976).

veyed in person, over the telephone, or by mail. The National Lead Company, for example, makes five-year forecasts of product sales using both personal interviews and mail questionnaires to collect the required data.

Most of the National Lead's products are not end-products, in themselves, but raw materials purchased by other firms as ingredients for the products they manufacture. For this reason, it is National Lead's objective to determine the business outlook of its consumer or customer industries. . . .

For example, one product the company processes is titanium, a pigment used in volume in the paint, paper, rubber, and hard surface flooring industries. In order to obtain a five-year forecast of its sales of titanium, the company attempts to determine three things: (a) whether the products in which titanium is an ingredient will increase in sales; (b) whether the average rate of the use of titanium is expanding or contracting in each of the using industries, and (c) what share of the resultant market the company can reasonably expect to get over the five-year period covered by the forecast. . . .

In order to forecast the market for any large volume product, the marketing research department goes directly to the users of the product. Executives of about 100 companies are interviewed in person, and as many as 300 to 500 more are surveyed by mail.[10]

The respondents in a user's expectations survey do not necessarily have to be the ultimate consumers. Rather, the firm may find it advantageous to secure the reactions of wholesalers and retailers that serve the channel. Ownes-Corning Fiberglas, for example, conducted a series of focus group interviews among dealers when it introduced glass radial tires. It hoped to determine the key benefits and merchandising aids that would help dealers sell radials and the kind of reaction the tires would generate.[11]

The users' expectations method of forecasting sales provides demand estimates that are probably closer to market or sales potential estimates than they are to sales forecasts since user groups would have difficulty anticipating the industry's or a particular firm's marketing efforts. Rather, the estimate users provide reflects their anticipated needs. From the sellers' standpoint, they provide a measure of the opportunities available among a particular segment of users.

Advantages

The users' expectations method offers several advantages to a firm. First, the forecast is based on estimates obtained directly from firms whose buying actions will actually determine the sales of the product. Second, the manner by which the information is collected—projected product use by customer— allows the prepa-

---

[10] *Forecasting Sales* (New York: National Industrial Conference Board, 1963), p. 31. The reader interested in greater detail regarding the forecasting techniques used by industry would do well to consult this excellent report. Although published in 1963, many arguments regarding the advantages and disadvantages of the various forecasting techniques are as valid now as they were then. See, for example, David. L. Hurwood, Elliott S. Grossman, and Earl L. Bailey, *Sales Forecasting* (New York: The Conference Board, 1978).

[11] "Owens Corning Listens to Dealers," *Sales Management: The Marketing Magazine,* March 3, 1975, p. 3. Owens Corning makes the glass belts but not the tires. However, dealer acceptance and support of the tires were felt to be critical to the company's success in selling the glass belts to tire manufacturers.

ration of forecasts in great detail—for example, by product, by customer, or by sales territory. Third, the method often provides some insight into the buyer's thinking and plans. This is helpful in planning the marketing strategy. Finally, this technique can be used when other techniques may be impossible, such as when forecasting sales of a brand new product.

Disadvantages

The users' expectations method is limited to situations where the potential customers for the product are few and well defined. The technique becomes difficult to implement and can result in serious error when there are many customers and they cannot be readily identified. Thus, the technique works well in forecasting sales for a product like compressors for natural gas transmission where there are probably no more than two dozen potential customers in the whole world. It would not work well at all for a company that manufactures paper clips. The technique also depends on the sophistication of the potential customers in anticipating their needs. Buyer intentions are subject to change, particularly when the buyer is the household; thus, the users' expectations method does not work particularly well for consumer goods.[12] It is sometimes difficult to determine the firmness of intentions to purchase, particularly when the person being queried is uninformed or uncooperative. Finally, the users' expectations method requires a considerable expenditure of money, time, and manpower. The survey instruments and sampling plan have to be designed; a field staff has to be recruited and trained; and the data must be collected, edited, coded, and tabulated before the forecast can be prepared.[13]

Sales Force Composite

The *sales force composite method* of forecasting sales gets its name from the fact that the initial input is the opinion of each member of the field sales staff. Each person states how much he or she expects to sell during the forecast period. These estimates are typically adjusted at various levels of sales management. They are likely to be checked, discussed, and possibly changed by the branch manager, and so on up the sales organization chart until the figures are finally

---

[12] "How Good Are Consumer Pollsters," *Business Week*, November 9, 1969, pp. 108–10. For a discussion of the use of the users' expectations method for forecasting sales of industrial products, see Richard Rippe, Maurice Wilkinson, and Donald Morrison, "Industrial Market Forecasting with Anticipations Data," *Management Science* 22 (February 1976), pp. 639–51.

[13] Most introductory marketing research texts discuss what is involved in each of these tasks. The effort can be substantial, and it is not unusual for a market survey to take two or three months. See, for example, Gilbert A. Churchill, Jr. *Marketing Research: Methodological Foundations*, 3d. ed. (Hinsdale, Ill.: Dryden Press, 1983).

accepted at corporate headquarters. The Harris-Intertype Corporation, a manufacturer of printing equipment and electronic products headquartered in Cleveland, uses a series of reviewers and revisions.

The district manager asks each of his salesmen for territorial estimates, customer by customer and product by product. The salesman is asked to estimate the number of units that he expects to sell in the following 6-, 12-, and 18-month periods. In addition, he is expected to record the names of large accounts with whom he expects to conclude transactions in the year to come. The district sales manager then compiles the overall sales forecast for his district from these territorial estimates. . . .

Each district manager, together with one or more of his leading salesmen, receives a visit from the staff sales forecaster at division headquarters, who reviews the district manager's estimates in detail. Reasons for variations from historical patterns are discussed, and estimates are examined product by product. This procedure enables the sales forecaster to evaluate the quality of the estimate and to get an impression of the general trend in the market. . . .

Subsequently, each district manager's forecast is forwarded to division headquarters. Here a committee composed of the division's forecaster, marketing executives, and those responsible for planning, budgeting, and production scheduling reviews the overall forecasts in the light of such additional factors as the economic outlook, trends in the industry and in related industries, competitive conditions, market survey results, promotion plans, and new product expectations. From the review, a preliminary sales forecast for the overall division is derived.

The preliminary forecast of divisional sales is then reviewed in conference with the division president and sales vice president for further possible modification. They bring to the conference broad industry and management experience, as well as special knowledge of planned sales-promotion or advertising programs.[14]

Ex-Cell-O Corporation also places heavy reliance on the sales force composite method of sales forecasting. Ex-Cell-O manufactures a variety of industrial items, including machinery, precision parts and assemblies, aerospace and electronic parts, and expendable tools and accessories. The company manufactures machine tools that range in price from a few thousand dollars to $400,000 or more. The products are sold by the machine tool group's own sales force which consists of approximately 50 salespeople and 100 independent distributors. Each sales person and distributor is required to forecast the proposals that are outstanding that they expect will be converted into orders during each of the upcoming five quarters. The process is repeated every three months. The regional manager reviews the forecasts with the individual salesperson or distributor and secures agreement on any necessary adjustments. When the manager is satisfied that all of the individual forecasts in the region are as realistic as can be, the manager forwards them to the marketing staff at group headquarters.[15]

---

[14] *Forecasting Sales*, p. 26.
[15] *Sales Forecasting*, pp. 40–44.

Advantages

A primary advantage of the sales force composite method of forecasting sales is that it uses the specialized knowledge of the people closest to the market. The final sales forecast often becomes one basis for establishing quotas for individual sales representatives. The sales force composite method puts the responsibility for those forecasts in the hands of those who will eventually have to produce the results. When they better understand how the quotas were established, they are much less likely to look on them with disdain and distrust. Their commitment to the sales forecast and quota can have beneficial effects on their performance. It is also argued that the size of the sample used to develop the forecast tends to produce estimates that are fairly accurate. Whereas individual sales representatives may err in producing estimates, with some forecasting high or low, the errors should cancel to produce a reasonably stable, accurate forecast when the judgments of 20, 50, 100, or more salespeople are combined.[16] Finally, the method lends itself to the easy development of customer, product, territory, or sales force breakdowns, which are a distinct plus in controlling the sales effort.

Disadvantages

A main complaint of those who are opposed to the sales force composite method is that sales representatives are notoriously poor estimators. They tend to be overly optimistic when the economy is booming and overly pessimistic when things are not so good. Furthermore, they tend to be unaware of broad economic conditions that shape the demand for the product, and they may even be unaware of the firm's planned marketing program when preparing their estimates.[17] If the sales forecast they prepare is going to be an input in setting their quotas, they have a vested interest in estimating low. This makes the quota easier to achieve, which makes them look good. Some companies pay bonuses to all who meet or exceed their quota, so forecasting low can have monetary advantages as well.[18] Thus, elaborate schemes are sometimes necessary to keep the estimates realistic

---

[16] Whether the errors do in fact balance is an empirical question. Staelin and Turner suggest that the total forecast error in judgmental sales forecasts consists of two components: (1) an expertise effect, which reflects each individual's accuracy; and (2) a contagion effect, which reflects the correlation among forecasts prepared by different individuals. They use the magnitude of one versus the other to suggest where in the sales organizational hierarchy the forecast should be prepared to minimize total forecast error. See Richard Staelin and Ronald E. Turner, "Error in Judgmental Sales Forecasts: Theory and Results," *Journal of Marketing Research* 10 (February 1973), pp 10–16.

[17] For sales managers' reports on the accuracy of forecasts prepared by their sales force, see Thomas R. Wotruba and Michael L. Thurlow, "Sales Force Participation in Quota Setting and Sales Forecasting," *Journal of Marketing* 40 (April 1976), pp. 11–16.

[18] Ibid., p. 16. Among sales managers in the San Francisco and Los Angeles areas in the Wotruba and Thurlow study, only one respondent in 20 reported that his salespeople forecast low to earn more money.

and free from bias. Such schemes can be expensive; they require a good deal of time from highly paid, highly placed people. Therefore, the cost of the sales force composite method is typically higher than that of other methods.

Jury of Executive Opinion

The *jury of executive* or *expert opinion method* either informally or formally polls the top executives of the company for their assessment of sales possibilities. The separate assessments are combined into a sales forecast for the company. Sometimes this is done by simply averaging the individual judgments; but other times disparate views are resolved through group discussion. The initial views may reflect no more than the executive's hunch about what is going to happen, but in other instances, the opinion may be based on considerable factual material, sometimes even an initial forecast prepared by other means. For example, in the Sealright-Oswego Falls Corporation, a manufacturer of food containers and closures, the sales forecast is prepared with a two-step process. First, a preliminary forecast is prepared by the manager of the sales analysis and statistics department in collaboration with the manager of sales-production coordination. Before this forecast becomes final,

it is submitted to a committee composed of the director of sales, manager of sales administration, director of finance, comptroller, manager of trade relations, budget director, manager of sales analysis and statistics, and manager of sales-production coordination. This committee reviews and analyzes the forecast and makes whatever judgments may be dictated by its collective judgment. There are often divergent views among committee members as to the general sales outlook, and these are argued back and forth until mutual agreement is achieved. The result is an official forecast.[19]

Advantages

Some advantages of this method of forecasting are the ease and quickness with which it may be made. Although the preparation of vast and elaborate statistics may improve the accuracy of the forecast, this method does not absolutely require them. Furthermore, the method brings together a variety of specialized viewpoints. The "collective wisdom" that results reflects the thinking of the top people in the company—those most aware of company plans, as well as external forces affecting those plans and the consequent impact on the plans. Finally, when there is an absence of adequate data or experience, such as with innovative products, this may be the only means of sales forecasting available to the company.

---

[19] *Forecasting Sales*, p. 15.

Disadvantages

One important disadvantage of the jury of executive opinion is that it produces an aggregate forecast. This forecast must be broken down by product and by time to plan production and financing. It also must be broken down by territory and by salesperson to schedule and control the personal selling effort. Generating these breakdowns is extremely difficult, sometimes impossible, and usually expensive. The method is also expensive because of the large amounts of highly paid executives' time it consumes. Furthermore, the pooling of opinion disperses the responsibility for the forecast. If it proves to be grossly inaccurate, it is hard to pinpoint exactly what went wrong and who is at fault. Also, the forecast may not properly weight the expertise of those most informed. Group dynamics do operate. Those who have most intensively studied the available statistics and facts may not have their judgment weighted more than another executive whose "best guess" has been much more casually derived but who is more eloquent in the discussion or higher in the management hierarchy.

Delphi Technique

One method that is becoming increasingly popular for modifying the operation of group dynamics to produce a more accurate forecast is the Delphi technique. Delphi uses repeated measurement and controlled feedback instead of direct confrontation and debate among the experts preparing the forecast.[20] Figure 5–4

Figure 5–4
Operation of Delphi process

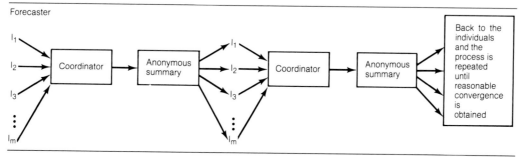

[20] The technique was originally devised at the Rand Corporation to assist in forecasting the likely state of technology in the future. See Norman C. Dalkey, *The Delphi Method: An Experimental Study of Group Opinion* (Santa Monica, Calif.: The Rand Corporation, 1969). The method has been adopted for sales forecasting and other types of marketing decision making. See Marvin A. Jolson and Gerald Rossow, "The Delphi Method in Marketing Decision Making," *Journal of Marketing Research* 8 (November 1971), pp. 443–48; and Roger J. Best, "An Experiment in Delphi Estimation in Marketing Decision Making," *Journal of Marketing Research* 11 (November 1974), pp. 447–52.

depicts how the method operates. First, each individual prepares a forecast using whatever facts, figures, and general knowledge of the environment he or she has at his or her disposal. Second, these forecasts are collected, and an anonymous summary is prepared by the person supervising the process. Third, the summary is distributed to each person who participated in the initial phase. Typically, the summary lists each forecast figure, the average (median), and some summary measure of the spread of the estimates. Quite often, those whose initial estimates fell outside the mid-range of responses (defined by the interquartile range or mid-50 percent) are asked to express their reasons for these extreme positions. These explanations are then incorporated in the summary. Those participating in the exercise are asked to study the summary and submit a revised forecast. The process is then repeated. There will typically be a number of these iterations. The method is based on the following two premises:

1. The range of responses will decrease, and the estimates will converge with repeated measurements.
2. The total group response or median will move successively toward the "correct" or "true" answer.[21]

The Delphi technique does seem to have advantages over the jury of executive opinion, in which group discussion and interaction are used to produce the forecast. The experience of TRW, where it has been used extensively for technological forecasting, is insightful in this regard.

This method seeks to take full advantage of the "committee" approach to forecasting, while avoiding some of the disadvantages of the typical brain-storming session. Our approach permitted us to circumvent group activity altogether and to deal with each member of our team of predictors directly and individually. Thus, we were able to eliminate the negative factors associated with group action—for example, the "aggressive expert" who feels called upon to defend his publicly stated opinions, the senior executive with whom subordinates are reluctant to differ, and the silver-tongued salesman who can sell refrigerators to Eskimos.[22]

The strategy of forcing those whose forecasts lie at the ends of the distribution to justify their estimates seems to have benefits in the sense that "informed" experts have greater opportunity to influence the final forecast. "The effect of placing the onus of justifying relatively extreme responses on the respondents had the effect of causing those without strong convictions to move their estimate closer to the median, while those who felt they had a good argument for a deviationist opinion tended to retain their original estimate and defend it."[23] Those who feel strongly about their estimates tend to feel more comfortable with Delphi because of the anonymity it provides. Since their forecasts are not neces-

[21] Jolson and Rossow, "The Delphi Method," p. 444.
[22] Harper Q. North and Donald L. Pyke, "Probes of the Technological Future," *Harvard Business Review* 47 (May-June 1969), p. 70.
[23] Olaf Helmer, *The Use of the Delphi Technique: Problems of Educational Innovations* (Santa Monica, Calif.: The Rand Corporation, 1966), pp. 2–3.

sarily revised, this can help produce more accurate estimates. For example, at the American Hoist and Derrick Company, which produces construction equipment, the use of the Delphi method allowed the company in 1975 and 1976 to reduce errors from ±20 percent experienced in previous years to less than 1 percent.[24]

One of the problems with the Delphi technique is that the process of iteration and feedback can take a long time. For example, Corning Glass Works used the Delphi method to develop a 10-year market forecast for certain electronic components using three waves of estimation. The study took nine months to complete.[25] IBM uses an interesting variation of the Delphi technique that virtually eliminates the time lag between ballots to estimate "how ripe" a market is for new equipment the company is considering introducing. The Delphi panel is composed of IBM experts with diverse backgrounds who are isolated from interruption so that they can concentrate fully on the project. The panelists' judgments are typed directly into a computer where the summary statistics are prepared. With the instant feedback provided by the system, the panelists' are often able to reach near consensus in a few hours.[26]

Market Test

Market testing is a relatively recent phenomenon in demand estimation. Market tests to assess the demand for new products were rare before 1960. They have grown significantly in popularity since that time, so that now the expenditures for test marketing total more than $1 billion per year.[27]

The essential feature of a market test is that "it is a controlled experiment, done in a limited but carefully selected part of the marketplace, whose aim is to predict the sales or profit consequences, either in absolute or relative terms, of one or more proposed marketing actions."[28] Note that the market test applies to assessing consequences of any change in the marketing strategy and not just to estimating the potential sales of a new product. For example, Welch Foods uses test marketing to measure the impact on demand of prices, coupons, advertising or any other elements in its marketing mix, while Union Carbide uses it to measure its share of market for individual products, to project sales potential, and to measure the effects of a new product on the company's other products.[29]

---

[24] Shanker Basu and Roger C. Shroeder, "Incorporating Judgments in Sales Forecasts: Applications of the Delphi-Method at American Hoist & Derrick," *Interfaces,* May 1977, p. 27.

[25] Jeffrey L. Johnson "A Ten-Year Delphi Forecast in the Electronics Industry," *Industrial Marketing Management,* March 1976, pp. 45–55.

[26] *Sales Forecasting,* pp. 16–17. For a sample of other users of Delphi and a 60-page semiannotated bibliography of the Delphi literature, see Harold Sackman, *Delphi Critique* (Lexington, Mass.: D. C. Heath, 1975.

[27] For a recent assessment of what is happening in test marketing, see the special supplement "Test Marketing" in *Advertising Age,* February 9, 1981, pp. S1–S28.

[28] Alvin R. Achenbaum, "Market Testing: Using the Marketplace as a Laboratory," in *Handbook of Marketing Research,* ed. Robert Ferber (New York: McGraw-Hill, 1974), pp. 4–31 to 4–54.

[29] "Testing Shows Marketers Where to Put Big Bucks," *Sales and Marketing Management,* March 16, 1981, p. 51.

2

Advantages

The potential for a new product is typically estimated by placing the product in several "representative" cities to see how well it performs and then projecting that experience to the United States as a whole. The Parker Pen Company, for example, test-marketed its Big Red ballpoint pen in Columbus, Ohio, and Phoenix, Arizona. It wanted to determine potential sales and assess whether the pen had a different appeal to the young and the old.[30] Similarly, Parker Pen used Winnipeg, St. Paul, Minneapolis, and St. Louis as test markets when estimating demand for its Systemark line of writing instruments.[31] For many firms, the test market is the final gauge of consumer acceptance of a new product and is the ultimate measure of market potential.

> Test marketing. . . still remains the only gauge we have to determine a new product's future (Dr. Edwin Berky, director of marketing research for Bristol-Myers Hillside Division).

> We are for it because it is the only way you can find out if you are in fact filling a real consumer need (Harrison F. Dunning, president, Scott Paper Company).[32]

Disadvantages

Test marketing to assess market potential is used much more by manufacturers of consumer products than by makers of industrial products. Many of the latter do not use it at all. This is partially because there are fewer potential customers for their products and also because they are more intimately familiar with their customer's needs, likes, and dislikes due to more direct contact involved in industrial transactions. Although the test market may be the ultimate gauge of consumer reaction to a new product, it is not without its disadvantages. Three of the more important ones are cost, time, and control.

Test markets are expensive. In addition to the normal costs associated with any kind of marketing research, such as designing the study and paying the field staff, there are costs associated with producing the product for the test market. To produce the product on a small scale is typically inefficient. To gear up immediately for large-scale production, however, can be tremendously wasteful of resources if the test market signals that the product is likely to fail. Furthermore, if the ultimate goal is to provide an accurate measurement, it is important that the small-scale environment reflect the marketing strategy likely to be used in the actual introduction. This requires designing the promotional effort and securing the proper distribution outlets, and both these efforts can be expensive.

---

[30] Don Morris, "Pen Not Only Mightier Than Sword: It Proliferates, Doesn't Grow Obsolete," *Marketing News* 11 (July 15, 1977), p. 1.

[31] "Testing Shows Marketers," p. 51.

[32] J. Weingarten, "The Most Dangerous Game in Marketing," *Dun's Review and Modern Industry* 89 (June 1967), p. 45.

The design of the marketing program and the actual conduct of the test market can also take substantial time. A minimum of a year is often recommended to allow for repeat purchasing behavior and seasonal influences to exert their impacts. This is necessary before any kind of go/no-go decision is made.[33] Experiments conducted over such a long time, however, invite competitive reaction, raise problems of control, and increase the cost. Yet market tests that are conducted over a short time do not accurately assess the cumulative impact of the marketing actions.

The problems associated with control manifest themselves in several ways. First, there are the control problems associated with the experiment itself. The firm must decide what specific test markets will be used. This raises the question of how product distribution will be organized in those markets. Can the firm elicit the necessary cooperation from wholesalers? From retailers? Can the test markets and control cities be matched sufficiently to rule out market characteristics as the primary determinant of the different sales results? Can the rest of the elements of the marketing strategy be controlled so as not to induce unwanted aberrations in the experimental setting? Second, there are control problems associated with competitive reaction. While the firm might be able to coordinate its own marketing activities and even those of intermediaries in the distribution channel so as not to contaminate the experiment, it can exert little control over its competitors. Competitors can, and do, sabotage marketing experiments by cutting the prices of their own products, gobbling up quantities of the test marketer's product and thereby creating a state of euphoria and false confidence within the test marketer, and by other devious means.[34]

Although test marketing may be the ultimate gauge of market potential, it can also be a dangerous one. Some have called it the most dangerous game in marketing because of the problems associated with it, particularly with respect to competitive reaction.

Time Series Analysis

Time series approaches to sales forecasting rely on the analysis of historical data to develop a prediction for the future. The sophistication of these analyses can vary widely. At one extreme, the forecaster might simply forecast next year's sales to be equal to this year's sales. Such a forecast might be reasonably accurate for a mature industry that is experiencing little growth. If there is growth, however, the forecaster might allow for it by predicting the same percentage increase for next year that the company experienced this year. Still further along the spectrum, the forecaster might attempt to break historical sales into basic components by isolating that portion due to trend, cyclical, seasonal, and irregular influences.

---

[33] Achenbaum, "Market Testing" p. 4–46.

[34] Gilbert A. Churchill, Jr., *Marketing Research: Methodological Foundations*, 3d ed. (Hinsdale, Ill.: Dryden Press, 1983), pp. 109–10. Copyright © 1983 by the Dryden Press, a division of Holt, Rinehart & Winston. Reprinted by permission of Holt, Rinehart & Winston.

The trend, cyclical, and seasonal components could all be forecast separately and then combined to produce the aggregate forecast. There are a number of time series approaches to sales forecasting, but only the moving average, exponential smoothing, and decomposition methods are discussed here.[35]

Moving Averages

The method of moving averages is conceptually quite simple. Consider the forecast that next year's sales will be equal to this year's sales. Such a forecast might be subject to large error if there is a great deal of fluctuation in sales from one year to the next. To allow for such randomness, we might consider using some kind of average of recent values. For example, we might average the last two years' sales, the last three years' sales, the last five years' sales, or any number of other periods. The forecast would simply be the average that resulted. "The obser-

Table 5–1
Annual sales and forecasted sales using two-year and four-year moving averages for a manufacturer of pens and pencils

| Year | Actual Sales | Forecasted Sales | |
		Two-Year Moving Average	Four-Year Moving Average
1970	4,200		
1971	4,410		
1972	4,322	4,305	
1973	4,106	4,366	
1974	4,311	4,214	4,260
1975	4,742	4,209	4,287
1976	4,837	4,527	4,370
1977	5,030	4,790	4,499
1978	4,779	4,934	4,730
1979	4,970	4,905	4,847
1980	5,716	4,875	4,904
1981	6,116	5,343	5,128
1982	5,932	5,916	5,395
1983	5,576	6,024	5,684
1984	5,465	5,754	5,835
1985		5,520	5,772

[35] Those who wish a more comprehensive coverage of forecasting with time series should see one of the books specifically devoted to forecasting methods in general, such as Steven C. Wheelwright and Spyros Makridakis, *Forecasting Methods for Management*, 2d ed. (New York: John Wiley & Sons, 1977); or time series forecasting methods in particular, such as C. Chatfield, *The Analysis of Time Series: Theory and Practice* (New York: John Wiley & Sons, 1975) or Douglas C. Montgomery and Lynwood A. Johnson, *Forecasting and Time Series Analysis* (New York: McGraw-Hill, 1976).

vation included in the average is specified by the manager and remains constant. The term *moving average* is used because, as each new observation becomes available, a new average can be computed and used as a forecast."[36]

Table 5–1 presents 15 years of historical sales data for a manufacturer of pens and pencils and also the resulting forecasts for a number of years using two-year and four-year moving averages. Figure 5–5 displays the results graphically. The entry 4,305 for 1972 under the two-year moving average method, for example, is the average of the sales of 4,200 units in 1970 and 4,410 units in 1971. Similarly, the forecast of 5,520 units in 1985 represents the average of the number of units sold in 1983 and 1984. The forecast of 5,772 units in 1985 under the four-year moving average method, on the other hand, represents the average number of units sold during the four-year period 1981–84. Note that it takes more data to begin forecasting with four-year than with two-year moving averages. This is an important consideration when starting to forecast sales for a new product.

Observe also the impact of the number of periods on the fluctuations in the forecasted series. The larger the number of observations included, the greater is the smoothing of the forecasts. Thus, whereas the range of forecasted values is 1,815 (6,024 − 4,209) with the two-year moving average, it is only 1,575

Figure 5–5
Actual and forecasted sales using moving scales

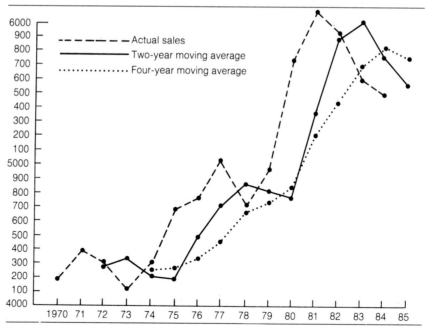

[36] Wheelwright and Makridakis, *Forecasting Methods for Management*, p. 29.

(5,835 − 4,260) with the four-year moving average—a difference of 420 units. When we desire a smoother value because we think there is little change in the underlying pattern and we are observing mainly random fluctuations, we should use a large number of periods to determine the moving average. Conversely, when we think the series is changing rapidly or when there is little randomness in sales, we would use a smaller number of periods to compute the moving average so that the forecast can react more quickly to the changes that are occurring.

Exponential Smoothing

The method of moving averages gives *equal* weight to each of the last n values in forecasting the next value. Thus, when $n = 4$ (the four-year moving average is being used), equal weight is given to each of the last four years' sales in predicting the sales for next year. No weight is given to any sales five or more years previous. The forecasting equation, in other words, is

$$\hat{X}_{t+1} = \frac{X_t + X_{t-1} + X_{t-2} + X_{t-3}}{n} = \frac{X_t + X_{t-1} + X_{t-2} + X_{t-n+1}}{n}$$

$\hat{X}_{t+1}$ = forecasted value for next year or next period
X_t = actual sales that resulted in year or period t

Exponential smoothing is a type of moving average. However, instead of weighting all observations equally in generating the forecast, exponential smoothing weights the most recent observations heaviest. There is a good reason for this. The most recent observations contain the most information about what is likely to happen in the future, and they should logically be given more weight. The general form of the exponential smoothing model is

$$\hat{X}_{t+1} = \alpha X_t + (1 - \alpha)\hat{X}_t$$

where the caret again indicates a forecasted value, and an X without a caret indicates an actual value. The exponential smoothing model thus suggests that next year's sales will be equal to this year's sales, X_t, times the constant, α, plus the forecasted value of this year's sales, $\hat{X}_t$, times the constant, $(1 - \alpha)$. It can be shown by successive substitution that the second term in this equation implicitly recognizes older values, thereby overcoming a second limitation of the moving average method, which ignores all those values more than n periods old.[37]

The key decision affecting the use of exponential smoothing is the choice of α, which is known as the smoothing constant, and which is constrained to be between 0 and 1. High values of α give great weight to recent observations and little weight to distant sales; low values of α, on the other hand, give more weight to older observations. If sales change slowly, low values of α work fine. When sales experience rapid changes and fluctuations, however, high values of α should be

[37] See Wheelwright and Makridakis, *Forecasting Methods for Management*, p. 36, for the derivation.

used so that the forecast series responds to these changes quickly. The value of α is normally determined empirically; various values of α are tried, and the one that produces the smallest forecast error when applied to the historical series is adopted. Table 5–2 and Figure 5–6 show what happens to forecasted values when α is set at 0.2, 0.5, and 0.8. Note two things. First, when the forecast is initialized, the first α forecast value is simply set equal to the prior year's actual sales.[38] Second, note the impact of α on the speed with which forecasted sales respond to changes in actual sales.

Table 5–2
Annual sales and forecasted sales using exponential smoothing and various values for the smoothing constant α

Year	Actual Sales	Forecasted Sales		
		$\alpha = 0.2$	$\alpha = 0.5$	$\alpha = 0.8$
1970 4,200				
1971 4,410		4,200	4,200	4,200
1972 4,322		4,242	4,305	4,368
1973 4,106		4,258	4,314	4,332
1974 4,311		4,228	4,210	4,151
1975 4,742		4,244	4,260	4,279
1976 4,837		4,343	4,501	4,649
1977 5,030		4,441	4,669	4,800
1978 4,779		4,559	4,849	4,984
1979 4,970		4,603	4,814	4,820
1980 5,716		4,676	4,892	4,940
1981 6,116		4,883	5,304	5,561
1982 5,932		5,129	5,710	6,005
1983 5,576		5,289	5,821	5,947
1984 5,465		5,346	5,699	5,650
1985		5,370	5,583	5,502

Decomposition

The decomposition method of sales forecasting is typically applied to monthly or quarterly data where there is some seasonal pattern evident and the manager wishes to forecast sales not only for the year but also for each period in the year. A

---

[38] The exponential smoothing approach to forecasting can be shown to be a subset of Box-Jenkins methods of forecasting. That approach involves: (1) postulating a model that might fit the data, (2) estimating the parameters in the model, (3) checking the adequacy of the model and repeating steps (1) and (2), if necessary, and (4) using the fitted model to generate forecasts. Box-Jenkins models are richer than exponential smoothing models in that they can be fitted to more complex data series. However, they are also more complicated for the manager to understand. See G. E. Box and G. M. Jenkins, *Time Series Analysis*, 2d ed. (San Francisco: Holden-Day, 1976). For a marketing application, see Richard M. Helmer and Johny K. Johansson, "An Exposition of the Box-Jenkins Transfer Function Analysis with an Application to the Advertising-Sales Relationship," *Journal of Marketing Research* 14 (May 1977), pp. 227–39.

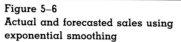

Figure 5–6
Actual and forecasted sales using
exponential smoothing

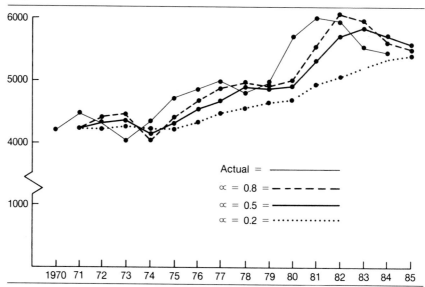

manufacturer of charcoal grills, for example, may notice a surge in sales every spring and might wish to determine what portion of that represents an overall, fundamental change in demand and what portion is due to seasonal aberrations.

The decomposition method attempts to isolate four separate portions of a time series: the *trend* factor, the *cyclical* factor, the *seasonal* factor, and the *random* factor. The trend reflects the long-run changes experienced in the series when the cyclical, seasonal, and irregular components are removed. It is typically assumed to be a straight line. The cyclical factor is not always present because it reflects the waves in a series when the seasonal and irregular components are removed. These ups and downs typically occur over a long period—perhaps two to five years. Some products experience little cyclical fluctuation (canned peas), whereas other experience a great deal (housing starts). The seasonal factor reflects the annual fluctuation in the series due to the natural seasons. The seasonal factor normally repeats itself each year, although the exact pattern of sales may be different from year to year.

Table 5–3, for example, shows the calculation of a simple seasonal index based on five years of sales history. Note that the data suggest there are definite seasonal and trend components in the series. The fourth quarter of every year is always the best quarter while the first quarter is the worst. At the same time, sales each year are higher than they were the year previous. Now one could calculate a seasonal index for each year by simply dividing quarterly sales by the yearly average per quarter. It is much more typical, though, to base the calculation of the seasonal index on several years of data so as to smooth out the random fluctua-

Table 5–3
Calculation of a seasonal index

Year	Quarter 1	2	3	4	Total
1980	82.8	105.8	119.6	151.8	460.0
1981	93.1	117.6	122.5	156.9	490.1
1982	92.0	122.4	132.6	163.2	510.2
1983	95.3	129.0	151.3	185.0	560.6
1984	120.1	138.1	162.2	180.2	600.6
5-year quarterly average.............	96.7	122.6	137.6	167.4	131.1
Seasonal index*	73.8	93.5	105.0	127.7	

*The seasonal index equals the quarterly average divided by the overall quarterly average times 100; for the first quarter, for example, the seasonal index equals (96.7 ÷ 131.1) × 100 = 73.8.

tions that occur by quarter. In the example, five years of sales history are used. To calculate the index, first determine the average sales for each quarter for the five years. Then divide these numbers by the average sales per quarter for the entire period to give the seasonal index for each quarter. The calculations suggest that the seasonal indices for the first and fourth quarters, for example, are 73.8 and 127.7. This means that sales in the first quarter are typically 26.2 percent less and those in the fourth quarter are 27.7 percent more than normal because of seasonal factors. A manager should not be upset therefore if the company experiences a 40 percent drop in sales from 200 units in the fourth quarter of last year to 120 units in the first quarter this year. That is natural because of the seasonal pattern to the business. Rather the appropriate way to interpret the figures is to deseasonalize them. This means that the actual sales figures should be divided by the appropriate seasonal index. The deseasonalized fourth quarter sales are 200 ÷ 127.7 × 100 = 156.6 while the deseasonalized first quarter sales are 120 ÷ 73.8 × 100 = 162.6. The deseasonalized sales per quarter times four gives the expected yearly sales if sales were to continue at the same rate. While the first inclination was to suggest that the company's sales performance was worse in the first quarter than it was in the prior fourth quarter, in fact, the first quarter was better. After accounting for the normal seasonal fluctuations in sales by comparing the deseasonalized values, the results suggest that sales in the first quarter were actually up.

In using the decomposition method, the analyst typically first determines the seasonal pattern and removes its impact to identify the trend. When the trend has been isolated and removed, the cyclical factor estimated. After the three components are isolated, the forecast is developed by applying each factor in turn to the historical data.[39]

[39] The entire process is illustrated in Wheelwright and Makridakis, *Forecasting Methods for Management*, pp. 91–97. The best-known decomposition method is the technique developed by Julius Shiskin, "Electronic Computers and Business Indicators," National Bureau of Economic Research, Occasional Paper 57, which is used in forecasting many national statistics.

Advantages

The time series approach to sales forecasting provides a systematic means for making quantitative projections of sales, and this is both its major advantage and disadvantage. The method is objective in the sense that two analysts working on the same data series using the same forecasting technique and the same model should produce the same forecast. This is not necessarily true with the subjective sales forecasting schemes discussed earlier. The time series approach allows the forecaster to take advantage of the particular repetitive patterns exhibited by historical sales. If there are trend, cyclical, or seasonal patterns, the analyst can attempt to isolate them. Such knowledge is often useful when developing company plans.

Disadvantages

Forecasts based on time series methods rest on the presumption that the factors that produced the historic fluctuations in sales will continue to operate in the future. This is often a heroic assumption because conditions change. New factors emerge while old ones diminish in importance. The competitor that was so vital a force in the marketplace several years ago may no longer have that same market clout. On the other hand, the new entrant two to three years ago may now be a potent force. In sum, even the most regular sales series are likely to vary because of changes in the economic environment, technology, or competition. The adage that "the only constant in life is change" applies; to blindly extrapolate the past to the future can be dangerous. Furthermore, the method may be difficult or even impossible to use when the series is very irregular because of aberrations induced by external shocks. The method also requires a good deal of technical skill and judgment, although the particular levels of these talents that are required depend on the type of time series forecasting method used. It is hard to break down forecasts developed by this scheme into estimates for individual salespeople and territories.

Statistical Demand Analysis

Time series analysis attempts to determine the relationship between sales and time and to use that as the basis of the forecast for the future. Statistical demand analysis attempts to determine the relationship between sales and the important factors affecting sales and uses that for forecasting the future. Typically, regression analysis is used to estimate the relationship. The emphasis is not on isolating all factors that affect sales but simply on identifying those that have the most dramatic impact and then estimating the magnitude of the impact.

Carlson and Umble, for example, used regression analysis to estimate the demand for various sizes of automobiles using quarterly historical data.[40] The general estimating equation was:

$$D_t^i = \beta_0 + \beta_1 Y_t^D + \beta_2 P_2^i + \beta_3 G_t + \beta_4 Z_t^E + \beta_5 Z_t + \epsilon_t$$

where

D_t^i = demand for car size i, seasonally adjusted and adjusted for population size, where

$i = 1$: subcompact
$i = 2$: compact
$i = 3$: intermediate
$i = 4$: standard
$i = 5$: luxury

Y_t^D = disposable income seasonally adjusted and adjusted for population size and to constant dollars (1967 = 100)

P_t^i = average price of car size i adjusted to constant dollars (1967 = 100)

G_t = gasoline price in current dollars

Z_t^E = 1 for the first and second quarter in 1974 when there was a gasoline shortage and 0 otherwise

Z_t = 1 for the fourth quarter of 1970 when there was a UAW strike and 0 otherwise;

ϵ_t = the disturbance term.

The best fitting equation for subcompacts, for example, turned out to be

$$D_t = -709,190 + 2570 Y_t^D - 275 P_t + 3470 G_t + 101,000 Z_t^E$$

The fit was good in that the equation accounted for 91 percent of the quarter-to-quarter variation in subcompact demand. The equation could consequently be used to estimate future demand for subcompacts.

Advantages

The use of statistical demand analysis to generate a sales forecast has many advantages. First, it has great intuitive appeal. It forces the forecaster and the manager to consider the major forces that affect sales. The analyst must identify these factors and must accurately model the relationship between the factors and sales. This can be a definite plus in understanding what is happening in the market and in planning future strategy. Second, the technique forces the forecaster to quantify the assumptions underlying the future sales estimates. This makes it easier for management to check the results. Third, this method provides a means of discovering factors affecting sales that intuitive reasoning may not

---

[40] Rodney L. Carlson and M. Michael Umble, "Statistical Demand Functions for Automobiles and Their Use for Forecasting in an Energy Crises," *Journal of Business*, 53 (1980), pp. 193–204.

uncover. The analyst may try suggested variables in the regression equation to see how well they work, since the method contains some statistics that can be used to assess whether the factor makes a "significant" difference.[41] Furthermore, the method is objective. The results can be reproduced by different analysts using the same model and variables.

Disadvantages

One fundamental weakness in using statistical demand analysis is that it presumes that historical relationships will continue into the future. Further, the analyst may have a false sense of security in this regard. Typically, an equation is only adopted after several variables have been tried and a number of equations estimated. The fit of the equation to the data, as measured by the proportion of variation explained, should then be good. Thus, it can prove extremely disconcerting to those involved when the forecast is badly in error. If the basic relationship between sales and the factor has changed, however, this is exactly what can happen. Even when the basic relationship between sales and the factor(s) has not changed, the method can prove troublesome. This occurs whenever the equation contains predictor variables with the same time specification as sales. Recall, for instance, that in the automobile demand example, subcompact sales in a given quarter were a function of disposable income, gasoline prices, and car prices in the quarter. Thus, to use the equation to forecast future sales, the price for subcompacts must be determined, and the level of disposable income and the price of gasoline must be predicted. Errors in predicting disposable income or the price of gasoline will affect the accuracy of the sales forecast, as will errors in predicting any quantities in a forecasting equation with the same time specification as sales. There is no problem, of course, when the relationship is between current sales and some *prior* level of the predictor variable, because the value of the predictor is then known. Statistical demand analysis does require a good deal of technical skill and judgment. Some managers do not possess the necessary expertise and are reluctant to use what they do not understand.

Choosing a Forecasting Method

The sales manager faced with a forecasting problem has a dilemma: Which forecasting method should be used and how accurate is the forecast likely to be? Each method has advantages and disadvantages, which are summarized in Table 5–4,

---

[41] To legitimately apply these tests, certain assumptions need to be satisfied. For a review of the assumptions, the tests, and what can be done if the assumptions are violated, see J. Johnston, *Econometric Methods*, 2d ed. (New York: McGraw-Hill, 1972).

Table 5–4
Summary of advantages and disadvantages of various forecasting techniques

Sales Forecasting Method	Advantages	Disadvantages
User expectations	1. Forecast estimates obtained directly from buyers 2. Projected product usage information can be greatly detailed 3. Insightful method aids planning marketing strategy 4. Useful for new product forecasting	1. Potential customers must be few and well defined 2. Does not work well for consumer goods 3. Depends upon the accuracy of user's estimates 4. Expensive, time consuming, labor intensive
Sales force composite	1. Involves the people (sales personnel) who will be held responsible for the results 2. Is fairly accurate 3. Aids in controlling and directing the sales effort	1. Estimators (sales personnel) have a vested interest and therefore may be biased 2. Elaborate schemes sometimes necessary to counteract bias 3. If estimates are biased, process to correct the data can be expensive
Jury of executive opinion	1. Easily done, very quick 2. Does not require elaborate statistics 3. Utilizes "collected wisdom" of the top people 4. Useful for new or innovative products	1. Produces aggregate forecasts that must be broken down 2. Expensive 3. Disperses responsibility for the forecast 4. Group dynamics operate
Delphi technique	1. Minimizes effects of group dynamics 2. Can utilize statistical information	1. Can be expensive and time-consuming
Market test	1. Provides ultimate test of consumers' reactions to the product 2. Allows the assessment of the effectiveness of the total marketing program 3. Useful for new and innovative products	1. Lets competitors know what firm is doing 2. Invites competitive reaction 3. Expensive and time consuming to set up 4. Often takes a long time to accurately assess level of initial and repeat demand
Time series analysis	1. Utilizes historical data 2. Objective, inexpensive	1. Not useful for new or innovative products 2. Factors for trend, cyclical, seasonal or product life-cycle phase must be accurately assessed and included 3. Technical skill and good judgment required 4. Final forecast difficult to breakdown into individual territory estimates

Table 5–4 (concluded)

Sales Forecasting Method	Advantages	Disadvantages
Statistical demand analysis	1. Great intuitive appeal 2. Requires quantification of assumptions underlying the estimates 3. Allows management to check results 4. Uncovers hidden factors affecting sales 5. Method is objective	1. Factors affecting sales must remain constant and be accurately identified to produce an accurate estimate 2. Requires technical skill and expertise 3. Some managers reluctant to use method due to the sophistication

and the decision of which to use will not always be clear.[42] If the company is typical, the decision will more than likely depend upon the level of technical sophistication available in the company as well as the existence of historic sales data. It will also likely depend upon the use to which the forecast will be put. A forecasting system designed to estimate production scheduling and inventory requirements may rely on a completely different set of procedures than one designed to plan marketing strategy. One guide which a manager might find useful when choosing a forecasting method is what other companies have done and what their experiences have been.

Data collected by The Conference Board are interesting in this regard. The Conference Board maintains a Senior Marketing Executive Panel. A survey of the members of this panel, with 161 companies reporting (including 93 industrial product manufacturers, 39 consumer product managers, and 29 service firms) produced the results shown in Table 5–5. Note the heavy reliance on the subjective methods, particularly sales force composite and jury of executive opinion, versus the quantitative, objective methods. There were some differences by type of industry to be sure, and many firms used a combination of approaches, but across all types the value of the subjective methods was evident. "Companies selling to consumer markets value the jury of executive opinion most highly of all, as do the companies in the service group. Firms selling to industrial markets generally give their top votes to the sales force composite method."[43]

Why would this be so, given the greater sophistication of the quantitative techniques? The latter would certainly seem capable of producing more accurate forecasts, and in fact, a 1975 survey among 175 midwestern businessmen

---

[42] For other comparisons of the advantages and disadvantages of the various forecasting techniques, see Vithala R. Rao and James E. Cox, Jr., *Sales Forecasting Methods: A Survey of Recent Developments* (Cambridge, Mass.: Marketing Science Institute, 1978); John C. Chambers, Satinder R. Mullick, and Donald D. Smith, *An Executive's Guide to Forecasting* (New York: John Wiley & Sons, 1974); and George C. Michael, *Sales Forecasting* (Chicago: American Marketing Association, 1979).

[43] PoKempner and Bailey, *Sales Forecasting Practices*, p. 15.

Table 5–5
Degree of company reliance and relative value of major sales forecasting methods in The Conference Board study

Forecasting Method	Percentage of All Companies Reporting				
	Heavy Reliance	Moderate Reliance	Very Little or No Reliance	Value Rated* 1st or 2d	Value Rated 3d to 5th
Users' expectations.........	18%	30%	52%	29%	55%
Sales force composite	42	33	25	56	32
Jury of executive opinion ...	48	32	20	54	36
Time series analysis	25	32	43	30	39
Demand analysis	15	19	66	15	51

Source: Adapted from Stanley J. PoKempner and Earl L. Bailey, *Sales Forecasting Practices: An Appraisal* (New York: National Industrial Conference Board, 1970), pp. 10 and 14.
*Many respondents did not give ratings for all five methods, usually because their companies do not make use of some of them, and thus the percentages do not sum to 100.

showed that the quantitative techniques produced forecasts that, on average, were more accurate than those produced by the subjective methods.[44] The comments of the executive vice president of a large insurance company who responded to The Conference Board survey are instructive in this regard.

The process of forecasting is stimulating to the committeemen [the company's forecasting committee] who participate. It forces them to think ahead, to evaluate opportunities for improving performance, and to mesh plans in a coordinated way. *These things are more important than the accuracy of the figures that emerge from the process.* [emphasis added].[45]

These sentiments were shared by a vice president of an equipment company, who stated:

We do not want to substitute a procedure which may be more accurate but would reduce the present in-depth involvement of the line and staff personnel.[46]

Apparently, these sentiments were as true in 1975 as they were in 1970; in spite of the greater accuracy of the objective methods, the study of midwestern businessmen at that time also indicated that the subjective methods were used more regularly. Table 5–6 displays the results and indicates how the use of the techniques varies by the forecasting time horizon. The jury of executive opinion and sales force composite still are most common. A national study of forecasting experiences in 127 companies at about the same time also indicated heavy reliance on these two methods; however, a large percentage of those responding who

---

[44] Douglas J. Dalrymple, "Sales Forecasting Methods and Accuracy," *Business Horizons*, December 1975, pp. 69–73.
[45] PoKempner and Bailey, *Sales Forecasting Practices*, p. 32.
[46] Ibid.

Table 5–6
Forecasting techniques used by the
sample of midwestern businessmen

Forecasting Method	Percentages Reporting					
	Use Regu- larly	Use Occa- sionally	No Longer Use	Never Tried	Use for Short Term (one year or less)	Use for Long Term (one to five years)
Users' expectations:						
Industry survey	22%	20%	2%	16%	17%	8%
Intention-to-buy survey	15	17	2	23	15	3
Sales force composite	48	15	3	9	37	6
Jury of executive opinion	52	16	1	5	27	16
Time series analysis:						
Moving average	24	15	2	15	18	7
Exponential smoothing	13	13	3	26	13	7
Decomposition (trend projection)	28	16	1	12	13	13
Statistical demand analysis:						
Regression	17	13	1	24	8	9
Leading index	12	16	1	24	12	5

Source: Adapted from Douglas J. Dalrymple, "Sales Forecasting Methods and Accuracy," *Business Horizons*, December 1975, p. 71. Used by permission.

were familiar with the techniques also used time series and regression methods almost as much.[47]

How accurate is a sales forecast likely to be? A *Sales Management* survey of sales forecasting programs at 182 companies indicated that "the deviation between forecasted and actual results averages 5 percent. . . . Consumer goods companies post the best record, primary and fabricated metal firms the poorest . . . the bigger the company, the more likely its forecast will be close to the target."[48] The Conference Board found a median difference of 4 percent between actual sales and the forecast prepared at the beginning of the year, with 93 percent of the companies having a forecast error of 10 percent or less. The study among midwestern businessmen produced an average error on a one-year forecast of 6.9 percent, with respondents attributing the errors to unstable business conditions, inflation, shortages of materials, and unstable customer demand, which were common at the time.[49] The more quantitative techniques tended to produce smaller errors than the more subjective, with those using the users' expectations method experiencing the largest average percentage errors. Another study among firms on the Fortune 500 list, however, which produced a 55 percent response

[47] Steven C. Wheelwright and Darral G. Clarke, "Corporate Forecasting: Promise and Reality," *Harvard Business Review*, November-December 1976, pp. 40 et. seq.

[48] "Sales Forecasting: Is 5% Error Good Enough?" *Sales Management*, December 15, 1967, p. 41.

[49] Dalrymple, "Sales Forecasting Methods," pp. 71–72.

rate, found that the accuracy of the forecast was: (1) relatively independent of the perceived sophistication of the method used and (2) positively related to desired accuracy.[50] Apparently, firms that strive for accurate forecasts can produce them. This may be partly because they are simply more willing to commit the necessary resources to the task.

There was one common finding across these studies. Most firms use a variety rather than simply one forecasting technique. Furthermore, the forecast error of firms that use a variety of techniques is generally less than for firms that rely on only one.

Developing Territory Estimates

Not only must firms develop global estimates of demand, but most also develop territory by territory estimates. The latter are particular important to the sales manager as they allow for more effective planning, directing, and controlling of salespeople in that they affect:

1. The design of sales territories.
2. The procedures used to identify potential customers.
3. The establishment of sales quotas.
4. Compensation levels and the mix of components in the firm's sales compensation scheme.
5. The evaluation of salespeople's performance.[51]

We will see how territory demand estimates allow sales managers to more effectively manage the salespeople under them in subsequent chapters, particularly in the chapters on territory design, quotas, motivation, and the three chapters on evaluation and control. For the moment, you should simply accept the fact that good territory demand estimates are a key ingredient to effective sales management.

This begs the question, of course, of how territory estimates can be derived. Some of the sales forecasting schemes provide them naturally. A survey of users or salespeople provide detailed estimates of demand, often by product by customer. These estimates can be combined easily into larger aggregates to produce demand estimates by product by territory. Similarly, the use of the sales history for a particular product in a particular territory in, say, a time series approach produces a forecast with the desired geographic detail. Some other forecasting schemes produce only aggregate forecasts which subsequently have to be broken down by appropriate geographical boundaries. The jury of executive opinion pro-

---

[50] Judy Pan, Donald R. Nichols, and Maurice O. Joy, "Sales Forecasting Practices of Large U.S. Industrial Firms," *Financial Management* 6 (Fall 1977), pp. 72–77. For an empirical investigation of the factors that seem to contribute to the forecast accuracy of objective methods, see Spyros Makridakis and Michele Hibon, "Accuracy of Forecasting: An Empirical Investigation" *Journal of the Royal Statistical Society* 142 (1979), pp. 97–145.

[51] For a discussion of these and other uses of sales territory demand estimates, see William E. Cox, Jr., *Industrial Marketing Research* (New York: John Wiley & Sons, 1979), pp. 146–148.

vides an obvious example. Statistical demand analysis also typically produces aggregate estimates that have to be apportioned to areas.

The use of market factors or market indices is the basic way by which aggregate estimates of demand are broken out by territory. A *market factor* is a feature or characteristic in a market that is related to the demand for the product. For example, the number of households in an area is one market factor influencing the demand for microwave ovens. A *market index* is a mathematical expression that combines two or more market factors into a numerical index. The market for microwave ovens might also be affected by income levels and whether both spouses work. Thus when assessing the likely demand for microwave ovens in a particular geographic area, we might wish to somehow combine the number of households in the area, the income level in the area, and the proportion of households with both spouses working. Typically this would be done by forming a linear combination of the factors where the weights assigned each factor would reflect their expected relative importance in affecting demand for microwave ovens. The amount of total demand that would be apportioned to the territory would reflect the relative size of the index versus the national total. Typically, this means treating the national total as 100 percent and assessing the portion of that 100 percent that lies within the particular geographic boundaries being considered.[52]

Industrial Goods

Territory demand estimates for industrial goods are typically developed by relating sales to some common denominator. The common denominator or market factor might be the number of total employees, number of production employees, value added by manufacture, value of materials consumed, value of products shipped, or expenditures for new plant and equipment. Say the ratio of sales per employee is developed for each of several identifiable markets. By then looking at the number of employees in a particular geographic area within each of those identifiable markets, one is able to estimate the total demand for the product that exists within the area.

The identifiable markets are usually defined using Standard Industrial Classification (SIC) codes, which is a system developed by the U.S. Census Department for organizing the reporting of business information, such as employment, value added in manufacturing, capital expenditures, and total sales. Each major industry in the United States is assigned a two-digit number, indicating the group to which it belongs. The types of businesses making up each industry are further identified by additional digits. Figure 5–7 displays a partial breakdown of the construction industry.

Consider a firm that wants to estimate the demand for its portable air compressors (those typically used on construction sites to power pavement breakers and

---

[52] The Buying Power Index (BPI) discussed below provides an example of a market index based allocation of total estimated demand to a territory.

Figure 5–7
Partial breakdown of Standard
Industrial Classification codes

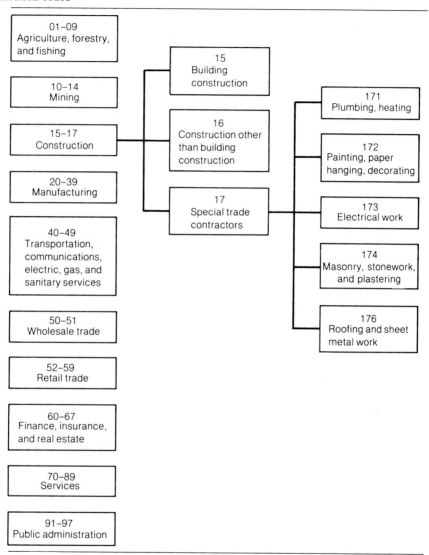

other equipment) in Providence County, Rhode Island. *A priori sales* of portable air compressors are logically related to the number of employees working in the industry and the number of employees serves as a direct indicator of the amount of construction activity in the area. At the same time, sales per employee would not be the same across the three major SIC construction categories. Those firms in road building (SIC 16) have much greater need for portable air compressors than those firms in building construction (SIC 15), and those firms in turn have greater need than special contractors (SIC 17). Suppose the historical evidence suggests that dollar sales of portable air compressors per employee in particular are $90, $28, and $13 for the SIC codes 16, 15, and 17, respectively. By knowing the number of construction employees of each type, one can estimate total market demand for portable air compressors in Providence County, Rhode Island. Table 5–7 illustrates the calculations. By then taking into account its competitive position in the Providence market, the firm could develop estimates for sales of its own brand. Alternatively, the firm could use total market demand to assess how well it is doing in the Providence market and could plan its marketing strategy accordingly.

Table 5–7
Estimation of market demand for portable air compressors by the construction industry in Providence County, Rhode Island

Industry	Number of Employees	Sales per Employee	Estimated Demand
15—Building construction................	2,989	28	83,692
16—Construction other than building	432	90	38,880
17—Special trade contractor............	5,697	13	74,061

A big advantage of a market factor method like this for breaking down total demand is that territory demand is derived objectively. The assumptions and calculations are obvious, and managers can readily follow the development of the estimates. They are likely to feel more confident with something they totally understand. Furthermore, the assumptions can be varied in systematic ways and the impact on estimated demand can be calculated. For example, the portable air compressor estimates might allow for the fact that the size of a firm affects potential by taking into account the number of firms of different sizes in Providence County. Thus, the method allows the calculation of not only area potentials but also customer potentials if the firm wishes to push the calculations that far. One key requirement of the method is that data is available in the detail required. This is one of the primary reasons firms selling to industrial consumers base their calculations on SIC codes as the Census Department publishes a great deal of detailed area data by SIC code.[53]

---

[53] For an overview of useful secondary data published by the Census Bureau and other public and private agencies, see Churchill, *Marketing Research,* pp. 158–67.

Consumer Goods

Whereas firms selling to industrial consumers rely most heavily on identifiable market segments using SIC codes when estimating territory demand, those selling consumer goods are more apt to rely on aggregate conditions in each territory. Sometimes this will be a single variable or market factor like the number of households, population, or perhaps the level of income in the area. In other instances, the firm attempts to relate demand to several variables combined in a systematic way. The demand for washing machines, for example, has been shown through regression analysis to be a function of: (1) the level of consumers' stock of washing machines, (2) the number of wired dwelling units, (3) disposable personal income, (4) net credit, and (5) the price index for house furnishings. Since these statistics are published by area, a firm can use the determined regression equation to estimate demand by area.

Many firms are willing to expend the effort necessary to develop an expression for the relationship between total demand for the product and several variables that are logically related to sales of the product. Many other firms, however, are content to base their estimates of territory demand on one of the standard multiple-factor indexes that have been developed.

One of the most popular standard indexes is the buying power index (BPI), which is generated and published by *Sales and Marketing Management*. The index considers income, population, and retail sales. These are weighted by the factors 5, 2, and 3, respectively, to generate a single number for a geographic region. This number is used to estimate the share of total market demand in the area. More specifically, the buying power index for an area can be calculated using the formula

$$BPI = \frac{5I + 2P + 3R}{10}$$

where I is the percentage of disposable personal income in the area, P is the percentage of U.S. population, and R is the percentage of total retail sales.

Table 5–8 shows the basic statistics and the BPI for the Atlanta, Georgia, area. Statistics are provided for the city itself, the county in which it is located, and the total metropolitan area. These statistics, as well as some category details such as how retail sales break out by store group, are published each year in *Sales and Marketing Management*'s Survey of Buying Power. Firms using the BPI would concentrate their analysis on the total percentage of the BPI found in the territory in question. The Atlanta metropolitan area, for example, has a BPI of .9613. This means that .0096 percent of the total potential for the product could be expected to be within the Atlanta metropolitan area. If the total demand for hair spray, for example, was anticipated to be $400 million, the BPI suggests that the demand within the Atlanta metropolitan area would be $3,845,000 (400,000,000 × .009613). Thus, even though the Atlanta metropolitan area contains less than 1

Table 5–8
Basic components and BPI for the
Atlanta, Georgia, area

Area	Total Population (000)	Percentage of U.S.	Total Retail Sales (000)	Percentage of U.S.	Total Effective Buying Income (000)	Percentage of U.S.	Buying Power Index
Atlanta........	412.2	.1784	2,192,258	.2076	3,874,417	.1926	.1942
Fulton County .	587.1	.2542	3,240,722	.3069	6,222,310	.3092	.2975
Atlanta metropolitan area	2,109.6	.9132	10,545,436	.9985	19,361,631	.9623	.9613
Total U.S.	231,009.5	100	1,056,106,658	100	2,012,116,899	100	

Source: Adapted from "1981 Survey of Buying Power," *Sales and Marketing Management* 129, no. 2 (July 27, 1982), pp. C–55 and C–58, Section C.

percent of the people, it could be expected to account for almost 1 percent of the total demand for the product.

As one might expect, the BPI is not especially useful for estimating territory potentials for industrial products. Nor is it especially useful for infrequently purchased, high-priced consumer goods. It is very popular, though, when estimating territory potential for frequently purchased lower-priced convenience goods. One strategy for a firm selling consumer goods is to determine empirically if the BPI correlates with industry sales by area. A firm is fortunate when it does because the BPI index is convenient to use—it is updated annually and is available by small geographic area. If the index does not correlate well with sales of the product, then the firm is probably better off (1) using a single market factor or (2) developing its own index using factors logically related to sales and some *a priori* or empirically determined weights regarding their relative importance, rather than blindly using the BPI to develop territory demand estimates.

Summary

This chapter reviewed the analysis of market opportunity, a pivotal ingredient in the design of marketing plans in general and sales plans in particular. Market opportunity analysis involves: (1) estimation of market potential or the expected sales of a commodity by the entire industry serving the market during a stated period, (2) estimation of sales potential or the share likely to be realized by the company, and (3) preparation of the sales forecast or the estimate of sales for a specified future period under an assumed marketing plan. The difference between potential estimates from forecasts is that potential estimates reflect maximum demand under ideal conditions, while a forecast reflects a specific marketing plan; thus, potential reflects opportunities while a forecast reflects expectations.

While the notions of potential and forecast are conceptually distinct, they become blurred when estimates of demand are actually developed as the various techniques available for estimating demand emphasize the proposed marketing effort differently. While all are called "sales forecasting methods," some ignore the marketing plan completely when estimates are developed, while others incorporate the proposed effort directly.

The main methods for preparing sales forecasts are users' expectations, sales force composite, jury of executive opinion, market test, time series analysis, and statistical demand analysis. The users expectations method is also known as the buyers' intentions method because it relies on answers from customers regarding their expected consumption or purchases of the product. The sales force composite method requires estimates of expected sales from each member of the sales force. These estimates are typically discussed, revised, and then pooled to form estimates for other levels of the sales organization hierarchy—for example, salesperson, branch, region, district, and overall. The jury of executive or expert opinion polls top executives of the company for their assessment of sales possibilities for the coming period. The forecast may be developed using face-to-face discussion or through anonymous interaction using Delphi procedures, in which each person in the group submits a forecast to the group coordinator. The coordinator, in turn, prepares a summary of these estimates, which is distributed to all those who submit forecasts. They then have the opportunity to revise their estimates. The process continues until a reasonable consensus is reached. The market test is a controlled experiment in which the product is placed in several representative cities, where its performance is monitored; the results are then projected to the area in which the firm operates. Time series analysis relies on the analysis of historical sales data to isolate the underlying pattern and the use of that pattern to predict the future. Statistical demand analysis rests on determining the relationship between sales and the important factors affecting sales. That relationship is then used to forecast the future.

Several recent surveys indicate that the subjective methods, particularly the jury of executive opinion and the sales force composite, are currently used more than the quantitative techniques, time series and statistical demand analysis in spite of the greater accuracy of the latter. Most firms, however, use a variety of techniques in combination. These surveys also indicate that the average forecast error is probably 4 to 5 percent, with most companies experiencing 10 percent error or less.

It is quite common to divide the total estimate of demand among the geographic areas the company serves. Typically this is done using a market factor or a market index. A market factor is a feature or characteristic in a market that is related to the demand for the product. An often used market factor for estimating territory demand for industrial goods, for example, is the number of employees in each of several industries (denoted by their SIC codes) that the company serves.

A market index is a mathematical expression that combines two or more market factors into a numerical index. The buying power index, for example, which combines income, population, and retail sales in an area into a single number, is an index that is often used to estimate territory potentials for frequently purchased, lower-priced consumer goods.

Discussion Questions

1. Define market potential, sales potential, and sales forecast. Under what conditions would sales potential and market potential be the same?

2. For the following products, indicate what factor(s) you would use to estimate market potential.
   a. Skippy peanut butter.
   b. Rolex watches.
   c. Waterford crystal.
   d. Power riding lawnmowers.
   e. Ektelon racquetball racquets.
   f. Calvin Klein designer jeans.
   g. Frye boots.
   h. Bayer aspirin.
   i. Muzak Corporation background music.

3. Komplete Kable TV offers movies to home viewers for showing on television. To obtain a movie on a given night, the viewer dials a number, which then allows the movie to be shown on the television set. The cost is $4.50 and is added to the telephone bill. How would you estimate the market potential for this service?

4. To estimate market potential for the garden tractor division of the M-F Implement Co., Mark Haynes, the statistician, estimated the following relationship using multiple regression analyses:

$$Y = a + b_1X_1 + b_2X_2 + b_3X_3 + b_4X_4$$

where:

   Y = unit sales of U.S. garden tractors
   X_1 = number of single-family homes
   X_2 = disposable personal income
   X_3 = index of food prices
   X_4 = family size

   Using data for 1970–80, $R^2 = 65$ was obtained. Should this method be used to predict market potential?

5. A new cake mix is to be introduced by Miracle Foods. To develop territory potentials, a corollary index has been proposed. The index contains several factors, such as income, population, and retail food sales. Can you justify

these factors? Does it make sense to use retail food sales, which means that cake sales are a function of food sales?

6. The PTF Corporation, a manufacturer of lawn and garden equipment, relies on trend analysis for determining future sales. Historically, the cost of marketing has been 58 percent of sales. Thus, with 1985 sales predicted to be $750,000, the resulting marketing budget will be $435,000. Comment.

7. Salespeople are either terribly pessimistic or hopelessly optimistic and therefore cannot be expected to make accurate sales forecasts. Comment.

8. The sales manager of a large manufacturer of photographic equipment stated: "The sales forecast is the most important document in the corporate planning process." How can you justify this statement?

9. The Crystal Pure Bottled Water Company has experienced explosive growth in recent years unlike the steady trend in earlier years. What would you suggest as a forecasting technique using the following sales data?

Year	Sales
1969	$ 2,843
1970	3,523
1971	4,507
1972	5,576
1973	6,462
1974	7,115
1975	7,928
1976	9,371
1977	10,054
1978	11,256
1979	16,074
1980	19,831
1981	28,764
1982	34,093
1983	39,420
1984	47,325

10. The value of the Delphi technique depends to a considerable extent on the panelists chosen. What criteria would you use to pick the panelists?

11. One executive of a large multinational corporation suggests that bonuses paid to the sales force should be related to the accuracy of the sales force's forecasts. Do you agree?

12. How do you account for the statement in the chapter that most firms use a variety of forecasting techniques? If a firm has one technique that is very accurate, why would other techniques be used?

13. The sales manager of the Draw-K-Cab Company states: "We never make sales forecasts, we are just too busy making money to worry about eyeballing the future." What are the implications of this comment? Can companies actually survive without making a sales forecast?

14. The Flambeau Corporation manufactures plastic parts for a variety of customers. Past attempts at sales forecasting have not met with success. Sales patterns display considerable fluctuations. Using the data below, develop a sales forecast for the first quarter of 1986.

	1981	1982	1983	1984	1985
Quarter 1	202	367	576	520	607
Quarter 2	75	158	278	295	309
Quarter 3	157	287	353	326	437
Quarter 4	476	659	901	1007	988

15. CBS Record Division needs to make a forecast for a new group known as the Austin City Roundup. The group is very popular in Texas but has never made an album. CBS planners have to schedule production runs for both the record and record jacket. What forecasting techniques would you recommend that they adopt?

16. The Madison Alarm Company manufactures burglar alarms for businesses. Executives want to enter the home market and need to estimate the demand. What factors would you include? How would you break your estimates down by region?

Chapter **6**

Sales Territories

As mentioned in Chapter 1, the design of sales territories is a key element in the formulation of a strategic sales program. Poorly designed territories can increase the cost of doing business and produce other negative consequences as well. These impacts are reviewed in the first part of this chapter. The remainder of the chapter looks at how a sales manager can determine how many sales territories the firm needs and then what each territory should be like.

The Need for Sales Territories

A sales territory is a group of present and potential customers that are assigned to a salesperson, branch, dealer, or distributor for a given period of time. The key word in the preceding definition is *customers*. "Good" sales territories are made up of customers who have money to spend and the willingness to spend it.

While the key to sales territory design is customers, the notion of a territory is operationalized using geographical boundaries in many firms. The salesperson might be assigned the state of Pennsylvania or the city of Philadelphia as his or her sales territory, for example. This is because there are certain advantages, discussed below, that a firm realizes with geographically defined territories. There are exceptions, though, when firms are unlikely to realize the advantages that arise with geographic territories.

When the firm is small or just getting started, for example, management can plan and control the sales operation without the benefit of territories. As a firm increases in size and its markets expand geographically, the advantages of geographically defined sales territories become clearer.

Sometimes firms forego geographic territories when their products are highly technical and sophisticated, choosing instead to rely on product specialists. The argument for this arrangement is that any given field representative could not be expected to have the technical expertise to sell all of the firm's complex equipment. Rather than using salespeople who might not be able to answer the customer's highly technical questions, the firm uses technical specialists who have the necessary expertise. The disadvantage of this scheme is that each of several field salespeople might call on the same account. An alternative scheme some firms use is to have a single salesperson responsible for the account, with the salesperson having the option of calling in home-office technical specialists when needed.

Still another situation in which sales territories are not geographically specified is when personal relationships and friendships have an important bearing on the sale, such as with the sale of securities or real estate. It would be dysfunctional to tell a customer that he or she had to deal with a salesperson other than the one the customer knew and liked.

Other than the exceptions noted above, geographically defined sales territories are the norm in most companies, and sales territory design is one of the most critical decisions for sales managers. A 1977 survey, for example, indicated that time and territory management was ranked as the number one problem for salespeople, which confirmed the results of a similar survey conducted three years earlier.[1] The design of sales territories affects sales force morale, the firm's ability to serve the market, and the firm's ability to evaluate and control the selling effort.

Sales Force Morale

The territory to which a salesperson is assigned can dramatically influence the individual's interest and morale.

In trying to gear a staff to peak effort in this age of frenzied competition, perhaps nothing a company does is more important to morale than dividing its sales territories fairly . . . the problem of setting up separate but equal sales territories is a particularly difficult one, because it is so closely tied to a company's product line and marketing policies, the type and location of its customers, and the compensation of its sales force. Territories are often a bone of contention between management and the men in the field, yet a fair resolution of the conflict is essential to both. The company must have effective coverage of its accounts, and a salesman must have the opportunity to earn an adequate living. The salesman's territory, obviously, can have great influence on his success. Certainly no man will be content with what he considers an inferior assignment while his colleagues seem to be making more money with less effort because of superior territories. Unequal sales territories, in short, are a prime cause of poor morale.[2]

Just as poor sales territory design can have a negative impact on morale, good territory design can affect it positively. There are advantages for salespeople who have their own territories; in some ways, they are in business for themselves. Since they have responsibility for the accounts in their district, they can take personal pride in what their customers buy and the effectiveness with which their customers are served.

Clearly defined territories lead to clarified responsibilities. Sales representatives can more readily appreciate the goals assigned them and can better visualize the effort that will be necessary to achieve those goals. Conflicts among salespeople over who is responsible for a given account, and who is entitled to the commission from the sales to a particular customer, can be reduced when responsibilities are delineated by territories. If disputes arise, as they always do among customers who transact business in more than one territory, they can be more amicably settled when sales territories are clearly defined. Many firms have developed some very standard divisions; for example, half the commission goes to the sales representative serving the account's national office, and half goes to the representative serving the plant to which the merchandise is shipped. Salespeo-

---

[1] The survey was conducted among members of the Research Institute for Sales Executives; 60 percent of those responding checked time and territory management as the most critical problem with which they must contend. See "Salespeople Disclose the Help They Need in 1977," *Research Institute for Sales Executives* February 3, 1977, p. 6.

[2] M. A. Brice, "Art of Dividing Sales Territories." Reprinted with the special permission of *Dun's Review*, May 1967, p. 93. Copyright 1967, Dun & Bradstreet Publications Corporation.

ple understand these ground rules. Although they realize that on a particular sale the home office may have no influence, perhaps on another it will be very important. Thus, they can more readily appreciate the necessity and even the desirability of such division of compensation.

Market Coverage

Soundly designed sales territories can improve the effectiveness with which the market is served. Consider the statement made by Richard Dixon, director of field service for Mutual of New York (MONY):

> We have the most sophisticated computer setup in the insurance industry today. It not only provides up-to-date sales lead information but also serves as a guide for making territorial decisions and opening new offices. The names of our 16 million policyholders have been registered in the computer by state and by county. The computer generates statistics that tell us the share of the market we are getting in any given county. If that share isn't big enough, we may decide to open another office, as we recently did in Walnut Creek, California.[3]

It is much easier to pinpoint customers and prospects and to determine who should call on them and how often when the market is geographically divided than when the market is considered a large aggregate of potential accounts. Salespeople who are restricted to a geographic area are more likely to get more out of that territory than when they can roam at will. Instead of simply skimming the cream off the top, they are more likely to develop small accounts that have the potential to become important accounts. When sales territories are designed to force such effort, salespeople cannot meet their performance goals calling on only "easy accounts."

Customer service can also be improved with properly designed sales territories. Because sales representatives call on the accounts in their territory on a regular basis, they have an opportunity to develop in-depth understanding of their customers' problems and needs. They can better anticipate products that will help the customer and those that will be less effective. They also understand the account better and learn who is involved in the purchasing decision. This helps the representative sell more effectively and service the account better, thereby producing greater long-term customer satisfaction.

Still another market-coverage benefit that arises with good territory design is the integration of the personal selling effort with other elements in the marketing program, particularly the communications program. In territories that have little potential, the manager may decide to emphasize advertising and supplement that with a telephone sales program; he or she may place only minimal emphasis on personal visits by field representatives. In a territory that has good potential and a concentration of customers, the manager may wish to completely forego the tele-

---

[3] Ibid., p. 98.

phone-call program, relying instead on personal sales calls while committing fewer dollars to advertising. Before launching a new product, salespeople may be instructed to call on distributors and dealers and to supply them with sufficient point-of-purchase display materials and other marketing aids. Sales representatives could also help to assure that middlemen have adequate inventories of the product so that they are not caught short, and they know how the product operates and should be serviced.

Evaluation and Control

Effective territory design can improve management's evaluation and control of the field selling effort. Geographically defined sales territories allow sales and cost data to be collected and analyzed by geographic area. This permits area comparisons—an important benefit because the strength of the competition often varies by area. One can compare market shares across areas in total and by product; thus, companies can more accurately pinpoint competitive strengths and weaknesses. Perhaps in one metropolitan area the company is doing poorly because of a dominant distributor that handles a competitor's product. The remedy might involve committing more resources to assist the distributor handling the firm's product. In a territory where the problem is simply awareness of the company and its products, however, the remedy could be decidedly different.

Managers can also evaluate the sales force better when there are geographically defined sales territories. Salespeople can be compared with respect to their sales versus potential, and thereby those who may need training can be spotted. The problem may be knowing how to sell to a particular type of account, or it may be linked to less than satisfactory sales of a particular product. In any case, a more effective cure can be formulated when the exact nature of the problem can be pinpointed.

There are also cost-control advantages that accrue to the firm with defined sales territories. Again, the ability to compare sales representatives in terms of the number of calls they make, their travel and other expenses, and the proportion of time spent in face-to-face customer contact versus other related selling activities can provide important insights into how the job can be done more efficiently. What may be considered slight, incremental differences can have important profit implications for the firm. Consider that, in 1981, the average cost of an industrial sales call was $137.02[4] while the number of calls per day was approximately 5.0.[5] Furthermore, industrial salespersons spend only 39 percent of their

---

[4] Study conducted by McGraw-Hill's Laboratory of Advertising Performance and reported in *Marketing News*, May 1, 1981, Section 2, p. 2. This cost compares with $9.02 in 1942, the first year in which the survey was conducted, and $42.92 just 14 years earlier.

[5] This 5.5 average calls per day is for a sales engineer in a metropolitan market in which the customers are concentrated and the salesperson can make several calls at one location. In territories where customers are dispersed, the average number of calls per day is only 3.5. For different types of salespeople and the two types of territories, the averages range from three to eight calls per day. See "1983 Survey of Selling Costs," *Sales and Marketing Management*, February 21, 1983, p. 38.

typical nine-hour, 32-minute work day, or 3.72 hours, in face-to-face selling;[6] the remainder is spent driving to interviews, waiting for interviews, making service calls, attending meetings, and making reports. If one considers face-to-face time as the real "productive" time of the salesperson, the average industrial sales representative's productive time costs its firm $184 per hour (5.0 calls/day × $137.02/call × 1 day ÷ 3.72 hours)—roughly comparable to that of a $370,000-a-year executive. Of course, some of this other time is also productive time—for example, planning a sales presentation. Yet to the extent that the firm can reduce the unproductive portions through more effective coverage of accounts and more efficient routing within territories, it can achieve substantial cost economies. Small incremental cost improvements for each salesperson for a firm that employs 50 to 100 or more representatives can produce significant contributions to profit.

Sales Force Size

Salespeople are among the most productive assets of a company; they are also among the most expensive. The firm that attempts to determine the optimal number to employ faces several fundamental dilemmas. On the one hand, increasing the number of salespeople will increase sales; on the other hand, it will also increase costs. Achieving the optimal balance between these considerations, although difficult, is vitally important. Complicating the decision is the fact that the optimal number of territories depends on the design of the individual territories. Different assignments of accounts to salespeople and even different call patterns on assigned accounts can produce different levels of sales. Of course, the number of calls the salesforce is required to make directly affects the number of salespeople the firm needs to employ. In sum, the number of sales territories and the design of individual territories must be looked at as interrelated decisions whose outcomes affect each other. The decisions need to be made jointly and not sequentially. At the same time, it is useful for discussion purposes to separate the issues. Consequently, the subsequent discussion first addresses the issue of sales force size and then the issue of sales territory design. However, the size of the sales force may need to be revised as a result of the sales territory design.[7]

---

[6] Study conducted by McGraw-Hill Publications' Research Department and reported in *Business Week* September 26, 1977, p. 158. This percentage has remained constant over the last decade; it was 42 percent in 1970. See *Allocating Field Sales Resources, Experiences in Marketing Management* 23 (New York: National Industrial Conference Board, 1970), p. 92.

[7] There are several computer models available that try to simultaneously treat the complex interactions that arise between the discussion of sales force size and sales territory design. Most of these models incorporate other variables as well, such as the allocation of selling effort to customers or products. See, for example, Charles A. Beswick and David W. Cravens, "A Multistage Decision Model for Salesforce Management," *Journal of Marketing Research* 14 (May 1977), pp. 135–44 and Leonard M. Lodish, "A User-Oriented Model for Sales Force Size, Product and Market Allocation Decisions," *Journal of Marketing* 44 (Summer 1980), pp. 70–78. For an overview of the thrust of the various sales territory computer decision models, see David W. Cravens, "Salesforce Decision Models: A Comparative Assessment," in *Sales Management: New Developments from Behavioral and Decision Model Research*, ed. Richard P. Bagozzi (Cambridge, Mass.: Marketing Science Institute, 1979), pp. 310–24.

There are several techniques for determining the size of the field sales force. Three of the more popular are the (1) breakdown, (2) workload, and (3) incremental methods.

Breakdown Method

The breakdown method is conceptually one of the simplest. An average salesperson is treated as a salesperson unit, and each salesperson unit is assumed to possess the same productivity potential in terms of the amount of sales he or she is likely to produce in a given year. To determine the size of the sales force needed, divide total forecasted sales for the company by the sales likely to be produced by each individual. Mathematically,

$$n = \frac{s}{p}$$

where

n = number of sales personnel needed
s = forecasted sales volume
p = estimated productivity of one salesperson unit

Thus, a firm that had forecast sales of $5 million and in which each salesperson unit could be expected to sell $250,000 would need 20 salespeople. Although conceptually simple, the breakdown method is not without its problems. For one thing, it uses reverse logic. It treats sales force size as a consequence of sales. Yet the logical causation is in the opposite direction. As discussed in Chapter 5, the level of sales expected should depend on the level of the marketing effort. The number of salespeople in the field is an important part of that marketing effort—in some companies the most important part. Determining the number of sales representatives to cover the market in a given year should logically precede forecasting final sales.

A second problem with the breakdown method is that it depends on the estimate of productivity per salesperson. The firm can certainly compute the average of what each salesperson sold, say, in the previous year. However, such averages can obscure important facts. They fail to take account of different ability levels of salespeople, differing potentials in the markets they service, and different levels of competition in sales territories. Perhaps the "most productive" salesperson had lower sales than average because the particular market area had below-average potential and intense competitive pressure. The technique fails to allow for such differences.

Also, this simple expression of the formula does not allow for turnover in the sales force. New salespeople are usually not as productive as those who have been on the job for several years. The formula can be modified to allow for sales force turnover, but it loses some of its simplicity and conceptual appeal.

Finally, a key shortcoming of the breakdown method is that it does not allow for profitability. It treats sales as the end in itself rather than as the means to an end. The number of salespeople is determined as a function of the level of forecast sales, not as a determinant of targeted profit.

Despite these shortcomings, the breakdown method is used. Emery Air Freight estimated the approximate sales volume per representative by multiplying the revenue per person per day by the number of working days.[8]

Workload Method

The basic premise underlying the workload approach (or, as it is sometimes called, the buildup method) is that all sales personnel should shoulder an equal amount of work. The method requires that management estimate the work required to serve the entire market. The total work calculation is typically treated as a function of the number of accounts, how often each should be called on, and for how long. This estimate is then divided by the amount of work an individual salesperson should be able to handle to determine the total number of salespeople required.[9] More specifically, the method consists of the following six steps:[10]

1. *Classify all the firm's customers into categories.* Often the classification is based on the level of sales to each customer. The ABC Rule of Account Classification holds that the first 15 percent of a firm's customers will account for 65 percent of the firm's sales, the next 20 percent will yield 20 percent of the sales, and the last 65 percent will produce only 15 percent of the sales.[11] The top group is categorized as A accounts, the middle group as B accounts, and the bottom group as C accounts. Although many firms do classify their accounts by level of sales, classification could be based on other criteria. One firm, for example, established the priority rating assigned each customer by taking into account each prospect's type of business, credit rating, and product line.[12] The important point is that any classification system should reflect the different amounts of selling effort that will be required to service the different classes of accounts and consequently the attractiveness of each class of accounts to the firm.[13] Suppose, for example, that the firm had 1,030 accounts that could be classified into three basic types or classes, as follows:

---

[8] Robert F. Vizza, *Measuring the Value of the Field Sales Force* (New York: Sales Executives Club of New York, 1963), p. 25.

[9] The method was first proposed by Walter J. Talley, Jr., "How to Design Sales Territories," *Journal of Marketing* 25 (January 1961), pp. 7–13.

[10] The steps are adapted from Richard R. Still, Edward W. Cundiff, and Norman A. P. Govoni, *Sales Management: Decisions, Policies, and Cases,* 4th ed. (Englewood Cliffs, N.J.: Prentice-Hall, 1981), pp. 99–101.

[11] Porter Henry, "The Important Few—The Unimportant Many," *1980 Portfolio of Sales and Marketing Plans* (New York: Sales and Marketing Management, 1980), pp. 34–37.

[12] Jeffrey H. Wecker, "An Approach to Higher Profits with Reduced Selling Costs," *Industrial Marketing,* December 1977, pp. 57–58.

[13] We will have more to say about the attractiveness of accounts when discussing sales territory design.

Type A—large or very attractive—200
Type B—medium or moderately attractive—350
Type C—small or relatively attractive—480

2. *Determine the frequency with which each type of account should be called upon and the desired length of each call.* These inputs can be generated in several ways. They can be based directly on the judgments of management as to what is desirable or the judgments of experienced salespeople as to what is necessary. Alternatively, the firm may wish to do some controlled experiments in which the frequency of contact and the length of each contact are systematically varied to determine what is optimal.[14] Still another possibility is to analyze historical data using appropriate statistical methods like regression analysis.[15] Suppose that the firm, using one of these methods, estimates that Class A accounts should be called on every two weeks, Class B accounts once a month, and Class C accounts every other month. It also estimates that the length of the typical call should be 60 minutes, 30 minutes, and 20 minutes, respectively. The number of contact hours per year for each type of account is thus calculated as:

Class A—26 times/year × 60 minutes/call = 1,560 minutes, or 26 hours
Class B—12 times/year × 30 minutes/call =   360 minutes, or   6 hours
Class C— 6 times/year × 20 minutes/call =   120 minutes, or   2 hours

3. *Calculate the workload involved in covering the entire market.* The total work involved in covering each class of account is given by multiplying the number of such accounts by the number of contact hours per year. These products are subsequently summed to estimate the work entailed in covering all the various types of accounts.

Class A—200 accounts × 26 hours/account = 5,200 hours
Class B—350 accounts ×   6 hours/account = 2,100 hours
Class C—480 accounts ×   2 hours/account =   960 hours
Total   =8,260 hours

4. *Determine the time available per salesperson.* For this calculation, estimate the number of hours the typical salesperson works per week and then multiply that by the number of weeks the representative will work during the year. Suppose the typical workweek is 40 hours and the average salesperson can be expected to work 48 weeks during the year, after allowing for vacation time, sickness, and other emergencies. This suggests that the average representative has 1,920 hours available per year—that is,

40 hours/week × 48 weeks/year = 1,920 hours/year

[14] See, for example, Arthur A. Brown, Frank T. Hulswet, and John D. Kettelle, "A Study of Sales Operations," *Operations Research* 4 (June 1956), pp. 296–308, involving a printing company; and Clark Ward, Donald F. Clark, and Russell L. Ackoff, "Allocation of the Sales Effort in the Lamp Division of General Electric Company," *Operations Research* 4 (December 1956), pp. 629–47.
[15] See, for example, the model developed by General Electric Company for one of its industrial divisions in *Allocating Field Sales Resources*, pp. 98–99.

5. *Apportion the salesperson's time by task performed.* Unfortunately, not all the salesperson's time is consumed in face-to-face customer contact. A large part of it is devoted to nonselling activities such as making reports, attending meetings, and making service calls. Another major portion is spent traveling. Suppose a time study of salespeople's effort suggested the following division:

Selling	40 percent =	768 hours/year	
Nonselling	30 percent =	576 hours/year	
Traveling	30 percent =	576 hours/year	
	100 percent	1,920 hours/year	

6. *Calculate the number of salespersons needed.* The number of salespeople the firm will need can now be readily determined. It is found by dividing the total number of hours needed to serve the entire market by the number of hours available per salesperson for selling—that is, by the calculation

$$\frac{8,260 \text{ hours}}{768 \text{ hours/salesperson}} = 10.75$$

or 11 salespeople.

The workload or buildup method is probably the most common way of determining sales force size. It has several attractive features. It is easy to understand, and it explicitly recognizes that different types of accounts should be called on with different frequencies. The inputs are readily available or can be secured without a great deal of trouble.

Unfortunately, it also possesses some weaknesses. For one thing, it does not allow for differences in sales response among accounts that receive the same sales effort. Two Class A accounts might respond quite differently to sales effort. One may be content with the products and services of the firm and continue to order even if the salesperson does not call every two weeks. Another, which does most of its business with a competitor, may willingly switch some of its orders if it receives more frequent contact. Furthermore, the method does not explicitly consider the profitability of the call frequencies. It does not take into account such factors as the cost of servicing and the gross margins on the product mix purchased by the account. Finally, the method assumes that all salespeople use their time with equal efficiency—for example, that each will have 768 hours available for face-to-face selling. This is simply not true. Some are better able to plan their calls to generate more direct selling time; others in smaller geographic territories can spend less time traveling and more time selling. Some simply make better use of the selling time they do have available. "As experienced sales executives assert, the 'quality of time invested in a sales call' is at least as important as the 'quantity of time spent on a sales call.'"[16] Yet the buildup method does not explicitly consider this dimension. The workload method to determine sales force size is popular and has been used by such companies as Celanese Corporation,[17] AT&T, and IBM.[18]

---

[16] Still, Cundiff, and Govoni, *Sales Management*, p. 101.
[17] Brice, "Art of Dividing," p. 93.
[18] Vizza, *Measuring the Value*, pp. 23–24.

Incremental Method

The basic premise underlying the incremental method of determining sales force size is that sales representatives should be added as long as the incremental profit produced by their addition exceeds the incremental costs. The method recognizes that there will probably be decreasing returns associated with the addition of salespeople; that is, whereas one more might produce $300,000, two more might produce only $550,000 in new sales.

One of the earliest demonstrations of the decreasing-returns principle in the sales management literature was reported by Semlow, who used this observation to outline a method for determining the size of the sales force.[19] His method is illustrated here because it is widely quoted and, in some ways, provides the basis for today's more sophisticated applications of the incremental method. Semlow's method relies on an estimate of what the average salesperson could reasonably be expected to sell, while simultaneously acknowledging that this estimate will vary as a function of the number of salespeople. He found, for example, that when he plotted sales volume per 1 percent of potential (y-axis) versus percentage of potential per territory (x-axis), the smoothed curve was shaped like a hyperbola. This indicated that sales representatives in territories with greater sales potential produced more sales but that their sales were less than proportionate to the increase in potential sales volume. For example, sales in territories with 1 percent of total national potential were $160,000, whereas total sales in territories with 5 percent of national potential averaged $200,000. Thus, only $40,000 of sales per 1 percent of potential were realized in the higher-potential territories versus $160,000 per 1 percent of potential in lower-potential territories. The obvious conclusion was that a higher proportion of sales per 1 percent of potential could be realized if the territories were made smaller by adding salespeople. The key question, though, was to determine the optimum number, since costs would also increase as the number of salespeople increased.

An analyst must execute three steps to determine the proper size of the sales force using Semlow's scheme:

1. *Determine the sales potential in each sales territory.* This can be determined using one of the methods for estimating market potential described in Chapter 5. They are presented for a sample of 10 hypothetical territories in the second column of Table 6–1. Note that total potential across all the territories including those not listed is $20 million. Column 3 expresses each territory's potential as a percentage of total national potential.

2. *Determine sales per 1 percent of territory potential.* This number is estimated by dividing the total sales in the territory (the fourth column in Table 6–1) by the percentage of total potential within the territory (the third column). Total sales are determined from company financial records. This means that a firm that wishes to use this scheme must already be using sales territories. Although the

---

[19] Walter J. Semlow, "How Many Salesmen Do You Need," *Harvard Business Review* 37 (May-June 1959), pp. 126--32.

Table 6–1
Determination of sales per 1 percent
of potential

Territory	Potential ($000)	Potential Percent of Total	Total Sales ($000)	Sales per 1 Percent of Potential ($000)
1	400	2.0%	$ 80	$40
2	1,000	5.0	175	35
3	200	1.0	50	50
4	400	2.0	80	40
5	2,000	10.0	300	30
6	2,000	10.0	300	30
7	1,000	5.0	175	35
8	4,000	20.0	560	28
9	400	2.0	80	40
10	1,000	5.0	175	35
....				
....				
....				
Total	20,000	100.0	3,200	

figures come out even in the example (each territory with 2 percent of potential produces the same total sales of $80,000), one should not expect this in practice. Rather, aberrations above and below some "average" figure can occur. An analyst then needs to generate a "smoothed" figure such as the mean or median sales per 1 percent of potential for territories with equal potential. Note also that the hypothetical figures, while exaggerating the relationship, do show that although salespeople in low-potential territories sell less absolutely, they can logically be expected to achieve more of their available potential than salespeople in higher-potential territories.

3. *Estimate the total sales expected for various numbers of equal-potential territories.* If all territories are equal, each can be expected to contain the same share of total national potential. Thus, if there were 100 territories, each would have 1 percent, whereas if there were 20 territories, each would contain 5 percent of total national potential. We know the expected sales per 1 percent of potential from Table 6–1. To estimate the total sales that could be realized from various numbers of salespeople, then, we simply multiply the contemplated number of salespeople by the relative potential by the sales per 1 percent of potential likely to be realized. With 20 equal territories, for example, each could be expected to contain 5 percent of the total national potential, and Table 6–1 indicates that each territory with 5 percent of potential produces $175,000 in sales or $35,000 per 1 percent of potential. Multiplying 20 territories each with 5 percent of the total potential by 35,000 per 1 percent of potential produces a total sales estimate of $3,500,000 (20 × 5 × $35,000). Table 6–2 indicates that the greatest total sales of $5 million will be realized if the firm employs 100 representatives. If it employs only 50 salespeople, only $4 million in sales will be realized, and even less with fewer people. The firm would want to consider the costs associated with supporting a

Table 6–2
Determination of total sales
expected with various numbers of
equal-potential customers

Number of Territories	Relative Potential (percent)	Sales per 1 Percent of Potential (000)	Total Sales (000)
100	1%	$50	$5,000
50	2	40	4,000
20	5	35	3,500
10	10	30	3,000
5	20	28	2,800

field representative to determine the exact number to employ to maximize profits after taking account of the cost of goods sold. Alternatively, the company might wish to focus on some other objective criterion—for example, the maximization of market share. In that case, the firm would consider the profit implications of such a strategy.

The Semlow method for determining the size of the sales force has several attractive features. The conclusion that a sales representative in a low-potential territory is expected to achieve more of his or her potential than a colleague in a higher-potential territory is intuitively appealing. So is the notion that territories should be structured to contain equal potential. Unfortunately, there is a technical flaw in Semlow's procedure. As Weinberg and Lucas demonstrate, it is incorrect to use an equation in which the dependent variable is sales in the territory divided by the potential in the territory.[20] The procedure is important nonetheless because it was the forerunner of the more modern, sophisticated applications of the incremental method of determining sales force size.

Recent evidence confirms that decreasing returns can be expected with additional salespeople.[21] Furthermore, the firm can expect decreasing returns with other territory design features, such as the market potential per salesperson, the number of buyers per salesperson, the number of calls each salesperson makes, and the actual time the representative spends in face-to-face contact.[22] At the same time, the firm can expect increasing costs as the number of calls the salesperson makes, the number of buyers seen per call, or the length of each sales call are increased. These findings imply that, although firms may wish to increase (or decrease) these factors, they should do so only within reasonable limits. There

---

[20] Charles B. Weinberg and Henry C. Lucas, Jr., "Semlow's Results are Based on a Spurious Relationship," *Journal of Marketing* 41 (April 1977), pp. 146–47.

[21] Zarrell Lambert and Fred W. Kniffen, "Response Functions and Their Applications in Sales Force Management," *Southern Journal of Business* 5 (January 1970), pp. 1–9.

[22] Ibid., p. 5, contains an excellent figure summarizing what the relationships should look like.

have been several attempts to determine statistically the optimal combination of the number of territories as well as these other factors.[23]

The incremental approach to determining sales force size is most conceptually correct, although it is also the most difficult of the three to implement. The inputs necessary for its successful application are harder to generate.

Sales Territory Design

After the number of sales territories has been determined, the sales manager can address territory design questions. The general issues with which he or she must deal and the process that should be followed are illustrated in Figure 6–1. The sales manager strives for the ideal of making all territories equal with respect to the amount of sales potential they contain and the amount of work it takes a salesperson to cover them effectively.[24] When territories are equal in potential, it is easier to evaluate each representative's performance and to compare one salesperson with another. When all territories have equal workloads, it tends to improve sales force morale and diminish disputes between management and the sales force. While considering these questions, the sales manager should take into account the impact on market response of particular territory structures and call frequencies. Obviously, it is going to be difficult, if not impossible, to achieve an optimal balance with respect to all these factors. The sales manager should constantly strive for the proper balance, however.

Select Basic Control Unit

The basic control unit is the most elemental geographic area that is used to form sales territories—county or city, for example. As a general rule, small geographic control units are preferable to large ones. The disadvantage of using large units is that areas with low potential may be hidden by their inclusion in areas with high potential, and vice versa. This makes it difficult to pinpoint geographic potential, which is one of the primary reasons for forming geographically defined sales territories in the first place. Also, the use of small control units makes it easier to adjust sales territories when conditions warrant. It is much easier to

---

[23] See, for example, David W. Cravens, Robert B. Woodruff, and Joe C. Stamper, "An Analytical Approach for Evaluating Sales Territory Performance," *Journal of Marketing* 36 (January 1972), pp. 31–37; C. Davis Fogg and Josef W. Rokus, "A Quantitative Method for Structuring a Profitable Sales Force," *Journal of Marketing* 37 (July 1973), pp. 8–17; Henry C. Lucas, Jr., Charles D. Weinberg, and Kenneth W. Clowes, "Sales Response as a Function of Territorial Potential and Sales Representative Workload," *Journal of Marketing Research* 12 (August 1975), pp. 298–305; and Zarrel V. Lambert, "Determining the Number of Salesmen to Employ: An Empirical Study," in *Changing Marketing Systems: Consumer Corporate, and Government Interfaces*, ed. Reed Moyer (Chicago: American Marketing Association, 1967), pp. 338–41.

[24] William J. Stanton and Richard H. Buskirk, *Management of the Sales Force*, 6th ed. (Homewood, Ill.: Richard D. Irwin, 1983, p. 443.

Figure 6–1
Stages in territory design

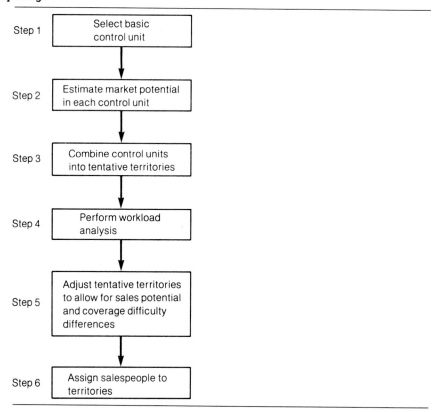

Step 1 — Select basic control unit

Step 2 — Estimate market potential in each control unit

Step 3 — Combine control units into tentative territories

Step 4 — Perform workload analysis

Step 5 — Adjust tentative territories to allow for sales potential and coverage difficulty differences

Step 6 — Assign salespeople to territories

reassign the accounts in a particular county from one salesperson to another, for example, than it is to reassign all the accounts in a state. Some commonly used basic control units are states, trading areas, counties, cities or MSAs, and ZIP code areas.

States. Although it has become less popular, some companies still use states as basic control units. There are some advantages in doing so. State boundaries are clearly defined and thus are simple and inexpensive to use. There is a good deal of statistical data accumulated by state, which makes it easy to analyze territory potential.

One primary weakness of using states as control units is that buying habits do not reflect state boundaries. The state represents a political rather than an economic division of the national market. Consumption patterns in Gary, Indiana, for example, may have more in common with those in Chicago than with those in other parts of Indiana. Another difficulty is that the size of states makes it extremely difficult to pinpoint problem areas. A problem in Ohio may be localized in Cincinnati, but it is hard to determine this if the only figures available are for

Ohio as a whole. States also contain great variations in market potential; the potential in New York City alone, for example, might be greater than the combined potential of all the Rocky Mountain states.

State units are sometimes used by firms that do not have the sophistication or staff to use counties or smaller geographic units—for example, firms at the early stages of territory design. States are also used by firms that cover a national market with only a few sales representatives, particularly when they can specify potential accounts by name—e.g., a firm selling dryers to paper mills.

Trading Areas. Trading areas include a principal city and the surrounding dependent area. A trading area is an economic unit that ignores political and other noneconomic boundaries. Trading areas recognize that consumers who live in New Jersey, for example, may prefer to shop in New York City rather than locally and that the trading area for a food processor in western Iowa may be wholesalers located in the upper Midwest rather than those in nearby Kansas.

One advantage of using trading areas as basic control units is that they do reflect economic factors and they are based on consumer buying habits and normal trading patterns. Thus, they facilitate sales planning and control and diminish the likelihood of disputes among sales representatives. "For instance, there is little danger that after a manufacturer's sales rep does considerable missionary work with retailers, they will buy the product from a wholesaler in another man's territory."[25] This is not apt to happen because all retailers called on by the missionary salesperson ordinarily will be in the same wholesale trading area served by the sales rep.

A major disadvantage of using trading areas as basic control units is that they vary from product to product and must be referred to in terms of specific products. To see this, compare the wholesale Grocery Trading Area Map published by the Department of Commerce with the Retail Trading Area Map put out by Rand McNally. The boundaries for two products may not coincide, and this can sometimes prove awkward and cumbersome for a multiproduct company. Another difficulty with trading areas is that it is often difficult to obtain detailed statistics for them. This in turn makes them expensive to use as geographic control units, although some firms adjust the boundaries of the trading areas so they coincide with county lines. Whether or not a firm formally uses trading areas as basic control units, it should consider the logical trading areas for the products it produces when specifying the boundaries of each sales territory.

Counties. Counties are probably the most widely used basic control unit. They permit a more fine-tuned analysis of the market than do states or trading areas, given that there are 3,133 counties and only 50 states and a varying number of trading areas depending on the product. One dramatic advantage of using counties as control units is that there is a great wealth of statistical data available by county. The county is the smallest geographic unit for which many data series are available. The *County and City Data Book*, which is published biennially by the Bureau of the Census, provides statistics by county on such things as popula-

---

[25] Ibid., p. 447.

tion, education, employment, income, housing, banking, manufacturing output and capital expenditures, retail and wholesale sales, and mineral and agricultural output. Another advantage of counties is that their size permits easy reassignment from one sales territory to another. Thus, sales territories can be altered to reflect changing economic conditions without major upheaval in basic service to the market. Furthermore, potentials do not have to be recalculated before doing so.

The most serious drawback to using counties as basic control units is that for some purposes they are still too large. Los Angeles County or Cook County (Chicago), for example, may require several sales representatives. In such cases, it is necessary to divide these counties into even smaller basic control units.

Cities and MSAs. Historically, firms that planned sales territories used the city as the basic control unit when most of the market potential was within city boundaries. Cities are rarely satisfactory anymore, however. For many products, the area surrounding a city now contains as much or more potential than the central city. Consequently, many firms that formerly used cities now employ Metropolitan Statistical Areas (MSAs) as basic control units.

MSAs are the new name adopted by the federal government to replace the former Standard Metropolitan Statistical Area (SMSAs) designation.[26] They are integrated economic and social units with a large population nucleus. An area can qualify as an MSA in either of two ways:

1. If it contains a city of at least 50,000 people or
2. If it includes a census defined urbanized area of 50,000, with a total metropolitan population of at least 100,000 people (75,000 in New England).

An MSA includes the county containing the central city and any counties having close social and economic ties to the central county. MSAs always include entire counties except in New England. MSAs are clearly important. Table 6–3, which ranks them in order of size, shows the concentration of population within MSAs, particularly within the largest MSAs. The concentration of economic activity matches the concentration of people. As a group, the 314 largest MSAs account for the following percentages of U.S. totals:

76 percent of the population.

81 percent of the effective buying income.

80 percent of total retail sales.

78 percent of food store sales.

83 percent of eating and drinking place sales.

86 percent of general merchandise store sales.

83 percent of furniture/home furnishing/appliance store sales

78 percent of automotive dealer sales.

---

[26] The Office of Management and Budget adopted the new designation and new standards for defining MSAs in 1980 although the changes did not go into effect until June 30, 1983.See "OMB Revises Metropolitan Statistical Area Definitions," *Data User News* 18 (April 1983), p. 3.

Table 6–3
100 Largest MSAs in decreasing order of size

Rank	Area	1980 Population	Rank	Area	1980 Population
1	New York-Northern New Jersey-Long Island	17,539,344	51	Orlando	700,055
2	Los Angeles-Anaheim-Riverside	11,497,568	52	Tulsa	657,173
3	Chicago-Gary-Lake County	7,937,326	53	Syracuse	642,971
4	Philadelphia-Wilmington-Trenton	5,680,768	54	Allentown-Bethlehem	635,481
5	San Francisco-Oakland-San Jose	5,367,925	55	Toledo	616,864
6	Detroit-Ann Arbor	4,752,820	56	Grand Rapids	601,680
7	Boston-Lawrence-Salem	3,971,736	57	Omaha	585,122
8	Washington	3,250,822	58	West Palm Beach-Boca Raton-Delray Beach	576,863
9	Houston-Galveston-Brazoria	3,101,293	59	Greenville-Spartanburg	569,066
10	Dallas-Fort Worth	2,930,516	60	Knoxville	565,970
11	Cleveland-Akron-Lorain	2,834,062	61	Raleigh-Durham	561,222
12	Miami-Fort Lauderdale	2,643,981	62	Harrisburg-Lebanon-Carlisle	555,158
13	Pittsburgh-Beaver Valley	2,423,311	63	Austin	536,688
14	St. Louis-East St. Louis-Alton	2,376,998	64	Tucson	531,443
15	Baltimore	2,199,531	65	Youngstown-Warren	531,350
16	Atlanta	2,138,231	66	Springfield	515,259
17	Minneapolis-St. Paul	2,137,133	67	Fresno	514,621
18	Seattle-Tacoma	2,093,112	68	New Haven-Meriden	500,474
19	San Diego	1,861,846	69	Baton Rouge	494,151
20	Cincinnati-Hamilton	1,660,278	70	El Paso	479,899
21	Denver-Boulder	1,618,461	71	Little Rock-North Little Rock	474,484
22	Tampa-St. Petersburg-Clearwater	1,613,603	72	Las Vegas	463,087
23	Milwaukee-Racine	1,570,275	73	Flint	450,449
24	Phoenix	1,509,052	74	Mobile	443,536
25	Kansas City, MO-Kansas City, KS	1,433,458	75	Johnson City-Kingsport-Bristol	433,638

Table 6–3 (concluded)

Rank	Area	1980 Population	Rank	Area	1980 Population
26	Portland-Vancouver	1,297,926	76	Charleston	430,462
27	New Orleans	1,256,256	77	Chattanooga	426,540
28	Columbus	1,243,833	78	Saginaw-Bay City-Midland	421,518
29	Buffalo-Niagra Falls	1,242,826	79	Lansing-East Lansing	419,750
30	Indianapolis	1,166,575	80	Albuquerque	419,700
31	Norfolk-Virginia Beach-Newport News	1,160,311	81	Wichita	411,313
32	Sacramento	1,099,814	82	Columbia	410,088
33	Providence-Pawtucket-Fall River	1,083,139	83	Canton	404,421
34	San Antonio	1,071,954	84	Bakersfield	403,089
35	Hartford-New Britain-Middleton	1,013,508	85	Worcester	402,918
36	Charlotte-Gastonia-Rock Hill	971,391	86	Davenport-Rock Island-Moline	383,958
37	Rochester	971,230	87	York	381,255
38	Louisville	956,756	88	Beaumont-Port Arthur	375,497
39	Dayton-Springfield	942,083	89	Des Moines	367,561
40	Memphis	913,472	90	Peoria	365,864
41	Salt Lake City-Ogden	910,222	91	Lancaster	362,346
42	Birmingham	883,946	92	Jackson	362,038
43	Oklahoma City	860,969	93	Fort Wayne	354,156
44	Greensboro-Winston-Salem-High Point	851,851	94	Stockton	347,342
45	Nashville	850,505	95	Augusta	345,918
46	Albany-Schenectady-Troy	835,880	96	Spokane	341,835
47	Honolulu	762,565	97	Huntington-Ashland	336,410
48	Richmond-Petersburg	761,311	98	Shreveport	333,079
49	Scranton-Wilkes-Barre	728,796	99	Corpus Christi	326,228
50	Jacksonville	722,252	100	Madison	323,545

77 percent of gasoline service station sales.

83 percent of apparel and accessories store sales.

71 percent of building materials/hardware store sales.

79 percent of drugstore sales.[27]

The heavy concentration of population, income, and retail sales in the MSAs explains why many firms are content to concentrate their field selling efforts on MSAs. Some assign all their field representatives to such areas, omitting coverage of geographic areas outside the MSAs. Such a strategy tends to minimize travel time and expense because of the geographic concentration of MSAs (see Figure 6–2).

ZIP Code Areas.   Some firms, for which city or MSA boundaries are too large, use ZIP code areas as basic control units. The ZIP code areas were devised by the Post Office Department to facilitate mail delivery. It defined more than 36,000 five-digit ZIP code areas. The first three digits in each code identify the sectional center, while the last two identify the particular post office.

A particular advantage of ZIP code areas is that they are relatively homogeneous with respect to basic socioeconomic data. Whereas residents within an MSA might display great heterogeneity, those within a ZIP code area are likely to be relatively similar in age, income, education, and so forth and to even display similar consumption patterns. At first there were problems in using ZIP code areas as basic control units because there were little detailed data available on them; however, this is changing. While the Census Bureau typically does not publish data by ZIP code area, it does provide data from the census and surveys of population and housing to individual companies on a reimbursable basis. Some firms have purchased the Census Bureau tapes and have in turn gone into the business of preparing reports by ZIP code areas to client specifications. In sum, while firms now have access to some economic and demographic data by ZIP code area, there is not as much data available nor is it as accessible as when counties or MSAs are used as basic control units.

Industrial marketers received a particular benefit with the establishment of ZIP code areas as one of their major sources of market data, Dun's "Market Identifiers" (DMI), contains ZIP code information. DMI is a special name given by Dun & Bradstreet to its marketing information service. DMI is a roster of U.S. and Canadian firms updated daily so that the record of each company is accurate and current. Figure 6–3 is an example of a card record, which is available on each industrial establishment—an establishment is a single physical location such as a manufacturing plant or a nonmanufacturing headquarters address. Records are also available as printed tabulating cards, magnetic tape, or standard punched cards. The ability to locate establishments by geographic area can greatly facilitate estimating market potential in planning territory design.

In addition to the more limited amount and lower accessibility of data, another major disadvantage of using ZIP code areas as basic control units is that the boundaries change over time.

---

[27] "1983 Survey of Buying Power," *Sales and Marketing Management,* July 25, 1983, pp. B9–B52.

Figure 6–2
Map of Metropolitan Statistical
Areas

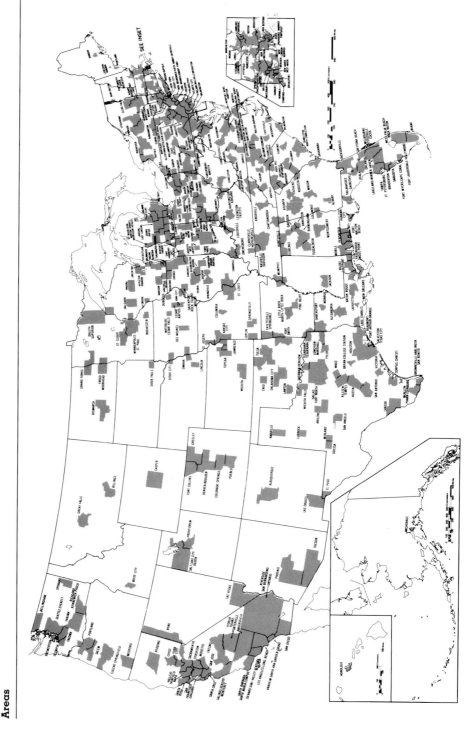

Figure 6–3
DMI sales prospecting record

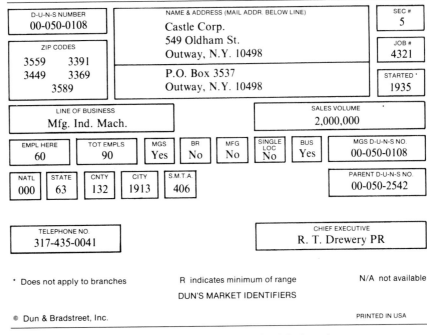

D-U-N-S NUMBER	NAME & ADDRESS (MAIL ADDR. BELOW LINE)	SEC #
00-050-0108	Castle Corp.	5

ZIP CODES: 3559 3391 3449 3369 3589

549 Oldham St.
Outway, N.Y. 10498

JOB #: 4321

P.O. Box 3537
Outway, N.Y. 10498

STARTED *: 1935

LINE OF BUSINESS: Mfg. Ind. Mach.

SALES VOLUME: 2,000,000

EMPL HERE	TOT EMPLS	MGS	BR	MFG	SINGLE LOC	BUS	MGS D-U-N-S NO.
60	90	Yes	No	No	No	Yes	00-050-0108

NATL	STATE	CNTY	CITY	S.M.T.A.	PARENT D-U-N-S NO.
000	63	132	1913	406	00-050-2542

TELEPHONE NO.: 317-435-0041

CHIEF EXECUTIVE: R. T. Drewery PR

* Does not apply to branches   R indicates minimum of range   N/A not available

DUN'S MARKET IDENTIFIERS

© Dun & Bradstreet, Inc.   PRINTED IN USA

Source: Reprinted with permission from Dun's Market Identifiers, © Dun & Bradstreet, Inc.

Estimate Market Potential

Step 2 in territory design involves estimating market potential in each basic control unit. This is done using one of the schemes suggested in Chapter 5. If a relationship can be established between sales of the product in question and some other variable or variables, for example, this relationship can be applied to each basic control unit. Data must be available for each of the variables for the small geographic area, though. Sometimes the potential within each basic control unit is estimated by taking account of the likely demand from each customer and prospect in the control unit. This works much better for industrial goods manufacturers than it does for consumer goods producers. The consumers of industrial goods are typically fewer in number and more easily identified—for example, using Dun's "Market Identifiers." Furthermore, each typically buys much more product than is true with consumer goods. This makes it worthwhile to identify at least the larger ones by name, to estimate the likely demand from each, and to add up these individual estimates to produce an estimate for the territory as a whole.

Form Tentative Territories

Step 3 in territory design involves combining contiguous basic control units into larger geographic aggregates. Units next to each other are combined to prevent salespeople from having to crisscross paths while skipping over geographic areas covered by another representative. The basic emphasis at this stage is to make the tentative territories as equal as possible in market potential. The premise is that each territory should provide an opportunity for the same standard of living for sales representatives. Differences in workload or sales potential (the share of total market potential a company expects to achieve) because of different levels of competitive activity are not taken into account at this stage. It is also presumed that all sales representatives have relatively equal abilities. All these assumptions are relaxed at subsequent stages of the territory planning process. The attempt at this stage is simply to develop a first approximation of the final territory alignment. The total number of territories defined equals the number of territories the firm has previously determined it needs. If the firm has not carried out such a calculation before, it needs to do so now.

Perform Workload Analysis

Once tentative initial boundaries have been established for all sales territories, it is necessary to determine how much work is required to cover each. Ideally, firms like to form sales territories equal in both potential and workload. Although Step 3 should produce territories roughly equal in potential, the territories will probably be decidedly unequal with respect to the amount of work necessary to cover them adequately. In Step 4, the analyst tries to estimate the amount of work involved in covering each.

Typically, the workload analysis is conducted by explicitly considering each customer (most assuredly, the larger ones) in the territory. The analysis is often conducted in two stages. First, the sales potential for each customer and prospect in the territory is estimated. This step is often called an account analysis. The sales potential estimate derived from the account analysis is then used to decide how often each account should be called on and for how long. The total effort required to cover the territory can be determined by considering the number of accounts, the number of calls to be made on each, the duration of each call, and the estimated amount of nonselling and travel time.

Table 6–3 contains an account analysis for a small sample of accounts in a single territory. Note several things in the table. First, the analysis is carried out customer by customer. Although the firm may not want to do this for every customer in the territory, it would for the potentially larger ones. Second, the potentials in the "Potential by Product" columns are market potentials. Thus, they represent the expected sales of each product to the customer for the entire industry for the period in question. While the analysis here is broken out by product, it is sometimes simply computed in aggregate. Third, the "Estimated Share" columns show the firm's competitive positions with each customer. The firm is particularly entrenched with respect to product Y to Pelton Industries, but it has a reasonable share of sales of all three products to all three customers. The multiplication of market potential by estimated market share produces an estimate of the firm's sales potential with each customer. The sum of sales potentials by product is the total sales potential of the account.

Total sales potential is one criterion used to classify accounts into attractiveness categories dictating the frequency and length of sales calls. There are a number of other criteria that have been suggested as well for determining the attractiveness of an individual account to the firm. The key is to identify those factors likely to affect the productivity of the sales call effort. Some of these other factors include competitive pressures for the account, account familiarity in terms of the firm's historic relationship with the account, the prestige of the account, how many products the firm produces that the account buys, and the number and level of buying influences within the account.[28] The specific factors that affect the productivity of an individual sales call are likely to change from firm to firm.

Once the specific factors affecting the productivity of a sales call have been isolated, they can be treated in various ways. One way is to use the ABC Rule of Account Classification discussed earlier and illustrated in Table 6–4. Another way is to employ a variation of the matrix concept of strategic planning, which suggests that accounts like strategic business units or markets can be divided along two dimensions reflecting the overall opportunity they represent and the firm's abilities to capitalize on those opportunities. In the case of accounts, the division should reflect (1) the strategic importance or attractiveness of the account to the firm and (2) the likely difficulties to be encountered in managing the account.[29] The accounts are then sorted into either a four- or nine-cell strategic planning matrix, like that shown in Figure 6–4, and call frequencies are established for each cell. The heaviest call rates in the sample matrix depicted in Figure 6–4 would be on accounts in cells 1, 2 and possibly 3, depending on the firm's abilities to overcome its competitive disadvantages. The lowest planned call rates would be on accounts located in cell 4.

It is not necessary that accounts be divided into classes and call frequencies be set at the same level for all accounts in the class. Rather, the firm might want to determine the workload in each tentative territory on an account-by-account basis. There are several ways of doing this. One scheme requires that the firm

---

[28] A. Parasuraman, "An Approach for Allocating Sales Call Effort," *Industrial Marketing Management* 11 (1982), pp. 75–79; Renato Fiocca, "Account Portfolio Analysis for Strategy Development," *Industrial Marketing Management,* 11 (1982), pp. 53–62. For an empirical assessment of the factors that affect the call frequency of a sample of salespeople representing 34 different firms, see Rosann L. Spiro and William D. Perreault, Jr., "Factors Influencing Sales Call Frequency of Industrial Salespersons," *Journal of Business Research,* January 1978, pp. 1–15.

[29] Fiocca, "Account Portfolio Analysis." La Forge and Cravens argue similarly that it is useful to classify all PCUs (planning and control units, in this case, accounts) according to two criteria: (1) PCU opportunity reflecting the potential available to all firms from the PCU, and (2) sales organization strength or the ability of the sales organization to take advantage of the opportunity. See Raymond La Forge and David W. Cravens, "Steps in Selling Effort Deployment," *Industrial Marketing Management* 11 (1982), pp. 183–194.

Table 6-4
Sample account analysis

Account Name	Potential by Product			Estimated Share			Sales Potential				
	X	Y	Z	X	Y	Z	X	Y	Z	Total	Classification
Helen Crosby Manufacturing...	$200,000	$140,000	$300,000	0.15	0.30	0.10	$ 30,000	$ 42,000	$ 30,000	$102,000	C
Pelton Industries	420,000	310,000	100,000	0.20	0.40	0.10	84,000	124,000	10,000	218,000	B
The Blattner Company	650,000	180,000	480,000	0.20	0.30	0.25	130,000	54,000	120,000	304,000	A

Classification	Number of Accounts
A	20
B	60
C	150

Source: Adapted from Robert F. Vizza and Thomas E. Chambers, *Time and Territorial Management for Salesmen* (New York: The Sales Executive's Club, 1971), p. 12. Used by permission.

Figure 6–4

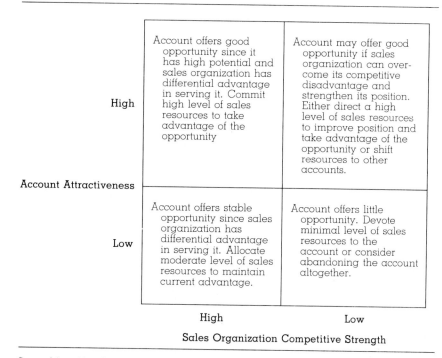

	High	Low
High	Account offers good opportunity since it has high potential and sales organization has differential advantage in serving it. Commit high level of sales resources to take advantage of the opportunity	Account may offer good opportunity if sales organization can overcome its competitive disadvantage and strengthen its position. Either direct a high level of sales resources to improve position and take advantage of the opportunity or shift resources to other accounts.
Low	Account offers stable opportunity since sales organization has differential advantage in serving it. Allocate moderate level of sales resources to maintain current advantage.	Account offers little opportunity. Devote minimal level of sales resources to the account or consider abandoning the account altogether.

Account Attractiveness

Sales Organization Competitive Strength

Source: Adapted from Raymond La Forge and David W. Cravens, "Steps in Selling Effort Deployment," *Industrial Marketing Management* 11 (1982), pp. 183–94; and Renato Fiocca, "Account Portfolio Analysis for Strategy Development," *Industrial Marketing Management* 11 (1982), pp. 53–62.

rate each account on each factor previously deemed as being critical to the success of the sales call effort and then develop a sales effort allocation index for each account.[30] The sales effort allocation index is formed by multiplying each rating score by its factor importance weight, summing over all factors, and then dividing by the sum of the importance points. The resulting sales effort allocation index reflects the relative amount of sales call effort that should be allocated to the account in comparison to other accounts—the larger the index, the greater the number of planned calls on the account.

Still another scheme is to have someone in the sales organization, typically the salesperson or the salesperson in conjunction with his or her sales manager, estimate the likely sales to be realized from each account as a function of the number of calls on the account. The actual sales response function is, of course, the key in determining the optimal number of sales calls to be made on any account and the workload in each tentative territory. A typical sales response function is shown in Figure 6–5. The figure shows that there are first increasing, then diminishing, and finally decreasing returns to the number of sales calls. The

[30] Parasuraman, "An Approach for Allocating."

Figure 6-5
Hypothetical sales response function

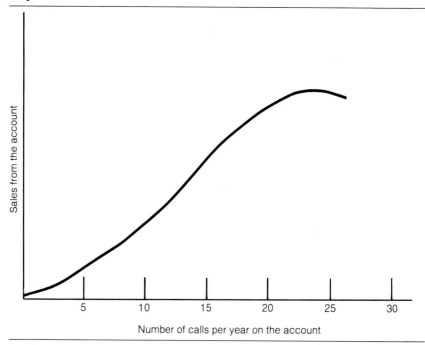

Sales from the account

Number of calls per year on the account

increasing returns are realized at low levels of sales force effort. The account, never having been contacted previously or only on rare occasions, responds positively and places some orders with the saleperson as the number of salesperson calls increases. At first, the rise in sales is swift but then begins to flatten out as the number of sales calls is increased. Decreasing returns set in when the number of calls becomes excessive and the salesperson becomes a nuisance to the account. In the hypothetical example in Figure 6-5, this occurs when the salesperson calls on the account more than twice a month. The costs associated with calling on the account are directly proportional to the number of calls, and the dilemma facing the firm is to balance sales/cost considerations to determine the optimal call level on each account taking into consideration the sales response functions of all the accounts in the territory.

There are interactive computer programs available for making the determination of the optimal number of calls to make on each account. One of the more popular of these is the CALLPLAN program in which the response function for each account is generated from the salesperson's own inputs.[31] The program operates in the following way. The salesperson assigned to the territory is asked the sales that will result from each current customer and prospect if:

[31] Leonard M. Lodish, "CALLPLAN: An Interactive Salesman's Call Planning System," *Management Science* 18 (December 1971), pp. 25–40.

No calls are made.

One half the present calls are made.

The present level of calls is continued.

50 percent more calls are scheduled.

A saturation level of calls are made.

The salesperson is also asked the probabilities that prospects will be converted into customers with different call frequencies. CALLPLAN then fits curves to these data points and prints out the expected sales for all feasible call frequencies and the optimal number of calls and the length of each call to be made on each client and prospect during an average effort period. In one experiment designed to test the CALLPLAN assignment scheme, 20 representatives from United Airlines were matched and then one from each pair was randomly assigned to one of two groups. The 10 control group salespeople were asked to manually estimate their optimal call frequency on each account. The 10 experimental group salespeople were asked their inputs via the CALLPLAN interactive system, and their optimal call levels were determined by the program. Both groups then called on their accounts at these predetermined levels during the course of the experiment. "After six months, the average CALLPLAN salesperson had sales 8.1 percent higher than his matched counterpart."[32] CALLPLAN seems best suited to repetitive selling situations where the amount of time spent with an account is an important factor in the amount of sales generated.

When the account analysis is complete, a workload analysis can be performed for each territory. The procedure parallels that discussed previously for determining the size of the sales force using the workload method. The total amount of face-to-face contact is computed by multiplying the frequency with which each type of account should be called on by the number of such accounts. The products are then summed. This figure is combined with estimates of the nonselling and travel time necessary to cover the territory to determine the total amount of work involved in covering that territory.[33] A similar set of calculations is made for each tentative territory.

Adjust Tentative Territories

Step 5 in territory planning involves adjusting the boundaries of the tentative territories established in Step 3 to compensate for the differences in workload found in Step 4. It is almost axiomatic that differences will be found.

---

[32] William K. Fudge and Leonard M. Lodish, "Evalution of the Effectiveness of a Model Based Salesman's Planning System By Field Experimentation," *Interfaces,* 8 (November 1977), p. 104.

[33] Some writers suggest that the travel time involved in servicing each account should be estimated from the location of the account and its proximity to other accounts. See Robert F. Vizza and Thomas E. Chambers, *Time and Territorial Management for Salesmen* (New York: The Sales Executives Club, 1971), pp. 11–15, for the details as to how such an analysis would be conducted. See also Robert Vizza, "Managing Time and Territories for Maximum Sales Success," *Journal of Business Research* 1 (March 1972), pp. 18–23.

It is possible, for example, that the states of Nevada, Utah, and Arizona together contain the same sales potential as the single state of Washington. Since considerably less travel time would be necessary to cover the Washington territory, the workload in the two territories would be far from equal.[34]

While attempting to balance potentials and workloads across territories, the analyst must constantly keep in mind the fact that the sales potential per account is not necessarily fixed. Rather, it is likely to vary with the number of calls made on the account. While this fact is explicitly considered in computer call allocation models like CALLPLAN,[35] it is not taken into account when, for example, the firm uses the ABC Rule of Account Classification and relies exclusively on historic sales when making account classifications. Clearly there is reciprocal causation between account attractiveness and account effort. Account attractiveness affects how hard the account should be worked. At the same time, the number of calls and length of the calls in turn affect the sales that are likely to be realized from the account. Yet, this reciprocal causation is only implicitly recognized in some of the other schemes used to determine workloads for the previously determined territories. The firm thus needs some mechanism for achieving a balance between potentials and workloads by territory when adjusting the initial territories if it is not using one of the available computer models to design them.

There are several ways to accomplish this balance. One way is to formally estimate the function that relates sales in a territory to the potential and workload in the territory.[36] Another way is through subjective judgment, whereby executives decide on all changes in call frequency to achieve some specific objective. For example, a midwestern wholesaler of farm machinery used this approach: it classified all accounts into three categories A, B, and C, according to potential. It then changed the frequency with which salespeople called on farm equipment dealers.

As a result of management emphasis on building volume with A and B dealers, the customer mix shifted from 1970 to 1973. . . . It is interesting to note that the shift in emphasis resulted in the growth of average sales per territory from $368,000 in 1970 to $640,000 in 1973. The sales growth was substantially greater than the increase in field sales expense. Hence, the field cost ratio was reduced, and the savings went to net profit.[37]

Another subjective scheme is to restructure the tentative territories so that each territory involves relatively equal amounts of work, since the tentative areas already reflect equal amounts of potential. The Celanese Plastics Division, for example, listed each account in each territory and then estimated the number of calls required to serve each account.

---

[34] Gerald Parkinson, "350 Miles for One Call: How to Make It Count," *Industrial Distribution* April 1967, p. 79.

[35] The response function linking sales to the number of calls made on the account is expressly built into most computer models that help determine how much time should be spent on each account. See, for example, Gary M. Armstrong, "The SCHEDULE Model and the Salesman's Effort Allocation," *California Management Review* 18 (Summer 1976), pp. 43–51.

[36] This is the approach that was used by a major national ready-to-wear apparel company. See Lucas, Weinberg, and Clowes, "Sales Response."

[37] William P. Hall, "Improving Sales Force Productivity," *Business Horizons*, August 1975, pp. 32-42.

Using these three factors—number of calls, call hours, and travel hours—the total time to be spent on each account per year was estimated and all the accounts in each territory totaled. Fifteen hundred man-hours per territory were used as a benchmark. Those that came close to this figure were equalized, while those that varied sharply from the norm were revised.

We found in the Chicago district that we had to make substantial geographic reassignments. The men who complained that they were overloaded really were. Conversely, some of those not complaining didn't have enough to do. However, there have been no complaints recently.[38]

Whether an analytical, subjective, or trial-and-error approach is taken, some realignment of the tentative territories should be expected and those involved should allow for this when planning territories.

Assign Salespeople to Territories

After the boundaries of territories are established, the analyst can determine which salesperson should be assigned to which territory. Up to now, it has generally been assumed that there are no differences in abilities among salespersons or in the effectiveness of different salespeople with different accounts or different products.[39] Such differences do arise, however. All salespeople do not have the same ability, nor are they equally effective with the same customers or products. At this stage in the territory planning progress, the analyst should consider such differences and follow the general guide: "Assign each salesperson to the particular territory where his relative contribution to profit is the highest."[40]

Unfortunately, the ideal cannot always be met. It would be too disruptive to an established sales force with established sales territories to change practically all account coverage. If the firm is currently operating without assigned sales territories, then a closer approximation of the ideal realignment might be achieved. The firm with established territories typically must be content to change assignments on a more limited basis.

One way of allowing for differences in general ability among salespeople is by converting each representative's ability to index form. The best salespersons may

---

[38] Statements made by Thomas Brydon, general sales manager. See Brice, "Art of Dividing," p. 93.

[39] Some of the computer call allocation models allow for product and customer mix considerations. They determine the optimal number of sales territories, which salespeople should cover which customers, and which products salespeople should emphasize, in addition to determining how often and for how long each account should be called on. See, for example, Sidney W. Hess and Stuart A. Samuels, "Experience with a Sales Districting Model: Criteria and Implementation," *Management Science* 18 (December 1971), pp. 41–54; Andres A. Zoltners, "Integer Programming Models for Sales Territory Alignment to Maximize Profit," *Journal of Marketing Research* 13 (November 1976), pp. 426–30; Leonard M. Lodish, "Assigning Salesmen to Accounts to Maximize Profit," *Journal of Marketing Research* 13 (November 1976), pp. 440–44; A. Parasuraman and Ralph L. Day, "A Management Oriented Model for Allocating Sales Effort," *Journal of Marketing Research* 14 (February 1977), pp. 22–33; and Charles A. Beswick and David W. Cravens, "A Multistage Model for Salesforce Management," *Journal of Marketing Research* 14 (May 1977), pp. 135–44. For a review of these models and others as to their basic differences, see David W. Cravens, "Sales Force Decision Models: A Comparative Assessment," in *Sales Management: New Developments from Behavioral Decision Model Research*, ed. Richard Bagozzi (Cambridge, Mass.: Marketing Science Institute, 1979), pp. 310–24.

[40] James G. Huak, "Research in Personal Selling," in *Science in Marketing*, ed. G. Schwartz (New York: John Wiley & Sons, 1965), pp. 241–42.

be rated 1.0, for example, and all other salespeople rated relative to them. One such relative scheme is to consider that a salesperson with a rating of 0.8 could secure 80 percent of the business in the territory that a representative with a rating of 1.0 could obtain. One can then systematically vary the assignments of salespeople to territories to determine which assignment maximizes the company's return.[41]

Summary

This chapter reviewed the important sales management planning decisions involving the number of sales territories needed and the process that can be used to decide upon the design of each. A sales territory represents a group of present and potential customers assigned to a salesperson, branch, dealer, or distributor for a given time. Although territories are often defined by their geographic boundaries, the key distinguishing component is customers. Good territory design can positively influence sales force morale and the firm's ability to serve the market and to evaluate the selling effort, whereas poorly designed territories can have the opposite effect.

One key question the sales manager must address in sales territory design is how many territories there should be. The three primary methods for answering this question are the breakdown, workload, and incremental methods. The breakdown method relies on an estimate of what an average salesperson could be expected to sell; the number of salespeople required is then determined by dividing forecasted sales by this average. The workload method rests on the premise that all sales personnel should shoulder an equal amount of work. Management estimates the total amount of work required to serve the market, taking into account the number of customers, how often each should be called on, and for how long. This estimate is then divided by the amount of work an individual salesperson should be able to handle to determine the total number of salespeople required. The basic premise underlying the incremental method of determining sales force size is that sales representatives should be added so long as the incremental profit produced by their addition exceeds the incremental cost. While conceptually correct, this is the most difficult method to implement.

Once the number of territories is determined, the sales manager can design the individual territories. The general process he or she might be expected to follow is: (1) select the basic control unit, (2) estimate market potential in each control unit, (3) combine control units into tentative territories, (4) perform a workload analysis for each territory, (5) adjust tentative territories to allow for sales potential and coverage difficulty differences, and (6) assign salespeople to territories.

---

[41] For an example of this approach, see Still, Cundiff, and Govoni, *Sales Management*, pp. 632–35.

Discussion Questions

1. Customer density varies—one Metropolitan Statistical Area can contain the same number of customers as might be found in entire states. When designing territories, what should a sales manager do to create territories that have equal work loads? How can the CALLPLAN method help?

2. One sales manager said, "The whole process of motivation and morale is made out to be too complicated. It's not. All I have to do is increase compensation and my salespeople's motivation, morale, *and* performance improve." Do you agree or disagree? Why?

3. What is the relationship between the measurement and control of marketing activities and geographically defined sales territories?

4. The breakdown method for determining the size of the sales force suffers from many shortcomings; for example, it does not account for turnover and profitability. How would you modify the equation $n = s \div p$ to account for these shortcomings?

5. A common problem experienced by most sales organizations is that too much time is spent on accounts that are small and not too profitable. Yet small accounts may develop into large and very profitable accounts. What techniques would be useful for identifying small accounts that have the potential of becoming large accounts?

6. What are the advantages and disadvantages of the workload approach to determining sales force size? How would you change the technique to overcome the disadvantages? For example, the workload method does not consider the time spent calling on prospective customers. Could this limitation be incorporated into the method?

7. Although the incremental approach for determining sales force size is conceptually appealing, it is the least-used approach. Why is this so?

8. Many sales managers dislike changing either territories or compensation plans unless it is absolutely necessary. Why is this so? What evidence does a sales manager need to determine if a territory change is needed?

9. Some companies have developed computer models, such as CALLPLAN, for determining the call patterns to be used by their sales personnel. Determining call patterns (routing plans) is very much like deciding how you would visit the 10 largest cities in your state while traveling the least amount of miles or time. In what situations would computer-determined call patterns be appropriate? Have you ever had a job where routing plans were applicable?

10. Referring to the last question, identify the 10 largest cities in your state and develop a routing plan that visits all cities while traveling the least number of miles. Do time of day for traveling or customer preferences affect your routing plan?

11. How have technological developments such as the introduction of micro computers and telemarketing affected such sales management issues as territory development and sales force size determination?

12. You have been hired as a sales representative by Interconics, Inc., and assigned to the Ohio territory. The customers are located in the following cities: Columbus, Newark, Springfield, Marion, Findlay, Toledo, Mansfield, Cleveland, Akron, Youngstown, and Warren. Prepare a routing plan that will minimize the number of driving miles. One possible approach is described in: John P. Norback and Robert F. Love, "Geometric Approaches to Solving the Traveling Salesman Problem," *Management Science* 23 (July 1977), pp. 1208–33.

13. The ABS Company presently uses the services of 25 manufacturers' agents. The sales manager feels that circumstances are right for ABS to have its own company sales force. Since 25 manufacturers' agents have met ABS's sales goals, the sales manager feels that ABS needs to hire 25 sales reps. Do you agree?

14. The John Deere Company is a multiproduct manufacturer of farm implements, machinery, snowmobiles, and home lawn and garden machinery. What problems are the Deere Company likely to experience in establishing sales territories? Should it establish the same territories for each product line?

15. The Home Furniture Company designed its sales territories so that each has approximately the same population. This approach, according to the sales manager, results in equal potential for each territory and is therefore very equitable. Comment.

Chapter 7

Sales Quotas

The last major element in sales management planning is establishing goals for each sales representative. The goals assigned to salespeople are called *quotas*.

Although one writer has called quotas the "traditional enemy of salesmen,"[1] quotas are a valuable planning and controlling device for the field selling effort. Some would argue that they are indispensable. For instance, John C. Emery, Jr., executive vice president of Emery Air Freight Corporation, said "I don't see how you can have any semblance of long-range planning without quotas. We have to know how much profit will be available at the end of [the planning period]. The only way to make any reasonable estimate is by carefully using short- and long-term sales quotas."[2]

As defined previously, a sales quota is a sales goal assigned to a marketing unit for use in managing sales efforts. The marketing unit in question might be an individual sales representative, a sales territory, a branch office, a region, a dealer or distributor, or a district, to name a few. Each salesperson in each sales territory might be assigned a sales volume goal for the next year, for example. This quota, while obviously related to each, is not the sales forecast or the estimate of potential for the territory. While it stems from potential, it is typically less than potential for example. Sales potential reflects what the company could sell in the territory under ideal conditions. Yet conditions are rarely ideal. The territories may not have been designed optimally, or it may not be possible for a firm to assign the best person for a particular territory to that territory because the individual is needed elsewhere. Differences in salesperson characteristics such as age, experience, energy, initiative, and physical condition should and do make a difference in the quotas assigned to the territory. Nor is the sales quota equal to the sales forecast for the territory. The sales forecast is the best estimate of what the company can sell with a particular planned level of marketing effort. It is an aggregate estimate that may or may not even be broken down by product line, customer, or territory. The ideal forecast is one that is perfectly accurate because that facilitates planning. Thus while a firm would not want to reward a salesperson for exceeding her forecast, they would want to reward her for exceeding her quota. Quotas are management devices and not planning tools. They are typically used to motivate salespeople and the prime concern is their effect on performance, and not their accuracy or precision except insofar as their accuracy or reasonableness affects motivation levels. As a practical matter, sales territory volume quotas are typically set to a level that is less than the sales potential in the territory and equal to or slightly above the sales forecast for the territory, although they also can be set less than the sales forecast if conditions warrant.

Sales quotas apply to specific periods and may be expressed in dollars or physical units. Thus, management can specify quarterly, annual, and longer-term quotas for each of the company's field representatives in both dollars and physical units. It might even specify these goals for individual products and customers. The product quotas can be varied systematically to reflect the profitability of dif-

---

[1] Leslie Rich, "The Controversy in Sales Quotas," *Duns Review* May 1966, p. 47.
[2] Ibid.

ferent items in the line, and customer quotas can be varied to reflect the relative desirability of serving particular accounts.

The full set of quota assignments is called the quota plan.[3] The full specification of the quota plan requires decisions about the types of quotas that will be used, the relative importance of each, and the target levels for each salesperson or other marketing unit.

Purposes of Quotas

Quotas facilitate the planning and control of the field selling effort in a number of ways. One useful way of viewing the benefits is by assessing their contribution in (1) providing incentives for sales representatives, (2) evaluating salespeople's performance, and (3) controlling salespeople's efforts.

Provide Incentives for Salespeople

Quotas serve as incentives for sales representatives in several ways. At a most elementary level, they are an objective to be secured, a challenge to be met. Many people are motivated by such challenges. For example, the definite objective of selling $200,000 worth of product A this year is more motivation to most salespeople than the indefinite charge to go out and do better. It seems one can always do better, but what standard is a reasonable goal? How hard should one push product A in relation to other products in the line? Sales quotas provide an answer to these questions. As one source aptly put it, "Without a standard of measurement, a football team cannot tell whether it made a first down, golfers cannot tell whether they shot par, and sales reps cannot be certain their performance is satisfactory."[4] One study that investigated the incentive created by quotas found that most sales personnel are "quota achievers" rather than "dollar maximizers." The salesperson's motivation tended to decline when he or she had an easily attainable goal.[5]

Quotas also influence salespeople's incentive through sales contests. The contest is a key element in the incentive programs of many firms. A key notion underlying such contests is that those who perform "best" will receive the contest prizes. Unfortunately, not all salespeople have the same opportunity to win unless some allowance is made for differences in sales abilities and in territorial potential and workload. These differences exist in spite of the company's best efforts to the

---

[3] Thomas R. Wotruba, *Sales Management: Planning Accomplishment, and Evaluation* (New York: Holt, Rinehart & Winston, 1971), p. 195.

[4] William J. Stanton and Richard H. Buskirk, *Management of the Sales Force*, 6th ed. (Homewood, Ill.: Richard D. Irwin, 1983), p. 475.

[5] Leon Winer, "The Effect of Product Sales Quotas on Sales Force Productivity," *Journal of Marketing Research* 10 (May 1973), pp. 180–83.

contrary. Thus, the company needs to design the sales contest so that all sales representatives have a chance to win. Sales quotas provide a common denominator by which territory and personal differences can be neutralized, so that all sales representatives have a relatively equal chance.

Quotas can also create incentive via their key role in the compensation systems of most firms. More will be said about compensation in later chapters, but it should be noted here that many firms use a commission or bonus plan, sometimes in conjunction with their base salary plan. In such schemes, salespeople are paid in direct proportion to what they sell (commission plan) or receive some percentage increment for sales in excess of target sales (bonus plan). Typically such plans are tied directly to the sales quotas established for the sales representative or branch. Even when salespeople are compensated with salary only, quotas can provide incentive when salary raises are tied to the extent of quota attainment in the previous year.

Evaluate Sales Performance

Quotas provide a quantitative standard against which the performance of individual sales representatives or other marketing units can be evaluated. They allow management to pinpoint the marketing units that are performing above average and those that are experiencing difficulty. They can be used relatively easily and lend themselves nicely to management by exception. Salespeople who miss their quotas by some appreciable amount, either above or below, can be singled out for more intensive investigation. Perhaps salespersons who perform far above quota are doing something especially right from which all salespeople might profit. Alternatively, perhaps others are having difficulty selling one type of product or to one type of customer.[6] Again there may be something the company can do to assist them. Maybe they are facing some intense competition from a regional competitor that is not being experienced elsewhere. Perhaps it is necessary for the firm to assume a more aggressive price posture in this region or to increase its advertising effort to neutralize the competitor's impact. The point is that quotas localize spots that need more intensive investigation, which would be hard to do without these quantitative standards.

Control Sales Efforts

Quotas can be used not only to evaluate salespeople's performance but also to evaluate and control their efforts. As part of their job, salespeople are expected to engage in specific activities. Although the activities and the time devoted to them vary by company and industry, some typical ones are calling on new accounts,

---

[6] We will have more to say about how sales quotas pinpoint potential marketing strategy deficiencies in the chapter on sales analysis.

selling a certain percentage of high-margin items, collecting past-due accounts, and planning and developing sales presentations. Activity quotas allow the company to monitor whether sales representatives are engaging in these activities to the extent desired. If they are not, corrective action can be taken early rather than waiting for these small activity problems to become large sales and profit problems.

Problems with Quotas

There are many advantages to using quotas, but there are also some problems. For one thing, they sometimes prove to be a difficult comparative yardstick. Many sales are the results of several people. One salesperson may call on corporate headquarters and another on the plant where the equipment will be installed. Both may play important but different roles in securing the order. In such cases, it is hard to decide what share of the total sale should be allocated to each salesperson; thus, it is hard to decide how well the salesperson did in relation to quota. It is equally troublesome when a salesperson's influence is relatively minor in obtaining a sale. Finally, quotas can be costly to establish, particularly if they are to be done well.

Characteristics of a Good Quota Plan

For a quota plan to produce its potential benefits, it is necessary that the quotas be (1) attainable, (2) easy to understand, and (3) complete. There is a great deal of controversy regarding the level at which quotas should be set. Some argue that quotas should be set high so that they can be achieved only with extraordinary effort. Although most salespeople may not reach them, the argument is that they are thereby spurred to greater effort than they would have expended in the absence of such a "carrot." Although perhaps intuitively appealing, high quotas can cause problems. They cause irritation among salespeople for one thing.[7] They can also cause salespeople and others in the organization to cheat in one way or another in order to make their quotas, sometimes with disastrous consequences for the firm as the example in Figure 7–1 indicates.

The use of very high "carrot" quotas seem to be the exception rather than the rule. In a Conference Board study, only 4 of 82 companies surveyed used them.[8] Rather, the predominant posture seems to be that quotas should be realistic and

---

[7] *Incentive Plans for Salesmen*, Studies in Personnel Policy, No. 217 (New York: The National Industrial Conference Board, 1970), pp. 27–29.

[8] Ibid.

Figure 7–1
Example of what can happen with
very high "carrot" quotas

Itel Corp.'s 1979 junket to Acapulco feted its hottest marketing men with fireworks and bugle fanfares, champagne, and showers of rose petals. "It was like *Fantasy Island*," recalls a former Itel man, who says he was so moved by the splendor and tequila that he tipped Mexican bartenders for a company disco party $600.

And that was but a flourish in an extravaganza that wined and dined some 1,300 employees and spouses at a month-long show that cost the company some $3 million.

For this was Itel in January 1979, the champagne of West Coast companies, buoyant, elegantly packaged and giddy with its success. Investors were giddy too. The stock of the computer and transportation-leasing company had soared to $39 from $18 in a six-month period of 1978, and the company saw 1979 as its first billion-dollar year in volume.

But 1979 proved to be the year Itel's bubble burst. Today, the company is a sober, stripped-down shell. Its shareholder equity has been dissipated by losses totaling $226 million in the nine months ending September 30 (the lastest figures available). Its employee rolls have been slashed by layoffs and divestitures from last year's high of 7,000 to an estimated 1,000 this year. Its shares led the list of New York Stock Exchange glamour losers last year, plunging 79 percent to $5.375. In addition, there are almost a dozen security-holder lawsuits and an investigation by the Securities and Exchange Commission. Vulnerable and debt-ridden, Itel is carefully negotiating its survival with the company's creditors.

The reasons for Itel's swift and stunning collapse surely will be debated from boardrooms to barrooms for years to come . . . probably most important was the supremacy of marketing in the power centers at Itel. In confrontations between the freewheeling marketing people and the more conservative legal and financial staffs, marketing almost always won.

"The salesman at Itel was exalted," a former employee says "A good one could make $100,000 a year, a great one $150,000. So long as he was productive, he was a demigod." Itel's fabled perks—the bonuses, cruises, and junkets (called "marketing-incentive trips")—were all designed to fuel the marketing machine, to inspire salesmen to meet and exceed *ambitious growth quotas* [emphasis added].

Given these high incentives, the pressure to produce and the laxity of controls, some sources contend that sleight of hand was inevitable and that it helped undo the company in the end. "If you couldn't meet your sales quota, you might as well submit your resignation," a former Itel attorney close to Itel's lease business says. "So at some point, somebody starts showing a profit that doesn't exist. The guy at the top accepts it. Where the duplicity comes in, I don't know." There isn't any indication that top management knew of such activity prior to Itel's collapse.

The attorney says that salespeople in Itel's complex third-party lease business began to enter false or exaggerated profits. He recalls, "I had salesmen tell me, 'I don't care how you close this deal, just close it. By the time it's discovered the money's not there, I'll be gone. I've got my commission.'"

Source: Adapted from Marilyn Chase, "How a Red-Hot Firm in Computer Business Overheated and Burned," *The Wall Street Journal*, February 22, 1980, p. 1.

attainable with "normal" effort. For example, E. P. Sheekon, as general sales manager of the York Division of Borg-Warner Corporation, suggested that a sales-person's quota should be an "attainable goal which he can achieve with justifiable pride."[9] This was also the position embraced by firms responding to the

---

[9] *Incentives for Salesmen*, Experiences in Marketing Management, No. 14 (New York: National Industrial Conference Board, 1967), p. 69.

Conference Board survey; 67 of 82, or 82 percent of the companies, used realistic quotas.

Quotas should be not only realistic but also easy to understand. Quota plans that are complex and difficult to comprehend may cause suspicion and mistrust among sales representatives and thereby discourage rather than motivate them. It helps when salespeople can be shown exactly how their quotas were derived. They are much more likely to accept quotas that are related to market potential when they can see the explicit assumptions that were made in translating the potential estimate into sales goals.

Quotas should also be easy to understand definitionally. If a salesperson's quota is 50 calls on new accounts within a quarter, it is important for the representative to be told exactly what customers qualify as new accounts. Does a call on a customer who has not placed an order within the past year qualify as a new-account call? How about a customer who has not placed an order within the last three years but before that was a steady customer? What about a call this quarter on an account that placed its first small order the previous quarter? Does the call qualify if an account makes only a partial payment? To avoid future conflicts, it is important that both the sales manager and all sales personnel understand the quota and the conditions under which various activities qualify as contributing to quota.

A third desirable feature of a quota plan is that it is complete. This means that it effectively covers the many criteria on which sales representatives are to be judged. Thus, if all sales representatives are supposed to engage in new account development, it is important to specify how much. Otherwise that activity will likely be neglected while the salesperson pursues volume and profit goals. Similarly, volume and profit goals should be adjusted to allow for the time that the representative has to spend identifying and soliciting new accounts. Carlisle Tire and Rubber, for example, develops quotas for each salesperson using both bottom-up and top-down sales forecasts as a basis. The bottom-up sales forecast requires each district manager, "to make a detailed, account-by-account analysis, which is the basis for establishing account sales objectives with specific plans and strategies for their achievement."[10] The top-down forecast is prepared at the same time by the product management group, and any differences in the two forecasts are reconciled by the national sales manager who then negotiates a final quota with each district manager in line with the company total. Salespeople receive 80 percent of their bonuses for achieving their sales volume quotas. "The remaining 20 percent can be earned through the completion of various nonsales quotas. These nonsales quotas are not standard but tailored to each district manager to encourage specific growth."[11]

---

[10] Benjamin G. Ammons, "Get Greater Commitment by Letting Salespeople Help Set the Quotas," *Sales and Marketing Management*, April 7, 1980, p. 90.

[11] Ibid., p. 93.

The Quota-Setting Process

Quota setting actually involves the three-step process shown in Figure 7–2.[12] First, the sales manager or someone else must decide on the types of quotas the firm will use. Next the person must determine the relative importance of each type of quota. Finally, the sales manager needs to determine the specific quota levels that will be used.

Figure 7–2
Quota-setting process

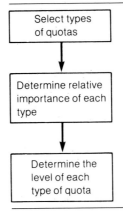

Source: Adapted from Thomas R. Wotruba, *Sales Management: Planning, Accomplishment, and Evaluation* (New York: Holt, Rinehart & Winston, 1971), p. 201.

Select Types of Quotas

There are three basic types of quotas: (1) those emphasizing sales or some aspect of sales volume, (2) those that focus on the activities in which sales representatives are supposed to engage, and (3) those that examine financial criteria such as gross margin or contribution to overhead.

Sales Volume. Quotas that emphasize total dollar sales or some other aspect of sales volume are undoubtedly the most common. Their popularity is understandable. They can be related directly to market potential and thereby be made more credible. They are easily understood by those who must achieve them. They are consistent with what most salespeople envision their jobs to be—that is, to sell. Furthermore, they are consistent with the old adage, "Someone must sell something before the other functions of business can be brought to bear." The

---

[12] Figure 7–2 and much of the surrounding discussion is adapted from Wotruba, *Sales Management*, pp. 201–23, which provides an excellent discussion of the subject.

production, finance, and personnel functions depend on a certain amount of the product being sold.

Sales volume quotas can be expressed in dollars, physical units, or points. Dollars have the convenient advantage of providing a common measure for all products. This helps to reduce communication problems when each sales representative handles a wide variety of products. In such instances, the establishment of physical volume quotas for each product for each sales representative can be very complex. Dollar volume quotas permit a more direct analysis of salespeople's expenses in relation to quota. The ratio of expenses to sales for each salesperson can be calculated directly, and salespeople can be compared in terms of these expense ratios. Dollar volume quotas are also advantageous when sales representatives have some discretion over price. Sales managers can see immediately whether they are using the discretion wisely or whether they are cutting prices so drastically that it cuts into the profits of a sale. To accomplish the same kinds of analyses with physical volume quotas, it would be necessary to estimate the total dollars of targeted sales by assuming some average price per sale.

Physical volume quotas express a salesperson's goals in some physical unit of measurement such as number of specific items, weight in pounds or tons, or some volume measure such as gallons. Physical volume quotas are especially attractive when sales representatives handle only a few products. Thus, a sales quota for a salesperson who works for a chemical manufacturer might be expressed as so many gallons of toluene, whereas that for a cement manufacturer might be expressed as so many pounds of cement, and that for a steel sales representative as so many tons of carbon steel and so many tons of stainless. Physical volume quotas are also attractive when prices fluctuate widely because of cyclical and competitive factors. In a price-intensive, competitive market, it may not be unusual for a normal $100 drum of chemicals to sell for $75. The impact on a salesperson's quota is obvious. Whereas before the representative might have had to sell 500 barrels to reach the quota of $50,000, the salesperson would now have to sell 667 drums. The change, however, could not be controlled personally by the representative. Dollar quotas in such situations can have a demoralizing effect on salespeople. Physical volume quotas are also attractive when unit prices are high. A dollar quota of $2 million, for example, might be psychologically overwhelming to a salesperson, whereas a quota of 20 units might not seem nearly so imposing even though each unit sells for $100,000.

Point quotas are another variation of sales volume quotas. A certain number of points is given for each dollar or unit sales of particular products. For example, each $100 of sales of product X might be worth three points; of product Y, two points, and product Z, one point; alternatively, each ton of steel tubing sold might be worth five points, while each ton of bar stock might be worth only two points. The total sales quota for the salesperson is expressed as the total number of points he or she is expected to achieve. The point system is typically used when a firm wants to give selective emphasis to certain products in the line. Those that are more profitable, for example, might be assigned more points.

Porter-Cable Machine Company, for instance, once used dollar-volume quotas exclusively. On analysis, however, management found that sales personnel often attained most of their quotas through selling only one or two easy-to-sell products. Management initiated a program whereby Porter-Cable products were put into eight different categories, according to their relative profitability. Then, individual point-volume quotas were set for each product category, and bonus points were awarded for sales over quota in each category. Sales personnel were required to meet all the point-volume quotas before becoming eligible for any bonus points. Furthermore, in appraising performance, management regarded a 150 percent total point-volume attainment with four points as less good than a 120 percent point-volume attainment with five bonus points. This quota system led to the selling of a considerably more profitable mixture of products.[13]

There are other uses of point quotas to promote selective emphases. New products might receive more points than old ones to encourage sales representatives to push them. A given dollar of sales to new accounts might be worth more points than the same level of sales to more established accounts to stimulate salespeople to call on them. Point quota systems allow sales managers to design quota systems that promote certain desired goals; yet, point quotas also can be easily understood by salespeople.

Activity.   Activity quotas attempt to recognize the investment nature of a salesperson's efforts. For example, the letter to a prospect, the product demonstration, and the arrangement of a display may not produce an immediate sale. On the other hand, they may have considerable influence on a future sale. If the whole emphasis in the quota system is on sales, however, salespeople may be inclined to neglect these activities and emphasize those with more immediate payout in the form of a sale. As one writer put it, "A volume quota becomes an obsession with salesmen, resulting in a break-down in control of other activities."[14]

An advantage of activity quotas is that they are directly related to factors that sales representatives can actually control. Whereas salespeople can perhaps influence sales volume, for example, they cannot control it; economic conditions and competitive behavior may thwart the salesperson's best efforts. Yet salespeople can control the number of new accounts they call on, the number of service calls they make, the call reports they complete, and so on. Thus, it is reasonable to judge their performance with respect to these activities. Furthermore, if these activities are important to the future success of the company, it is reasonable to judge salespeople on whether their performance meets or exceeds these criteria.

Some common types of activity quotas are listed in Table 7–1 . A salesperson's performance can easily be compared with respect to each activity in the list. However, much effort is required to measure each salesperson's efforts. The number of proposals a salesperson develops or the number of demonstrations he

---

[13] Richard R. Still, Edward W. Cundiff, and Norman A. P. Govoni, *Sales Management: Decisions, Strategies, and Cases,* 4th ed. (Englewood Cliffs, N.J.: Prentice-Hall, 1981), p. 598. Reprinted by permission.

[14] Gilbert J. Black, *Motivation of Salesmen through Compensation and Sales Quota* (New York: Sales and Marketing Executives International, 1968), p. 7.

Table 7–1
Common types of activity quotas

1. Number of calls on new accounts.
2. Number of letters to potential customers.
3. Number of proposals submitted.
4. Number of field demonstrations arranged.
5. Number of service calls made.
6. Number of equipment installations supervised.
7. Number of displays arranged.
8. Number of dealer sales meetings held.
9. Number of meetings and conventions attended.
10. Number of past-due accounts collected.

or she arranges is not recorded in the normal accounting cycle. This information has to be developed by requiring salespeople to complete activity reports. This increases salespeople's paper work and represents time away from their primary activity of face-to-face selling. Furthermore, since sales representatives complete the activity reports themselves, there is great opportunity for sloppiness and misrepresentation unless this function is closely supervised. The activity report reflects only the amounts of effort expended on various activities; that the salesperson called on 20 new accounts in the period says nothing about the quality of these calls. They may have represented nothing more than a salesperson spending five ineffective, or perhaps even detrimental, minutes with a new customer.

All these problems are reduced when a sales volume measure is used for quotas. The figures that are necessary to compare performance with the established standard arise in the normal accounting cycle. The amount of sales produced, although not perfect, is a somewhat direct measure of the quality of the effort expended on the client. A sales volume quota decreases the amount of paperwork necessary and increases the amount of time sales representatives have available for selling.

Financial. Financial quotas are used to make salespeople conscious of the cost and profit implications of what they sell. Being human, sales representatives left to their own devices often take the easy way out. They emphasize products that are easiest to sell or concentrate on customers with whom they feel most comfortable. Unfortunately, these products, while easy to sell, may be costly to produce and have a lower-than-average return. Similarly, the customers with whom the representative feels comfortable may not purchase much and may be less profitable than other potential accounts because of the services they require. Financial quotas attempt to make salespeople aware of these conditions so that they direct their efforts to more profitable products and customers.

Financial quotas are often stated in terms of direct selling expenses, gross margin, or net profit. They are most applicable when the firm's market penetration approaches saturation levels. In such instances, it is hard to increase sales or market share, and an emphasis on selling efficiency and cost control becomes a logical mechanism for increasing profit.[15]

A key to improving profits is to control the field selling expenses incurred in generating a given level of sales. Expense quotas are typically stated as a certain percentage of sales, although they are sometimes expressed in absolute dollar amounts. Although expense quotas force sales representatives to recognize the costs of what they are doing and to be aware of their responsibilities for controlling expenses, they can also have dysfunctional effects. This is particularly so when they cause salespeople to do other than what they should because they are worried about expenses. Instead of calling four times in a quarter, for example, the salesman may call only twice because he feels the chances for purchase are low. Thus, he loses the opportunity to secure a big equipment purchase. Field sales expenses, on the other hand, contribute substantially to the difference in profitability of firms in the same industry, and their control is important.[16]

Gross margin quotas are useful when there are significant differences in gross margins by product, since they can be set so that salespeople concentrate on items with higher returns. Unfortunately, gross margin quotas are somewhat difficult to administer. Some firms simply do not wish to disclose production cost information to sales representatives.[17] Even among those that do, it is hard for salespeople to tell how they are doing with respect to their gross margin quotas at any given time and thus the quotas do not produce the desired motivation effects. In one study among medical supply wholesalers, for example, it was found that firms using gross margin commissions were less efficient than firms using other compensation programs.[18] Margin information is typically not provided in the normal accounting cycle by a unit of analysis so small as a salesperson. At the same time, the same objective can be accomplished for all practical purposes with a well-designed point quota system. Products that bear higher gross margins can simply carry more points. Point quota systems are much easier for salespeople to understand and thereby make it easier for them to monitor their progress.

Some managers feel that net profit quotas are the ultimate because they emphasize what the selling effort should be—profitable sales volume and not sales volume for its own sake. It is true that net profit quotas are tied directly to a major goal of top management. It is also true that net profit quotas can be superior to gross margin quotas in instances where products with high gross margins require extensive effort and thereby produce higher field selling expenses and lower net profit.

Net profit quotas also have some disadvantages. First, they are harder than the

---

[15] Wotruba, *Sales Management*, p. 205.

[16] William P. Hall, "Improving Sales Force Productivity," *Business Horizons*, August 1975, pp. 32–42.

[17] One of the authors personally worked for a firm whose policy was not to disclose any price or other sales information to the production people or cost information to field sales personnel, but rather to restrict the possession of both types of information to a few selected people in the company. Top management felt that this arrangement provided some strong advantages when the company was forced to compete on price to secure a major installation.

[18] Douglas Dalyrymple, P. Ronald Stephenson, and William Cron, "Gross Margin Sales Compensation Plans," *Industrial Marketing Management* 10 (1981), pp. 219–24.

other types for the salespeople to understand, thereby making it difficult for them to monitor their progress. The net profit they produce depends on the product mix they sell, the margins on these products, and the expenses they incur. At any given time, it is tremendously difficult for sales representatives to determine just how they are doing. This can prove frustrating to them and thereby stifle motivation. Second, net profit quota schemes are difficult to administer. Again, the information required to operate them—net profit produced by a given salesperson in a given time period—is simply not produced in the normal accounting cycle in most firms. It can be acquired, to be sure, but it is typically very expensive to do so. Finally, the profit a salesperson produces is affected by many factors beyond his or her control—competitive reaction, economic conditions, and the firm's willingness to negotiate on price, for example. Some would argue that it is unreasonable to hold the individual salesperson responsible for all these external influences.

Determine Relative Importance of Each Type

As the preceding discussion indicates, each main type of quota system has advantages and disadvantages. In some situations, the firm may feel that the advantages of one scheme completely outweigh the disadvantages and therefore may use it without even considering the other options. Although quota schemes with a single basis can work well in relatively stable situations, they can prove disastrous in dynamic environments.[19] For example, a sales-volume quota may work well for an established product with an established market. That same scheme, however, can lead to an overconcentration of calls on existing accounts and the neglect of new accounts with new products for which new uses are being discovered. In such instances, the sales manager may want to use a combination of criteria that produces the best balance of goals for each salesperson. Furthermore, the conditions from territory to territory and from customer to customer may be different, and the sales manager might wish to reflect such differences in the quota plan. A key question that must be addressed is how the various quotas should be combined to produce a single criterion by which performance can be evaluated.

The problem is illustrated in Table 7–2. The example assumes that there are three criteria, one of each of the three main types, on which each salesperson should be evaluated. Note that each sales representative performed best with respect to a single criterion. Thus, if the emphasis were placed on sales volume quota attainment, Curtain would be considered the top performing salesperson. She is, in fact, the only one who made her sales volume quota. On the other hand, if it were placed on the activity measure, number of new account calls, Michael

---

[19] Allan Easton, "A Forward Step in Performance Evaluation," *Journal of Marketing* 30 (July 1966), pp. 26–32.

Table 7–2
Performance evaluation with multiple quotas

Salesperson/ Quota Basis	Quota	Actual	Percent Quota	Weight	Percent Quota × Weight
Leslie Curtain:					
Sales volume $150,000		$150,000	100.0	3	300.0
New account calls ... 22		20	91.0	1	91.0
Gross margin........$ 50,000		$ 40,000	80.0	2	160.0
Average			90.3		91.8
David Michael:					
Sales volume $200,000		$180,000	90.0	3	270.0
New account calls ... 20		24	120.0	1	120.0
Gross margin........$ 66,000		$ 70,000	106.1	2	212.2
Average			105.4		100.4
Carol Suchomel:					
Sales volume $170,000		$160,000	94.0	3	282.0
New account calls ... 18		21	117.0	1	117.0
Gross margin........$ 56,000		$ 60,000	107.1	2	214.2
Average			106.0		102.2

would be rated best. Suchomel would be rated best if the emphasis were on the financial measure, gross margin. The example illustrates Finagle's rule of management, which holds "that if you look long enough, you can find a ratio which makes any performer look good—or bad."[20] Rather than simply "looking hard enough" and becoming confused as to who truly performed best, management needs some objective mechanism for determining which representatives satisfied their quota responsibilities.

One way is simply to average the ratios reflecting percent quota achievement. Suchomel performed best using the simple average; her performance was 106.0 percent of quota, while Michael's was 105.4 percent and Curtain's was 90.3 percent.

One problem with the simple average is that it weights all three performance criteria equally when they might not be equally important to the firm. While the firm may want to place formal emphasis on the number of new account calls a salesperson makes by including it in the quota system, for example, it may not want to place as much emphasis on this activity as it does on actual sales volume produced by the salesperson. In situations where the firm may want to give unequal emphasis to the different quota bases, a linear combination can be used to provide a useful summary measure of each representative's overall performance. A linear combination is a weighted average of the results on the individual dimensions, where the weights reflect the importance of each component to management. In the example in Table 7–2, a weight of 3 was assigned to sales volume

---

[20] Richard I. Levin "Who's on First?" *Sales Management: The Marketing Magazine*, July 17, 1964, p. 56.

(SV), a weight of 2 to gross margin (CM), and a weight of 1 to new account calls (C). Thus, the weighted average for overall performance (OP) is:

$$OP = \frac{3SV + 1C + 2GM}{6}$$

The sum is divided by 6 to reduce the weighted combination to a basis of 100. Note that using the weighted criterion, Suchomel performed best and Curtain worst. Michael was almost right on target, with an aggregate index of 100.4 versus a 100.0 if he had simply met quota.

Although the weights 3, 2, and 1 were used in the example, other weights could be used as well. The point is that the weights should reflect the importance of performance on each component to the firm. The weights can be determined in a number of ways. They might simply be set by the sales manager using his or her own best judgment. Alternatively, they might reflect the collective opinion of a group of top managers, or they might be based on some objective analysis of the importance of each component to the firm's long-run goals.[21] One attractive feature of the linear combination as a measure of overall performance versus quota is that it allows differential weights to reflect unique territory or customer differences. Another advantage is that it can be easily explained to salespeople.

Determine Level of Each Type

The final stage in determining the quota plan assigned to each marketing unit is to decide the level at which each type of quota is to be set. In establishing these levels, the sales manager must balance a number of factors, including the potential available in the territory, the impact of the quota level on the salesperson's motivation, the long-term objectives of the company, and the impact on short-term profitability. When discussing quota levels, it is useful to separate sales volume, activity, and financial quotas.

Sales Volume Quotas. As mentioned, sales volume quotas are the most commonly used. Unfortunately, some firms do not use them very intelligently. Some, for example, simply set these quotas on the basis of past sales. The charge "beat last year's sales" is given to each marketing unit. Sometimes the standard is the average of sales in the territory over some past time period—five years, for example. Sometimes the admonition is expressed more concretely. Thus, if the company's sales forecast suggests a 7 percent sales increase this year, each marketing unit is assigned a quota 7 percent higher than last year's or the average of the past five years' sales.

The most attractive feature of this quota-setting scheme is that it is easy to administer. One does not have to engage in an extensive analysis to determine what the quotas should be. This makes it inexpensive to use. Furthermore, salespeople readily understand it.

---

[21] For discussions of how one might go about generating the necessary weights, see Easton, "A Forward Step"; and C. West Churchman, Russell L. Ackoff, and E. Leonard Arnoff, *Introduction to Operations Research* (New York: John Wiley & Sons, 1957), pp. 139–42.

Unfortunately, such schemes forego many potential advantages of using sales volume quotas. For one thing, such quotas ignore current conditions in the territory. A territory may be rapidly growing and the influx of many new potential customers could justify a much larger increase in quota than the 7 percent established by the overall company's sales forecast. Alternatively, the territory might be so intensely competitive or depressed that any increase in the assigned sales quota is not justified.

A quota based solely on past sales ignores territory potentials and therefore provides a poor yardstick for how individual sales representatives are doing. Two salespersons, for example, might each have generated $300,000 in sales last year. It clearly makes a difference in what one can expect from each of them this year if the market potential in one territory is $500,000 while that in the other is $1 million. The firm may be foregoing some tremendous market opportunities simply because it is unaware of them.

A quota based solely on past years' sales can also have demoralizing effects on salespeople and cause them to engage in undesirable behaviors. For example, a salesperson who has realized quota for one year may be tempted to delay placing orders secured at the end of the year until the new accounting cycle begins. This accomplishes two things: it makes his quota for the next year lower and it gives him a start on satisfying that quota.

Although sales quotas should not be based solely on sales in prior years, there is no question that historic sales should be taken into account when quotas are established. Historic sales provide some indication of how competitive a firm is within a territory. By comparing historic sales with potential sales, one can localize trouble spots and determine the problem and what action should be taken.

Territory potentials provide a useful start for establishing quotas for territory sales volume. However, the firm should go beyond strict adherence to a formula relating quota to potential and should attempt to reflect the special situations within each territory. Determining how to go about this is the key difficulty. On one hand, the sales representative who serves the territory should be involved in setting the territory quota, because he or she should have the most intimate knowledge of the conditions in the territory. On the other hand, since the representative will be substantially affected by the quota established, he or she may not be impartial with respect to the process. More specifically, one might expect sales representatives to understate potential to generate lower, easier-to-reach quotas.

In one study conducted in the San Francisco and Los Angeles areas to investigate sales-force bias when establishing quotas, it was found that the extent of overestimation versus underestimation was "about equal, and the degree of error in each direction is 10 percent or less in more than three quarters of the responding firms."[22]

Some firms have resolved the problem of potential bias when salespeople are used to help set their own quotas by tying their compensation into the process. For example, IBM of Brazil established a system that takes into account territory

---

[22] Thomas R. Wotruba and Michael L. Thurlow, "Sales Force Participation in Quota Setting and Sales Forecasting," *Journal of Marketing* 40 (April 1976), p. 16.

potential differences and company objectives for the territory. It also encourages good forecasts by rewarding sales representatives according to how close their actual results are to the company's objectives. The system rewards good planning because it simultaneously incorporates the company objectives, O, a salesman's forecast, F, and the results the salesman actually achieves, A, in a compensation grid. The system works in the following way (see Table 7–3).

After receiving his objective, O, a salesman must turn in his forecast; F divided by O determines the column in which the salesman's bonus percentage will fall. For instance, the 1.0 column represents a forecast equal to the quota, the 0.5 column means the forecast is half the objective, and the 1.5 column indicates a forecast 50 percent larger than the objective. The letter "A" stands for actual sales results. Thus A divided by 0 and multiplied by 100 is the percentage of the objective that was actually achieved by the salesman; 100 percent means full achievement of the company's objective, not of the salesman's forecast.

Now let us see how it works. John sells photographic equipment. His quota is 500 cameras. Let us assume that John fully agrees to his quota and turns in a 500-units forecast. (On the Grid, F/O equals 1.0). If John sells 500 cameras, he makes 100 percent of his objective and is entitled to 120 percent of his bonus. In other words, he gets a 20 percent premium for his good planning capability. How much that represents in dollars depends on John's personal value, namely, his experience, time with the company, and merit.

If John sells 750 cameras, which is 150 percent of his objective, he is entitled to 150 percent of his bonus; the more he sells the more he earns. But now John realizes that if his forecast has been 750 instead of 500 units (1.5 on the grid), then he would have received 180 percent of his bonus instead of 150 percent. Bad planning on his part has deprived him of a good chunk of money. If John had sold 250 units, half of his objective, he would have earned just 30 percent of his incentive. Here again, John sees that it would have been better to have forecasted 250 instead of 500 for his earnings would have been 60 percent.

In other words, the best earnings lie in the diagonal that goes down from left to right in the grid. For a given result, A, the more precise John's forecast is, the higher his earnings. But John will always earn most if his forecast is perfect.

After being introduced to the grid, John goes back to study his territory. This time he does not want to return a faulty forecast—his earnings are at stake. He may still complain that the objective set up by his manager is too high—there is no solution to that—but for the first time he can enhance his earnings through a good work plan. If he comes in with a low forecast, he may damage his earnings in exchange for safety. On the other hand, a high forecast may plunge him into trouble if his sales are too low. John understands that he must be precise. This is exactly what his manager is waiting for.

From that moment on, John becomes committed to the number he forecasts. The grid tells him that his sales should be equal to or higher than the forecast in order for his earnings to increase. Soon, John sees that, because of the new interactive approach, the headquarters staff begins to really understand the market and sets sales objectives that approach his own forecast. Total accuracy will never happen, but for practical purposes the three main objectives of the system—sales volume, payment for performance, and good field information for planning—will be brought about.[23]

---

[23] Jacob Gonik, "Tie Salesmen's Bonuses to Their Forecasts," *Harvard Business Review,* May-June 1978, pp. 119–20. The St. Regis Paper Company has also used a scheme in which the salesman's compensation was tied to potential quota differences. See *Managing By- and With-Objectives,* Studies in Personnel Policy, No. 212 (New York: The National Industrial Conference Board, 1968), pp. 43–45.

Table 7–3
Basis of OFA system

A/O × 100 (actual results divided by objective then multiplied by 100)	F/O (forecast divided by objectives)										
	0	0.5	1.0	1.5	2.0	2.5	3.0	3.5	4.0	4.5	5.0
0	—	—	—	—	—	—	—	—	—	—	—
50	30	60	30	—	—	—	—	—	—	—	—
100	60	90	120	90	60	30	—	—	—	—	—
150	90	120	150	180	150	120	90	60	30	—	—
200	120	150	180	210	240	210	180	150	120	90	60
250	150	180	210	240	270	300	270	240	210	180	150
300	180	210	240	270	300	330	360	330	300	270	240
350	210	240	270	300	330	360	390	420	390	360	330
400	240	270	300	330	360	390	420	450	480	450	420
450	270	300	330	360	390	420	450	480	510	540	510
500	300	330	360	390	420	450	480	510	540	570	600

Calculation of grid numbers:

If F equal to A, then OFA $= 120 \times FO$
If F smaller than A, then OFA $= 60 \times (AF)/O$
If F bigger than A, then OFA $= 60 \times (3AF)/O$

Activity Quotas. The levels for activity quotas are most likely to be set according to the conditions in the territory. They require a detailed analysis of the work required to cover the territory effectively. Activity quotas are affected by the size of the territory, as well as by the physical number of accounts and prospects the salesperson is expected to call on. The size of the representative's customers can also make a difference, as can their purchasing patterns. These factors affect the number of times the salesperson needs to call on them in the period, the number of service calls or calls to demonstrate the use of the firm's equipment he or she must make, and so on.

The inputs for establishing the activity quotas can come from at least three sources: (1) discussions between the sales representative serving the territory and the sales manager, (2) the salesperson's reports, and (3) marketing research. The sales manager and territory salesperson can use past experience as a basis for determining what activities are necessary to cover the territory effectively. Such a discussion typically revolves around key accounts and what needs to be done to serve them better. In some cases, it may mean more frequent calls, whereas in others, it may mean that the number of calls may be reduced. The specification for a potential account might be simply to bid on three equipment installations during the next year. These assessments are then combined with estimates of other activities—for example, traveling—to determine the total activity level in the territory, from which a judgment can be made as to whether that level is reasonable. If not, some modification is warranted. The iterative process ceases when reasonable activity levels have been determined. They must be reasonable in the sense of being consistent with the objectives of the firm for the territory and with the time available from the salesperson.

Sometimes activity quotas can be established from salespeople's reports. Suppose, for example, that one main duty of field representatives is erecting displays in retail outlets. An analysis of historic call reports can often indicate how long it takes to set up a display on average and the variation in times as a function of the size of the display. Suppose further that different sizes of accounts typically receive different size displays. It is then relatively easy to determine the number of displays and the time required to erect them by analyzing the number of accounts of each class size in the salesperson's territory.

The firm might also rely on marketing research to determine activity level quotas. The firm might systematically vary the number of calls per account to determine the optimal number to be made on each account in any time period, as was done by the Lamp Division of General Electric.[24] Alternatively, it might do a study of past bid behavior to establish some rules of thumb as to when the firm should bid on some equipment request. [25]

Financial Quotas. The levels of financial quotas are typically set to reflect the financial goals of the firm. For example, a firm may want a particular net

[24] R. Gwinner, "Base Theories in the Formulation of Sales Strategy," *MSU Business Topics*, Autumn 1968, p. 37–44.

[25] Marvin A. Jolson, "Should the Sales Presentation Be 'Fresh' or 'Canned'?" *Business Horizons*, October 1973, pp. 80–86.

profit or gross margin on all sales in a territory. Suppose the potential for a representative is basically concentrated in two products—one with a gross margin of 30 percent and one with a gross margin of 40 percent. The sales manager could shift the relative attention given to one versus the other by assigning a gross margin goal of 37 percent. The salesperson would then have to sell a greater proportion of the products with 40 percent margin to achieve that goal than if the goal were 34 percent.

A field-selling expense quota may be based on last year's ratio of field selling expenses to sales. The sales manager might analyze these ratios across territories and on this basis establish a target for the territory given the potential in the territory. Although there is always some temptation to use the historic average across territories as the target, the unique conditions of the territory should be considered. Perhaps the field selling expense target should be less than the average because of the geographic concentration of customers. Perhaps it should be higher than average because of the intense competition in the territory. Perhaps the accounts require more entertaining at first-class restaurants and social events if the firm is going to have any chance of remaining competitive.

Summary

The last major element in sales management planning is the establishment of sales quotas. A sales quota is the sales goal assigned to a marketing unit in a specified period. Sales quotas may be expressed in aggregate or broken down by customers and products. The full set of quota assignments is called the quota plan.

Sales quotas are used to motivate salespeople, evaluate their performance, and control their efforts. For a quota plan to produce its potential benefits, the quotas must be attainable with normal effort, easy to understand, and complete.

Setting quotas involves a three-step process. First, the sales manager must decide on the types of quotas the firm will use. This choice entails determining whether the firm will use quotas that emphasize: (1) sales or some aspect of sales volume, (2) the activities in which salespeople are supposed to engage, or (3) financial criteria such as gross margin or contribution to overhead. These are known as sales volume, activity, and financial quotas, respectively. Typically, firms use some combination of these quotas rather than relying exclusively on one type because each has advantages and disadvantages. The second step in the process involves specifying the relative importance of each type of quota. Then most firms seek some mechanism for combining the individual quotas into a single summary measure that serves as the standard for each representative's performance. Quite often a linear combination or weighted average is used in which the weights reflect the importance of each component to management.

The final step in determining the quotas assigned to each marketing unit is to determine the level at which each type of quota is to be set. In establishing these levels, the sales manager must balance a number of factors, including the potential available in the territory, the impact of the quota level on the salesperson's motivation, the long-term objectives of the company, and the impact on short-term profitability.

Discussion Questions

1. During the high inflationary years in the late 1970s and early 80s, some firms assumed that, if inflation rose by 12 percent, sales quotas should at least increase by the same amount. Do you agree or disagree?

2. Mike Blake, the sales representative for the Milwaukee district office of the Monarch Machine Tool Corp., has failed to meet his sales quota for the first half of 1985. The regional sales manager has sent a warning letter to Blake, telling him that, unless he achieves his quota by year-end 1985, he will be terminated. Is this action justified?

3. If territories are established with equal potential, it stands to reason that the quotas for the sales territories should be equal. Do you agree?

4. Some companies start to pay bonuses when sales reps reach 75 percent of quota rather than when 100 percent of quota is reached. Is this evidence that quota setting is an art and not a science?

5. Sales representatives for the Feminique Cosmetic Company are paid a 40 percent commission on sales volume. To date, management has not been able to persuade the sales force about the value of putting up store displays and encouraging retailers to utilize Feminique's cooperative advertising. What do you suggest?

6. Quotas at the Acme Feed Corporation are set equal to the average of sales for the last three years plus 5 percent. Sales reps who exceed quota are paid bonuses according to the following schedule:

Percent of Quota	Bonus Percent
106–110	5%
111–115	7
116–120	10
121–125	12
Over 125	15

   What are the advantages and disadvantages of this approach? What is likely to happen? How would you change the method?

7. The sales manager of the Clearline Paper Company has tried unsuccessfully to develop a quota system for the sales force. To simplify the procedure, sales volume for the last five years will be averaged for each representative, and a flat percentage increase—10 percent, for example—will be added to this average to determine next year's quota. The process will be repeated for future years by changing the five-year base. What is your opinion of this approach?

8. According to one sales manager, "The sales force should not participate in quota-setting activities. The typical sales representative is either overly optimistic or pessimistic and, as a result, is ill-equipped to set quotas." Comment.

9. Sales representatives and their district sales manager from the Minneapolis office of the Standard Computer Corporation recently persuaded the national sales manager to adjust the unit volume quota for their district. Word of this has spread to other districts, causing unrest. Personnel from these districts are requesting similar adjustments. How would you respond if you were the national sales manager?

10. One approach for handling sales representatives who fail to make their quotas is to add to next year's quota the amount by which they fell short. The opposite approach deducts this amount from next year's quota. Which approach is the most reasonable?

11. According to the vice-president of finance at the Mason Corporation, all sales reps ought to have profit quotas. She feels that volume quotas fail to direct the sales force to sell the more profitable products or pay attention to expenses. She advocates the following method:

Sales
Less Cost of Goods Sold
Gross Margin
Less:
Salary
Commission
Bonus
Travel Expenses
Contribution to Profit Quota

Cases for Part 1

Case 1–1
Gildersleeve Furniture Enterprises[*]

In June 1984, Gildersleeve Furniture Enterprises merged with Bon-Quer Industries, a manufacturer of upholstered furniture for living and family rooms. The merger was not planned in a conventional sense. Bruce Ahlers' father-in-law died suddenly in February 1984, leaving his daughter with a controlling interest in the firm. The merger proceeded smoothly since the two firms were located on adjacent properties. The general consensus was that the two firms would maintain as much autonomy as was economically justified. Moreover, the upholstery line filled a gap in the Gildersleeve product mix, even though it would retain its own identity and brand names.

The only real issue that continued to plague Ahlers was merging the selling effort. Gildersleeve had its own sales force, but Bon-Quer Industries relied on sales agents to represent it. The question was straightforward in his opinion: Do we give the upholstery line to our sales force or do we continue to use the sales agents? Don Lott, Gildersleeve's sales vice president, said the line should be given to his sales group; Tom Frost, national sales manager of Bon-Quer Industries, said the upholstery line should remain with sales agents.

Bon-Quer Industries

Bon-Quer Industries is a small manufacturer of upholstered furniture for use in living and family rooms. The firm is more than 85 years old. The company has some of the finest fabrics and frame construction in the industry, according to trade sources. Net sales in 1983 were $3 million. Total industry sales of 1,500

---

[*]This case was prepared by Professor Roger Kerin, Southern Methodist University, as a basis for class discussion and is not designed to illustrate appropriate or inappropriate handling of administrative situations. It is being used with permission.

upholstered furniture manufacturers in 1983 were $2.5 billion. Company sales had increased 15 percent annually over the last five years, and company executives believed this growth rate would continue for the foreseeable future.

Bon-Quer Industries employed 15 sales agents to represent its products. These sales agents also represented several manufacturers of noncompeting furniture and home furnishings. Often a sales agent found it necessary to deal with several buyers in a store to represent all lines carried. On a typical sales call, a sales agent would first visit buyers. New lines would be discussed in addition to any promotions offered by manufacturers. New orders were sought where and when it was appropriate. A sales agent would then visit a retailer's selling floor to check displays, inspect furniture, and inform salespeople about furniture. Bon-Quer Industries paid an agent commission of 5 percent of net company sales for these services. Frost thought sales agents spent 10 to 15 percent of their in-store sales time on Bon-Quer products.

The company did not attempt to influence the type of retailers that agents contacted. Yet it was implicit in the agency agreement that agents would not sell to discount houses. All agents had established relationships with their retail accounts and worked closely with them. Sales records indicated that agents were calling on furniture and department stores. An estimated 1,000 retail accounts were called on in 1983.

Gildersleeve Furniture Enterprises

Gildersleeve Furniture Enterprises is a manufacturer of medium- to high-priced living and dining room wood furniture. The firm was formed in 1902. Net sales in 1983 were $50 million. Total estimated industry sales of wood furniture in 1983 were $9.4 billion at manufacturers' prices.

The company employed 10 full-time sales representatives who called on 1,000 retail accounts in 1983. These individuals performed the same function as sales agents but were paid a salary plus a small commission. In 1983, the average Gildersleeve sales representative received an annual salary of $40,000 and a ½ percent commission on net company sales. Total sales administrator costs were $212,500.

The Gildersleeve sales force was highly regarded in the industry. It was known particularly for its knowledge of wood furniture and willingness to work with buyers and retail sales personnel. Nevertheless, Ahlers knew that all retail accounts did not carry the complete Gildersleeve furniture line. He had, therefore, instructed Don Lott to "push the group a little harder." At present, sales representatives were making 10 sales calls per week, with the average sales call lasting three hours. The remaining time was accounted for by administrative activities and travel. Ahlers recommended that the call frequency be increased to seven calls per account per year, which he thought was the industry norm.

Merging the Sales Effort

In separate meetings with Lott and Frost, Ahlers was able to piece together a variety of data and perspectives on the question. These meetings also made it clear that Lott and Frost differed dramatically in their views.

Lott had no doubts about assigning the line to the Gildersleeve sales force. Among the reasons he gave for this approach were the following. First, Gildersleeve had developed one of the most well-respected, professional sales groups in the industry. Sales representatives could easily learn the fabric jargon, and they already knew personally many of the buyers responsible for upholstered furniture. Second, selling the Bon-Quer line would require only about 15 percent of the present sales call time. Thus, the new line would not be a major burden, he thought. Third, more control over sales efforts was possible. He noted that Bruce Ahlers' father-in-law developed the sales group 25 years earlier because of the commitment it engendered and the service "only our own people are able and willing to give." Moreover, these people have the Gildersleeve "look" and presentation style, which is instilled in every person. Fourth, he said it would not look right if both Gildersleeve and Bon-Quer representatives and agents called on the same stores and buyers. He noted that the firms overlapped on all their accounts. He said: "We'd be paying a commission on sales to these accounts when we would have gotten it anyway. The difference in commission percentages would not be good for morale."

Frost advocated keeping sales agents for the Bon-Quer line. His arguments were as follows. First, all sales agents had established contacts, were highly regarded by store buyers, and most had represented the line in a professional manner for many years. He too had a good working relationship with all 15 agents. Second, sales agents required little, if any, costs beyond commissions. Frost noted: "Agents get paid when we get paid." Third, sales agents were committed to the Bon-Quer line: "The agents earn a part of their living representing us. They have to service retail accounts to get the repeat business." Fourth, sales agents were calling on buyers who were not contacted by Gildersleeve sales representatives. He noted: "If we let Gildersleeve people handle the line, we might lose these accounts, have to hire more sales personnel, or take away 25 percent of the present selling time given to Gildersleeve product lines."

As Ahlers reflected on the meetings, he felt that a broader perspective was necessary beyond the views expressed by Lott and Frost. One issue was profitability. Existing Gildersleeve furniture lines typically had gross margins that were 5 percent higher than Bon-Quer upholstered lines. Another factor was the "us and they" references apparent in the meetings with Lott and Frost. Would merging the sales efforts overcome this, or would it cause more problems? Finally, the idea of increasing the sales force to incorporate the Bon-Quer line did not set well with him. Hiring a new salesperson would require restructuring sales territories, a potential loss of commission to existing people, and "a big headache."

Case 1–2
Sidex Corporation: The
Dynasty Proposal*

Carrington, president of Sidex Corporation, was reviewing the proposals submitted by several staff members. In a recent memo, Carrington had requested each staff member to come up with a proposal that would contain a recommendation as to how Sidex should market their line of home computers consisting of the smart-ALEC Jr. and the smart-ALEC II. With one exception, the proposals were not very complete. The exception contained a rather detailed proposal suggested by Sidex's vice-president in charge of marketing.

Sidex's line of computers, described in Exhibit 1, have been marketed in Europe for the last two years under a different name. Sales fell off dramatically due to import restrictions and other problems, and Carrington had high hopes that their newly named line of personal computers could be introduced into the U. S. market. So far, there has been very little interest from retailers expressing a desire to carry the smart-ALEC line.

Publicity about personal computers has been very high. Despite this, personal computers in the home are rare: approximately 5 percent of the nation's 84 million households have them. This situation, along with the favorable prospects for future growth, is responsible for attracting many manufacturers of both hardware and software into the market. Carrington wanted Sidex to become heavily involved in the personal home computer market. Prior to developing the smart-ALEC line, Sidex had served primarily as a supplier of components to other manufacturers of personal computers. The product line was marketed in Europe under the brand name Digitex before its withdrawal.

To help develop a strategy to enter the U.S. market, Carrington hired a consultant. The consultant's first task was to review the volumes of literature which Carrington had been collecting for several months. The purpose of this review was to help the consultant and Carrington to be fully aware of developments occurring in the fast growing personal computer market. Next, the consultant advised Carrington to get Sidex's staff involved in the process so that they would be part of the planning process. As a result, Carrington asked the staff to suggest how Sidex should enter the U.S. market.

Members of Carrington's staff had different ideas about how Sidex should enter the fiercely competitive personal computer market. In fact, one staff member, Colby, vice-president of finance, felt that Sidex should ignore the personal

*The assistance of Pamela Grothman, MBA–Marketing, University of Wisconsin, Madison, in the preparation of this case is greatly appreciated.

Exhibit 1
Components of the smart-ALEC line
of personal computers

THE smart-ALEC JR.—THE PERFECT HOME COMPUTER FOR BEGINNERS

Functional Specifications

Memory: 16K-120K ROM
        -4K   RAM
        Expandable to 64K

Language: Microsoft BASIC
        Includes full screen editor

Video: 2 modes-text: 32 characters x 16 lines—9 colors
        Graphics: 128 x 64 dots (pixels)—8 colors

Colors: Black, green, yellow, blue, red, buff, magenta, cyan, orange
Sound: User note and frequency controlled

Keyboard: Full size, moving rubber keys
        45 automatic repeat keys with "beep" sound for key entry
        Single key commands for most often used programming words
        16 pre-defined graphic keys

Cassette Interface: 600 baud—includes cable for connection to any standard cassette
        recorder

Video Connect: RF output to home TV (adapter included)
        Direct connect to monitor built in
        Video cable included

Manufacturer's Suggested Retail Price: $129.95

THE smart-ALEC II—THE FAMILY COMPUTER

Functional Specifications

The system includes:
        The smart-ALEC II computer, 64K
        Video display, green standard
        smart-STAND with plug strip
        DUAL 5¼" disc drives with CP/M operating system handbook
        JRT PASCAL with manual
        Math Tutor
        Modem Link I
        Checkbook Balancer
        Amortization Schedule
        Mortgage Analysis

Manufacturer's Suggested Retail Price: $2,995

computer market completely since the market already contained several casualties. Colby pointed out that companies much larger than Sidex had failed in the personal computer market. One staff member, Dexter, the service manager, believed that the only way Sidex could become a force in the market would be to persuade existing computer stores such as ComputerLand to carry the smart-

ALEC. Dexter also pointed out that such a move would require a very extensive advertising campaign by Sidex.

Jennings, Sidex's production manager, also favored retail distribution but felt that the best chances would be through large discount chains such as K-Mart and ShopKo. Jennings conceded that extensive advertising would be an absolute necessity. Retail distribution via department store chains such as Macy's or Sears Roebuck but using a private brand was suggested by Jennings as a way to get around the need for heavy advertising expenditures.

Stevens, Sidex's marketing research specialist, advocated direct mail as the best approach. Stevens indicated that several mail order catalogs, The Sharper Image, for instance, were carrying rather expensive merchandise and would be compatible with the smart-ALEC line.

Carrington, personally opposed to the private brand idea, was not committed to any specific approach. He had wondered about the feasibility of establishing their own retail franchise operation, similar to Tandy's Radio Shack, but on a much smaller scale since Sidex did not manufacture a broad product line like that carried in the Radio Shack outlets.

Fallon, director of marketing, opposed any type of retail distribution and reminded Carrington that, despite the quality of the smart-ALEC line, Sidex had failed to generate any interest from retailers in carrying the line. Fallon knew that other personal computer manufacturers are struggling to obtain shelf space and that some have lost space. And, as Fallon pointed out, these other manufacturers had been advertising extensively, unlike Sidex which was a virtual unknown in the personal computer market. It was Fallon who had gone to considerable lengths to investigate how Sidex should enter the market with the smart-ALEC line.

Fallon proposed that Sidex should enter the U.S. market by selling the line of personal computers directly to the consumers. Fallon argued that many consumers would need personal attention and service when buying a home computer, and that direct selling methods would be very appropriate. Since nobody else used direct methods, Sidex would be in a unique position. Fallon suggested that there must be a sizable number of consumers who were skittish about going to a computer outlet for fear that they would make a wrong decision: people were afraid of computers and "handholding" would be a necessary part of the strategy. This handholding could be best obtained by using direct marketing methods. When asked if direct marketing meant door-to-door selling, Fallon said yes, but added that the proposal would be more along the party plan approach successfully used by Tupperware for many years. In fact, Fallon proposed calling the method the "seminar plan."

Fallon discussed the idea with several associates and one person mentioned the idea to Larry Hagerty, president of Dynasty Corporation, a Dallas-based direct selling organization specializing in the sales of telecommunications equipment to the home market. Fallon contacted Hagerty to learn more about Dynasty's program and to see if there might be a fit between Sidex and Dynasty.

Industry Overview

The consultant retained by Carrington had been asked to present a brief summary of the personal computer industry in the United States to help Carrington to better understand the nature of the challenge before Sidex. The consultant's report follows.

The personal computer industry represents a classic industry profile. Product technology prevails in the early years of rapid growth, but as the technology matures, those manufacturers with superior marketing strategy and tactics take the lead. As a result, the number of computer manufacturers lessens, leaving a few large suppliers. The predicted shakeout for 1985 happened earlier than expected. With little to no opportunity to make it in the mainstream of the personal computer market, the majority of small manufacturers must find market niches that the major suppliers do not pursue in order to survive.

Personal computers are aimed at two distinct markets—home and office. The 1983 sales of the major players in the home computer market, in which Sidex operates, are illustrated in Exhibit 2. As shown, Commodore has taken the lead

Exhibit 2
1983 home computer sales
(estimated share of $2 billion retail
market)

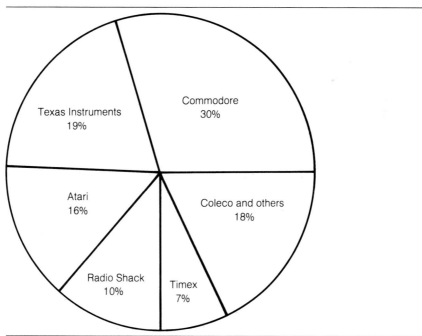

Source: Future Computing Inc.

with 30 percent. A brief discussion of the competition is found in Appendix A.

Home computers have sold well to those consumers who are quick to buy the latest thing, for example the early adopters and innovators. However, because of frequent price cuts and continuous improvement, the consumer is never sure if now is the time to buy. In addition, buyers are hesitant to buy a model, even if superior, from a small producer. Consumers worry about the producer's staying power and question if service and updating will be available in the future. Furthermore, standardization has had a big effect on the home market. Consumers want a variety of popular software programs which are often written for only the top brands.

In the home computer market, the question is whether the consumer will want any computer at all. Underpriced and oversold, home computers have disappointed purchasers who have discovered how hard it was to make them do anything besides play games. Many machines have ended up beside abandoned board games such as Monopoly and Parchesi. Of the four major producers of inexpensive home computers, only Commodore was making money in 1983. One problem confronting the industry is that a basic system does not do much: To build a capable system costs more than most consumers want to pay.

A continuing challenge will be to persuade customers that by paying more they get more. The biggest challenge will be telling people **why** they need a computer in their homes. Presently, the average consumer does not know what to do with a home computer.

Advertising will play an ever-increasing role for survival according to one expert. Advertisers search for the "hot button" or sales pitch that will work with consumers. One example of this is the advertising tactic which dwells on parents' fears that their children will be left behind in life if they do not have a computer. This same theme was used successfully by encyclopedia sales reps, a tactic criticized by consumer advocates. Coleco's "We made obsolescence obsolete" illustrates one attempt to create a "hot button." Yearly advertising budgets for the major competitors run as high as $20 to $25 million for Coleco and $45 million for Commodore.

The Dynasty Program

After meeting with Fallon, Hagerty prepared a proposal for representing Sidex's smart-ALEC line of home computers. In addition, Hagerty provided more information about Dynasty.

Dynasty Corporation, a Dallas-based company, was established in 1980 by Hagerty to sell telecommunications equipment. Presently, Dynasty covers 23 states with the bulk of their sales coming from Texas, Arkansas, and Louisiana. Dynasty successfully uses a direct-to-consumer approach to market various telephone models ranging from standard telephones to novelty telephones. The future looks bright since there are 130 million telephones in operation, but only 5 percent are personally owned by users. With the deregulation of AT&T, the changeover to ownership will not be immediate but longterm. Those who move—one in five families move each year—will find that owning their telephones will be more economical.

Fallon is favorably impressed with Hagerty's enthusiasm. Hagerty has responded to Fallon's request by developing a direct selling marketing plan. Hagerty wants to change the name of his company to Dynasty Computer Corporation, provided that Sidex accepts his proposal. He envisions Dynasty becoming the "Tupperware of the computer industry" because its sales program would utilize the same technique. Word-of-mouth advertising works well for Tupperware, Avon, Amway, and Shaklee, and it should work for Dynasty. Hagerty feels that people are influenced to buy computers primarily by word-of-mouth. Home demonstration is important for many products and the smart-ALEC line would be a natural. He has expressed some concern about Fallon's "seminar plan" but is willing to evaluate the idea. Since handholding is a must, Hagerty wonders if a one-on-one approach might be more effective than a seminar plan. Fallon suggests that the seminar plan might be appropriate at first as a technique to measure degree of interest of potential buyers and then use a one-on-one approach to complete the sale.

Fallon conveyed to Hagerty the concern expressed by others about the image of the direct selling industry. Hagerty indicated that Dynasty is equally concerned about past and present abuses and that he personally works very closely with the Direct Selling Association in their attempts to correct some of the problems. Hagerty showed Fallon the following statement which appears on many of the brochures passed out to consumers:

Dynasty is a member of the Direct Selling Association (DSA). The DSA is a national trade association comprised of the leading firms which manufacture and distribute goods and services marketed by independent sales people using the party plan or person-to-person methods. DSA seeks to serve the public interest and promote the direct selling method of marketing.

Consumer advocacy is in the interest of legitimate business. The public and the direct selling industry benefit from DSA's support of local, state and national consumer organizations. DSA provides such support by lobbying for consumer protection, legislation and regulations. The industry believes the four million independent salespeople, in conducting their business, should be held accountable to the highest level of ethic within the business community because they are guests in people's homes.

Hagerty anticipated that this statement would not satisfy everybody's concern and provided Fallon with a summary of a report on the direct selling industry (Appendix B).

Hagerty also provided Fallon with a detailed sales plan which he had prepared on the assumption that Dynasty would be given the exclusive right to sell the smart-ALEC line of personal computers along with Dynasty's line of telecommunications equipment (Appendix C). Before leaving Fallon with the proposal and other related material he explained to Fallon how Dynasty sales reps operate. All

Dynasty Computer Consultants will be self-employed, as is common in direct selling. They are not employees of Dynasty, but are independent contractors. Consequently, they are free to select their own means, methods and manners of operation. In other words, Dynasty has no right of control over its dealers and dealers have no power or authority to incur any debt, obligation, or liability or to make any representation or contract on behalf of the company. Hagerty pointed out that Dynasty incurs little to no risk when adding to its sales force. As a matter of fact, new salespeople are likely to buy a system for their own use (although this is not a requirement) as well as selling them to relatives and friends.

With this, Hagerty left Fallon and asked when he might expect a decision from Sidex. Fallon indicated that the Dynasty proposal would have to be reviewed by Carrington and others before a decision could be reached. Fallon stated that the Dynasty proposal looked very promising but that it would be difficult to persuade certain people on its merits.

Appendix A: Competitive Analysis

Commodore

The Commodore 64 has been called the hottest product in the home computer market. In February of 1983, Commodore began selling the 64 to mass merchandisers; K mart and Sears are two of its major retailers and distributors. Not surprisingly, Commodore is the industry's low cost producer. One reason for this is that their disk drives are produced in the Far East, enabling Commodore to save approximately $15 million per year. Because of this saving and cost tactics, Commodore was able to drop the basic computer's introduction price from $595 (September 1982) to $193 (Summer 1983). Needless to say, the demand sky-rocketed. At the end of 1983, it had captured 40 percent of the market share.

Commodore believes that its targeted market (i.e., young America), who may have little disposable income, want to "build a system" rather than to buy the whole system in a single transaction. Furthermore, it plans and uses well-timed selling propositions. For example, during the video game rage in the autumn of 1982, Commodore's inexpensive Vic 20 full computer was positioned against mere video-game consoles—at the same price. Subsequently, the superior Commodore 64 was introduced to meet the consumer's growing demands for more elaborate machines. When the 64's limitations were realized, Commodore introduced a $200 disk drive attachment.

As successful as Commodore has been, it does not lack problems. For instance, with the great demand for the 64, Commodore experienced a shortage of disk drives. In addition, its sales force is not well-structured. In March of 1983, its national network of independent sales representatives was replaced by an in-house sales staff. Three months later, it fired that staff too. Furthermore, in August of 1983, Commodore stopped offering small retailers advertising money.

Texas Instruments

Holding the second largest share in the home computer market in 1983 was Texas Instruments, with its 99/4A. TI separated its home computer operations from its business computer operations organizationally and geographically. Having the broadest range of outlets in the home computer industry, TI announced that it was not interested in simply being a niche player and would cooperate with re-sellers and vertical marketers to develop specific markets. Furthermore, TI acknowledged the fact that marketing is the key element in the home computer contest. It determined to position itself as a serious, credible source in the consumer's consciousness. Consequently, it directed its marketing efforts toward two goals—establishing quality distribution and creating customer awareness.

Unfortunately, despite its second place standing in the midst of the over-populated home computer market, the 99/4A resulted in a 119 million dollar deficit in the second quarter for TI. Keeping up with frequent price cuts, over-estimating the influence of its price reductions, and inventory back up contributed to these red figures.

In an attempt to save itself, it tried advertising more and laying off workers. However, with numerous competitors vying for second place, its position was not likely to change—unless it obtained a new product. Consequently, TI is contemplating surrendering in the home computer business—at least temporarily.

Tronics Sales Corporation

Tronics Sales Corporation, based in Fort Worth, actually uses direct selling tactics to sell home computers. In July 1981, it got a multiyear contract to distribute Texas Instrument's 99/4A home computer. Its multilevel organization is set up similarly to Amway Corporation's. Distributors earn a commission on each computer they sell, plus commission on software and peripherals. In addition, distributors get 2 to 3 percent of the sales made by people as far removed as five levels in their down-line networks (i.e., sales people they have brought into the organization). Tronics' distributors are not required to buy a computer for themselves. However, they must pay full price for everything they buy for resale and then receive a 10 percent refund, which serves as their commission.

The Tronics pyramidal-structure consists of approximately 15,000 distributors. The majority of them sell the TI 99/4A in their spare time. They comprise a diverse group—school teachers, engineers, airline pilots, and many husband-

and-wife teams. Actually, anyone with a desire to sell home computers door-to-door or at parties can become a Tronics distributor. He/She simply has to pay $20 for sales brochures and is encouraged to buy a kit of seven programs (i.e., market motivational tapes) for $106.25. To ensure that the sales force maintains its enthusiasm, motivational seminars and sales incentives are offered.

Two major problems exist within Tronics' framework. First, it must compete with all of the other channels that carry the TI 99/4A, such as department stores and mail order operations. What's more, Tronics charges $30 or more beyond what other retailers charge for the same system. Of course, customers do receive personal attention and handholding throughout this trying decision process. Secondly, Tronics is presently operating at the mercy of TI. If TI decides not to renew the contract, Tronics will be in a real predicament and will have to make some drastic business decisions. In addition, as mentioned earlier, TI may pull out of the home computer market altogether.

Others

Timex

During the fall of 1982, Timex introduced a home computer for less than $100. At that price, it was an instant success. However, by the same token, at that price it did not do too much. Consequently, "the Timex buyers got such a little taste of what computers are all about and a big taste of what frustration is all about." As might be expected, sales fell drastically after a few months. Many home computer consumers were frightened away, as well.

Atari (Warner Communications, Inc.)

Atari has unsuccessfully tried to market a keyboard that would attach to its video-game units. In February of 1983, the "My First Computer" keyboard was not well received. After renaming it the "Graduate" and making a second valiant attempt to sell the consumers on it, Atari abandoned it. In addition, Atari failed to match its competitors' price cuts in the 1983 price war. Consequently, it dropped 150 of its 190 distributors and experienced a disturbing loss of more than $500 million dollars in the last three quarters of 1983.

Despite this rather bleak scenario, Warner Communications' Atari intends to remain a competitor in the market. As a matter of fact, Atari has informed its dealers of a scheduled price increase (for its 600XL and 800XL computers) early in 1984, in response to the predicted home computer shortage (yet they will stay below IBM's PCjr's price).

Coleco

Coleco is making an admirable attempt at survival in the home computer jungle. They have developed Adam, a milestone in home computers. It provides a complete computer system (digital-tape memory storage, full typewriter keyboard, built-in word processing software, and a central processor which can store up to 80,000 characters) at a mass market price (i.e. approximately $700). However, like Atari, a price increase is planned to exploit the anticipated home computer market. It will be sold at retail stores like J.C. Penney. Coleco plans on stressing the longevity and expansibility of Adam.

Future Competitive Threats

IBM

IBM, the master of the business personal computer segment, has begun to weave its way into the home computer tapestry. IBM has disclosed its contender, the PCjr., but will not formally launch it until early 1984. Its debut will put IBM in every major niche of the computer market. In keeping with its tradition, IBM is predicted to stabilize the shambles called the home computer market and, in addition, is expected to significantly increase the size of this market. Hesitant customers are expected to overcome their indecision over buying a home computer.

The IBM PCjr will sell for $669 (vs. the 64's $200) or $1269 depending on accessories and memory. Since this is considerably more than competitors' machines, the effect is uncertain. It may tap a different market or simply move the market towards more-expensive home computers.

It will be marketed through IBM's more than 1000 authorized dealers (e.g. ComputerLand, Macy department stores). However, it is expected to be in short supply during its introductory period. Consequently, this may create an unmet home computer demand which could be welcomed by competitors armed with a good sales pitch.

Internationals

Currently, foreign competitors do not pose a serious threat to the U.S. computer market. The Japanese hold only about 2 percent. The dynamic state of the market accounts for this surprisingly low figure. Japanese companies usually enter the market after designing a product comparable to the competition—but more reliable, more spectacular, and less expensive. As frequently mentioned, the volatile prices and tastes in the home computer market make finding a standard for comparisons and imitation nearly impossible. As the market stabilizes, perhaps with the entrance of PCjr, this problem for the Japanese may disappear. Until then, the majority of competing foreign firms (European and Japanese) are resorting to targeting specific niches, such as the education market (e.g. Acorn Computers Ltd.) or appealing to the hobbyist with technical advances.

Appendix B: Direct Selling Research
Results and Information

A.   The DSA has comprised the following general facts and statistics concerning the direct selling industry. Direct selling is defined as a dynamic and vital form of direct-to-consumer marketing through personal explanation and demonstration of products and services to consumers, primarily in their homes.

1.   The direct selling industry contributes approximately $7.5 billion to the national economy.
2.   The direct selling industry offers more than four million income-earning opportunities each year. Interestingly, direct-sales outfits often do more poorly in recruiting in economic recoveries than in recessions, as other jobs become more available.
3.   Females comprise 80 percent of the sales force; almost 15 percent are minorities, about 5 percent are over 65, and 10 percent are disabled.
4.   90 percent of salespersons work on a part-time basis; 80 percent work less than half-time; 60 percent work less than ten hours a week.
5.   8 percent of the homes in the U.S. include someone who has been a direct seller some time during the year, and an additional 15 percent include people who have been direct sellers at some point in the past.
6.   Most consumers consider direct selling as good as in-store shopping when it comes to helpfulness of salespeople, product quality, honesty of salespeople and guarantees and warranties.
7.   Most companies have satisfaction guarantee and many offer unconditional money-back guarantees.
8.   Customers having had contact with direct salespeople have much praise for the salespeople and their products.
9.   75 percent of U.S. homes are contacted by direct salespeople each year and 50 percent of the households make a purchase. Over a five year period, 88 percent of all American homes are contacted, and 63 percent make a purchase.

B.   Following are the findings of the 1982 Nowland Organization, Inc.'s study concerning consumer experiences and attitudes with respect to direct selling. The question is whether these results can be generalized to the home computer market.

Overall, the study suggests that there is an increasing opportunity for direct selling in the marketplace. Presently, consumers tend to be dissatisfied with retail sales help (i.e., unhelpful and/or uninformed), the quality of the merchandise offered, and the inconveniences and tension associated with the retail environment. The prime opportunities are seen to reside with middle America (i.e., high school graduate, moderate income, middle class). Furthermore, many of the industry's most successful products relate to the home. About half of American consumers are now or would be open to the direct buying idea.

With regard to sales approaches, the findings suggest that presolicited meetings, appointments, and establishing seller-buyer relationships result in markedly more purchases. Furthermore, non-repetitive (generally high-ticketed, infrequently purchased items) buyers consider product relevance or usefulness, appeal and quality/brand reputation more than price.

In summary, both recent exposure to direct selling and particularly buying leads to higher appraisals of direct selling. However, a fundamental problem is the still prevalent negative view of the field at large, which creates a widespread resistance to direct selling. Many consumers do not accept it as a basic channel of distribution. The main dislikes about this type of selling are its lack of relevance for much of one's buying and a fear that the sales contacts will cause the buyer to lose his/her autonomy.

With regard to loss of relevance, the products are often not immediately available; there is often a lack of accessibility and continuity with the buyer; comparison shopping is difficult; and a negative, "door-to-door", old-fashioned image still exists. Loss of control refers to such things as pressure and obligation, invasion of privacy, and the risk of deception.

Despite these drawbacks related to the image of direct selling, direct buying (the preferred term) has great potential as an alternative for retail buying. In particular, non-repetitive direct buying could be very useful if consumers realized its capacity as an informative, individualized and pleasurable way of selecting items in the home environment, where the product will ultimately be used.

Appendix C: The Dynasty Sales Plan

In a marketing plan such as that provided by Dynasty Computer Corporation, it is necessary that every computer consultant, distributor, and senior distributor understands fully the relationship with the company. As a Dynasty consultant or distributor handling Dynasty products and associated literature you are a self-employed person and remain so for all federal tax purposes. You purchase merchandise and sales aids from Dynasty Computer Corporation at wholesale prices and sell to ultimate consumers of your own choosing at retail. . . the difference between wholesale and retail being your basic income.

All orders sent in by you are subject to acceptance by Dynasty at its Home Office in Dallas, Texas. You are expected to read and fully understand the Independent Dealer Agreement, which you entered into upon becoming a Dynasty representative. You are not an employee of the company, but are an independent contractor and, as such, are free to select your own means, method, and manner of operation, and to choose the hours and location of your selling activities. The company has no right of control over you, and you have no power or authority to incur any debt, obligation or liability or to make any representation or contract on behalf of the company.

DYNASTY COMPUTER CORPORATION IS A MEMBER OF THE DIRECT SELLING ASSOCIATION AND ENDORSES ALL PRIVATE AND GOVERN-

MENTAL EFFORTS WHICH SEEK TO PROMOTE HIGH ETHICAL STAND-ARDS IN SELLING.

To better familiarize yourself with Dynasty, it is recommended that you read the Dynasty Concept Brochure (Form No. 8105) and, in particular, study the marketing plan section in that brochure. A more complete explanation of the Dynasty marketing plan now follows:

The Sales Plan

Take the four steps to the top . . . build your own Dynasty!

When a person first sees the Dynasty Opportunity, he or she is sometimes confused about the various income opportunities available as a dealer of Dynasty products. Taken a step at a time, however, it is really quite simple. Although there are six different sources of income available to you through Dynasty, they all are based on one thing: the sale of quality products to our customers. IT IS IMPOR-TANT TO NOTE THAT THERE ARE NO TIME RESTRICTIONS ON DYNASTY DEALERS. YOU CAN PROGRESS UP THE ORGANIZATION AS RAPIDLY AS YOU DESIRE. IN DYNASTY YOU CONTROL YOUR OWN DESTINY.

In order to fully understand the Dynasty Sales Plan, we will begin with the first step (Computer Consultant) and build from there.

Everyone begins their Dynasty career as a Computer Consultant, and, in fact, the majority of our dealers operate at the Consultant level. For an individual seeking an extra $200 or $300 per month to supplement their current income, this is an excellent opportunity.

Getting Started

Becoming a Computer Consultant Is Easy:

1. Find a Distributor to sponsor you.
2. Fill out your Independent Dealer Agreement.
3. Purchase a "Registration Kit" for $25.

Note: Your Registration Kit consists of the following items:

1 Year subscription to Family Computing Magazine

1 Dynasty Sales Manual

1 Pad of Retail Sales Receipts

3 Wholesale Order Forms

3 Dynasty Concept Brochures

1 Price List

. . . YOU ARE NOW A COMPUTER CONSULTANT

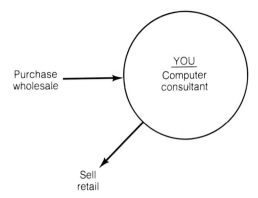

Income Opportunity: Profit from retail sales

Example: Sell one "Home Pak" and one "Voice Phone" per week and earn over $200 per month

That is an extra $2,400 a year!

By demonstrating our telephone products to several families at once, a consultant's time can be maximized thus creating very large hourly returns on the time one spends working their Dynasty business. (See the section of the Sales Manual dealing with group demonstrations.)

The Second Step: Becoming a Dynasty Distributor

Once a person has registered as a computer consultant, the next step is to become a distributor. Here's how:

1.   Submit wholesale orders for products you sell. Once your cumulative volume reaches $500 in wholesale (commissionable) volume you are eligible to submit your Dealer Advancement Application (Form No. 8001/4) requesting promotion to Distributor status.

2.   Indicate on your Dealer Advancement Application whether you wish to receive your Dealership Activation Package immediately (cost $250) or whether you wish to apply future commissions towards purchase of this package. If you elect to apply commissions towards the cost of your Activation Package, it will be shipped once $250 in overrides have accumulated towards your account.

What's Included in Your Dealership Activation Package

a. How to Master Direct Sales.   A complete cassette home study course covering the ten keys to success in direct sales.

The 8 basic steps towards success

How to motivate yourself and set personal goals

The key to earning a large income

How to handle "No's"

Building name lists and referral lists

How to make a successful sales presentation

How to get speedy decisions from prospects

Handling questions and objections

Time management, setting priorities

Becoming a leader

(This course normally retails for $125.00)

b. The Dynasty Slide and Sound Presentation.   Presents the "big picture" of what Dynasty is all about. This slide presentation normally retails for $75.

c. Computer Service Fee.   This $50 annual fee covers state sales tax handling for you and your consultants as well as accounting services on your computer consultant organization. (This allows your consultants to order direct from the company and frees you from handling their orders and product shipments). This $50 annual fee is due each year a distributor elects to renew his or her distributorship.

. . . YOU ARE NOW A DYNASTY DISTRIBUTOR

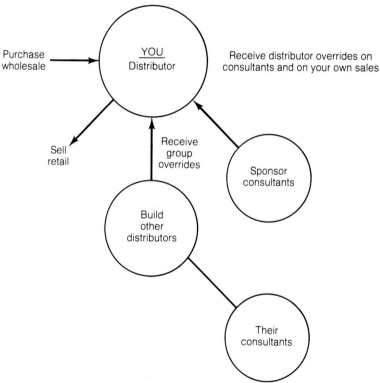

Income Opportunities: Profit from retail sales

Distributor Overrides

Group Overrides

Example: An organization consisting of YOU, one personal consultant and one personal distributor who has one consultant.

If all sell one "Home Pak" and one "Voice Phone" per week, your combined income would exceed $500 per month.

That is over $6,000 per year!

The Third Step: Becoming a Senior Distributor

After qualifying as a distributor, you continue accumulating sales volume to qualify as a senior distributor. All of your previous volume counts. In Dynasty, we look at cumulative sales volume from the first day you begin with us. Therefore, you can go as fast, or slow as you like. You are your own boss!

Senior Distributor Requirements:

1. Be a fully qualified Distributor.

2. Continue submitting wholesale orders for products you sell. Once your additional cumulative volume reaches $3,000.00 in wholesale (commissionable) volume, you are eligible to submit your Dealer Advancement Application (Form No. 8001) requesting promotion to senior distributor status.

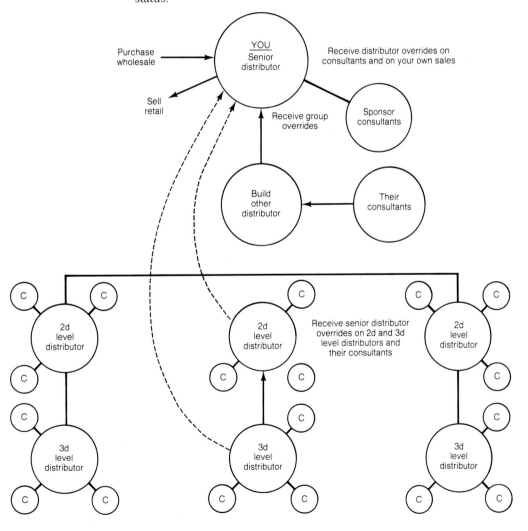

Note: All cumulative volume requirements are based on personal sales.

Alternate Qualifications for Senior Distributor:

1. Be a fully qualified Distributor.

2. Personally sponsor TWO other persons who qualify as full distributors within thirty days of the time you first were shown the Dynasty Sales Plan.

3. Sponsor FIVE (5) new distributors over ANY PERIOD OF TIME.

. . . YOU ARE NOW A SENIOR DISTRIBUTOR

Income Opportunities: Profit from retail sales
Distributor Overrides
Group Overrides
Senior Distributor Overrides

Example: An organization consisting of YOU, one personal consultant, one personal distributor who has one consultant and three personal distributors etc. as shown above.

If all sell one "Home Pak" and one "Voice Phone" per week, your combined income would exceed $800 per month.

That is over $9,600 per year.

The Fourth Step: Earning Your Own Pin Number

Once an individual qualifies as a senior distributor, they receive a senior distributor pin. The next step is to earn the One Emerald Pin and along with it your own unique Pin Number. The impact of a Pin Number can be awesome!

Here Is How the Pin System Works. When a person registers with Dynasty, they are assigned the "Pin Number" of their sponsor. This number remains with an individual and is passed on to people they sponsor on down-line indefinitely. Once a person receives their One Emerald Pin they are assigned their own unique Pin Number which they then begin passing on down the line. Upon qualification for receipt of one's own Pin Number, only the qualifying individual's number is changed, NOT the numbers of any other persons previously sponsored.

Everyone in your sponsorship chain would carry your Pin Number until such time as they qualified for their own number.

How to Qualify for a Pin Number and Higher Pin Levels.

1. Be a fully qualified senior distributor.
2. Add an additional $3,000 (wholesale) in cumulative volume to your total after the date you became a senior distributor.

Alternate Qualifications for A Pin Number.

1. Be a fully qualified senior distributor.
2. Personally sponsor FIVE Dynasty distributors in any 30 consecutive days.

Note: If all five distributors are sponsored within thirty days of the time you first were shown the Dynasty Sales Plan, then you may count the two distributors sponsored under senior qualifications in your Alternate Pin Qualification.

3. Have a personally sponsored consultant qualify as a distributor with an order of $2,500 or more.

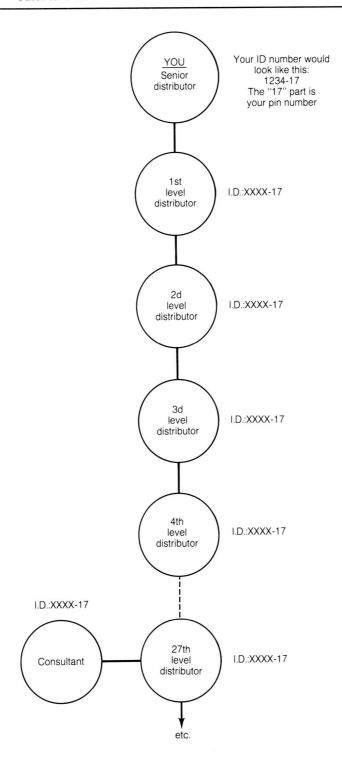

Each time you meet either the cumulative volume requirement or the Alternate requirement, you will move up in the pin structure. To receive your advancement, send in your qualifications on a Dealer Advancement Application, Form No. 8001/4. Pin levels are shown below:

PV Commission Level

Senior Distributor	–0–
One Emerald	1%
Two Emerald	2%
One Ruby	3%
Two Ruby	4%
Diamond (up to 3 diamonds)	5%

Income Opportunities: You continue to receive ALL
Senior Distributor income sources
PLUS
Pin Money

Pin Money is extra commission paid to pin holders of One Emerald and up. You will note a column on the Wholesale Price List entitled "Pin Volume."

Each month, the Pin Volume (PV) on all the orders submitted by everyone holding your Pin Number is totaled. That amount is then multiplied by the PV Commission Level you hold (e.g., 5 percent for a Diamond Pin Holder). PROVIDED YOU HAVE MET THE PIN MONEY QUALIFICATIONS FOR THAT MONTH, you will receive your Pin Money for the entire sponsorship chain holding your Pin Number no matter how many levels deep.

Look at the example on page 249. This organization does not even take into account the fact that Pin Money is paid all the way down your organization, not just on the first three levels. Yet, if you were at the Diamond Pin level (5 percent) based on this example, your Pin "Money" would exceed $10,000 per year!!! Not counting sales made by dealers with your Pin Number below the third level.

Diamond Special: All Diamond Pin holders will receive 5 percent of the PV of all persons coded under their Pin Number. PLUS they will receive 1 percent of the PV of individuals they Personally Sponsored who now have their own pin numbers. (Example: Joe (No. XXXX-18) sponsors Bill (No. XXXX-18). Bill earns his own pin and his pin number is changed (XXXX-35). When Joe earns his Diamond Pin he receives 5 percent of the PV of all persons whose I.D. Number ends in -18, plus 1 percent of the PV of all persons whose I.D. Number ends in -35 until such time as Bill earns his own Diamond Pin.

Qualifications to Receive "PV" Commissions. In order to be eligible to receive the monthly PV commissions, a distributor must have sold at least $500 (PV) worth of product during the month in question OR during the previous month. This volume may be either personal sales or the sales of personally sponsored computer consultants. This volume requirement may be carried forward for up to 12 months. (Example: In January, three personal consultants meet the requirements for distributor and all have a total of $1,500 PV. This is enough to qualify their sponsor for the next four months of Pin Commissions . . . $500 towards January, $500 towards February, $500 towards March, and April is free since March was qualified).

Case 1–3
Omega Medical Products, Incorporated[*]

Omega Medical Products (OMP), located in Denver, Colorado, is one of the top manufacturers of life-support medical equipment and surgical pharmaceuticals. In fiscal year 1983, OMP recorded sales of $230 million (See Exhibit 1). Over the past three years, sales have increased at an annual rate of 18 percent. The company currently employs 175 sales representatives, including a separate sales force of 40 that handles the company's anesthesia line exclusively. As the result of a recent staff reorganization, a decision was made to realign the sales and marketing department to better meet the future goals of the company.

Exhibit 1
1983 Sales ($000)

Patient care		$ 84,270
Anesthesia equipment	$40,100	
Anesthesia disposables	20,450	
Nursing products	13,720	
Infant care	10,000	
Respiratory therapy		40,418
Architectural products		35,980
Anesthesia (gases)		50,055
Other (government, OEM, service, military)		20,000
Total		$230,723

Five years ago, Omega's president retired, and the top position was filled by the executive vice president, Christopher John. Subsequently, several other major changes occurred in the executive staff hierarchy. The most important were the elimination of the executive vice president position and the creation of the position of vice president, marketing and sales. Reporting to the new vice president would be the current vice president of sales, service, and distribution, the vice president of international sales, the general manager of medical equipment marketing, the general manager of distribution, customer services and gases, the director of market research and strategic planning, the director of communications, and the marketing manager of architectural products (See Exhibit 2).

The vice president of marketing and sales, destined to be one of the most powerful positions at OMP, was ultimately filled by Earl Callahan. Callahan had previously held the top marketing job in a firm that manufactured medical products unrelated to those sold by Omega. Filling this position with an "outsider" generated noticeable discontent among several executives who had been considered as top contenders. Shortly after he began work, Callahan was pressured by

[*]The assistance of Bonnie J. Queram, MBA–Marketing, University of Wisconsin, Madison in the preparation of this case is greatly appreciated.

Exhibit 2

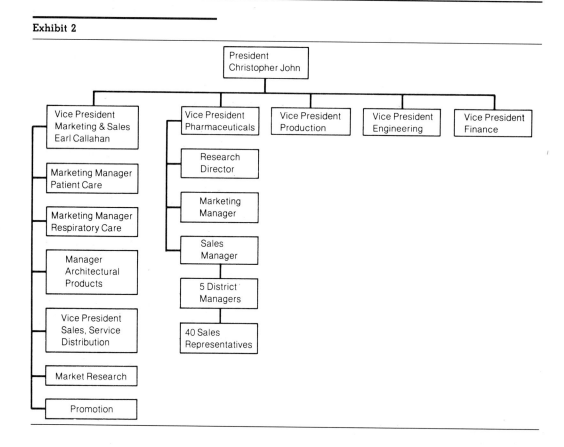

John to have a revised sales organization chart completed prior to Omega's new fiscal year, beginning July 1. After reviewing Omega's current organization charts, sales figures, and marketing plans for new products, Callahan realized there were several major problems.

Marketing Activities

Omega's marketing function was divided into four separate product areas. The patient care group consisted of anesthesia equipment and disposables, nursing equipment, and infant care supplies. The anesthesia equipment and disposables line accounted for the greatest dollar volume, with 1983 sales of $60 million. With new products as the primary growth factor in the portable patient monitoring area, sales were expected to be $115 million by 1987. Product prices ranged from a few cents for disposables to several thousand dollars for equipment.

The respiratory therapy line accounted for $40 million sales in 1983. The line had experienced only slight growth over the last few years but was expected to generate $58 million by 1987 with the introduction of one major new critical care ventilator, priced as high as $35,000 with all accessories. The prime market for this do-everything machine was the small to medium-size hospital. Although Omega was the leader in the anesthesia field, they did not enjoy the same position in respiratory care. In fact, due to several major failures with new products during the last 10 to 15 years, the Omega name was still associated by many therapists with inferior quality, poor product design, and inadequate service.

The architectural product line, composed of pipelines and gas outlets, had sales of $36 million in 1983, while the anesthesia line (gases), sold by a separate sales organization, accounted for $50 million. The major product was a liquid that, when converted to gas, was used to anesthetize patients for surgery.

Sales Activities

The general sales force, consisting of 135 representatives in the United States and Canada reporting to 16 district managers, and six regional vice presidents (See Exhibit 3) were currently expected to call on four major departments in each hospital: operating room, recovery room, emergency room, and nursery. Additionally, they were expected to keep in contact with purchasing and, if one existed, with the biomedical engineering department. The latter, usually present only in larger hospitals, was often responsible for reviewing and testing potential new equipment. Biomedical engineers were becoming instrumental in the purchase of sophisticated electronic monitoring devices. Also, the sales force was expected to sell bulk oxygen and nitrous oxide as well as Omega's architectural product line equipment to new hospitals or those being remodeled. This required that they work very closely with architects and construction contractors, usually a very time-consuming endeavor, ranging from several months to over one year. The anesthesia sales force called on the anesthesia staff exclusively. Close and frequent contact was necessary in most cases. The members of the sales force, all with chemical backgrounds, were expected to keep abreast of technological developments in the field. Some sales representatives were formerly anesthetists.

Although Omega's products covered a wide variety of medical applications and necessitated sales calls to many different departments, the general line sales force had to date handled the lines very well. Callahan felt that one primary reason they had done so well was that the majority of Omega's products were not particularly complicated and the sales force could be adequately trained by product managers when new products were introduced. Additionally, although Omega sold several thousand items, which realistically is a line much too broad for a sales representative to handle effectively, Callahan knew that many products sold with little or no sales effort because of the Omega name and strong dealer network. Most dealers handled low-cost, easy-to-sell products, although some of the very large dealers sold high priced equipment. Callahan also felt, however, that this would not continue in the future because many products planned for market introduction in the

Exhibit 3

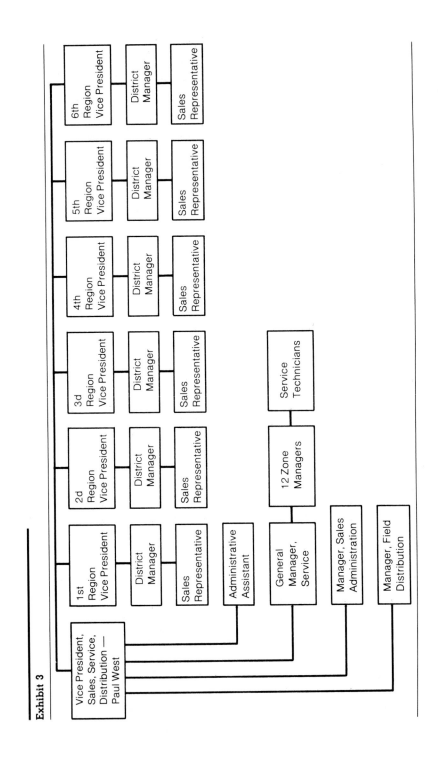

next five years were state-of-the-art electronic monitoring equipment. Most of these products were in the anesthesia line. Omega's lack of experience in the medical electronics field would mean that an intensive sales effort would be required to enter the market profitably, as there were several formidable competitors controlling the market.

Unfortunately, it was generally known that perhaps as many as half of Omega's sales representatives did not have the training or experience to sell these kinds of products. In view of the need to deal with hospital biomedical engineers on a very technical level, in the long run, Callahan surmised, it would be better to use only sales personnel experienced in selling electronic equipment rather than attempt to train the entire force. Besides, he knew from personal conversations that no more than 10 percent of the representatives had any interest in learning about or selling the new equipment. Thus, he wondered about augmenting the sales force with specialists who would be able to provide technical assistance to sell portable patient monitoring equipment. But, since there were already general line and anesthesia sales representatives calling on hospital personnel, he did not want a third party calling on the same personnel. Callahan felt this would be more confusing than advantageous.

Other Information

For the last year, the marketing manager of respiratory care, Bill Griese, had been attempting to convince Callahan that, in spite of the line's history, real growth potential existed in respiratory therapy. He wanted the company to spend more time and money pursuing this market. Griese had also indicated that to sell and service the products adequately—particularly the new critical care ventilator—the line should be handled by separate sales force. He argued that because most of Omega's products were in the anesthesia field, the representatives were spending a disproportionate amount of sales time in that area. Thus, Omega's relatively poor sales and image in respiratory therapy were perpetuated.

Callahan knew that Jeff Hardy, marketing manager for patient care, would lobby for a separate sales group for anesthesia products since that line represents one quarter of the company's sales. Apparently this request had been made several times over the past five years. One proposal had included plans for the anesthesia (gases) sales force to also handle the anesthesia equipment because both were sold to the same department. Another proposal had called for a separate anesthesia equipment force altogether. Callahan felt that drugs and equipment required substantially different sales techniques and that one force could not adequately handle both. But he also had reservations about two different representatives calling on the same customer, as was currently the case. On the other hand, a separate anesthesia equipment force would result in substantially more sales time spent on respiratory products by the general line sales force.

Anesthesia Sales Organization

Approximately 10 years ago, Omega's chemical research department discovered a revolutionary new drug (a gas) to anesthetize patients safely for surgery. Following two years of testing for the Food and Drug Administration, the drug was approved and successfully introduced to the marketplace. It is currently used on 60 percent of all surgical patients, and it continues to capture market share. The drug has a very high gross margin, and in 1983, it had profits of $21 million on sales of $50 million. Its patent runs through 1990.

To develop the surgical drug market fully and lead the marketing and sales activities, a vice-presidential position was created at the time of discovery of the new drug. Ronald Hagen was hired for this position. He, in turn, put together a separate sales organization with 40 persons by 1983. Most of the sales representatives were hired away from pharmaceutical companies and thus demanded and were paid salaries and commissions somewhat above those paid to Omega's general line sales force (See Exhibit 4.)

Exhibit 4
Sales compensation plans

	General Line Representatives	Anesthesia Representatives
Base salary	$1,500–$1,850	$1,650–$2,100
Commission on sales up to quota (percent)	1	1
Commission on sales over quota (percent)	2–5	2–5
1982 salary range	$24,200–$35,800	$29,800–$42,750
Average salary	$38,100	$42,000

Hagen is very proud of his organization, believing that his sales representatives are a cut above the general line organization. Consequently, he wants no part of any plans to join the two forces. Besides, other new drugs are scheduled for introduction in the 1985–86 period and will provide the drug sales group with a sufficient product load for several years into the future.

General Line Sales Organization

The general line sales organization, reporting to Paul West, consisted of 135 representatives, 16 district managers, and six regional vice presidents. The service department, also under West, consisted of a total of 172 technicians reporting to 16 zone managers. Also reporting to West were the manager of sales administration, the manager of field distribution, and an administrative assistant.

West was initially quite upset about the apparent demotion of his position as a result of the reorganization; he had reported directly to John before Callahan was hired. Knowing that further reorganization was imminent, West felt he would ultimately lose control of the service and distribution areas. Although this would narrow his responsibilities somewhat, West was not particularly concerned. In fact, because of the need to update both the service organization and the distribution organization to handle the new portable patient care monitoring products, those areas had been commanding a disproportionate amount of his time for the last few months. West would prefer to hire a general manager for service and distribution and have that new individual, reporting to him, handle most of the responsibility in those two crucial areas. He intended to propose this to Callahan.

In the meantime, West was most interested in studying the sales force reorganization and conveying his ideas to Callahan. West had always been interested in developing a separate sales force for anesthesia equipment and disposables. He felt there was sufficient sales volume to support it and customers would be receptive to the extra attention and service. When selling this equipment, the representative would call on the anesthesia staff, a group typically more difficult to deal with and more technically oriented than personnel from other hospital departments. Often the sale also involved the hospital's biomedical engineers, which was not true of Omega's other products. A separate force could be more intensely trained, thus ensuring better customer service.

West also felt that a strong case could be made for putting architectural products under the mandate of a small but specialized sales force. General line sales representatives tended to ignore architectural products because their sales consumed too much time and involved contact with non-hospital personnel.

If a separate anesthesia equipment force were developed, the remaining general line would be left with nursing, infant care, respiratory therapy, and architectural products. This seemed reasonable because many of these products were sold in the same hospital departments even though they were categorized in different product lines. West also felt that the dealers should be encouraged to handle more low-cost products, giving the general line sales force more time for other products.

The real problem with splitting out the anesthesia products, West thought, was that each group would remain responsible for the new portable patient monitoring equipment. West further thought that since each force would be responsible for a smaller number of the new products, they could be sufficiently trained to do this work. Since most of the new portable patient monitoring equipment was in the anesthesia area, the selection of this group would come from those with the most training and experience with electronics products. Additionally, West felt there was a strong case to be made for having 'monitoring specialists' in both sales groups. These persons would handle all the products of their groups but would place more emphasis on the new equipment and would be available for dual sales calls with their colleagues who were not so well versed in the items.

At a recent convention, West briefly discussed his ideas with Tom Reinke, the western regional vice president and one of West's closest friends. Reinke had, at one time, worked for a company that manufactured sterilization equipment for hospitals. Following the development of a new, very sophisticated unit, it had divided the sales organization into two groups. One handled the existing line, and the other group specialized in the new equipment. Reinke indicated the sales force division proved disastrous, leading to duplicate sales calls, customer confusion, and increased expenses. He felt the same would occur with West's monitoring specialists. He recommended that Omega should hire more technically qualified personnel for the general line sales force. West left the convention somewhat less enthusiastic about his sales force proposal.

Case 1–4
Olsen Seed Farms[*]

After graduating from Iowa State University with degrees in Agronomy and Business, Jon Olsen assumed responsibility for the management and marketing of Olsen Seed Farms, a family business, located in Mount Horeb, Wisconsin. Founded by Jon's grandfather 76 years ago, Olsen Seed Farms now produces and sells a full line of agriculture seeds including corn, alfalfa, beans, and sorghum. As shown in Table 1, sales of seed corn, which is Olsen's main product, totaled $2,500,000 or 39,803 bushels in 1983.

Table 1
Unit sales of seed (bushels)

Year	Corn	Soybeans	Alfalfa	Total Sales
1979	30,665	4,657	1,066	36,388
1980	31,956	4,175	1,130	37,261
1981	32,873	6,075	1,122	40,070
1982	38,914	5,815	1,053	45,782
1983	39,803	7,120	1,210	48,133

In 1982, under Jon's direction, Olsen Seed Farms embarked upon an expansion program. The production facilities were upgraded and production acreage was expanded by 60 percent to 3,500 acres.

After improvements to the production facilities were completed, Jon focused on the marketing function of the business. Olsen's market share has remained unchanged for the past six years. In contrast, the market share of the three dominant national seed companies, Pioneer, DeKalb, and Jacques, has increased steadily.

Jon feels that Olsen's lack of growth is primarily due to inefficiencies within the sales organization. In addition, he has identified three conditions in the environment that affect the demand for Olsen's products. First, the seed corn industry is in the mature stage of its life cycle and saturated with competitors. In Wisconsin, for example, more than 35 firms sell agriculture seeds. Consequently, Olsen's sales can only increase at the expense of the competitors. Second, while the number of acres planted to corn has stabilized, acreage planted to soybeans and alfalfa is rapidly increasing. Lastly, acreage planted to crops is dependent on government and export programs.

---

[*]This case was prepared especially for this text by Regina Downey and Linda Drew, MBAs—Marketing, University of Wisconsin, Madison.

Sales Territories

In 1975, Olsen Seed Farms expanded outside its home state. Jon's father, Joseph, logged over 60,000 miles in one year establishing new territories. As a result, Olsen seed is presently available in seven states including Illinois, Iowa, Michigan, Minnesota, Nebraska, South Dakota, and Wisconsin. Exhibit 1 details Olsen's distribution area. However, market share in 1984 varies widely from a high of 11.26 percent in their home county to less than 0.52 percent in several counties in Michigan and Nebraska.

To improve operations, Jon established market share and profitability objectives for each territory. In developing the objectives, he considered the higher costs of servicing and delivering to areas outside Wisconsin. Because the areas south and west of Wisconsin differ in soil conditions and length of growing season, Jon concluded that seed more suitable to those regions needs to be developed

Exhibit 1
Distribution of Olsen Seed

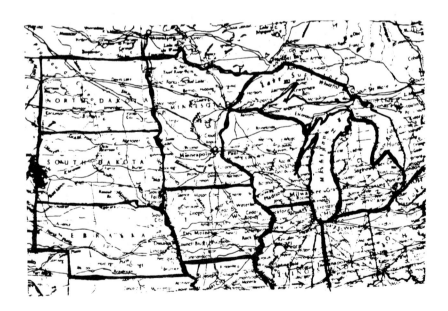

to obtain significant share improvement. However, he is uncertain whether the existing research and production facilities can accommodate these changes.

Sales Force

Olsen Seed Farms employs a sales manager and 18 district supervisors who manage 576 dealers in seven states. Jon feels that poor organization and control of the sales force contributes to Olsen Seed Farms' marketing problems.

Dealers

Like other agriculture seed companies, Olsen Seed Farms sells seed through the company dealer organization. More than 50 percent of the dealers are located in Wisconsin, as shown in Table 2.

The dealers are farmers who agree to sell Olsen Seed to their friends and neighbors in exchange for a discount based on the number of bushels sold. The 1984 dealer discount schedule is shown in Table 3.

Table 2
Location and size of current dealers

Sales Area*	Number of Dealers	Bushels Sold by Dealers	Average Dealer Size (Bushels)
1	27	300	11
2	22	1,086	49
3	15	759	51
4	18	320	18
5	92	2,970	32
6*	124	10,851	88
7	25	2,340	94
8*	91	4,014	44
9*	39	2,243	58
10*	21	1,544	74
11	5	110	22
12*	47	2,123	45
13	5	109	22
14	4	204	51
15	9	634	70
16	20	498	25
17	12	308	26
18	—	—	—
Total	576	30,413	53

*Wisconsin territories.

Table 3
1984 dealer discount schedule

Number of Bushels	Discount Percent
1–24	9
25–49	14
50–99	16
100–199	18
200–349	20
350–499	21
500–999	22
1,000–1,499	23
1,500+	24

To aid Jon in discovering problems and opportunities in the organization of the sales force, a dealership audit was conducted. The audit revealed that, although the dealers' associations with Olsen Seed Farms varies from less than one year to over 19 years, the majority have been with the company for three to four years. Over 60 percent of the dealers are over 50 years old and are full-time farmers. The chief reasons cited for becoming dealers were:

"I was asked."

Free seed (sample bags)

Liked the supervisor and/or Joseph Olsen

Olsen Seed Farms is a small family operation

As shown in Table 4, categorizing the dealers by number of bushels sold confirmed Jon's suspicion that most of the dealers do not sell seed. Since over half of the dealers sell less than 49 bushels of seed, some farmers are becoming dealers to get the discount on their own seed rather than to sell seed.

The audit also showed that, while some dealers do plant 100 percent of their total seed requirements with Olsen Seed, most only plant 30 to 50 percent of their total seed requirements with Olsen Seed. When questioned, dealers said they purchase the remaining 50 to 70 percent of their seed from other companies for

Table 4
Dealer size

Bushels Sold	Number of Dealers
0–24	169
25–49	203
50–99	169
100–199	88
200+	41

comparison purposes. Others replied that they purchase seed from other companies because they are unaware that crop seed, besides corn, is available from Olsen Seed Farms. Many dealers, for example, do not know that Olsen Seed Farms sells alfalfa seed.

A breakdown of the size of the dealers in relation to company sales, as shown in Table 5, indicated to Jon that a small percent of the dealers account for more than half of total sales.

Table 5
Dealer sales as a percent of company sales

Bushels Sold	Percent of Dealers	Percent of Total Sales
1–49 55		20
50–99 25		24
100+ 19		55

Jon is considering reclassifying the small dealers who account for only 20 percent of total sales and probably only purchase seed for their own planting needs as customers.

Supervisors

Eighteen district supervisors manage territories in Olsen Seed Farms' seven state market area, as detailed in Exhibit 2.

After a careful analysis of the supervisor structure at Olsen Seed Farms and competing seed companies, Jon identified four major problems.

First, a lack of contact exists between the dealers and supervisors. In 1983, 70 percent of the dealers had not seen their supervisors in six months. One dealer had not been contacted by his supervisor for two years. In the seed industry, close communication between supervisors, dealers, and customers is critical, especially during the growing season, so that timely information about the crop can be conveyed to the farmers. For example, in 1982, disease affected most of the corn crop in Wisconsin. The stalk disease hurt the standability of the corn during the later harvesting weeks. Olsen supervisors and dealers were able to warn their customers with longer maturing hybrids to harvest early. Thus, although the hybrids were harvested at less than their maximum yield potential, the farmers avoided harvesting a crop that had fallen over and was rotting in the fields. Because Olsen's supervisors are typically not very involved with their dealers and customers, Jon feels extremely fortunate that Olsen had been able to catch this problem in time. He thinks a more formal communication channel between the

Exhibit 2
Supervisor territories

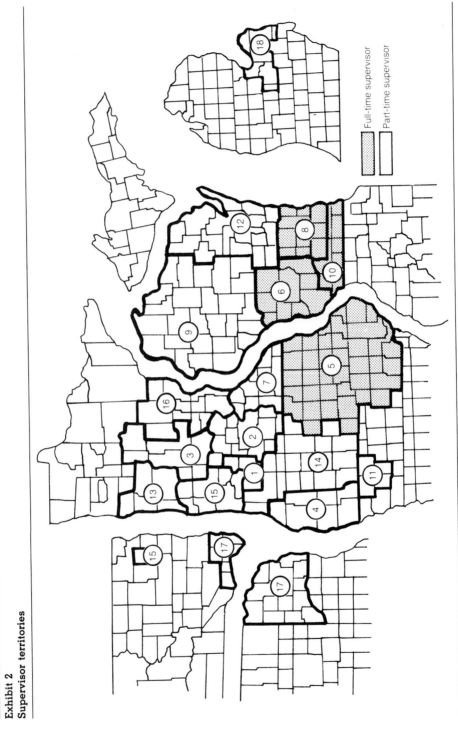

Full-time supervisor

Part-time supervisor

dealers, supervisors, and customers should be implemented to guarantee this timely communication in the future.

Second, the supervisors have varying abilities and commitments to selling Olsen seeds. Unlike the Pioneer Seed Company's sales force, whose supervisors are primarily full-time supervisors with agronomy degrees, fourteen of Olsen's supervisors are part-time supervisors and full-time farmers. Because the supervisors' main source of income is farming, not selling, Jon is experiencing difficulty in starting a formalized sales structure based on goals and objectives as well as motivating the supervisors to sell and work with their dealers. Many promotional and sales programs are never implemented because unless a supervisor is "sold" on an idea, he will not pass it on to the dealer. As a result, the supervisors do not inform the dealers and the dealers, in turn, cannot inform their customers. Of the dealers Jon surveyed:

40 percent were unaware of Olsen's PEN (special deal) program

20 percent were unaware of the early order discount program

Most requested information on soil tests, fertilizers, and herbicides.

Third, company figures show that Olsen's highest market share is in counties in which the supervisors reside. Other counties in the supervisors' assigned territories have very low market share. Jon suspects that the sales territories may be too large for the supervisors to cover adequately. He also wonders if the lack of a formal agronomy education hampers the supervisors' efforts to effectively service the dealers beyond the basic sale of seed. Because the company is a small family business, Jon feels that Olsen Seed Farms' distinct advantage over its competitors is high quality service and seed. Thus, the dealers and supervisors contact with the customers is critical to Olsen's image.

Finally, the supervisor commission structure encourages the formation of "front dealerships," especially among the part-time supervisors. Dealers can receive up to a 24 percent discount, while supervisors can only receive a 14 percent discount.

Part-time supervisors designate another family member as a dealer. Then the supervisor concentrates his efforts on servicing and obtaining customers for the dealership rather than on servicing and attracting new customers for the existing dealers. The establishment of front dealerships also prevents Jon from gaining an accurate picture of Olsen Seed Farms' customer base.

Based on his analysis of the company's sales force, Jon feels that reorganization of the force is necessary to gain greater market share. He is wondering how to develop a plan to meet the market share objectives established.

Case 1–5
HOMAP, Inc.

HOMAP, Inc., manufactures major household appliances such as refrigerators, ranges, washers, dryers, and dishwashers. Recently, the company decided to enter the room air conditioner market on a nationwide basis.

HOMAP executives felt confident that this new product would be successful for several reasons. First, the suggested retail price was very competitive. Second, the units had the lowest energy requirements of any competitive model on the market. Third, the HOMAP name was already well known. Fourth, HOMAP's appliances were widely distributed in the United States. There were dealers in all Standard Metropolitan Statistical Areas. Production capacity was available as well as the necessary production personnel. In addition to production alignment, there was marketing alignment. HOMAP's sales staff would have no problem encouraging dealers to carry the new line of room air conditioners. Most dealers carried one or more lines of room air conditioners, but many would switch to HOMAP. Marketing support to dealers was a strong feature of HOMAP's marketing strategy. Rapport between HOMAP and dealers was very strong.

HOMAP's marketing research department had prepared an industry sales forecast for the United States for the first year. Factors used in preparing the industry sales forecast were:

1.   Number of housing units.
2.   Level of personal income.
3.   Appliance sales.
4.   Number of households with air conditioners.
5.   Industry sales of room air conditioners.

Government statistics existed for the first four variables and industry sales were provided by National Data Corporation, a firm specializing in providing companies with analytical reports of past and future trends for a variety of products.

Using multiple regression analysis, HOMAP's marketing research department was able to measure the degree of correlation between industry sales of room air conditioners and the four independent variables: (1) number of housing units, (2) level of personal income, (3) appliance sales, and (4) number of households with air conditioners. The coefficient of multiple regression was quite strong: $R = 0.92$. Thus, 85 percent of the variation in industry sales was explained by the four variables. The regression analysis also provided data that indicated the relative importance of the four variables. After modest adjustment, the following weights were applied:

Independent Variable	Weight
Number of housing units	0.1
Level of personal income	0.2
Appliance sales	0.3
Number of households with air conditioners	0.4

HOMAP's marketing analyst felt confident that this same relationship would hold true for HOMAP. Based on the industry sales forecast, HOMAP derived a nationwide sales forecast of $63 million for its first year. HOMAP's existing market share for its other products was a factor used to determine what share of the market it might expect for the new line of room air conditioners. HOMAP also considered that this would be a new product and that its normal market share would not be reached until three to four years after introduction.

The next problem facing HOMAP was to develop sales forecasts for each of the 48 contiguous states. It was decided to use the same regional groups that existed for other products. Washington, Oregon, Idaho, and Montana constituted the northwestern region. HOMAP knew that after making regional and state forecasts, forecasts for SMSAs within each state would be needed.

Case 1–6
Delaware Paint and Plate Glass
Industries, Inc.

The Strategic Forecasting and Planning Committee had just completed its review of the company's activities for all of its divisions for the last 15 years. The committee was reasonably pleased with its ability to prepare forecasts of sales, recognizing how important forecasts are to division heads for planning cash flows, production scheduling, personnel planning, budgeting, inventory control, purchasing, and other purposes. However, the committee was perplexed by problems that had been experienced in the Glass Division.

The Glass Division has confronted rather uncertain times due mainly to fluctuations in the economic environment. As a result, inventories are bloated, and the division is operating at less than 60 percent of capacity. Karl Backes, president of the Glass Division, is concerned about these problems and has assigned to his forecasting and planning group the responsibility for reviewing past forecasting procedures and for developing new methods that offer greater accuracy. Heading up the forecasting and planning group is Jackie Vandenberg. Although Jackie was transferred recently from another division, she has managed to impress her peers in the Glass Division with her knowledge of the industry and of the various methods available for forecasting. Her first activity involved a careful review of past methods and results. It was very apparent that the division's forecasting procedures needed revamping in order to be more useful to the numerous departments relying on the forecasts for their own planning and scheduling activities.

The Company

Delaware Paint and Plate Glass incorporated in Delaware in 1895. Delaware P&PG wholly owns a variety of companies which have been integrated into four basic business segments. In addition, Delaware P&PG has entered several joint ventures with other corporations in such areas as oil and gas exploration, iodine production, and ethylene glycol production.

The company is concentrated in four basic business segments: glass, chemicals, coatings and resins, and fiber glass. The diversity of Delaware's markets helped to soften the effects of the economic downturn which had started in 1980. Major markets are transportation and construction, which are served in varying degrees by the business' four segments. Other industrial and agricultural markets are served by the basic business lines. Foreign markets comprise the same basic categories as the domestic mix.

Domestic sales in 1980 were divided about equally among Delaware's major markets: transportation, primarily automotive; residential and commercial construction, including building and remodeling; chemical processing and refining, and other industrial and agricultural areas.

The continuing slump in the automobile industry had a substantial impact on the glass and fiber glass business segments. Manufacture of original equipment glass parts was affected by the decline in U.S. car production falling to one of the lowest levels in recent years. Sales of fiber glass products declined due to poor economic conditions, which affected the recreational vehicle and pleasure boat markets. The low level of domestic auto production also affected Delaware's factory-applied automotive finishes business. The company's leading position in several areas of technology, which provided superior products, helped offset some of this effect.

Delaware's strong position in the aircraft market remained fairly stable. Sales were strong for windshields and other transparencies for business aviation and military aircraft. The company also provides coatings for specialty ballistics glazing.

Housing starts were at their lowest level in 35 years which had an adverse effect on Delaware P&PG's insulating glass units, as well as sales of fiber glass products for such items as bathtubs and shower enclosures. On the other hand, the use of fiber glass roofing products and shingles increased dramatically in 1984.

In contrast to the depressed residential construction market, commercial construction continued strong in 1984. Demand grew for Delaware's energy-efficient architectural glass products.

Because of weak economic conditions, demand for most of Delaware's chemical products was down. Sale of farm fertilizers declined along with most of their industrial chemicals. Demand was strong for the company's line of chemicals used in the oil- and gas-exploration markets.

The Glass Division

Delaware P&PG is one of the nation's largest producers of flat glass, manufacturing about one third of total domestic industry output. The company's major markets are automotive original equipment, automotive replacement, residential construction, commercial construction, and aircraft transparencies. Delaware also supplies the furniture industry and other markets. Most glass products are sold to other manufacturing and construction companies, although some are sold directly to independent distributors and to consumers through Delaware's franchised distribution centers.

The Forecasting and Planning Group

In addition to Jackie Vandenberg, the group was composed of Clair Voyance, sales analyst, Gregg O. Strander, national sales manager, and Scott Wilson, production planning. The group could rely on a staff statistical group that reported to corporate headquarters for technical assistance, if needed.

Specifically, the group was expected not only to come up with an overall sales forecast of division sales, but also to break down this forecast by market, product, quarter, and major account. Its first task concerned the development of a sales forecast for the glass division.

Some differences over what methods to use arose within the group. Gregg felt that the group should rely on the sales force composite method, arguing that the end result would be more receptive to the sales force as a result of their involvement in its preparation. Scott, on the other hand, felt that sales force input should be minimal since they have little impact on OEM contracts. These contracts are determined at the top. Clair felt that, regardless of method used, it is mandatory that the group be able to provide forecasts for each major market. Then, by adding up the forecasts, a total estimate of dollar sales for the division would result.

Despite these differences, Jackie felt that the group would be able to work together without any major problems. She was aware that numerous techniques existed for making forecasts and was pondering which would be most appropriate. Believing that simplicity is an advantage, she hoped the group would not allow the process to become overly complicated. For example, she knew that trend analysis, using either simple regression analysis or exponential smoothing, would be easier than more complicated methods.

At their first meeting, she initiated the discussion by asking the group to identify factors that they thought would have a significant effect on glass sales. Gregg's immediate response was that sales were dependent on efforts of the sales force. Although the rest of the group agreed, Jackie pointed out that external variables were desired for purposes of developing a sales forecasting model. To illustrate, she suggested that some national economic variables would be appropriate, such as gross national product, personal income, per capita income, employment, etc. Clair suggested variables that would closely reflect activities in the division's major markets, such as automobile production, automobile repair, and construction. Scott pointed out that construction is too broad and that this variable needs to be separated into types of construction, such as residential, nonresidential, and nonbusiness. Housing starts would be useful as well. Jackie suggested accident rates as a proxy for automobile repair. Buildings are remodeled and repaired, and some index reflecting this might be useful. In addition, since weather causes various kinds of damage some measure of weather, such as the incident of tornadoes, could be of value.

Realizing that the group was headed in the right direction, Jackie suggested that an attempt to use these variables be initiated and that the results be examined for their forecasting effectiveness. She proposed that regression analysis be

Exhibit 1
Statistical 1965–1982

Year	Plate Glass Sales ($ millions)	Automobile Production Units (thousands)	New Housing Units Started (thousands)	Per Capita Personal Income ($)	Motor Vehicle Accidents (millions)	Residential Construction ($ billions)	Nonresidential Construction ($ billions)	Nonbuilding Construction ($ billions)	Tornadoes (units)
1965	$337	9,306	1,510	$2,782	13.2	$21.2	$17.2	$10.8	899
1966	375	8,598	1,196	2,987	13.6	17.8	19.4	12.9	570
1967	396	7,437	1,322	3,167	13.7	21.2	20.1	13.2	912
1968	439	8,822	1,545	3,433	14.6	24.8	22.5	14.4	661
1969	481	8,224	1,500	2,705	15.5	25.6	25.9	16.7	604
1970	459	6,547	1,469	3,955	16.0	24.8	24.6	19.0	649
1971	520	8,585	2,085	4,283	15.9	31.6	26.7	20.7	888
1972	586	8,824	2,379	4,513	16.3	42.4	29.8	21.3	741
1973	665	9,658	2,057	5,026	16.6	45.7	31.4	22.1	1102
1974	665	7,331	1,352	5,463	15.6	33.6	33.2	27.0	947
1975	641	6,713	1,171	5,857	16.5	31.3	31.6	29.8	920
1976	800	8,500	1,548	6,379	16.8	44.2	30.0	35.9	835
1977	872	9,201	1,990	6,993	17.6	62.0	35.1	42.6	852
1978	995	9,165	2,023	7,783	18.3	74.9	45.0	39.9	788
1979	1097	8,419	1,749	8,668	18.1	74.6	50.2	43.7	852
1980	1174	6,400	1,313	9,510	17.9	63.7	52.5	31.2	866
1981	1210	6,255	1,100	10,591	18.0	60.2	60.1	33.2	783
1982	1261	5,049	1,072	11,109	—	58.1	59.2	37.3	—

Source: For plate glass sales, company records; all other data, *Statistical Abstract of the United States, 1984* (Washington, D.C.: U.S. Government Printing Office, 1984). p. 615.

used at first along with trend analysis over time and exponential smoothing. She felt that multiple methods were more effective than trying to rely on a single approach.

Collecting data for the suggested variables was relatively simple. Exhibit 1 contains information for division sales and for per capita income, auto production, housing starts, accidents, residential construction, nonresidential construction, nonbusiness construction, and tornadoes. In case these variables were not useful, Jackie instructed the group to be prepared to discuss the addition of extra variables. This, she hoped, would not be necessary, since more variables violated her principles of parsimony.

Before scheduling another meeting with her group, she met with Karl Backes to discuss progress to date. He was pleased with her efforts and expressed confidence that the group's results would be useful in helping to improve some of the Glass Division's problems. Karl mentioned other factors that Jackie's group may want to consider. For example, Karl suggested the following data series and/or sources: *Business Conditions Digest, Standard & Poor's Index of Stock Prices, The Conference Board's Index of Help-Wanted Advertising, The Federal Reserve Board's Index of Industrial Production,* and several of the indices from *Forbes* and *Business Week.* He indicated that these sources have been useful as predictors of sales for other Delaware P&PG divisions.

Case 1–7
National Manufacturing Company (A)*

Roy Arnold, National's sales manager, considered the high price of gasoline to be a leading factor in the rising cost of sales. In recent years, National's selling expenses have risen dramatically, especially those associated with travel. Arnold needed to find a way to increase the productivity of the sales force or to decrease the sales expenses.

National Manufacturing produced a full line of builders' hardware. Corporate objectives directed that sales would be made only to retailers or to retail voluntary chain organizations. Customers ranged from small hardware stores to large franchised operations, such as True Value and Ace Hardware. Occasionally, a sales representative would make a sale to a hardware wholesaler, only to have the sales canceled by his sales manager. National settled on this account management strategy in order to ensure that its retailers would have access to hardware supplies at reasonable prices, which would enable them to stay competitive and to stay in business.

To better understand what was happening to sales expenses, Arnold asked his sales analyst, Nancy Lindberg, to compile information that would help clarify the issues. Some of the information that National had been collecting for years included data on:

Number of customers

Orders by customers

Number of calls by salesperson by customer

Sales by customer

National's sales force of 48 people was divided into eight districts with an average of six sales representatives for each district. Depending upon location, a sales representative was assigned an entire state, parts of several states, parts of one state, or in some cases, a single metropolitan area. Large metropolitan areas, such as Chicago, were divided into two or more territories.

The size of a territory and the number of accounts in it were factors considered in determining territory potential and the need for territory modification. Arnold hoped that Lindberg could develop a market index for determining territory potential.

Lindberg began by compiling information on call activity for each sales representative by district for the last five years. Table 1 shows these results.

A cursory analysis of Table 1 shows that District 4 experienced a sizable increase in number of calls from 1980 to 1984. Since selling expenses in this district, located in the Midwest, had also increased above average, Nancy Lindberg decided to begin her detailed analysis with this district.

---

*The assistance of Wally Rachmaciej, MBA—Marketing, University of Wisconsin, Madison in the preparation of this case is greatly appreciated.

Table 1
Number of calls made by district

District	Year				
	1980	1981	1982	1983	1984
1	6,326	6,390	6,415	6,383	6,358
2	4,020	4,115	4,110	4,180	4,200
3	5,812	5,750	5,803	5,791	5,876
4	5,581	5,965	6,658	6,837	7,025
5	3,905	4,118	4,150	4,109	4,008
6	7,132	7,100	7,085	7,110	7,145
7	6,028	6,085	6,115	5,990	6,163
8	4,930	4,918	5,112	5,138	5,035
Totals	43,734	44,441	45,458	45,538	45,810

She produced a table showing the number of calls made per year for each
District 4 sales representative over the last five years. As Table 2 indicates, the
sales representative's number of calls per year had increased since 1980. This
was the result of Roy Arnold's insistence that National's sales force call on all
retail hardware and lumber dealers. In order to comply with Arnold's wishes,
most sales representatives paid close attention to their routing patterns. Dramatic
improvements resulted. Some sales representatives increased both calls and sales
without a corresponding increase in selling expenses. Some representatives,
however, probably increased the number of calls by spending less time on each
call. This is what Nancy Lindberg suspected had happened in District 4, where
calls had increased substantially, but sales had remained fairly constant. She
decided to examine 1984 sales totals by sales representative. The results appear
in Table 3.

Nancy calculated sales and calls for each representative relative to the total
and discovered that J. Harrison accounted for 19 percent of the district's sales and

Table 2
Number of calls made by District 4
sales representatives

Sales Representative	Year				
	1980	1981	1982	1983	1984
L. Daniel	1,050	1,074	1,198	1,231	1,245
D. Malley	893	954	998	957	1,001
J. Christopher.............	895	894	965	1,094	1,120
J. Harrison................	1,116	1,193	1,332	1,367	1,407
P. Tonneson	1,010	1,104	1,215	1,246	1,267
M. Leary	662	746	950	942	985
Totals	5,581	5,965	6,658	6,837	7,025

Table 3
Annual sales and number of calls
for District 4, 1984

Sales Representative	Sales	Number of Calls	Sales/Call
L. Daniel	$ 288,840	1,245	$232
D. Malley	220,220	1,001	220
J. Christopher	254,240	1,120	227
J. Harrison.	295,470	1,407	210
P. Tonneson	291,410	1,267	230
M. Leary	224,580	985	228
Totals	$1,574,760	7,025	$224

made 20 percent of the district's calls. While this may seem reasonable, according to Nancy's calculations, all other sales representatives had a percent of sales equal to or greater than their percent of calls. For example, L. Daniel accounted for 18 percent of both district sales and calls. Nancy decided to zero in her analysis on Harrison's territory.

With existing data, Nancy was able to identify calls and sales of Harrison's 23 counties, located in south-central Wisconsin (Exhibit 1). Table 4 shows the county breakdown for J. Harrison. He lived in the district in Beloit (Rock County), a city that borders the state of Illinois.

Before she could complete her analysis, Lindberg was promoted to a market research analyst position and Joseph Kubb was promoted from his position as National's sales representative in Houston, Texas to fill her spot. Lindberg worked with Kubb to provide further direction for the sales analysis he was to complete. They agreed that in order to understand the recent increase in selling expenses, Kubb needed to first develop an index that could be used as a guide for planning the number of calls that should be made in each territory. He could then compare the salesmen's actual performance versus this benchmark performance. Kubb wondered if Arnold had been correct in urging the salesmen to increase their calls. He thought they might be working pretty hard already. Kubb agreed with Nancy's idea of focusing on J. Harrison's case. Because Kubb remembered a similar problem situation that had occurred in Texas that had been the result of inadequate territory coverage and poor routing, he decided to see if Harrison was effectively covering his 23-county territory.

Kubb examined the table that Lindberg had constructed that showed the actual number of calls per year made by Harrison in each county (Table 4). The fact that Harrison made absolutely no calls in three counties (i.e., Crawford, Green Lake, and Richland) immediately caught Kubb's eye. When asked about this, Harrison replied, "I go where the business is." However, a conversation with a former colleague of Harrison's (now a sales representative in Texas) revealed that Harrison considered himself an urban-type and preferred calling on larger stores located in bigger cities. Harrison often admitted to his colleagues that he had a

Exhibit 1
Harrison's 23-county territory

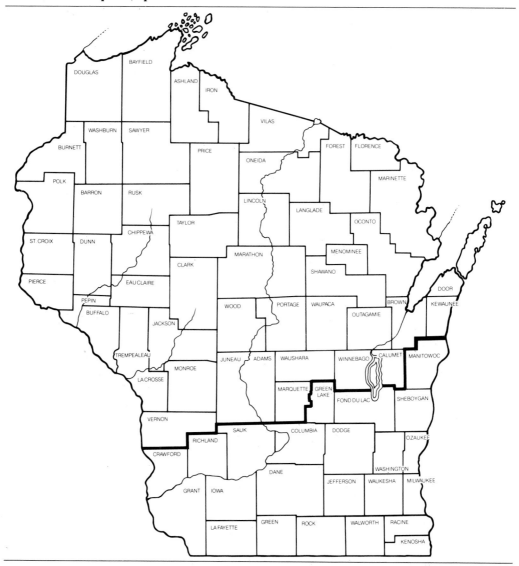

hard time developing good rapport with many of the managers of small town retail outlets. Instead of trying harder to develop good rapport with these store managers, Harrison often ignored them, rationalizing that he should spend more time at the larger stores since "that's where the business is."

**Table 4
Sales and calls for J. Harrison's
territory, 1984**

County	Calls	Sales
Columbia	9	$ 3,875
Crawford	0	0
Dane	157	32,379
Dodge	55	8,412
Fond du Lac	28	8,387
Grant	17	4,903
Green	17	4,053
Green Lake	0	0
Iowa	10	3,152
Jefferson	52	7,797
Kenosha	80	14,991
Lafayette	19	1,850
Manitowoc	37	789
Milwaukee	403	99,812
Ozaukee	30	8,131
Racine	100	19,894
Richland	0	0
Rock	83	14,772
Sauk	10	4,563
Sheboygan	44	12,206
Walworth	45	7,579
Washington	46	8,223
Waukesha	165	29,702
Total	1,407	$295,470

The conversation with Harrison's former colleague made Kubb further suspect that Harrison was not covering his territory properly. Being unfamiliar with the 23 county territory, Kubb sought out a proxy measure that would give him a basic idea of where business potential existed for Harrison. Kubb used the *1983-County and City Data Book* and the *1977 Census of Retail Trade* to generate the data found in Table 5. Column 1 lists the total sales by county for *all* retail sales accounted for by the kind of business that is most closely related to National's products (i.e., building materials, hardware, garden supply, mobile homes dealers).

Column 3 lists the number of business establishments of this business type in each county. Kubb hoped to use this information as a benchmark to evaluate Harrison's coverage.

Kubb next requested a copy of Harrison's monthly itinerary (see Table 6). Each member of National's sales force was required to develop a standard monthly itinerary, based on 21 working days per month and six calls per day. Since National's sales calls were not made by appointment, the salesman could develop his itinerary according to his personal preferences. For example, Harrison liked to

Table 5
Sales and calls for J. Harrison's territory, 1984

County	Total Retail Sales, All Establishments ($000)*	Sales by Kind of Business ($000)†	Number of Kind of Business Establishments†
Columbia	$ 136,022	$ 13,422	35
Crawford	48,748	3,939	14
Dane	1,221,180	82,001	119
Dodge	164,825	(D)	44
Fond du Lac	270,418	(D)	41
Grant	137,600	12,332	40
Green	139,313	10,259	23
Green Lake	69,029	(D)	18
Iowa	44,101	(D)	13
Jefferson	168,860	7,572	31
Kenosha	340,956	13,246	44
Lafayette	25,402	(D)	14
Manitowoc	217,163	10,058	36
Milwaukee	3,453,803	104,878	254
Ozaukee	175,756	13,672	28
Racine	531,580	30,939	59
Richland	37,878	3,973	14
Rock	483,599	31,186	56
Sauk	151,170	15,807	40
Sheboygan	286,544	20,888	42
Walworth	209,091	19,596	46
Washington	203,444	21,270	38
Waukesha	957,851	53,434	114

D = Unable to disclose information due to competitive situation.
*Source: *1983-County and City Data Book*, A Statistical Abstract Supplement, U.S. Department of Commerce, Bureau of the Census.
†Source: *1977 Census of Retail Trade*, Vol. II Geographic Area Statistics, Part 3., U.S. Department of Commerce, Bureau of the Census.

work a full day in Milwaukee county on the first day of each week. Notice that this itinerary allows for 126 calls per month (21×6). Harrison was making only about 117 calls per month (1407 calls/year divided by 12). The difference may be due to holidays, vacations, occasional sales meetings, etc.

Kubb found it interesting that, according to his itinerary, Harrison scheduled only one overnight stay each month. Company policy dictated that salesmen with large enough territories (such as Harrison's territory) could spend up to four overnights per month. Harrison preferred not to exercise this option. When questioned, he replied somewhat defensively, "I really don't like staying overnight in some strange city. If I could, I would come home every day. I like driving, too. What does it matter, as long as I get my work done? I would think that the company would appreciate me keeping my overnight stays to the bare minimum."

Table 6
Harrison's current monthly itinerary

Call	Day 1	Day 2	Day 3	Day 4	Day 5
1	Milwaukee	Green	Dane	Kenosha	Dane
2	Milwaukee	Green	Dane	Kenosha	Dane
3	Milwaukee	Lafayette	Jefferson	Kenosha	Dane
4	Milwaukee	Grant	Waukesha	Kenosha	Rock
5	Milwaukee	Grant	Waukesha	Kenosha	Rock
6	Milwaukee (home)	Rock (home)	Waukesha (home)	Kenosha (home)	Rock (home)

Call	Day 6	Day 7	Day 8	Day 9	Day 10
1	Milwaukee	Jefferson	Manitowoc	Sheboygan	Dane
2	Milwaukee	Jefferson	Manitowoc	Sheboygan	Dane
3	Milwaukee	Dodge	Manitowoc	Fond du Lac	Dane
4	Milwaukee	Dodge	Manitowoc	Fond du Lac	Rock
5	Milwaukee	Dane	Sheboygan	Fond du Lac	Rock
6	Milwaukee (home)	Dane (home)	Sheboygan (overnight)	Columbia (home)	Rock (home)

Call	Day 11	Day 12	Day 13	Day 14	Day 15
1	Milwaukee	Jefferson	Kenosha	Racine	Waukesha
2	Milwaukee	Jefferson	Racine	Racine	Waukesha
3	Milwaukee	Dodge	Racine	Racine	Waukesha
4	Milwaukee	Dodge	Racine	Racine	Waukesha
5	Milwaukee	Dane	Racine	Milwaukee	Walworth
6	Milwaukee (home)	Dane (home)	Racine (home)	Washington (home)	Walworth (home)

Call	Day 16	Day 17	Day 18	Day 19	Day 20
1	Milwaukee	Ozaukee	Milwaukee	Dodge	Waukesha
2	Milwaukee	Ozaukee	Milwaukee	Sauk	Waukesha
3	Milwaukee	Ozaukee	Milwaukee	Iowa	Waukesha
4	Milwaukee	Washington	Waukesha	Lafayette	Waukesha
5	Milwaukee	Washington	Waukesha	Dane	Walworth
6	Milwaukee (home)	Washington (home)	Waukesha (home)	Dane (home)	Walworth (home)

Call	Day 21
1	Milwaukee
2	Milwaukee
3	Milwaukee
4	Milwaukee
5	Milwaukee
6	Milwaukee

Table 7
Distance from Rock County (Beloit)

County/Major City	Miles from Beloit
Columbia (Portage)	83
Crawford (Prairie du Chien)	136
Dane (Madison)	51
Dodge (Beaver Dam)	75
Fond du Lac (Fond du Lac)	104
Grant (Lancaster)	101
Green (Monroe)	33
Green Lake (Green Lake)	106
Iowa (Dodgeville)	75
Jefferson (Fort Atkinson)	33
Kenosha (Kenosha)	67
Lafayette (Darlington)	64
Manitowoc (Manitowoc)	153
Milwaukee (Milwaukee)	73
Ozaukee (Port Washington)	101
Racine (Racine)	70
Richland (Richland Center)	109
Rock (Beloit)	0
Sauk (Baraboo)	93
Sheboygan (Sheboygan)	125
Walworth (Lake Geneva)	34
Washington (West Bend)	96
Waukesha (Waukesha)	57

To get a better understanding of the mileage distances involved, Kubb completed Table 7. This table lists distances from Beloit, Wisconsin (Harrison's home) to a major city (usually the county seat) of each county in Harrison's territory.

Kubb now felt that he was armed with enough information to closely analyze Harrison's territory coverage. If problems were found, he realized that corrective recommendations would be expected.

Case 1-8
Midwest Medical Equipment Corporation

Mervin Stipp, sales manager of Midwest Medical, was examining the results of an extensive data collection activity concerning Midwest's weak market position. Midwest sells in a regional market and has a market share of 8.1 percent. Midwest's products are sold primarily to hospitals and medical supply houses, which in turn sell to hospitals, clinics, doctors, convalescent centers, and other health care operations. According to the results in Exhibit 1, Midwest has 2,032 active accounts in a regional market containing 4,670 potential accounts. Stipp is concerned about an account penetration of almost 44 percent that produces only 8 percent in market share. Moreover, wide differences in market share among the sales force suggest that problems might exist concerning territory size.

Midwest sales representatives had territories composed of several counties, although two representatives, Moore and Houston, shared the Chicago metropolitan area. On the other hand, Tyler had a territory that included Dallas-Fort Worth, Houston, San Antonio, and New Orleans. Nelson's territory was the Denver area. The Detroit metropolitan area was Reitman's assignment. Minneapolis-St. Paul, Rochester, Madison, and Milwaukee comprised Myers's territory. Sikes was responsible for St. Louis, Kansas City, Omaha, Tulsa, and Oklahoma City. Finally, Hester covered Washington, D.C., Baltimore, and Philadelphia.

Each Midwest sales representative was expected to make five to 10 calls each day, although circumstances permitted considerable variation. Compensation was comprised of a base salary ranging from $12,500 to $18,750. Bonuses were paid quarterly and were based on the gross margin of each representative's sales. Gross margin was used to discourage price cutting by the sales force. Gross margin also provided an incentive for the sales force to sell more profitable products.

The sales force is expected to develop new accounts, although Stipp wonders whether the sales force has enough time. He suspects that some territories may be either too large or have too many accounts for one person to cover adequately. Realignment of territories may be a partial solution, although increasing the size of the sales force is also a possibility. Finally, Stipp feels that call patterns are not closely related to size of account. He is convinced that 20 percent of Midwest's customers provide 80 percent of the sales but that some sales representatives spend too much time calling on small accounts. He recalls reading call reports prepared by Tyler and being amazed that one customer who does an annual business of $2,500 was called on two times in one month. When questioned about this apparent misallocation of time, Tyler's response was unnerving. Tyler said, "I was in the area so I decided to drop in and see what was happening."

Analysis of account size for the active accounts produced the following breakdown:

Exhibit 1
Territory sale analysis, 1983

Sales Representative	Territory	Sales Potential ($000)	Sales Volume ($000)	Market Share	Potential Accounts	Active Accounts	Sales Calls	Base Salary	Bonus	Sales Expenses
D. Myers	Minneapolis-St. Paul, Rochester, Madison, Milwaukee	$ 6,861	$1,036	15.1%	433	117	2,192	$ 17,500	$ 2,240	$ 4,375
J. Hester	Washington, D.C., Baltimore, Philadelphia	9,603	864	9.0	728	400	2,138	15,000	1,950	3,750
B. Moore	Chicago	11,300	893	7.9	685	343	1,855	16,250	1,825	5,125
M. Houston	Chicago	10,468	806	7.7	673	370	2,040	13,750	1,740	3,375
W. Reitman	Detroit	6,838	1,087	15.9	498	289	2,027	18,750	2,375	4,125
S. Tyler	Dallas–Ft. Worth, Houston, San Antonio, New Orleans	24,230	703	2.9	770	208	1,782	13,750	1,600	4,625
D. Nelson	Denver	6,585	1,060	16.1	428	205	2,096	15,625	2,200	3,875
T. Sikes	St. Louis, Kansas City, Tulsa, Oklahoma City	9,374	478	5.1	455	100	1,514	12,500	1,010	5,375
Totals		$85,259	$6,927	8.1%	4,670	2,032	15,644	$123,125	$14,940	$34,625

Large	400
Medium	715
Small	917
Total	2,032

Stipp suspected that this distribution was unlike the distribution by size for the remainder of the accounts. He was sure that the distribution among territories was not the same. Further analysis showed the following distribution by each sales representative:

Distribution of Active Accounts

	Large	Medium	Small	Total
D. Myers	40	47	30	117
J. Hester	90	130	180	400
B. Moore	53	102	188	343
M. Houston	62	105	203	370
W. Reitman	70	130	89	289
S. Tyler.............	17	77	114	208
D. Nelson	52	99	54	205
T. Sikes	16	25	59	100
Total	400	715	917	2,032

Further investigation by Stipp led him to believe that the following call frequencies should be adopted as guidelines:

Large accounts	24 times/year
Medium accounts	12 times/year
Small accounts	6 times/year
Prospective accounts...................................	6 times/year

Stipp realized that not all prospective accounts should be called the same number of times a year. Some represent more substantial opportunities than others and may deserve more than six calls a year.

Case 1–9
The Goldman Chemical Company[*]

"A substantial growth in sales and a shift in market strength from the Northeast to the South and Southwest have knocked our sales territories completely out of line," said Bill King, sales manager of the Goldman Chemical Company. "The morale of the sales force is low," he continued, "because some of the salespeople feel that the present territories don't afford an equal opportunity to earn commissions."

The Company

Goldman Chemical was a wholesale chemical house supplying specialized chemicals to paper processors throughout the country. The several thousand potential users of the company's products ranged in size from small operators to giants such as International Paper and Crown Zellerbach. Competition was intense, with sales going to the firms offering the best combination of quality, service, and price.

The company's sales increased significantly between the years 1976 and 1979. A continuation of this trend was expected in 1980, although there was some concern about general economic conditions. The company started in the East and extended operations westward after 1960. Twenty-four states were serviced in 1979.

The Sale

The typical Goldman customer purchased $17,000 in chemicals yearly, although the range was from $50 to over $120,000. Some sales were contracted, but most were solicited directly by the company's 10-man sales force. About 70 percent of the Goldman line consisted of standard items for which purchasing agents made the final buying choice. The remaining items were specialized "brand" products and required the approval of production personnel. The chemical companies, in 1979, faced a buyers' market, thus the demands for service were heavy. A purchasing agent from one of the larger paper firms recently said to a Goldman salesman, "We might as well get one thing straight. You know as well as I do that your competitors can beat you in price and quality, so if you want our business we had better see some real service."

---

[*]This case was prepared by Professor Robert T. Davis, Stanford University, Graduate School of Business. Reprinted from *Stanford Business Cases 1980* with permission of the publishers, Stanford University Graduate School of Business, © 1980 by the Board of Trustees of the Leland Stanford Junior University.

Salespeople, during their calls, checked the performance of products sold previously, followed up delivery promises, and sought to introduce the customer to new uses for existing products as well as to new products. Goldman salespeople were expected to have a chemical engineering background because of the technical orientation of their customers.

Salesmen/women averaged five calls daily in metropolitan centers and four in non-metropolitan areas. Typically, they spent four days in each week on metropolitan calls. Accounts were classified by purchases as A, B, or C, the limits for A accounts being "over $50,000;" for B accounts, "between $10,000 and $50,000;" and for C accounts, "below $10,000." A accounts were called on weekly, B accounts monthly, and C accounts quarterly. About 10 percent of a salesperson's time was devoted to "service call-backs."

The Salesmen

The Goldman Company employed 10 salesmen/women, ranging in experience from six months to 25 years. Mr. King was generally satisfied with his sales force and thought them technically qualified to sell the full line.

Each salesperson had a monthly drawing account of between $1,000 and $1,200. "This," said Mr. King, "is justified for the missionary work that they are required to do." Above the draw, compensation was by straight commission. Commission rates varied with the profitability of products, and according to the sales manager, there was no apparent tendency for salespeople to overlook the full-line in favor of higher-margin items. "The nature of our selling is such," said Mr. King, "that the salesperson first has to establish him/herself with the account. Once this is done, full-line selling is not a problem."

Mr. King was convinced that differences in compensation (see Exhibit 1) arose from the distribution of territories rather than the individual abilities of the salespeople. Of this, he said, "I would expect some variations in commissions earned, but not to the extent we've experienced. I don't see that much difference among the members of our sales force."

Mr. King gave the following appraisal of his 10 salespeople: *Phil Haney* is our "oldtimer," having been with us since 1955. He is one year from our mandatory retirement age of 65, and he likes to remind people of his 20-odd years of seniority. He hasn't been particularly easy for me to work with. Phil has strong personal ideas about selling, many of which are "academically" outdated but which are apparently accepted by his customers. He has what you might call an old-time personality and has been tremendously successful over the years. I often wonder what kind of volume could be generated by combining Phil's personality with some of our new merchandising techniques. Phil has always worked Manhattan, although initially he sold to all of New York City.

Mary Whalen is in her sixth year with the company and sells to accounts in the New Jersey-Pennsylvania area. Whalen is an excellent saleswoman who is obvi-

Exhibit 1
Performance of salespeople, 1978–1979*

Salesman	Territory	Terr. No.	Sales Record† 1978	Sales Record† 1979*	Number of Accounts Metro	Number of Accounts Nonmetro	Number of Accounts Total	Compensation	Cost Percent to Sales 1979*	Planned Sales 1980†	Planned Accounts 1970	Estimated Share of Market 1969*	Estimated Share of Market 1970	Selling Cost Percent to Planned Sales
Ives	Me, N.H., Ver.	1	not covered under present territory arrangement							$ 82	7	—	26.0%	
	Mass.		$ 972	$ 816	54	13	67			648	54	24.0%	18.6	
	R.I.		240	180	13	—	13			82	7	39.7	49.6	
	Conn.		240	240	13	7	20			180	13	21.2	19.9	
	Total terr.		$ 1,452	$ 1,216	80	20	100	$ 25,200	2.1%	$ 972	81	23.2	19.9	2.6%
Gordon	N.Y. State	2	488	408	27	7	34	13,200	3.2	324	27	50.2	50.3	4.1
Haney	Manhattan	3	4,054	3,888	162	—	162	37,200	0.96	3,408	142	18.7	18.6	1.1
Richards	Other N.Y. City & L.I.	4	1,452	1,608	61	6	67	28,800	1.8	1,784	74	25.3	25.2	1.6
Whalen	New Jersey	5	324	406	27	7	34			488	40	10.6	16.5	
	Pennsylvania		2,592	2,424	88	13	101			2,112	88	18.2	17.0	
	Total terr.		$ 2,916	$ 2,830	115	20	135	$ 30,000	1.1	$2,600	128	16.9	17.0	1.2
Ericson	Del., Md., Wash., D.C.	6	not covered under present territory arrangement							160	13	—	20.0	
	Va., WVa.		240	324	13	13	26			324	27	19.9	16.2	
	N. Carolina		240	324	20	7	27			408	34	16.5	16.3	
	S. Carolina		82	160	7	7	14			324	27	11.0	16.5	
	Georgia		240	240	7	13	20			240	20	18.5	14.9	
	Florida		160	324	27	0	27			408	34	20.2	16.1	
	Total terr.		$ 962	$ 1,372	74	40	114	$ 20,400	1.5	$ 1,864	155	16.3	16.4	1.1

Division		State												
Davey	7	Mississippi	82	160	7	7	14			160	13	16.7	16.6	
		Alabama	240	324	13	13	26			324	27	18.3	18.3	
		Kty. & Tenn.	—	82	7	—	7			82	7	16.5	16.5	
		Total terr.	$ 322	$ 566	27	20	47	$ 16,800	3.0	$ 566	47	17.4	17.4	3.0
Owens	8	Ohio & Ind.	not covered under present territory arrangement							160	13	—	14.1	
		Illinois	$ 1,534	$ 1,370	51	7	58			1,214	51	16.2	16.2	
		Michigan	564	564	40	7	47			480	40	15.1	15.1	
		Wisconsin	not covered under present territory arrangement							82	7	—	16.6	
		Total terr.	$ 2,098	$ 1,934	91	14	105	$ 27,600	1.4	$ 1,936	111	15.1	15.7	1.4
Billings	9	Minn., Iowa, N. Dak., S. Dak., Nebraska	not covered under present territory arrangement							240	20	—	18.6	
		Missouri	160	564	40	7	47			730	61	11.4	15.1	
		Kansas	—	82	7	—	7			160	13	8.3	16.6	
		Ark., La., Okla.	not covered under present territory arrangement							160	13	—	16.7	
		Texas	160	324	20	7	27			816	67	6.6	14.6	
		Total terr.	$ 320	$ 970	67	14	81	$ 18,000	1.9	$ 2,106	174	7.9	15.5	.85
Sharp	10	Mont., Wyo., Idaho	not covered under present territory arrangement											
		Utah, Col., Az., N.M.	not covered under present territory arrangement							240	20	—	18.7	
		Wash., Ore.	$ 160	$ 240	7	13	20			324	27	18.9	16.6	
		California	564	648	38	7	45			816	67	11.3	14.3	
		Nevada	not covered under present territory arrangement											
		Total terr.	$ 724	$ 888	45	20	65	$ 18,000	2.0	$ 1,380	114	15.2	15.4	1.3
		Grand total, United States	$14,788	$15,680	749	161	910	$235,200	1.5	$16,940	1,053	16.6	17.8	1.4

*Projected.
†000s omitted.

ously aware of the "smoothness" of her sales approach. She carries this self assurance to the extent that she often becomes very indifferent whenever I offer a few suggestions for improvement in her sales techniques.

Norman Ives is probably the most ambitious, aggressive, and argumentative salesman we have. He has been with the company since 1966, following his discharge from the Army. He reached the rank of Lt. Colonel at the age of 30 but had no interest in a military career. Norman really stormed into his present territory in 1969 and, in the first year, doubled its volume. He's extremely independent but will work hard to implement any sales program that he agrees with. If he doesn't agree, though, I get absolutely no cooperation. In 1976, Norman's territory began to slip—primarily, I think, because of a shift in market strength. Moreover, his compensation fell from $30,000 in 1976 to $25,000 in 1979.

Bob Ericson has been with the company three years now and I still get the feeling that he is unsure of himself. He seems somewhat confused and overworked, probably because he's trying to serve too many accounts in too large an area. Surprisingly enough, though, the general growth in the territory has given Bob a significant increase in sales in 1979.

Dick Richards is the "mystery man" of the sales force. Neither the other salespeople nor I know very much about Dick's personal life. He's quiet and unassuming and knows the Goldman line amazingly well. I've often wondered why Dick chose sales over research work. Sales in his territory have continued to grow, which is unusual, considering an opposite trend in neighboring territories.

Warren Sharp is the guy on the sales force who keeps the rest of us going. Warren is slightly rotund and always good-natured. His accounts seem genuinely happy to see him when he makes a call. He worked the New York State territory for his first two years and then moved into the West Coast when we took on Joe Gordon. At first, I worried about Warren's ability to get serious long enough to make a sale. However, this has not proved to be a problem.

Gus Billings joined the company in 1973, after four years with a competitor. Gus is easygoing, even-tempered, and very popular with his customers. Despite his even temperament, Gus was somewhat upset the last time I saw him. We plan to activate five more states in his territory during 1980. This would make Gus responsible for a geographic area covering roughly one fourth of the United States. He is already calling on 81 accounts in six states, and this keeps him away from home much of the time.

Barbara Owens joined us in 1975 after receiving an M.S. degree in chemistry from the University of Pennsylvania. After the normal three-month training program, during which time Barbara traveled with Mary Whalen, she stepped into her territory and was immediately successful. Barbara is earnest and conscientious, and has increased her sales volume each year. She's not what you would call the "sales type," but she is always exceedingly successful in using the merchandising techniques that I try to implement.

Joe Gordon is the youngster of our sales force at 23. Joe went into New York State in the spring of 1978. The territory is relatively inactive and we usually try to assign it to new salespeople. Sales have dropped from the time that Joe took

Exhibit 2
Number of customers by $ volume for the year 1979

Salesperson	0 to 1,999	2,000 to 4,499	4,500 to 9,999	10,000 to 19,999	20,000 to 29,999	30,000 to 49,999	50,000 to 99,999	100,000 to 199,999	Total
Ives	32	30	15	10	5	5	2	1	100
Gordon	10	5	4	12	1	2	—	—	34
Haney	26	30	20	31	22	20	10	3	162
Richards	9	3	13	15	15	8	4	—	67
Whalen	16	40	30	10	10	21	6	2	135
Ericson	34	32	21	8	8	7	4	—	114
Davey	14	10	6	7	9	—	1	—	47
Owens	33	11	19	13	15	9	3	2	105
Billings	30	6	13	14	16	2	—	—	81
Sharp	10	12	24	8	10	—	—	1	65
Total	214	179	165	128	111	74	30	9	910
Dollar volume totals (000)	256	730	1,488	2,304	3,328	3,552	2,700	1,620	15,978
Cumulative dollar total (000)		986	2,474	4,778	8,106	11,658	14,358	15,978	
Cumulative percent dollar volume	1.6	6.2	15.5	29.9	50.7	73.0	89.8	100	
Cumulative percent accounts	23.5	43.2	61.3	75.4	87.6	95.7	99.0	100	

over and he is very apologetic about the situation. I've told him that he would have to expect some tough moments, and I think his determination to "make a go of it" will be realized because of his conscientiousness. He's always receptive to any help that is offered and tries hard to put suggestions to use. That territory has always been a "dog."

Jim Davey is in his third year and I'd say he's good at selling. Jim always dresses impeccably in Ivy League fashion and he has good bearing. He responds well to any suggestion that I make to him. It's a funny thing, but whenever I travel with Jim the sales in the territory increase for the next several months. After that, right back to the previous level. Accounts within the territory are scattered, which keeps Jim on the road most of the time.

Aside from the morale problem, Bill King had other reasons for wanting to change the territories. "We expect continued growth," he said, "and at least for the time being, I plan to add no new people. I'm positive that by redistributing the sales territories, we can get more sales effort from the sales force as a group and thus handle our growth."

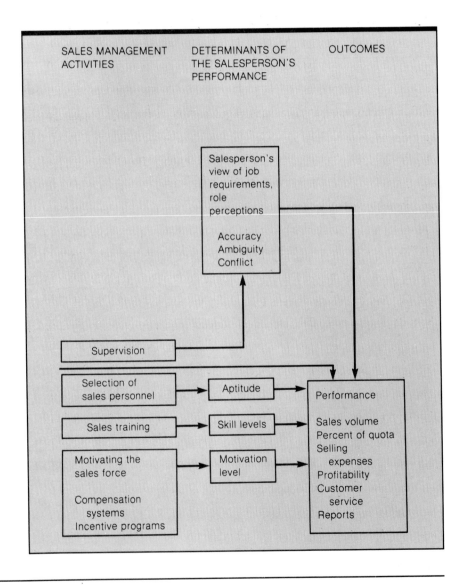

SALES MANAGEMENT ACTIVITIES

DETERMINANTS OF THE SALESPERSON'S PERFORMANCE

OUTCOMES

Salesperson's view of job requirements, role perceptions

Accuracy
Ambiguity
Conflict

Supervision

Selection of sales personnel

Aptitude

Sales training

Skill levels

Motivating the sales force

Compensation systems
Incentive programs

Motivation level

Performance

Sales volume
Percent of quota
Selling
  expenses
Profitability
Customer
  service
Reports

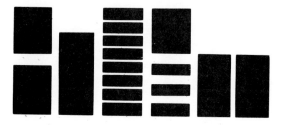

Implementation of the Sales Program

Part 2 explores the policies and procedures involved in implementing a firm's sales program. Chapter 8 provides a model that incorporates the main factors that affect a salesperson's performance and job behavior. The remaining chapters then elaborate on the factors and sales management decisions that influence them. Chapter 9 describes the demands salespeople receive from their customers, managers, and families. It also discusses how supervisory policies can be designed to help them deal with ambiguous and conflicting demands. Chapters 10 and 11 examine the personal characteristics that are related to sales aptitude, and the ways in which recruiting and selection procedures can be designed to build a sales force with the abilities needed to carry out the required selling tasks and activities. The objectives of sales training and a variety of training techniques are examined in Chapter 12. Finally, Chapters 13 and 14 discuss the kinds of rewards that motivate people to expend effort on various aspects of their jobs and how these rewards can be incorporated into effective sales compensation and incentive programs.

Chapter 8

Model of Salesperson Performance

In Chapter 1, it was suggested that the task of sales management involves three interrelated processes: (1) formulation of a strategic sales program, (2) implementation of the sales program, and (3) evaluation and control of sales force performance. Part 1 of the book concentrated on the first of these processes; this part concentrates on the second.

For sales managers to implement a sales program, they must motivate and direct the behavior of sales representatives. This requires that sales managers understand why people in the sales force behave the way they do so that policies and procedures can be devised to direct that behavior toward desired objectives. This chapter offers a model by which sales force behavior can be understood. The model highlights the links between a salesperson's performance and the determinants of that performance. Do not be surprised if you do not completely understand the model upon reading this chapter as the purpose of the chapter is only to outline the model and to highlight the various components. Complete model understanding should develop as you study the remaining chapters in this section which discuss the basic components of the model in detail.

The Model

The literature on industrial and organizational psychology suggests that a worker's job performance is a function of five basic factors: (1) motivation, (2) aptitude, (3) skill level, (4) role perceptions, and (5) personal, organizational, and environmental variables.[1] Figure 8-1 presents an overall model of a salesperson's performance, which includes these factors as primary determinants.

Although not pictured in the model, there is substantial interaction among the determinants. Much of the published literature, for example, holds that the various factors combine multiplicatively to influence performance. The rationale is that if a worker is deficient in any of these factors, the individual could be expected to perform poorly. If the salesperson had native ability and the motivation to perform but lacked understanding of how the job should be done, for example, he or she could be expected to perform at a low level. Similarly, if the salesperson had the ability and accurately perceived how the job should be performed but lacked motivation, the representative is likely to perform poorly. The empirical research is somewhat equivocal about whether the factors do combine multiplicatively, but it is fairly certain that the determinants are not independent. There are substantial interaction effects among and between them. Although we know very little about the form or the magnitude of those interactions, we need to recognize that they do exist.

---

[1] This chapter borrows heavily from the following articles: Orville C. Walker, Jr., Gilbert A. Churchill, Jr., and Neil M. Ford, "Motivation and Performance in Industrial Selling: Present Knowledge and Needed Research," *Journal of Marketing Research* 14 (May 1977), pp. 156–68; and Orville C. Walker, Jr., Gilbert A. Churchill, Jr., and Neil M. Ford, "Where Do We Go From Here? Selected Conceptual and Empirical Issues Concerning the Motivation and Performance of the Industrial Salesforce," in *Critical Issues in Sales Management. State of the Art and Future Research Needs*, ed. Gerald Albaum and Gilbert A. Churchill, Jr. (Eugene: University of Oregon, 1979), pp. 10–75.

Figure 8–1
Model of the determinants of
salesperson's performance

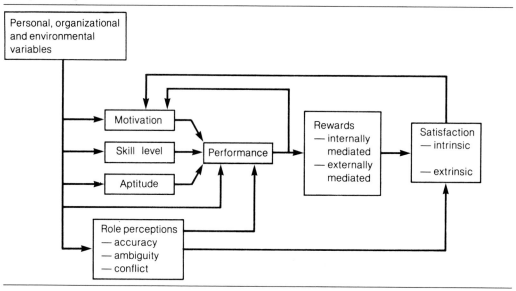

The Role Perceptions Component

The *role* attached to the position of salesperson in any firm represents the set of activities or behaviors to be performed by any person occupying that position. This role is defined largely through the expectations, demands, and pressures communicated to the salesperson by his or her role partners. These partners include persons both outside and within the individual's firm who have a vested interest in how the salesperson performs the job—top management, the individual's supervisor, customers, and family members. The salesperson's *perceptions* of these expectations strongly influence the individual's definition of his or her role in the company and behavior on the job.

The role perceptions component of the model has three dimensions: role accuracy, perceived role conflict, and perceived role ambiguity. The term *role accuracy* refers to the degree to which the salesperson's perceptions of his or her role partners' demands—particularly company superiors—are accurate. Does what the salesperson thinks his superiors want him to do on the job correspond to their actual expectations and demands?

Perceived role conflict arises when a salesperson believes that the role demands of two or more of his or her role partners are incompatible. Thus, he or she cannot possibly satisfy them all at the same time. A saleswoman suffers from perceptions of conflict, for example, when a customer demands a delivery schedule or credit terms that the saleswoman believes will be unacceptable to her company superiors.

Perceived role ambiguity occurs when the salesman feels he does not have the information necessary to perform his job adequately. The salesman may be uncertain about what some role partners expect of him in certain situations, how he should go about satisfying those expectations, or how his performance will be evaluated and rewarded.

The model indicates that the three role perception variables have psychological consequences for the individual salesperson. They can produce dissatisfaction with the job. They can also affect the salesperson's motivation to perform. All these effects can in turn produce higher turnover within the sales force and poorer performance.

Industrial salespeople are particularly vulnerable to role inaccuracy, conflict, and ambiguity because of the nature of their jobs. Yet several personal and organizational variables can exert some impact on people's role perceptions. Fortunately, many of these variables can be controlled or influenced by sales management policies and methods, thus allowing the sales manager to influence the performance of individual salespeople.

The entire role perceptions component of the model is explored more fully in Chapter 9. That chapter includes a more detailed look at the consequences of inaccuracy, conflict, and ambiguity and the factors that affect these role perceptions.

The Motivation Component

Over the years, *motivation* has meant various, and often inconsistent, things in the literature, although some recent consensus seems to be emerging.[2] For our purposes, *motivation* is viewed as the amount of effort the salesperson desires to expend on each activity or task associated with the job. These include calling on potential new accounts, developing sales presentations, and filling out reports.

The salesperson's motivation to expend effort on any task seems to be a function of the person's (1) *expectancies,* or estimates of the probability that expending a given effort on the task will lead to improved performance on some specific dimensions, and (2) *valences for performance,* or perceptions on the desirability of attaining improved performance on these dimensions. The salesperson's valence for performance on a specific dimension in turn seems to be a function of the salesperson's (1) *instrumentalities,* or estimates of the probability that achieving improved performance on that dimension will lead to increased attainment of particular rewards, and (2) *valences for rewards,* or perceptions of the desirability of receiving increased rewards as a result of improved performance.

---

[2] John P. Campbell and Robert D. Pritchard, "Motivation Theory in Industrial and Organizational Psychology," in *Handbook of Industrial and Organizational Psychology,* ed. Marvin D. Dunnette (Chicago: Rand McNally, 1976), p. 65.

The salesperson's expectancy, instrumentality, and valence perceptions are not directly under the sales manager's control. They can certainly be influenced, however, by things the sales manager does, such as how he or she supervises the salesperson or rewards the individual. Since the salesperson's motivation strongly influences subsequent performance, the sales manager must be sensitive to how various factors exert their impact. These issues are explored more fully in Chapter 13.

The Aptitude Component

The overall model of sales performance in Figure 8-1 treats the sales aptitude of an individual largely as a constraint on the person's ability to perform the sales job. This assumes there is an adequate understanding of the role to be performed, motivation, and learned skills and an absence of other constraints. In other words, two people with equal motivation, role perceptions, and skills might perform at very different levels because one has more aptitude or ability than the other.

Aptitude and its impact on sales performance have historically received the greatest amount of research attention. Sales ability has been thought to be a function of such personal and psychological characteristics as the following:

1. Physical factors, such as age, height, sex, and physical attractiveness.
2. Mental abilities, such as verbal intelligence and mathematical ability.
3. Personality characteristics, such as empathy, ego strength, sociability, aggressiveness, and dominance.

Numerous studies have attempted to predict variations in sales performance using one or more of these aptitude variables. Many of these studies have found statistically significant relationships between the aptitude variables and performance. However, the broad measures of aptitude by themselves have not been able to explain a very large proportion of the variation in sales performance.[3]

There are several reasons why broad measures of aptitude may not predict sales performance. Consider first the motivation component of the overall model. Motivation has been defined as the desire to expend effort on specific sales tasks. This effort should lead to improved performance on one or more dimensions. The link between the effort a salesperson expends on any task and the resulting performance achieved is affected by that salesperson's ability to carry out the task successfully. In other words, the *concept of sales ability or aptitude is very task-specific.* Therefore, the appropriate definition of aptitude, and the appropriate measures of the construct, may vary greatly from industry to industry, firm to firm, and product line to product line. It depends on what specific tasks must be

[3] For a summary of the results of these studies, see Edwin E Ghiselli, *The Validity of Occupational Aptitude Tests* (New York: John Wiley & Sons, 1966), pp. 41–43. For a recent example, see Lawrence M. Lamont and William J. Lundstrom, "Identifying Successful Industrial Salesmen by Personality and Personal Characteristics," *Journal of Marketing Research* 14 (November 1977), pp. 517–29.

performed and what dimensions of performance are considered important. The broad measures of aptitude may simply fail to capture the task-specific nature of the construct.

Second, aptitude may affect performance in more ways than by simply moderating an individual's ability to do the job. It may also affect the salesperson's motivation to perform. It seems, for example, that the salesperson's *perceived* ability to perform a task and general self-confidence influence the magnitude of the person's expectancy estimates.[4] Furthermore, the salesperson's intelligence and feelings as to whether he largely controls his own destiny or whether this destiny is largely controlled by outside forces (internal versus external locus of control) affect the magnitude of the individual's instrumentality estimates.[5] Thus, the salesperson's intelligence and perceptions of his or her own ability as a salesperson may strongly influence the individual's motivation to expend effort on various aspects of the job. All this suggests that objective measures of sales aptitude may be insufficient by themselves. Predictions of sales performance could be improved by including measures of perceived aptitude as well.

The Skill Level Component

Whereas role perceptions determine how well the salesperson knows what must be done in performing a job, and aptitude determines whether the person has the necessary native abilities, skill level refers to the individual's *learned proficiency at performing the necessary tasks*. Aptitude and skill level are thus related constructs. Aptitude, though, consists of relatively enduring personal abilities, while skills are proficiency levels that can change rapidly with learning and experience.

The skills needed for good sales performance include:

1. Salesmanship skills, such as knowing how to make a sales presentation and how to close a sale.
2. Interpersonal skills, such as knowing how to cope with and resolve conflicts.
3. Technical skills, such as knowledge of product features and benefits, engineering skills, and the procedures required by company policies.

The relative importance of each of these skills, and the necessity of having other skills as well, depends on the selling situation. It is likely that different kinds of skills are needed for different types of selling tasks in various selling situations. Unfortunately, we know very little about which skills are most critical for certain selling environments.

The salesperson's past selling experience and the extensiveness and content of the firm's sales training programs influence skill level. While American compa-

---

[4] See Abraham K. Korman, "Expectancies as Determinants of Performance," *Journal of Applied Psychology* 55 (1971), pp. 218–22; or Edward E. Lawler III, "Job Attitudes and Employee Motivation: Theory, Research and Practice," *Personnel Psychology* 23 (1970), pp. 223–37.

[5] See Julian B. Rotter, "Generalized Expectancies for Internal versus External Control of Reinforcement," *Psychological Monographs: General and Applied* 80 (1966); or Lawler, "Job Attitudes."

nies spend large amounts of money on sales training, there is almost no published research concerning the effects of these training programs on salespeople's skills, behavior, and performance.

There are a number of articles on training in the sales literature, but they are typically how-to-do-it or experiential pieces. Few studies have evaluated the psychological or behavioral effects of alternative training methods.

The Personal, Organizational, and Environmental Variable Component

The sales performance model in Figure 8–1 suggests that personal, organizational, and environmental variables influence sales performance in two ways: (1) by directly facilitating or constraining performance, and (2) by influencing and interacting with the other performance determinants, such as the role perceptions and motivation.

Part 1 of the book described how these variables can influence sales performance directly. In discussing the organization of the sales force and the design of sales territories, much of the evidence and logic supporting the relationship between performance and organizational factors was reviewed. These factors include company advertising expenditures, the firm's current market share, and the closeness with which the sales force is supervised. There is a relationship between performance and environmental factors like territory potential, concentration of customers, the salesperson's workload, and the intensity of competition. The direct impact of the personal, organizational, and environmental variables on performance is thus rather clear.

Unfortunately, there has been less empirical work investigating the interactions among personal, organizational, and environmental variables and other determinants of performance. As discussed, studies have had modest success in identifying personal characteristics associated with sales aptitude and relating them to variations in sales performance.

A few studies have found significant relationships between personal and organizational variables—such as job experience, closeness of supervision, performance feedback, influence in determining standards, and span of control—and the amount of role conflict and ambiguity perceived by salespeople.[6] One study related personal characteristics to variations in motivation by showing that salespeople's desires for different job-related rewards (e.g., pay, promotion) differ with age, education, and family size.[7] Overall, though, many questions concerning the effects of personal, organizational, and environmental variables on the other determinants of sales performance remain unanswered.

---

[6] Orville C. Walker, Jr., Gilbert A. Churchill, Jr., and Neil M. Ford, "Organizational Determinants of the Industrial Salesman's Role Conflict and Ambiguity." *Journal of Marketing* 39 (January 1975), pp. 32–39; and Eric N. Berkowitz, "Role Strain and Ambiguity: Performance Implications in a Sales Organization," working paper, Graduate School of Business Administration, University of Minnesota, 1978.

[7] Gilbert A. Churchill, Jr., Neil M. Ford, and Orville C. Walker, Jr., "Motivating the Industrial Salesforce: The Attractiveness of Alternative Rewards," *Journal of Business Research* 7 (1979), pp. 25–50.

Rewards

The performance model in Figure 8–1 indicates that the salesperson's job performance affects the rewards the representative receives. The relationship between performance and rewards is very complex, however. For one thing, there are different dimensions of sales performance that a firm may choose to evaluate and reward. A company might evaluate its salespeople on total sales volume, quota attainment, selling expenses, profitability of sales, new accounts generated, services provided to customers, performance of administrative duties, or some combination of these. Different firms are likely to use different dimensions. Even among firms that use the same performance criteria, there are likely to be different relative emphases.[8]

In addition to the multidimensional character of sales performance, there are a variety of rewards that a company might bestow for any given level of performance. The model distinguishes between two broad types of rewards—extrinsic and intrinsic. *Extrinsic rewards* are those controlled and bestowed by people other than the salesperson, such as managers or customers. These include such things as pay, financial incentives, security, recognition, and promotion—rewards that are generally related to lower-order human needs. *Intrinsic rewards* are those that salespeople primarily attain for themselves. They include such things as feelings of accomplishment, personal growth, and self-worth—all of which relate to higher-order human needs.

As the model in Figure 8–1 suggests, salespeople's perceptions of the rewards they will receive in return for various types of job performance, together with the value they place on those rewards, strongly influence their motivation to perform.

Satisfaction

The job satisfaction of salespeople refers to all the characteristics of the job itself that representatives find rewarding, fulfilling, and satisfying, or frustrating and unsatisfying. There seems to be seven different dimensions to sales job satisfaction: (1) the job itself, (2) fellow workers, (3) supervision, (4) company policies and support, (5) pay, (6) promotion and advancement opportunities, and (7) customers. Salespeople's total satisfaction with their jobs is a reflection of their satisfaction with each of these elements.[9]

As Figure 8–1 suggests, the rewards received by a salesperson have a major impact on the individual's satisfaction with the job and the total work environment. The seven dimensions of satisfaction can be grouped, like rewards, into two

---

[8] Bill R. Darden and Warren French, "An Investigation Into the Salesman Evaluation Practices of Sales Managers," *Southern Journal of Business* 5 (July 1970), pp. 47–56.

[9] See Gilbert A. Churchill, Jr., Neil M. Ford, and Orville C. Walker, Jr., "Measuring the Job Satisfaction of Industrial Salesmen," *Journal of Marketing Research* 11 (August 1974), pp. 254–60.

major components—intrinsic and extrinsic. Intrinsic satisfaction is related to the intrinsic rewards the salesperson obtains from the job, such as satisfaction with the work itself and with the opportunities for personal growth and accomplishment which the job provides. Extrinsic satisfaction is associated with the extrinsic rewards bestowed on the salesperson, such as satisfaction with pay, company policies and support, supervision, fellow workers, chances for promotion, and customers.

The amount of satisfaction salespeople obtain from their jobs is also influenced by their role perceptions. Salespeople who perceive large amounts of conflict in the demands placed on them tend to be less satisfied than those who do not. So do those who experience great uncertainty in what is expected from them on the job.

Finally, a salesperson's job satisfaction is likely to have an impact on the individual's motivation to perform, as suggested by the feedback loop in Figure 8–1. The relationship between satisfaction and motivation is neither simple nor well understood, though. It is explored more fully in the discussion of the motivation component of the model in Chapter 13.

Importance for Sales Management

Understanding the model of salesperson performance in Figure 8–1 can be extremely important to the sales manager. As mentioned in Chapter 1, sales management involves three interrelated processes:

1. The formulation of a strategic sales program.
2. The implementation of the sales program.
3. The evaluation and control of sales force performance.

Almost everything the sales manager does can influence sales performance. For example, the way the sales manager organizes and deploys the sales force can affect salespeople's perceptions of the job. Similarly, how the manager selects salespeople and the kind of training to which they are exposed can affect the aptitude and skill that sales personnel bring to the job. The compensation program and the way it is administered can influence motivation levels and overall sales performance. The model offers the sales manager a tool for visualizing the effects of the activities in which he or she might engage. It frees the sales manager from operating without proper appreciation of the interrelated roles of the options under his or her command.

As mentioned earlier, do not be surprised if you have difficulty comprehending the full implications of the model or the suggested links. The purpose of this chapter was only to outline the model and to highlight the various components. The remaining chapters in this section elaborate on the components. Chapter 9 discusses the role component and the evidence supporting its effects and the influences on it. Chapter 10 on aptitude and Chapter 11 on selection provide background understanding on aptitude and its implications for effective sales management. Chapter 12 delves into sales training programs; these directly affect skill levels but can also influence the role component. Chapters 13 and 14 then look in more detail at motivation, rewards, and the design of compensation systems. These are key elements that the sales manager can control that can profoundly affect the motivation level of the sales force.

Summary

This chapter, the first on implementing the sales program, sought to present a model by which the performance of salespeople can be understood. This chapter was an overview of the model and the important links, whereas the emphasis in the remaining chapters in this section is on detailing the components of the model.

The model suggests that a salesperson's performance is a function of five basic factors: (1) motivation, (2) aptitude, (3) skill level, (4) role perceptions, and (5) personal, organizational, and environmental variables. There is substantial interaction among the components. A salesperson who is sorely deficient with respect to any one of them could be expected to perform poorly.

The role of the salesperson is defined largely through the expectations, demands, and pressures communicated by his or her role partners. Role partners are people both within and outside the company who are affected by the way the salesperson performs the job. The three major variables in the role perception component are role accuracy, perceived role ambiguity, and perceived role conflict. Role accuracy refers to the degree to which the salesperson's perceptions of his role partners' demands are accurate. Perceived role ambiguity occurs when the salesperson does not feel that she has the information to perform the job adequately. Perceived role conflict arises when a salesperson believes that the demands of two or more of his role partners are incompatible.

Motivation refers to the effort the salesperson desires to expend on each activity or task associated with the job. These include calling on potential new accounts, developing sales presentations, and the like. The motivation to expend effort on any particular task depends on: (1) expectancy—the salesperson's estimate of the probability that expending effort on the task will lead to improved performance on some dimension, and (2) valence for performance—the salesperson's perception of the desirability of improving performance on that dimension. The valence for performance on any dimension is, in turn, a function of: (1) instrumentality—the salesperson's estimate of the probability that improved performance on that dimension will lead to increased attainment of particular rewards, and (2) valence for rewards—the salesperson's perception of the desirability of receiving increased rewards as a result of improved performance.

Aptitude refers to the salesperson's native ability to do the job and includes such things as physical factors, mental abilities, and personality characteristics. Aptitude is a constraint on the person's ability to perform the sales job given an adequate understanding of the role to be performed, motivation, and learned skills and the absence of other constraints.

Skill level refers to the person's learned proficiency at performing the necessary tasks. It is distinguished from aptitude. Whereas aptitude consists of relatively enduring personal abilities, skills are proficiency levels that can change rapidly with learning and experience.

The personal, organizational, and environmental variables influence sales performance in two ways: (1) by directly facilitating or constraining performance, and (2) by influencing and interacting with other performance determinants, such as role perceptions and motivation.

The performance of the salesperson affects the rewards the individual receives. There are two basic types of rewards: extrinsic rewards, which are controlled and bestowed by people other than the salesperson, and intrinsic rewards, which are those that people primarily attain for themselves.

The rewards received by a salesperson have a major impact on the individual's satisfaction with the job and the total work environment. Satisfaction can also be of two types. Intrinsic satisfaction is related to the intrinsic rewards the salesperson obtains from the job, such as satisfaction with the work itself and the opportunities it provides for personal growth and sense of accomplishment. Extrinsic satisfaction is associated with the extrinsic rewards bestowed upon the salesperson, such as pay, chances for promotion, and supervisory and company policies.

Discussion Questions

1. The sales manager of a nationwide corporation commented: "There's no such thing as a sales representative who can't be motivated by money." Do you agree or disagree? Why?

2. Explain the relationship between motivation, performance, and satisfaction. Which causes which?

3. "Show me a person who is motivated and I'll produce a super sales representative." Do you agree with this comment?

4. Define intrinsic and extrinsic rewards. To what extent, if any, are they related?

5. Is it possible for a sales representative to want rewards that are not provided by the employer? What impact does this have on motivation? Performance? Satisfaction?

6. Although many aptitude tests exist, their ability to predict sales performance has been weak. How do you account for this?

7. Is it possible for a person to be highly motivated, possess the necessary aptitude, have a high skill level, and still not be able to sell?

8. Frequently, sales managers use contests and recognition rewards to motivate the sales force. If sales managers understand salesperson performance, then why is it necessary to employ these additional techniques?

9. The national sales manager of the C&N Bearing Corporation feels that poor sales performance is the reason for the recent decline in sales. It has been recommended that sales commissions be raised as a solution to the problem. Comment.

10. What aptitudes should be possessed by sales representatives who sell the following products and services?
    a. Electric typewriters.
    b. Business forms.
    c. Product liability insurance to manufacturers.
    d. Financial services to corporations.
    e. Electronic computers.
    f. Software programs.
    g. Flour to bakeries.
    h. Pension programs for employees.
    i. Paper to printers.

11. What is the relationship between aptitude and skill levels.

12. Sales management involves three interrelated processes: formulation, implementation, and evaluation and control of sales performance. What are the essential points a manager must consider and work with if the sales program, once formulated, is to be effectively implemented?

13. With regard to the role perceptions component of the overall performance model, how is it defined? What affects it and what does it affect?

14. From a sales representative's point of view, what are the determinants of sales performance? In what way is management able to direct and control these determinants? What are the consequences of management supervision; that is, what are the outcomes of managerial direction?

Chapter 9

The Salesperson's Role Perceptions

The model of salesperson performance in Figure 8–1 suggests that a primary influence on how salespeople perform is their perceptions of the demands placed on them. Are these perceptions accurate? Are salespeople fairly certain about what they should do? Are the demands of different people consistent?

This chapter elaborates on the role perceptions variable in the model. More particularly, the first part of the chapter reviews the notion of role and the process by which the salesperson's role is defined. The second highlights some key aspects of the salesperson's role that make it particularly susceptible to conflicts, ambiguities, and inaccurate perceptions. The third part of the chapter then focuses on role conflict and ambiguity. It discusses some common demands salespeople receive and the consequences and causes of the conflict and ambiguity they feel. The fourth part of the chapter takes a similar approach with respect to role inaccuracy. It reviews the specific nature of the effort-performance and performance-reward linkages salespeople perceive and the consequences and causes of their expectancy and instrumentality estimates.

The Salesperson's Role

Every employee occupies a position within the firm to which a *role* is attached. This role is like a prescription in that it represents the activities and behaviors that are to be performed by *any person* who occupies that position.

The salesperson's role is defined through a three-step process.[1] First, expectations and demands concerning how the salesperson should behave, together with pressures to conform, are communicated to the salesperson by members of that person's *role set*. The salesperson's role set consists of people who have a vested interest in how the representative performs the job. These people include the individual's immediate superior, other executives in the firm, purchasing agents and other members of customers' organizations, and the salesperson's family. They all try to influence the person's behavior, either formally through organizational policies, operating procedures, training programs, and the like, or informally through social pressures, rewards, and sanctions.

The second part of the role definition process involves the perceived role. This is salespeople's perceptions of the expectations and demands that are communicated to them by their role-set members. Salespeople perform in accordance with what they think the role-set members expect even though their perceptions of those expectations may not be entirely accurate. To really understand why salespeople perform the way they do, it is necessary to understand what salespeople *think* the members of the role set expect.

At this stage of the role definition process, three factors can wreak havoc with a salesperson's job performance and mental well-being. As Figure 9–1 suggests,

---

[1] Gilbert A. Churchill, Jr., Neil M. Ford, and Orville C. Walker, Jr., "The Social Psychology of Industrial Selling: The Salesman's View of His Job," *Perspectives in Business*, Winter 1975–76, pp. 18–28.

Figure 9–1
Salesperson's perceptions of the job

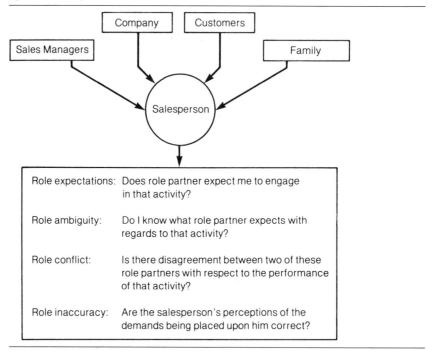

the salesperson may suffer from perceptions of role ambiguity, role conflict, or role inaccuracy.

Perceived role ambiguity occurs when representatives do not feel they have the necessary information to perform the job adequately. They feel uncertain about how to do a specific task, what the members of the role set expect in a particular situation, or how their performance is evaluated by members of the role set.

Perceived role conflict exists when a salesperson believes that the role demands of two or more members of the role set are incompatible. A customer, for example, may demand unusually liberal credit terms or delivery schedules that are unacceptable to the salesperson's superiors. The representative's perception that it is not possible to simultaneously satisfy all members of the role set creates conflicting role forces and psychological conflict within the salesperson.

Perceived role inaccuracy arises when the salesperson's perceptions of the role partners' demands are inaccurate. Does the salesperson's idea about what the role partners desire correspond to their actual expectations? Role inaccuracy differs from role ambiguity in that, with role inaccuracy, the salesperson feels fairly certain what should be done except that he or she is wrong. It differs from role conflict in that the salesperson does not see any inconsistencies in the expectations and demands communicated. Furthermore, it differs from both in that it is unrealized. The representative does not know that the perceptions he or she holds are inaccurate.

The final step in the role definition process involves the salesperson's conversion of these role perceptions into actual behavior. Both the salesperson's job behavior and psychological well-being can be affected if there are perceptions of role ambiguity or conflict or if these perceptions are inaccurate. There is a good deal of evidence, for example, that both perceived ambiguity and conflict are directly related to high mental anxiety and tension and low job satisfaction.[2] Also, the salesperson's feelings of uncertainty and conflict and the actions taken to resolve them can have a strong impact on ultimate job performance.[3] At a minimum, the salesperson's performance is less likely to be consistent with management's expectations and desires when the representative is uncertain about what those expectations are, or believes that the customers or family hold conflicting expectations, or has inaccurate perceptions of those expectations.

Susceptibility of the Salesperson's Role

Several characteristics of the salesperson's role make it particularly susceptible to role conflict, role ambiguity, and the development of inaccurate role perceptions. (1) It is at the boundary of the firm. (2) The salesperson's performance affects the occupants of a large number of other positions. (3) It is an innovative role.[4]

Boundary Position

Salespeople are likely to experience more role conflict than most other organization members because they occupy positions at the boundaries of their firms. Some members of each salesperson's role set—the customers—are in external organizations. As a result, the salesperson receives demands from organizations that have diverse goals, policies, and problems.[5] Since each role partner wants the salesperson's behavior to be consistent with the partner's own goals, the demands they communicate are diverse and often incompatible.[6]

---

[2] Robert L. Kahn et al., *Organizational Stress* (New York: John Wiley & Sons, 1964), pp. 57–71; Charles N. Greene and Dennis W. Organ, "An Evaluation of Causal Models Linking Received Role and Job Satisfaction," *Administrative Science Quarterly* 18 (March 1973), pp. 95–103; and John R. Rizzo, Robert J. House, and Sidney I. Lirtzman, "Role Conflict and Ambiguity in Complex Organizations," *Administrative Science Quarterly* 15 (June 1970), pp. 150–63.

[3] Henry O. Pruden and Richard M. Reese, "Interorganizational Role-Set Relations and the Performance and Satisfaction of Industrial Salesmen," *Administrative Science Quarterly* 17 (December 1972), pp. 601–9.

[4] Orville C. Walker, Jr., Gilbert A. Churchill, Jr., and Neil M. Ford, "Reactions to Role Conflict: The Case of the Industrial Salesman," *Journal of Business Administration* 3 (Spring 1972), pp. 25–36.

[5] Henry O. Pruden, "Interorganizational Conflict, Linkage, and Exchange: A Study of Industrial Salesmen," *Academy of Management Journal* 12 (September 1969), pp. 339–50.

[6] James A. Belasco, "The Salesman's Role Revisited," *Journal of Marketing* 30 (April 1966), pp. 6–8.

A customer, for example, might request that a product be modified to make it more suitable for her company's specific needs. The representative's company, however, may balk at making the modification because of the additional design and production costs it involves.[7] The salesperson becomes literally caught in the middle. To satisfy the demands of one role partner, the sales representative must ignore or attempt to change the demands of the other.

Another problem that arises from the salesperson's boundary position is that the role partners in one organization often have little appreciation for the expectations and demands made by role partners in another. A customer, for example, may not know the policies of the salesperson's company or the constraints under which the salesperson must operate. The sales representative's superiors, on the other hand, may formulate company policies without an adequate understanding of the particular requirements of some customers. Even a role partner who is aware of another's demands may not understand the reasoning behind them and may thus consider them arbitrary or illegitimate.

The fact that the position is a boundary one also increases the likelihood that the salesperson will experience role ambiguity or form inaccurate perceptions. Contact with many of the salesperson's role partners, though regular, is probably infrequent. When personal interaction does occur, it is often brief. Under such conditions, it is easy for the salesperson to feel uncertain about what the customer really expects in the way of delivery, service, or credit or how the customer really feels about how well the representative is servicing the account. Furthermore, the salesperson's perceptions with respect to these issues may be inaccurate.

Large Role Set

The salesperson's role set includes many diverse individuals. The representative may sell to hundreds of different customers, and each expects its own particular needs and requirements to be satisfied. In addition, people within the representative's own firm rely on him for executing company policies in dealings with customers and for the ultimate success of the firm's revenue-producing efforts. The specific design-performance criteria that a product is supposed to satisfy, and the delivery and credit terms the salesperson quotes, can directly influence people in the engineering, production, and credit departments, for example. All these people may hold definite beliefs about how the salesperson should perform the job, and they all will pressure the individual to conform to their expectations.[8] Salespeople for a Fortune 500 subsidiary that manufactured automotive components, for example, were recently caught up in one such disagreement. Engineer-

[7] Product design is only one of the areas where there is often conflict between marketing and engineering departments with respect to how best to serve customers' needs. See J. Donald Weinrauch and Richard Anderson, "Conflicts Between Engineering and Marketing Units," *Industrial Marketing Management* 11 (October 1982), pp. 291–301.

[8] Richard E. Walton, John M. Dutton, and H. G. Fitch, "A Study of Conflict in the Process, Structure, and Attitudes of Lateral Relationships," in *Some Theories of Organization*, rev. ed., ed. Albert H. Rubenstein and Chadwick J. Haberstroh (Homewood, Ill.: Richard D. Irwin, 1966), pp. 444–65.

ing wanted salespeople to emphasize the technical consistencies among the items in the product line as a prelude to their redesigning the line to make it simpler and more consistent. At the same time, marketing wanted salespeople to downplay the consistencies so as to maintain some technical mystique which marketing felt was needed for product differentiation.[9]

The large number of people from diverse departments and organizations who depend on the salesperson increases the probability that at least some role demands will be incompatible. It also increases the probability that the salesperson's perceptions of some demands will be inaccurate and that he or she will be uncertain about others.

Innovative Role

The salesperson's role is frequently innovative in that she is often called upon to produce new solutions to nonroutine problems. This is particularly true when the salesperson is selling highly technical products or engineered systems that are designed to the customer's specifications. Even when the salesperson is selling standardized products, she must display some creativity in matching the company's offerings to the customer's particular needs. With potential new accounts, this is an extremely difficult, but critical, task.

Occupants of innovative roles tend to experience more conflict than other organization members because they must have flexibility to perform their roles well. Such people must have the authority to develop and carry out innovative solutions.[10] This need for flexibility often brings the salesperson into conflict with the standard operating procedures of the firm and with the expectations of organization members who want to maintain the status quo. The production manager, for example, may frown on orders for nonstandard products because of their adverse effects on production costs and schedules.

Occupants of innovative roles also tend to experience more role ambiguity and inaccurate role perceptions than occupants of noninnovative roles. This is because they frequently face unusual situations where they have no standard procedures or past experience to guide them. Consequently, they are often uncertain about how their role partners expect them to proceed. The perceptions they do have are more likely to be inaccurate because of the nonroutine nature of the task. The flexibility that is needed to fulfill an innovative role can consequently have unforeseen, negative consequences.

A salesman of a major manufacturer of heating, ventilating and air conditioning equipment was recently embarrassed during a sales demonstration. Since the product was higher priced than the competition, the salesman decided to prove that there would be less labor costs for installation. On the field demonstration day, engineering sent the prototype with a last-minute design change without notifying the salesman. The alteration made the product

---

[9] Weinrauch and Anderson, "Conflicts Between."
[10] Kahn et al., *Organizational Stress*, pp. 125–36.

similar to the competition. Thus, the customer was indifferent during the sales installation demonstration, and more importantly, because of the last minute engineering change, there was no labor advantage. Besides experiencing a demeaning demonstration, the salesman lost the potential sale.[11]

Role Conflict and Ambiguity

In discussing the causes and consequences of the various role perceptions, it is useful to separate the concepts of role conflict and role ambiguity, on the one hand, and inaccurate role perceptions, on the other. This section concentrates on role conflict and role ambiguity, and the next section emphasizes role inaccuracy. More particularly, this section looks at some common expectations of industrial salespeople, the consequences of perceived conflict and ambiguity, and the primary organizational factors that affect the amount of conflict and ambiguity salespeople feel.

Common Expectations and Key Areas of Conflict and Ambiguity

Different sales jobs require different tasks and place different demands on salespeople. The person selling dresses to a woman's fashion store may have to be concerned most with follow-up service to make sure the reorders for styles, colors, or sizes arrive in time for the current selling season. The representative selling pumps to a refinery may have to be concerned most with making sure the equipment can handle the load, chemicals, and other harsh conditions to which it will be subjected. Thus, it is next to impossible to develop one set of expectations common to all sales jobs. Even firms within the same industry often place different demands on their salespeople. Nevertheless, to develop a feel for some common expectations that are important sources of conflict and ambiguity, one extensive study aimed at measuring the demands placed on salespeople will be reviewed.

The study involved only industrial sales representatives. It was conducted among 265 salespeople from 10 companies in seven different industries.[12] All the firms were manufacturers of relatively technical equipment and materials, ranging from computers and machine tools to cleaning supplies. Each participating

---

[11] Weinrauch and Anderson, "Conflicts Between," p. 292.

[12] Actually, 479 salespersons were mailed questionnaires, but only 265 returned both questionnaires used in the study—a response rate of 55 percent. For details of the study and the data collection instrument that was used, see Neil M. Ford, Orville C. Walker, Jr., and Gilbert A. Churchill, Jr., "Expectation-Specific Measures of the Intersender Conflict and Role Ambiguity Experienced by Industrial Salesmen," *Journal of Business Research* 3 (April 1975), pp. 95–112. For another study that attempted to develop an understanding of the salesperson's role in a building materials sales situation, see Lawrence M. Lamont and William G. Lundstrom, "Defining Industrial Sales Behavior: A Factor Analytic Study," in *1974 Combined Proceedings*, ed. R. C. Curhan (Chicago: American Marketing Association. 1974), pp. 493–98.

salesperson completed a questionnaire which listed the various activities in which he or she might be expected to engage by each role partner. The activities were organized into four groups, reflecting each primary role partner: (1) sales manager, (2) the company (other organizational superiors), (3) customers, and (4) family. The salesperson was asked to indicate whether he or she thought the role partner expected the salesperson to engage in each activity by checking one of five points on a scale from "strongly agree" to "strongly disagree."

Perceived role conflict was measured by the difference in the salesperson's response between each pair of role partners on each common activity item. For example, the salesperson might "agree strongly" (score 5) that the customers expected him to expedite orders but "disagree strongly" (score 1) that the sales manager held the same expectations. Then the perceived role conflict score for that activity would be 4. All possible conflicts between all possible pairs of role partners were examined in this way.

Each salesperson's role ambiguity was measured with another scale that included 41 items regarding the requirements of the salesperson's job. The representative was asked to indicate his level of confidence or ambiguity concerning the expectations and evaluations of the various role partners on a six-point scale from "absolutely certain" to "absolutely uncertain."

Role Expectations. Figure 9–2 presents salespeople's perceptions concerning what each group of role partners expects of them on the job. It shows the proportion of salespeople in the sample who "agree" or "agree strongly" that the role partner expects them to engage in each activity. Because of the large number of activities examined, Figure 9-2 displays only those that a relatively large or unusually small proportion of salespersons feel they were expected to perform. The figure prompts the following two major conclusions.

1. Different role partners emphasize different types of expectations. Some seem to have more expectations about the functional aspects of the job, whereas others are more likely to have expectations about salespeople's personal relations and performance "style." In other words, salespeople see some role partners as being concerned with what they do—company superiors focus on the functional aspects of the job such as handling back charges and adjustments, expediting orders, and supervising installations. Others are more concerned with how they do it—family members are concerned about the salesperson's hours of work and personal relations with customers.

2. Perceived role expectations are consistent among salespeople. One might expect a great deal of variation in the role demands perceived by salespeople in different firms and industries; however, Figure 9–2 suggests that a large proportion of sales representatives are consistent in their perceptions of what their company superiors and sales managers expect of them. The largest number of common perceptions relate to style, but there are also functional activities that three quarters or two thirds of the salespeople say their superiors expect them to perform. The major area where sales representatives do not perceive similar role expectations involves the demands of family members. These demands are much more likely to differ from one salesperson to the next than are the expectations of

Figure 9–2
Salespeople's perceptions of role partners' expectations

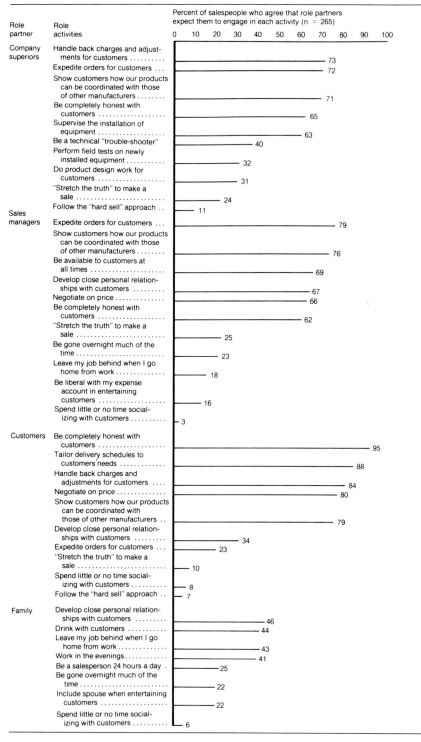

Role partner	Role activities	Percent of salespeople who agree that role partners expect them to engage in each activity (n = 265)
Company superiors	Handle back charges and adjustments for customers	73
	Expedite orders for customers	72
	Show customers how our products can be coordinated with those of other manufacturers	71
	Be completely honest with customers	65
	Supervise the installation of equipment	63
	Be a technical "trouble-shooter"	40
	Perform field tests on newly installed equipment	32
	Do product design work for customers	31
	"Stretch the truth" to make a sale	24
	Follow the "hard sell" approach	11
Sales managers	Expedite orders for customers	79
	Show customers how our products can be coordinated with those of other manufacturers	76
	Be available to customers at all times	69
	Develop close personal relationships with customers	67
	Negotiate on price	66
	Be completely honest with customers	62
	"Stretch the truth" to make a sale	25
	Be gone overnight much of the time	23
	Leave my job behind when I go home from work	18
	Be liberal with my expense account in entertaining customers	16
	Spend little or no time socializing with customers	3
Customers	Be completely honest with customers	95
	Tailor delivery schedules to customers' needs	88
	Handle back charges and adjustments for customers	84
	Negotiate on price	80
	Show customers how our products can be coordinated with those of other manufacturers	79
	Develop close personal relationships with customers	34
	Expedite orders for customers	23
	"Stretch the truth" to make a sale	10
	Spend little or no time socializing with customers	8
	Follow the "hard sell" approach	7
Family	Develop close personal relationships with customers	46
	Drink with customers	44
	Leave my job behind when I go home from work	43
	Work in the evenings	41
	Be a salesperson 24 hours a day	25
	Be gone overnight much of the time	22
	Include spouse when entertaining customers	22
	Spend little or no time socializing with customers	6

customers or company superiors. This suggests that no matter what the company expects in terms of hours of work, relations with customers, travel, and the like, a substantial number of its salespeople are likely to be placed in conflict with the expectations of their families.

Role Ambiguity. Figure 9–3 shows the proportion of salespeople in the sample who felt ambiguity or uncertainty about how to perform various aspects of their jobs and about the expectations and evaluations of the members of their role set. Again, the figure presents only those items about which relatively many or unusually few salespeople feel uncertain.

Most industrial salespeople do not seem uncertain about what they are expected to do or how their performance is being evaluated. However, a substantial proportion are plagued by ambiguity concerning some aspects of their job and some role partners. Sales representatives say they are particularly uncertain about company policies, how their performance is being evaluated by company superiors, and what their sales managers expect. In comparison, very few are uncertain about the expectations or evaluations of customers or family members. This suggests that customers and family members communicate their role expectations more effectively than the salesperson's company superiors do. Perhaps this is not surprising since a representative faces customers and family members almost daily, whereas company policies are communicated through infrequent sales meetings, written memos, and other less effective means.

Role Conflict. Figure 9–4 shows the proportion of salespeople who believe the expectations of their role partners are in conflict. Again, the figure includes only those activities where either very many or unusually few salespeople experienced conflict.

A comparison of Figure 9–4 with Figure 9–3 suggests that many more industrial salespeople experience role conflict than role ambiguity. Compared with other conflicts, intraorganizational conflict—where the role demands of the sales manager are incompatible with those of other organizational superiors—is experienced by few salespeople. Still, as many as one quarter of all representatives perceive conflicts between the demands of their sales managers and other company executives.

Most salespeople perceive conflicts between some company policies or expectations and their customers' demands. Customers are usually seen as demanding more functions performed by the salesperson, more services, more honesty, more liberal use of the expense account, and so forth. Sales managers and other company executives, on the other hand, are seen as demanding that the salesperson hold down selling expenses and customer concessions.

Most salespeople agree that their company superiors and customers expect them to travel, work flexible hours, and be available to customers in the evenings and on weekends. Unfortunately, more than half the representatives in the sample feel that these expectations conflict with the desires of their families. Although job-family conflicts are not unique to salespeople, their pervasiveness in the sales force should be recognized as a major influence on job satisfaction and performance.

Figure 9–3
Salespeople's feelings of role ambiguity

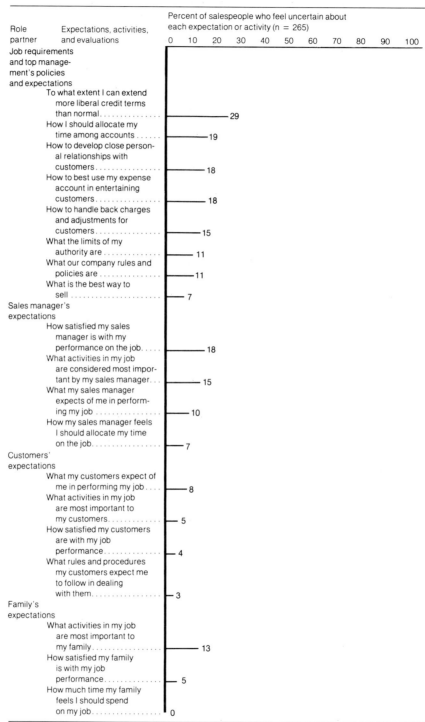

Role partner	Expectations, activities, and evaluations	Percent of salespeople who feel uncertain about each expectation or activity (n = 265)
Job requirements and top management's policies and expectations		
	To what extent I can extend more liberal credit terms than normal.	29
	How I should allocate my time among accounts	19
	How to develop close personal relationships with customers.	18
	How to best use my expense account in entertaining customers.	18
	How to handle back charges and adjustments for customers.	15
	What the limits of my authority are	11
	What our company rules and policies are	11
	What is the best way to sell	7
Sales manager's expectations		
	How satisfied my sales manager is with my performance on the job.	18
	What activities in my job are considered most important by my sales manager.	15
	What my sales manager expects of me in performing my job	10
	How my sales manager feels I should allocate my time on the job.	7
Customers' expectations		
	What my customers expect of me in performing my job	8
	What activities in my job are most important to my customers.	5
	How satisfied my customers are with my job performance.	4
	What rules and procedures my customers expect me to follow in dealing with them.	3
Family's expectations		
	What activities in my job are most important to my family.	13
	How satisfied my family is with my job performance.	5
	How much time my family feels I should spend on my job.	0

Figure 9–4
Salespeople's perceptions of role conflict

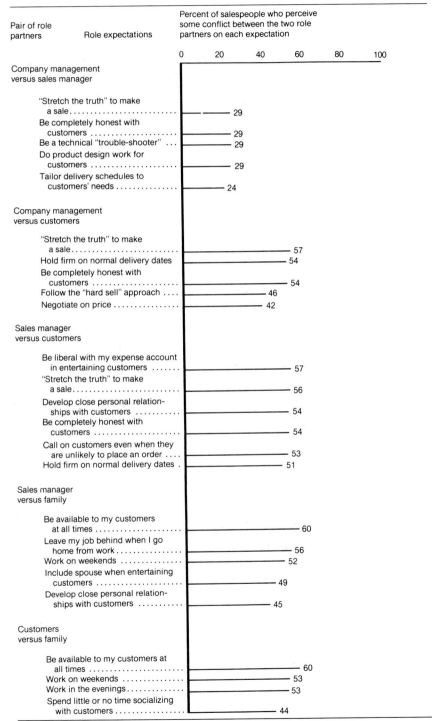

Pair of role partners	Role expectations	Percent of salespeople who perceive some conflict between the two role partners on each expectation

Company management versus sales manager

- "Stretch the truth" to make a sale 29
- Be completely honest with customers 29
- Be a technical "trouble-shooter" . . . 29
- Do product design work for customers 29
- Tailor delivery schedules to customers' needs 24

Company management versus customers

- "Stretch the truth" to make a sale 57
- Hold firm on normal delivery dates 54
- Be completely honest with customers 54
- Follow the "hard sell" approach 46
- Negotiate on price 42

Sales manager versus customers

- Be liberal with my expense account in entertaining customers 57
- "Stretch the truth" to make a sale 56
- Develop close personal relationships with customers 54
- Be completely honest with customers 54
- Call on customers even when they are unlikely to place an order 53
- Hold firm on normal delivery dates . 51

Sales manager versus family

- Be available to my customers at all times 60
- Leave my job behind when I go home from work 56
- Work on weekends 52
- Include spouse when entertaining customers 49
- Develop close personal relationships with customers 45

Customers versus family

- Be available to my customers at all times 60
- Work on weekends 53
- Work in the evenings 53
- Spend little or no time socializing with customers 44

Consequences of Conflict and Ambiguity

Most people experience some occasional role conflict and ambiguity. In small doses, role conflict and ambiguity may be good for the individual and the organization.   When there are no disagreements and no uncertainty associated with a role, people can become so comfortable in the position that they constantly strive to preserve the status quo. Some role stress, therefore, can lead to useful adaptation and change. In sum, there is a level of hostility below which conflict and ambiguity may be benign but above which they will be malign. Excessive role stress can have dysfunctional consequences, both psychological and behavioral, for the individual and the organization, as Figure 9–5 indicates. Consider first the psychological consequences.

Figure 9–5
Causes and consequences of a salesperson's role perceptions

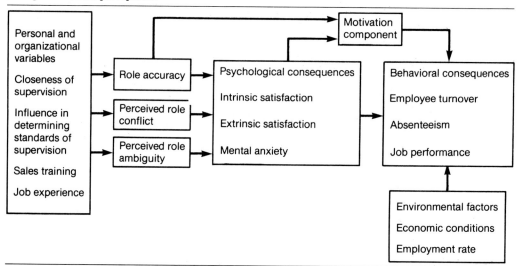

Psychological Consequences.   When a salesperson perceives that role partners have conflicting expectations about how the job should be performed, the salesperson becomes the "person in the middle." How can she satisfy the demands of one role partner without incurring the wrath of others? This situation can produce psychological conflict, which is uncomfortable for the individual and which can produce various kinds of emotional turmoil. The tensions associated with the job increase, and the salesperson tends to worry more about conditions and events at work than she otherwise would. As a result, the salesperson's overall feelings of anxiety increase, and she is likely to become less satisfied with role partners, the company, and the job.[13]

Perceived role ambiguity can have similar negative consequences for salespeople. When the salesperson feels he lacks the necessary information to perform the job adequately, when he does not know what role partners expect of him, or when he is uncertain about his ability to perform, the salesperson is likely to lose confidence in his ability to perform the sales role successfully. The salesperson tends to worry more about whether he is doing the right thing and about how role partners will react to his performance. The representative may also lose confidence in role partners and blame them for failing to communicate their expectations and evaluations adequately. Like conflict, then, perceived role ambiguity is likely to increase a salesperson's mental anxiety and decrease job satisfaction.[14]

Although conflict and ambiguity both affect job satisfaction negatively, they affect it somewhat differently.[15] Perceived role conflict primarily affects extrinsic job satisfaction, but has little or no effect on the intrinsic satisfactions the salesperson derives from the job. The salesperson's ability to obtain extrinsic rewards, such as more pay, a promotion, praise, and recognition is influenced by role partners. Therefore, conflicts among the expectations and demands of those role partners not only make it more difficult for the salesperson to satisfy their demands but also jeopardize the representative's ability to earn desired extrinsic rewards.[16] On the other hand, such conflicts may not restrain the salesperson's ability to obtain intrinsic satisfactions from the job. Even when two or more role partners cannot agree on how the representative should be performing, the salesperson may still gain a sense of accomplishment from working or improving personal abilities.

Unlike perceived conflict, ambiguity has a negative impact on the intrinsic components of a salesperson's job satisfaction as well as the extrinsic components.[17] When a salesperson is uncertain about how she should be doing the job, whether she is doing it right, and how others are evaluating her performance, the salesperson is likely to lose confidence in her abilities and her self-esteem suffers.[18] Ambiguity, therefore, reduces the salesperson's ability to obtain intrinsic rewards and satisfactions from the job. Similarly, if the salesperson is uncertain about how role partners are evaluating his performance, he is likely to be uncertain about his chances for promotion or pay increases in the future. Finally, the salesperson is likely to be dissatisfied with role partners when they have failed

---

[13] Grady D. Bruce, Charles M. Bonjean, and J. Allen Williams, Jr., "Job Satisfaction among Independent Businessmen: A Correlative Study," *Sociology and Social Research* 52 (April 1968), pp. 195–204; and Neil M. Ford, Orville C. Walker, Jr., and Gilbert A. Churchill, Jr., "The Psychological Consequences of Role Conflict and Ambiguity in the Industrial Salesforce," in *Marketing: 1776–1976 and Beyond,* ed. Kenneth L. Bernhardt (Chicago: American Marketing Association, 1976), pp. 403–8.

[14] Kahn et al., *Organizational Stress,* pp. 72–95; and Rizzo, House, and Lirtzman, "Role Conflict and Ambiguity."

[15] Ford, Walker, and Churchill, "Psychological Consequences."

[16] Pruden and Reese. "Interorganizational Role-Set Relations."

[17] James H. Donnelly, Jr., and John M. Ivancevich, "Role Clarity and the Salesman," *Journal of Marketing* 39 (January 1975), pp. 71–74; and Eric N. Berkowitz, "Role Strain and Ambiguity: Performance Implications in a Sales Organization," working paper, Graduate School of Business Administration, University of Minnesota, 1978.

[18] Richard P. Bagozzi, "The Nature and Causes of Self-Esteem, Performance, and Satisfaction in the Sales Force: A Structural Equation Approach," *Journal of Business* 53 (1980), pp. 315–31.

to make clear their expectations and evaluations, thus causing the salesperson emotional discomfort.

Behavioral Consequences.   Perceived role conflict and ambiguity not only have negative psychological consequences for sales representatives but also can produce dysfunctional behavioral consequences. It is naive to think that a happy worker is invariably a productive worker, but much evidence collected from a variety of occupations suggests that a worker's satisfaction does influence job behavior. For instance, a negative relationship consistently appears between job satisfaction and absenteeism and employee turnover.[19]

Low satisfaction may also be related to high turnover among salespeople, although the relationship is likely to be moderated by economic conditions and the availability of alternative jobs. Unfortunately, no research has been done on this relationship in industrial sales occupations. This lack of research is surprising because turnover is a major problem in sales management. The costs of recruiting and training a new sales representative may be as high as $50,000 before the individual achieves a productive status.[20]

Another relationship that appears in many studies in other occupations is a positive correlation between satisfaction and performance, although there is controversy concerning the nature of the relationship. Some theorists argue that high satisfaction leads to good performance, whereas others argue that good performance makes workers more satisfied with their jobs.[21] More research is needed to define more accurately the nature of the relationship between satisfaction and performance. The available sales management literature seems to suggest, however, that a salesperson's job satisfaction is directly related to performance on the job[22] and that conflict and ambiguity are negatively related to sales performance.[23]

Causes of Conflict and Ambiguity

Given that conflict and ambiguity produce dysfunctional psychological and behavioral consequences for salespeople, the next question is whether sales management can do anything to hold conflicts and ambiguities at a manageable level or to aid the salesperson in dealing with them when they occur. In one study of this question, it was found that there was little management could do to reduce

[19] Charles N. Greene, "The Satisfaction-Performance Controversy," *Business Horizons,* October 1972, pp. 31–41; and Donald P. Schwab and Larry L. Cummings, "Theories of Performance and Satisfaction: A Review," *Industrial Relations,* October 1970, pp. 408–30.

[20] William J. Stanton and Richard H. Buskirk, *Management of the Sales Force,* 6th ed. (Homewood, Ill.: Richard D. Irwin, 1983), p. 86.

[21] For a review of the evidence as well as the controversy, see Green, "Satisfaction-Performance Controversy," or Schwab and Cummings, "Theories of Performance."

[22] Richard P. Bagozzi, "Salesforce Performance and Satisfaction as a Function of Individual Difference, Interpersonal, and Situational Factors," *Journal of Marketing Research* 15 (November 1978) pp. 517–31.

[23] Pruden and Reese, "Interorganizational Role-Set Relations"; Donnelly and Ivancevich, "Role Clarity"; Berkowitz, "Role Strain," and Bagozzi, "The Nature and Causes."

conflict in the sales force. This was because the only variable that was related significantly to perceptions of conflict was the amount of time the salesperson had been on the job.[24] More experienced salespeople perceived less conflict than less experienced representatives. Perhaps this is because salespeople who experience a great deal of conflict become dissatisfied and quit, whereas those who stay on the job do not perceive much conflict. On the other hand, sales representatives may learn with experience how to deal with conflict. They may learn that demands that initially appear to be in conflict may turn out to be compatible. They may learn how to resolve or cope with conflicts so that they are no longer so stressful. Finally, they may build up psychological defense mechanisms to screen out conflicts and protect themselves from tension. If these learning hypotheses are correct, perhaps sales training programs can prepare new salespeople to deal with the conflicts they will encounter on the job. Training, after all, is an attempt to compress the learning that occurs with experience into a shorter time period.

In contrast to conflict, there does seem to be something management can do to reduce role ambiguity among salespeople. It too depends on experience, and thus sales training should be effective in helping salespeople cope with it. Perhaps more important, it seems to depend on the manager's supervisory style. Less ambiguity is experienced when salespeople are closely supervised and have some influence over the standards by which their performance is controlled and evaluated.[25] Salespeople who are closely supervised are more aware of the expectations and demands of their supervisors, and those behaviors that are inconsistent can be more quickly brought to their attention. Similarly, salespeople who have an input in determining the standards by which they are evaluated are more familiar with these standards, which tends to reduce role ambiguity. One direct way of affecting the closeness with which salespeople feel supervised is by altering the sales manager's span of control. An increase in the span of control tends to increase salespeople's perceived role ambiguity while reducing it tends to allow closer supervision which, in turn, tends to make things clearer to salespeople as to how they should do their jobs.[26]

Close supervision can be a two-edged sword, however. While it can reduce ambiguity, supervision that is too close can increase a salesperson's job dissatisfaction. This occurs when the salesperson no longer feels enough latitude to deal effectively with the customer or enough creativity to service the account. The problem is particularly acute when sales managers use coercion and threats to direct the salespeople under them.[27] Sales managers must walk a very fine line indeed with respect to how closely and by what means they supervise the people under them.

---

[24] Orville C. Walker, Jr., Gilbert A. Churchill, Jr., and Neil M. Ford, "Organizational Determinants of the Role Conflict and Ambiguity Experienced by Industrial Salesmen," *Journal of Marketing* 39 (January 1975), pp. 32–39.

[25] Ibid.

[26] Lawrence B. Chonko, "The Relationship of Span of Control to Sales Representatives, Experienced Role Conflict and Role Ambiguity," *Academy of Management Journal* 25 (June 1982), pp. 452–56.

[27] Paul Busch, "The Sales Manager's Bases of Social Power and Influence Upon the Sales Force," *Journal of Marketing* 44 (Summer 1980), pp. 91–101.

Role Accuracy

The role component of the model contains three variables: role conflict, role ambiguity, and role accuracy. It is convenient to highlight role accuracy for separate discussion for two reasons. First, role accuracy can be viewed both generally and from the standpoint of specific linkages. When it is viewed generally, its impact and antecedents are similar to those for role conflict and ambiguity. What was stated previously also applies to role accuracy then. Nothing is lost, therefore, and some additional insight is gained by looking at role accuracy with respect to specific linkages. Second, role accuracy influences the motivation component of the model, whereas role conflict and role ambiguity do not. To understand role accuracy, therefore, it is necessary to assess its impact on the salesperson's motivation to perform.

In this section, the nature of role accuracy is examined first. Next, the consequences of inaccurate perceptions are reviewed and the personal, organizational, and environmental factors that affect the accuracy of a salesperson's perceptions are highlighted.

Nature of Role Accuracy

A salesperson has accurate role perceptions when he accurately understands what role partners expect when performing the job. Role inaccuracy can be either *general* or *linkage*-specific. *General* role inaccuracy involves considerations like whether the salesperson correctly thinks he can negotiate on price, promise shorter delivery times than normal, and handle back charges and adjustments for customers. General role inaccuracy can arise with respect to almost any job dimension that also gives rise to role ambiguity and conflict (see Figures 9–2 and 9–3). Its antecedents and consequences are also similar.

Linkage role inaccuracy, on the other hand, recognizes that salespeople must engage in certain activities to perform well and that they will receive certain rewards based on their performance on each of the dimensions. *Linkage* role inaccuracy arises when the salesperson has incorrect perceptions with respect to the relationships between (1) the activities and performance dimensions, or (2) the performance dimensions and the rewards. In terms of the model in Figure 8–1, linkage role inaccuracy relates to the motivational component and more particularly to the expectancy and instrumentality estimates.

There is great potential for linkage role inaccuracy among salespeople because all three components—activities, performance dimensions, and rewards—are multidimensional. There are consequently a great many linkages, which increases the chances that a salesperson will have inaccurate perceptions about at least some of them. Some common activities in which salespersons are expected to engage, the criteria used to evaluate their performance, and the rewards that

Table 9–1
Common activities, performance criteria, and rewards for industrial salespeople

Activities

1. Supervise installation and field testing of equipment.
2. Troubleshoot technical problems.
3. Expedite orders.
4. Train customers in the use of equipment.
5. Prepare sales presentations and equipment quotations.
6. Handle back charges and adjustments.
7. Tailor delivery schedules to customers' needs.
8. Handle price and credit negotiations.
9. Design products and/or systems for customers.
10. Call on potential new accounts.
11. Make a specified number of calls on existing accounts.
12. Socialize with and/or entertain customers.
13. Study the company's product line.
14. Study customers' situations and problems.
15. Fill out reports.
16. Attend company training programs.
17. Attend company sales meetings.
18. Attend professional conferences and conventions.

Performance criteria

1. Total sales volume and increase over last year.
2. Degree of quota attainment.
3. Selling expenses and decrease versus last year.
4. Profitability of sales and increase over last year.
5. New accounts generated.
6. Improvement in performance of administrative duties.
7. Improvement in service provided customers.

Rewards

1. Pay.
   a. Increased take-home pay.
   b. Increased bonuses and other financial incentives.
2. Promotion.
   a. Higher-level job.
   b. Better territory.
3. Nonfinancial incentives (contests, travel, prices, etc.).
4. Special recognitions (clubs, awards, etc.).
5. Job security.
6. Feeling of self-fulfillment.
7. Feeling of worthwhile accomplishment.
8. Opportunity for personal growth and development.
9. Opportunity for independent thought and action.

are typically used to motivate them are listed in Table 9–1. Obviously, not all salespeople in every firm are expected to engage in all these activities, nor are they evaluated on each performance dimension. Neither do all firms provide the same rewards to the same degree. This makes it very difficult to discuss linkage inaccuracy in a way that is useful to sales managers in general. One has to get down to the level of the individual firm and the linkages operating there in order to discuss the notion.

One salesperson activity that is common across many firms is an emphasis on new account calls. Similarly, the number of new accounts generated is often used as one criterion for evaluating how salespeople performed. In spite of these emphases, it is not unusual to find that salespeople do not spend enough time calling on new accounts, even when they recognize that there are many such opportunities in their territories and that their sales managers want them to spend much more time on such accounts. The two primary reasons given for the lack of emphasis on new account development in one study that investigated the question using reasonably large samples of salespeople and salesmanagers (over 400 of each) were: (1) salespeople fail to see the payoff to themselves in new account development, and (2) they did not know what it takes to perform these activities successfully.[28] Further,

the difference in priorities between sales representatives and sales managers appear to start very early in the sales planning process. At the very basic step of classifying accounts, 80 percent of sales managers state that this should be done on the basis of potential volumes, whereas only 54 percent of sales representatives indicate that they do so. The other 56 percent, if they classify their accounts at all, prefer to utilize other factors such as historic volumes or geography.[29]

Clearly, the sales managers in the study did not effectively communicate to the sales force their perceptions of the linkages between activities and performance, and performance and rewards. Yet the accuracy of a salesperson's expectancy and instrumentality estimates, as well as their magnitude, can influence a salesperson's performance and consequently have important implications for sales managers. The next section reviews some causes and consequences of inaccurate role perceptions and highlights what this implies for sales managers.

Causes, Consequences, and Management Implications of Perceived Linkages

For purposes of discussion, it would be best to separate expectancy and instrumentality estimates and to break down each category into considerations of accu-

---

[28] Terry Deutscher, Judith Marshall, and David Burgoyne, "The Process of Obtaining New Accounts," *Industrial Marketing Management* 11 (July 1982), pp. 173–81.
[29] Ibid., p. 175.

Table 9–2
Important questions and management implications of salespeople's expectancy estimates

Question	Management Implications
Accuracy of expectancy estimates	
Are salespeople's views of the linkage between activities and performance outcomes consistent with those of sales managers?	If substantial variation exists, salespeople may devote too much effort to activities considered unimportant by management, and vice versa. This might indicate a need for:
	More extensive/explicit sales training.
	Closer supervision.
	Evaluation of salesperson's effort and time allocation as well as performance.
Are there large variations in expectancy perceptions between high performers and low performers in the sales force?	If high-performing salespeople hold reasonably consistent views concerning which activities are most important in producing good performance, those views might be used as a model for sales training/professional development programs.
Magnitude of expectancy estimates	
All other things equal, the higher the salesperson's expectancy estimates, the greater the individual's motivation to expend effort.	If such relationships are found, they may suggest additional criteria for recruitment/selection.
Do personal characteristics of salespeople influence the size of their expectancies?	
Overall self-esteem?	
Perceived competence?	
Mental ability? (Intelligence?)	
Previous sales experience?	
Do perceptions of uncertainty or constraints in the environment (e.g., materials shortages, recession, etc.) reduce salespeople's expectancy estimates?	During periods of economic uncertainty, management may have to change performance criteria, evaluation methods, and/or compensation systems to maintain desired levels of effort from the sales force (e.g., lower quotas, reward servicing rather than selling activities, etc.).

racy and magnitude. Table 9–2 outlines some questions and management implications surrounding a salesperson's expectancy estimates, and Table 9–3 does the same for instrumentality estimates.[30]

Accuracy of Expectancies. As pointed out, it is possible for a salesperson to misjudge the true relationship between the effort expended on a particular task

---

[30] The tables and much of the discussion are taken from Orville C. Walker, Jr., Gilbert A. Churchill, Jr., and Neil M. Ford, "Measuring and Improving Salesmen's Motivation and Performance," in *Marketing Looks Outward: 1976 Proceedings of International Marketing Conference*, ed. William Locander (Chicago: American Marketing Association, 1977), pp. 25–32.

Table 9–3
Important questions and management implications of salespeople's instrumentality estimates

Question	Management Implications
Accuracy of instrumentality estimates	
Are salespeople's views of the linkage between performance on various dimensions and the rewards they will receive consistent with those of sales managers?	If substantial variation exists, salespeople may concentrate on aspects of performance considered relatively unimportant by management, and vice versa. This might indicate the need for: More extensive/explicit sales training. Closer supervision. More direct feedback to salespeople concerning how performance is evaluated and how rewards are determined.
Magnitude of instrumentality estimates	
How are salespeople's instrumentality estimates influenced by their compensation system (salary versus commission)?	If such relationships are found, managers should select the type of compensation plan that maximizes instrumentality estimates for those performance dimensions considered most crucial.
Do salespeople on commission have higher instrumentality estimates for performance dimensions related to short-term sales volume?	
Do salaried salespeople have higher instrumentalities for performance dimensions not directly related to short-term sales volume?	
Do personal characteristics of salespeople influence the size of their instrumentality estimates?	If such relationships are found, they may suggest additional criteria for recruitment/selection.
Feelings of internal control? Mental ability? Sales experience?	

and resulting performance. When this happens, the salesperson will misallocate his efforts. The representative will spend too much time and energy on activities that have relatively little impact on performance and not enough on activities with greater impact.

In most industrial psychology literature concerning work expectancies, it is assumed that a worker's immediate superior, by virtue of greater knowledge and experience, will more accurately perceive the linkages between effort and performance in the worker's job than the worker himself. If this is also true in the selling profession, it suggests that inaccurate expectancy perceptions in the sales force can be improved through closer contact between salespeople and their supervisors. Expanded sales training programs, closer day-to-day supervision of the sales force, and periodic review of each salesperson's time and effort allocation by the supervisor might improve the accuracy of expectancy estimates.

One often hears salespeople complain that their superiors have an unrealistic view of conditions in the field and that they do not realize what is necessary to make a sale.[31] If these complaints are valid, managers' perceptions of the linkages between effort and performance may not be appropriate criteria for judging the accuracy of salespeople's expectancies. It may be better to use the expectancy estimates of the highest performing salesperson in the company as a model for sales training and supervision.

Magnitude of Expectancies. The magnitude of a salesperson's expectancy estimates indicates the degree to which the representative believes that the effort expended on various job activities affects her level of performance. In other words, it reflects the salesperson's perceptions of her ability to control or influence her own job performance.

Several individual and environmental characteristics are likely to affect these expectancies. Some psychologists suggest that a worker's overall level of self-esteem and perceived ability to perform necessary tasks are positively related to the magnitude of the person's expectancy estimates.[32] Similarly, the salesperson's general intelligence and previous sales experience may influence the individual's perceived ability to improve performance through his own efforts. If these relationships are also true for salespeople, the characteristics may be useful supplementary criteria for the recruitment and selection of salespeople.

A salesperson's perceptions of the linkages between effort and performance are also likely to be influenced by environmental characteristics. How the salesperson perceives general economic conditions, territory potential, the strength of competition, restrictions on product availability due to energy shortages, and so forth are all likely to affect her thoughts on how much sales performance can be improved by simply increasing efforts. Without attempting to identify all the relevant environmental factors, it can be said that the greater the environmental constraints a salesperson sees as restricting performance, the lower the salesperson's expectancy estimates will be. Consequently, managers may find it desirable to change performance criteria and/or evaluation methods during periods of economic uncertainty to maintain desired levels of effort from the sales force.

Accuracy of Instrumentalities. The true linkages between performance on various dimensions and the attainment of rewards are determined by management practices and policies concerning how sales performance is evaluated and

---

[31] The argument is often advanced, for example, that salespeople should be given pricing flexibility in that they are closest to the customers and have the best perspective on the price that will be needed to make the sales. Interestingly, one study that investigated the admonition found that among a sample of 108 firms that those firms that gave salespeople the highest degree of pricing authority generated the lowest sales and profit performance. See P. Ronald Stephenson, William L. Cron, and Gary L. Frazier, "Delegating Pricing Authority in the Sales Force: The Effects on Sales and Profit Performance," *Journal of Marketing* 43 (Spring 1979), pp. 21–28.

[32] Abraham K. Korman, "Expectances as Determinants of Performance," *Journal of Applied Psychology* 55 (1971), pp. 218–22; and Edward E. Lawler, III, "Job Attitudes and Employee Motivation: Theory, Research and Practice," *Personnel Psychology* 23 (1970), pp. 223–37.

what rewards are given for various levels of performance. These policies and practices may be misperceived by the salesperson. As a result, the salesperson may concentrate on improving performance in areas that are relatively unimportant to management, and the representative may ultimately become disillusioned with his ability to attain rewards.

Thus, it would seem useful to compare salespeople's instrumentality perceptions with stated company policies and management perceptions of the true or desired linkages between performance and rewards. If many salespeople misperceive how performance is rewarded in the firm, it may be desirable to improve the accuracy of those perceptions. This can be done through closer supervision and more direct feedback concerning evaluation and the determination of rewards.

Magnitude of Instrumentalities. One organizational variable that obviously has an impact on the magnitude of some of a salesperson's instrumentality estimates is the compensation plan used by the firm. A salesperson who is compensated largely or entirely by commission is likely to perceive a greater probability of attaining more pay if he improves performance on those dimensions directly related to total sales volume (e.g., increase in total sales dollars or percentage of quota). On the other hand, the salaried salesperson is more likely to perceive a greater probability of receiving increased pay for improving performance on dimensions not directly related to short-term sales volume (e.g., new account generation, reduction of selling expenses, or performance of administrative duties).

Additionally, the salesperson may be rewarded with things other than pay, such as promotion, recognition, and feelings of accomplishment. The representative may value these other rewards more highly than an increase in pay. In any case, the company's compensation plan is unlikely to have any effect on the salesperson's perceptions of the linkages between performance and these nonfinancial rewards. Therefore, a compensation plan by itself is inadequate for explaining differences in motivation among salespeople.

Personal characteristics of the salesperson may also influence the magnitude of instrumentality estimates. One such characteristic is the individual's perception of whether he controls life events or whether these events are determined by external forces beyond the individual's control. Specifically, the greater the degree to which a salesperson believes he has internal control over life, the more likely the representative is to feel that an improvement in performance will result in the attainment of rewards.[33] Similarly, some evidence in industrial psychology suggests that a worker's intelligence is positively related to the individual's instrumentality estimates. Once again, if such relationships hold true for industrial salespeople, these personal characteristics may be useful criteria for the recruitment and selection of salespeople.

---

[33] Lawler, "Job Attitudes"; and Julian B. Rotter, "Generalized Expectancies for Internal Versus External Control of Reinforcement," *Psychological Monographs: General and Applied* 80 (1960), pp. 1–28.

The Role Component and the
Sales Manager

As this chapter suggests, the role component of the model has some important implications for sales managers. Feelings of ambiguity, conflict, and inaccurate role perceptions can cause psychological stress and job-related anxiety for salespeople. These, in turn, can lead to lowered performance. All are dysfunctional consequences as far as sales managers are concerned. Thus, sales managers have a vested interest in keeping salespeople's role perceptions within tolerable limits.

Fortunately, there are things the sales manager can do to accomplish that goal. The kind of salespeople that are hired, the manner in which they are trained, the kinds of incentives used to motivate them, the criteria used to evaluate them, and the manner in which they are supervised can all affect perceptions of role. These factors can also determine whether these perceptions are ambiguous, in conflict, or inaccurate. That is why the role component of the salesperson performance model was discussed first. Its early discussion allows a fuller appreciation of the significance of the sales manager's primary duties, which were outlined in Chapter 1 and discussed more fully in subsequent chapters.

Summary

The purpose of this chapter was to elaborate on the role perceptions variable in the model of salesperson's performance. A person's role represents the set of activities and behaviors that are to be performed by anyone who occupies that position. The role of salesperson is defined through a three-step process: (1) Expectations and demands concerning how the salesperson should behave in various situations, together with pressures to conform, are communicated to the salesperson by members of the individual's role set. (2) The salesperson perceives these expectations and demands that are communicated by members of the role set. (3) The salesperson converts these perceptions into actual behavior.

Perceived role ambiguity arises when the salesperson is uncertain about the expectations and demands being communicated. Perceived role conflict exists when a representative believes that the role demands of two or more members of the role set are incompatible. Perceived role inaccuracy arises when the salesperson's perceptions of the role partner's demands are inaccurate.

The role of salesperson is particularly susceptible to feelings of ambiguity and conflict and to forming inaccurate perceptions. There are three reasons for this: (1) it is at the boundary of the firm, (2) the salesperson's relevant role set includes many other people both within and outside the firm, and (3) the position of sales representative often requires a good deal of innovativeness.

Important managerial consequences are associated with salespeople experiencing feelings of ambiguity or conflict or having inaccurate perceptions. Such feelings can cause psychological stress, produce low satisfaction and lead to poorer performance. Fortunately, the sales manager can affect these consequences through decisions on the type of salespeople that are hired, the manner in which they are trained, the incentives used to motivate them, the criteria used to evaluate them, and the way they are supervised and controlled.

Discussion Questions

1. "I want sales representatives who can stand on their own. Once a representative has been through training and shows how to apply this knowledge, it shouldn't be necessary for me to constantly tell them how they are doing. The stars always shine; it's the other sales representatives that need my attention." Comment on this statement. Do you agree or disagree?

2. Discuss the three problems that occur in the perception of salespeople. What effect do they have on a salesperson's performance or mental well-being? How do these problems differ?

3. Salespeople are likely to experience more role conflict than most other organizations' members because they occupy positions at the boundaries of the firm. Is this true? Explain.

4. "In small doses, role conflict and ambiguity may be good for the individual—and therefore for the organization—since stress is often associated with adaptation and change." Do you agree? Explain why or why not.

5. Some sales managers tell married applicants that they would like to interview their spouses before making the hiring decision. Why would a sales manager make such a request? Do you approve?

6. A sales representative for the Railroad Equipment Corporation is faced with a demand from an important customer that is in direct conflict with company policies. The customer wants several product modifications with no change in price. What can the sales representative do to handle this conflict?

7. Most sales representatives are expected to complete a variety of reports—some daily, some weekly, and some annually. However, research indicates that most sales representatives perceive that very few rewards result from having timely and carefully prepared written reports. Why is this so? What are the implications of this result?

8. The sales force for the Ansul Company, a manufacturer of fire prevention systems for industrial applications, has been told that they will now have to sell small fire extinguishers to the retail market. What role problems are likely to occur?

Chapter 10

Personal Characteristics and Sales Aptitude: Criteria for Selecting Salespeople

The Dallas Cowboys professional football team was formed in 1960. The team did not win any of the 12 games it played during that first year. For each of the next four years, it lost more games than it won. Finally, in 1965, it broke even in the won-lost column. Since that time, though, its record has been phenomenal. It has never had a losing season, and its record for 1966–82 was 171 games won, 59 lost, and 2 tied—a winning percentage of 73.7. Experts attribute much of the Cowboys' continuing success to the team's talent scouts and director of player personnel. They have shown an uncanny ability to locate and select college players—often players overlooked by other teams—who have the ability to be successful professional ballplayers. As a result, Dallas has seldom had to seek replacements for its older, retiring players through costly trades with other teams. Also, the Cowboys have never had to suffer through an extended period of "rebuilding." The ability to accurately assess the aptitude and ability of young players has enabled the team to draft and train its own replacements with great success.

Identifying and selecting personnel who have the aptitude necessary for future success is as important in staffing a sales force as it is in a sports organization. Just as it would be useless for a team to hire and train players who are too small or too slow to be successful in the National Football League, it would be futile for a firm to hire, train, and attempt to motivate salespeople who lack the basic mental capacity or personality characteristics to be successful. Unfortunately, many firms are not very adept at recruiting and selecting salespeople with the talent and ability for future selling success.

One indication that firms do not always make wise decisions is the relatively high proportion of recruits who either become disillusioned and quit their jobs or are discharged a short time after joining a company. One survey reported in *Sales Management* found that, on the average, 15 percent of a firm's salespeople either quit or are fired during their first year on the job. Sales-force turnover approaches 50 percent during the first five years of employment.[1]

The results of another recent survey of 319 large manufacturing firms are shown in Table 10–1. Although this study found that quit rates and discharge rates vary by type of product sold—with consumer goods firms having somewhat higher rates than industrial goods manufacturers—overall, the rates are highest in firms where the average age of the sales force is relatively young.[2] Again, this suggests that companies are not always successful in identifying and hiring people—particularly those who are younger and inexperienced—who have the personal characteristics and abilities to become satisfied and successful salespersons.

Mistakes in recruitment and selection are very expensive, given that it costs between $10,000 and $50,000 to recruit, train, and develop one productive industrial salesperson. When that person lacks the aptitude to be successful, those

---

[1] "Some Stay and Some Go, but Which Salesmen Stay with You Longest?" *Sales Management*, May 1, 1972, p. 74.
[2] Charles A. Peck, "Compensating Field Sales Representativeness," Report No. 828 (New York: The Conference Board, 1982), pp. 34–35.

Table 10–1
Median salesperson quit rates and discharge rates by average age of the sales force

Average Age of Sales Force (years)	Median Quit Rates	Median Discharge Rates
25–34	5.4%	3.0%
34–39	6.0	2.0
40–44	4.0	1.0
45–54	3.0	0.0

Source: Charles A. Peck, "Compensating Field Sales Representatives," Report No. 828 (New York: The Conference Board, 1982), p. 35.

recruiting and training dollars go down the drain. Indeed, one authority estimates that it costs American firms more than $5 billion a year to recruit and train *replacements* for salespeople who either quit or are fired.[3]

There is another hidden cost when a firm is unable to attract and select new recruits with the greatest possible selling aptitude. Even though such people may turn out to be adequate, they will never be as productive as people with greater natural ability, regardless of how well the firm's sales managers train, supervise, and motivate them. Thus, the firm that does an inadequate job of recruitment and selection incurs opportunity costs in the form of sales and profits that are lower than they could have been.

In view of these problems, many sales managers consider the recruitment and selection of new sales recruits to be among the most important aspects of their jobs. The remainder of this chapter, consequently, examines some personal and psychological characteristics that are thought to be related to, or determinants of, an individual's aptitude.

What Is Sales Aptitude?

Sales aptitude is one of the five major determinants of a person's sales performance. Aptitude is typically viewed as the overall limit of an individual's ability to perform a given sales job. In other words, two people with equal motivation, role perceptions, and training might perform at different levels because one does not have the personal characteristics necessary to do the job as well as the other. The question is: What personal characteristics enable a person to achieve good sales performance? What are the determinants of sales aptitude?

---

[3] Barton A. Weitz, "A Critical Review of Personal Selling Research: The Need for Contingency Approaches," in *Critical Issues in Sales Management: State-of-the-Art and Future Research Needs*, ed. Gerald Albaum and Gilbert A. Churchill, Jr. (Eugene: College of Business Administration, University of Oregon, 1979), p. 76.

The Characteristics that Sales Managers Look for

One way to answer these questions is to identify the personal characteristics that sales managers look for when selecting new salespeople. Imagine that you are sales manager for a major manufacturer and you must judge applicants for a position in your sales force. Which of the following characteristics would you consider to be most important for your new salesperson to have? Just for fun, rank the relative importance of those characteristics from one to 10. You can then compare your responses with those of 44 top sales executives from major manufacturing organizations, which are displayed in Table 10–2.

_____ High persuasiveness	_____ Follows instructions
_____ Sociability	_____ Highly recommended
_____ Enthusiasm	_____ High verbal skill
_____ Well organized	_____ General sales experience
_____ Obvious ambition	_____ Specific sales experience

As you can see, "enthusiasm" is ranked as the most important characteristic to look for in new recruits by twice as many sales executives surveyed than any

Table 10–2
Importance rankings of ten indicators of sales aptitude by top sales executives in 44 major manufacturing firms

Attribute	Rank Assigned by Respondents*										Total Points
	1 (10)	2 (9)	3 (8)	4 (7)	5 (6)	6 (5)	7 (4)	8 (3)	9 (2)	10 (1)	
Enthusiasm	16	5	8	5	1	5	—	1	—	—	338
Well organized	6	8	11	3	5	5	1	2	—	—	304
Obvious ambition	8	6	5	7	4	3	2	3	3	—	285
High persuasiveness	2	10	3	1	10	4	5	3	1	2	254
General sales experience	3	2	4	6	6	2	8	8	5	4	226
High verbal skill	2	3	3	6	2	7	7	6	4	1	215
Specific sales experience	2	4	2	8	6	1	5	4	4	5	214
Highly recommended	1	—	1	4	3	3	7	2	7	2	149
Follows instructions	—	2	—	3	4	4	2	9	9	8	142
Sociability	—	1	1	2	—	7	6	6	8	10	134

*The top numeral in each column is the ranking given by executives, with 1 being most important and 10 least important. Numbers in parentheses are point ratings assigned to each rank. Numbers in the table show the number of respondents who assigned each rank to each attribute.
Source: Stan Moss, "What Sales Executives Look For in New Salespeople," *Sales and Marketing Management*, March 1978, p. 47.

other attribute. Other characteristics the respondents consider relatively important are "well organized," "ambition," and the two related attributes of "high persuasiveness" and "verbal skill." Although many executives consider previous sales experience to be important in indicating the sales aptitude of new employees, general experience in selling is viewed as being more relevant than specific product or industry experience.

The results of this survey seem to contradict some beliefs that are widely held among people who apply for sales jobs. Glowing recommendations from previous employers or professors are not seen as relevant indicators of a candidate's potential for future selling success. Also, the highly sociable, "hail-fellow-well-met" type of personality is often not considered a very important attribute.

Surveys like this are instructive, but they do not provide a definitive answer to the question of what personal characteristics make some individuals better salespeople than others. One major weakness of such surveys is that their results merely reflect the perceptions of the sales executives who responded. Although those perceptions are based on years of practical experience, they may still be biased or inaccurate. A more objective way to identify which personal characteristics are strongly related to sales aptitude is to examine a large cross section of salespeople. From this, one can determine whether a statistically significant relationship exists between the possession of a particular personal trait and actual sales performance among the members of the sample. Fortunately, many such studies have been conducted among salespeople. The first published study, which examined the usefulness of vocational tests in selecting retail salespeople, appeared in 1918.[4] Since then, more than 400 studies have been published.[5] Conclusions from the results of these studies are discussed next.

The Relationship between General Personal Characteristics and Sales Performance

Most studies of sales aptitude have related salespeople's performance to their scores on standard personality tests, ability tests, and application form information commonly used in the selection process. In other words, these studies have attempted to find one or more general personal traits that are related to—and perhaps explain—individual differences in sales performance. The personal traits examined in these studies generally fall into one of three broad categories:

1. Aptitude Characteristics—relatively stable and unchanging psychological characteristics of a person that enhance or constrain his or her *ability* to

[4] Elsie Oschrin, "Vocational Tests for Retail Saleswomen," *Journal of Applied Psychology* 2 (June 1918), pp. 148–55.
[5] Gilbert A. Churchill, Jr., Neil M. Ford, Steven W. Hartley, and Orville C. Walker, Jr., "The Determinants of Salesperson Performance: A Meta Analysis," Working Paper (Madison: Graduate School of Business, University of Wisconsin, 1984).

perform a sales job effectively. Aptitude characteristics can be broken down into:

    a. Mental abilities, such as general intelligence, verbal intelligence and mathematical ability.

    b. Personality characteristics, such as empathy, aggressiveness, dominance, need for achievement, and sociability.

2. Skill Level—an individual's level of sales-related knowledge or proficiency at carrying out the specific tasks necessary to perform a sales job. While aptitude consists of relatively enduring personal abilities, skill levels can change rapidly with training and years of selling experience.

3. Personal Characteristics—other individual factors that might affect a salesperson's performance, but which are not direct determinants of the person's aptitude or skill. These factors include physical traits like age, sex, height and physical attractiveness, level of formal education, and "life style" characteristics, such as the person's interests and family situation.

One problem with most existing studies, however, is that they are atheoretical; that is, anticipated relationships between particular personal traits and sales performance are rarely specified in formal hypotheses. Even studies that do test explicit hypotheses seldom offer any explanation for why a given personal trait is expected to lead to better performance. The lack of an explicit theoretical framework makes it difficult to compare the results of the existing studies or to summarize their findings.

On the basis of common sense and experience, however, it is possible to state some theoretical relationships between a number of personal characteristics, skills and aptitude characteristics, and a salesperson's ultimate performance.[6] We can then use these relationships as a framework for summarizing and evaluating the existing research findings.

Personal Characteristics

We might hypothesize that older salespeople will be perceived by customers as relatively more experienced and knowledgeable than younger people. Therefore, they may be seen as more credible sources of information. Also, older salespeople may have a better understanding of the selling process and, thus, may be more effective in their dealings with customers.

Sex and *race* are other physical traits of particular interest to sales managers, particularly in view of government regulations concerning equal opportunity in hiring and promotion. Although only a few studies have examined the relationships between these two characteristics and sales performance, those relation-

---

[6] The following discussion draws heavily from material in Weitz, "Critical Review," and Barton A. Weitz, "Effectiveness in Sales Interactions: A Contingency Framework," *Journal of Marketing*, Winter 1981, pp. 85–103.

ships are of so much concern that we will examine them separately in a later section of this chapter.

Other personal variables may influence sales performance indirectly through their effects on other major determinants of performance. *Formal education,* for example, might be related to the attainment of basic mental and interpersonal skills necessary for effective selling, while a person's *family situation* might affect his or her motivation level and desire for financial rewards.

Skill Levels

As with older salespeople, one would expect that individuals with a large amount of *sales-related knowledge* will be perceived by their customers as more useful and believable sources of information than less knowledgeable salespeople. This knowledge may be obtained through years of *experience,* extensive *training,* or *familiarity with the products* being sold. Salespeople who know more should be better able to influence their customers and achieve a high level of sales perform- ance.

Aptitude—Mental Abilities

It seems likely that relatively intelligent salespeople and those with relatively high levels of *mental ability* should be better able to analyze their customers and understand their needs. Such individuals may also have the communications skills to develop and deliver effective sales presentations. After all, verbal intelli- gence is a major component of overall intelligence.

Aptitude—Personality Characteristics

Salespeople with personality characteristics that make them relatively out- going and *sociable*—such as other-directedness, extroversion, and social adapta- bility—might be expected to be more successful. They should be better able to develop close personal relationships with their customers than less sociable sales- people. Such close personal relationships, in turn, should enable them to learn more about their customers' needs and be more effective in influencing purchase decisions.

Salespeople with personality traits that help them to be relatively *forceful* in their dealings with other people—such as ego drive, dominance, aggressiveness, and need for achievement—should also be more effective. It is reasonable to expect forceful salespeople to be more persistent at overcoming objections from customers and more successful at closing sales.

Finally, *empathetic* personality types should be more successful as salespeople. They are likely to be more sensitive to their customers' needs and more flexible in tailoring their sales presentations to address each customer's unique problems and concerns.

Specific Research Evidence

While all the preceding propositions seem to make common sense, the question is whether they are supported by the findings of recent research studies. Table 10–3 summarizes the results of 21 studies conducted since 1950 that investigate the relationship between one or more of the personal, mental, and personality traits discussed earlier and the performance of salespeople. For each of the seven characteristics, studies that found that people with more of the characteristic performed significantly better than those with less are listed in the middle column of Table 10–3, together with a description of the type of firm or sales job examined in the study. Studies that found no significant relationship between possession of the characteristic and sales performance are listed in the right-hand column.

As you can see, the relationships between the general characteristics of salespeople and their sales performance are not very consistent across studies in different industries and job settings. Both age and education were significantly related to performance in three studies, but they were not related in six other studies. Sales-related knowledge and performance were significantly related in one study, but not in six others. Intelligence was positively related to performance in two studies, not related to performance in one, and negatively related in another study. Similarly, a positive relationship was found between sociability and sales performance in three studies, a negative relationship was discovered in one, and no relationship in six others. Forcefulness was positively related to performance in eight studies, but not in four others. Finally, although empathy and performance were positively related in four studies, one study found a negative relationship and another found no relationship at all.

A Comprehensive Overview of
Past Research

Inconsistencies in the relationships between various characteristics of salespeople and their sales performance were also found in a recent comprehensive review of past studies of sales success.[7] The review examined more than 400 published and unpublished studies conducted between 1918 and 1983, 116 of

---

[7] Churchill, et al., "The Determinants of Salesperson Performance."

Table 10–3
Research findings concerning the relationship of selected personal characteristics of salespeople to sales performance in various industries and selling jobs

Personal Characteristic	Studies in Which Characteristic Was Related to Performance at a Statistically Significant Level	Studies in Which Characteristic Was Not Related to Performance at a Statistically Significant Level
1. Age (Kirchner et al., 1960)	Industrial goods Retail sales (Mosel, 1952) Retail sales (Weaver, 1969)	Industrial goods (Lamont and Lundstrom, 1977) Retail sales (French, 1960) Retail appliance sales (Cotham, 1969) Stockbroker (Ghiselli, 1969) Life insurance (Meranda and Clarke, 1959) Life insurance (Tanofsky et al., 1969)
2. Education	Life insurance (Meranda and Clarke, 1959) Retail sales (Mosel, 1952) Retail sales (Weaver, 1969)	Life insurance (Tanofsky et al., 1969) Retail sales (French, 1960) Retail appliance sales (Cothan, 1969) Specialty food manufacturing (Baehr and Williams, 1968) Stockbroker (Ghiselli, 1969) Industrial goods (Lamont and Lundstrom, 1977)
3. Sales-related knowledge (experience, amount of training, and/or amount of product knowledge)	Life insurance (Baier and Duggan, 1957)	Life insurance (Meranda and Clarke, 1959) Life insurance (Tanofsky et al., 1969) Specialty food manufacturer (Baehr and Williams, 1968) Stockbroker (Ghiselli, 1969) Retail sales (French, 1960) Retail appliance sales (Cotham, 1969)
4. Intelligence	Stockbroker (Ghiselli, 1969) Oil company (Miner, 1962) Industrial goods (Bagozzi, 1978)*	Oil company (Harrell, 1960)
5. Sociability (extroversion, adaptability, other-directedness, etc.)	Life insurance (Meranda and Clarke, 1959) Technical reps. (Howells, 1968)* Retail sales (Howells, 1968) Van sales (Howells, 1968)	Oil company (Harrell, 1960) Oil company (Miner, 1962) Real estate (Scheibelhut and Albaum, 1973) Utility (Scheibelhut and Albaum, 1973) Industrial goods (Pruden and Peterson, 1971) Industrial goods (Bagozzi, 1978)

Table 10–3 *(concluded)*

Personal Characteristic	Studies in Which Characteristic Was Related to Performance at a Statistically Significant Level	Studies in Which Characteristic Was Not Related to Performance at a Statistically Significant Level
6. Forcefulness (dominance, ego drive, need for achievement, aggressiveness, etc.)	Oil company (Harrell, 1960) Life insurance (Meranda and Clarke, 1959) Life insurance (Greenberg and Mayer, 1964) Van sales (Howells, 1968) Mutual fund (Greenberg and Mayer, 1964) Automobile (Greenberg and Mayer, 1964) Trade (Dunnette and Kirchner, 1960) Industrial goods (Dunnette and Kirchner, 1960)	Oil company (Miner, 1962) Life insurance (Zdep and Weaver, 1967) Technical reps. (Howells, 1968) Retail sales (Howells, 1968)
7. Empathy	New automobile (Tobolski and Kerr, 1952) Automobile (Greenberg and Mayer, 1964) Life insurance (Greenberg and Mayer, 1964) Mutual fund (Greenberg and Mayer, 1964) Industrial goods (Lamont and Lundstrom, 1977)*	Used automobile (Tobolski and Kerr, 1952)

*Statistically significant but negatively related to performance.

List of studies cited:

Melany E. Baehr and Glenn B. Williams, "Prediction of Sales Success from Factorially Determined Dimensions of Personal Background Data," *Journal of Applied Psychology* 52 (April 1968), pp. 98–103; Richard P. Bagozzi, "Salesforce Performance and Satisfaction as a Function of Individual Difference, Interpersonal and Situational Factors," *Journal of Marketing Research* 15 (November 1978), pp. 517–31; Donald E. Baier and Robert D. Duggan, "Factors in Sales Success," *Journal of Applied Psychology* 41 (1957), pp. 37–40; James C. Cotham III, "Using Personal History Information in Retail Salesman Selection," *Journal of Retailing* 45 (Spring 1969), pp. 31–38; Marvin D. Dunnette and Wayne K. Kirchner, "Psychological Test Differences between Industrial Salesmen and Retail Salesmen," *Journal of Applied Psychology* 44 (April 1960), pp. 121–25; Cecil L. French, "Correlates of Success in Retail Selling," *American Journal of Sociology* 66 (1960), pp. 128–34; Edwin E. Ghiselli, "Prediction of Success of Stockbrokers," *Personnel Psychology* 22 (Summer 1969), pp. 125–30; Herbert Greenberg and David Mayer, "A New Approach to the Scientific Selection of Successful Salesmen," *Journal of Psychology* 5 (1964), pp. 113–23; Thomas W. Harrell, "The Relation of Test Scores to Sales Criteria," *Personnel Psychology* 13 (1960), pp. 65–69; G. W. Howells, "The Successful Salesman Personality Analysis," *British Journal of Marketing* 2 (1968), pp. 13–23; Wayne K. Kirchner, Carolyn S. McElwain and Marvin D. Dunnette, "A Note on the Relationship Betweem Age and Sales Effectiveness," *Journal of Applied Psychology* 44 (April 1960), pp. 92–93; Lawrence M. Lamont and William J. Lundstrom, "Identifying Successful Industrial Salesmen by Personality and Personal Characteristics," *Journal of Marketing Research* 14 (November 1977), pp. 517–29; Peter F. Merenda and Walter V. Clarke, "Predictive Efficiency of Temperament Characteristics and Personal History Variables in Determining Success of Life Insurance Agents," *Journal of Applied Psychology* 43 (1959), pp. 360–66; John B. Miner, "Personality and Ability Factors in Sales Performance," *Journal of Applied Psychology* 46 (February 1962), pp. 6–13; James N. Mosel, "Prediction of Department Store Sales Performance from Personnel Data," *Journal of Applied Psychology* 36 (1952), pp. 8–10; Henry O. Pruden and Robert A. Peterson, "Personality and the Performance-Satisfaction of Industrial Salesmen," *Journal of Marketing Research* 8 (November 1971), pp. 501–504; John H. Scheibelhut and Gerald Albaum, "Self-Orientation Among Salesmen and Non-Salesmen," *Journal of Marketing Research* 10 (February 1973), pp. 97–99; Robert Tanofsky, R. Ronald Shepps, and Paul J. O'Neill, "Pattern Analysis of Biographical Predictors of Success as an Insurance Salesman," *Journal of Applied Psychology* 53 (April 1969), pp. 136–39; Frances P. Tobolski and Willard A. Kerr, "Predictive Value of the Empathy Test in Automobile Salesmanship," *Journal of Applied Psychology* 36 (1952), pp. 310–11; Charles N. Weaver, "An Empirical Study to Aid in the Selection of Retail Salesclerks," *Journal of Retailing* 45 (1969), pp. 22–26; S. M. Zdep and H. B. Weaver, "The Graphoanalytic Approach to Selecting Life Insurance Salesmen," *Journal of Applied Psychology* 51 (June 1967), pp. 295–99.

Source: Adapted from Barton A. Weitz, "A Critical Review of Personal Selling Research: The Need for Contingency Approaches," in Gerald Albaum and Gilbert A. Churchill, Jr., eds., *Critical Issues in Sales Management: State-of-the-Art and Future Research Needs* (Eugene: College of Business Administration, University of Oregon, 1979), pp. 87–88.

which reported some empirical evidence regarding the strength of the relation-ship between one or more characteristics of salespeople and their performance. Since most of those studies investigated more than one variable, the review actu-ally summarized a total of 1,653 reported relationships between various individ-ual characteristics and sales performance. For purposes of analysis, the individ-ual characteristics were grouped into six categories. Three categories were the same as those discussed above—(1) personal characteristics, (2) skill levels, and (3) aptitude (including mental abilities and personality traits)—while the other three consisted of (4) role perceptions, (5) motivational factors, and (6) character-istics of the organization and its environment.

The review found that, on the average across all 116 studies, people's role perceptions had the strongest relationship with their sales performance, followed by skill levels, motivation, personal characteristics, aptitude, and organizational and environmental factors. As was the case with the findings reported in Table 10-3, however, the size of the relationships between each category of individual characteristics and sales performance varied widely across studies. The strengths of those relationships also varied according to the type of goods or services being sold. Aptitude variables, for example, were found to be more positively related to performance for people selling industrial products than for those selling services.

Another disconcerting finding of the review was that while many studies have reported relationships between particular individual attributes and sales success, those relationships are typically not very strong. On the average, each of the six categories of variables accounted for less than 10 percent of the variation in per-formance, although some stronger relationships were reported in individual stud-ies. This suggests that, in order to identify potentially successful sales recruits, a sales manager should pay attention to a variety of individual characteristics in-stead of giving too much weight to only one or a few, such as past experience, formal education, or an outgoing personality.

Possible Reasons for Inconsistent Research Findings

Why have some studies found significant relationships between particular personal characteristics and sales performance, whereas others have not? One reason may be that different research methods and procedures have been used in different studies. For example, different tests—such as the Edwards Personal Preference Schedule and the Jackson Personality Profile—have been used to measure personality traits such as sociability and forcefulness. Similarly, sales performance has been defined and measured in a variety of ways in different studies. Consequently, a given personal characteristic may actually be an impor-tant determinant of sales aptitude, but because of variations in the accuracy and reliability of the measures used in different studies, researchers have not always found a statistically significant relationship between the characteristic and sales performance.

This argument, however, cannot explain *all* the inconsistency in the research findings. Some personal characteristics—such as age and job experience—have been measured objectively and consistently across a number of studies. Such characteristics are significantly related to sales performance in some of those studies but not in others.

Another plausible explanation for the lack of consistent relationships is that different types of sales jobs require salespeople to perform different activities and to deal with different types of customers. Thus, people with particular traits and abilities may have the aptitude for success in some sales jobs but not others. This explanation is consistent with the finding reported above that the strength of relationships between various individual attributes and sales performance varies with the type of product or service being sold. Consequently, it may be futile to look for a single "type" of person who is most likely to be successful in all kinds of selling jobs. Instead, sales managers may have to identify specific characteristics and abilities that will enable a salesperson to handle competently the particular selling tasks faced by his or her sales force.

Similarly, different salesperson characteristics and abilities may be needed for dealing successfully with different kinds of customers. As one authority suggests, a successful sale is the result of the "dyadic interaction" between a given salesperson and prospect rather than the individual qualities of either alone.[8]

With these thoughts in mind, a number of recent research efforts have attempted to identify specific aspects of sales aptitude that are related to successful selling performance involving interactions with particular types of customers. The results of these studies are discussed in a later section of this chapter. First, though, there is an examination of two other general physical characteristics that may be related to sales aptitude: race and sex. These two attributes deserve special attention because of recent changes in the social and legal environment. The question of whether a person's race or sex influences his or her ability to be successful in selling has become an issue of great interest to sales managers.

Race, Sex, and Sales Aptitude

Black Americans make up about 12 percent of our country's population, yet statistics gathered from the 1980 U.S. Census show that only about 6 percent of all sales jobs were held by blacks. The proportion of blacks in the more prestigious and rewarding industrial sales positions was even lower.

Historically, women have experienced a similar lack of opportunity in selling. A survey conducted in the mid-1970s by the Research Institute of America found that 81 percent of the responding companies did not employ any saleswomen.[9] A study sponsored by the 3,000-member Sales Executive Club of New York revealed

---

[8] Franklin Evans, "Selling as a Dyadic Relationship—A New Approach," *American Behavioral Scientist* 6 (May 1963), pp. 76–79.

[9] "RIA-SECNY Study Finds 81% of the U.S. Businesses Employ No Saleswomen," *Marketing News*, July 15, 1974, p. 1.

that women accounted for only 4 percent of the member firms' sales forces.[10] Companies that have traditionally hired women for sales jobs are concentrated in the retailing and real estate industries. This is reflected in the fact that, according to the 1980 Census, 2.9 million women were employed as "sales workers," but their average annual income was only $9,748—only 42 percent as much as the average income earned by all male "sales workers" and only a third as much as was earned by senior industrial salespeople in 1980.[11]

One major reason for this history of unequal employment was that many sales managers felt that women and racial minorities would face disadvantages in performing selling jobs and would not do as well as white men. It was widely believed that some customers, particularly those with racial prejudices, would be reluctant to deal with or buy from minority salespeople. Similarly, many sales managers felt that women were generally too emotional and lacking in aggressiveness and self-confidence to be effective salespeople. Some managers thought that turnover rates would be higher for women due to marriage and childbirth, and that women would be less willing to travel and entertain. Consequently, 80 percent of the 180 top sales and marketing executives surveyed by *Sales Management* in the late 1960s admitted that they were unwilling to hire women for outside sales positions.[12]

Legal Requirements for Equal Employment Opportunities. Despite past negative attitudes, employment opportunities for women and minorities in selling have improved in recent years as the result of environmental changes and pressures. These include such things as the civil rights movement, changing attitudes concerning women's roles, increasing career orientation among women, and changes in the law. Indeed, the rights of women and minorities to equal employment opportunities in selling, as well as in other occupations, are strongly protected by federal laws. Title VII of the 1964 Civil Rights Act prohibits discrimination in hiring, promotions, and compensation. It covers all private employers of 15 or more persons. The Equal Employment Opportunity Commission administers Title VII. Since 1972, it has had broad enforcement powers. The commission's guidelines prohibit withholding jobs or promotions because of either customer preferences for salespeople of a particular race or sex or assumed differences in turnover rates. They also prohibit separate promotional paths or seniority lists.

Firms with federal contracts are further regulated by the Office of Federal Contract Compliance. Supply contractors with 50 or more employees and a federal contract worth $50,000 or more are required to develop written affirmative action plans. Title VII requires such plans only after the Equal Employment Opportunity Commission determines that a firm has shown a pattern of discrimination.

---

[10] John Costello, "Ms. Star in Sales," *Marketing Times,* March-April 1975), pp. 4–9.

[11] Daphne Spain and Suzanne M. Bianchi, "How Women Have Changed," *American Demographics* 5 (May 1983), pp. 18–25; and "Compensation," *Sales and Marketing Management,* February 21, 1983, p. 71.

[12] Eleanor Schwartz, "Women in Sales: Will the Walls Come Tumbling Down?" *Sales Management,* August 15, 1969, pp. 39–40.

Research evidence. As firms have hired more minorities and women for sales positions, have the old concerns about the possible shortcomings of such individuals been supported or disproved? Have sales managers' attitudes changed as more women and minorities have been added to their sales forces? Do sex and race have anything to do with a person's sales aptitude and ultimate performance?

Unfortunately, the existing research evidence relevant to such questions is neither very extensive nor conclusive. Very few published studies have compared the job performance of minority salespeople with that of whites, or examined sales managers' attitudes or perceptions of minority salespeople.[13] One reason for this lack of empirical evidence is that there are still relatively few minorities employed in industrial selling. Consequently, it is difficult for researchers to obtain a large enough sample to make statistically valid comparisons of their performance with that of whites.

On the other hand, several firms—such as IBM, Procter & Gamble, General Mills, Hallmark Cards, Inland Steel, and General Foods—have been active and successful in recruiting minorities for their sales forces.[14] The experiences of these companies suggest that, given adequate training and solid company support, minority salespeople have no major difficulties gaining access to customers. Also, their job performance is not systematically different from that of the rest of the sales force. Furthermore, there are some selling situations in which minority salespeople have actually performed better than whites. For example, some food companies, such as Armour, have found that minority salespeople are more effective than white salespeople in calling on retail stores in minority neighborhoods.

As for saleswomen, there have been no published studies comparing objective measures of the actual sales performance of men and women. However, several recent studies have examined the attitudes and perceptions of sales managers concerning the abilities and job performance of women in their sales forces.[15]

The perceptions of 100 top sales executives from firms in the paper and chemical industries concerning the relative job performance of men and women in their sales forces are shown in Table 10–4. A large majority of managers feel there is no difference between men and women in their rates of absenteeism and sales performance. However, one quarter of the respondents believe that women have higher rates of job turnover than men.

In the study reported in Table 10–4, respondents were also asked what they believed their customers' reactions were to having women in the sales force. Nearly 75 percent of the respondents thought their customers' attitudes were

---

[13] For a review of these studies, see William A. Strang, Gilbert A. Churchill, Jr., and Robert H. Collins, "Blacks in Sales: Why Are There So Few?" *The Review of Black Political Economy* 6 (Winter 1976), pp. 200–212.

[14] "The Negro in Sales: Color Him Out," *Sales Management*, February 15, 1968, pp. 32–36.

[15] Sally Scanlon, "Ms. Is a Hit!" *Sales Management*, February 5, 1973, p. 24; Don H. Robertson and Donald W. Hackett, "Saleswomen: Perceptions, Problems and Prospects," *Journal of Marketing* 41 (July 1977), pp. 66–71; John E. Swan, Charles M. Futrell, and John T. Todd, "Same Job—Different Views: Women and Men in Industrial Sales," *Journal of Marketing* 41 (January 1977), pp. 92–98; and Leslie Kanuk, "Women in Industrial Selling," *Journal of Marketing* 42 (January 1978), pp. 87–91.

Table 10–4
Sales managers' perceptions of the relative job performance of men and women in sales forces

Performance Dimension	Perception	Percent of Response*
Sales volume	Men make more sales	22%
	No difference between men and women	76
	Don't know or no response	2
Absenteeism	Women have greater absenteeism	8
	No difference between men and women	60
	Don't know or no response	32
Turnover	Women have greater turnover	26
	No difference between men and women	43
	Don't know or no response	31

*There were 100 respondents.
Source: Adapted from Leslie Kanuk, "Women in Industrial Selling." *Journal of Marketing* 42 (January 1978), p. 90.

positive, 25 percent thought it made no difference to customers, and only 3 percent felt there had been any negative reactions from customers.

When asked whether they thought their saleswomen faced any special problems on the job compared with men, 70 percent of the respondents said yes. These problems were primarily concerned with necessary adjustments in "traditional" female roles. For instance, 62 percent felt that women might have difficulty entertaining male prospects, more than 40 percent believed saleswomen must sometimes deal with sexual advances from their customers, and 25 percent felt that the job demands created more marital discord for saleswomen than for salesmen.[16]

On the other hand, 22 percent of the respondents in the study thought that saleswomen have some advantages over salesmen. Indeed, this is a common finding from all surveys of managers' perceptions of saleswomen. Three commonly cited advantages of women in the sales force are:

1. The buyer nearly always sees them—even when he has refused to see male reps from the same company.
2. Women sales reps are highly memorable. Thus, their companies and product lines tend to stick in the buyer's mind.
3. Women tend to be better listeners than men, so buyers often will open up to them about their problems.[17]

Another recent study examined the job behavior of salesmen and women from the customer's point of view. One hundred and twenty-five industrial buyers were asked to rate the salesmen and saleswomen who call on them on 23 behav-

---

[16] Kanuk, "Women in Industrial Selling," p. 90.
[17] Scanlon, "Ms. Is a Hit," p. 24.

ioral attributes. The buyers' responses, as shown in Table 10–5, indicate that they perceive salesmen to be better than saleswomen on some dimension—such as product knowledge and technical assistance—but that saleswomen are perceived to be superior on a larger number of attributes, including preparation for sales presentations and follow-through. In the eyes of the buyers surveyed in this study, at least, the performance of saleswomen is perceived to be as good or better than that of salesmen.[18]

The existing studies do not provide an objective comparison of the actual sales

Table 10–5
Industrial buyers' perceptions of salesmen and saleswomen

Attribute	Sales Men	Women	M > W	M < W
1. Understanding of other people	4.90	4.96		x
2. Friendly	5.67	5.84		x
3. Regarded by the buyer as a person	5.36	5.54		x
4. Willingness to go to bat for the buyer within the supplier firm	5.03	5.13		x
5. Vigorous, has a lot of drive	4.83	5.40		x*
6. Know how to listen	4.62	4.98		x*
7. Stability of judgment	4.60	4.66		x
8. Inquisitiveness	4.95	5.15		x
9. Knowledge of companies she's selling to	4.37	4.23	x*	
10. Knowledge of buyer's product line	4.29	4.02	x	
11. Imagination in applying supplier products to buyer's product line	4.29	4.14	x	
12. Confidence	5.11	5.16		x
13. Self-reliance	4.86	5.02		x
14. Product knowledge	5.13	4.93	x*	
15. Preparation for sales presentation	4.57	5.05		x*
16. Understanding of buyer's problems	4.10	4.02	x	
17. Follow-through on deliveries	3.34	4.61		x*
18. Regularity of sales calls	4.55	4.37	x	
19. Has a personalized presentation for each buyer	3.85	4.10		x*
20. Providing technical assistance	4.54	3.92	x*	
21. Presents many new ideas to the buyer	4.03	3.90	x*	
22. Willingness to handle rush orders	4.62	5.11		x*
23. Does not bypass purchasing with back door selling	4.33	5.57		x*

Note: Each attribute was scaled on a 7-point scale, with 7 = very descriptive and 1 = very undescriptive.
*Difference in ratings is statistically significant at the $p < .05$ level.
Source: Adapted from John E. Swan, David R. Rink, G. E. Kiser, and Warren S. Martin, "Industrial Buyer Image of the Saleswoman," *Journal of Marketing* 48 (Winter 1984), p. 114.

---

[18] John E. Swan, David R. Rink, G. E. Kiser, and Warren S. Martin, "Industrial Buyer Image of the Saleswoman," *Journal of Marketing* 48 (Winter 1984), pp. 110–16.

performance of men and women, but they clearly support one major conclusion: As more women have found employment in selling over the past decade, sales managers' attitudes and perceptions of the sales aptitude of women have changed in a positive way. Whereas early surveys indicated that most sales executives were reluctant to hire women for outside sales jobs, recent studies show that most managers do not believe a person's sex has any important influence on job performance. While many executives feel that women may face some unique problems in selling, they also believe they may enjoy some offsetting advantages over salesmen. There is one final indication of how attitudes toward—and opportunities for—women in industrial selling have changed. When executives were asked in a recent study whether they would encourage female college students to consider a career in sales, 88 percent responded with a definite yes.[19]

Personal Characteristics of the Salesperson, Customer Characteristics, and Sales Performance

General personal characteristics do not seem to be consistently related to sales performance across different types of selling jobs. One reason for this may be that particular characteristics enable a salesperson to deal more effectively with some kinds of customers than with others. Consequently, a number of more recent studies have taken a "dyadic" approach to try to explain variations in performance among salespeople. Most of the studies test a very simple hypothesis: Salespeople are more likely to be successful when they are dealing with prospects who are *similar to themselves in demographic characteristics, personality traits, and attitudes* than when their prospects have characteristics different from their own. The rationale for this is that we tend to understand, have empathy for, and be attracted to other people more when they are like us. Therefore, a salesperson may be better able to understand a customer's problems and needs, communicate a sales message, and persuade the prospect to make a purchase when he or she has physical characteristics, personality traits, and attitudes similar to those of the prospect.

Research Evidence

The first study to explore this "similarity" hypothesis was conducted by Franklin Evans in 1963. He surveyed dyads consisting of life insurance salespeople and their customers. Half the dyads consisted of customers who had purchased insur-

[19] Kanuk, "Women in Industrial Sales," p. 91. It should be pointed out that women have performed so well as salespeople that they are moving into sales management positions in increasing numbers. For several case studies of female sales managers and how they achieved their positions, see Sally Scanlon, "Manage Sales? Yes, She Can," *Sales and Marketing Management*, June 13, 1977, pp. 33–36.

ance from the salesperson, and the other half included customers who had decided not to purchase. Evans concluded that the dyads consisting of salespeople and customers who had purchased life insurance were more similar on the following characteristics:

1. Age.
2. Height.
3. Education.
4. Income.
5. Religion.
6. Political affiliation.
7. Smoking habits.

In addition, customers who had purchased insurance were more likely to (1) consider the salesperson as a friend, (2) believe that the salesperson liked them, (3) have enjoyed their conversations with the salesperson, and (4) think that the salesperson enjoyed his or her job.[20]

Evans's findings seem to offer strong support for the similarity hypothesis. Subsequent studies have produced similar results in other types of selling situations, although their findings have usually not been so clear cut and unequivocal as the original. For instance, many studies have found that other attributes of the salesperson—such as expertise—are more strongly related to selling success than similarity with the customer.[21]

Implications and Problems

The implications of these research findings seem quite simple and straightforward. Managers should attempt to hire salespeople with demographic and personality characteristics that are as similar as possible to those of the prospects they will be calling on. Thus, a department store might try to hire young female salesclerks for the "junior miss" department and people who are experienced in a variety of sports for the sporting goods department. Similarly, an industrial goods firm with salespeople who must call on engineers and technically oriented purchasing agents should seek salespeople with technical educations. They should also implement sales training programs that emphasize the technical attributes of the company's products.

These guidelines seem simple enough; however, they pose two fundamental

---

[20] Evans, "Selling as a Dyadic Relationship."

[21] M. S. Gadel, "Concentration by Salesmen Congenial Prospects," *Journal of Marketing* 28 (April 1964), pp. 64–66; Timothy C. Brock, "Communicator-Recipient Similarity and Decision Change," *Journal of Personality and Social Psychology* 1 (June 1965), pp. 650–54; H. Lee Mathews, David T. Wilson, and John F. Monoky, Jr., "Bargaining Behavior in a Buyer-Seller Dyad," *Journal of Marketing Research* 9 (February 1972), pp. 103–5; Arch G. Woodside and William J. Davenport, "The Effect of Salesman Similarity and Expertise on Consumer Purchase Behavior," *Journal of Marketing Research* 11 (May 1974), pp. 198–202; Paul Busch and David T. Wilson, "An Experimental Analysis of a Salesman's Expert and Referent Bases of Social Power in the Buyer-Seller Dyad," *Journal of Maketing Research* 13 (February 1976), pp. 3–11; and Dale Doreen, Donald R. Emery and Robert W. Sweitzer, "Selling as a Dyadic Relationship Revisited," Paper presented at the 1979 National AIDS Conference, New Orleans.

problems. For one thing, they are often impossible to implement. Because buyers and purchasing agents come in all shapes and sizes and vary widely in characteristics, it can be difficult to match a salesperson's attributes with those of all or even most of the potential customers. Matching salesperson and customer characteristics can sometimes be accomplished in retail selling, where different types of consumers tend to patronize different stores or departments within a store. It is much more difficult, however, in industrial or trade selling where purchasing organizations and their buyers are more diverse.

A second problem is that some recent research has cast doubt on the validity of the similarity hypothesis. One authority suggests that there is another explanation for the findings that customers who have made a purchase tend to see themselves as more similar to the salesperson than customers who did not make a purchase.[22] Since customers generally were not contacted until *after* they had made their decision to purchase, their feelings toward the product and toward the salesperson may have been relatively positive as a result of their attempts to reduce postpurchase cognitive dissonance.[23] Furthermore, it has been shown that people who have positive feelings toward another individual tend to perceive that individual as being similar to themselves. Thus, customers who had decided to purchase may have developed more positive feelings toward the product and the salesperson and, subsequently, came to perceive the salesperson as having the same attitudes and personal characteristics as themselves. Using the same reasoning, customers who did not make a purchase may have developed more negative attitudes toward the product and the salesperson after their decision. As a result, they may have perceived the salesperson as being relatively different from themselves.

One recent empirical study has attempted to eliminate the effects of such potentially biased perceptions. In this study, only *objective* characteristics were measured, such as education, religion, political preference, age, height, nationality, sex, and race. Measures of these characteristics were obtained separately from each customer and salesperson rather than relying on one person's perceptions of the other. Four similarity indexes were calculated for dyads composed of retail salesclerks and their customers. *None* of the indexes was significantly related to whether or not the customer in the dyad made a purchase from the salesperson. Two similarity indexes were positively related to the amount that customers purchased (that is, customers tended to purchase more from salespeople who were objectively similar to themselves); however, only 2 percent of the variance in the purchase amount could be explained by salesperson-customer similarity.[24]

In view of the conflicting theoretical explanations, research findings, and practical problems involved in implementation, choosing salespeople who have

---

[22] Weitz, "Effectiveness in Sales Interactions," pp. 88–89.

[23] Leon Festiger, *A Theory of Cognitive Dissonance* (Stanford, Calif.: Stanford University Press, 1957).

[24] Gilbert A. Churchill, Jr., Robert H. Collins, and William A. Strang, "Should Retail Salespersons Be Similar to Their Customers?" *Journal of Retailing* 51 (Fall 1975), pp. 29–42.

characteristics similar to those of their potential customers does not appear to be a viable method of sales force selection. There is still another approach, however, which may prove useful for defining and measuring sales aptitude and for predicting the likelihood of a given salesperson's future success.

Task-Specific Determinants of Sales Aptitude

Each different type of selling job requires the salesperson to perform a variety of different tasks and activities under different circumstances. It might be wise to develop task-specific definitions and measures of sales aptitude and ability, since the abilities needed to be successful at one sales job may be irrelevant for another. Indeed, one authority suggests that sales effectiveness depends on the closeness of the *match* between a salesperson's characteristics, skills and activities on the one hand, and the nature of the needs, buying tasks and relationships with the customers he or she is trying to sell to on the other.[25]

As discussed in Chapter 11, this kind of task-specific or "contingency" approach is the one sales managers should use. Unfortunately, however, there is little published research to guide sales managers in deciding what personal characteristics and abilities are likely to be most important in enabling salespeople to perform specific selling tasks or what criteria they should use in selecting new sales employees.

Indeed, only one survey compares the characteristics of successful and unsuccessful salespeople in specific sales jobs across a large number of organizations. In this study, responses were obtained from a sample of 1,029 sales executives in a wide variety of manufacturing, wholesaling, and service firms. These firms were classified according to the type of selling their salespeople were primarily engaged in. The four categories of industrial sales jobs discussed in Chapter 1 were used, specifically: (1) trade selling, (2) missionary selling, (3) technical selling, and (4) new business selling. The study then compared some personal characteristics of successful and unsuccessful salespeople in each of the four kinds of sales jobs. The results of this survey are summarized in Table 10–6 and discussed here.[26]

Trade Selling

The primary responsibility of the trade sales force is to increase the volume of a firm's sales to its customers (usually wholesalers or retailers). It does this by providing them with merchandising and promotional assistance to aid them in

---

[25] Weitz, "Effectiveness in Sales Interactions."

[26] Derek A. Newton, "Get the Most Out Your Salesforce," *Harvard Business Review*, September-October 1969, pp. 130–43.

Table 10–6
Characteristics related to sales performance in different types of sales jobs

Type of Sales Job	Characteristics That Are Relatively Important	Characteristics That Are Relatively Less Important
Trade selling	Age, maturity, empathy, knowledge of customer and business methods	Aggressiveness, technical ability, product knowledge, persuasiveness
Missionary selling	Youth, high energy and stamina, verbal skill, persuasiveness	Empathy, knowledge of customers, maturity, previous sales experience
Technical selling	Education, product and customer knowledge—usually gained through training, intelligence	Empathy, persuasiveness, aggressiveness, age
New business selling	Experience, age and maturity, aggressiveness, persuasiveness, persistence	Customer knowledge, product knowledge, education, empathy

becoming more effective at selling to their customers. The trade sales force, then, *sells through*, rather than *sells to*, its customers. Trade selling is common in many industries, but it predominates in such consumer goods fields as food and apparel and in selling to wholesalers in general.

Products sold through trade selling tend to be well established; thus, a company's personal selling effort is often less important than its advertising and promotion efforts. The exception is when a new item is being introduced and the trade must be persuaded to stock it. Trade salespeople are usually not so highly pressured by management as salespeople in some other fields, such as new business selling. However, the trade sales job can become dull and repetitious if it involves nothing but stocking shelves or taking orders.

The development of long-term personal relationships is critical for successful trade selling. The salesperson must have empathy and experience to understand his or her customers. Technical competence is less important than getting along well with customers, and aggressiveness is less important than maturity. Consequently, successful trade salespeople tend to be older on the average than successful salespeople in other types of sales jobs.

Missionary Selling

The primary responsibility of the missionary salesperson is to provide the firm's *direct* customers (wholesalers, retailers) with personal selling assistance.

This is done by providing product information to *indirect* customers and persuading them to buy from the firm's direct customers. For example, a brewer's sales representative might call on bar owners and attempt to persuade them to order the company's brand from its local distributor.

Like trade selling, missionary selling is low key and low pressure, but it differs in its primary objective; the missionary force sells for its direct customers, whereas the trade sales force sells through them. This type of selling is common in many industries, particularly foods, pharmaceuticals, chemicals, transportation, and the utilities.

Good coverage of potential indirect customers and the ability to make a succinct, yet persuasive, presentation of product benefits is vitally important to success in missionary selling. Missionary salespeople tend to be more communicators and persuaders than problem solvers. Consequently, missionary salespeople should be energetic and articulate. They need not be particularly aggressive at closing sales because the people they talk to do not buy directly from them. Also, while it helps to have a pleasing personality, missionary salespeople need not be particularly empathetic to customers because the development of long-term relationships is not so important. Indeed, the lack of an opportunity to develop satisfying relationships with customers and the lack of intellectually challenging problem-solving activities are often cited as two unattractive aspects of the missionary sales job. In view of all this, successful missionary sales forces tend to consist of young people with the energy and stamina to make a lot of calls. After a few years, such people commonly move into other marketing jobs or other more challenging types of sales work.

Technical Selling

The major job of the technical sales force is to increase the volume of sales to existing customers by providing them with technical advice and assistance. These salespeople sell directly to the firms that use their products. Technical selling is especially important in industries such as chemicals, machinery, and heavy equipment.

Technical selling is much like management consulting in that the ability to identify, analyze, and solve customer problems is vitally important. Technical competence and knowledge of both product and customer are necessary for such salespeople since they need to discover customer problems and then explain the product's benefits for solving the problems. However, too much aggressiveness can undermine the customer's confidence in the objectiveness of the salesperson. Because of the need for technical competence, the successful technical sales force tends to be relatively young, with a high proportion of recent college graduates. To provide product knowledge, successful firms provide their technical salespeople with extensive training and company support.

New Business Selling

The primary responsibility of the new business sales force is to seek out and persuade new customers to buy from the firm for the first time. Persuasiveness, aggressiveness, and persistence are important attributes for success in this kind of job. The greatest difficulty in new business selling is the frequent rejection, and consequent deflation of the ego, that salespeople experience. Young, inexperienced people typically do not perform well in this kind of selling; they are too easily discouraged and their turnover rate is very high. Consequently, successful new business salespeople tend to be older persons with substantial sales experience. They like the challenge and independence from supervision that goes along with "cold canvassing" potential new accounts.

Implications for Sales Management

What has this review of the wisdom accumulated through experience and published research taught us about the personal characteristics that are related to sales aptitude and the potential for selling success? For one thing, there do not appear to be any general physical characteristics, mental abilities, or personality traits that are consistently related to sales aptitude and performance in all companies and selling situations. Also, the evidence suggests that it is probably neither wise nor practical for a sales manager to try to select salespeople with characteristics that match those of their potential customers. (The possible exception is in retail selling.) Instead, the most potentially useful approach to defining sales aptitude and evaluating a person's potential for future success is first to determine the kinds of tasks involved in a specific sales job. Then, one can evaluate the relevance of particular characteristics and abilities for enabling a person to carry out those tasks successfully.

Unfortunately, few published studies have either analyzed the tasks and activities unique to particular types of selling or identified the personal traits and abilities that are important for success in different sales jobs. Some marketing theorists and researchers have begun to develop such task-specific or contingency approaches to defining and measuring sales aptitude.[27] However, it will probably take years before such efforts produce much information of practical use to front-line sales executives.

For now, each sales executive must try to develop his or her own specifications concerning what to look for in new sales recruits. Those specifications should be developed after a careful analysis and description of the tasks and activities in-

---

[27] For example, see the theoretical framework for a contingency theory of sales performance developed in Weitz, "Effectiveness in Sales Interactions."

volved in selling the firm's products to its target market. There should also be an evaluation of the characteristics and qualifications that new salespeople must have to perform those tasks and activities. Therefore, Chapter 11 examines the methods and procedures involved in sales force recruitment and selection. It begins with a discussion of how to carry out a job analysis and develop a list of qualifications to use in evaluating recruits.

Summary

This chapter, the first of two dealing with salesperson selection, sought to review the evidence regarding what personal and psychological characteristics are related to an individual's aptitude in performing well as a salesperson. Aptitude is typically viewed as the overall limit, or constraint upon, an individual's ability to perform a given sales job.

Several factors are thought to affect this ability to perform, including:

1. Aptitude characteristics, including—
    a. mental abilities, such as general intelligence or mathematical ability, and
    b. personality traits, such as empathy, aggressiveness, need for achievement and sociability.
2. Skill levels—such as product knowledge or communications skills—gained through training or experience.
3. Personal characteristics, including physical traits, education and life style factors.

Although a number of reasons can be advanced as to why these factors might be related to sales performance, the available evidence suggests that none are consistently related to performance when examined across industries and job settings.

One of the more persuasive reasons for these inconsistent relationships is that particular characteristics of salespeople enable them to deal more effectively with some kinds of customers than with others. Consequently, some recent studies have used a dyadic approach to explain variations in performance among salespeople. The basic hypothesis is that salespeople are more likely to be successful when they deal with prospects who are similar to themselves in terms of demographic characteristics, personality traits, and attitudes. The implication of the dyadic perspective for sales managers is that they should hire salespeople with characteristics similar to the customers they will call upon. Not only is such a strategy hard to implement in industrial selling, but the research evidence does not consistently support the proposition.

The most important conclusion regarding salespeople selection is that there are many different types of selling jobs. Each type requires the salesperson to perform a variety of different tasks and activities under different circumstances.

Consequently, the most useful approach to defining sales aptitude and evaluating a person's potential for future success is, first, to determine the kinds of tasks involved in a specific sales job. Then, one can evaluate the relevance of particular characteristics and abilities for enabling a person to carry out those tasks successfully.

Discussion Questions

1. What are the opportunity costs resulting from a firm having a poor recruitment and selection policy? Can these costs be measured?

2. For the following sales positions, indicate the characteristics, traits, skill levels, and aptitudes that a sales manager should look for in recruiting and selection.
   a. Representatives selling high-priced computers.
   b. Representatives selling petroleum lubricants to manufacturers.
   c. Representatives selling paper products used for cleaning, wiping, and drying to companies and institutions.
   d. Representatives selling copying equipment and supplies.
   e. Representatives selling telephone communications systems.
   f. Representatives selling telephone directory advertising.

3. Table 10–2 shows that enthusiasm is one of the most important attributes sales executives look for in new salespeople. How would you go about measuring or determining whether an applicant possessed enthusiasm? If an applicant lacks enthusiasm but shows a positive interest in sales, would it be possible to "teach" enthusiasm?

4. There is evidence that some sales managers prefer to hire tall, good-looking, well-proportioned people for their sales force. How do you justify this practice? Does it constitute discrimination?

5. How valuable are aptitude tests in selecting sales personnel? What problems are associated with their use in sales selection? What specific questions would you ask to measure the trait of "sociability"?

6. An article in the *Wall Street Journal* (2-5-81, p. 21) states: "Women's commissions were 10% to 15% higher than men's at Exxon's Qyx typewriter division. Semispecialists of America, a Farmingdale, N.Y. electronic products distributor, says its average saleswoman earned $31,500 last year, compared with about $25,000 for men." What traits do women possess that might account for these results? Would these companies be justified in hiring only women?

7. "Sure, I'm willing to hire minorities and women for my sales force," said Marvin C. Procter, "but they'll be treated the same as everybody else; no special training programs or differential treatment." Comment on this statement. Do you agree?

8. An article in the *Wall Street Journal* (5-11-81, p. 25) states: "According to the Life Insurance Marketing and Research Association: Women agents, as a group, sell 20 percent less insurance than male agents of comparable experience." What might explain the performance difference? Can life insurance companies use sex as a criterion when hiring agents?

9. The sales manager of a company manufacturing metal castings attempts to hire salespeople based on the personalities of the customers. The sales manager uses the same process when assigning salespeople to customers. In other words, the Evans' similarity hypothesis is being applied. Does this process make sense? Does this procedure agree with Weitz's contingency theory?

10. A few companies have organized their sales forces into two groups. One group calls only on existing customers and the other calls only on prospective customers. Are the selling jobs different enough to justify this approach? What differences in traits would you expect to discover between the two groups?

11. A district sales manager made the following statement when asked about hiring procedures:

    I have a rule I never break. I only hire salesmen who are in their thirties, married with three or more kids, and are carrying mortgages as big as the Ritz. I want them up to their ears in debt. That way, they'll need me more than I need them, and I know for a fact that they'll be back on the job each and every morning!

    Obviously, this district sales manager wants to avoid turnover as much as possible. How can a sales manager control turnover? Do you agree with the preceding statement? What are the controllable costs of turnover in the sales force?

12. According to one sales manager: "As far as I am concerned, the most important personal characteristic related to sales success is age. Younger people, those under thirty, do not accept the Protestant Ethic." What is the Protestant Ethic? Do you agree with this viewpoint?

Chapter **11**

Sales Force Recruitment and Selection

Several years ago, an MBA student at one of the authors' schools was recruited for a sales job with a major manufacturer of outdoor and garden equipment. She was interviewed extensively and "wined and dined," not only by the sales manager, who was her prospective supervisor, but also by higher-level executives in the firm, including the vice president of marketing. All this attention from top-level managers surprised the candidate. "After all," she said, "it's only a sales job. Is it common for so many executives to be involved in recruiting new salespeople?"

Who Has the Responsibility for Recruiting and Selecting Salespeople?

The student's question raises the issue of who should have the primary responsibility for recruiting and selecting new salespeople. The way in which a company answers this question typically depends on (1) the size of the sales force, and (2) the kind of selling involved. In firms with small sales forces, the top-level sales manager commonly views the recruitment and selection of new people as a primary responsibility. In larger, multilevel sales forces, however, the job of attracting and choosing new recruits is usually too extensive and time-consuming for a single executive. In such firms, authority for recruitment and selection is commonly delegated to lower-level sales managers.

In companies where the sales job is not very difficult or complex, new recruits do not need any special qualifications, and turnover rates in the sales force are high—as in firms that sell consumer goods door to door—first-level sales managers often have sole responsibility for hiring their own salespeople. When a firm must be more selective in choosing new recruits with certain qualifications and abilities, however, a recruiting specialist may advise and assist first-level managers in evaluating new recruits and making hiring decisions. These staff positions are usually filled by sales managers who are being groomed for higher-level executive positions.

In some firms, members of the personnel department assist and advise sales managers in hiring new salespeople instead of assigning such duties to a member of the sales management staff. This approach helps to reduce duplication of effort and avoids friction between the sales and personnel departments. One disadvantage is that personnel specialists may not be as knowledgeable about the job to be filled and the qualifications necessary as a member of the sales management staff. When the personnel department is involved in sales recruiting and hiring, it usually helps to attract applicants and aid in evaluating them. The sales manager, however, typically has the final responsibility for deciding who to hire.

Finally, when the firm sees its sales force as a training ground for sales and marketing managers, either personnel executives or other top-level managers may take part in the recruiting effort to ensure that the new hirees have management potential. This was the situation in the firm that interviewed our MBA student. Although they wanted to hire her for "just a sales job," company executives saw that job as a stepping-stone to management responsibilities.

Recruitment and Selection Procedures

Regardless of who has the responsibility for recruiting new members of the sales force, certain procedures should be followed to ensure that the new recruits have the aptitude for the job and the potential to be successful. As discussed in Chapter 10, there do not seem to be any general characteristics that make some people better performers in all types of sales jobs. Therefore, the starting point in the recruitment process should be a thorough analysis of the job to be filled and a description of the qualifications that any new hiree should have.

The next step is to find and attract a pool of job applicants. The methods used for this should be selective and chosen with an eye to drawing applicants with the qualifications for which the firm is looking. The objective, in other words, usually is not to maximize the number of job applicants but to attract a few good applicants.

The final stage in the hiring process is to evaluate each applicant through personal history information, interviews, reference checks, and formal tests. The purpose is to determine which applicants have the personal characteristics and abilities that are most likely to lead to success in the job. During this stage of the evaluation and selection process, however, managers must be especially careful not to violate the requirements and guidelines of equal employment opportunity laws and regulations.

The remaining sections of this chapter discuss the specific methods and procedures that managers might use at each stage of the recruitment and selection process. Although the primary focus is on "how to do it" from a manager's point of view, some material in this chapter should be useful for learning what is expected if you ever apply for a sales job.

Job Analysis and Determination of Selection Criteria

Research relating salespeople's personal characteristics to sales aptitude and job performance suggests that there is no single set of traits and abilities that sales managers can use as criteria in deciding what kind of recruits to hire. Different sales jobs require the performance of different activities, and this suggests that people with different personality traits and abilities should be hired to fill them. The first activities in the recruitment and selection process thus should be:

1. *Conduct a job analysis* to determine what activities, tasks, responsibilities, and environmental influences are involved in the job to be filled.
2. *Write a job description* that details the findings of the job analysis.
3. *Develop a statement of job qualifications* that determines and describes the personal traits and abilities a person should have to perform the tasks and responsibilities involved in the job.

Job Analysis and Description

Most companies—particularly larger ones—have some type of written job descriptions for positions within their sales forces. Unfortunately, often those job descriptions are out of date and do not accurately reflect the current scope and content of the positions. The tasks and responsibilities involved in a given sales job change as the customers, the firm's account management policies, the competition, and other environmental factors change. But too often, firms do not conduct new analyses and prepare up-dated descriptions to reflect those changes. Also, firms create new kinds of sales positions from time to time, and the tasks to be accomplished by people in these newly created jobs may not be thoroughly spelled out. Consequently, a critical first step in the hiring process is for management to make sure that the job to be filled has been analyzed *recently* and that the findings have been *written* out in *great detail*. Without such a detailed and up-to-date description, the sales manager will have more difficulty deciding what kind of person is needed to perform the job adequately. In addition, prospective recruits will not really know for what position they are applying.

Who Conducts the Analysis and Prepares the Description?   In some firms, the task of analyzing and describing sales jobs is assigned to someone in the sales management ranks. In other firms, the task is assigned to a job analysis specialist, who is either someone from the company's personnel department or an outside consultant. Regardless of who is responsible for analyzing and describing the various selling positions within a company, however, it is important that he or she collects information about the job's content from two sources: (1) the current occupants of the job, and (2) the sales managers who supervise the people in the job.

Current job occupants should be observed and/or interviewed to determine what they actually do in performing the job. Sales managers at various levels should be asked what they think the job occupant should be doing in view of the firm's strategic sales program and account management policies. It is not uncommon for the person who analyzes a job to discover that the salespeople are doing things that management is not aware of and that they are "slacking off" on some activities management feels are important. Such misunderstandings and inaccurate role perceptions illustrate the need for accurate and detailed job descriptions.

Job descriptions written to reflect a consensus between salespeople and their managers concerning what a job should entail can serve several useful functions in addition to guiding the firm's recruiting efforts. They can guide the design of a sales training program that will provide new salespeople with the skills to do their job effectively and that will improve their understanding of how the job should be done. Similarly, detailed job descriptions can serve as standards for evaluating each salesperson's job performance, as discussed in Chapter 17.

Content of the Job Description.   Good descriptions of sales jobs typically cover the following job dimensions and requirements:

1.   The *nature of the product(s) or service(s)* to be sold.

2. The *types of customers* to be called on, including the policies concerning the frequency with which calls are to be made on different types of customers and the types of personnel within customer organizations who should be contacted (e.g., buyers, purchasing agents, plant supervisors).

3. The *specific tasks and responsibilities* to be carried out, including planning tasks, research and information collection activities, specific selling tasks, other promotional duties, customer servicing activities, and clerical and reporting duties.

4. The *relationships between the job occupant and other positions* within the organization. To whom does the job occupant report? What are the salesperson's responsibilities to his or her immediate superior? How and under what circumstances does the salesperson interact with members of other departments, such as production or engineering?

5. The *mental and physical demands* of the job, including the amount of technical knowledge the salesperson should have concerning the company's products, other necessary skills, and the amount of travel involved.

6. The *environmental pressures and constraints* that might influence performance of the job, such as market trends, the strengths and weaknesses of the competition, the company's reputation among customers, and resource and supply problems.

An example of a job description that addresses most of these job dimensions is presented in Table 11–1.

Determining Job Qualifications and Selection Criteria

Determining the qualifications that a prospective employee should have to perform a given sales job is the most difficult part of the recruitment and selection process. The sales manager—perhaps with assistance from a manpower planning specialist or a vocational psychologist from the firm's personnel department—should consider the relative importance of all the personal traits and characteristics discussed previously. These include physical attributes, mental abilities and experience, and personality traits. The problem is that nearly all these characteristics are of at least some importance in choosing new salespeople. No firm, for instance, would actively seek sales recruits who are unintelligent or lacking in self-confidence. It is unlikely, though, that many job candidates will possess high levels of all these desirable characteristics. The task, then, is to decide which traits and abilities are most important in qualifying an individual for a particular job and which are relatively less critical. Also, some thought should be given to whether there can be tradeoffs among the qualification criteria. Will a person with a deficiency on one important attribute still be considered acceptable if he or she has outstanding qualities in other areas? For example, will the firm be willing

Table 11–1
Job Description

JOB TITLE SALES REPRESENTATIVE	JOB CODE
ESTABLISHMENT—DEPARTMENT MARKETING BD SALES	DATE

FUNCTION

Promotes and consummates the sale of office systems and related equipment, paper, accessories and other supplies within an assigned geographic territory, for the Business Division.

MAJOR ACTIVITIES

A. Establishes and maintains close liaison between the company and customers within an assigned geographic territory, for the ultimate purpose of selling Business Division products.

B. Establishes and maintains a working rapport with customers by providing expertise in the analysis of systems problems and the application of BD products and services to the solution of these problems.

C. Provides service to customers by recommending changes in operating procedures, assisting them in planning for office systems applications, recommending equipment purchases and supervising their installation, suggesting methods of quality control, and checking to determine that equipment and systems function properly.

D. Provides accurate and timely information on office products and demonstrates to customers the benefits derived from utilizing these products in his business. Keeps customers and prospects updated on new products and office systems.

E. Assists customers in achieving the high quality capabilities of the company's office products.

F. Prepares a variety of reports and correspondence including data reports on activities, expenses, market acceptance of office products, product problems, market needs, etc.

G. Studies customers systems needs and formulates written proposals to satisfy these with the general philosophies established by BD. Outlines systems recommendations incorporating products in customer proposals, cites advantages and operating cost reductions resulting from the proposed system.

H. Maintains a thorough familiarity of the products of other manufacturers in order to deal with questions posed by customers and prospects in daily activities.

I. Participates and/or originates customer seminars and education programs by instructing customers and their personnel in the capabilities of office systems and the proper application and operation of BD products. Provides information and assistance at trade shows and exhibits to interested persons.

J. Keeps abreast of the new developments and trends in office equipment and systems in order to be capable of understanding customer needs and to be better prepared to provide workable solutions to customer systems requirements.

K. Handles product complaints, and makes recommendations to the marketing center regarding goodwill replacements of products.

L. Advises district, and/or regional, and/or BD management of any information pertinent to BD activities, gathered as a result of observations made in the field. Reports include new systems applications, activities of other manufacturers, equipment modifications and improvements, customer needs, etc.

M. Follows up on all sales leads as quickly as possible. Makes new calls on potential customers to stimulate interest in BD products.

N. Plans activities in a manner that provides for adequate territory coverage. Allocates time on the basis of maximum potential yield and/or priorities established by the district sales manager.

SCOPE OF THE POSITION

A. Accountability

1. Reports to the district sales manager of the marketing center to which assigned. May direct the activities of less experienced sales representatives assigned to assist on a project basis or for training and development purposes.

Table 11-1 (concluded)

2. Responsible for reviewing unusual complex and/or sensitive problems, proposals, or controversial matters with supervision prior to taking any action. Manages the assigned territory with considerable independence.

3. The assigned territory is in the middle range in relation to others in the region in overall dollar accountability, and/or customers have complex installations with sophisticated systems and product applications with which the sales representative must be familiar.

4. Responsible for having a thorough knowledge of all BD products and services and is capable of effectively analyzing, from a systems viewpoint, customers' problems and needs, in developing new business by demonstrating the capabilities of Business Systems products to satisfy these needs.

5. Is capable of independently meeting expected sales goals for all categories of products in the assigned territories.

6. Responsible for submitting knowledgeable reports on emerging trends in the marketplace, market needs and ideas for new products which demonstrate a thorough understanding of the company's position in the marketplace, and the direction it must pursue to maintain and improve this position.

7. Shows increasing expertise and professionalism in: customer contracts; diagnosis of customer needs; analysis of systems; preparation and presentation of proposals for new systems based on sound economic evaluations.

8. Is expected to exhibit maturity and competence in running the assigned territory with a minimum of direction. Has demonstrated the ability of developing large accounts, multiple sales, etc.

B. Innovation
1. Has a thorough understanding of the capabilities of other manufacturers' product and effectively uses this information to serve customers needs.

2. Demonstrates originality and creativity in solving systems problems and meeting needs of the market.

3. Responsible for consistently aiding customers by disseminating information on new methods, systems, and techniques which are applicable to their operations.

JOB KNOWLEDGE
A. Has a college degree or the equivalent in applicable training and experience.
B. Requires completion of the basic BD training program.
C. Requires a thorough knowledge of all billing, credit and distribution procedures, paperwork, and policies and is capable of resolving complex problems in these areas with a minimum of confusion, frustration, and inconvenience for all parties concerned.
D. This level of activity is generally achieved with four years' selling experience, or the equivalent, with the assigned products where the individual is subjected to all types of problems and challenges covering the entire product line.

WRITTEN BY	APPROVED	DATE	APPROVED	DATE

to hire someone with only average verbal ability and persuasiveness if that person has an extremely high degree of ambition and persistence?

Methods for deciding on selection criteria. Decisions about the qualifications that should be looked for in selecting new employees can often be made by simply *examining the job description.* If the job requires extensive travel, for instance, management might look for applicants who are young, have few family responsibilities, and want to travel. Similarly, statements in the job description concerning the necessary level of technical knowledge and skill can help managers determine the educational background and previous job experience to look for when selecting hirees.

Most larger firms go one step further and *evaluate the personal histories of their existing salespeople* to determine what characteristics differentiate between good and poor performers. As seen in Chapter 10, this kind of analysis seldom produces consistent results across different jobs and different companies. It can produce useful insight, however, when applied to a single type of sales job within a single firm. The job-specific study conducted by Derek Newton and reported at the end of Chapter 10 illustrates the guidance that such an analysis can give managers in choosing selection criteria.[1]

Current sales employees might be divided into two groups according to their level of performance on the job—one group of high performers and one group of low performers. Then, the characteristics of the two groups can be compared on the basis of information from job application forms, records of personal interviews and intelligence, aptitude, and personality test scores. Alternatively, statistical techniques might be used to look for significant correlations between variations in the personal characteristics of current salespeople and variations in their job performance. In either case, management attempts to identify personal attributes that differ significantly between high-performing and low-performing salespeople. The assumption is that there may be a cause-and-effect relationship between such attributes and job performance. If new employees are selected who have attributes similar to those of people who are currently performing the job successfully, they also may be successful.

In addition to improving management's ability to specify relevant criteria in selecting new salespeople, there is another compelling reason why a firm should conduct a personal history analysis. Such analyses are necessary to validate the selection criteria that the firm is currently using, as required by government regulations on equal employment opportunity in hiring. This issue is discussed later in this chapter.

Besides comparing the characteristics of good and poor performers in a particular job, management might also try to *analyze the unique characteristics of employees who have failed*—people who either quit or were fired. One consulting firm—the Klein Institute for Aptitude Testing—suggests that the following characteristics are frequently found among salespeople who fail:

1. Instability of residence.
2. Failure in business within the past two years.
3. Unexplained gaps in the person's employment record.
4. Recent divorce or marital problems.
5. Excessive personal indebtedness; for example, bills could not be paid within two years from earnings on the new job.

---

[1] Derek A. Newton, "Get the Most Out of Your Salesforce," *Harvard Business Review*, September-October 1969, pp. 130–43.

The firm might attempt to identify such characteristics among its own sales failures by conducting exit interviews with all salespeople who quit or are fired. Although this sounds like a good idea, it seldom works very well in practice. Salespeople who quit are often reluctant to discuss the real reasons for leaving a job, and people who are fired are not likely to cooperate in any research that will be of value to their former employer. However, some useful information about ex-salespeople can often be obtained from the application forms and test scores that were recorded when they were hired. They may also have spoken with the managers who were their supervisors at the time they left the company.

On the basis of these kinds of information, a written statement of job qualifications should be prepared that is both detailed and specific enough to guide the selection of new salespeople. An example of such a statement is shown in Table 11–2.

Table 11–2

Business Division
Applicant Interview Form

Applicant name: _____ Date: _____

Interview with: Time

1. _____   _____

2. _____   _____

3. _____   _____

4. _____   _____

Rating:
5—Excellent
4—Above average
3—Average
2—Fair
1—Poor

Directions: Check square that most correctly reflects characteristics applicable to candidate. An outstanding candidate would score 95 to 100.

	1	2	3	4	5
General appearance					
1. Neatness, dress					
2. Business image					
Impressions					
3. Positive mannerisms					
4. Speech, expressions					
5. Outgoing personality					
6. Positive attitude					

Table 11–2 *(concluded)*

Potential sales ability	1	2	3	4	5
7. Persuasive communication					
8. Aggressiveness					
9. Sell and manage large accounts					
10. Make executive calls					
11. Organize and manage a territory					
12. Work with others					
13. Successful prior experience					
14. Potential for career growth					

Maturity	1	2	3	4	5
15. General intelligence, common sense					
16. Self-confidence					
17. Self-motivation, ambition					
18. Composure, stability					
19. Adaptability					
20. Sense of ethics					

General comments: _____

_____

_____

_____

Overall rating (total score): _____

Would you recommend this candidate for the position? _____

Why or why not? _____

Recruiting Applicants

Some firms do not actively recruit salespeople. They simply choose new employees from applicants who come to them and ask for work. Although this may be a satisfactory policy for a few well-known firms with good products, strong positions in the market, and attractive compensation policies, today's labor market makes such an approach unworkable for most companies. Firms that seek well-educated people for industrial sales jobs must compete with many other occupations in attracting such individuals. To make matters worse, people with no selling experience often tend to have negative attitudes toward employment in sales. Also, the kinds of people who do seek employment in sales often do not have the qualifications a firm is looking for, particularly when the job involves relatively sophisti-cated selling, such as technical or new business sales. Consequently, the com-pany may have to evaluate a large number of applicants to find one person who is fully qualified. Unfortunately, this is one area where some firms are "penny-wise but pound-foolish." They attempt to hold down recruiting costs on the assump-tion that a good training program can convert marginal recruits into solid sales performers. As we saw in the last chapter, however, some of the determinants of sales success—such as aptitude and personal characteristics—are difficult or impossible to change through training or experience. Therefore, spending the money and effort necessary to find well-qualified candidates can turn out to be a profitable investment for the firm.[2] Indeed, one authority estimates that for a routinized and closely supervised sales job, it is necessary to consider 20 to 50 applicants to find one who meets company requirements. For more demanding positions that call for a higher caliber of salesperson, it may be necessary to screen 50 to 100 prospects before finding one who is qualified.[3]

In view of the difficulties in attracting qualified people to fill sales positions, a well-planned and effectively implemented recruiting effort is usually a crucial part of the firm's hiring program. The primary objective of the recruiting process should *not* be to maximize the total number of job applicants, however. As one expert points out:

Many sales managers believe that the more recruits they have to select from, the better their selection will be. This is not at all true. Large numbers of recruits tend to hurt the selection process because they overload it. . . . (Also) numbers do not ensure quality. The question is not how many recruits but how many good recruits.[4]

Therefore, the recruiting process should be designed to be the first step in the selection process. Self-selection by the prospective employees themselves is the most efficient means of selection. The recruiting effort should thus be imple-mented in a way that discourages unqualified people from applying for the job. To accomplish this, recruiting communications should point out both the attractive and unattractive aspects of the job to be filled, spell out the qualifications, and state the likely compensation. This will help ensure that only qualified and inter-ested people apply for the job. Also, recruiting efforts should be focused only on sources of potential applicants where fully qualified people are most likely to be found.

There are a number of places where sales managers can go to find recruits or leads concerning potential recruits. These sources include: (1) people within the company, (2) people in other firms (e.g., customers and competitors), (3) educa-tional institutions, (4) advertisements, and (5) employment agencies. Each

---

[2] Rene Y. Darmon and S. J. Shapiro, "Sales Recruiting—A Major Area of Underinvestment," *Industrial Marketing Management* 9 (1980), pp. 47–51; and Gregory B. Salsbury, "Properly Recruit Salespeople to Reduce Training Cost," *Industrial Marketing Management* 11 (1982), pp. 143–46.

[3] Robert N. McMurry, "Why You Must Plan Now to Meet Your Sales Manpower Needs for Tomorrow," *Sales Manage-ment*, November 10, 1957, p. 86.

[4] Benson P. Shapiro, *Sales Program Management: Formulation and Implementation* (New York: McGraw-Hill, 1977), p. 457.

source is likely to produce candidates with somewhat different backgrounds and characteristics. Therefore, although most firms seek recruits from more than one source, a company's recruiting efforts should be concentrated on sources that are most likely to produce the kinds of people needed.

People within the Company

People in nonsales departments within the firm, such as manufacturing, maintenance, engineering, or the office staff, sometimes have latent sales talent and are a common source of sales recruits. One study found that 60 percent of the industrial organizations surveyed had hired salespeople from other internal departments, and 37 percent of the salespeople responding to the same survey "revealed that their previous jobs were of a nonsales nature."[5]

Recruiting current company employees for the sales force has some distinct advantages:

1. Company employees have established performance records and they are more of a known quantity than outsiders.
2. Recruits from inside the firm should require less orientation and training because they are already familiar with the company's products, policies, and operations.
3. Recruiting from within can bolster company morale as employees become aware that opportunities for advancement are available outside of their own departments or divisions.

As a result of these advantages, recruiting from within can produce handsome dividends. In one West Coast manufacturing firm, 5 of the top 10 salespeople and field sales managers were recruited from the company's own production department.[6] To facilitate successful internal recruiting, the company's personnel department should always be kept abreast of sales manpower needs. Because the personnel staff is familiar with the qualifications of all employees and continuously evaluates their performance, they are in the best position to identify people with the attributes necessary to fill available sales jobs.

On the other hand, internal recruiting has some limitations. People in nonsales departments seldom have much previous selling experience. Also, internal recruiting can cause some animosity within the firm if supervisors of other departments feel that their best employees are being pirated by the sales force.[7]

In addition to being potential sales employees themselves, company personnel can provide management with leads to potential recruits from outside the firm. Current salespeople are in a particularly good position to provide their superiors

---

[5] *Finding the Superior Salesman* (New York: The Research Institute of America, 1967), p. 6.

[6] Ibid., p. 7.

[7] Sometimes latent talent inside a firm is hidden from sales managers. For a discussion of the reasons for this and of ways around the problem, see Raymond O. Loen, "How to Spot Potential Salesmen," *Sales Management,* November 15, 1963, p. 53.

with leads to new recruits. They know the requirements of the job, they often have contacts with other salespeople who may be willing to change jobs, and they can do much to help "sell" an available job to potential recruits. Consequently, many sales managers make sure their salespeople are aware of the company's recruiting needs. In the survey conducted by the Research Institute of America, 76 percent of the respondents felt that current employees and salespeople were either "good" or "excellent" sources of new recruits.[8] Indeed, some companies, such as IBM, offer bonuses as incentives to their salespeople to recruit new prospects. Of course, such referrals from current employees must be handled tactfully so as not to cause hard feelings if the applicant is rejected later in the selection process.

People in Other Firms

Customers can be a source of sales recruits. Sometimes a customer's employees have the kinds of knowledge that make them attractive as prospective salespeople. For instance, department store employees can make good salespeople for the wholesalers or manufacturers who supply the store because they are familiar with the product and the procedures of store buyers.

Customers with whom a firm has good relations may also serve as a source of leads concerning potential recruits who are working for other firms, particularly competitors. Purchasing agents know what impresses them in a salesperson, they are familiar with the abilities of the sales representatives who call on them, and they are sometimes aware when a sales representative is interested in changing jobs.

The question of whether a firm should recruit salespeople from its competitors, however, is controversial. On one hand, such people are knowledgeable about the industry from their experience. They also might be expected to "bring along" some of their current customers when they switch companies. Frequently this does not happen, however, since customers are usually more loyal to a supplier than to the specific individual who represents that supplier.

On the other side of the argument, it is sometimes difficult to get salespeople who have worked for a competing firm to unlearn old practices and to conform to their new employer's account management policies. Also, some managers feel that recruiting a competitor's personnel is unethical. They believe it is unfair for firm B to recruit *actively* someone from firm A after A has spent the money to hire and train that person. Such people may be in a position to divulge A's company secrets to B. Consequently, some firms refuse to recruit their competitor's salespeople, although whether such policies are due to high ethical standards, the expense of retraining, or fear of possible retaliation is open to question.

---

[8] *Finding the Superior Salesman*, p. 7.

Educational Institutions

College and university placement offices are a common source of recruits for firms that require salespeople with sound mental abilities or technical backgrounds. They are used particularly when the sales job is viewed as a first step toward a career in management. College graduates are often more socially poised than people of the same age without college training, and good grades are at least some evidence that the person can think logically, budget time efficiently, and communicate reasonably well.

On the other hand, college graduates seldom have much selling experience, and they are likely to require more extensive orientation and training in the basics of salesmanship. Also, college-educated sales recruits have a reputation for "job hopping," unless their jobs are challenging and promotions are rapid. Equitable Life Assurance Society, for instance, stopped recruiting college graduates when it found that such recruits did not stay with their jobs for very long.[9] Another drawback of college recruiting is that some graduates have negative attitudes toward sales jobs. Consequently, college recruiting can require a great deal of time and effort to attract a relatively few interested applicants.

Junior colleges and vocational schools are another source of sales recruits that has expanded rapidly in recent years. Many such schools have programs of study explicitly designed to prepare people for selling careers. Thus, firms that recruit the graduates of such programs do not have to contend with the negative attitudes toward selling that they sometimes encounter in four-year college graduates. Junior colleges and vocational schools are particularly good sources of recruits for sales jobs that require reasonably well-developed mental and communications abilities, but where advanced technical knowledge or a four-year degree is not essential.

Advertisements

A less selective means of attracting job applicants is to advertise the available position. When a technically qualified or experienced person is needed, an ad might be placed in an industry trade or technical journal. More commonly, advertisements are placed in the personnel or marketplace sections of local newspapers to attract applicants for relatively less demanding sales jobs where special qualifications are not required. A well-written ad can be very effective for attracting applicants. For example, one firm boasts of an applicant-to-job ratio of 120 to 1 as a result of its newspaper ads.[10] As suggested, however, this is not necessarily a good thing. When a firm's advertisements attract large numbers of applicants

---

[9] "How Do You Find More Salesmen Just Like the Successful Salesmen You Now Have?" *Sales Management*, April 15, 1966, p. 108.

[10] "The Recruitment of College Graduates for Sales Careers," *Journal of Business—Manhattan College* 1 (1972), p. 4.

who are unqualified or only marginally interested, the firm must engage in an extensive and costly process of screening and selection to "separate the wheat from the chaff." Consequently, most sales executives who responded to the Research Institute of America's survey of recruiting methods were not enthusiastic about advertisements as a source of recruits. Only 15 percent of the salespeople who responded said that they had applied for their present job as a result of seeing an ad.[11]

If a firm does use newspaper advertising in its recruiting efforts, it faces a related question concerning how much information about the job should be included in its ads. Many sales managers argue that "open" ads, which disclose the firm's name, product to be sold, compensation, and specific job duties (see Figure 11–1 for an example) generate higher-quality applicants, decreased turnover

Figure 11–1

A. Example of an "Open," Full-Disclosure Newspaper Recruitment Ad

SALES ENGINEER

Responsible for the sale of highly engineered materials and components to electronic, computer, and other original equipment manufacturers. Seeks new product opportunities and new applications for present products. BSEE or the equivalent in a combination of schooling and experience, plus 2 years experience in applications engineering or technical sales. Salary plus commission guaranteed in the first year. Car and expenses provided. Will be located in Minneapolis. Send resume, salary history and requirements to: L. D. Schutz, Corporate Personnel Director, Kennesaw Corp., Kennesaw, AL 21940.

Equal Opp. Employer M/F

B. Example of a "Blind" Newspaper Recruitment Ad

SALES, national company needs 4 salespersons. High income, local territory, paid insurance, fringe benefits. We train. Phone Employment Manager, 689-4112.

---

[11] *Finding the Superior Salesman*, pp. 9–11. Interestingly, though, two thirds of the salespeople responding to this study said they did not read the recruiting ads of other people.

rates, and lower selection costs than ads without such information. However, for less attractive, high-turnover sales jobs—such as door-to-door selling—some sales managers prefer "blind" ads (see Figure 11–1). These maximize the number of applicants and give the manager an opportunity to explain the attractive features of the job in a face-to-face meeting with the applicant.

In a study that compared the effectiveness of blind versus open ads for recruiting salespeople, it was found that blind ads did result in higher selection costs and a lower ratio of hirees to applicants. On the other hand, the blind ads produced three times as many applicants. Consequently, the number of successful salespeople hired per ad was higher. Also, the total recruiting and selection costs per successful salesperson were slightly lower for blind ads than for open ads, as shown in Table 11–3.[12] Keep in mind, however, that this study was conducted in a firm that was hiring people for routine selling jobs where the turnover rate was high. Blind ads are much less attractive when the company must be relatively selective in recruiting and hiring people who meet a detailed set of job qualifications.

Table 11–3
Comparison of cost and personnel data by type of newspaper recruitment ad

	Blind Ads	Open Ads
Cost per ad	$ 46.42	$ 35.34
Number of applicants per ad	3.9	1.2
Selection costs per ad	$ 77.90	$ 24.07
Ratio of hirees to applicants	0.46	0.66
Number of successful salespersons per ad*	0.25	0.10
Total recruitment and selection cost per successful salesperson*	$492.60	$584.17

*A successful salesperson is defined as someone who was still producing sales for the company one year later.
Source: Adapted from Marvin A. Jolson, "A Comparison of Blind vs. Full-Disclosure Ads for Sales Personnel," *Akron Business and Economic Review* 5 (Winter 1974), p. 17.

Employment Agencies

Employment agencies are sometimes used to find recruits, usually for more routine sales jobs such as retail and door-to-door sales. However, a few agencies specialize in finding applicants for more demanding jobs in technical and industrial sales. Some sales managers have had unsatisfactory experiences with employment agencies. They charge that the agencies are sometimes overzealous in

---

[12] Marvin A. Jolson, "A Comparison of Blind vs. Full-Disclosure Ads for Sales Personnel," *Akron Business and Economic Review* 5 (Winter 1974), pp. 16–18.

attempting to earn their fees, and that they tend to send applicants who do not meet the qualifications for the job to be filled. Consequently, many firms turn to employment agencies only as a last resort.

Others argue, however, that when a firm has problems with an employment agency, it is often the fault of the company for not understanding the agency's role and not providing sufficient information about the kinds of recruits it is looking for. When a firm carefully selects an agency with a good reputation, establishes a long-term relationship, and provides detailed descriptions of job qualifications, the agency can perform a valuable service. It locates and screens job applicants and reduces the amount of time and effort that the company's sales managers must devote to the recruiting process.

Selection Procedures

After the qualifications necessary to fill a job have been determined and some applicants have been recruited, the final task is to determine which applicants best meet the qualifications and have the greatest aptitude for the job. To gain the information needed to evaluate each prospective employee, firms typically use the following selection tools and procedures:

1. Application blanks.
2. Face-to-face interviews.
3. Reference checks.
4. Physical examinations.
5. Tests.
   a. Intelligence.
   b. Aptitude.
   c. Personality.

In a survey of firms with large sales forces, top sales executives were asked to rank each selection tool on the basis of: (1) helpfulness in selecting salespeople, (2) cost, and (3) order in which it is typically used in the selection process. The results of this study are shown in Table 11–4. Managers rated personal interviews and application forms as the most useful selection tools, whereas aptitude and personality tests were viewed as the least helpful.

These perceptions of the usefulness of various selection tools are reflected in the actual practices of many firms. The results of a recent survey of selection procedures followed by a sample of 121 industrial firms indicate that personal interviews are almost universally employed while psychological tests are the least used selection tools. As Table 11–5 shows, however, larger firms are somewhat more thorough in their use of job descriptions and psychological tests than smaller companies.

Table 11-4
How sales executives rank selection tools on helpfulness, order of use, and cost

	Rankings on		
	Helpfulness	Order of Use	Cost*
Interviews 1		2	1
Application blanks 2		1	6.5
Physical examinations.............. 3		6.5	2
Intelligence examinations.......... 4		3	3.5
Reference checks 5		4.5	6.5
Aptitude tests..................... 6		4.5	3.5
Personality tests 7		6.5	5

*Rank of 1 = most costly.
Source: Thomas R. Wotruba, "An Analysis of the Salesmen Selection Process," *Southern Journal of Business* 5 (January 1970), p. 47.

Table 11-5
Percentage of small and large firms that "extensively use" the following selection tools

Selection Items	Percentage of Small Firms	Percentage of Large Firms
Personal interviews 91		96
Application blanks 73		70
Personal reference checks 70		62
List of job qualifications 34		45
Job descriptions* 30		51
Psychological tests 22		32

*A statistically significant difference ($p < 0.05$) exists between the percentage of small and large firms that "extensively use" this sales management tool. In this survey, "small" firms were defined as those with annual sales of less than $40 million ($n = 74$), and large firms were those with sales over $40 million ($n = 47$).
Source: Alan J. Dubinsky and Thomas E. Barry, "A Survey of Sales Management Practices," *Industrial Marketing Management* 11 (1982), p. 136.

Application Blanks

Although professional salespeople often have resumes to submit to prospective employers, many personnel experts believe that a standard company application form makes it easier to assess applicants. A well-designed application blank helps ensure that the same information is obtained in the same form from all candidates.

The primary purpose of the application form is to collect information about the recruit's physical characteristics and personal history. Forms typically ask for facts about the candidate's physical condition, family status, education, business experience, military service, participation in social organizations, and outside interests and activities. This information can be reviewed to determine whether the applicant is qualified for the job on such dimensions as age, education, and experience.[13]

A second function of the application form is to help managers prepare for personal interviews with job candidates. Often a recruit's responses to items on the application form raise questions that should be explored during an interview. If the application shows that a person has held several different jobs within the past few years, for example, the interviewer should attempt to find out the reasons for these changes. Perhaps he can determine whether the applicant is a "job hopper" who is unlikely to stay with the company for very long.

Personal Interviews

In addition to probing deeper into the applicant's history, personal interviews enable managers to gain insight into the applicant's mental abilities and personality. An interview provides a manager with the opportunity to assess a candidate's communication skills, intelligence, sociability, aggressiveness, empathy, ambition, and other traits related to the qualifications necessary for the job. Different managers use many different interviewing approaches to accomplish these objectives. These methods of conducting personal interviews, however, can all be classified as either structured or unstructured.

In *structured interviews*, each applicant is asked the same predetermined set of questions. This approach is particularly good when the interviewer is inexperienced at evaluating candidates. The standard questions help guide the interview and ensure that all factors relevant to the candidate's qualifications are covered. Also, asking the same questions of all candidates makes it easier to compare their strengths and weaknesses. To facilitate such comparisons, many firms use a standard interview evaluation form like the one shown in Table 11–6 (pages 380–81). The interviewer rates each applicant's response to each question together with his or her overall impressions of each candidate.

One potential weakness of structured interviews is that the interviewer may rigidly stick to the prepared questions and fail to identify or probe the unique qualities or flaws of each candidate. In practice, though, structured interviews are often not so inflexible as this criticism implies. As a manager gains interviewing experience, he or she often learns to ask additional questions when an applicant's response is inadequate without disturbing the flow of the interview.

At the other end of the spectrum of interviewing techniques is the *unstructured interview*. The objective of such interviews is to get the applicant talking

---

[13] For example, see James C. Cotham III, "Using Personal History Information in Retail Salesman Selection," *Journal of Retailing* 45 (Summer 1969), pp. 31–38.

freely on a variety of subjects. The interviewer asks only a few questions to direct the conversation to topics of interest, such as the applicant's work experiences, career objectives, and outside activities. The rationale for this approach is that significant insights into the applicant's character and motivations can be gained by allowing him or her to talk freely with a minimum of direction. Also, the interviewer is free to spend more time on topics where the applicant's responses are interesting or unusual.

Successful, unstructured interviewing requires interviewers with experience and interpretive skills. Because there is no predetermined set of questions, there is always a danger that the interviewer will neglect some relevant topic areas. It is also more difficult to compare the responses of two or more applicants. Consequently, since most firms' sales managers have relatively little experience as interviewers, structured interviews are much more common in selecting new salespeople than unstructured approaches.

Within the interview itself, particularly those that are relatively unstructured, some sales managers use additional techniques to learn as much as possible about the applicant's character and aptitude. One such technique is the *stress interview*. The interviewer puts the applicant under stress in one of many ways, ranging from silence or rudeness on the part of the interviewer to constant, aggressive probing and questioning. The rationale for this technique is that the interviewer may learn how the applicant will respond to and deal with the stress he or she will encounter in selling situations.

Another approach is for the interviewer to ask the applicant to sell something. "Hand the prospect a stapler, a pencil, or any other object that's handy and ask him to 'sell' it. . . . A pro should be able to sell anything," says one sales manager. "The one thing he's got to do is to ask for the order. Seven of ten fail to do so."[14]

Techniques like these can be useful to assess a candidate's character and selling skills, but they should be used as only one part of the interview. Sometimes sales managers become so obsessed with finding the "one best way" to assess candidates that they allow interviewing gimmicks to get in the way of real communication. After all, another purpose of job interviews is to provide candidates with information about the job and company so that they will be interested in taking the job. One real danger with gimmicky interviewing techniques is that the applicant will be "turned off" and lose interest in working for the firm.

Reference Checks

If an applicant passes the face-to-face interview, a reference check is often the next step. Some sales managers question the value of references because "they always say nice things." However, with a little resourcefulness, reference checks can be a valuable selection tool.

---

[14] How Fredrich's McElveen Finds Super Salesmen," *Sales Management*, August 5, 1974, p. 4.

Table 11–6
Structured interview evaluation form

Name _____ Date of Interview _____

Position sought _____ Conducted by _____

Educational Background

	Low		High
1. Level attained	High school passing marks	———————	Ph.D. honors
2. Intellectual accomplishments		———————	
3. Outside activities	None	———————	Many, varied
4. Athletic abilities	No sports	———————	Varsity competition
5. Subject taken	Not job related	———————	Highly suitable

Job Experience

	Low		High
1. Past responsibilities	None	———————	Heavy, varied
2. Skills	Unskilled	———————	Competent professional
3. Past accomplishments	None	———————	Top-flight manager
4. Career progress	None	———————	Steadily upward
5. Motivation	Happy with routine	———————	Works under pressure, ambitious
6. Pertinence of past jobs		———————	Highly suitable

Suitability for Available Position

	Low		High
1. Future ambitions	Unplanned, confused	———————	Realistic, objective
2. Reasons for applying	No clear reason	———————	Qualified by past experience and desire
3. Promotion potential	None	———————	Highly promotable

Individual Characteristics

			Positive
1.	Appearance	Awkward, homely	——— ——— ———	Poised, cleancut
2.	Diction	Grammar bad	——— ——— ———	Well spoken, cultivated
3.	Verbal facility	Difficulty expressing self	——— ——— ———	Excellent
4.	Tone of voice	Sharp, unpleasant	——— ——— ———	Well modulated, pleasant
5.	Attitude	Timid, nervous	——— ——— ———	Confident, at ease
6.	Grooming	Badly dressed	——— ——— ———	Well groomed, in good taste

Social Relationships

1.	Family status	Parents divorced, unstable home	——— ——— ———	Enjoys home life
2.	Marriage relationship	Unhappy, divorced	——— ——— ———	Successful marriage
3.	Social interests	None	——— ——— ———	Outgoing, sociable
4.	Outside interests	None	——— ——— ———	Civic leader
5.	Hobbies	None	——— ——— ———	Several active hobbies

Final Disposition

(1) Reject (2) Hire on trial (3) Hire with caution if no better candidate appears
(4) Recommend (5) Recommend highly

Remarks: _____

Source: From James Menzies Black, *How to Get Results from Interviewing* (New York: McGraw-Hill, 1970), pp. 60–61. Copyright © 1970 McGraw-Hill Book Company. Used with permission.

One purpose of checking references is to ensure the accuracy of factual data about the applicant. It is naive to assume that everything a candidate has written on his or her resume or application form is true. Facts about previous job experiences and college degrees should be checked. The discovery of false data on a candidate's application raises a question about his or her basic honesty as well as about what the candidate is trying to hide.

References can supply additional information and opinions about a prospect's aptitude and past job performance. Although it is important to respect an applicant's request not to prejudice his or her position with a current employer, useful information can be obtained from previous employers and supervisors. Even though most applicants try to provide only "good references," a resourceful interviewer can probe beyond a reference's positive biases with questions such as, "If you were hiring this individual today, what qualities would you think it most important to develop?" Also, some firms require applicants to supply as many as six or seven references on the theory that it is unlikely that so many people will all have strong personal biases in favor of the applicant. Calling a large number of references and probing them in depth can be time-consuming and costly, but it can also produce worthwhile information and protect against making expensive hiring mistakes.

Physical Examinations

One typically does not think of selling as physically demanding, yet sales jobs often require a great deal of stamina and the physical ability to withstand large amounts of stress. Consequently, even though physical examinations are relatively expensive compared with other selection tools, many sales managers see them as valuable aids for evaluating candidates, as indicated by the survey results shown in Table 11–4.

If a firm does require a physical examination, the company should designate either a company doctor or a private physician. In either case, the sales manager should inform the doctor about the nature and physical requirements of the job. The physician should be asked to be particularly vigilant concerning indications of chronic diseases, heart ailments, digestive troubles, and respiratory difficulties.

Tests

A final set of selection tools used by many firms consists of tests aimed at measuring an applicant's mental abilities and personality traits. The most commonly used tests can be grouped into three types: (1) intelligence, (2) aptitude, and (3) personality tests. Within each category, there are a variety of different tests used by different companies.

Intelligence Tests. Intelligence tests are useful for determining whether an applicant has sufficient mental ability to perform a job successfully. Sales managers tend to believe that these are the most useful of all the tests commonly used in selecting salespeople. General intelligence tests are designed to measure an applicant's overall mental abilities by examining how well he or she comprehends, reasons, and learns. The *Wonderlic Personnel Test* is one common general intelligence test. It is popular because it is short; it consists of 50 items and requires only about 12 minutes to complete.

When the job to be filled requires special competence in one or a few areas of mental ability, a specialized intelligence test might be used to evaluate candidates. There are tests available for measuring such things as speed of learning, number facility, memory, logical reasoning, and verbal ability.

Aptitude Tests. Aptitude tests are designed to determine whether an applicant has an interest in, or the ability to perform, certain tasks and activities. For example, the *Strong Vocational Interest Blank* asks the respondent to indicate whether he or she likes or dislikes a variety of situations and activities. This can determine whether the applicant's interests are similar to those of people who are successful in a variety of different occupations, including selling. Other tests measure skills or abilities that might be related to success in particular types of selling jobs, such as mechanical or mathematical aptitude.

One problem with at least some aptitude tests is that, instead of measuring a person's native abilities, they measure his or her current level of skill at certain tasks. At least some skills necessary for successful selling can be taught, or improved, through a well-designed training program. Therefore, rejecting applicants because they currently do not have the necessary skills can result in losing people who could be trained to be successful salespeople. This may account, at least in part, for the low rating given to aptitude tests by sales managers in Table 11–4.

Personality Tests. Many general personality tests evaluate an individual on a large number of traits. The *Edwards Personal Preference Schedule,* for instance, measures 17 traits such as sociability, aggressiveness, and independence. Such tests, however, contain a large number of questions, require substantial amounts of time to complete, and gather information about some traits that may be irrelevant for evaluating future salespeople. Consequently, more limited personality tests have been developed in recent years that concentrate on only a few traits thought to be directly relevant to a person's future success in sales. *The Multiple Personal Inventory,* for example, uses a small number of "forced-choice" questions to measure the strength of two personality traits: empathy with other people and ego drive.[15]

Concerns Regarding the Use of Tests. The results in Tables 11–4 and 11–5 suggest that, on the average, sales managers do not think test scores are as helpful as other selection tools in evaluating potential salespeople. Indeed, many companies do not use tests at all. There are a number of reasons for these negative attitudes.

For one thing, some sales managers doubt that test scores are valid for predict-

---

[15] Leslie Rich, "Can Salesmen Be Tested?" *Dun's Review* 87 (March 1966), pp. 40–41 and 63–65.

ing the future success of salespeople in their companies. As discussed in Chapter 10, no mental abilities or personality traits have been found to be positively related to performance across a wide variety of selling jobs in different firms. Thus, specific tests that measure such abilities and traits may be valid for selecting salespeople for some jobs, but invalid for others. To make matters worse, tests for measuring specific abilities and characteristics of applicants do not always produce consistent scores. Some commercially available tests have not been developed according to the most scientific measurement procedures; as a result, their reliability and validity are questionable. Consequently, even when a firm believes that a particular trait, such as empathy or sociability, is related to job performance, there is still a question concerning which test should be used to measure that trait.

A related concern, particularly in the case of personality tests, is that some creative and talented people may be rejected simply because their personalities do not conform to the test norms. Many sales jobs require creative people, particularly when those people are being groomed for future management responsibilities. Yet these people seldom fit an average personality profile because the "average" person is not particularly creative.

Another concern about testing involves the possible reactions of the people who are tested. A reasonably intelligent, "test-wise" person can "fudge" the results of many tests by selecting answers that he or she thinks management will want. These answers may not accurately reflect his or her own feelings or behavior. Also, many prospective employees view extensive testing as an onerous burden and perhaps an invasion of their privacy. Therefore, some managers fear that requiring a large battery of tests may "turn off" a candidate and reduce the likelihood that he or she will accept a job with the firm.

Finally, a given test may discriminate between people of different races or sexes, and the use of such tests is illegal. Consequently, some firms have abandoned the use of tests entirely rather than risk getting into trouble with the government.

Guidelines for the Appropriate Use of Tests. To avoid, or at least minimize, the preceding testing problems, managers should keep the following guidelines in mind.

1. Test scores should be considered only one input to the selection decision. Managers should not rely on them to do the work of other parts of the selection process—such as interviewing and checking references. Candidates should not be eliminated solely on the basis of test scores.
2. Applicants should be tested only on those abilities and traits that management, on the basis of a thorough job analysis, has determined to be relevant for the specific job. Broad tests that evaluate a large number of traits not relevant to a specific job are probably inappropriate.
3. When possible, tests with built-in "internal consistency checks" should be used. Then the person who analyzes the test results can determine whether

the applicant responded honestly or was faking some answers. Many recently designed tests ask similar questions with slightly different wording several times throughout the test. If a respondent is answering honestly, he or she should always give the same response to similar questions.

4. A firm should conduct empirical studies to ensure that the tests are valid for predicting an applicant's future performance in the job. This kind of hard evidence of test validity is particularly important in view of the government's equal employment opportunity requirements.

Equal Employment Opportunity Requirements in Selecting Salespeople

Title VII of the 1964 Civil Rights Act forbids discrimination in employment on the basis of race, sex, color, religion, national origin, or age. This means that the selection procedures a firm uses—particularly its interviewing and testing procedures—should not be biased against any subgroup of the labor force.

Requirements for Tests

Section 703(h) of the 1964 Civil Rights Act specifically approves the use of "professionally developed ability tests," provided that such tests are not "designed, intended, or used to discriminate because of race, color, religion, sex, or national origin." Suppose, however, that an employer innocently uses a test that does discriminate in that a larger proportion of men than women, or a larger of whites than blacks, receives passing scores. Has the employer violated the law? Not necessarily. In such cases, the burden of proof is on the employer to show that the test scores are valid predictors of successful performance on the job in question. In other words, it is legal for a firm to hire more men than women for a job if it can be proven that men possess more of some trait or ability that will enable them to do the job better. This requires that the employer have *empirical evidence* showing a significant relationship between scores on the test and actual job performance. The procedures a firm might use to produce this kind of evidence were described earlier in this chapter when discussing how to determine whether particular job qualifications are valid.[16]

---

[16] For a detailed discussion of the procedures required to validate employment tests, see Equal Employment Opportunity Commission, "Guidelines on Employee Selection Procedures," 35 Fed. Reg. 1233 (29 C.F.R. Sec. 1607.1–1607.14, 1971). For a discussion of recent court interpretations of these guidelines, see David E. Robertson, "Update on Testing and Equal Opportunity," *Personnel Journal*, March 1977, pp. 144–47.

Table 11–7
Illegal discriminatory questions
must be omitted from employment
applications and interviews

Nationality and race	Comments or questions relating to the race, color, national origin or descent of the applicant—or his or her spouse—must be avoided. Applicants should not be asked to supply a photo of themselves when applying for a job. If proficiency in another language is an important part of the job, the applicant can be asked to demonstrate that proficiency but cannot be asked whether it is his or her native language. Applicants may be asked if they are U.S. citizens, but not whether they—or their parents or spouse—are naturalized or native-born Americans. Applicants who are not citizens may be asked whether they have the legal right to remain and work in the United States.
Religion	Applicants should not be asked about their religious beliefs or whether the company's workweek or the job schedule would interfere with their religious convictions.
Sex and marital status	Except for jobs where sex is clearly related to job performance—as in a TV commercial role—the applicant's sex should not enter the hiring discussion. Applicants should not be asked about their marital status, whether or not their spouse works, or even whom the prospective employer should notify in an emergency. A woman should not be asked whether she would like to be addressed as Mrs., Miss, or Ms. Applicants should not be asked any questions about their children, baby-sitting arrangements, contraceptive practices, or planned family size.
Age	Applicants may be asked whether they are minors or age 70 or over, because special laws govern the employment of such people. With those exceptions, however, applicants should not be asked their age or date of birth.
Handicaps	The U.S. government and its contractors are prohibited by law from discriminatory hiring because of physical or mental handicaps. Some states already have such laws; and Congress is considering extending such requirements to all employers. Once an employer has described the job to be performed, an applicant can be asked whether he or she has any physical or mental limitations that would prevent him or her from performing the job.

Requirements for Interviews and Application Forms

Because it is illegal to discriminate in hiring on the basis of race, sex, religion, age, and national origin, there is no reason for a firm to ask for such information on its job application forms or during personal interviews. Indeed, it is wise to completely avoid all questions that are in any way related to such factors. Then there will be no question in the applicant's mind about whether the hiring decision was biased or unfair. This is easier said than done, however, because some seemingly innocent questions can be viewed as attempts to gain information that might be used to discriminate against a candidate. Table 11–7 offers some guidelines concerning the kinds of questions managers should avoid when conducting employment interviews or designing application forms.

Summary

This chapter sought to review the issues that surround the recruitment and selection of new salespeople. The issues discussed ranged from who has the responsibility for these tasks to the impact of the Equal Employment Opportunity Act on selection procedures.

Two factors are primary in determining who has the responsibility for recruiting and selecting salespeople: (1) the size of the sales force, and (2) the kind of selling involved. In general, the smaller the sales force, the more sophisticated the selling task. The more the sales force is used as a training ground for marketing and sales managers, the more likely it is that higher-level people, including the sales manager, will be directly involved in the recruiting and selection effort. To ensure that new recruits have the aptitude for the job, it is useful to look at the recruitment and selection procedures as a three-step process. The steps are: (1) a job analysis and description, (2) the recruitment of a pool of applicants, and (3) the selection of the best applicants from the available pool.

The job analysis and description phase includes a detailed examination of the job to determine what activities, tasks, responsibilities, and environmental influences are involved. This analysis may be carried out by someone in the sales management ranks or by a job analysis specialist. Regardless of who does it, it is important for that person to prepare a job description that details the findings of the job analysis. Finally, the job description is used to develop a statement of job qualifications, which lists and describes the personal traits and abilities a person should have to perform the tasks and responsibilities involved in the job.

The pool of recruits from which the firm finally selects can be generated from a number of sources, including: (1) people within the company, (2) people in other firms, (3) educational institutions, (4) advertisements, and (5) employment agencies. Each source has its own advantages and disadvantages. Some, such as advertisements, typically produce a larger pool. The key question the sales manager needs to address is which source or combination of sources is likely to produce the largest pool of good, qualified recruits.

Once the qualifications necessary to fill a job have been determined and applicants have been recruited, the final task is to determine which applicant best meets the qualifications and has the greatest aptitude for the job. To make this determination, firms often use most, and in some cases all, of the following tools and procedures: (1) application blanks, (2) face-to-face interviews, (3) reference checks, (4) physical examinations, and (5) intelligence, aptitude, and personality tests. Although most employers find the interview and then the application blank most helpful, each device seems to perform some functions better than the other alternatives. This may explain why most firms use a combination of selection tools.

Title VII of the 1964 Civil Rights Act forbids discrimination in employment on the basis of race, sex, color, religion, or national origin. A firm must be careful, therefore, about how it uses tests, how it structures its application form, and the questions it asks during personal interviews so as not to be charged with noncompliance with the act. A firm that uses tests, for example, must be able to demonstrate empirically that the attributes measured are related to the salesperson's performance on the job.

Discussion Questions

1. The *Wall Street Journal* (10-26-82, p. 1) carried an article on handwriting analysis. A quote from the article reads: "Graphodynamics, Paramus, N.J., says it works regularly with many insurance companies to screen prospective sales people." What evidence exists that shows that sales performance is related to handwriting? What does handwriting analysis reveal?

2. According to one recruiter, "Selling requires skills in being persuasive. The best way to see if a person is persuasive is to ask them to sell me something during the interview, a pen, an ashtray, or even a coffee cup, anything." Do you approve of this tactic? What would you do if you were asked to sell something during the interview?

3. "When I am interviewing applicants for sales positions, I make it a practice to allow interruptions, answering the phone or letting others enter the room to conduct their business, while the interview is going on." Is this approach justified?

4. The Allen Corporation, manufacturers of industrial valves, does little outside recruiting, relying instead on recommendations from existing members of the sales force. What are the advantages and disadvantages of this method?

5. The national sales manager of the Quick-Change Tool Co. recruits people for the position of driver-sales representative. Duties involve calling on service stations, garages, and automobile dealers. To be considered, all applicants must be high school graduates and pass both the Bennett Mechanical Comprehension Test and the Wonderlic Personnel Test. The personnel manager has advised the national sales manager that this procedure may violate equal employment opportunity regulations. Do you agree?

6. "Honesty is one of the most important characteristics that a stockbroker must have to be successful. In order to ensure that this trait exists, all applicants must pass a lie-detector test." What are the risks associated with giving a lie-detector test? What does the evidence show about the value of lie-detector tests (polygraphs) as a selection device?

7. One potential source of applicants for sales positions is sales representatives who work for competitors. One sales manager indicated: "Pirating sales representatives from other companies makes sense. Let them do the training, then we'll hire them." Is this ethical? Does this practice make good business sense?

8. "I'm glad that our legal department has advised us not to use all of those time-consuming tests. Show me a man and I can tell you after one interview whether he can sell or not." Comment.

9. The Irvine Corporation has had little success in recruiting and hiring women for its sales force. Should direct techniques be adopted? If so, does this constitute discrimination?

10. The CASCO Feed Co. prefers to hire older sales representatives to call on farmers. The youngest sales representative is 53. A weighted application blank treats age as follows:

Age	Points
Under 30	− 2
30–39	− 1
40–45	+ 1
46–49	+ 2
50–59	+ 4
60–69	+ 3
70 and over	+ 1

Is CASCO in violation of EEOC requirements? How can CASCO justify this practice?

11. "I don't care what the law says," retorted the sales manager for National Products, Ltd., "selling for National involves some travel and evening work, and I want to know whether the applicant is married or not. If married, then I want to discuss the job with the applicant's spouse." Comment.

12. The applicant left the question concerning religion blank. The district sales manager insisted that this information be provided. The applicant refused to comply. Who is right? Are there situations where religion would be a Bona Fide Occupational Qualification (BFOQ)? What about sex?

Chapter **12**

Sales Training: Objectives, Techniques, and Evaluation

At a recent sales management seminar, one of the authors asked the participants to describe their experiences and reactions to the need for and the problems with sales training. Initially, the response was rather limited, possibly due to the reluctance of the various sales managers to admit that they were not comfortable with this subject. All of them, however, agreed that sales training is needed for everybody, new sales reps and experienced sales reps alike. One sales manager said, "In our company, it's a continuous process. Anytime we introduce a new product or change our basic procedures, we incorporate this into our training programs." Another stated, "There's no doubt that some sort of training is needed, but my top management keeps asking if its worth the cost. And I don't know how to answer them." Finally, a sales manager from a company that manufactures medical equipment claimed, "My biggest problem is trying to justify what we are doing in sales training. We spend a bundle and see no change in market share."

These comments reveal several points about sales training. First, there is universal agreement that some sales training is needed. Second, sales training is an on-going or continuous process. Third, measurement of the benefits of sales training is a difficult process. And fourth, there is uncertainty over what sales training should accomplish.

Next, the sales managers were asked to identify the characteristics of successful salespeople in their own companies. The responses were typical and seemed to follow a somewhat disturbing pattern. One sales manager said, "In my company, the really good reps are problem solvers. They know how to determine the customer's problem and come up with a solution." Another took a different approach, stating, "The successful sales rep has many traits. He knows how to listen, he is enthusiastic, he is persuasive, and he can put himself into the customer's shoes." A recently appointed sales manager pointed out that in her company the good sales reps meet quota as a rule and ". . . always seem to be on top of things, well organized, and good planners." Responses tended to be rather broad and failed to give much direction as to what a sales training program should accomplish. Presumably, sales reps should be trained to be problem solvers, good listeners and enthusiastic. They should know how to understand the customer's needs, as well as being persuasive, well organized, and good planners.

Finally, the sales managers were asked if their sales-training programs had been successful in teaching sales reps—both new and experienced ones—the characteristics they associated with being successful. Their answers varied; some said they thought that their sales training programs did contribute to better sales performance, while others were less enthusiastic about the value of their training programs. One sales manager replied, "We go through the motions. But without job descriptions, it is difficult to develop a training program that answers our needs. We do it anyway, though." At this point, the discussion leader asked if their sales training programs attempted to teach sales reps how to be enthusiastic, or to be problem solvers, or to be good listeners, or to be well organized. Most of the participants said that their programs paid some heed to time and territory management and that this would help develop good organizational skills. For the other traits, one sales manager spoke for the rest of the group: "You don't teach people how to listen or to be enthusiastic. They either have it, or they don't." It was only when the sales managers were asked to describe an enthusiastic sales representative did it occur to them that maybe what is wrong with sales training programs is that they assume too much. The programs do not deal with basic issues. In fact, the sales manager who said problem solving was an attribute associated with sales success admitted that he preaches to his reps that this is a key to success. But he did not bother to identify *how* a problem solver behaves. Thus, one problem with sales training programs based on this group is that they assume too much and that they do not deal with the basics.

What's Wrong with Sales Training Programs?

There are a variety of problems found in most sales training programs. One commonly cited criticism is that there has been too much rah-rah, too many bells and whistles. According to Michael Cook, editor of *Training and Development Journal*, "simple sales formulas and 'sell-your-socks-off' mesmerization are no longer sufficient in the face of increased customer sophistication and product-service complexity."[1] While this represents a positive finding, many companies still follow the belief that bringing in the so-called enterTRAINER will produce desired results. According to one industrial psychologist, "Traditional sales-training programs are based on the assumption that increased motivation leads to a change in attitude, which changes the way salespeople perform. Experience shows that programs which aim head-on to increase motivation generally produce dismal results."[2]

Another criticism of conventional sales-training programs is that they rely too much on passive learning techniques. One expert feels that there has been too much emphasis on lectures, the "spray and pray" method, and not enough emphasis on techniques that require participant involvement, using such techniques as role-playing, simulations, and case analyses.[3] Related to this is the argument that traditional sales training concentrates too much on ensuring that the trainees understand various selling situations, rather than on how they will perform or behave in those situations.[4]

Too often, top management approves a training program, hoping that it will be a panacea for all of the company's sales problems, and then sends the sales force back into the field without planning any follow-up activities. During the program— often an expensive multimedia extravaganza—interest and morale do build up, only to disappear one week later. All is forgotten, and sales reps are selling the

---

[1] Michael H. Cook, "Sales Training Today: "Less Rah-Rah, Fewer Bells & Whistles"," *Training and Development Journal*, November 1981, p. 4.

[2] Bernard L. Rosenbaum, "Modeling vs. Motivation," *Industrial Marketing*, January 1981, p.76.

[3] Frank W. Bonheim, "Dual-Purpose Training," *Training and Development Journal*, May 1978, pp. 40–42.

[4] Carl D. Riegel, "Behavior Modeling for Management Development," *Cornell Hotel and Restaurant Administration Quarterly*, August 1982, pp. 77–81.

same way they did before the training took place. And sales managers are not coaching or helping the sales reps apply the new techniques.[5] This is similar to training a football team before the season gets underway and then not using the coach for the rest of the season. Another major weakness of many sales training programs is that there is often no planning for follow-up activities.

The content of sales training programs has been criticized as not being relevant. One of the sales managers mentioned earlier commented, "There is too much emphasis on product knowledge. Why, I can't even think of a case where a sale was lost due to inadequate product knowledge. Not in my company anyway. But we have lost sales because the sales rep did not know how to sell." His position was supported by another who said, "The same thing happens in my company. When I pleaded for more training on selling skills, they added a session onto the already too-long session on product knowledge. And then it was nothing more than a lecture." Thus, both the content and method of instruction in sales-training programs have been criticized.[6]

Other criticisms of many sales-training programs exist: They lack direction, they are not relevant, they cost too much, benefits are too hard to measure, and so on. The problems of sales training programs raises the question: What can be done to make sales training more effective?

Improving Sales Training

Many of the problems overlap and can be resolved by adopting a more objective approach. First, sales training often lacks credibility. Programs fail to deliver what they promise and, as a result, are viewed by many as being a waste of time and money. Second, the level of approach assumes too much: "Trainees already know how to listen or to be enthusiastic, so why spend time on such basic areas?" Or, "Sales veterans already know how to sell, so time is not needed on this subject." Third, once techniques have been taught, it is not necessary to worry about the use of reinforcers or rewards to stimulate sales reps to continue to use them.

Creating Credibility in Sales Training.[7] A problem often discussed among sales trainers is that they feel their programs lack credibility. Budget cutting efforts are too often directed at existing sales-training programs. This may reflect management's feeling that these programs are accomplishing little and are expendable. Sales-training programs have to be sold, just like any other product or service. Well-designed programs are easier to sell to management than those put together with little thought.

The starting point is to analyze the needs of the sales force. One way to do this

---

[5] Jack R. Snader, "Most Sales Training Doesn't Work," *SalesReport, vol. 1*, no. 3 (Chicago: SYSTEMA CORPORA-TION), pp. 1–4.

[6] For an excellent discussion of sales training problems, see: John J. Falvey, "Myths of Sales Training," *Sales and Marketing Management,* April, May, June 1978.

[7] The following discussion is based to a large extent on Gene Hahne, "Creating Credibility for Your Sales Training," *Training and Development Journal,* November 1981, pp. 34–38.

is to travel with sales reps, observing what they are doing and asking them what they need to know that will help them to perform more effectively. Discussions with field sales managers is a useful source of information since they are closest to the sales reps. Interviews with key members of management are productive ways to identify training needs. One expert advocates sending anonymous questionnaires to customers asking: What do you expect of a salesperson in this industry? How do salespersons disappoint you? Which company in the industry does the best selling job? In what ways are its salepersons better?[8] Other sources include company records showing turnover data, performance evaluations, and sales and cost analyses. Attitudinal studies conducted with the sales force are useful sources of information. This analysis of needs answers three basic questions: Where in the organization is training needed, what should be the content of the training program, and who needs the training.[9]

Next, setting specific, realistic, and measurable objectives adds to the credibility of a sales-training program. The objectives may include learning about new products, new techniques, or new procedures. It pays to keep the objectives simple. Management may want a 10 percent sales increase, which then becomes the broad objective of the training program. The specific objective might be to teach sales reps how to call on new accounts which, if improved, will help lead to the broad objective. Measurability is critical in sales training. More will be said about this later.

At this point, a decision has to be made concerning developing the training program or hiring an outside organization to conduct it. There are many companies, large and small, that use outside agencies for sales training purposes. Small companies may farm out most of their training needs. Large companies develop most of their own programs and will use outside agencies to handle specialized needs. Lack of careful investigation of outside suppliers can lead to problems. One of our sales managers mentioned how he was embarrassed by retaining a company that put on an "entertaining song-and-dance routine" that cost $5,000 but failed to have any lasting effect. Use of outside sources is encouraged if they meet the objectives of the company.

Designing a system of measurement is the next step. Questions that need to be asked include: What do we want to measure? When do we want to measure? How do we do it? Or, what measuring tools are available? Using tests to measure learning is not that difficult, measuring application in the field is difficult. Training a sales rep how to demonstrate a product can be evaluated during the training session. But whether the sales rep provides effective demonstration in front of a customer is harder to evaluate. This is why field sales managers are an important link: They can provide follow-up and feed-back information on how well the sales rep demonstrates the product. The field sales managers can coach the salesperson on how to demonstrate the product. Finally, performance evaluations of sales

---

[8] James F. Carey, "Assess Your Personnel Needs," in *Sales Training and Motivation Special Report, Sales and Marketing Management*, 1977.

[9] Kenneth N. Wexley, "Personnel Training," *Annual Review of Psychology*, 1984, pp. 519–51.

performance provides additional evidence on the value of training although such information must be used carefully. Changes in performance, like sales increases, may be due to factors not related to sales training. To claim that they are casts doubt on the sales-training efforts.

Larger companies must decide which group to train. It is wrong to assume that everyone in the sales force needs training. Certainly, newly hired recruits must have some training, whether it's on-the-job at first and then more centralized later or some other arrangement. When changes in procedures or products exist, it is fairly safe to assume that training needs are universal. However, if only certain sales reps are having a problem, such as a sales slump, then the training needs to directed at them and not everybody. To include the entire force may create problems, especially among those not experiencing the sales slump. This latter group may resent being included and let others know as well. In the case where a new training method is being tested, it is wise to use a group that will be most receptive. In this way, credibility increases, creating a favorable climate for continuation.

Since measurement is crucial, the sales trainer needs to collect data before training starts. The needs analysis provided relevant information pertaining to program content. For example, if it was observed that some salespeople had difficulty managing their sales calls, then observation by the trainer or the field sales manager after the program should provide data indicating the value of the training. Call reports would be another source of information. Follow-up must continue beyond the initial check since the use of new skills may drop off. If this happens, some form of reinforcement is necessary.

The data collection process should provide sales trainers with information that will justify the program. Top management wants to know if the benefits exceed or equal the costs. Keeping top management informed about the success of training programs contributes to the overall credibility. Sales managers do not want to have training programs canceled due to faulty communications with top management about the value of sales training efforts.

Continuous follow-up and evaluation of all sales-training efforts is mandatory. Gene Hahne, manager of training for Shell Oil Company, comments, "We used one program for seven years in our company. We used it because nobody evaluated it. Nobody followed up on it. Nobody ever took the time out to go out in the field and ask participants, 'What did you get out of the program?'"[10] In this case, the program had attempted to teach sales reps how to probe for information during a sales call. Although most sales reps identified the subject matter, very few were able to identify the skills that had been taught. The program was not working and probably had been written off as a poor investment by management.

Sales-training programs, whether being sold to the sales manager or to top management, must be credible. Management can always find other alternatives for spending resources. Proof of the value of new programs is a function of past experiences.

---

[10] Ibid., p. 38.

Needed: A Back-to-the-Basics Approach. Traditional sales training programs concentrate on teaching factual information about new products or services, new company procedures, and important changes in the market. For the most part, these programs have been successful. They have been less successful in developing sales skills. Characteristics of the firm's superstars are portrayed as the ideal, and all others are told that they should try to emulate these high performers. It's as if the goal of the program is to produce clones of the superstars. According to one authority, "The problem in trying to produce superseller clones is that it just doesn't work. One of the best examples I've encountered in trying to clone a superseller was provided by a mid-sized insurance company. The company's most productive agent was asked to develop a sales presentation. The agent was a fast-paced, quick-witted, distinctively New York, New Yorker. He wrote a presentation which was distributed at a national sales training seminar to other insurance agents who were instructed to 'learn it' (i.e., memorize it)."[11] The program failed since it ignored regional, cultural, and personality differences not only of the participants but of their customers. In a sense, the program was saying that there exists a single personality type that applies to all salespeople and to all of their customers. Unfortunately, this image is hard to dispel. There is no one type of personality or selling style that works in all cases. People are different, regardless of whether they are selling or buying. To assume otherwise leads to the development of meaningless sales training programs.

The back-to-the-basics approach rests on a key assumption: Selling is a process of influence.[12] The salesperson influences the customer, who in turn influences the salesperson. For the salesperson to control the selling process he or she must accurately assess the buying situation to determine the approach most likely to work. In some cases, being persuasive works, in others, being quietly persistent and forceful is more effective. The conclusion: There is no one selling style or personality that works in all cases. Successful salespeople alter their approach to meet the needs of specific customers and specific selling situations. Successful selling is situation-specific. This conclusion leads to the development of a more general basis of sales training, namely a behavioral approach or behavior modeling.

What is behavior modeling? How does it influence salesperson behavior? How can modeling be used in a sales training program? Psychologists define behavior modeling as a process by which new patterns of behavior can be acquired, or existing patterns of behavior altered. The fundamental idea is that learning takes place, not through actual experiences, but through observation of others. Thus, modeling is a vicarious process that takes place through observing others, copying, matching, or imitation.[13] Figure 12–1 contrasts traditional sales training with behavior modeling.

---

[11] Laura L'Herisson, "Teaching the Sales Force to Fail," *Training and Development Journal,* November 1981, pp. 78–82.

[12] The following discussion is based to a large extent on Malcolm E. Shaw, "Sales Training in Transition," *Training and Development Journal,* February 1981, pp. 74–83.

[13] Henry P. Sims, Jr. and Charles C. Manz, "Modeling Influences on Employee Behavior," *Personnel Journal,* January 1982, pp. 58–65.

Figure 12–1
Traditional sales training models
versus behavior modeling

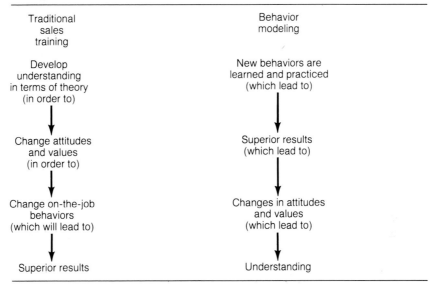

Source: Adapted from: A. I. Kraut, "Developing Managerial Skills via Modeling Techniques: Some Positive Research Findings—A Symposium," *Personnel Psychology*, 1976, p. 326.

If we can assume that salespeople need to know a variety of selling skills to be successful, then it follows that behavior modeling would be an appropriate method. A behavioral sales-training program should help the sales rep to acquire a wide range of desirable selling behaviors like giving information, asking questions, listening, and solving problems in order to influence the process. Shaw identifies two basic patterns of behavior: "First, the sales representative may choose to *act* upon the customer . . . in ways which are aimed at shaping the customer's viewpoints, feelings, and reactions. Secondly, the sales representative may *reach* to the customer in ways which are aimed at drawing out the customer's views and demonstrating empathy and responsiveness.[14] Two choices exist for a salesperson: to *act* or to *react*. In a sales transaction, the rep combines these two resources in order to influence the transaction. Remember, earlier, when our sales managers described successful salespeople broadly as being "problem solvers" and narrowly as being "persuasive." Further probing revealed a series of behavioral terms that defined persuasiveness. Salespeople who are behaving in a persuasive manner use gestures, vary the pitch and tempo of their voice, make eye contact, smile, and use positive words and phrases.

There are three tiers of behavior according to Shaw, who states, "Since problem-solving behavior is a different order of concern than giving information which is, in turn, of a different order than 'making eye contact,' it was found that

---

[14] Shaw, "Sales Training in Transition," p. 75.

three tiers were useful in clarifying the relationship between means and ends."[15] They are: (1) behavioral strategies, (2) behavioral skills, and (3) behavioral tactics. Behavioral strategies can be defined as a basic selling approach comprised of a set of skills that, when used together, form an approach for dealing with a specific customer. Different strategies are used with different customers. Behavioral skills are the competencies needed to execute a specific strategy. To use a problem-solving strategy, a term too broad to be meaningful, it is necessary to use specific skills such as listening carefully, asking the right questions, and presenting solutions. It is skills such as these upon which behavioral sales training must concentrate. Behavioral tactics are subsets of skills. For example, persuasiveness is a skill requiring tactics such as using gestures, varying voice tempo and pitch, making eye contact, etc. Can these tactics be acquired via observation and practice? Behavior modeling assumes that they can be learned, as illustrated back in Figure 12–1.

Skills and tactics can be combined into two categories: "A" or *act* skills and tactics, and "R" or *react* skills and tactics. A partial listing of each class follows:[16]

A—SKILLS AND TACTICS
Give Information by:
  Being brief and specific.
  Making eye contact.
  Avoiding apologies or equivocations.

Be Persuasive by:
  Talking benefits.
  Using affirmative words.
  Varying voice dynamics—tempo.
  Gesturing.

Be Convincing by:
  Being deliberate and emphatic.
  Using facts.
  Being "grounded."

R—SKILLS AND TACTICS
Explore the Other's Views by:
  Asking direct questions.
  Asking open-ended questions.
  Sustaining eye contact.

Support the Other by:
  Summarizing his/her viewpoint.
  Reflecting feelings.
  Identifying with customer's feelings.

[15] Ibid., p. 76.
[16] Ibid., p. 78.

Adapt to Other's Views by:
Seeking compromise.
Seeking alternatives.
Modifying your behavior.

It should be clear that the sales manager who urges the sales rep to be more persuasive without telling the rep *how* to be persuasive is not providing training. Persuasiveness must be broken down into subsets before training can occur.

Selling strategies, the last idea, consist of: (1) interactive or problem-solving strategies using A and R skills, (2) proactive or controlling strategies primarily using A skills, (3) reactive or adaptive strategies primarily using R skills, and (4) mixed or negotiating strategies combining A and R skills. The skilled sales rep acquires skills and tactics and is able to blend them to meet the needs of specific situations. Remember that customers have different needs and personalities and that one selling strategy will not work in all cases.

How can behavior modeling help train sales representatives to acquire the necessary tactics, skills, and strategies? Once desired behaviors have been identified, the next stage is to provide a means whereby sales trainees can observe and experience these activities. Figure 12–2 illustrates the process.

Figure 12–2
Modeling processes and methods

Processes	Methods
Attention	Appropriate models Appropriate rate of presentation Appropriate complexity Repeated exposure to model
Retention	Covert rehearsal Learning points Discussion Role-playing
Motor reproduction	Role-playing On-the-job practice
Motivation	Positive feedback Sharing positive on-the-job experiences

Source: Carl D. Riegel, "Behavior Modeling for Management Development," *Cornell Hotel and Restaurant Administration Quarterly*, August 1982, p. 79.

The starting point then is to present or display the desired behavior using demonstrations or models employing live or filmed methods of presentation, written examples, case problems, exercises, etc. Shaw argues that only desired behavior should be demonstrated so that negative habits are avoided.[17] This view coin-

---

[17] Ibid., p. 80.

cides with one of Falvey's concerns expressed in "Myths of Sales Training" where he states that it is wrong to "Let Old Joe Train the New Rep." Old Joe has acquired many tactics that work for him, some right and some wrong, and its erroneous to have him teach bad habits.[18] The next step in the training process is to have the sales rep experience the desired behavior by actually doing it, not in front of everybody, but alone or with a trainer or manager in a one-on-one setting. This is followed by practice and more practice coupled with coaching. On-the-job practice with a field sales manager present provides an opportunity for instant feedback and reinforcement. Reinforcement is critical to the success of all behavior modeling programs and must occur during all phases. Meeting quota provides rewards to salespeople but incentives must be available during training. The sales rep who learns how to be persuasive by practicing various tactics needs reinforcing as the tactics are learned.[19] Eventually acquiring the necessary skills and tactics will lead to higher order rewards, such as a promotion. In the interim, management needs to provide a support system which reinforces and supports positive behavior. An important ingredient of behavior modeling as a sales-training method is follow-up and reinforcement. Snader advocates allocating 50 percent of the budget to the training program and 50 percent to reinforcement and follow-up of the program.[20] Without this, sales managers may be inclined to assume that training is over and they can turn their attention to other issues.

Throughout this discussion, attention has focused primarily on the development of selling skills for salespeople, including new recruits and experienced reps as well. One issue left concerns the practices of small and large companies. Table 12–1 presents the results of a recent study of 121 firms.

The results in Table 12–1 clearly indicate that there is much room for improvement in the sales-training practices of the companies represented in the study. Product knowledge obviously is needed, however, if one has to question whether the respondents are placing enough emphasis on the development of selling skills. The unanswered question concerns what methods the companies are using to teach selling skills. The promises of behavior modeling are so strong that hopefully more companies will use this method to teach selling skills. Next, we examine other objectives of sales-training programs.

Objectives of Sales Training

Although the specific objectives of sales training may vary from firm to firm, there is some agreement on the broad objectives. Sales training is undertaken to: (1) increase productivity, (2) improve morale, (3) lower turnover, (4) improve customer relations, and (5) produce better management of time and territory.

---

[18] Falvey, "Myths of Sales Training," p. 80.

[19] For an excellent example of behavior modification in marketing, see Walter R. Nord and J. Paul Peter, "A Behavior Modification Perspective on Marketing," *Journal of Marketing,* Spring 1980, pp. 36–47.

[20] Snader, "Most Sales Training Doesn't Work," p. 4.

Table 12–1
**Percentage of small and large firms
that "extensively use" the following
sales training tools and practices**

Training Practices	Percentage of Small Firms	Percentage of Large Firms
Type of training program:		
Product knowledge training	74	79
Field/on-the-job training	66	68
Selling skills training	43	64
Market/competition training	28	55
Company information training	14	34
Type of trainer:		
Sales manager	55	55
Senior salesperson	30	33
Full-time (staff) sales trainer	5	38
Outside training cosultant	1	9
Training program procedure:		
Establishment of training program objectives	37	64
Evaluation of training program effectiveness	19	53

Note: A statistically significant difference ($p < 0.05$) exists between the percentage of small and large firms that "extensively use" this sales management tool or practice.
Source: Adapted from: Alan J. Dubinsky and Thomas E. Barry, "A Survey of Sales Management Practices," *Industrial Marketing Management*, vol. 11, 1982, p. 137, copyright by Elsevier Science Publishing Co., Inc.

Increase Productivity

One objective of sales training is to provide trainees with the necessary skills so that their selling performance makes a positive contribution to the firm. Sales trainees need to know about company products and policies, the nature of the market, and selling techniques if they are to represent the company adequately and achieve both company and personal goals. In a relatively short time, sales training attempts to teach the skills possessed by the more experienced members of the sales force. The time it takes for a new member of the sales force to achieve satisfactory levels of productivity is thus shortened considerably.

Improve Morale

Although the precise nature of the relationship between productivity and morale is controversial, they are related. Productive salespeople tend to have higher morale.[21]

---

[21] Charles N. Green, "The Satisfaction-Performance Controversy," *Business Horizons*, October 1972, pp. 31–41; and Donald P. Schwab and L. L. Cummings, "Theories of Performance and Satisfaction: A Review," *Industrial Relations*, October 1970, pp. 408–30.

How does sales training lead to better morale? Remember that one objective of sales training is to prepare trainees to perform tasks so that their productivity increases as quickly as possible. If sales trainees know what is expected of them, they will be less likely to experience the frustrations that arise from trying to perform a job without adequate preparation. Without sales training, customers may ask questions that sales representatives cannot answer. This leads to frustration and lower morale. Available evidence indicates that salespeople who are uncertain about their job requirements tend to be less satisfied with their jobs.[22] This same evidence shows that representatives who are most aware of the job requirements are also more satisfied with their company's sales-training activities.

Lower Turnover

If sales training can lead to improved morale (greater job satisfaction), then this should result in lower turnover. Younger, inexperienced salespeople are more likely to get discouraged and quit as a result of not being prepared for the task. Turnover rates are higher for younger salespeople than for older salespeople. When salespeople quit, the company must spend money and effort to find replacements, thus raising the cost of recruiting and selection. Turnover can also lead to customer problems, since many customers prefer some continuity with the sales representatives who call on them. A customer who is called on by a sales representative who suddenly quits may transfer business to other suppliers rather than wait for a new representative. Sales training, by leading to lower turnover, alleviates such problems.

Improve Customer Relations

One benefit of sales training that accompanies lower turnover is continuity in customer relationships. When the same sales representative calls on customers on a regular basis, it helps to promote customer loyalty, especially when the salesperson is adequately prepared to handle customer questions, objections, and complaints. Conversely, a sales representative who calls on a customer over a period of time but is not proficient in handling the customer's problems or cannot provide the products and services the customer needs will not foster customer loyalty. Customers place orders for their own benefits. Inadequately trained salespeople are usually not able to provide these benefits, and customer relations subsequently suffer.

---

[22] Neil M. Ford, Orville C. Walker, Jr., and Gilbert A. Churchill, Jr., "The Psychological Consequences of Role Conflict and Ambiguity in the Industrial Salesforce," in *Marketing: 1776-1976 and Beyond*, ed. Kenneth L. Bernhardt (Chicago: American Marketing Association, 1976), pp. 403–8.

Manage Time and Territory Better

A subject in many sales-training programs is how salespeople should spend their time. How much time should be devoted to calls on existing accounts and how much time to calls on potential new accounts? How often should each class of account be called on? What is the most effective way of covering the territory to ensure that the routes traveled are the most efficient with respect to miles driven and time spent? One important objective of many sales-training programs is to provide salespeople with ways to answer these questions.

The Timing of Sales Training

Although sales training is a continuous process, exactly when firms accept sales trainees into the formal sales training program varies considerably. A common practice is to have sales trainees work in the field, calling on accounts, before any formal sales training occurs. It is also common to start with formal training followed by a field assignment. In either case, the length of the formal training program can vary from a few days to more than a year, depending on company needs.

Training of experienced sales personnel varies just as much. Some companies have annual programs, whereas others have programs only when the need arises. The length of both types of programs varies from firm to firm. Training of experienced sales personnel may be routine, such as when it is associated with an annual sales convention. It may be nonroutine or remedial and may occur as a result of problems experienced by one or more members of the sales force. For example, several sales representatives may be experiencing a decline in sales. These reps may need to be retrained so they can relearn skills needed to correct the problem. They may be retrained as a group or individually by their field sales manager or sales trainer.

Training the New Sales Recruit

Most larger companies have programs for training new sales recruits. These programs differ considerably in length and content, however. The differences often reflect variations in company policies, nature of the selling job, and types of products and services.[23] Even within the same industry, sales training programs vary in length, content, and even technique.[24]

---

[23] David S. Hopkins, *Training the Sales Force: A Progress Report* (New York: The Conference Board, 1978), p. 4. The material in this section has been adapted from this source.

[24] Ibid., pp. 31–43, for a more detailed discussion.

Although a few companies have no preset period of time for training sales recruits, most firms have embraced the notion of a fixed time period for formal training. The time varies "from just a couple of days in the office, followed by actual selling combined with on-the-job coaching, to as long as two or three years of intensive training in a number of fields and skills."[25]

What accounts for this variation? First, training needs vary from firm to firm and even within a firm. For example, one manufacturer of drugs has a seven-week program for new recruits who will sell conventional consumer products. For those recruits destined to sell more technical products, the training lasts two years.

Second, training needs vary as a result of differences in the needs and aptitudes of the recruits. Experienced recruits have less need for training than inexperienced recruits, although most large firms require everyone to go through some formal training. One industrial firm requires a one-week program for experienced recruits, whereas inexperienced recruits may require a two- to three-year program.

A final reason for variation in the length of training programs is company philosophy. Some sales managers feel that training for new recruits should be concentrated at the beginning of a sales career, but others feel that it should be spread over a longer time, including a large dose of "learning by doing."[26]

Figure 12–3 illustrates the differences in the length of sales training programs for new recruits. The training programs for new recruits tend to be shorter for manufacturers of consumer products than for manufacturers of industrial products. Service firms, which include insurance, banking, public utilities, and transportation companies, generally have longer sales training programs than manufacturers.

Content of Training Programs for New Recruits

Training programs for new recruits vary not only in length but also in content and not only among industries but within industries as well. For example, among the 17 manufacturers of food, beverages, and tobacco products that participated in the 1978 Conference Board study, the time devoted to teaching product knowledge varied from 10 percent to 50 percent of the total time available for training. A sales manager from one insurance company revealed that 70 percent of the training program was spent on product knowledge; as little as 10 percent was spent in another insurance company.

---

[25] Ibid., p. 4.
[26] Hopkins, *Training the Sales Force*, p. 4.

Figure 12–3
Length of training programs for
new salespeople

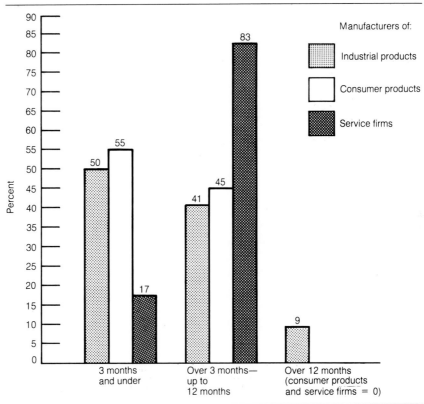

Source: Adapted from *Sales & Marketing Management*, February 20, 1984, p. 73.

Table 12–2 shows how companies generally allocate time to various subjects in formal sales-training programs. Product knowledge receives the most emphasis, followed by selling techniques, market/industry orientation, and company orientation. The quartiles show that considerable divergence exists, however; 25 percent of the firms spend 5 percent of the time on company orientation, but 75 percent spend 20 percent of the total time on this subject. Individual company differences are even more extreme.

Deciding what to teach new recruits should coincide with the information that is most needed by the new salesperson. Typically this means that at least some information should relate to one of the training objectives cited earlier. Telling recruits about company service policies gives them information for answering customer questions. Training recruits on handling objections from customers can therefore lead to more sales and more satisfied customers.

Table 12–2
Distribution of training time by subject matter for newly hired sales personnel

	Percentage of Time Devoted to			
Values*	Company Orientation	Market/Industry Orientation	Selling Technique	Product Knowledge
First quartile...... 5	10	15	30	
Median 10	15	20	40	
Third quartile..... 20	20	30	60	

*Based on 152 sales units.
Source: Adapted from: David S. Hopkins, *Training the Sales Force: A Progress Report* (New York: The Conference Board, 1978), p. 6.

The four orientations in Table 12–2 do not fully capture the range of issues in modern sales-training programs. In an attempt to overcome the negative image associated with the selling profession and to improve overall effectiveness, many sales managers have modified training programs to develop more well-rounded business professionals who are "beyond the stage of being just an inventory counter or an order taker."[27]

A *metals producer* has upgraded its program to provide what is termed "in-depth training" so that sales personnel will in fact "represent our company and our industry to the highest levels of their customers." On completing the program, trainees are said to be able to comprehend and handle all types of financial, marketing, and operational discussions.

At a *rubber products company,* training of field sales personnel has been directed toward business counsel, inventory management, and similar programs to reinforce knowledge of product-line profitability.

For a *railroad,* ". . . the most dramatic and significant improvement in our sales training efforts . . . has been to change the traditional concept of our field personnel selling rail service only, into making them transportation and distribution consultants with knowledge of marketing concepts and advanced distribution techniques that can benefit the customer as well as our company."

At a tobacco company, there has been a shift in training emphasis from "selling" to "merchandising." . . . Says the vice president of sales, ". . . those sales representatives who are the most knowledgeable about the customer's whole business, as well as about the category in which his products fit, will be the most successful"[28]

Developing sales representatives with the skills described in these examples places a heavy burden on sales training. Sales training programs must include more topics than just selling skills, but what is the most appropriate mix of subjects? Although this determination must always be made by the individual firm, an appreciation for the "whys" of some general industry techniques should be helpful.

---

[27] Hopkins, *Training the Sales Force,* p. 13.

[28] Ibid. For an excellent discussion of the growing professionalism in selling, see "The New Supersalesman: Wired for Success," *Business Week,* January 6, 1973, pp. 44–49.

Product Knowledge

Product knowledge is one of the most important topics. More time is typically spent on it than any other subject, although the time spent varies with the commodity sold. Companies that produce technical products, such as computer manufacturers, spend more time on this subject than do manufacturers of nontechnical products. One manufacturer of specialized industrial components allocates 90 percent of its sales training program to application engineering and product knowledge for graduate engineers recruited directly from campuses.[29] Producers of personal care products and toiletry preparations spend less time on product knowledge. In the service industry, the complexity of the service influences the amount of time needed to learn the service, such as with various types of insurance.

Product knowledge involves not only knowing how the product is made but also how the product is used and, in some cases, how it should not be used. One producer of machine tools gives newly hired sales engineers extensive in-plant exposure to technical and engineering matters. Before field assignment, they spend time in a customer's plant, where they are taught machine setup and operations under realistic conditions.[30] In yet another situation, "A sales trainee in an electrical utility destined for a position as a consultative salesman to eating establishments obtained his end-use knowledge by working in a restaurant kitchen for several months."[31] Dodge cautions that finding one customer who is both representative and cooperative may be difficult, however.[32]

Training in product knowledge is not limited to only those products that the sales trainee will eventually sell. Customers often want to know how competitive products compare on price, construction, performance, and compatibility with each other. Customers expect representatives to show them how the seller's products can be coordinated with competitive products, such as in a computer installation that involves products made by different manufacturers. One paper products manufacturer that supplies paper towels to industrial firms exposes sales trainees to competitive towel dispensers so they will know which dispensers handle their paper towels.

A major objective of training in product knowledge is so that a salesperson can provide potential customers with the information needed for rational decision making. Some benefits that accrue to salespeople as they acquire product knowledge include:

1. Pride and confidence in product quality.
2. Self-assurance emanating from technical knowledge of product makeup.

---

[29] Hopkins, *Training the Sales Force*, p. 5.
[30] Ibid., p. 8.
[31] Dodge, *Field Sales Management*, p. 227.
[32] Ibid.

3. Communication with customers through the use of the operational vocabulary peculiar to the industry.
4. Understanding of product functioning that allows effective diagnosis of customer problems.[33]

All these benefits contribute to improved salesperson-customer interaction.

Market/Industry Orientation

Sales training in market/industry orientation covers both broad and specific factors. From a broad viewpoint, salespeople need to know how their particular industry fits into the overall economy. Economic fluctuations affect buying behavior, which in turn affects selling techniques. Information about inflationary pressure, for example, may be used to convince prospective buyers to move their decision dates ahead. If the sales force is involved in forecasting sales and setting quotas, knowledge of the industry and the economy is essential.

From a narrower viewpoint, salespeople must have detailed knowledge about present customers. They need to know their customer's buying policies, patterns, and preferences; and the products or services these companies produce. In some cases, sales representatives need to be knowledgeable about their customers' customers. This is especially true when sales representatives sell through wholesalers or distributors who often want sales representatives to assist them with their customers' problems. Missionary salespeople are expected to know the needs of both wholesalers and retailers, even though the retailers buy from the wholesalers.

Company Orientation

Sales trainees must be aware of company policies that affect their selling activities. Like all new employees, they need indoctrination in personnel policies on such items as salary structure and company benefits.

Sales representatives can expect customers to request price adjustments, product modifications, faster delivery, and different credit terms. Most companies have policies on such matters arising from legal requirements or industry practices. Too often, however, avoidable delays and possibly lost sales result from inadequate sales training in company policies. Two practices provide salespeople with knowledge of company policies. The first requires sales trainees to spend time in the home office, learning about company policies and procedures by working in various departments, such as credit, order processing, advertising, sales promotion, and shipping. The second approach has the trainee work as a sales

---

[33] Ibid., p. 226.

correspondent for a time. The trainee processes customer orders, maintains mail and telephone contact with customers, and sometimes serves as the company contact for a group of customers.

Major corporations provide the sales force with sales manuals that cover product line information and company policies. A well-prepared sales manual can give a sales representative a quick answer to a customer's question.

Time and Territory Management

Along with sales training in product knowledge, sales skills, market/industry orientation, and company policies, sales trainees need assistance in how to manage their time and territories. Several recent surveys suggest that salespeople perceive this as their number one problem.[34]

The familiar 20:80 ratio, where 20 percent of a company's customers account for 80 percent of the business, applies to time and territory management in the reverse direction. It is not unusual to find sales representatives who are skilled in all areas except efficient time management, spending 80 percent of their time with customers who account for only 20 percent of sales.

Poor assignment of customers and development of territories contribute to the time management problem. Sales managers need to know how to develop territories to enhance the sales representative's efficiency. Assigning a sales representative too many accounts or a territory that is too large leads to time and territory management problems.

The program for a manufacturer of micrographic equipment and supplies trains salespeople to "plan your work—work your plan." Although some instruction in time management is provided by this company during home-office classroom training, the major responsibility rests with the district sales managers. Effective time management is more likely to be achieved via on-the-job training. Sales representatives turn in their projected activities every two weeks and review with their district sales managers past plans and performance. The district sales manager helps them modify the projected plans for greater efficiency. The desire for more effective time and territory management has led to greater usage of the telephone. Telemarketing sales training courses provide sales representatives with knowledge about effective use of the telephone.

Other Subjects

The discussion so far has emphasized the typical subjects in most sales training programs. Some companies go beyond these basic areas to include subjects such as *transactional analysis* (TA) in their training programs.

---

[34] "Research Institute Marketing for Sales Executives," published by Research Institute of America, New York, (February 3, 1977), p. 6. A similar survey taken three years before in 1974 produced the same conclusion.

One popular subject in sales training programs in recent years has been transactional analysis. The book by Thomas A. Harris, *I'm OK—You're OK*,[35] has had a tremendous impact on popularizing Eric Berne's original theory developed in *Games People Play*.[36] Although advocates of TA claim that it will make a sales representative better able to analyze transactions and thus "keep the communication lines open between him and his customers,"[37] the technique is not without its critics. It is viewed by one sales personnel development manager as "one of a variety of methods that have found their way into business procedure. Sensitivity Training has had its disastrous run; Transcendental Meditation is the latest fad."[38] The main purpose in discussing TA is to point out that whatever techniques are used or whatever subjects are taught, they need to be evaluated in terms of their costs and benefits in such areas as skill development, improved performance, and sales growth.[39]

Control Data Corporation offers a program called, "Selling: The Psychological Approach," using their PLATO system. PLATO is a computer-based learning system that can be used at one of their learning centers or at the trainee's residence or facility. The program examines the psychology of both the salesperson and the customer and describes how to develop a sales strategy that builds on this knowledge. Learning occurs at a pace determined by the trainee.

Location of Training Programs

The location of training programs and the various training approaches are highly interrelated. The content of the training program influences the location as well. In deciding on the location, one must consider the advantages and disadvantages of centralized versus decentralized sales training.

Table 12–3, which identifies the sites most frequently used and the median length of training time at different sites. Table 12–3 includes training for experienced salespeople, as well as for new trainees. Although home-office training is used by most companies, more time is spent in sales training at field and regional offices. For example, one manufacturer of photographic and copying equipment and supplies has sales trainees first spend time at a district or field office. Then, they move to a regional office with a central training facility, and finally, they spend a short time at the home office. The sales trainee usually returns to the same district office for additional on-the-job training. Thus, there is a progression from the initial assignment to a district office, where the trainees are closely supervised until they demonstrate the ability to work on their own.

---

[35] Thomas A. Harris, *I'm OK—You're OK* (New York: Harper & Row, Publishers, 1967).
[36] Eric Berne, *Games People Play* (New York: Grove Press, 1964).
[37] Ed Musselwhite, "TA in Selling," in *Contemporary Readings in Sales Management*, ed. Marvin A. Jolson (New York: Petrocelli/Charter, 1977), pp. 207–22.
[38] Falvey, "Myths of Sales Training," p. 71.
[39] Ibid.

Table 12–3
Sites most frequently used for
sales training

Location	Percent of Companies Conducting Training at This Location			Median Length of Training Time at This Location (in weeks)*		
	Industrial Products	Consumer Products	Services	Industrial Products	Consumer Products	Services†
Home office 75%	44%	67%	4	2	6
Field office 50	78	67	3	6	11
Regional office..............42	78	17	2	2	1
Plant locations.............. 8	11	0	2	1	0
Central training facility (away from home office)...33	22	50	2	3	1
Noncompany site (hotel, restaurant, club) ... 8	11	17	2	2	1

*Length of time should not necessarily be considered cumulative because not all training procedures include all locations.
†Includes insurance, financial, utilities, transportation, retail stores, etc.
Source: Sales and Marketing Management survey reported in "1979 Survey of Selling Costs," *Sales & Marketing Management*, February 20, 1984, p. 73. Reprinted by permission from *Sales & Marketing* magazine, © 1979.

The Conference Board study illustrates the variability in location and technique in sales training programs.

Most newly hired sales personnel of a specialized equipment producer spend considerable time with the inside sales group before going into the field. "Working for a year in a sales correspondent position," says an executive of the firm, "provides excellent product knowledge, as well as exposure to company procedures and industry business methods."

According to another equipment producer, the first three months of a training program that extends over a year is spent by trainees in one of the operating divisions, learning not only marketing procedures but also key elements of manufacturing and engineering. The next three months are spent in a district sales office; and the year is rounded out with about six weeks in each of the company's five divisions—primarily to acquire product knowledge.

Recruits to the sales force of a paper producer are channeled through several departments, spending considerable time in the laboratory and six months in the customer service department to familiarize themselves with product features, accounting, pricing and distribution. Only then do the recruits begin to make field trips in the company of experienced sales representatives.[40]

Other examples of sales training programs can be found in Table 12–4. Perhaps the most important conclusion to be derived from these examples is that sales training is an ongoing and time-consuming activity. Good training consumes resources that might be used elsewhere, and consequently it is necessary that the benefits derived from training justify the costs.

---

[40] Hopkins, *Training the Sales Force*, pp. 7–8.

Table 12–4
Examples of training programs for sales trainees

A drug company

1 to 5 weeks

After a new sales representative is hired and has filled out the preliminary paper work, he or she then reports to a field sales trainer to begin an intensive five-week field training program.

The field sales training program is broken down into five distinct phases, which are outlined below.

Phase 1: Introduction and observation

This phase of the sales representative's training includes orientation to training program; orientation to company policy, hospitals, distributors,and company organization; observation of trainer's calls; introduction to territory organization; acquaintance with competitive products; instruction on preparing reports; general study of product line, and an introduction to planned sales presentations.

Phase 2: In-service training

Four days of orientation, observation, and participation in routine procedures in a general hospital (preceptorship).

Phase 3: Study of products, policies, and programs

Continued observation of the trainer's calls; establishing opportunities for trainee to converse with hospital and dealer personnel; specific study of all product features, advantages, and benefits; specific sales presentation to customers; study of policies regarding territory administration; and the preparation of all routine papers.

Phase 4: Trainee participation

Continued observation of trainer's calls; participation in trainer's calls; specific sales presentation to customers; participation in program selling (i.e., in-service programs, demonstrations, dealer meetings); planning and execution of all territory administration under supervision of trainer; and distributor training in the field and in dealer's facilities.

Phase 5: General review

A general review and testing on all policies, procedures, programs and product features, advantages and benefits with the trainer; and a general review with the district manager.

Each day of this five-week field training program is structured with discussion topics that must be checked off by the trainer as they are discussed with the trainee. The trainee and the trainer inform the district manager by written report of the progress made each week, with copies going to the regional manager, sales training manager, and director of sales.

6 to 8 weeks

After completing the initial five weeks, the same representative then spends two weeks with the representative being replaced, or the district manager, who introduces the new representative to his or her accounts.

The sales representative's primary objective during this time is to develop knowledge of his or her customers.

9 to 19 weeks

In the next ten weeks, the sales representatives are on their own, working with close supervision from their district manager. The primary objective during this time frame is developing customer knowledge, selling skills, product knowledge, territory management skills,customer service skills,and strengthening communication skills.

Initial sales training seminar

Sometime between the 10th and 19th week, if the trainee is progressing at an acceptable rate, the district manager and regional manager will nominate him or her for the initial Sales Training Seminar. This is an intensive three-week course consisting of three distinct learning sections:

Table 12–4 *(continued)*

Week one—Selling skills. The first week is devoted to courses in effective listening and professional selling skills. The trainee uses these skills to develop selling points—some feature, advantage, or benefit to support the sale of particular products.

Week two—Product knowledge. In the second week, the trainee is exposed to the anatomy, physiology, and pharmacology of the product line; disease states and related therapeutics; medical terminology; and basic medical techniques by the company's medical, nursing, and pharmacy staff.

Week three—Combining of selling skills and product knowledge. In this section, selling skills and product knowledge are combined into an effective sales presentation, emphasizing benefits that are important to the customer. The pertinent government regulations and legal requirements in promoting company products are reviewed by the legal department.

The sales representative then returns to his or her territory under the direction of the district manager. Additional sales training is carried on at district and regional meetings. At least 25 percent of the meeting time is used for sales training and updating the field sales force in selling skills, product knowledge, and product presentation.

A forest products company

Persons hired as sales trainees join the company without being assigned to an operating division. Within a few days to a few weeks in a group of five to ten (maximum), they begin the Marketing Personnel Development program, a basic group sales training program. During the next nine weeks they learn:

Company organizations, policies, procedures; the business of each operating division. During a four-day classroom lecture session, corporate department heads and representatives of all organizational units of the company (service, products, manufacturing facilities, markets, field selling efforts, and so on) discuss the nature, function, and objectives of their units.

The technology of pulp and paper manufacture. A four-day lecture, including programmed instruction and supported by slides and sound movies, teaches the important properties of industrial papers and how these properties are achieved, controlled, and measured in manufacture. A three-day tour of an integrated pulp and paper mill concludes this instruction.

The nature of major markets for the company's products. Sales and sales management representatives discuss major markets for each division.

Selling skills and communication skills in general (approximately two weeks). Films followed by discussion, printed programmed instruction, recorded cassettes (a commercially packaged program), and role-playing exercises before CCTV camera and recorder provide instruction and application to develop selling and persuasive communication skills. Case problems indigenous to the company's operating divisions supply the framework for selling exercises.

Principles of time and territory management. Programmed instructions, supplemented by lecture and discussion, develop the principles of sales time management in accordance with profit opportunities.

This program concludes with a week or two of individual meetings and interviews between trainees and division management personnel interested in adding to their sales staff.

Thus begins a competitive selection process, the outcome of which both trainee and division management can influence. Upon accepting the invitation of a division to join it, the trainee now begins a six-to-nine-month program of on-the-job training and instruction to learn how to sell specific products to particular markets.

A chemicals company

Our new field salespersons are recruited on the campus. After screening at headquarters, successful candidates report to one of 26 field sales offices. Almost immediately the new salesperson breaks in on an office sales job (sales order handling) at the same time receiving basic training in telephone skills, order entry, and basic company orientation. He or she goes through a self-study (programmed) instruction course on chemistry and distribution and traffic functions. After 30 to 60 days, the candidate is now ready for the next step.

Table 12–4 *(concluded)*

Four times a year, a three-week training session is conducted at headquarters. This consists of a one-week chemistry course and two weeks of basic company orientation, basics of business, and office selling skills. Our salesperson now returns to his or her field office.

For the next six months, the salesperson performs an office sales job and is rated accordingly. Here the individual is in constant phone contact with customers and, at the same time, participates on occasion in some field calls with field sales people.

Following successful completion of the office assignment, the salesperson attends a one-week field sales session at headquarters, oriented toward doing the field sales job. Subjects include territory analysis, account analysis, account strategy, legal aspects, pricing, and, of course, call skills and presentations.

Some of our people then have temporary field assignments (60–90 days). Here the project consists of making market surveys or implementing new promotions. It gives the field salesperson valuable experience in polishing call skills.

The whole process requires 12 to 18 months, depending on the progress of the individual.

Source: David S. Hopkins, *Training the Sales Force: A Progress Report* (New York: The Conference Board, 1978), pp. 9–12.

Centralized Training versus Decentralized Training: Pros and Cons

Centralized Training. Training programs held at central locations possess several advantages.[41]

1. They are easier and less expensive to operate since they are held at one location rather than at several.
2. Skilled sales trainers are more likely to be available.
3. Sales trainees can meet home-office personnel and sales trainees from other locations.
4. Generally, better training facilities are available.
5. Product knowledge is more effectively taught by viewing production operations.
6. Evaluation of the benefits of sales training is easier as a result of greater control.
7. It is easier for company executives to become involved in sales training activities.
8. Sales trainees do not have to contend with distractions of home life and can concentrate on the program.

Centralized training programs also have some serious drawbacks.

1. They are very expensive. Sales trainees must be brought to a central location, which requires provisions for meals, lodging, transportation, and recreation.

---

[41] The discussion of centralized and decentralized training is largely based on: William J. Stanton and Richard H. Buskirk, *Management of the Sales Force,* 5th ed. (Homewood, Ill.: Richard D. Irwin, 1978), pp. 227–29.

2. Any sales productivity possessed by the trainees is lost during centralized training.

3. It is difficult to keep trainees at a centralized location for long periods of time. Short sessions become cram sessions and learning is less effective.

Decentralized Training.   Some advantages of decentralized training are:

1. It is less expensive since provisions for transportation, lodging, and meals are not necessary.

2. Sales trainees can work while learning, which gives them an opportunity to apply the sales training instruction.

3. Branch managers may be more knowledgeable about field conditions and adjust the content of sales training accordingly.

4. Training can proceed at a more normal pace, thus avoiding the problems associated with cramming.

Some of the more serious disadvantages of decentralized training are:

1. Product training may be less realistic and effective than when conducted at in-plant locations.

2. Facilities are less likely to be designed specifically for training.

3. Sales managers may not be highly skilled as sales trainers.

4. Evaluation and control are less effective due to variations in instructional methods, content, and location.

5. Trainees may not have the opportunity to meet executives from other company divisions or sales trainees from other areas.

Which approach should a company adopt? No definite answer is possible. As Table 12–4 reveals, companies use both centralized and decentralized locations to accomplish their objectives.

Relative Importance of Methods

The most commonly used methods for training new sales personnel are on-the-job training (OJT), classroom instruction, coaching, observation, home study, and special courses provided by consulting organizations that specialize in sales training.[42] Table 12–5 summarizes industry preferences for these methods. Note that 90 of the 154 sales units (58 percent) cited OJT as the most important training method. Moreover, 94 percent placed OJT in the top three ranks, thus further emphasizing its perceived importance.

Formal classroom training ranks second in importance and is used by most (83 percent) companies. Coaching and observation are rated next. Home-study training is perceived as being less important, yet two thirds of the companies use this

---

[42] The following discussion is based to a large extent on David S. Hopkins, *Training the Sales Force: A Progress Report* (New York: The Conference Board, 1978), pp. 5–14.

Table 12–5
Importance of various training approaches for newly hired sales personnel

Training Approach	Rank Order of Importance in Company*						
	1st	2d	3d	4th	5th	6th	NR†
On-the-job	90	41	14	4	2	1	2
Classroom	46	22	27	24	7	2	26
Coaching	17	42	47	34	5	—	9
Observation	9	32	54	37	10	1	11
Home study	5	7	7	24	52	9	50
Special outside courses	1	3	5	12	21	33	79

*Based on 154 sales units.
†NR = preferences not reported or training approach listed not used.
Source: David S. Hopkins, *Training the Salesforce: A Progress Report* (New York: The Conference Board, Inc., 1978), p. 6.

approach. With the introduction of microcomputers and VCR equipment, the popularity of home study has increased. Half the companies use special outside courses. Most companies use a variety of approaches and, in fact, use several, such as coaching and on-the-job training, at the same time.

Which approach to sales training should be used first? "A common view is that at least a part of the formal training in a classroom setting is better deferred until after recruits have spent some time in on-the-job training."[43] Actual field experience exposes trainees to the problems and opportunities associated with selling the company's products and services. They ask more intelligent questions and can more readily apply what is being taught based, on their personal experiences.

Descriptions of Methods

On-the-Job Training

The mere mention of OJT sometimes scares new sales recruits. The thought of "learning by doing" is psychologically discomforting to many. Quite often, this is due to their incorrect perceptions of what is involved in OJT. On the-job training is not a "sink or swim" approach in which the trainee is handed an order book, maybe a sales manual, and told to "go out and sell." OJT should be a carefully planned process in which the new recruit learns by doing and, at the same time, is productively employed. Furthermore, a good OJT program contains established

---

[43] Ibid., p. 6.

procedures for evaluating and reviewing a sales trainee's progress, as noted in the following example:

> . . . critiques are held after each OJT sales call and are summarized daily. The critiques cover effectiveness, selling skills, communication of information in a persuasive manner, and other criteria.[44]

A key aspect of on-the-job training is the coaching that sales trainees receive from trainers, who may be experienced sales personnel, sales managers, or personnel specifically assigned to do sales training.

On-the-job training and coaching often occur together; this is referred to as one-on-one training. Observation is an integral part of the process. The structure at R. J. Reynolds is typical.

> The recruit spends the first four to six weeks traveling with the division manager or his assistant for one-on-one training. When the manager believes the recruit is ready, he is allowed to make a call. After that, man and manager alternate calls, with the manager critiquing between calls.[45]

One-on-one training should not become "two-on-one" selling, where the objective becomes getting the order, not training the recruit. The sales manager or trainer is supposed to be a coach, not a player, and should stay out of the game no matter what the score. When the manager jumps in and says, "Let me take it from here," the recruit knows that training has stopped and two-on-one selling has begun.[46] Some suggestions for making one-on-one training most effective are as follows:

1. Set pre-call objectives with the trainee.
2. Practice actual questions to be used to accomplish objectives (such as informational, directional, and closing).
3. Make the call (manager as a nonparticipating observer).
4. Contribute only positive reinforcement and act as a resource only on specific points and only on the request of the trainee.
5. Conduct the post-call analysis by letting the sales representative do the majority of the talking.[47]

OJT often involves job rotation-assigning trainees to different departments over a period of time where they learn about such things as manufacturing, marketing, shipping, credits and collections, and servicing procedures. After on-the-job training, many sales trainees proceed to formal classroom training.

---

[44] Ibid., p. 7.
[45] Sally Scanlon, "Richard Joshua Reynolds Would Be Proud," *Sales & Marketing Management*, November 8, 1976, p. 45.
[46] Falvey, "Myths of Sales Training," p. 78.
[47] Ibid., p. 79.

Classroom Training

For most companies, formal classroom training is an indispensable part of sales training, although very few of them rely solely on it.[48] Classroom training has several advantages. First, each trainee receives standard briefings on such subjects as product knowledge, company policies, customer and market characteristics, and selling skills. Second, formal training sessions often save substantial amounts of executive time because executives can meet an entire group of trainees at once. Third, classroom sessions permit the use of audiovisual materials such as movies and video tape. Lectures, presentations, and case discussions can also be programmed into a classroom setting. The opportunity for interaction between sales trainees is a fourth advantage. Such interaction is beneficial, since reinforcement and ideas for improvement can come from other sales trainees. Interaction is so important that many companies divide sales trainees into teams for case presentations, which results in interaction and forces trainees to become actively involved in the education process.

Classroom training also has its disadvantages. It is expensive and time-consuming. It requires recruits to be brought together and facilities, meals, transportation, recreation, and lodging to be provided for them. Sales managers, who are cognizant of these costs and time demands, sometimes attempt to cover too much material in too short of a time. This results in less retention of information: many sessions become merely cram sessions. Sales managers must avoid the natural tendency to add more and more material because the additional exposure is often gained at the expense of retention and opportunity for interaction.

Lecture. The lecture method is very efficient for presenting factual knowledge. Subjects such as market/customer orientation, company history, company policies, and product history are suitable for the structured lecture. Experience suggests that, to be most effective, lectures should be carefully planned with liberal use of audio visual aids. Most sales training programs use lectures sparingly and rely more heavily on methods that produce group involvement.

Conferences/Discussions. This method parallels a graduate school seminar. Small groups of trainees along with a conference leader discuss various problems and issues. Conferences are usually aimed at developing problem-solving and decision-making skills and modifying attitudes.[49]

Case Analyses. Instruction in handling problems with customers may be more effective if sales trainees are required to read a case report that describes the details of the problem. Lectures on problem-solving techniques may precede the case presentations. In one case, sales trainees were lectured on the subject of time and territory management. A case analysis was then prepared by the train-

[48] Hopkins, *Training the Sales Force*, p. 9.

[49] John P. Campbell, Marvin D. Dunnette, Edward E. Lawler III, and Karl E. Weick, Jr., *Managing Behavior, Performance, and Effectiveness* (New York: McGraw-Hill, 1970), p. 236.

ees. Finally, the sales trainees presented their recommendations, which were discussed and critiqued.

Role-Playing. A popular technique used in most companies has the trainee act out the part of a sales representative in a simulated buying session. The buyer may be either a sales instructor or another trainee. Role-playing is widely used to develop selling skills, but it can also be used to determine whether the trainee can apply knowledge taught via other methods of instruction. Immediately following the role-playing session, the trainee's performance is critiqued by the trainee, the trainer, and other trainees.

The use of videotape records (VTRs) is very prevalent in role-playing training. The role-playing session can be played back several times, in private, thus, ensuring that *all* the positive and negative traits are identified. This allows sales trainees to evaluate their own performance.

Another VTR approach requires the sales trainee to watch several types of contacts between various sales representatives and buyers. These tapes may show different situations and ways of handling these problems. A drug company uses videotape in the following way:

In addition, during this four-week program, each representative will have completed 25 to 30 simulated physician interviews of "detail calls" on videotape. The representative will also have observed and critiqued with the sales training instructor and all other participants in the school another 60 to 70 videotaped physician and pharmacist calls.[50]

Role-playing using VTR where a sales trainee performs in front of others and where that performance is subsequently critiqued can be harsh. One sales training expert compares VTR with the guillotine, pointing out that:

The victims are kept in line and forced to witness the execution of others.

The victims' fates are published and scheduled in advance with much fanfare and an apprehensive countdown to kick off.

The VTR seems to be designed for surgical incisiveness and spectator enjoyment.[51]

Some of these problems disappear if the critique is conducted only in the presence of the sales trainee and then only by the sales instructor. When handled well, most trainees can still identify their own strengths and weaknesses.

Home Study

The many changes in sales training fostered by technological developments in the audiovisual field have affected home study. These advances have certainly made home study more viable. VTR helps to overcome the disadvantages of lack

---

[50] Hopkins, *Training the Sales Force*, p. 51.

[51] John J. Falvey, "Myths of Sales Training," *Sales & Marketing Management*, April 3, 1978, p. 64.

of control over program content that are often found in decentralized training programs. Programmed instruction is another technique that provides control over content and permits trainees to learn at their own pace at home.

The advantages of home study using programmed instruction, audio cassettes, and videotape are described by the marketing training manager of an office equipment company: "Training costs are reduced; individuals can proceed at their own speed; and less disruption occurs to personal life by lessening the need to travel for these courses."[52]

Training Experienced Sales Personnel

After sales trainees are assigned to field positions, they quickly become involved in customer relationships, competitive developments, and other related matters. Over time, their knowledge of competitive developments and market conditions becomes dated. Indeed, even their personal selling styles may become stereotyped and less effective. Finally, as a result of so-called minor changes in company policies and product line, sales representatives may be ill-equipped to handle customer inquiries in these areas. Companies recognize these problems and provide refresher or advanced training programs for experienced sales personnel. Few companies are willing to halt training after the trainee has completed the basics. Most managements endorse the view that the need to learn is a never-ending process, and that even the most successful of their sales representatives can benefit from refresher training from time to time.

Additional training often occurs when a sales representative is being considered for promotion. In many companies, a promotion is more than moving from sales representative to district sales manager. A promotion can include being assigned better customers, transferring to a better territory, moving to a staff position, or being promoted to the ranks of sales management. Whenever salespeople are assigned better customers or better territories, additional sales training acquaints them with their increased responsibilities.

Most companies promote personnel who are already in the sales force to sales management positions. This requires that sales personnel with managerial talent be identified early so they can be groomed for eventual promotion. This grooming process may include a wide variety of training techniques, such as special conferences, home study, management development courses, and role-playing. Table 12–6 illustrates the procedure and techniques used by a consumer products company.

---

[52] Hopkins, *Training the Sales Force*, p. 13.

Table 12–6
One company's procedures for identifying and training potential sales managers

Existing managers are asked to submit names of individuals who, they feel, demonstrate the emotional maturity, intelligence, and goal orientation to manage others successfully. When chosen from the ranks of the sales force, their past performance is carefully reviewed. After review by the home office, the group selected attends a two-day introductory school for sales managers. Here they are introduced to the theories and techniques of sales management and are evaluated by the group instructors (sales training specialists). They are also given a manpower evaluation test that provides a measure of one's human assets and allows predictable comparisons, based on personality dimensions related to sales management success. Based on validated individual and group profiles and the information developed through observation, top management receives recommended candidates for further development and possible advancement selection.

Each successful candidate then begins a 16- to 20-week self-study program which provides a solid foundation of sales management theory with substantial reinforcement. Final selection is made by the vice president of sales.

Each individual is introduced to the foundation of sales management through an advanced, eclectic approach to the continuous development of sales management prepared by an outside organization. This program ranges from 18 to 20 weeks of daily participation via taped cassette lessons and workbooks. Periodic seminars, workshops, and learning labs are conducted to assure maximum benefits from the program. Emphasis is directed toward a comprehensive program of corporate and individual goal setting—one which integrates the needs of the individual and the achievement of the company's objectives.

Three or four additional seminars are held annually in conjunction with scheduled sales meetings on specific topics (e.g., time management or personal organization). This approach has been found to be highly motivational and has won wide acceptance from the management team.

Marketing; vice president,
a consumer products company

Source: David S. Hopkins, *Training the Sales Force: A Progress Report* (New York: The Conference Board, 1978), p. 20.

Training Sales Managers

Sales managers must become an integral part of the total sales-training process. No longer can sales managers, from the district level to the national level, be content to sit back and assume that sales training is a self-fulfilling event that does not require their follow-up. They need to be trained in a variety of subjects, such as learning how to train their salespeople, knowing how to coach, learning how to give praise or to suggest different methods, and learning how to give a performance evaluation. Unless sales managers receive training in these areas, money invested in sales training for the sales force will have been wasted.

Today's sales forces are very different. They bring to the job a different set of expectations and values than did their predecessors. Rosenbaum and Ward identify four critical changes which lead to the need for more and better training for sales managers.[53] The first change shows that salespeople are no longer the independent loners as dramatized by Willy Lohman in *Death of a Salesman*. Several research studies reveal that salespeople expect a close and candid relationship with their sales managers. To provide this, sales managers need training in how to conduct pre- and post-call reviews with sales reps. "High-potential salespeople not only expect formal sales training, but also a close, ongoing relationship with a coach who is demanding, competent and supportive."[54] To do this requires training.

The second change reveals that self-esteem has become as important as money. Salespeople today place greater value on achieving higher order rewards, such as personal growth and development, need for achievement, and self-actualization. Discussions with sales managers indicate some concern on their part as to how to provide these rewards. Sales managers usually rank these rewards below promotions and pay increases. This is not surprising since most sales managers understand how to provide these rewards. Thus, sales managers need training to ". . . help them find ways to use the limitless supply of self-esteem incentives that are available."[55]

The third change: Salespeople expect to be managed professionally and to participate in this process. High-potential salespeople are attracted to companies with well-planned procedures that include strong training programs, complete job descriptions, and sound performance appraisal procedures. Performance appraisal requires the careful development of forms, as described in Chapter 17, and sales managers must be trained in the administration of these forms and in the process itself. Sales managers must be trained to engage in such activities as establishing goals with the sales rep, holding progress reviews, and conducting performance reviews. Sales managers have to know how ". . . to "go beyond the numbers' and assess performance across a broad range of activities. Sales managers need to know how to reinforce effective behavior while clearly identifying deficiencies."[56]

The last change reveals that successful salespeople are more difficult to identify. Sales managers need to learn the skills necessary to identify sales aptitudes that are related to sales success. They need to be trained how to interview prospects and to ask the right questions, replacing their old "gut-feeling" approach with a more logical procedure. Rosenbaum and Ward conclude: "The message is clear—sales managers who are able to meet the challenge of this decade will be training professionals responsive to the changing psychological profile and needs of today's salesperson."[57]

---

[53] Bernard L. Rosenbaum and Nick Ward, "Why Sales Managers Need More and Better Management Training," *Training/HRD*, August 1982, pp. 44–49. The following discussion is based on this article.

[54] Ibid., p. 45.

[55] Ibid.

[56] Ibid., p. 46.

[57] Ibid., p. 49.

Recent Developments in Sales Training

As a result of technological changes, the sales force now needs training in new areas. Technicians, whose primary responsibilities involve equipment installation, troubleshooting, and training users, need training in selling. Service organizations, such as public accounting firms, now require sales training, the result of competitive changes.

The introduction of micro computers has already had a significant impact on the activities of the sales force. This impact will grow significantly in the future. For example, *Sales & Marketing Management* now carries a column in the biweekly magazine titled, "The Computer in Sales & Marketing." In their December 5, 1983 issue, *S&MM* devoted a special section to the subject of computerizing the sales force. The introduction reads: "Giving the sales force electronic tools to help it sell more effectively is a high priority in both industrial and consumer goods companies. Marketers also learn that direct involvement by sales personnel in the planning phase is the best way to insure that the computers will be useful."[58] Detailing all of the benefits would take too much space. One major benefit will be more time for selling activities and less time needed for administrative activities due to the computer. Call reports, the bane of many sales reps, will become paperless. Computerized ordering reduces the time required for this task. One sales rep, who works for a company selling non-grocery products to grocery stores, uses a scanner to read universal product codes on the shelves to record product number and quantity needed. At the end of the day, he scans the company catalog to record additional ordering data. Next, he connects his computer, measuring 4" × 8" × 2", to the telephone to transmit the order to his home office. Not all salespeople are leaping at the chance to learn how computers can increase their effectiveness. Jerry M. Kohl, president of Leegin Creative Leather Products, a company that gave each of its 35 reps a portable computer, was not sure the gift was welcome: "The average sales person is scared to death of computers . . . and they want to be salesmen, not computer people."[59] Obviously, training is needed if the personal computer is to become an effective tool as illustrated.

Companies selling technologically advanced products use technicians to provide installation and advisory services. IBM, for instance, calls these people systems engineers, and their job descriptions identify marketing responsibilities. This, in turn, has sales-training implications. The problem that companies face when training their technical people ". . . is how to turn them into salespeople without turning them off."[60] According to one expert, "In providing sales and

---

[58] "Computerizing the Sales Force," an S&MM Special Section, *Sales & Marketing Management*, December 5, 1983, p. 51.

[59] Liz Murphy, "Getting the Sales Force to Think About Computers," *Sales & Marketing Management*, December 5, 1983, p. 59.

[60] Thomas C. Ways, "Training the Technicians to Sell," *Training and Development Journal*, November 1982, p. 54.

marketing training for technical employees, it is best to start off with the premise that you are not attempting to turn them into "salespeople." The best way to approach this type of employee is to provide the skill training on the basis of: explaining exactly what the salesperson's job consists of; discussing how you will help them become better communicators by providing them with sales skills."[61] Training technicians to sell is beneficial since they do have extensive customer contact.

Sales training has been introduced into many service firms such as public accounting firms. Public accountants are more marketing oriented as a result of changes in the American Institute of CPAs Code of Professional Ethics which prohibited advertising and other marketing tactics. One source states, "A good marketing program starts in-house by transforming every staff member into a potential 'salesperson' for your firm's professional services."[62] As with technicians, the need for sales training in CPA firms is obvious. Competitive pressures and legal changes dictate a more aggressive response.

Measuring the Costs and Benefits of Sales Training

Sales training is a time-consuming and very costly activity. Is all this effort worth the cost? Does sales training produce enough benefits to justify its existence?

Sales training and increased profits have an obscure relationship at best. In the beginning of Chapter 12, we identified some broad objectives of sales training: improved selling skills, increased productivity, improved morale, lower sales-force turnover, better customer relations, and better time and territory management. Unfortunately, pinning down the relationship between sales training and these broad objectives is not easy. Very little research has been done to determine what effect, if any, sales training has on the sales force. It appears that most sales organizations simply assume on blind faith that their sales training programs are successful. After all, if a company has high sales and high profits, why should a sales manager assume that sales training is anything but effective?

Sales Training Costs

Business firms spend millions of dollars each year on sales training in hopes of improving overall productivity. Table 12–7 shows that direct sales-training costs rose steadily from 1980 to 1983. Costs increased 22 percent for industrial products, 22 percent for consumer products, and 25 percent for services. The statistics

---

[61] Ibid., p. 56.
[62] Ruth J. Dumesic and Neil M. Ford, "Internal Practice Development: An Overlooked Strategy for Marketing Professional Services," *The Practical Accountant*, December 1982, p. 39.

Table 12–7
Average annual cost of sales training per salesperson (including salary)*

Type of Company	1983	1982	1981	1980	Percent change, 1980–83
Industrial products	$24,600	$22,490	$21,017	$20,093	22.4%
Consumer products ...	16,600	15,090	14,294	13,625	21.8
Services†	16,000	14,720	12,864	12,772	25.3

*In addition to salary, these costs cover such items as instructional materials prepared, purchased, and rented for the training program; transportation and living expenses incurred during training course; instructional staff; outside seminars and management time spent with the salesperson when it is a part of the training budget.
†Includes insurance, financial, utilities, retail stores, etc.
Source: Adapted from "Survey of Selling Costs," *Sales & Marketing Management*, February 1981, 1982, 1983, and 1984. Reprinted by permission from *Sales & Marketing* magazine.

suggest that only the largest companies can afford to support a full-scale training program, yet all firms need sales training, regardless of size. The statistics suggest that business has a relatively generous attitude toward sales training. It allocates funds for training with minimal regard for the results. Clearly, some attention needs to be given to measuring the benefits of sales training.

Is the measurement process that difficult? After all, if sales training is supposed to lead to better productivity, improved morale, and lower turnover, then why not measure the changes in these variables after training has taken place? Indeed, some sales managers have done just that. They have assumed: We instituted sales training and shortly thereafter sales increased. Therefore, sales training was the reason. Right? Wrong! Unless appropriate procedures are used to design the research by which the benefits are assessed, it is hard to say what caused the sales increase. Sales may have increased as a result of improved economic conditions, competitive activity, environmental changes, seasonal trends, or other reasons. Consequently, research must be carefully designed to isolate these contaminating effects, to identify the benefits directly attributable to training.

Measurement Criteria

Even though intervening variables such as changes in competitive activities make evaluation of sales training programs difficult, some measurement must take place. This raises the question of what characteristics of sales training should be assessed. The following criteria seem appropriate:

1. Reaction: How well did the trainees like the program?
2. Learning: To what extent did the trainees learn the facts, principles, and approaches that were included in the training?

3. Behavior: To what extent did salespeople's job behavior change as a result of the program?
4. Results: What performance results were achieved?[63]

One could certainly single out one of these criteria as the measure of effectiveness, but a strong argument can be made that several criteria should be used in assessing the results of any sales training program. Measuring what was learned, for example, seems inappropriate because the obtained knowledge may not produce desired behavior changes. Not to assess what was learned is inadequate, however, because the program might be considered a failure if nothing was learned or if what was learned is inappropriate. The solution rests in the proper specification of the objectives and content of the sales training program, the criteria used to evaluate the program, and the proper design of the research so that the benefits can be unambiguously determined.

Measuring Broad Benefits

Broad benefits of sales training include improved morale and lower turnover. Morale can be partially measured by studies of job satisfaction. This approach is feasible with experienced sales personnel. Suppose, for instance, that a company measured job satisfaction as part of a needs analysis and found evidence of problems. Conducting a follow-up job satisfaction study after finishing the corrective sales training program would determine if there were any noticeable changes in morale.

Measuring reactions and learning is important in sales training for both new and experienced personnel. Most companies measure reactions by asking those attending the training to complete an evaluation form either immediately after the session or several weeks later. Emotions and enthusiasm may be high right after a session, but sales-training effectiveness is much more than a "warm feeling."

Measuring what was learned requires the use of tests. To what extent did sales trainees learn the facts, concepts, and techniques that were included in the training session? Objective examinations are appropriate.

Measuring Specific Benefits

Liking the program and learning something is not enough. Specific measures to examine behavior and results are needed to assess effectiveness. The effectiveness of a sales-training program aimed at securing more new customers, for example, can be partially assessed by examining call reports to see whether more

---

[63] Ralph F. Catalanello and Donald L. Kirkpatrick, "Evaluating Training Programs: The State of the Art," *Training and Development Journal,* May 1968, pp. 2–9.

new customers are being called on. Results can be measured by tracking new account sales to see whether they have increased. If the specific objective of sales training is to increase the sales of more profitable items, subsequent evidence that this has been accomplished provides a partial measure of training effectiveness. Finally, if reducing customer complaints was an objective, then the appropriate specific measure is whether customer complaints decreased.

The measurement of both specific and broad benefits presumes that the sales training program is designed to achieve certain objectives. The objectives might include such goals as:

To break in new sales representatives.

To provide marketing training for existing sales representatives.

To reduce sales force turnover.

To develop new markets.

To introduce new products.

To integrate advertising and promotional efforts.

To locate new distribution.[64]

It is important that the goals must be established before sales training begins. When specific objectives have been determined, the best training program can be developed to achieve these objectives. Most training programs have several objectives. Multiple measurements of the effectiveness of the training program are then a necessary part of evaluating the benefits.

Sales-training evaluation is still in its infancy. The little experimental research evidence available is generally favorable; sales training produces positive results. The unanswered question is whether or not the value is enough to justify the costs. If sales managers are called on to defend their training programs, they must be able to provide evidence on the cost/benefit tradeoffs. After all, there are alternative uses for the money spent on sales training. Experimental designs provide a powerful methodology by which the trade-off question can be answered.

Summary

Sales training programs have been criticized for emphasizing the wrong subjects and for using techniques that are not effective. The actual process of selling is one of the neglected subjects. Behavior modeling differs from traditional sales training programs and offers significant advantages. A Chinese proverb expresses the concept of behavior modeling well: "Tell me, I'll forget. Show me, I may remember. But involve me and I'll understand." Indeed, behavior modeling involves not only the sales representative but field sales managers as well. An essential ingre-

---

[64] R. A. Gopel, "A Basic Guide to Training Industrial Salesmen," in *Sales Management: Roles and Methods*, ed. James M. Comer (Santa Monica, Calif.: Goodyear, 1977) pp. 119–41.

dient of sales training programs is the follow-up activities required of sales management and sales trainers.

Sales training is a varied and on-going activity that is time-consuming and expensive. Most companies engage in some type of sales training. In fact, most sales managers feel that sales training is such an important activity that they require it for everybody, regardless of their experience. Some common objectives of sales training are to teach selling skills, increase productivity, improve morale, lower turnover, improve customer relations, and improve time and territory management.

Considerable variability exists in the length of sales training programs. Industry differences account not only for variations in length but also variations in program content. Company policies, the nature of the selling job, and the types of products and services offered also contribute to differences in time spent and on topics covered.

Product knowledge receives the most attention followed by selling techniques, market/industry orientation, and company orientation. This allocation is the subject of considerable criticism, as described in the chapter.

The location of training programs and the approaches used are interrelated. On-the-job training takes place in the field and is decentralized. Classroom training occurs at company headquarters and at field offices as well. Firms do not rely strictly on one approach or location but use a combination. Other methods of instruction in decreasing order of use are: classroom instruction, coaching, observation, home study, and special courses. Coaching and observation are important components of the behavior modeling approach. OJT often occurs before formal classroom training. This helps to prepare the trainee for the more formalized approach. The sales trainee can appreciate the value of sales training and can identify how training would have helped during on-the-job training.

As a result of various environmental changes, the content and method of sales training has changed. How to use the telephone in selling is a commonly taught subject. Salespeople receive instruction on how to use a microcomputer to better plan their activities. And, salespeople are now being trained via personal computers and VCR systems. Companies recognize that their technical people need sales training. Sales training is now part of training programs for firms that felt that such training was unnecessary, for example, public accounting firms, banks, and hospitals and clinics.

Sales training is very expensive and generally considered beneficial. Accurate measurement of the benefits is difficult. It is hard to isolate the effects produced solely by sales training from those that might have been produced by other factors such as changes in the economy or the nature of competition.

Sales training provides managers with the opportunity to convey their expectations to the sales force. A well-designed training program shows the sales force how to sell. Sales managers can communicate high performance expectations through training and equip the force with the skills needed to reach high performance levels.

Discussion Questions

1. The sales training manager of I. Klug Co., a manufacturer of office equipment, was debating the merits of the firm's recent decision to add eight women to its sales force. The debate centered on whether or not the content of the training program should be the same for the women as for the men. I. Klug's sales manager was opposed to any differential treatment, arguing that to do so constituted special treatment. The sales training manager felt otherwise. With whom do you agree? Are there different subjects that should be taught?

2. The sales analyst for the Blotter Paper Company has informed the sales manager that selling expenses relative to sales were higher than expected for the last quarter. What might cause this problem? Does this problem have any implications for sales training?

3. The sales manager of a large insurance company feels that sales training is too expensive and a waste of money. Turnover rates have increased recently, and many of those leaving went to work for other insurance firms. To this, the sales manager replied: "Nuts to sales training. All we're doing is training salespeople for our competitors. What we need to do is hire experienced people." Do you agree?

4. Many times, salespeople are put into conflict situations resulting from customers having expectations that differ from expectations of others. Can sales training reduce the conflict encountered by salespeople?

5. Behavior modeling has been described by one expert as a technique that holds great promise in sales training. A critic, however, views the concept as another faddish subject that will soon be substituted by yet another buzzword approach. To what extent has the promise of behavior modeling been fulfilled? What are the limitations of the technique?

6. Over the years, students have indicated a strong preference for formal training programs and an equally strong dislike for on-the-job training. Yet, as noted in the chapter, OJT is the most preferred method of sales managers. How do you account for this difference?

7. What techniques of instruction would you use for the following situations?
   a. Handling customer's objections.
   b. Training sales personnel about the technical and operational features of a new product.
   c. Teaching company history and policies.
   d. Improving time and territory management.
   e. Introducing a new sales call reporting system using personal computers.
   f. Explaining a minor change in the commission schedule.

8. Sales training programs need constant monitoring to ensure their effectiveness. What monitoring techniques would you propose?

9. A consulting organization is trying to convince the sales manager to use its program for training their salespeople. The program's thrust involves trans-actional analysis. The cost is $250 per salesperson. The company employs 150 sales reps who have been experiencing a decline in sales. How should the sales manager decide whether to adopt the program?

10. Telemarketing is a new subject found in many sales training programs. What telemarketing skills do salespeople need to know? What is the best way to teach these skills?

11. There is general agreement that empathy is a needed trait to be successful in sales. What is empathy? How would you teach empathy to salespeople?

12. Older sales representatives often resent being told that they need more sales training. They contend that they have been through all of this before and it is a waste of time. How would you handle this problem?

Chapter **13**

Motivating the Sales Force

Fitwell's Fashion Shop

"The Fitwell Company" is a fictitious name given to a well-known manufacturer of women's apparel by Professor Benson Shapiro of Harvard Business School. Shapiro reports that several years ago, the Fitwell Company employed 50 salespeople and had annual sales of about $40 million in the medium- to medium—high-priced dress lines.[1]

Fitwell's salespeople were paid on a variable commission rate, receiving a 7 percent commission on dresses with the highest gross margins and 5 percent on those with the lowest gross margins. The salespeople called on retail stores, paid their own out-of-pocket expenses, and averaged about $46,000 each in gross compensation per year.

To keep pace with the market and improve its margins, Fitwell introduced a higher-priced line of dresses. Extra high commissions of 9 percent were offered to the company salespeople to motivate them to devote substantial efforts in selling the new line. Despite these high commissions and relatively high advertising, however, the new line did not sell well, much to the chagrin of the top executives who had developed it.

The immediate reaction of Fitwell's sales managers was to push harder. The annual sales meeting included speeches by the board chairman, the president, the marketing vice president, and the national sales manager on the importance of the new line to the company and to the salespeople. Regional sales managers were urged to motivate their salespeople to "push the line." Contests offered substantial prizes, such as a trip to Europe for the salesperson with the largest percentage of sales and a car for the person with the largest dollar volume of sales in the new line. Unfortunately, the more Fitwell's sales managers "motivated," the more they were frustrated. New-line sales did not improve, and increasingly "powerful" speeches to the sales force were met with yawns.

What Went Wrong?

One reason for the failure of Fitwell's new line was that the firm was using a product-oriented, rather than a customer-oriented marketing strategy. The decision to develop the new line was based largely on considerations of competition and gross margins. Little analysis was done to determine if consumers wanted to buy the new dresses or if retailers were interested in stocking a new line in the upper price range—so Fitwell ended up trying very hard to sell a product no one wanted to buy. One lesson to learn from Fitwell's experience, then, is that sales

---

[1] The Fitwell example is based on material found in Benson P. Shapiro, "Manage the Customer, Not Just the Sales-force," *Harvard Business Review* 52 (September-October 1974), pp. 127–36.

force motivation—like other sales performance determinants—does not operate in a vacuum. No matter how highly motivated salespeople are, they will not be successful unless supported by a marketing strategy geared to customer needs, a well-designed strategic sales program, and effective account-management policies. A second possible reason for the failure of Fitwell to generate sales for its new dress line was management's programs for motivating the sales force. While one would suppose that large commissions and valuable contest prizes would effectively motivate salespeople to expend much effort selling a product, this is not necessarily true. Perhaps Fitwell's salespeople were so well satisfied with their current pay that the opportunity to earn even more was not worth the additional effort. Perhaps other kinds of rewards, such as promotions or opportunities for personal development, would have been more appealing. Perhaps the salespeople felt that the new line would not sell—and that they would not be able to earn the big commissions and win the contests—no matter how much effort they expended.

In other words, motivating a sales force is a very complicated process. The success or failure of a given compensation system or incentive program is influenced by many factors, including (1) environmental conditions, (2) the firm's other management policies and programs, and (3) the personal characteristics of the salespeople. Fitwell's managers failed to consider these factors in deciding to motivate their staff to sell the new line. Instead, they simply offered common compensation and incentive packages and a lot of "inspirational" speeches.

In view of the complicated nature of motivation and its critical role in sales management, the rest of this chapter and all of Chapter 14 are devoted to the subject. This chapter examines what is known about motivation as a psychological process, and how a person's motivation to perform a given job is affected by environmental, organizational, and personal variables. Chapter 14 discusses compensation plans and incentive programs sales managers use to stimulate and direct salespeople's efforts. The chapter explores the strengths and weaknesses of these programs and examines the conditions under which each is most likely to be an effective motivational tool.

The Psychological Process of Motivation

The term *motivation* produces severe stomachaches for many psychologists. The reason for this gastric distress is the wide variety of different and often inconsistent meanings that have been attached to the term. In recent years, though, some consensus seems to be emerging. Most industrial and organizational psychologists now view *motivation* as a general label for the choice (1) to initiate action on a certain task, (2) to expend a certain amount of effort on that task, and (3) to persist in expending effort over a period of time.[2]

---

[2] John P. Campbell and Robert D. Pritchard, "Motivation Theory in Industrial and Organizational Psychology," in *Handbook of Industrial and Organizational Psychology*, ed. Marvin D. Dunnette (Chicago: Rand McNally, 1976), p. 65.

For our purposes, *motivation* is viewed as the amount of effort the salesperson desires to expend on each activity or task associated with the job. This may include calling on potential new accounts, developing sales presentations, and filling out reports. The psychological process involved in determining how much effort a salesperson will want to expend, and some variables that influence the process, are shown in Figure 13–1.

The model in Figure 13–1 suggests that the effort expended by a salesperson on each task associated with his or her job will lead to some level of achievement on one or more dimensions of job performance. These dimensions include total sales volume, profitability of sales, and new accounts generated. It is assumed that the salesperson's performance on some of these dimensions will be evaluated by superiors and rewarded with one or more rewards. These might be externally mediated rewards, like a promotion, or internally mediated rewards, such as feelings of accomplishment or personal growth. A salesperson's motivation to expend effort on a given task, then, is determined by three sets of perceptions: (1) expectancies—the perceived linkages between expending more effort on a particular task and achieving improved performance, (2) instrumentalities—the perceived relationship between improved performance and the attainment of increased rewards, and (3) valence for rewards—the perceived attractiveness of the various rewards the salesperson might receive.

Expectancies—Perceived Links between Effort and Performance

Expectancies are the salesperson's perceptions of the link between job effort and performance. Specifically, an expectancy is the person's estimate of the probability that expending effort on some task will lead to improved performance on a dimension. The following statement illustrates an expectancy perception: "If I increase my calls on potential new accounts by 10 percent (effort), then there is a 50 percent chance (expectancy) that my volume of new account sales will increase by 10 percent during the next six months (performance level)."

When attempting to motivate salespeople, sales managers should be concerned with two aspects of their subordinates' expectancy perceptions: magnitude and accuracy. The *magnitude* of a salesperson's expectancy perceptions indicates the degree to which that person believes expending effort on job activities will influence his or her ultimate job performance. Other things being equal, the larger a salesperson's expectancy perceptions, the more willing he or she is to devote effort to the job in hopes of bettering performance.

The *accuracy* of a salesperson's expectancy perceptions refers to how clearly he or she understands the relationship between effort expended on a task and the resulting achievement on some performance dimension. When salespeople's expectancies are inaccurate, they are likely to misallocate job efforts. They spend too much time and energy on activities that have little impact on performance and not enough on activities with a greater impact.

Figure 13–1
The psychological determinants
of motivation

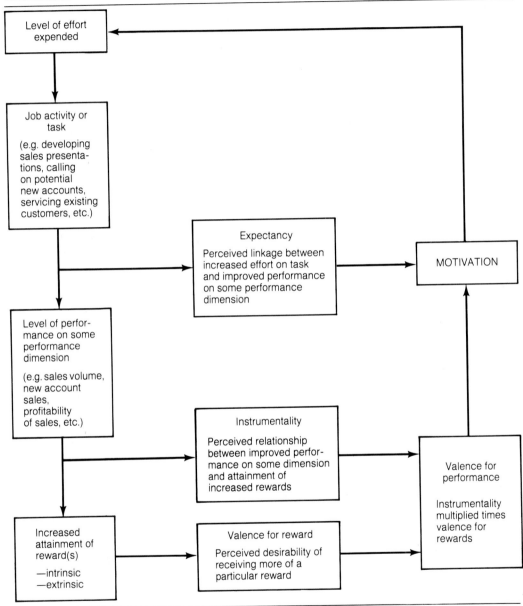

As Figure 13–2 indicates, personal and organizational characteristics affect the magnitude and accuracy of salespeople's expectancy perceptions. Managers must take these factors into account when deciding on supervisory policies, compensation, and incentive plans so that their subordinates' expectancies will be as large and as accurate as possible. The factors that affect salespeople's expectancy estimates, along with their managerial implications, are discussed later in this chapter.

Instrumentalities—Perceived Links between Performance and Rewards

Like expectancies, instrumentalities are probability estimates made by the salesperson. They are the individual's perceptions of the link between job performance and various rewards. Specifically, an instrumentality is a salesperson's

Figure 13–2
Factors influencing the motivation process

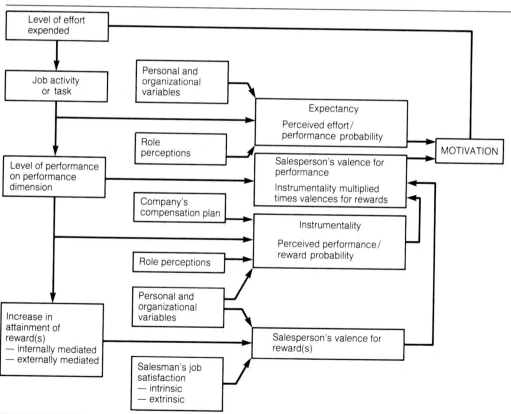

estimate of the probability that an improvement in performance on some dimension will lead to a specific increase in the amount of a particular reward. The reward may be more pay, winning a sales contest, or promotion to a better territory.

As with expectancies, sales managers should be concerned with both the magnitude and the accuracy of their subordinates' instrumentalities. When the magnitude of a salesperson's instrumentality estimates is relatively large, he or she believes there is a high probability that improved performance will lead to more rewards. Consequently, he or she will be more willing to expend the effort necessary to achieve better performance.

The true link between performance and rewards in a firm are determined by management policies about how sales performance is evaluated and what rewards are conferred for various levels of performance. These policies may be inaccurately perceived by the salespeople. As a result, salespeople may concentrate on improving their performance in areas that are relatively unimportant to management; and they ultimately may become disillusioned with their ability to attain desired rewards.

Besides the firm's compensation policies, other organizational factors and the personal characteristics of the salespeople themselves can influence both the magnitude and the accuracy of their instrumentality estimates. These factors and their managerial implications are explored in a later section of this chapter and in Chapter 14.

Valence for Rewards

Valences are the salesperson's perceptions of the desirability of receiving increased amounts of the rewards he or she might attain as a result of improved performance. One question about valences that has always interested sales managers is whether there are consistent preferences among salespeople for specific kinds of rewards. Are some rewards consistently valued more highly than others?

Historically, many sales managers and most authors of books and articles on motivating salespeople have assumed that monetary rewards are the most highly valued and motivating rewards. They feel that recognition and other psychological rewards are less valued and serve only to spur additional sales effort under certain circumstances.[3] As one sales executive said, "Money isn't everything, but it's so far ahead of what's in second place that it's simply 'no contest' as a reward . . ."[4] However, few empirical studies have been conducted to test whether salespeople typically have higher valences for more pay than for other rewards.

[3] For example, see Albert Haring and Robert H. Meyers, "Special Incentives for Salesmen," *Journal of Marketing* 18 (October 1953), pp. 155–59; or Richard C. Smyth, "Financial Incentives for Salesmen," *Harvard Business Review* 46 (January-February 1968), pp. 109–17.
[4] "Managing and Motivating Industrial Salesmen," *Industrial Marketing*, October 1965, p. 112.

Rather, the assumption has been based largely on the perceptions of sales managers rather than on any evidence obtained from salespeople themselves.

Surveys conducted among employees in other occupations often find that increased pay is *not* always the most highly desired reward. For example, one psychologist recently reviewed 43 surveys of nonsales workers in which the importance of more pay was rated relative to other rewards. Pay was ranked most important in only 25 percent of these studies, and its average importance across all studies was third.[5]

In view of this evidence, is the "conventional wisdom" that salespeople desire money more than other rewards wrong—or are salespeople different from workers in other jobs? One recent study of 106 salespeople in three industrial products companies supports the conventional view. On the average, those salespeople placed a higher value on receiving more pay than any other reward.[6]

But increased pay is not always seen as the most attractive reward by salespeople in all companies. An illustration of this point is provided by a study of 481 salespeople in two large manufacturing organizations who ranked seven different rewards according to their relative attractiveness and rated them on a 100-point scale.[7] Table 13–1 shows the results.

More pay was not universally seen as the most desirable reward by all the salespeople in the study. Although more pay was by far the most attractive reward for salespeople in Company A, it ranked only third behind "opportunities for personal growth" and "sense of accomplishment" for those in Company B.

Table 13–1
Valence ratings and rankings of alternative rewards by salespeople in two manufacturers

	Company A (n = 151)		Company B (n = 76)	
	Valence Rating	Rank	Valence Rating	Rank
More pay	90.8	1	80.9	3
Sense of accomplishment	74.8	2	84.6	2
Opportunities for personal growth	74.7	3	87.9	1
Promotion	64.7	4	74.6	4
Liking and respect	62.2	5	64.8	5
Security	60.3	6	57.4	6
Recognition	50.3	7	53.9	7

Source: Adapted from Gilbert A. Churchill, Jr., Neil M. Ford, and Orville C. Walker, Jr., *Motivating the Industrial Salesforce: The Attractiveness of Alternative Rewards*, Report #76–115 (Cambridge, Mass.: The Marketing Science Institute, 1976), p. 14.

[5] Edward E. Lawler III, *Pay and Organizational Effectiveness: A Psychological View* (New York: McGraw-Hill, 1971).
[6] Neil M. Ford, Orville C. Walker, Jr., and Gilbert A. Churchill, Jr., "Differences in the Attractiveness of Alternative Rewards Among Industrial Salespeople: Additional Evidence," *Journal of Business Research*, 1984.
[7] Gilbert A. Churchill, Jr., Neil M. Ford, and Orville C. Walker, Jr., *Motivating the Industrial Salesforce: The Attractiveness of Alternative Rewards*, Report #76-115 (Cambridge, Mass.: The Marketing Science Institute, 1976).

Why did the salespeople in one company value a pay increase more than those in the other? One plausible answer is that the average total compensation received by salespeople in Company B was about $5,000 higher than that of salespeople in A at the time of the study. Also, there had been a sharp decline in the proportion of salespeople reaching quota and qualifying for bonuses in Company A in the year preceding the study due to quota increases of as much as 25 percent over the year before. No such changes had occurred in Company B. It is possible, then, that the salespeople in Company A had a higher valence for more pay because they were less satisfied with the financial compensation they were currently receiving.

In other words there are no universal statements to be made about what kinds of rewards are most desired by salespeople and most effective for motivating them. Salespeople's valences for rewards are likely to be influenced by their satisfaction with the rewards they are currently receiving. Their satisfaction with current rewards, in turn, is influenced by their personal characteristics and by the compensation policies and management practices of their firm.

Can the Motivation Model Predict Salesperson Effort and Performance

Several studies have tested the ability of motivation models such as the one outlined in Figures 13–1 and 13–2 predict the amount of effort workers will expend on various job activities. The findings provide positive support for the validity of such expectancy models of motivation, explaining as much as 25 percent of the variation in effort among workers.[8]

The salesperson model of performance discussed previously suggests that motivation is only one determinant of job performance. Thus, it seems inappropriate to use only motivation to predict differences in job performance among workers. Nevertheless, several studies have attempted to do just that, and with surprising success. Some studies have found that predictions of workers' motivation to expend effort can explain as much as 40 percent of the variation in their overall job performance.[9]

It is nice to know that there is evidence that models like Figure 13–1 are valid descriptions of the psychological processes that determine a salesperson's motivation. However, there is a question of even greater relevance to sales managers as

---

[8] For a detailed review of a large number of such studies, see Campbell and Pritchard, "Motivation Theory," pp. 63–130. For a study that tests the model with a sample of salespeople, see Gilbert A. Churchill, Jr., Neil M. Ford, and Orville C. Walker, Jr., "Predicting a Salesperson's Job Effort and Performance: Theoretical, Empirical and Methodological Considerations," in *Sales Management: New Developments from Behavioral and Decision Model Research*, ed. Richard P. Bagozzi (Cambridge, Mass.: Marketing Science Institute, 1979), pp. 3–39.

[9] Campbell and Pritchard, "Motivation Theory." For a study focused on industrial salespeople, see Richard P. Oliver. "Expectancy Theory Predictions of Salesmen's Performance," *Journal of Marketing Research* 11 (August 1974), pp. 243–53.

they struggle to design effective compensation and incentive programs. The question is how the three determinants of motivation—expectancy perceptions, instrumentality perceptions, and valences for rewards—are affected by (1) differences in the personal characteristics of individuals, (2) environmental conditions, and (3) the organization's policies and procedures. Therefore, the impact of each of these variables on the determinants of motivation is now examined in greater detail.

The Impact of a Salesperson's Personal Characteristics on Motivation

When placed in the same job with the same compensation and incentive programs, different salespeople are likely to be motivated to expend widely differing amounts of effort. This is because people with different personal characteristics have divergent perceptions of the links between effort and performance (expectancies) and between performance and rewards (instrumentalities). They are also likely to have different valences for the rewards they might obtain through improved job performance. The personal characteristics that affect motivation include: (1) the individual's satisfaction with current rewards, (2) demographic variables, (3) job experience, and (4) psychological traits. The impacts of each characteristic on expectancies, instrumentalities, and valences are summarized in Table 13–2 and discussed in more detail.

Table 13–2
Influence of personal characteristics on the determinants of motivation

| | Motivation Variables | | | | | |
| | Expectancies | | Instrumentalities | | Valences | |
Personal Characteristics	Magnitude	Accuracy	Magnitude	Accuracy	High Order	Low Order
Demographic variables						
Age......................					+	−
Family size..............						+
Education					+	
Job Experience.............	+	+		+		
Personality traits						
High need achievement ...					+	
Internal locus of control ...	+		+			
Verbal intelligence	+	+	+	+		
General self-esteem	+				+	
Task-specific self-esteem ...	+				+	

Satisfaction

Is it possible to pay a salesperson too much? After a salesperson reaches a certain satisfactory level of compensation, does he or she lose interest in working to obtain still more money? Does the attainment of nonfinancial rewards similarly affect the salesperson's desire to earn more of those rewards? The basic issue underlying these questions is whether a salesperson's satisfaction with current rewards has any impact on the valence for more of those rewards or on the desire for different kinds of rewards.

The relationship between satisfaction and the valence for rewards is different for rewards that satisfy lower-order needs (e.g., pay and job security) than for those that satisfy higher-order needs (e.g., promotions, recognition, opportunities for personal growth, self-fulfillment). Maslow's theory of a need hierarchy,[10] Herzberg's theory of motivation,[11] and Alderfer's "existence, relatedness, and growth theory"[12] all suggest that lower-order rewards are valued most highly by workers currently dissatisfied with their attainment of those rewards. In other words, the more dissatisfied a salesperson is with current pay, job security, recognition, and other rewards related to lower-order needs, the higher the valence he or she attaches to increases in those rewards. In contrast, as salespeople become more satisfied with their attainment of low-order rewards, the value of further increases in those rewards declines.

The theories of Maslow, Herzberg, and Alderfer further suggest that high-order rewards are not valued highly by salespeople until they are relatively satisfied with their lower-order rewards. The greater the salesperson's satisfaction with lower-order rewards, the higher the valence of increased attainment of high-order rewards.

Perhaps the most controversial aspect of Maslow's and Alderfer's theories is the proposition that high-order rewards have increasing marginal utility. The more satisfied a salesperson is with the high-order rewards he or she is receiving from the job, the higher the value he or she places on further increases in those rewards.

Several studies in industrial psychology have provided at least partial support for these suggested relationships between satisfaction and the valence of lower-order and higher-order rewards.[13] Some evidence is equivocal, though, and some propositions—particularly the idea that high-order rewards have increasingly marginal utility—have not been tested adequately.

---

[10] Abraham Harold Maslow, "A Theory of Human Motivation," *Psychology Review* 50 (1943), pp. 370–96; and Abraham Harold Maslow, *Motivation and Personality*, 2d ed. (New York: Harper & Row, 1970).

[11] Frederick Herzberg, Bernard Mausner, and Barbara Snyderman, *The Motivation to Work*, 2d ed. (New York: John Wiley & Sons, 1959).

[12] Clayton P. Aldefer, "An Empirical Test of a New Theory of Human Needs," *Organizational Behavior and Human Performance* 4 (1969), pp. 142–75.

[13] Alderfer, "Empirical Test"; H. Peter Dachler and Charles L. Hulin, "A Reconsideration of the Relationship Between Satisfaction and Judged Importance of Environmental and Job Characteristics," *Organizational Behavior and Human Performance* 4 (1969), pp. 252–66; and Edward E. Lawler III and J. Lloyd Suttle, "A Casual Correlation Test of the Need Hierarchy Concept," *Organizational Behavior and Human Performance* 7 (1972), pp. 265–87.

Two studies of valence for rewards conducted among salespeople provide some support for the preceding hypotheses. One survey of salespeople in two manufacturing firms found that salespeople relatively satisfied with current pay (a lower-order reward) had significantly lower valences for attaining more pay than those dissatisfied with current pay. Also, salespeople satisfied with their overall attainment of higher-order rewards had significantly higher valences for more of those rewards than those dissatisfied with their higher-order rewards. Salespeople satisfied with their lower-order rewards, however, did not have significantly higher valences for higher-order rewards, as the theories would predict.[14] On the other hand, a second study of salespeople in three companies did find that the desire for higher order rewards like personal growth and promotion was highest among those individuals who were most satisfied with their current pay and other lower-order rewards.[15]

Demographic Characteristics

Demographic characteristics, such as age, family size, and education, also affect a salesperson's valence for rewards. At least part of the reason for this is that people with different demographic characteristics are likely to have different levels of satisfaction with their current rewards. Although there is only limited empirical evidence with respect to salespeople in this regard, some conclusions can be drawn from studies conducted in other occupations.[16]

It is generally true that older, more experienced salespeople obtain higher levels of lower-order rewards (e.g., higher pay, a better territory) than newer members of the sales force. Thus, it could be expected that more experienced salespeople are more satisfied with their lower-order rewards. Consequently, they also should have lower valences for lower-order rewards and higher valences for higher-order rewards than younger and less experienced salespeople.

A salesperson's satisfaction with the current level of lower-order rewards may also be influenced by the demands and responsibilities he or she must satisfy with those rewards. The salesperson with a large family to support, for instance, is less likely to be satisfied with a given level of financial compensation than the single salesperson. Consequently, the more family members a salesperson must support, the higher the valence for more lower-order rewards and the lower the valence for higher-order rewards.

Finally, individuals with more formal education are more likely to desire opportunities for personal growth, career advancement, and self-fulfillment than those with less education. Consequently, highly educated salespeople are likely to have higher valences for higher-order rewards.

---

[14] Churchill, Ford, and Walker, *Motivating the Industrial Salesforce.*

[15] Ford, Walker and Churchill, "Additional Evidence."

[16] See Lawler, *Pay and Organizational Effectiveness,* especially pp. 46–59; Gilbert A. Churchill, Jr., Neil M. Ford, and Orville C. Walker, Jr., "Personal Characteristics of Salespeople and the Attractivenss of Alternative Rewards," *Journal of Business Research* 7 (1979), pp. 25–50; and Ford, Walker, and Churchill, "Additional Evidence."

Job Experience

As an individual gains experience on a job, he or she is likely to gain a clearer idea of how expending effort on particular tasks affects performance. The experienced salesperson is also likely to understand better how his or her superiors evaluate performance and how particular types of performance are rewarded in the company. Consequently, as suggested by Table 13–2, there is likely to be a positive relationship between the years a salesperson has spent on the job and the accuracy of his or her expectancy and instrumentality perceptions.

In addition, the magnitude of a salesperson's expectancy perceptions may be affected by experience. As they gain experience, salespeople have opportunities to sharpen their selling skills; and they gain confidence in their ability to perform successfully. As a result, experienced salespeople are likely to have larger expectancy estimates than inexperienced ones.

Psychological Traits

An individual's motivation also seems to be affected by psychological traits. People with strong achievement needs are likely to have higher valences for such higher-order rewards as recognition, personal growth, and feeling of accomplishment. This is particularly true when they see their jobs as being relatively difficult to perform successfully.[17]

The degree to which individuals believe they have internal control over the events in their lives or whether those events are determined by external forces beyond their control also affects their motivation. Specifically, the greater the degree to which salespeople believe they have internal control over events, the more likely they are to feel that they can improve their performance by expending more effort. They also feel that improved performance will be appropriately rewarded. Therefore, salespeople with high "internal locus of control" are likely to have relatively high expectancy and instrumentality estimates.[18]

There is some evidence that intelligence is positively related to feelings of internal control.[19] Therefore, more intelligent salespeople may have higher expectancy and instrumentality perceptions than those less intelligent. Those with relatively high levels of intelligence—particularly verbal intelligence- are especially likely to understand their jobs and their companies' reward policies more

---

[17] David C. McClelland, John W. Atkinson, Russell A. Clark, and Edgar L. Lowell, *The Achievement Motive* (New York: Appleton-Century-Crofts, 1953); and John W. Atkinson, *An Introduction to Motivation* (Princeton, N.J.: Van Nostrand, 1964).

[18] See, for example, E. E. Lawler III, "Job Attitudes and Employee Motivation: Theory, Research, and Practice," *Personnel Psychology* 23 (1970), pp. 223–37; or Julian B. Rotter, "Generalized Expectancies for Internal versus External Control of Reinforcement," *Psychological Monographs: General and Applied* 80 (1966).

[19] Ibid.

quickly and accurately. Thus, their instrumentality and expectancy estimates are likely to be more accurate.

Finally, a worker's general feeling of self-esteem and perceived competence and ability to perform job activities (task-specific self-esteem) are both positively related to the magnitude of expectancy estimates.[20] Since such people believe they have the talents and abilities to be successful, they are likely to see a strong relationship between effort expended and good performance. Also, people with high levels of self-esteem are likely to attach greater importance to, and receive more satisfaction from, good performance. Consequently, such people probably have higher valences for the higher-order, intrinsic rewards attained from successful job performance.

Management Implications

The relationships between salespeople's personal characteristics and motivation levels have two broad implications for sales managers. First, they suggest that people with certain characteristics are likely to understand their jobs and their companies' policies better. They also should perceive higher expectancy and instrumentality links. Such people should be easier to train and be motivated to expend greater effort and achieve better performance. Therefore, as researchers and managers gain a better understanding of these relationships, it may be possible to develop improved selection criteria for hiring salespeople easy to train and motivate.

More important, some personal characteristics are related to the kinds of rewards salespeople are likely to value and find motivating. This suggests that sales managers should examine the characteristics of their salespeople and attempt to determine their relative valences for various rewards when designing compensation and incentive programs. Also, as the demographic characteristics of a sales force change over time, the manager should be aware that salespeople's satisfaction with rewards and their valences for future rewards may also change.

The Impact of Environmental Conditions on Motivation

Environmental factors such as variations in territory potential and strength of competition can constrain a salesperson's ability to achieve high levels of performance. Such environmental constraints can cause substantial variations in performance across salespeople. In addition to placing actual constraints on performance, however, environmental conditions can affect salespeople's *percep-*

---

[20] Abraham K. Korman, "Expectancies as Determinants of Performance," *Journal of Applied Psychology* 55 (1971), pp. 218–22; and Lawler, "Job Attitudes," pp. 223–37.

tions of their likelihood of succeeding and thus their willingness to expend effort on their jobs.

Although management can do little to change the environment faced by its salespeople (with the possible exception of rearranging sales territories), an understanding of how and why salespeople perform differently under varying environmental circumstances is useful to sales managers. It provides some clues about the compensation methods and management policies that will have the greatest impact on sales performance under specific environmental conditions. Consequently, the effects of various environmental factors on salespeople's perceptions and motivations are now discussed. These effects are summarized in Table 13–3.

Table 13–3
Influence of environmental factors
on the determinants of motivation

| | Motivation Variables | | | | | |
| | Expectancies | | Instrumentalities | | Valences | |
Environmental Factors	Magnitude	Accuracy	Magnitude	Accuracy	High Order	Low Order
Stability of product offerings ...		+				
Output constraints	−		−			
Superiority of competitive position	+					
Territory potential	+					

In some industries, the pace of technological change is very rapid, as recent advances in the computer and office machine industries show. Sales people in such industries must deal with a constant flow of product innovations, modifications, and applications. Salespeople often look with favor on a constantly changing product line because it adds variety to their jobs, and their markets never have a chance to become saturated and stagnant. However, *a rapidly changing product line* can also cause problems for the salesperson. New products and services may require new selling methods and result in new expectations and demands from role partners. Consequently, an unstable product line may lead to less accurate expectancy estimates among the sales force.

In some firms, salespeople must perform in the face of *output constraints*. These can result from short supplies of production factors, including shortages of raw materials, plant capacity, or labor. Such constraints can cause severe problems for the salesperson. In one paper-products firm a few years ago, salespeople were given quotas that they were penalized for exceeding. In general, salespeople operating in the face of uncertain or limited product supplies are likely to feel relatively powerless to improve their performance or rewards through their own efforts. After all, their ultimate effectiveness is constrained by factors beyond their control. Therefore, their expectancy and instrumentality estimates are likely to be low.

There are many ways of assessing the strength of a firm's competitive position in the marketplace. One might look at its market share, the quality of its products and services as perceived by customers, or its prices. Regardless of how competitive superiority is defined, though, when salespeople believe they work for a strongly competitive firm, they are more likely to feel that selling effort will result in successful performance. In other words, the stronger a firm's competitive position, the higher its salespeople's expectancy estimates are likely to be.

Sales territories often have very different potentials for future sales. These potentials are affected by many environmental factors, including economic conditions, competitors' activities, and customer concentrations. Again, though, the salesperson's *perception* of the unrealized potential of his or her territory can influence that person's motivation to expend selling effort. Specifically, the greater the perceived potential of a territory, the higher the salesperson's expectancy estimates are likely to be.

The Impact of Organizational Variables on Motivation

Company policies and characteristics can directly facilitate or hinder a salesperson's effectiveness. Such organizational variables may also influence salespeople's performance indirectly, however, by affecting their valences for company rewards and the size and accuracy of their expectancy and instrumentality estimates. These relationships between organizational variables and the determinants of motivation are summarized in Table 13–4.

Table 13–4
Influence of organizational variables on the determinants of motivation

	Motivation Variables					
	Expectancies		Instrumentalities		Valences	
Organizational Variables	Magnitude	Accuracy	Magnitude	Accuracy	High Order	Low Order
Closeness of supervision		+		+		
Span of control		−		−		
Influence over standards				+		
Frequency of communication ..		+		+		
Opportunity rate					Curvilinear	
Recognition rate					Curvilinear	
Compensation rate...........						−
Earnings opportunity ratio						+

Supervisory Variables and Leadership

According to one highly regarded theory of leadership, a leader attains good performance from his or her work unit by increasing subordinates' personal rewards from goal attainment and by making the path to those rewards easier to follow—through instructions and training, reducing roadblocks and pitfalls, and by increasing the opportunities for personal satisfaction along the way.[21] This theory suggests that effective leaders are the ones who tailor their style and approach to the needs of their subordinates and the kinds of tasks those subordinates must perform. When the subordinates' task is well-defined, routine, and repetitive, the leader should seek ways to increase the intrinsic rewards of the task. This might be accomplished by assigning subordinates a broader range of activities or by giving them more flexibility to perform tasks in their own way. When the subordinate's job is complex and ambiguous, on the other hand, he or she is likely to be happier and more productive when the leader provides relatively high levels of guidance and structure.

In most occupations, workers perform relatively well-defined and routine jobs, and they prefer to be relatively free from supervision. They do not like to feel their superiors "breathing down their necks." Industrial salespeople, however, are different. They occupy a position at the boundary of their companies, dealing with customers and other nonorganization people who may make conflicting demands. Salespeople frequently face new, nonroutine problems. Consequently, there is some evidence that industrial salespeople are happier when they feel relatively closely supervised.[22] Closely supervised salespeople can learn more quickly what is expected of them and how they should perform their job. Consequently, such individuals should have more accurate expectancies and instrumentalities than less closely supervised salespeople. On the other hand, close supervision can lead to more role conflict since it can reduce flexibility in accommodating and adapting to customers' demands.

Another organizational variable related to the closeness of supervision is the firm's first-level sales managers' span of control. The more salespeople each manager must supervise (the larger the span of control), the less closely he or she can supervise each person. Therefore, the impact of span of control on role perceptions and motivation variables should be the opposite of the expected impact of close supervision.

Another related supervisory variable is the frequency with which salespeople communicate with their superiors. The greater the frequency of communication, the less role ambiguity salespeople are likely to experience and the more accurate their expectancy and instrumentality estimates should be. Again, however, fre-

---

[21] Robert House, "A Path-Goal Theory of Leadership Effectiveness," *Administrative Science Quarterly* (1971), pp. 321–39; and Valarie A. Zeithaml and Carl P. Zeithaml, "The Contingency Approach to Theory Building: Its Foundations and Relevance to Marketing Theory and Research," paper presented at the American Marketing Association's Winter Theory Conference, Ft. Lauderdale, Florida, 1984.

[22] Gilbert A. Churchill, Jr., Neil M. Ford, and Orville C. Walker, Jr., "Organizational Climate and Job Satisfaction in the Sales Force," *Journal of Marketing Research* 13 (November 1976), pp. 323–32.

quent contact with superiors may increase the individual's feelings of role conflict.

Management by objectives (MBO) is a popular supervisory technique in sales management. Specific procedures vary from firm to firm, but one basic principle of MBO is to give the individual a voice in determining the standards and criteria by which performance will be evaluated and rewarded. Salespeople who feel that they influence such standards are likely to have a clearer understanding of how to perform their jobs and how performance will be rewarded.

Incentive and Compensation Policies

Management policies and programs concerning higher-order rewards, such as recognition and promotion, can influence the desirability of such rewards in the salesperson's mind. For these rewards, there is likely to be a curvilinear relationship between the perceived likelihood of receiving them and the salesperson's valence for them. For example, if a large proportion of the sales force receives some formal recognition each year, salespeople may feel that such recognition is too common, too easy to obtain, and not worth much. If very few members receive formal recognition, however, salespeople may feel that it is not a very attractive or motivating reward simply because the odds of attaining it are so low. The same curvilinear relationship is likely to exist between the proportion of salespeople promoted into management each year (the *opportunity* rate) and salespeople's valence for promotion.

A company's policies on the kinds and amounts of financial compensation paid to its salespeople are also likely to affect their motivation. As seen, when a person's lower-order needs are satisfied, they become less important and the individual's valence for rewards that satisfy such needs—such as pay and job security—is reduced. This suggests that in firms where the current financial compensation (compensation rate) is relatively high, sales people will be satisfied with their attainment of lower-order rewards. They will have lower valences for more of those rewards than people in firms where compensation is lower.

The *range* of financial rewards currently received by members of a sales force also might affect their valences for more financial rewards. If some salespeople receive much more money than the average, many others may feel underpaid and have high valences for more money. The ratio of the total financial compensation of the highest paid salesperson to that of the average in a sales force is the *earnings opportunity ratio*. The higher this ratio is within a company, the higher the average salesperson's valence for pay is likely to be.

Finally, the kind of reward mix offered by the firm is a factor. Reward mix is the relative emphasis placed on salary versus commissions or other incentive pay and nonfinancial rewards. It is likely to influence the salesperson's instrumentality estimates and help determine which job activities and types of performance will receive the greatest effort from that salesperson. The question from a manager's viewpoint is how to design an effective reward mix for directing the sales force's efforts toward the activities felt to be most important to the overall success of the firm's sales program. This leads to a discussion of the relative advantages and weaknesses of alternative compensation and incentive programs—the topic of Chapter 14.

Summary

The amount of effort the salesperson desires to expend on each activity or task associated with the job—the individual's *motivation*—can strongly influence his or her job performance. This chapter reviewed the factors that affect an individual's motivation level. More specifically, the chapter suggested that an individual's motivation to expend effort on any particular task is a function of his or her (1) expectancy, (2) instrumentality, and (3) valence perceptions.

Expectancy refers to the salesperson's estimate of the probability that expending a given amount of effort on some task will lead to improved performance on some dimension. Expectancies have two dimensions that are important to sales managers—magnitude and accuracy. The magnitude of a salesperson's expectancy perceptions indicates the degree to which the individual believes that expending effort on job activities will directly influence job performance. The accuracy of expectancy perceptions refers to how clearly the individual understands the relationship between the effort expended on a task and the performance on some specific dimension that is likely to result.

Instrumentalities are the person's perceptions of links between job performance and various rewards. Specifically, an instrumentality is a salesperson's estimate of the probability that a given improvement in performance on some dimension will lead to a specific increase in the amount of a particular reward. A reward can be more pay, winning a sales contest, or promotion to a better territory. As with expectancies, sales managers need to be concerned with both the magnitude and accuracy of their subordinates' instrumentalities.

In the expectancy model of motivation, there are two valences of interest: valences for rewards and valences for performance. The former is a measured quantity, and the latter is a derived quantity. More specifically, the salesperson's valence for a specific reward is the individual's perception of the desirability of receiving increased amounts of that reward. This valence, along with the individual's valence for all other rewards he or she finds attractive and the person's instrumentality perceptions, determines how attractive it is to perform well on some specific dimension. These valences, in combination with the individual's expectancy estimates, determine how much effort he or she is willing to expend on some task.

Several factors influence salespeople's expectancy, instrumentality, and valence perceptions. Three major forces are: (1) the personal characteristics of the individuals in the sales force, (2) the environmental conditions they face, and (3) the company's own policies and procedures. The chapter reviewed some major influences and their likely impacts on each of the three categories.

Discussion Questions

1. What sales manager has not had the problem of motivating the older sales representative? The once-valuable producer has dried up and is not meeting quotas. He or she is a drag on the rest of the district sales team. What do you do? Fire the sales rep? Baby him or her? What can a sales manager do to turn the older sales rep into a valuable asset?

2. A situation different from the above concerns how to motivate the sales representative when money or merchandise is not the question. When ordinary incentives no longer work—commissions, incentives, or cars—what can a sales manager do to motivate the successful salesperson?

3. Marketing segmentation has become a significant part of marketing terminology. According to two writers, the sales force should be segmented or divided into several discrete units, with each unit being treated according to consumer needs. These two authors claim that this approach will motivate the sales force to better performance. What is the relationship between performance and segmentation?

4. The desirability of an increase in personal growth and development was ranked second by the sales representatives of a "Fortune Top 500" corporation. Sales managers ranked this reward eighth. What explains the apparent discrepancy? How can sales managers motivate the sales force that desires personal growth and development?

5. Many companies use so-called "motivational" speakers to "hype up" the sales force. Athletic stars are frequently used for this purpose. How and where do these motivational techniques impact the motivational process depicted in Figure 13–1?

6. Sales representatives and sales managers from one company were asked to state their valence for earning points in a sales contest. Out of a total 13 rewards, the sales reps ranked this reward 10th, and the sales managers ranked it 11th. What might explain this relatively low ranking for sales contests, considering their popularity?

7. Define motivation as it is used in this chapter. What is the psychological process used in determining how much effort a salesperson will spend on the job? What variables influence this process?

8. What is the relationship between sales force motivation and leadership? What can a sales manager do to lead the sales force to better performance?

9. What assumptions are sales managers making when they claim that all the sales force needs is a pat on the back? Thus, they bring in the so-called motivation expert to pep up the sales group to go out and apply more effort. What role do these entertaining experts play in the motivation of the sales force?

10. When recruiting, some sales managers treat the sales job as a stepping stone to management. Why do they do this? What are the long run implications?

11. Pygmalion, a sculptor in Greek mythology who carved a statue of a beautiful woman that was subsequently brought to life, became the basis for the musical hit, "My Fair Lady." Both have similar themes. In *My Fair Lady,* Eliza Doolittle explains, "You see, really and truly, apart from the things anyone can pick up (the dressing, and the proper way of speaking, and so on), the difference between a lady and a flower girl is not how she behaves, but how she's treated. I shall always be a flower girl to Professor Higgins, because he always treats me as a flower girl, and always will; but I know I can be a lady to you, because you always treat me as a lady, and always will." J. Sterling Livingston, in the *Harvard Business Review* (July-August 1969, pp. 81–89), discusses the Pygmalion effect in management. What is this effect and how does it relate to motivation of the sales force?

12. "If you ask me, there's entirely too much mystique about motivation. This stuff about valences, expectancies, and instrumentalities is nothing more than 'college-knowledge.' Either my sales force will be fired up with enthusiasm, or I'll fire them with enthusiasm." Comment.

Chapter 14

Designing Compensation and Incentive Programs

As Chapter 13 pointed out, when the Fitwell Company introduced a new line of dresses, a primary sales-management objective was to encourage the sales force to expend a large amount of selling effort on the line. The new line carried a higher gross margin than the firm's other products, and management naturally wanted salespeople to focus their efforts where the profit return would be maximized. To accomplish this, the company relied almost exclusively on a financial incentive—an extra large commission for sales of the new line.

One reason Fitwell's new line was not a success was the company's reliance on one reward, money, to motivate its sales force. Chapter 13 mentioned that money is highly valued as a reward by most salespeople. However, more money is not the only reward salespeople seek from their jobs. In many cases, more money is not even the reward salespeople value most. For instance, in one survey of 121 top sales executives, overall financial compensation was rated as only the sixth most effective of 17 types of rewards for motivating salespeople. The survey results are shown in Figure 14–1.[1]

Because most salespeople value more than one reward and people with different characteristics place different values on the same reward, most firms do not rely on a single reward to motivate their sales forces. Instead, they offer a mix of rewards, including both financial and nonfinancial incentives. The ideal motivation program would perhaps offer rewards that are tailor-made to the unique needs and characteristics of each member of the sales force. Such an approach might not be practical, however, because of the administrative complexities it would involve. Nevertheless, many firms have developed compensation and incentive programs that aim to achieve, at least in part, this personalized ideal. These firms offer a variety of rewards so that each member of the sales force has at least something he or she considers worth working for.[2]

In view of the trend toward using multiple rewards to motivate salespeople, this chapter examines a variety of financial and nonfinancial incentives. The financial rewards examined include the total level of compensation; incentive pay, such as commissions and bonuses; and short-term incentives, such as sales contests. Among the nonfinancial rewards discussed are promotion opportunities, programs for personal and career development, recognition programs, and sales meetings and conventions. The advantages and limitations of each reward are examined, and the most appropriate conditions for using each in a firm's motivation program are discussed.

One other crucial question addressed is how to choose among such a wide variety of rewards and integrate them into one effective compensation and incentive program. To answer this question, it is useful to examine the procedures that a sales manager should go through in designing an integrated compensation and incentive program.

---

[1] Mary Lynn Miller, "Motivating the Sales Force," *The Conference Board Information Bulletin* 64 (1979), pp.1–7.
[2] Ibid., p. 2. Also see David M. Gardner and Kenneth M. Rowland, "A Self-Tailored Approach to Incentives," *Personnel Journal* 49 (November 1979), pp. 907–12.

Figure 14–1
Sales force motivators, in order of average rated effectiveness

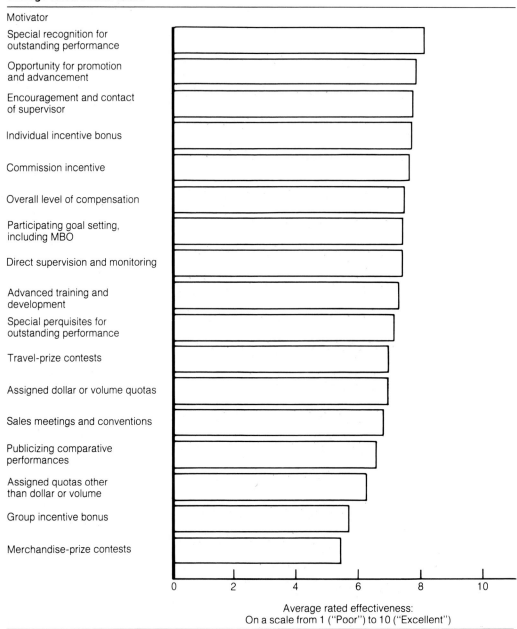

Motivator

Special recognition for outstanding performance

Opportunity for promotion and advancement

Encouragement and contact of supervisor

Individual incentive bonus

Commission incentive

Overall level of compensation

Participating goal setting, including MBO

Direct supervision and monitoring

Advanced training and development

Special perquisites for outstanding performance

Travel-prize contests

Assigned dollar or volume quotas

Sales meetings and conventions

Publicizing comparative performances

Assigned quotas other than dollar or volume

Group incentive bonus

Merchandise-prize contests

0 2 4 6 8 10

Average rated effectiveness:
On a scale from 1 ("Poor") to 10 ("Excellent")

Note: Based on judgments of 127 senior sales and marketing executives (on a scale of 1 to 10, ranging from "poor" to "excellent") in stimulating superior performance on the part of members of a manufacturing company's sales force.
Source: Mary Lynn Miller, "Motivating the Sales Force," *The Conference Board Information Bulletin*, no. 64, p. 20. Copyright 1979, The Conference Board, Inc.

Procedures for Designing a Compensation and Incentive Program

In the words of a top sales executive, "Finding the right combination of motivators is extremely tough."[3] The difficulty of designing and implementing effective compensation and incentive programs is further shown by a recent survey of 449 executives in charge of administering such programs. The study found that more than a third of the respondents were dissatisfied with their companies' programs.[4]

One reason for this dissatisfaction is that sales motivation programs tend to lose their effectiveness over time. The dynamic character of the market environment and the changing circumstances of those who participate cause motivation programs to lose their balance and power of stimulation. As salespeople become satisfied with the rewards offered by a particular plan, their valences for more of those rewards are likely to decline. Recognizing such problems, an increasing proportion of firms frequently review their compensation and incentive programs. Many firms adjust their total compensation levels at least annually, and they are increasingly willing to make more substantial alterations in their programs if required. Indeed, some firms have set up internal "compensation and incentive committees" to monitor their sales motivation programs for fairness and effectiveness.

The critical question, though, is this: How should a firm design a new compensation and incentive program when one is needed? What factors should be considered to help ensure that the program will effectively motivate the sales force to spend effort on activities that are most consistent with the firm's marketing and sales objectives? Figure 14–2 suggests a series of steps that managers should take in designing integrated and effective sales-motivation programs.

Assessing Company Objectives and Determining What Dimensions of Sales Performance to Encourage

A company's compensation and incentive programs, along with its selection policies, training programs, and supervision, can be used by managers to influence and direct a salesperson's behavior in the field. A major purpose of any sales compensation program is to influence the sales force to do what management wants, how they want it done, and within the desired time. Before a firm's managers can design a compensation and incentive package to accomplish this, however, they must have a clear idea of what they want the salesperson to do.

---

[3] Miller, "Motivating the Sales Force," p. 2.
[4] "There Has To Be a Better Way," *Sales & Marketing Management*, November 12, 1979, pp. 41–43.

Figure 14–2
Procedures for designing compensation and incentive programs

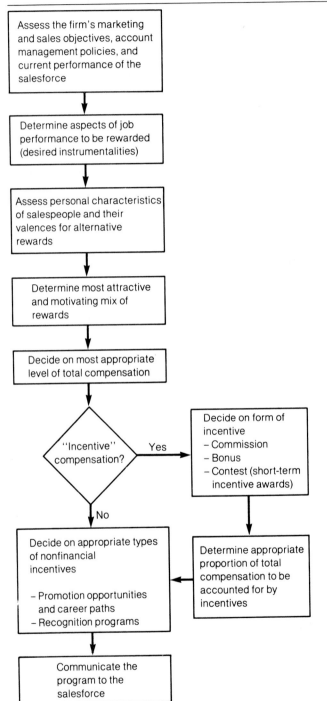

To determine what aspects of job behavior and performance a new or improved sales motivation program should be designed to encourage, managers should examine three issues.[5] First, they should determine how their salespeople now spend their time on the job. On what functions do they spend their time? What proportion of their time do they devote to each activity? How well do they perform on various dimensions, such as total sales volume, sales to new accounts, or sales of certain items in the line? Much of this information can be obtained from job analyses the company conducts as part of its sales-force selection procedures, as well as from performance evaluations and records.

Second, managers should carefully assess their firm's marketing and sales objectives, as outlined in the company's marketing plan, strategic sales program, and account management policies. Some thought should also be given to the order of importance of the firm's objectives.

Finally, in view of priorities in the company's marketing and sales objectives, managers should determine which selling functions and aspects of sales performance should be receiving greater attention from the sales force. The new compensation and incentive program can then be designed to reward desired activities more strongly, thus motivating members of the sales force to redirect their efforts. In terms of the motivation model discussed in Chapter 13, managers must decide which aspects of selling performance will be given the highest instrumentalities in the firm's compensation and incentive program. In the Fitwell Company, for example, management's primary objectives were to encourage sales of its new higher-priced line and to improve the profitability of sales. Therefore, the firm's compensation system was designed to offer bigger commissions for sales of the new, more profitable dresses than for sales of lower-priced items. Some specific selling activities and performance outcomes that a sales motivation program might be designed to encourage are listed in Table 14–1.

In most cases, managers would like salespeople to perform well on many of the performance dimensions listed in Table 14–1. One common mistake in designing sales compensation and incentive plans, however, is to rely solely on such plans to motivate salespeople to perform all the desired functions. Plans that try to motivate salespeople to do too many things at once tend to be ineffective. When rewards are tied to many different aspects of performance, the salesperson's motivation to improve performance dramatically in any single area is "watered down." Also, when rewards are based on many different aspects of performance, the salesperson is more likely to be uncertain about how total performance will be evaluated and about what rewards can be obtained as a result of that performance. In other words, complex compensation and incentive programs may lead to inaccurate instrumentality perceptions by salespeople. Consequently, most authorities recommend that compensation and incentive plans link rewards to only two or three aspects of job performance. They should be linked to those aspects

---

[5] The following discussion is based on Richard C. Smyth and Matthew J. Murphy, *Compensating and Motivating Salesmen* (New York: American Management Association, 1969), Chapter 5.

Table 14–1
Sales activities and performance
outcomes that might be ecouraged
by compensation and incentive
programs

Sell a greater overall dollar volume.
Increase sales of more profitable products.
Push new products.
Push selected items at designated seasons.
Achieve a higher degree of market penetration by products, kinds of customers, or
    territories.
Secure large average orders.
Secure new customers.
Service and maintain existing business.
Reduce turnover of customers.
Achieve full-line (balanced) selling.
Reduce direct selling costs.
Increase the number of calls made.
Submit reports and other data promptly.

Source: Richard C. Smyth and Matthew J. Murphy, *Compensating and Motivatng Salesmen* (New York: American Management Association, Inc., 1969), pp. 47–48.

consistent with the firm's highest-priority sales and marketing objectives.[6] Other aspects of the sales force's behavior and performance should be directed and controlled through effective training programs and supervision by field sales managers.

Assessing Salespeople's Valences and Choosing an Attractive Mix of Rewards

As mentioned, all salespeople do not find the same rewards equally attractive. Salespeople may be more or less satisfied with their current attainment of a given reward, and this causes them to have different valences for more of that reward. Similarly, people's needs for a particular reward vary, depending on their personalities, demographic characteristics, and lifestyles. Consequently, no single reward—including money—is likely to be effective for motivating all of a firm's salespeople. Similarly, a mix of rewards that is effective for motivating a sales force at one time may lose its appeal as the members' personal circumstances and needs change and as new salespeople are hired. In view of this, a wise preliminary step in designing a sales compensation and incentive package is for a firm to determine its salespeople's current valences for the various rewards that might be incorporated in such a package. This could be done with a simple survey in which

[6] Ibid., pp. 48–49.

each salesperson is asked to rate the attractiveness of specific increases of various rewards on a numerical scale, say from zero to 100. Also, one of the techniques specifically aimed at assessing a person's preferences could be used, such as conjoint analysis.[7]

Today, few managers actually carry out such surveys when designing motivation programs because they believe they know their salespeople's needs and desires well enough. Yet, when salespeople's actual valences for rewards have been compared with their managers' perceptions of those valences, the managers' perceptions sometimes turn out to be very inaccurate. For example, in one large firm, top sales executives believed that their recognition program was an important reward in the eyes of their salespeople. In a subsequent survey of those salespeople's actual valences, however, it was discovered that they rated recognition as the least attractive of seven alternative rewards. Rather than offering rewards that managers think their subordinates find attractive, it may well be worth the time and trouble to conduct a study of salespeople's actual valences for rewards before designing a motivation program.

Determining the Appropriate Level of Total Compensation

The total amount of compensation a salesperson receives affects his or her satisfaction with pay and with the company, as well as his or her valence for more pay in the future. Thus, the decision about how much total compensation (base pay plus any commissions or bonuses) a salesperson may earn is crucial in designing an effective motivation program. The starting point for making this decision is to determine the gross amount of compensation that is necessary to attract, retain, and motivate the right type of salespeople. This, in turn, depends on the type of sales job in question, the size of both the firm and the sales force, and the sales management policies of the company.

Average compensation varies substantially in different types of sales jobs. In general, more complex and demanding sales jobs, which require salespeople with special qualifications, offer higher pay than more routine sales jobs. To compete for the best talent, a firm should determine how much total compensation other firms in its industry or related ones pay people in similar jobs. Then the firm can consciously decide whether to pay its salespeople an amount average in relation to what others are paying or to pay above average. Few companies consciously pay below average (although some do so without realizing it) because below-average compensation generally cannot attract the right level of selling talent.

The decision about whether to offer average total pay or a premium level of compensation depends on the size of the firm and its sales force. Large firms with

---

[7] Rene Y. Darmon, "Setting Sales Quotas with Conjoint Analysis," *Journal of Marketing Research* 16 (February 1979), pp. 133–40.

good reputations in their industries and large sales forces (more than 75 or 100 salespeople) generally offer only average or slightly below average compensation. Such firms can attract sales talent because of their reputation in the marketplace and because they are big enough to offer advancement into management. Also, such firms can hire younger people (often just out of school) as sales trainees and put them through an extensive training program. This allows them to pay relatively low gross compensation levels, since they do not have to pay a marketplace premium to attract older, experienced salespeople. On the other hand, smaller firms with sales forces of fewer than 25 people often cannot afford extensive sales training programs. Consequently, they must often pay above-average levels of compensation to attract experienced salespeople from other companies. One survey found that firms with fewer than 25 salespeople paid total compensation that was about 5 percent higher than the average for other firms in their industries.[8]

Dangers of Paying Too Much

Some firms, regardless of their size or position in their industries, follow a deliberate policy of offering their salespeople opportunities to make very large amounts of financial compensation. For example, in the late 1960s, a paint and varnish company with $6 million in annual sales had 30 salespeople who were paid a straight commission. Six of those earned more than $40,000 a year, and two made more than $50,000—while the company president's salary and bonus amounted to only $42,000.[9] The rationale for this policy is that opportunities for high pay will attract the best talent and motivate members of the sales force to continue working for higher and higher sales volumes. As some managers say, "We don't care how much we pay our salespeople, since their compensation relates to their volume of sales."

Overpaying salespeople relative to what other firms pay for similar jobs and relative to what other employees in the same firm are paid for nonsales jobs can cause major problems, however. For one thing, compensation is usually the largest single element of a firm's selling costs. Therefore, overpaying salespeople unnecessarily increases selling costs and reduces the firm's profits. Also, it can cause resentment and low morale among the firm's other employees and executives when salespeople earn more money than even top management. It then becomes virtually impossible to promote good salespeople into managerial positions because of the financial sacrifice they would have to make. Finally, it is not clear that offering unlimited opportunities to earn higher pay is always an effective way to motivate continually increasing selling effort. "Need theory," for ex-

---

[8] Smyth and Murphy, *Compensating and Motivating Salesmen*, Chapter 3.
[9] Ibid., p. 26.

ample, suggests that when salespeople reach a compensation level that they consider satisfactory, their valences for still more money are likely to be reduced. Indeed, one empirical study found that most salespeople tend to work toward a "satisfactory" level of compensation rather than to maximize their pay.[10]

Dangers of Paying Too Little

Whereas overpaying salespeople can cause problems, it is equally important not to underpay them. Holding down sales compensation may appear to be a convenient way to hold down selling costs and enhance profits, but this is usually not true in the long run. When buying talent in the labor market, a company tends to get what it pays for. If poor salespeople are hired at low pay, poor performance will almost surely result. If good salespeople are hired at low pay, the firm is likely to have a high rate of turnover in the sales force, with higher costs for recruiting and training replacements and lost sales.

Choosing the Most Effective Form of Financial Compensation

The three major methods of compensating salespeople are: (1) straight salary, (2) straight commission, and (3) a combination of base salary plus incentive pay in the form of commissions, bonuses, or both. Over the past 30 years, there has been a steady trend away from using both straight salary and straight commission plans toward combination plans. Today, combination plans are the most common form of compensation, as the survey results in Table 14–2 show.

Table 14–2
Proportion of different types of firms using straight salary, straight commission, and combination compensation plans

Type of Plan	Manufacturers (n = 249)	Service Companies (n = 50)	Wholesalers and Distributors (n = 124)
Straight salary	18.6%	24.0%	7.3%
Straight commission	14.2	14.0	13.3
Commission plus draw	0.8	10.0	25.8
Salary plus incentive	66.3	52.0	43.2

Source: "There Has To Be a Better Way," *Sales & Marketing Management*, November 12, 1979, pp. 41–42.

[10] Rene Y. Darmon, "Salesmen's Responses to Financial Incentives," *Journal of Marketing Research* 38 (July 1974), pp. 39–46.

Another fact that you should note concerning the data presented in Table 14–2 is that the use of the various types of compensation plans varies greatly across different industries. This suggests that all three types of plans have unique advantages for motivating specific kinds of sales performance under particular circumstances. Therefore, the advantages and limitations of each type of compensation plan and the conditions under which each is most appropriate are now discussed.

Straight Salary

A *salary* is a fixed sum of money paid at regular intervals. The amount paid to the salesperson is a function of the amount of time worked rather than any specific performance.

Two sets of conditions favor the use of a straight salary compensation plan. These are (1) when management wishes to motivate salespeople to achieve objectives other than short-run sales volume, and (2) when the individual salesperson's impact on sales volume is difficult to measure in a reasonable time.

The primary advantage of a straight salary is that management can require salespeople to spend their time on activities that may not result in immediate sales. Therefore, a salary plan or a plan offering a large proportion of fixed salary is appropriate when the salesperson is expected to perform many account servicing or other nonselling activities. These may include market research, customer problem analysis, stocking, or sales promotion. Straight salary plans are also common in industries where a great deal of engineering and design services are required as part of the selling function, such as in the aerospace and other high-technology industries.

Straight salary compensation plans are also desirable when it is difficult for management to measure the individual salesperson's actual impact on sales volume or other aspects of performance. Thus, firms tend to pay salaries to their sales force when: (1) their salespeople are engaged in missionary selling, as in the pharmaceutical industry; (2) other parts of the marketing program, such as advertising or dealer promotions, are the primary determinants of sales success, as in some consumer packaged goods businesses; or (3) the selling process is complex and involves a team or multilevel selling effort, as in the case of computers or atomic reactors.

Straight salary plans have the advantage of providing salespeople with a steady, guaranteed income. Thus, salary compensation plans are often used when the salesperson's ability to generate immediate sales is uncertain, as in the case of new recruits in a field-training program or when a firm is introducing a new product line or opening new territories.

Finally, salary plans are easy for management to compute and administer.

Figure 14–3
Relative costs of salary and
commission compensation plans

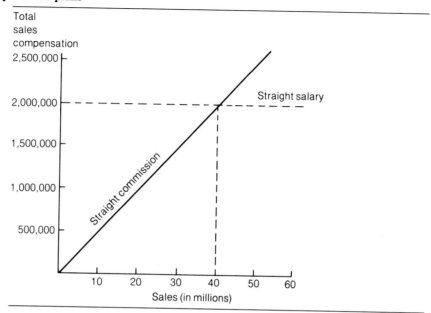

Note: This firm has 100 salespeople, and it has the option of paying each of them a salary of $20,000 per year or a 5 percent commission on net sales. As you can see, the salary plan results in higher compensation costs at sales volumes below $40 million, but lower costs at volumes above $40 million.

They also give management more flexibility. It is easy to reassign salespeople to new territories or product lines because they do not have to worry about how such changes will affect their sales volumes. Also, since salaries are fixed costs, the compensation cost per unit sold is lower at relatively high levels of sales volume, as shown in Figure 14–3.

The major limitation of straight salary compensation is that financial rewards are not tied directly to any specific aspect of job performance. Management should attempt to give bigger salary increases each year to the good performers than those given to the poor ones. However, the amount of those increases and the way performance is evaluated are subject to the whims of the manager who makes the decision. Consequently, the salesperson is likely to have lower and less accurate instrumentality perceptions about how much more money he or she is likely to receive as the result of a given increase in sales volume, profitability, or the like. In other words, salaries do not provide any direct financial incentive for improving sales related aspects of performance. Consequently, salary plans appeal more to security-oriented rather than achievement-oriented salespeople.

Straight Commission

A commission is payment for achieving a given level of performance. Salespeople are paid for results. Usually, commission payments are based on the salesperson's dollar or unit sales volume. However, it is becoming more popular for firms to base commissions on the profitability of sales to motivate the sales force to expend effort on the most profitable products or customers. The most common way of accomplishing this is to offer salespeople variable commissions, where relatively high commissions are paid for sales of the most profitable products or sales to the most profitable accounts. Likewise, lower rates are paid for sales of less profitable products or to less profitable customers. This was the kind of commission plan used by the Fitwell Company.

Direct motivation is the key advantage of a commission compensation plan. There is a direct link between sales performance and the financial compensation the salesperson earns. Consequently, salespeople are strongly motivated to improve their sales productivity to increase their compensation, at least until they reach such high pay that further increases become less attractive. Commission plans also have a built-in element of fairness (if sales territories are properly defined with about equal potential), because good performers are automatically rewarded, whereas poor performers are discouraged from continuing their low productivity.

Commission plans have some advantages from an administrative view point. Commissions are usually easy to compute and administer. Also, compensation costs vary directly with sales volume. This is an advantage for firms that are short on working capital because they do not need to worry about paying high wages to the sales force unless it generates high sales revenues.

On the other hand, straight commission compensation plans have some important limitations that have caused many firms to abandon them. Perhaps the most critical weakness is that management has very little control over the sales force. When all their financial rewards are tied directly to sales volume, it is difficult to motivate salespeople to engage in account management activities that do not lead directly to short-term sales. Consequently, salespeople on commission are likely to "milk" existing customers rather than work to develop new accounts. They may overstock their customers and neglect service after the sale. Finally, they have little motivation to engage in market analysis and other administrative duties that take time away from actual selling activities.

Straight commission plans also have a disadvantage for many salespeople. Such plans make a salesperson's earnings unstable and hard to predict. When business conditions are poor, turnover rates in the sales force are likely to be high because salespeople find it hard to live on the low earnings produced by poor sales.

To combat the inherent instability of commission plans, some firms provide their salespeople with a *drawing account*. Money is advanced to salespeople in months when commissions are low to ensure that they will always take home a specified minimum amount of pay each month. The amount of the salesperson's "draw" in poor months is subsequently deducted from his or her earned commissions when sales improve. This gives salespeople some secure salary, and it allows management more control over their activities. A problem arises, however, when a salesperson fails to earn enough commissions to repay his or her draw. Then the person may quit or be fired, and the company must absorb the loss.

Combination Plans

As indicated by the survey results in Table 14–1, compensation plans that offer a base salary plus some proportion of incentive pay are by far the most popular. They have many of the advantages but avoid most of the limitations of both straight salary and straight commission plans. The base salary provides the salesperson with a stable income and gives management some capability to reward salespeople for performing customer servicing and administrative tasks that are not directly related to short-term sales. At the same time, the incentive portion of such compensation plans provides direct rewards to motivate the salesperson to expend effort to improve his or her sales volume or profitability.

Combination plans combine a base salary with commissions, bonuses, or both. When salary plus commission is used, the commissions are tied to sales volume or profitability, just as with a straight commission plan. The only difference is that the commissions are smaller in a combination plan than when the salesperson is compensated solely by commission.

A *bonus* is a payment made at the discretion of management for achieving or surpassing some set level of performance. Whereas, commissions are typically paid for each sale that is made, a bonus is typically not paid until the salesperson surpasses some level of total sales or other aspect of performance. When the salesperson reaches the minimum level of performance required to earn a bonus, however, the size of the bonus might be determined by the degree to which he or she exceeds that minimum. Thus, bonuses are usually additional incentives to motivate salespeople to reach high levels of performance, rather than as part of the basic compensation plan.

Attaining quota is often the minimum requirement for a salesperson to earn a bonus. As mentioned in Chapter 8, quotas can be based on sales volume, profitability of sales, or other account-servicing activities. Therefore, bonuses can be offered as a reward for attaining or surpassing a predetermined level of performance on any performance dimensions for which quotas are set. Indeed, some complex bonus plans use a point system to tie the bonus to the accomplishment of two or more performance objectives. An example of such a point-bonus plan is described in Table 14–3.

Table 14–3
A point system for basing bonus payments on two performance dimensions

An industrial chemical manufacturer pays its salespeople a base salary of $15,000 per year. An annual sales quota is established for each salesperson, and the sum of the quotas equals the firm's annual sales forecast.

The incentive plan is divided into two parts. Part I provides that each salesperson who meets or exceeds quota receives 10 bonus points. In addition, for each 2 percent of sales in excess of quota, each salesperson receives an additional bonus point up to a maximum of 20 points per year on Part I of the plan.

Part II of the plan provides bonus points for bringing in new accounts. A new account is defined as one that has not placed an order during the preceding 36 months. Bonus points are granted to salespeople for new accounts as follows:

Annual Purchase Volume by New Account	Bonus points Received by Salesperson
$ 5,000–25,000	1
25,001–50,000	2
50,001–100,000	3
100,001 and up	4

Each salesperson is limited to a maximum of 20 bonus points per year on Part II of the plan.

Bonus earnings are calclulated and paid annually. For each bonus point earned, the salesperson receives 1 percent of his or her salary. Thus, each salesperson can earn bonus payments up to a maximum of 40 percent of the salary.

Source: Based on a plan described in Richard C. Smyth and Matthew J. Murphy, *Compensating and Motivating Salesmen* (New York: American Management Association, 1969), pp. 127–29.

Other Issues in Designing Combination Plans

Whether base salary is combined with commission payments or bonuses, managers must answer several other questions in designing effective combination compensation plans. These include: (1) the appropriate size of the incentive relative to the base salary, (2) whether there should be a ceiling on incentive earnings, (3) when the salesperson should be credited with a sale, and (4) how often the salesperson should receive incentive payments.

What proportion of total compensation should be incentive pay? One of the most common reasons that combination plans are not very effective at motivating salespeople is that the incentive portion is too small to generate much interest. After studying the reasons for the success or failure of 180 compensation plans, two researchers concluded that "if the average successful salesman working under a sales incentive plan cannot make at least 25 percent of his gross earnings as incentive pay in the form of bonus or commissions, the plan will never be truly successful."[11]

---

[11] Smyth and Murphy, *Compensating and Motivating Salesmen*, p. 58.

Table 14–4
Variations in incentive payments in industry

Industry	Bonus or Commission Payments as a Percentage of Annual Gross Earnings
Household furniture	52%
Special industrial machinery	39
Household appliances	35
Molded plastic products	27
Machine tools	23
Pharmaceutical preparations	16
Electronic components	11
Industrial chemicals	7
Portland cement	3
Cigarettes	0

Source: Reprinted by permission of the *Harvard Business Review*. Adapted from an exhibit in "Financial Incentives for Salesmen" by Richard C. Smyth (January–February 1968). Copyright © 1968 by the President and Fellows of Harvard College; all rights reserved.

The 25 percent figure may be a good rule of thumb, but the actual ratio of incentive pay to total compensation varies substantially by industry, as Table 14–4 suggests. Another recent survey of more than 200 combination compensation plans also found that the relative size of incentive pay varied by type of plan. Plans offering a salary plus bonus based on one or more dimensions of total performance contained incentive pay that averaged only 11 percent of total compensation, while "salary plus commission" plans averaged 33 percent incentive pay.[12]

A manager's decision concerning what proportion of the overall compensation package is represented by incentive pay should be based on the company's objectives and the nature of the selling job. When the firm's primary objectives are directly related to short-term sales, such as increasing sales volume, profitability, or new customers, a large incentive component should be offered. On the other hand, when customer service and other nonsales objectives are deemed more important, the major emphasis should be placed on the base salary component of the plan. This gives management more control over the sales force's account management activities.

Similarly, when the salesperson's selling skill is the key to sales success, the incentive portion of compensation should be large. However, when the product has been presold through advertising and the salesperson is largely an order taker, or when the salesperson's job involves a large proportion of missionary or customer service work, the incentive component should be relatively small.

Should there be a ceiling on incentive earnings? Some compensation plans impose ceilings on incentive earnings. This ensures that top salespeople will not make such high earnings that it causes low morale among other employees. It

---

[12] Charles A. Peck, *Compensating Field Sales Representatives*, Report No. 828 (New York: The Conference Board, 1982), p. 14.

also protects against "windfalls"—such as at the introduction of successful new products—where a salesperson's earning might become very large without corresponding effort.

A strong argument can be made, however, that such ceilings have a bad effect on motivation and dampen the sales force's enthusiasm. Also, some salespeople may reach their earning maximum early in the year and be inclined to take it easy for the rest of the year.

As a compromise, one authority suggests that it might be acceptable to limit incentive earnings to 100 percent of base salary.[13] This should give the firm adequate protection yet offer an attractive enough opportunity to motivate salespeople.

Another way that some functions of ceilings can be accomplished without arbitrarily limiting the motivation of the sales force is for management to pretest any new or revised compensation plan before it is implemented. One way to do this is to apply the plan to the historical sales performance of selected salespeople. Particular attention should be given to the amount of compensation that would have been earned by the best and poorest performers to ensure that the compensation provided by the plan is both fair and reasonable.

When Is a Sale a Sale? When incentives are based on sales volume or other sales-related aspects of performance, the precise meaning of a sale should be defined to avoid confusion and irritation. Most plans credit a salesperson with a sale when the *order* is accepted by the company, less any returns and allowances. Occasionally, though, crediting the salesperson with a sale only after the goods have been shipped or payment is received from the customer makes good sense. This is particularly true when the time between receipt of an order and shipment of the goods is long and the company wants its salespeople to maintain close contact with the customer during this time to prevent cancellations and other problems. As a compromise, some plans credit their salespeople with half a sale when the order is received and the other half when payment is actually made by the customer.

When Should the Salesperson Receive Incentive Payments? One survey of over 200 compensation plans found that 31 percent paid salespeople incentive earnings on an annual basis, 8 percent paid semiannually, 28 percent paid quarterly, and 32 percent made monthly payments. In general, plans offering salary plus commissions were more likely to involve monthly incentive payments, while salary plus bonus plans more often made incentive payments on a quarterly or annual schedule.[14]

Shorter time intervals between performance and the receipt of rewards increase the motivating power of the plan. However, short intervals add to the amount of computation required, increase administrative expenses, and may make the absolute amount of money received by the salespeople appear so small that they may not be very impressed with their rewards. Consequently, many authorities argue that quarterly incentive payments are an effective compromise.

---

[13] Smyth and Murphy, *Compensating and Motivating Salesmen*, p. 66.
[14] Peck, *Compensating Field Sales Representatives*, p. 10.

A Summary Overview of Financial Compensation Methods

The above discussion indicates that combination plans pose more prickly administrative and control problems than either straight salary or straight commission plans. This may be one reason why combination plans are more commonly found in larger firms than in smaller ones (i.e. firms with sales volume less than $40 million per year).[15] In spite of such problems, however, the offsetting advantages offered by combination plans make them the most popular method of compensating salespeople. But as we have seen, all three types of plans have some unique advantages and limitations that make each of them particularly well suited for use in certain circumstances. Those advantages, limitations and uses are summarized in Table 14–5.

The Reimbursement of Selling Expenses

The costs associated with the average field sales call rose faster than the overall rate of inflation during the 1970s and early 1980s. From 1974 to 1981, selling costs—including both compensation for salespeople and their travel, lodging, meals, entertainment and auto expenses—rose an average of almost ten percent a year. While the annual rate of increase fell to below six percent during the early 1980s, the cost of a sales call by 1982 had reached an average of between $80 and more than $150, as shown in Table 14–6.[16]

Of course, a large proportion of such selling costs consists of the compensation paid to the salespeople. Consequently, costs vary greatly across different kinds of selling jobs, with more highly skilled (and highly paid) types of salespeople generating higher annual selling costs, as indicated by the figures in Table 14–7. However, the table also indicates that a substantial part of total selling costs is made up of expense items incurred by the salesperson in the field, including travel, lodging, meals, entertainment, and the costs of an automobile. In some cases, such expense items can add up to an amount equal to the salesperson's total compensation.

As mentioned in Chapters 3 and 4, recent increases in and high levels of selling costs have caused many sales managers to question the economic feasi-

---

[15] Alan J. Dubinsky and Thomas E. Barry, "A Survey of Sales Management Practices," *Industrial Marketing Management* 11 (1982), p. 137.

[16] Thayer C. Taylor, "Sales Call Costs in a Holding Pattern," *Sales & Marketing Management*, February 21, 1983, p. 36. One reason why the various estimates of sales-call costs vary so widely is that different surveys focus on different types of selling. Cahners' survey, for example, samples only industrial firms whose selling costs per call tend to be high, while *Sales & Marketing Management* includes consumer goods and service firms in its study.

Table 14–5
Characteristics of compensation methods for sales personnel

Compensation Method	Frequency of Use	Especially Useful	Advantages	Disadvantages
Straight salary	18%	When compensating new salespersons; when firm moves into new sales territories that require developmental work; when salespersons need to perform many nonselling activities	Provides salesperson with maximum amount of security; gives sales manager large amount of control over salespersons; easy to administer; yields more predictable selling expenses	Provides no incentive; necessitates closer supervision of salespersons' activities; during sales declines, selling expenses remain at same level
Straight commission	9%	When highly aggressive selling is required; when nonselling tasks are minimized; when company cannot closely control sales force activities	Provides maximum amount of incentive; by increasing commission rate, sales managers can encourage salespersons to sell certain items; selling expenses relate directly to sales resources	Salespersons have little financial security; sales manager has minimum control over sales force; may cause salespeople to provide inadequate service to smaller accounts; selling costs less predictable
Combination	73%	When sales territories have relatively similar sales potentials; when firm wishes to provide incentive but still control sales force activities	Provides certain level of financial security; provides some incentive; selling expenses fluctuate with sales revenue; sales manager has some control over salespersons nonselling activities	Selling expenses less predictable; may be difficult to administer

Table 14–6
Estimates of the average cost of a sales call*

	Cost-per-Call Estimates			
	1979	1980	1981	1982
Sales & Marketing Management Survey....	$69.40	$ 72.65	$ 76.85	$ 81.25
Cahners	N.A.	128.53	142.95	152.75
Dartnell	71.90	N.A.	106.91	N.A.

N.A. = Not available.
*Includes salesperson's compensation, and travel, entertainment, meals, lodging, and auto expenses.
Source: Adapted from Thayer C. Tayler, "Sales Call Costs in a Holding Pattern," *Sales & Marketing Management*, February 12, 1983, p. 36.

Table 14–7
Annual direct sales costs for different types of selling jobs

	Range Of Yearly Direct Sales Costs			
Type of Salespersons*	Compensation		Average Expenses†	Total
	Range	Average		
Account representative	$19,100–51,600	$35,350	$7,000–13,900	$42,350–49,250
Detail salesperson	19,500–41,000	30,250	7,500–17,500	37,750–47,750
Sales engineer	25,500–51,000	38,250	8,800–22,100	47,050–60,350
Industrial products salesperson	20,400–60,000	40,200	5,800–31,300	46,000–71,500
Service salesperson	20,000–57,700	38,850	6,600–26,300	45,450–65,150

*Definitions:
Account representative—A salesperson who calls on a large number of already established customers. Much of this selling is low key and there is minimal pressure to develop new business.
Detail salesperson—A salesperson who, instead of directly soliciting an order, concentrates on performing promotional activities and introducing products.
Sales engineer—A salesperson who sells products for which technical know-how and the ability to discuss technical aspects of the product are extremely important. The salesperson's expertise in identifying, analyzing, and solving customer problems is another critical factor.
Industrial products salesperson, nontechnical—This salesperson sells a tangible product to industrial or commercial purchasers; no high degree of technical knowledge is required.
Service salesperson—A salesperson who sells intangibles, such as insurance and advertising.
†Includes average travel, entertainment, meals, lodging, and auto expenses.
Source: Thayer C. Taylor, "Sales Call Costs in a Holding Pattern," *Sales & Marketing Management*, February 12, 1983, p. 38.

bility of having field salespeople make face-to-face calls on smaller customers, and to turn to telemarketing and other account management policies for reducing the expenses involved in servicing smaller firms. A second response to cost increases has been a search for improved methods of expense control. To this end, many firms have experimented with a variety of expense reimbursement

Table 14–8
**Percentage of large and small
(annual sales less than $40 million)
firms that "extensively use" various
expense reimbursement plans**

Reimbursement Plans	Percent of Small Firms	Percent of Large Firms
Unlimited payment plan (full reimbursement, receipts and expense reports submitted)	85%	91%
Expense plan with adjustments for variations	11	26
Limited payment plan (advance lump sum for all expenses for a given time period)	11	16
Salespeople pay all their own expenses	11	19
Honor system (full reimbursement, no receipts nor expense reports submitted)	1	0
Flat allowance plan (fixed sum per expense item)	1	2

Source: Alan J. Dubinsky and Thomas E. Barry, "A Survey of Sales Management Practices," *Industrial Marketing Management* 11 (1982), p. 137.

plans. Such plans range from unlimited reimbursement for all "reasonable and allowable" expenses to plans where the salesperson must pay all expenses out of his or her total compensation. A number of variations in expense reimbursement plans and their frequency of use by large and small firms is shown in Table 14–8.

A major dilemma facing sales managers when deciding which form of expense reimbursement plan to use is that there are often tradeoffs involved between tight control aimed at holding down total expenses on the one hand, and the financial well-being—and the subsequent motivation level—of salespeople on the other. This is because some expense items—such as entertainment expenses, club dues, and the costs of personal services while the salesperson is away from home—can be considered either legitimate business expenses that should be reimbursed by the company or personal expenses that should be paid for by the salesperson. Obviously, company policies and reimbursement plans that treat such costs as business expenses have the effect of increasing the salesperson's total financial compensation but at the same time increase the firm's total selling costs. The issue of expense control, and some techniques that firms might use to improve their control over selling expenses are discussed in more detail in Chapter 16. Since different reimbursement plans have an impact on the effective financial compensation received by,and the motivation level of, a firm's salespeople, however, some of the relative advantages and limitations of alternative plans and policies are discussed now.

Direct Reimbursement Plans

As Table 14–8 shows, the most popular type of expense reimbursement plan among both small and large companies is one involving direct and unlimited reimbursement of all "allowable and reasonable" expenses. In almost all cases, however, reimbursement under such plans is contingent upon the salesperson submitting receipts or detailed records justifying his or her expense claims. The disadvantage of such plans is that the processing and evaluation of expense claims add to the firm's sales administration costs. On the other hand, the primary advantage is that such plans give the sales manager some control over both the total magnitude of sales expenses and over the kinds of activities his or her salespeople will be motivated to engage in. If a particular activity—such as entertaining potential new accounts—is thought to be an important ingredient of the firm's account management policies, salespeople can be encouraged to engage in that activity by being informed that all related expenses will be liberally reimbursed. On the other hand, managers can discourage their subordinates from spending time on unimportant tasks by refusing to reimburse expenditures for such activities. Thus, company policies concerning reimbursable expenses can be a useful tool for motivating and directing sales effort. Indeed, more than a quarter of the large firms surveyed in the study shown in Table 14–8 reported that they adjusted their expense reimbursement policies according to the differences in the territories covered or the job activities required of different members of their sales forces. For example, some firms reimburse a broader range and higher levels of expenses for their national account managers than for members of their regular field sales force. The results of a survey of company reimbursement policies concerning a variety of different expense items are displayed in Table 14–9.

Limited Reimbursement Plans

Some firms limit the total amount of expense reimbursement, either by setting maximum limits for each expense item (e.g., a policy which limits reimbursement for restaurant meals to $25 per person), or by providing each salesperson with a predetermined lump-sum payment to cover total expenses. This approach has the advantage of keeping total selling expenses within planned limits; limits which are often determined by the sales expense budget set at the beginning of the year. In some cases, budgeted expense amounts may vary across members of the sales force, depending on the past or forecasted sales volume or the requirements of their territories. Unless the budgeted limits are based on an accurate understanding of the costs associated with successful sales performance in each territory, however, these kinds of plans can have a negative effect on motivation

Table 14–9
Company policies regarding expense items

ITEMS USUALLY REGARDED AS REIMBURSABLE EXPENDITURES FOR SALESPEOPLE

Expense Item	Normally Percent	Only on Special Occasions Percent	Never Percent
Air transportation			
First class	7.3%	67.5%	25.1%
Coach	96.4	2.7	0.9
Charges for excess baggage	53.4	35.2	11.4
Travel insurance	12.6	5.4	82.0
Cocktails—salesperson alone	30.7	14.7	54.6
Cocktails—with customer	86.7	10.2	3.1
Taxis or other local transportation	96.9	2.6	0.4
Gratuities and tips	96.9	1.8	1.3
Temporary secretary while away from office	10.3	53.1	36.6
Office supplies/equipment while away from office	41.7	43.0	15.4
Personal entertainment	4.5%	20.5%	75.0%
Doctor/dentist while away from office	4.5	24.1	71.4
Travel expenses for wife	0.9	69.5	29.6
Postage/telephone/telegraphs to home	69.5	23.5	7.1
Valet/laundry while away from office	58.2	31.6	10.2
Barber/manicurist/bootblack while away from office	4.1	11.3	84.7
Theft/loss/damage to personal effects while away from office	17.2	41.2	41.6

ENTERTAINMENT EXPENSES REGARDED AS ALLOWABLE FOR SALESPEOPLE'S BUSINESS PURPOSES

Expense Item	Normally Percent	Only on Special Occasions Percent	Never Percent
Restaurants	96.5%	3.1%	0.4%
Nightclubs	39.0	48.9	12.1
Sporting events	37.7	46.6	15.7
Cocktail parties	30.5	55.2	14.3
Theatre	28.4	47.3	24.3
Club dues	25.2%	33.8%	41.0%
Movies	22.6	33.6	43.8
At home	14.5	55.5	30.0
Hunting/fishing trips	12.8	42.0	45.2

Note: May not add up to 100 percent because of rounding.
Source: "Survey of Selling Costs," *Sales & Marketing Management*, February 21, 1977, p. 21.

and sales performance. Individual salespeople may feel that their ability to do a good job is constrained by tight-fisted company expense reimbursement policies. Rather than pay for necessary activities out of their own pocket, salespeople are likely to avoid or cut back on certain expense activities in order to keep their costs within their budgets.

No Reimbursement Plans

A variation of the advanced lump-sum plan still found in some firms is a policy of requiring each salesperson to cover all of his or her own expenses. Such plans usually involve paying the salesperson a relatively high amount of total financial compensation to help cover necessary expenses. Indeed, such plans are most commonly associated with "straight commission" compensation plans involving high percentage commissions. The rationale is that salespeople will be motivated to spend both the effort and money necessary to increase sales volume as long as the resulting financial rewards are big enough to be worthwhile.[17] Since these plans are simply a variation of the "limited reimbursement" plans discussed previously, they have similar advantages and limitations. They help the firm limit sales expenses, or—in the case of commission plans—make them a totally variable cost which moves up and down with changes in sales volume. On the other hand, they sacrifice management control over the motivation and types of activities engaged in by members of the salesforce.

Sales Contests

Sales contests are short-term incentive programs designed to motivate sales personnel to accomplish very specific sales objectives. Although contests should not be considered part of the firm's ongoing compensation plan, they do offer salespeople the opportunity to gain financial, as well as nonfinancial, rewards. Contest winners often receive prizes in cash or merchandise or travel, which have monetary value. Winners also receive nonfinancial rewards in the form of recognition and a sense of accomplishment.

Successful contests require the following:

1. Clearly defined, specific objectives.
2. An exciting theme.
3. Reasonable probability of rewards for all salespeople.
4. Attractive rewards.
5. Promotion and follow-through.

---

[17] A comparison of expense practices by type of compensation plan is found in John P. Steinbrink, "How To Pay Your Salesforce," *Harvard Business Review* 56 (July-August 1978), pp. 114–21.

Contest Objectives

Since contests are designed to supplement the firm's compensation program and to motivate extra effort toward the accomplishment of some short term goal, their objectives should be very specific and clearly defined. One survey found that the following were the most common objectives of sales contests: (1) to obtain new customers (65 percent of the contests surveyed), (2) to promote the sale of specific items (44 percent), (3) to generate larger orders per sales call (42 percent), (4) to offset seasonal sales weaknesses (41 percent), and (5) to stimulate the introduction of a new product (37 percent).[18]

The period of time in which the contest's objectives are to be achieved should be relatively short. This ensures that the salespeople will maintain their enthusiasm and effort throughout the contest. On the other hand, the contest should be long enough to allow all members of the sales force to cover their territories at least once and to have a reasonable chance of generating the performance necessary to win. Therefore, the average sales contest lasts about three months.

Contest Themes

A sales contest should have an exciting theme to help build enthusiasm among the participants and promote the event. The theme should be designed to stress the contest's objectives and to appeal to all participants. Sports themes, such as "a sales superbowl" or "world series," are popular because they provide a competitive atmosphere.

Probability of Winning

There are three popular contest formats. In some contests, salespeople compete with themselves by trying to attain individual quotas. Everyone who reaches or exceeds quota during the contest period wins. A second form requires that all members of the sales force compete with each other. The people who achieve the highest overall performance on some dimension are the winners and everyone else loses. A third format organizes the sales force into teams, which compete for group and individual prizes.

Whichever format is used, every member of the sales force should have a reasonable chance of winning an award. If there are to be only one or a few winners, many salespeople may feel that their chances of coming out on top are

---

[18] Albert Haring and Malcolm L. Morris, "Sales Contests as a Motivating Device," in *Readings in Sales Management: Concepts and Viewpoints*, ed. Thomas R. Wotruba and Robert M. Olsen (New York: Holt, Rinehart & Winston, 1971), pp. 290–95.

remote. Consequently, their instrumentality perceptions of the likelihood of winning are low and they are not motivated to expend much effort to win. As one sales executive put it, "The percentage of winners you get is very important. If you have only a few winners, the salesmen say, 'See, I told you the goals were unrealistic.' You get much better reaction if you can come in with 40 percent to 50 percent of your men winners."[19] In this respect, contests that provide rewards to everyone who meets their quotas during the contest period are desirable. The number of possible winners is not arbitrarily limited, and everyone has a chance for a reward.

Type of Rewards

Contest rewards can take the form of cash, merchandise or travel. As Table 14–10 indicates, cash is the most commonly used form of reward because individual winners can spend it on whatever they find most attractive.

Table 14–10
Types of contest awards used by 168 firms

Type of Award	Percentage of Firms Using
Cash	62%
Merchandise	53
Travel	42

Source: *Sales & Marketing Management,* April 7, 1980, p. 58.

Whatever form of reward is used, the monetary value must be large enough to be attractive to the participants, given their level of compensation. A portable TV, for example, may be more attractive where the average salesperson makes $15,000 per year than where the average compensation is $40,000. One authority recommends that contest awards should be worth the equivalent of at least one week's compensation of the average person in the sales force.[20]

Promotion and Follow-through

To generate interest and enthusiasm, contests should be launched with fanfare. For this firms announce their contests at national or regional sales meetings. Follow-up promotion is also necessary to maintain interest throughout the con-

---

[19] Sally Scanlon, "A New Role for Incentives," *Sales and Marketing Management,* April 7, 1975, p. 43.
[20] Benson P. Shapiro, *Sales Program Management: Formulation and Implementation* (New York: McGraw-Hill, 1977), p. 309.

test period. As the contest proceeds, salespeople should be given frequent feedback concerning their progress so they know how much more they must do to win an award. Finally, winners should be recognized within the company and prizes should be awarded promptly.

Criticisms of Sales Contests

Although many sales managers believe that contests are effective for motivating special efforts from their salespeople, contests can cause a few potential problems, particularly if they are poorly designed or used.

Some critics argue that contests designed to stimulate sales volume may produce results that are largely illusory, with no lasting improvement in market share. Salespeople may "borrow" sales from before and/or after the contest to increase their volume during the contest. They may hold back orders prior to the start of the contest and rush orders that would normally not be placed until after the contest is over. As a result, customers may be overstocked, and sales volume falls off for some time after the contest is over.

Contests may also have a negative impact on the cohesiveness and morale of the company's salespeople. This is particularly true when plans force individual salespeople to compete with one another for rewards and when the number of rewards is limited.

Finally, some firms have a tendency to use sales contests to "cover up" faulty compensation plans. Sales personnel should not have to be compensated a second time for what they are already being paid to do. Thus, contests should be used only on a short-term basis to motivate special efforts beyond the normal performance expected of the sales force. If a firm conducts frequent contests to maintain an acceptable level of sales performance, it should reexamine its entire compensation and incentive program.

Nonfinancial Rewards

Promotion and Career Paths

As Table 14–1 suggests, sales managers consider opportunities for promotion and advancement second only to special recognition as an effective sales motivator. This is particularly true for young, well-educated salespeople who tend to view their jobs as stepping-stones to top management. Unfortunately, salespeople's valences for promotion tend to decline in many companies as they get older, particularly when they have been with the firm for 10 years or more.[21] One rea-

---

[21] Gilbert A. Churchill, Jr., Neil M. Ford, and Orville C. Walker, Jr., "Personal Characteristics of Salespeople and the Attractiveness of Alternative Rewards," *Journal of Business Research* 7 (1979), pp. 25–50.

son is that many firms do not provide many promotion opportunities for their salespeople. The common career path is from salesperson to district sales manager to top sales management. Thus, if a person has been with a firm for several years without making it into sales management, he or she may start to believe that such a promotion will never happen. Consequently, older salespeople may concentrate solely on financial rewards, or they may lose motivation and not work as hard at their jobs.[22]

To overcome this problem, some firms have instituted two different career paths for their salespeople. One leads to management positions for promising candidates, while the other leads to more advanced positions within the sales force. The latter usually involve responsibility for dealing with key accounts or leading sales teams. In this system, even though a salesperson may not make it into management, he or she can still work toward a more prestigious and lucrative position within the sales force. To make advanced sales positions more attractive as promotions, many firms provide people in those positions with additional perquisites ("perks"), including higher compensation, a better automobile, and better office facilities.

Recognition Programs

Contest awards and promotions provide recognition for good performance, but many firms also have separate recognition programs to provide nonmonetary rewards. As with contests, effective recognition programs should offer a reasonable chance of winning for everyone in the sales force. On the other hand, if a very large proportion of the sales force achieves recognition, the program is likely to lose some of its appeal because the winners feel no special sense of accomplishment.

Consequently, better recognition programs often recognize the best performers for several different performance dimensions. For example, winners might include persons with the highest sales volume for the year, the biggest percentage increase in sales, the biggest dollar increase, the highest penetration of territory potential, and the largest sales per account.

One thing that makes recognition attractive as a reward—besides the feeling of accomplishment—is that a person's peers and superiors are made aware of his or her outstanding performance. Therefore, communication of the winner's achievements, through recognition at a sales meeting, publicity in the local press, announcements in the company's internal newsletter, or other ways, is an essential part of a good program. Also, firms typically give special awards as part of their recognition program, as shown in Table 14–11.

---

[22] For a more detailed discussion of the problems involved in motivating older salespeple, see Marvin A. Jolson, "The Salesman's Career Cycle," *Journal of Marketing* 38 (July 1974), pp. 39–46.

Table 14–11
**Awards given in recognition
programs and their popularity**

	Percentage Who Use	Popularity Rating		
		Very Popular	Popular	Not Very Popular
Wall plaques	72.5%	43.2%	51.3%	5.5%
Trophies	39.2	45.0	50.0	5.0
Publicity—company	33.3	52.9	35.3	11.8
Membership in special sales club	25.5	38.5	61.5	0.0
Jewelry	23.5	50.0	33.3	16.7
Special meetings with top executives	21.6	63.6	27.3	9.1
Publicity—trade	19.6	60.0	30.0	10.0
Publicity—hometown	17.6	55.6	11.1	33.3
Special business cards	17.6	22.2	55.6	22.2
Other*	15.7	100.0	0.0	0.0

Who gives award?
Vice president, sales 42.3%
President 40.4
National sales manager 36.5
District manager 23.1
Vice president, marketing 1.9

Where is award given?
National sales meeting 67.3%
District sales meeting 28.8
Sales office 19.2
Other† 17.3

*Personalized gifts, cash, trips, nonpersonal merchandise, clothing.
†Regional sales meetings, home, parent-company dinner, trips, company publications, etc.
Source: "Leadership Panel—The Role of Recognition," *Sales & Marketing Management*, April 12, 1976, p. 45. Reprinted by permission from *Sales & Marketing* magazine, © 1976.

Summary

The sales manager concerned with motivating the members of the sales force needs to be concerned with the firm's compensation system. Which rewards do salespeople value? How much of each is optimum? How should the rewards be integrated in a total compensation system? This chapter sought to provide answers to these questions.

More specifically, the chapter suggested a framework that sales managers can use when designing compensation and incentive programs. The frame work includes the following steps: (1) assess the firm's marketing and sales objectives, account management policies, and current performance of the sales force; (2) determine the aspects of job performance that are to be rewarded; (3) assess personal characteristics of salespeople and their valences for alternative rewards; (4) determine the most attractive and motivating mix of rewards; (5) decide on the most appropriate level of total compensation; (6) decide whether incentive compensation is to be used and, if the answer is yes, what kind and proportion of total compensation it should represent; (7) decide on the appropriate types of nonfinancial incentives; and (8) communicate the program to the sales force.

A major purpose of any sales compensation program is to influence the sales force to do what management wants, the way they want it done, and within the desired time. These requirements are largely dictated by the firm's marketing and sales objectives and account management policies. The important first two steps, then, are to establish the most important objectives for the personal selling effort and to decide which priorities the compensation system should attempt to address.

The success of any compensation system depends heavily on whether those affected by it find the rewards attractive. Thus, the third and fourth steps in the process involve finding out exactly which rewards the company's salespeople value and what combination of rewards they find most attractive. These often vary by salesperson and can be determined by simple surveys or other research methods that assess a person's performance. Given this determination, the firm is in a position to weigh the benefits and costs associated with various combinations of rewards.

The fifth step in the process is determining the total amount of compensation. Here the firm often walks a fine line. If it overpays its salespeople, it incurs increased costs and runs the risk of creating low morale among other employees of the company. If it pays less than its competitors, it generally attracts lower quality recruits and experiences higher turnover and its attendant costs.

In determining the most effective form of financial compensation, the firm must decide whether it should use (1) straight salary, (2) straight commission, or (3) a combination of base salary and incentive pay such as commissions, bonuses, or both. Most companies today use the combination approach. The base salary provides the salesperson with a stable income while allowing the company to reward its salespeople for performing tasks not directly related to short-term sales. The incentive portion of combination plans provides direct rewards to motivate salespeople to expend effort to improve their sales volume or profitability of these sales. For the incentive pay portion of the combination plan to be effective, it has to be large enough to generate the necessary interest among salespeople. Although the opportunity to earn 25 percent of the base salary in incentive has been suggested as a good rule of thumb, the decision should logically be based on the company's objectives and the nature of the selling job.

Sales contests are often part of the incentive portion of compensation systems. To be successful a sales contest needs to have (1) clearly defined, specific objectives; (2) an exciting theme; (3) a reasonable probability of rewards for all salespeople; (4) attractive rewards; and (5) the necessary promotion and follow-through.

Nonfinancial incentives can play an important role in a firm's compensation system. In one survey of sales managers, it was found that they consider opportunities for promotion and advancement to be second only to special recognition as effective sales motivators. Because all salespeople cannot possibly move into sales management positions, some companies have dual career paths to maintain the motivating potential of promotion and advancement. One path leads to positions in the sales management hierarchy, while the other leads to greater responsibility in selling itself, such as a better territory or key account sales. For recognition programs to be effective, the salesperson's peers and superiors must be made aware of the representative's outstanding performance. This can be done through a formal recognition program at a sales meeting, publicity in the local press, announcements in the company's internal newsletter, or in other desirable ways.

The last stage in the process is to communicate the compensation program to the sales force. Salespeople need to have a clear understanding of its overall structure and what they specifically have to do to secure the elements in the total package that they find desirable.

Discussion Questions

1. "Look, Barb, the sales picture right now is not very good. A raise is not likely for the immediate future. For certain, if anyone deserves a raise it's you. Here's a suggestion: Since nobody watches expenses that closely, just add an additional amount to cover for the raise you didn't get, and I'll approve the voucher." What should Barb do in this situation? What would you do?

2. Discuss what you feel would be the greatest incentives to increase job performance for the following people and why.
   a. A 58-year-old sales manager for a large firm; married, no children at home.
   b. An MBA fresh out of college.
   c. A 35-year-old salesperson for an industrial goods manufacturer; married, three children.

3. The MoKay Company recently had its sales compensation program evaluated by a recognized consulting firm which indicated that the plan compared favorably with other plans offered by similar companies. Their analysis revealed that the program is more than competitive and that its mechanics and administration are equitable. Yet, MoKay still experiences a disturbing rate of turnover, and those that stay are not enthusiastic about their pay plan. What factors might be contributing to MoKay's problems?

4. "Most authorities recommend that compensation and incentive plans should link rewards to only two or three aspects of job performance." Discuss the reasoning behind this statement.

5. "Bill, I have some good news for you. The 'brass' authorized an increase in your salary from $27,500 to $29,500. But, there's a minor problem. You are not to discuss this with anybody else. We don't want to be bombarded by other sales reps asking for raises as well. This will be our secret." Comment. Are there any advantages in not keeping salary levels secret?

6. Large firms with good reputations and large sales forces generally offer only average or slightly below average compensation. Yet many of these firms are

much more financially sound than smaller firms that offer above-average compensation. Discuss the ethical considerations of this situation.

7. "We don't care how much we pay our salespeople, since their compensation relates to their volume of sales." What possible problems can result from this policy?

8. Compensation of field managers involves some rather difficult issues. How should this critically important individual be paid? Should field sales managers participate in an incentive program that is similar to that offered to the sales force? Or, should the field sales manager's compensation reflect—to a greater degree than the sales rep's—the overall profitability of the division? Should sales reps have the opportunity to earn more than their field sales manager?

9. Sales contests, although very popular, raise questions concerning their value. Questions asked include: Don't they simply shift into the contest period sales volume that would have occurred anyway? How can everyone be equally motivated when certain territories have a built-in edge because of customer and market characteristics? Won't the contest backfire if people feel they haven't had a fair chance to win? Will all sales representatives participate with equal enthusiasm when there can only be a few winners? How would you handle these objections?

10. The sales representative from the premium company was very positive about the benefits of his plan. He claimed that past users have experienced sales increases ranging from 15 percent to 25 percent. The sales manager was not so excited about the proposal. She wondered what would happen if the sales increase was less than 15 percent. Variable costs were 40 percent of sales and fixed costs were 50 percent. Added to this would be the cost of the incentive program which would average 7 percent. Should the incentive program be used?

11. When should a salesperson not be credited with a sale upon receipt of the customer's order?

12. What might be some appropriate contest themes for sales forces composed of the following?
    a. 50 percent women.
    b. Mostly young college graduates.
    c. Mostly experienced salespeople over 40 years old.

Cases for Part 2

Case 2–1
Crosby Flour Mills, Ltd.

Crosby Flour Mills, Ltd., is a Canadian-based producer of flour products sold primarily to bakeries of all sizes. A minor portion of the output is sold to institutions such as hospitals, large businesses, and educational institutions. A sales force of 32 covers all the provinces, although the bulk of Crosby's business is concentrated in metropolitan areas such as Montreal, Ottawa, Toronto, Winnipeg, Calgary, and Vancouver.

In recent years, Crosby has experienced a variety of problems. Sales have declined along with market share; turnover has increased, resulting in problems in recruiting and training; and customer complaints concerning sales force performance have increased dramatically.

Heading up the sales force is Helen Jane Crosby, general sales manager, and Susan M. Shelley, assistant to the sales manager. To help alleviate some of the problems, a consulting firm was hired by Crosby to investigate the attitudes of the sales force toward a variety of job-related factors. In particular, the sales force completed a questionnaire about job satisfaction, job expectations, task certainty, and attitudes toward various rewards. Both Crosby and Shelley completed questionnaires stating how they thought the sales force would respond to various questions. Thus, the sales force indicated what rewards they thought were important, and sales management indicated what rewards they thought would be important to the sales force.

Summary results of the job satisfaction measure revealed that considerable dissatisfaction existed in the following areas:

Pay.

Promotion.

Company policies and benefits.

Company support.

For the most part the sales force was satisfied with:

The job.

Fellow workers.

Customers.

487

Partial results of the expectation measures appear in Exhibit 1. The scale is a five-point Likert scale with the range "strongly disagree," "disagree," "neutral," "agree," and "strongly agree." "Strongly agree" is weighted 5, then 4, and so on down. Thus, the higher the score, the stronger is the agreement with the statement. For the first statement, the sales force mean score of 2.08 reveals that the sales force disagrees, whereas sales management agrees with the statement (4.18).

Exhibit 1
Sales manager expectations as stated by the sales force and sales management*

Item: My Sales Manager Expects Me:	Sales Force Mean	Sales Management Mean
1. To perform advisory services for my customers	2.08	4.18
2. To "stretch the truth" to make a sale	2.14	2.31
3. To call on customers even when they are unlikely to place an order	2.94	4.03
4. To expedite orders for my customers	4.42	2.73
5. To be gone overnight much of the time	2.53	2.41
6. To work on weekends	4.06	2.93
7. To "hold firm," on our normal delivery dates	1.30	2.42
8. To be available to my customers at all times	4.43	2.62
9. To work in the evenings	4.54	2.41
10. To be completely honest with my customers	2.96	3.61
11. To include my spouse when entertaining customers	4.64	2.91
12. To tailor credit terms to fit the needs of customers	1.35	3.23
13. To be available for customers' telephone calls at any hour of the day or night	4.57	2.51
14. To negotiate on price	3.35	1.44
15. To drink with my customers	4.13	3.26
16. To develop close personal relationships with my customers	4.45	2.68
17. To be liberal with my expense account in entertaining customers	3.47	1.57
18. To be a company sales representative 24 hours a day	3.82	2.85

*The sales force responded to the above items. Sales managers also revealed what they expected from the sales force for the same items.

Exhibit 2 presents the results for the task certainty measure. Sales representatives indicated how certain or uncertain they were about a variety of job activities using a six-point scale. In this case, the higher the score, the greater is the uncertainty. A score of 1.00 means "absolutely certain" and 6.00 means "absolutely uncertain."

The ranking of rewards data appears in Exhibit 3. The most important reward

Exhibit 2
Task certainty

Item: I Am _____ Certain/Uncertain:	Sales Force Mean
1. To what extent I can extend more liberal credit terms than normal.	3.40
2. How my sales manager expects me to allocate my time among accounts.	4.55
3. What is the best way to close a sale	3.39
4. How much time I should spend socializing with customers	3.60
5. About the frequency with which I should call on prospective customers	3.31
6. About our company rules and regulations	4.08
7. How to handle credits and adjustments for my customers	3.53
8. To what extent I can modify normal delivery schedules customers	3.85
9. What is the best way to sell	2.39
10. About where to go to get assistance to do my job	4.03
11. To what extent I can negotiate on price	4.40
12. About what activities in my job are most important to my sales manager	4.39
13. About what my sales manager expects of me in performing on my job	4.18
14. How satisfied my sales manager is with my performance on my job	5.53
15. How I should perform my job in order to satisfy my sales manager	4.23
16. How satisfied my customers are with my performance in my job	2.15
17. About what activities in my job are least important to my customers	2.57
18. About what activities in my job are most important to my customers	2.31
19. About the rules and procedures my customers expect me to follow in dealing with them	2.40
20. How I should perform my job in order to satisfy my customers	2.11
21. What my customers expect of me in performing my job	2.20
22. About how frequently my customers expect me to call on them	2.66

Exhibit 3
Importance of rewards

	Rank	
Reward	Sales Force	Sales Management
1. More job security	1	6
2. A promotion	6	1
3. A merit pay increase	2	3
4. More fringe benefits	3	2
5. An increase in your own feeling of worthwhile accomplishment	4	5
6. An increase in your own feeling of personal growth and development	5	4

is designated by 1 and the least important by 6. Sales management personnel were asked to rank the rewards according to how they thought the sales force would rank them.

Finally, the consulting organization conducted interviews with a limited number of salespeople to gain further insight into the nature of the jobs. Several salespeople commented that they did not know how the reward system worked. In other words, they were not sure which activities were most important and, moreover, if they performed well on various activities, they were not sure how this performance related to such things as promotions and pay increases.

Case 2–2
Agrisystem Farm Machines, Inc. (A)*

Agrisystem Farm Machines, Inc., is a large manufacturer of farm structures (silos) and grain-processing equipment, such as forage harvesters, burr mills, and recutters. The company has national distribution of its products and sells via an independent dealership network spread over 35 states.

The firm's dealers are serviced by a direct sales force that makes sales calls, provides product training, assists in qualifying prospective clients, and plans farm tours in conjunction with dealers and their customers. These sales representatives are known as area sales managers, and they operate under the direct supervision of regional sales managers.

In early 1984, Terry Benet, regional sales manager for the midcentral states, realized that some of his best area sales managers were overburdened with work and were having a difficult time fulfilling many of their sales and account management responsibilities. After identifying this problem, Benet decided that he would create a new position of assistant area sales manager. This person would be trained by the area sales manager and then assist in meeting the territory's sales and account objectives. Benet felt that this person would eventually be promoted to area sales manager when the opportunity or need arose. Thus, the position of assistant area sales manager would provide a steady source of sales talent that could be used to staff newly vacant area sales manager positions that opened up as the company grew and/or new territories were needed.

The job of assistant area sales manager was to have an annual salary of between $22,000 and $24,000. This figure included base salary plus incentives. Benet was told by management that he was not to exceed this salary benchmark and was further instructed that for now he could hire only one person for the new position. After evaluating the success of the experiment, management would decide whether the concept should be expanded throughout the company.

Benet quickly set out to hire the appropriate person for the new job. The first thing he did was study the job description of the area sales manager position (see Exhibit 1). Then, after talking to each of his area managers and receiving their input, he developed a detailed job description (see Exhibit 2) that outlined the responsibilities and qualifications of any assistant.

The next step was to attract a sizable pool of applicants and, from this pool, narrow the field to several of the best qualified candidates. Benet spent the next six weeks extensively interviewing and researching each applicant. Finally, he singled out four candidates as those that he felt had the greatest promise of being successful in the new job.

The four prospective hires were Ted Feldman, an experienced salesman with an impressive employment record; Jesse Barns, a dynamic man with a bachelor's

---

*This case was prepared especially for this text by Myron R. Lyskanycz, MBA—Marketing, University of Wisconsin at Madison.

Exhibit 1
Job description of area sales
manager position

Job Title: Area sales manager

Department: Marketing

Location: Western Region

Supervisor: Mr. Terrence Benet
Area consists of counties in northeastern Iowa and southeastern Minnesota. Travel away from home: estimated two nights per week.

General Description of Work:
Meet assigned MBO sales objectives in assigned sales territory by effective territory management including prospecting for, recruiting, training, motivating, and assisting Agrisystem Farm Machines Incorporated retailing dealers in the sales of Agrisystem structures and/or equipment manufactured by the company.
This is not a trainee position. Successful candidates will be expected to immediately assume full area sales management responsibility for meeting assigned sales objectives. While adequate product and sales training will be provided, the scope of this position requires a person who understands the sales and distribution of structures and farmstead equipment through a dealer organization as well as selling retail to farmers.

Major Responsibilities:
1. Make effective sales calls on existing dealers: train, motivate, and assist dealers in developing qualified sales prospects and selling plans that logically lead to the completed sale. Sell products on the farm as part of dealer training and assistance program.
2. With assistance from regional sales manager, analyze assigned territory for sales potential of assigned products; develop dealer prospects and/or effectively recruit new dealers for maximum product sales potential and service coverage within territory.
3. Train dealers in product features, benefits, effective selling techniques, installation, troubleshooting, and service, as required.
4. Collect accounts receivable from dealers and develop effective business relations between Agrisystem Farm Machine and dealerships as directed by regional sales manager.
5. Effectively implement Agrisystem Farm Machines' sales promotion programs, including local advertising, farm tours, field days, farmer meetings, and dealer meetings.
6. Prepare weekly written reports: territory sales progress, expense vouchers, promotion activity reports.
7. Develop annual Management by Objective plans for unit sales by product line, dealership area potential, county, etc., under direction of regional sales manager (revise plans quarterly).

---

degree in agricultural science and an almost completed master's degree in marketing; Ruth Spencer, a 33-year-old mother who had recently begun selling farm structures for one of Agrisystem's competitors; and Richard Werneth, a young man who was currently employed by a large dealer that stocked and sold Agrisystem Farm Machine products. Due to an extensive data-gathering effort, Benet was able to amass the following background material on the four prospective salespeople.

Exhibit 2
Notice of job opening

Job Title: Assistant area sales manager

Department: Marketing Group, Western Sales Region

Location: Southeastern Minnesota based—Travel in eastern Minnesota and northeastern Iowa in assigned sales territory. (Away from home: 1 or 2 nights per week.)

Supervisor: Regional sales manager—Mr. Terrence Benet

General Description of Work: This position involves working under the general direction of the regional sales manager to assist area sales managers in meeting assigned MBO sales objectives in assigned sales territories.

Major Responsibilities:
1. Make effective sales calls on existing dealers as assigned by area sales managers; trains, motivates, and assists dealers in developing qualified sales prospects and selling plans that logically lead to the completed sale. Sell products on the farm as part of dealer training and assistance program.
2. Train dealers in product features, benefits, effective selling techniques, installation, troubleshooting, and service, as required.
3. Work with area sales manager to collect accounts receivable from dealers and develop effective business relations between Agrisystem Farm Machines and dealerships.
4. Effectively implement Agrisystem Farm Machines' sales promotion programs, including local advertising, farm tours, field days, farmer meetings, and dealer meetings.
5. Prepare weekly written reports: territory sales progress, expense vouchers, promotion activity reports.

Qualification Requirements:
1. High school diploma required. Minimum of two years of college work in an agricultural science preferred. B.S. degree in agriculture preferred.
2. A broad, in-depth knowledge of dairy and beef production practices.
3. A general understanding of agribusiness distribution through local dealerships.
4. A minimum of one year of sales experience, dealing with a tangible product in agribusiness or equivalent in experience, which must include effectively dealing with farmers and/or agribusiness dealers, including proven successful experience in communicating to and with farmers, and convincing farmers to take action on some recommended plan or program.

Application Procedure:
Employees interested in applying for this position should complete a new application form for employment including his or her current job with Agrisystem Farm Machines.

Ted Feldman

Following a rural upbringing and graduation from high school, Ted enrolled at a large midwestern university where he intended to study agriculture. After one year, he became disillusioned with college and decided to enlist in the armed forces. Ted joined the Air Force, spent six years as a pilot, and was subsequently discharged as an Air Force captain.

At the age of 26, Ted returned to his home state of Illinois, got married, and found a job working as a salesman for one of the nation's largest manufacturers of farm tractors. He spent the next three years selling combines and tractors to the firm's dealers.

Ted performed impressively during this period and was quite content with his position. However, during his third year, a protracted labor strike against the company caused Ted to be laid off for several months. During this time, he began searching for a new position and was offered a job by a manufacturer of equipment used to store, process, and convey grain. The job provided Ted with a salary increase and a chance to be in a warm southern climate.

He accepted the offer and has been there for the past two years. Ted's job requires that he call on large farmers, grain elevator owners, and feed processors. He designs the entire job and then hires the subcontractors to actually install the equipment.

Ted has applied for the Agrisystem position because he sees no chance of getting into sales management with his present employer and feels that Agrisystem (because of its size) could eventually offer him that opportunity. His annual salary with the present employer will reach approximately $28,000 this year.

Jesse Barns

Jesse Barns is 27 years old. Although he has no actual sales experience in agribusiness, he does have impressive educational credentials and has been involved in several internship programs sponsored by companies that manufacture products for agricultural applications.

Jesse grew up in a small city in the South. He always had a fascination with animals and the rural countryside, so when he entered college he chose to major in agriculture. Jesse studied agriculture for four years and was the first black person in his university to graduate with a degree in agriculture.

During his studies, Jesse had the opportunity to spend a good deal of time at the university research farm and worked there full-time in his final two summers at the school.

After graduation from college, Jesse felt that he was not yet ready to begin a career so he enlisted in the Army for two years. After his discharge, Jesse returned to school to earn his MBA degree in business, using his GI benefits to cover the costs of the education.

While working toward his MBA degree, Jesse participated in an internship program sponsored by a manufacturer of dairy farm equipment. Here he was assigned to the marketing department and charged with developing promotional literature that the company provided to its dealers for distribution to farmers.

Jesse learned of the availability of the assistant area sales manager position with Agrisystem through a job posting at the placement office of his university.

He got in touch with Benet directly—who consequently interviewed him at his branch office. There Jesse informed Benet that he would be graduating within one month and would be willing to start work at that time. He also let it be known that his counterparts in the MBA program had been receiving offers with salaries of $21,000–$23,000 annually and that he would expect any offer from Agrisystem to be competitive.

During his interview with Benet, Jesse could not list any specific long-term career objectives. He made it clear, however, that he simply wished to be directly involved in the agricultural industry while having the opportunity to utilize his business-related educational skills.

Ruth Spencer

Ruth Spencer, an only child, was born and raised in a rural farm community in northern Wisconsin. Her father owned and operated a dairy farm; thus, Ruth learned farming and knew the lifestyle of the midwestern farmer.

After graduating from high school, Ruth went to college to study agriculture with the intent of some day returning to her father's farm and managing the operation. Following two years of college, Ruth got married at the age of 21 and left school to be with her husband, who had an engineering job with a company in Minneapolis. The Spencers settled in Minneapolis and had a child. Until recently, Ruth was content to be a housewife and a mother.

About a year ago, Ruth decided that she wanted to go to work and embark upon a career. She had several friends who worked for one of Agrisystem's competitors and through them was able to land a job as a sales representative selling silo equipment to dealers.

Ruth has been working for this firm for nearly 12 months. Her performance to this point has been lackluster but adequate. Spencer blames this mediocre performance on her relative inexperience and on her current employer's inferior product lines, which make them rather difficult to sell.

It is her belief that she can do a much better job selling for Agrisystem because of the quality of its products, her familiarity with the equipment, and because she now has a year of experience.

Ruth's current territory covers a relatively concentrated farming community and allows her to work out of her home each day. It includes a portion of the same area that Benet hopes to assign to the new assistant, but it is much smaller than the one she would be expected to cover for Agrisystem.

During their interview, Ruth told Benet that her earnings during the current year would approach $20,000, but that she expected to do much better working for Agrisystem.

Richard Werneth

Richard was born in the West. His father owns a large beef ranch in Montana. Richard worked on the farm until the age of 18. Then he decided he wanted to pursue the study of business at a large midwestern university.

Richard stayed in Chicago for two years and enrolled at Northwestern University. After completing his sophomore year, he decided to take a year off and travel around the country. Having done so, he returned to Montana and finished his requirements for a bachelor's degree in finance at his home state university.

After receiving his degree, Richard went back to his father's ranch and worked the cattle ranch for one year. At the age of 23, he left for Wisconsin to spend some time with a brother who owned a dairy farm in the south central part of the state. A month later, Richard heard of a job opening for an installer of farm structures being offered by an Agrisystem dealer. He applied for and got the job.

Richard has been employed by this dealer for the past two years. In that time, he has shown both the competence and strong ambition that resulted in his attaining responsibility over four of the dealer's assembly crews.

Recently, Richard discovered from the local Agrisystem area sales manager of the planned hiring of an assistant sales manager. Wishing to move up to a more professional level, Richard applied for the position and interviewed with Benet.

Benet has been very impressed by Richard's assertiveness, ambition, poise, and apparent leadership qualities. However, he has also been notified by Richard's current employer (who is one of the largest Agrisystem dealers in the region) that he does not wish to lose Richard because he needs his expertise and leadership skills to keep the assembly crews working efficiently and smoothly.

Richard's current salary with the dealer is $18,000 annually, and he is due for a $2,000 raise as of the end of the year.

Case 2–3
Reliable Meter Company

John Bailey, the recently hired national sales manager of Reliable Meter, was faced with problems of declining market share, unfilled back orders for new equipment and parts, a lethargic sales force, and low employee turnover. Most sales managers would not be upset with the low turnover rate, but Bailey felt differently. The average age of the sales force was 55. In the past, only applicants with experience were hired as sales engineers. Now five of the sales engineers were 69 years old, however, and Bailey was going to insist on retirement for all five, even though he knew that three of them wanted to continue working. Forcing retirement would create further personnel problems, which Bailey did not want.

Reliable was a wholly owned subsidiary of Hancock Industries, a large conglomerate. Bailey was hired from the Barber Corporation, where he was assistant sales manager. He had been very successful at Barber, but a lack of promotional opportunities prompted him to accept Reliable's position as sales manager. This position was vacated by Fred Lohman, who had retired unexpectedly at the age of 67 due to health problems.

Bailey had inherited a mess when he took the position at Reliable. Executives at Hancock knew that Bailey's appointment might create discontent, but they felt that appointing one of the two regional managers, both in their early 60s, would not bring about the needed changes. One Hancock executive hoped that Bailey's appointment would lead to a few departures.

Bailey also knew that his appointment would be viewed with some mistrust by the Reliable sales force. For one thing, Bailey's age of 38 caused him to be viewed as a "young upstart." He was, after all, younger than Reliable's two regional sales managers and the four district sales managers. Another problem for Bailey was that he was hired from outside the company. A third problem Bailey faced was his lack of experience in the meter business. Bailey's previous company was a manufacturer of pneumatic tools.

In Bailey's favor was his past experience in developing a strong sales organization. While at Barber, Bailey revamped the company's recruiting procedure, which he felt was ineffective. Bailey had been involved with other projects that helped to increase Barber's market share and profits.

One Hancock executive described John Bailey as a "real go-getter." Bailey knew of the high expectations and was now wondering whether he could handle the challenge. Improving the performance of the 47-man sales force was one problem for which Bailey was responsible. With the forced retirement of five sales engineers, Bailey felt the time was right to revamp the recruiting and selection process.

The Company

Reliable Meter, located in Buffalo, New York, manufactures a broad line of measuring instruments used in a wide variety of applications. Reliable makes gas meters, water meters, and electric meters for residential application. In addition, Reliable produces meters used by industrial firms, hospitals, and public utilities. Reliable's meters range in price from $40 to $12,500. Complexity varies considerably as well. More accurate meters are usually more complex, more fragile, and typically cost more.

The Selling Process

Approximately half of Reliable's sales are on a bid basis to public utilities and local governments. Reliable has recently lost several large bids, which Bailey felt was caused by deficiencies in the sales force. Not only were Reliable's bids too high, but the meter specifications favored competitive products. Bailey felt that the sales force could have an impact on how meter specifications are set so that they favor one company. If this happens, there is a cost advantage for the favored company. In some cases, a slightly higher bid can win because the product specifications are superior. Product knowledge is very useful in such situations.

Many of Reliable's meters are standard equipment. Bailey felt that sales of standard meters require more selling knowledge than product knowledge. To improve selling skills, Bailey planned to revamp the sales training program. More emphasis would be placed on selling techniques, and the time devoted to product knowledge was to be reduced. More frequent training sessions were to be scheduled and conducted at district or regional offices.

The Recruiting Process

Bailey recognized that with five sales vacancies, a new system for recruiting and selection would have to be established as soon as possible. The recruiting process was the first item Bailey reviewed with Reliable's personnel manager, Herb Aldag. "All job openings in the company are posted," Aldag indicated, "in order to comply with Reliable's promotion-from-within practice." Most existing members of Reliable's sales force were obtained using referrals from other sales representatives. It was not uncommon to find that a prospective sales engineer had been recommended by two or three present sales engineers. The system worked so well that Reliable did not have to advertise for sales applicants very often. Interviewing students graduating in engineering was not feasible because of their lack of sales experience in similar industries.

The Selection Process

Reviewing the actual selection procedure was not going to be so easy. Aldag indicated that Bailey's predecessor, Fred Lohman, used some techniques of his own to decide which applicant to hire. Aldag described the "official" procedure as follows:

1. Application blanks were completed by all applicants.
2. The initial interview was conducted by Aldag or one of his assistants. Completed application forms for those who survived the first interview were sent to the sales manager.
3. If the applicant got past the initial interview, then the next interview was with Reliable's sales manager and his assistant. Aldag indicated that one of Lohman's pet strategies was to ask the prospect to "sell" him something. "Something" usually was a mechanical pencil or a ball point pen. Aldag was not sure how much weight this tactic carried.
4. If the applicant survived this interview, then Lohman requested reference letters, a credit check, and testing. Testing involved the Strong-Campbell Vocational Interest Blank and the timed Wonderlic Personnel Test.
5. If references and test scores were satisfactory, another interview was scheduled with Fred Lohman. Lohman required applicants to write out in longhand their reasons why they wanted to be sales engineers for Reliable Meter.
6. If applicants successfully passed this step, then Lohman asked to meet married applicants' spouses for another interview. This was usually a dinner interview at a local restaurant. Occasionally, Lohman would meet with the couple at their home.
7. The final step in the selection process, assuming that an applicant had met all the previous requirements, was the company physical examination. Aldag indicated that this was usually a minor exam since most applicants passed.

Bailey knew that this procedure was not similar to the one he instituted at the Barber Company. He also knew that to bring about any changes, supporting evidence would be needed.

Sales Force Characteristics

Reviewing the sales engineers' personnel files was Bailey's next step. The files were fairly complete, although Bailey was unable to find any notes about what transpired during the interview where the applicant was asked to "sell" something to Lohman. There were no notes for the interview where the spouse was present. The handwritten statements containing reasons why the applicants wanted to be sales engineers were generally broad and not too informative. Bailey

Exhibit 1
Sales force characteristics

1984 Sales Performance (sales/quotas)	Wonderlic Personnel Test Score	Type of Engineering Degree*	Source of Application†	Age	Marital Status	Number of Years Selling Experience Prior	Reliable	Strong-Campbell Interest Inventory Basic Interest‡
1 132	38	I	I	44	M	1	10	58.90
2 130	36	I	I	56	M	7	12	68.34
3 129	31	M	E	43	S	—	11	62.11
4 129	25	I	I	57	M	13	8	63.92
5 128	37	E	E	64	M	2	17	73.83
6 126	38	E	E	63	M	8	16	65.38
7 123	32	M	I	34	S	—	5	61.52
8 122	38	M	I	53	M	11	8	62.30
9 120	31	I	E	44	M	—	11	78.76
10 119	36	I	I	59	M	7	12	56.86
11 119	31	M	I	44	S	4	6	61.65
12 118	35	I	I	48	S	3	5	63.13
13 117	24	I	E	65	M	14	10	55.80
14 116	32	M	E	58	M	9	12	52.01
15 113	30	M	E	45	M	2	9	54.87
16 110	33	E	I	69	M	8	21	51.79
17 106	30	M	I	51	M	6	13	53.95
18 105	26	E	I	40	M	1	9	55.43
19 104	26	I	E	52	M	7	15	50.63
20 104	25	E	I	63	M	14	11	55.89
21 104	28	M	I	63	M	8	22	45.57
22 103	34	M	I	42	M	—	6	53.33
23 102	25	I	I	49	S	4	8	58.33
24 101	33	E	I	69	M	12	14	49.38

25 100	E	I	43	M	2	7	49.05
26 100	I	I	54	M	7	8	39.24
27 100	M	I	59	S	9	13	49.18
28 100	M	I	48	M	4	6	44.79
29 99	E	I	57	M	11	11	45.86
30 99	I	I	69	S	10	17	46.00
31 98	E	E	69	S	12	14	47.04
32 97	I	I	56	M	6	4	42.62
33 95	M	I	59	M	5	12	41.19
34 92	M	I	63	M	10	12	40.68
35 91	M	I	50	M	4	10	40.67
36 90	E	I	58	M	8	16	46.19
37 90	M	I	64	S	12	21	45.83
38 89	E	I	57	M	7	8	47.81
39 88	E	I	69	M	14	12	42.50
40 82	M	I	48	S	3	7	41.17
41 78	I	I	52	M	8	12	35.55
42 77	M	I	45	S	8	6	44.36
43 75	I	E	38	M	—	2	53.34
44 71	I	I	57	S	11	10	33.61
45 65	M	I	68	M	14	22	40.18
46 62	E	I	57	M	10	14	36.11
47 57	E	I	60	M	9	17	55.43

*E = electrical, M = mechanical, I = industrial.
†I = internal, E = external.
‡The higher the score, the greater is the interest in sales.

did notice that all the statements showed good handwriting. "At least I'll be able to read their call reports," Bailey reflected. The statements did not show above-average communication skills.

The files contained reference letters, which were generally good. Results of the two tests and the physical exam were also in the personnel files. Bailey investigated the files for those who had applied but had not been hired. Files were complete for existing employees who had applied for the sales engineer position, but for outsiders, the files were very incomplete. Bailey wanted to compare those hired with those not hired to see what differences there were.

Based on a sketchy review of information presented in Exhibit 1, Bailey drew the following tentative conclusions:

1. All 47 sales engineers had undergraduate engineering degrees.
2. About three quarters of the sales engineers were married at the time of application. Those not hired were more likely to be single, widowed, or divorced.
3. A comparison of the handwritten statements did not reveal any significant differences between those hired and those not hired.
4. All 47 sales engineers were male, with an average age of 55.
5. Most of the 47 had been referred to Reliable by existing sales engineers.
6. The majority of the 47 sales engineers had selling experience before joining Reliable.

Bailey discussed these findings with Herb Aldag, who was not surprised at Bailey's tentative conclusions. Aldag expressed some concern that no women were in the sales force. Bailey agreed but pointed out that the recruiting process used by Lohman was unlikely to result in hiring women.

The handwritten statements caused Bailey to wonder if Lohman used graphology to aid him in making choices as to who should be hired. No evidence in the form of an analysis could be found. Possibly Lohman used this technique but did not want to retain any evidence due to the controversial nature of handwriting analysis. On the other hand, maybe Lohman felt that good handwriting was a necessity, since filling out forms is part of the job. Bailey was somewhat intrigued by the idea of using graphoanalysis as a selection device. Aldag pointed out another reason for requesting handwritten statements. The applicant's handwriting from the statement of reasons could be compared with the signature on the application to make sure they matched. This helped to ensure that the statement of reasons was the applicant's own effort and not someone else's.

Summary

At this point Bailey felt that a revamp of the recruiting and selection system was needed. He also knew that reversing Reliable's sales trends would involve much more than changing recruitment and selection procedures. For example, he felt that the compensation package, which was 90 percent salary plus 10 percent commission on all sales over quota, failed to provide sufficient motivation. He also questioned the promotional situation, since very few promotion opportunities existed.

Case 2–4
Golden Bear Distributors[*]

John Gray, president of Golden Bear Distributors (GBD), had been pleased with his company's performance, but felt that the lack of an extensive training program for his salesmen might be a limiting factor in the company's growth plans. Thus, in November 1979, Gray hired a San Francisco consulting firm to study the GBD sales force and to outline a sales-training program. Specifically, he wanted the consultants to define the training that would be best for his salesmen, to indicate the material which should be covered, and to recommend how it should be presented.

Background

Golden Bear distributed several nationally advertised brands of electrical home appliances as well as a line of home-entertainment equipment through more than 200 dealers in California. The product lines included stereos, automatic washers and dryers, vacuum cleaners, air conditioners, television sets, radios, ranges, refrigerators, garbage disposals, dishwashers, mixers, toasters, and complete kitchen installations.

GBD's sales organization included four product sales managers who reported to a general sales manager. (See Exhibit 1). Each product sales manager was assigned to three or four of the company's lines and was held responsible for sales and profits.

The sales force consisted of 25 salesmen, supervised collectively by the product sales managers. Each salesman was assigned a specific geographic territory made up of approximately 4 percent of the total Retail Distribution Index of GBD's trading area.[1] Each time a new man was hired, he was assigned a territory equal in potential to the other 24 salesmen.

There was little *formal* sales training. Whenever a new man was hired, the product sales managers took turns "going the rounds" with him to acquaint him with his territory and to introduce him to his customers. Each salesman sold all of the products in the company's line; if his sales fell off in one product area, that product sales manager usually discussed at regular biweekly meetings any problems the salesmen had encountered.

Each salesman could draw a salary of $250 a week against commissions. Since the average commission rate was 2½ percent, each salesman had to sell $520,000 of merchandise per year in order to cover his draw. Net annual commissions for the different salesmen varied between $15,000 and $25,000. All selling

[*]This case was prepared by Professor Robert T. Davis, Stanford University, Graduate School of Business. Reprinted from *Stanford Business Cases 1980* with permission of the publishers, Stanford University Graduate School of Business, © 1980 by the Board of Trustees of the Leland Stanford Junior University.
[1] Taken from *The Survey of Buying Power.*

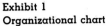

Exhibit 1
Organizational chart

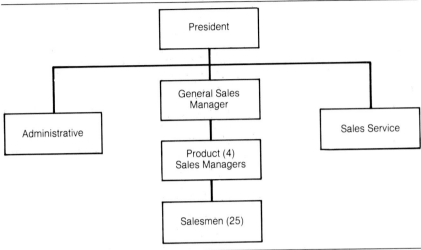

expenses were paid out of the salesmen's gross, although several salesmen received a mileage allowance when extensive travel was required.

The salesmen filled out detailed weekly route sheets describing all planned activities for the following week. In addition, they made out a daily call report which they mailed in to the home office at the end of each work day.

GBD's 200 outlets consisted primarily of small, independent merchants who accounted for perhaps one-third of the area's total volume. The other two-thirds was represented by discounters and mass merchandising chains who typically dealt directly with the suppliers, or bought through large buying groups. Although the discounters continued to grow, their increased share of the market was beginning to slow. The independents were presumably starting to offer a service alternative, as well as more aggressive pricing, which appealed to certain segments of the population. Price cutting, nonetheless, remained a serious problem for the independents.

Mr. Murphy's Interviews

The consulting firm assigned the GBD account to one of its top young men, Kelvin Murphy. Murphy has received an MBA from a leading western business school in 1975 and had taken a job with a large industrial equipment manufacturer upon graduation. He left his sales management job there four years later to join the consultant.

Shortly after John Gray's initial discussion with the consultants, Murphy contacted GBD's general sales manager, Lynn Philips, at the home office in Oakland. After getting some background data on the sales organization, Murphy asked Lynn for his views on sales training at GBD. He responded:

As far as I'm concerned, the training job has to be two-fold; retail salesmen need training just as much as distributor salesmen. Right now we have a policy whereby we invite dealer personnel to our home office in small groups for meetings to demonstrate and discuss all of the appliances that we carry. On the other hand, as I mentioned earlier, our salesmen's only on-the-job training is by the product sales managers. Such limited training probably isn't sufficient, but I'm not sure what kind of training they do need. That's what I expect *you* to tell *me* after you spend some time with them.

Lynn Philips then arranged for Murphy to "make the rounds" with several of the GBD's salesmen. Murphy first met Bob Boatwright, who serviced part of Monterey County, south of San Francisco. Bob was 32 years old and had been with GBD over four years. His initial reaction to Murphy was, "I never hear from the office unless my sales are down"; but when Murphy explained that he was merely interested in learning how he sold as part of a general study on sales training, Bob talked more freely:

You gotta learn to sell like a retailer sells. New salesmen oughta be given all kinds of product information, and the company should demonstrate the operation of our products to the new men.

Next, you gotta follow up on the new men, so they tell their story to the retailer *every* time they go into a store. The idea is to get 'em to give the story to the retailer and his salesmen so many times that when a customer walks in the store and asks about a dishwasher, the retailer goes into the pitch on our machines automatically.

According to the home office we're supposed to be "sales consultants" to the dealers, but I don't go for that much. I tried to help out a couple of small retailers once by showing 'em how I'd sell our product line, but they both thought I was trying' to run their business. I think the best way is to bring the retail salesmen into the home office every once in a while and show 'em how to operate our equipment and explain it thoroughly—just like we do now. That's how to train 'em to sell.

Bob's first stop Friday afternoon was at Harry's TV and Radio Shop. Before he and Murphy went in, Bob explained his sales approach.

I go in and say hello to the salesmen first because if there's any service problem with any of our stuff, they're sure to know about it. That way, the boss won't surprise me if something's gone wrong. Next, if I have a chance, I slip back into the stock room to see how many TVs they have left. This guy, Harry, sells TVs, and that's about all. Incidentally, most of my sales are on TVs—I can't sell many white goods down in this area.

Well, after that, I usually check with the service manager to make certain that anything I've promised him in the last week or so has been taken care of. Then, of course, I tip my hat to the secretary, and ask to see the boss.

When Bob entered the store, he greeted the two retail salesmen, walked over to a quiet corner of the store, and conversed with one of the salesmen in low tones. Shortly thereafter, he went downstairs for about ten minutes. When he came back upstairs, he headed for a desk at the back and motioned for Murphy to follow. He greeted the service manager and introduced Murphy as his helper. The service manager was apparently mad at GBD, and Bob in particular, because Bob had promised him a replacement transmission for an automatic washing machine which had not yet been delivered. After Bob stated that he had relayed the information to GBD's service department a week or so ago, he phoned the GBD service manager and a short, heated argument ensued. When Bob finished the call, he informed Harry's service manager that he would have to "check further." Although Harry's service manager was not satisfied, Bob explained that he wanted to see Harry first and that he would talk with him later.

Bob then knocked on a door marked "Private" and motioned Murphy to follow. As they entered, a man on the telephone looked up and waved them to a seat. After he hung up, Bob introduced Murphy and proceeded to ask Harry if there was anything he wanted in the line of TV sets. Harry answered by questioning Bob about the automatic transmission. When Bob assured him that he was following it up, Harry stated, "That's OK for me, Bob."

Bob then began to explain a new window display GBD had designed for its dealers for the Christmas holidays. Harry turned down the display because, "Panasonic pays me 100 bucks a year to put their line in the window during the first three weeks of December, so you can forget about that for me."

Bob glanced at his note pad and informed Harry that he needed to stock up on several models. Harry replied, "I'm OK for now, but I'll give you an order next week." After leaving Harry's office, Bob stopped by the service manager's desk and reviewed the transmission problem. Bob concluded by stating that he would check on the unit the following morning when he reported to the home office. He promised to call the service manager with a report.

As they left the store, Bob remarked, "Harry evidently wasn't in a buying mood today, but I'll definitely get an order from him next week." Since it was then nearly 4:30 p.m., Bob wanted to call it a day, but he offered to take Murphy to visit other stores on Monday if he wished.

The following week Murphy spent most of one day with Walt Warren. Walt was about 40 years old and had sold for GBD about 1½ years. He had left a comfortable job as a feed and seed wholesaler because a back injury prevented him from carrying and stacking the heavy bags of seed and grain. Walt had a large territory north of San Francisco, which covered a number of small towns. Murphy met Walt about 9:00 a.m. and they chatted over a cup of coffee before beginning their calls.

When Murphy explained that he was helping to do a study for GBD on methods of training salesmen, Walt evidently interpreted this to mean that he should talk about his job, for he started explaining his daily call routine. His suggested approach to the retailer was much the same as that voiced by Bob Boatwright.

Walt and Murphy first visited Anderson's Gas and Appliance Company, which sold butane and propane gases, as well as a large line of home appliances. Walt quickly introduced Murphy to Mrs. Anderson, listened to a complaint about a scratched cabinet on a television set, and checked the company's inventory. After discussing with Mrs. Anderson the aggressive price cutting initiated by a local discounter, Walt took an order for four mixers. The call lasted about 20 minutes.

As they walked toward the second stop several blocks away, Walt stated, "I always try to get on a first-name basis with my retailers as soon as I can because it helps me establish rapport with them. Another thing about calling on a territory that you haven't visited in a week or so is to walk along the main street and window shop and see who's got what bargains displayed. That helps you get a 'feel' for the town. I also buy a local paper most every time I come into these little towns to see who's advertising what. I think that helps me get a feel for my competition, too."

The second call, which lasted about 45 minutes, was at a large home service center. As soon as they entered the store, Walt introduced Murphy to Joe, the owner. The following conversation took place:

Walt: I see you're leasing a couple of our video recording systems, Joe. Great— that should help to boost your sales.

Joe: Yeah, that's true. But the reason I'm renting 'em is that I can't sell 'em. As long as the payments keep coming in, though, I should care.

Walt: Joe, portable radios and hi-fi's should be picking up pretty soon now— Christmas, you know. Over half of these sales should come in November and December.

Joe: What's good?

Walt: Everything, Joe.

Joe: [*Looking at display*] I've got some G.E.'s here, got 'em at a special price. But the last I sold was about three months ago.

(Walt began to talk about a new warranty program on the food mixer. Joe explained he was aware of it.)

Walt: Well, we do have a nice gift promotion on the mixers.

Joe: I don't need all that stuff. I've got plenty now.

Walt: We can send it to you prepaid you know, Joe, plus a 10 percent dating. These mixers will really go well . . .

Joe: I just don't need any.

Walt: Well, anything else? How about taking an ad in your local paper on the automatic washer. I've never seen your newspaper feature any of our products. What's the cost over there anyway?

Joe: $1.60 a line.

Walt: Well, of course, we'd split the cost fifty-fifty with you, Joe, on any ads you'd like to run.

Joe: Fifty-fifty?

Walt: Yep, on all the lines you run with our mats.

Joe: On everything?

Walt: That's right. Just send us the tear sheets.

Joe: Why don't you mail me some mats then? I can use 'em.

Walt: O.K. Now, how about those radios, Joe?

Joe: Send me a couple of those new brown FM sets—you know the ones I mean.

Walt: The FM-36B? Yeah, that's the popular one, Joe.

Joe: O.K. I'll see you next week.

Walt: Fine, Joe, see you.

As they left the store, Walt remarked, "Gee, sure looks like a good day. You know, the personal approach means everything in this business. I'm trying to build goodwill so that when I leave a store, those retailers will want to sell GBD because I'm a good guy. Now Joe there thinks that I'm a nice guy, so he tries to sell my line. Incidentally, the reason I pushed some advertising is that he's got to advertise if he wants to sell. These dealers often look upon advertising as a cost instead of an investment. Or they think the manufacturer should do it all."

The next stop was a new TV dealer. Walt had taken an order from the dealer for a new combination stereo TV and home recording system on the promise that it would be delivered in two days. Three days after taking the order, Walt had received a phone call from the dealer who stated that, unless the set were delivered that very day, Walt was to cancel the order. Walt commented to Murphy, "I checked with our delivery people yesterday after I got the call, and they weren't sure the set would go out. If it isn't there now, I'll be in trouble with him. Seeing as how he's a new dealer, I don't want to rock the boat."

In the TV dealer's window was the system distributed by GBD. "Well," remarked Walt, "I guess it's safe to go in." As soon as they entered the store, a thin man greeted Walt with, "The set arrived just as I was closing last night." Walt explained some of the features of the set to the dealer, and gave him some literature on several other models. Then Walt inquired about what other sets the dealer was planning to install. The dealer replied that he wouldn't carry any others until he had sold this one. After a few more words, Walt and Murphy left the store. Several minutes later Walt remarked, "You know, bringing people around with you hurts your sales . . . but he's a tough dealer to sell, anyway."

Murphy and Walt then drove twenty miles to another town further north. During the trip, Walt talked about why he had left his wholesaling business and why he liked selling. When they arrived at the next stop, Walt explained, "I have to try to collect a check from the dealer, and report my results back to the home office by telephone." Since the man he wishes to see was not in, he made arrangements to call back later that afternoon.

During lunch at a small diner, Walt talked more about the seed and grain business. He also expressed a desire to obtain a territory closer to the city. After lunch, as they began walking toward the next call, they passed a newly-renovated hardware store. Walt paused, "This is a new store. I haven't got them for an account. It's just possible they haven't got a kitchen line. I think I'll go in cold and see what I can do." They entered the store and looked around for a clerk. A woman came out and Walt explained the purpose of his call, stating that his company had just started up with a new line of complete kitchen installations.

When he mentioned the brand name, the woman remarked that the store carried that line, and added that she could show it to him. In a corner of the store, a complete kitchen was installed in a little room off the main part of the building. The woman explained that she and her husband had recently purchased the store, and were in the process of renovating it. Walt noticed the fixtures that she had, and explained that on his next call he would supply her with some promotional material on the line. He also added that the distributor who formerly handled the line had gone out of business and that GBD would gladly provide them with the components from now on. The woman thanked him, and they left the store.

* * * * *

After similar experiences traveling with three other salesmen, Kelvin Murphy felt that he had a good feeling for the GBD selling job and its requirements. Since two men were retiring soon from GBD's sales force, John Gray was very anxious that Murphy complete his recommendations for a sales training program before new men had to be hired to take over the territories. Thus, Murphy began outlining a training program for GBD which would include recommendations for training dealer sales personnel as well as the firm's own salesmen.

Case 2–5
General Typewriter Company

General Typewriter Company started operations in 1926, concentrating primarily on manufacturing typewriters. General has always been recognized as a leader in the industry. It was one of the first companies to introduce electric typewriters. General has dominated the industry in other areas, as well. Its most recent innovation was the magnetic card machine, which permits a typist to reproduce letters that are identical except for the recipient's name, address, and salutation. The letters appear as if they were individually typed.

As a result of a merger with a small electronics company, General developed a new system that combines a typewriter with a video screen and a printer. The system, sometimes called a text editor, interfaces with a small computer. The typist types a letter or manuscript page and the copy appears on the screen. With the image on the screen, the typist can reread the copy, make corrections, change sentences, add, and/or delete material. Once the final copy has been approved, the typist pushes a button and the printer reproduces the image onto typing paper. A memory unit allows the typist to retrieve any page for further modification or reproduction.

Since General's inception, it has sold directly to users including business firms of all sizes, government operations, and educational institutions. The sales force numbers 150 and is organized by customer groupings. There are four regional managers and 25 district managers.

General first used manufacturers' agents to handle its selling activities. As a result of product line expansion and the need for more control of the servicing area, General replaced the manufacturers' agents with a company sales force. Many of the manufacturers' agents were recruited by General; others were experienced salespeople from other typewriter manufacturers. General's strategy of hiring only experienced salespeople persisted for several years and was justified on the basis that such an approach alleviated the need for sales training.

Although servicing was handled separately, the sales force had to be well versed on the technical features of General typewriters. Knowledge of competitive products was important as well. The advantages of General Typewriter had to be explained to prospective customers. Complicating the sales task further was that not one but several people had to be contacted and sold on the General product. Buying and product interests varied, depending on whether the person was a purchasing agent, office manager, or secretary. Identifying the influential buyer in a customer's organization was an integral part of the sales force's activity. With these requirements, General preferred experienced salespeople.

With the introduction of each technological change, General found that it had to develop training programs to communicate the information needed by the sales force. Some members of the sales force were difficult to train due to the very technical nature of some of the innovations. For salespeople lacking technical ability, the training task took too long, and it was doubtful whether they remembered enough to sell effectively.

It was at this point, prior to the introduction of the new video typewriter, that Cory Maker, national sales manager, suggested that General no longer hire only experienced salespeople. The new source would be college graduates, preferably those with a business-engineering background. Based on past experience, Maker expected to lose 20 percent of the existing sales force this year for such reasons as retirements, quits, transfers, deaths, and dismissals. Maker knew that hiring inexperienced college graduates would result in the need for sales training programs. Sales training in the past had been handled on an ad hoc basis, so there was no sales training specialist. Business Research Associates, a midwestern consulting firm, was retained by Maker to help General hire a sales training specialist and to provide this specialist with assistance in establishing a program. Margaret Shore from Business Research Associates was assigned to work on the General project. Margaret has an M.S. degree in marketing and personnel management from Illinois and had worked on several similar projects since joining BRA.

Case 2–6
Mid-State Coat Company[*]

After 10 years of successive sales increases, Mid-State Coat Company experienced a leveling off in 1982. In 1983, sales continued to remain low and were $575,000 below estimated sales. Estimated sales are usually based on an average of the last three years' sales. While economic conditions were bleak in 82 and 83, Robert Grover, president, and John Carroll, national sales manager, believed that some of the problems with sales were due to poor performance on the part of Mid-State's sales force. Now that the 1984 sales results are available, Carroll was attempting to isolate the problems. In particular, Carroll was concerned about account coverage, new account efforts, and the high number of markdowns. Carroll believed the markdowns were excessive and were contributing to Mid-State's reduction in profits, which had dropped below the two percent mark in 1983.

The Company

Mid-State Coat Company was started by the Grover family in 1898. The company, which manufactures higher-priced coats, has remained in the Grover family since its founding. Over the years, Mid-State has built a reputation as being a manufacturer of a quality product line which consists primarily of leather and wool garments.

During the 1970s, company sales had shown a steady increase and during that time, after-tax profits ranged from 3 to 5 percent, which is average for the industry. The sales force has also continued to grow and Mid-State currently has 17 sales representatives who cover the entire country. These sales reps report to the national sales manager, John Carroll, and to the assistant sales manager, Jay Barr. Carroll reports directly to the president, Robert Grover.

The Sales Force

The sales force has played a major role in Mid-State's success. Turnover has been low and primarily the result of retirement. In hiring new representatives, Carroll looks primarily for experience in the garment industry. No one under 30 has ever been hired, as maturity and experience are considered key determinants of success. Carroll feels that, as a result, Mid-State's selling efforts are strong and continuous.

---

[*]The assistance of Gary Cohen, MBA—Marketing, University of Wisconsin, Madison, in the preparation of this case is greatly appreciated.

Since Mid-State does not pay for traveling and selling expenses, with the exception of costs involved with sales meetings, over one half of the sales reps carry additional lines to increase their yearly incomes. Mid-State's only requirements are that alternate lines do not directly compete against Mid-State products and that the rep's other lines still leave enough time to thoroughly sell Mid-State products.

The sales force has two major selling seasons. The spring season, in which they sell primarily lightweight jackets, begins on Labor Day and ends on January 1. The fall season, in which the sales force sells heavier winter garments, begins on March 1 and ends on June 1. While these are the two main seasons, Mid-State sales reps are supposed to be continually monitoring the company's 1100 accounts for possible reorders. These accounts consist largely of better department stores and specialty stores.

Mid-State compensates its sales force on a straight commission basis. All the reps are given draws, which must be repaid, to help stabilize monthly earnings. Sales reps are paid 7 percent commission on gross sales provided that these sales are made at the suggested selling price, which consists of production costs plus a 33 percent markup. Sales made at prices less than the suggested price are commissioned at 4 percent. The reps have little authority over price, and any deviations from the suggested price must be approved by the home office. Generally, it is difficult to deny a rep's request for a markdown, since sales at less than suggested selling price still represent a contribution to Mid-State's overhead. Mid-State encourages its sales reps to open new accounts and offers an additional one-half percent bonus to reps who open new accounts. The one-half percent bonus is paid on total sales to new accounts at the end of each season. Thus, total commission increases to 7½ percent when new accounts are obtained.

The Problem

An examination of 1984 sales records provided Carroll with some insight into Mid-State's problems. Carroll felt the drop in sales is particularly acute in certain midwest territories, as Table 1 illustrates. Carroll believed that much of the decrease in the midwest region was due to high unemployment, especially in the industrial areas. The reduction in discretionary income usually affects sales of higher priced coats and jackets. While he believed this explained decreases in Michigan and Ohio territories, he felt that it did not totally explain the sharp drop in the Illinois and Indiana territory, traditionally one of Mid-State's better areas. Furthermore, Carroll was concerned about the lack of new accounts, not only in the midwestern areas but in all other areas as well.

Carroll directed his attention to Irv Harper's performance in Illinois and Indiana. After working with Harper in the early part of 1983, Carroll found that Harper, who was Mid-State's oldest sales rep, was not adequately covering his territory. Harper was spending almost all his time in the Chicago area, while

Table 1
Selected sales statistics, 1984

Region/Sales Rep	Age	Estimated Volume*	Actual Volume	Increase/ (Decrease)	Salary
Eastern Region					
Jim Baker (New York City)	48	$950,000	$1,200,000	$250,000	$71,600
John Farmer (NY, west PA)	33	800,000	700,000	(100,000)	42,600
Ed Feinberg (MA, VT, NH, CT)	54	450,000	340,000	(110,000)	23,800
Lou Moon (Phila, DC, MD)	47	850,000	750,000	(100,000)	46,500
Martin Regan (NJ, suburban NY)	63	900,000	750,000	(150,000)	40,300
Eastern Region total		$3,950,000	$3,740,000	($210,000)	$224,800
Midwestern Region					
Tim Allen (WI, MN, ND, SD)	33	$820,000	$750,000	($70,000)	$44,500
Dale Enders (IA)	38	275,000	350,000	75,000	20,600
Irv Harper (IL, IN)	67	1,000,000	750,000	(250,000)	41,500
Tom Kelly (MI)	48	800,000	650,000	(150,000)	46,300
Max Smith (OH)	54	825,000	600,000	(225,000)	36,700
Midwestern Region total		$3,720,000	$3,100,000	($620,000)	$189,600
Southern Region					
Bill Jackson (NC, SC, LA, TN)	51	$350,000	$400,000	$50,000	$28,000
Arthur Kohn (FL, GA, AL)	57	325,000	350,000	25,000	20,400
Southern Region total		$675,000	$750,000	$75,000	$48,400
Western Region					
Steve Harmon (KA, MO)	42	$350,000	$350,000	—	$19,500
Lee Kline (UT, CO, ID, MT, WY)	45	420,000	300,000	($120,000)	16,400
Larry Trump (TX, OK)	35	850,000	1,100,000	250,000	69,800
Sandy Turner (Northern CA, OR, WA)	47	600,000	700,000	100,000	41,300
Western Region total		$2,220,000	$2,450,000	$230,000	$147,000
House accounts		$650,000	$650,000	—	—
Total		$11,815,000	$11,240,000	($575,000)	$642,200

*Based on the average of the last three years' sales.

practically ignoring the rest of Illinois and Indiana. Carroll suspected that Harper's age had reduced his mobility, and thus he was no longer able to cover his territory.

Another area of concern to Carroll was suburban New York and New Jersey, a territory whose sales had shrunk for the third consecutive year. This area was covered by Martin Regan, who had been with Mid-State for over thirty years. In working with Regan, Carroll found that although Regan was well liked by his customers and a good sales rep, he was basically lazy. Regan persuaded some of his accounts to visit him at his office to view merchandise because he refused to carry samples to the customer's store. Carroll felt this approach had cost the company several accounts over the last three years.

The other problem concerning Carroll was the high number of markdowns. He found this problem in all territories, although he felt that it was more of a problem in certain territories. Again, Carroll attributed much of the markdown problem to economic conditions, which had forced Mid-State to lower prices in order to stimulate sales. Carroll suspected that part of the problem resulted from the sales reps' failure to spend enough time with their accounts, particularly at the beginning of each season.

Case 2–7
Chips-to-Dip, Inc.[*]

During the past few months, regional management of the Chips-to-Dip Corporation has noticed an increasing negative attitude prevailing in their sales force. The focus of the complaints centers on the sales force's role in the performance of a recent addition to the Chips-to-Dip product line, Bakers' Choice Cookies.

For more than twenty years, Chips-to-Dip has been a national leader in the sales of salty snacks with market shares that run into the 60s and 70s throughout the country. Until recently, the Chips-to-Dip product line consisted exclusively of potato and corn chips, tortilla chips, cheese puffs and pretzels. Many of the salty snack products have developed over time to include flavor variations and alternative package sizes. Historically, they have faced little competition and have built a reputation for premium quality products sold at premium prices. However, in the past three to five years, several market characteristics have changed, causing Chips-to-Dip management some concern. Their salty-snack line has been challenged by an increasing number of lower priced salty snack brands entering the market. Store managers, believing that consumers favor lower priced products, have devoted significant shelf space to these new brands.

In response to these competitive inroads, Chips-to-Dip considered several new products that would be compatible with their present form of distribution. They acquired Bakers' Choice Cookies of Seattle, Washington. Management felt that the new cookie line would be sold to many of the same accounts as the salty snack line. The cookie line was added to the sales reps' existing line. Chips-to-Dip management did not alter either the existing route schedules or the account assignments for their sales reps. As a result, the route sales reps are responsible for selling, delivering and promoting two product lines. The Bakers' Choice line consists of five different types of cookies.

Sales projections for the new line of cookies have not met expectations. In fact, sales have plateaued at a less than optimal level, causing some disillusionment among the sales force. The national sales force numbers in excess of 10,000, and the company prides itself on its ability to provide daily service to its accounts. In fact, Chips' "99.5 percent service level" has been criticized by analysts as being excessive, especially for a commodity product such as salty snacks. The market share results, however, seem to support the feasibility of providing such high levels of service.

During this time, the Chips-to-Dip selling task was straightforward. Given a route in an urban or rural area, the sales rep was to sell to grocery stores, convenience·stores, taverns, and gas stations with the goal of achieving the highest possible volume while making the best use of their time. Because they dealt

---

[*]The assistance of Patricia Zarnstorff, BBA—Marketing, University of Wisconsin, Madison in the preparation of this case is greatly appreciated.

exclusively in salty snacks, the route sales reps ordered from and delivered to only one area of the store. This usually required only one trip to the delivery truck to get the product once the initial sales order was taken.

In order to provide excellent service, which is Chips-to-Dip's differential advantage, a well-planned distribution system exists in both rural and urban areas. In the rural areas, small warehouses, known as "bins" provide the products for one to two sales reps. Shipments arrive on a weekly basis. In urban areas, the facilities are known as "distribution centers" and supply one or more sales districts. Shipments arrive daily and in large quantities.

Many aspects of the route salesperson's job have since changed. First, their job task is larger. Sales reps are now required to not only introduce and sell the cookie line to all of their salty accounts, but in addition, set up displays and offer samples, discounts and coupons to encourage product trial. However, the salespeople are still expected to continue their excellent sales and service record in the salty snack line. Second, the addition of the Bakers' Choice line has naturally increased the time required by each salesperson to spend at each account. The existence of two order forms, separate grocery sections, different buyers in the larger stores and the frequent need for two trips from delivery truck to store door require additional time to complete each sales stop. Third, district sales managers require route sales reps to make substantial effort promoting sales of Bakers' Choice Cookies. Reports itemizing sales of cookies and the regular salty line are demanded by management on a daily basis. Frequent conferences between district sales managers and route sales reps are held to discuss sales efforts promoting the Bakers' Choice line. In addition, sales contests and dealer incentives have been used to further motivate the sales force.

When the Bakers' Choice line was added, very little attention was given to its impact on the length of the salesperson's day. Sales routes were not restructured to allow for the extra margin of time needed to properly promote both products. Those salespeople who were able to provide a satisfactory effort selling the cookie line found that their average workday increased by 1½ to 2½ hours.

Jeff Bartz, regional sales manager, believes that the existing financial incentive should be sufficient to motivate the sales reps. According to Jeff: "If my salespeople make an effort to sell Bakers' Choice Cookies, they will realize a substantial gain in their weekly commission." However, with cookie commissions equal to salty snack commissions—both are 10 percent of sales—the salespeople feel differently. As Jim Riley, a route salesman for ten years, said: "Why should I lengthen my sales day with a completely new product? It isn't worth hassling with store managers and elbowing for space in the cookie section. For the same 10 percent commission, I would rather spend my time selling the tried-and-true Chips-to-Dip salty snacks."

In an attempt to alleviate the time demands placed on the sales reps as a result of the additional product line, Chips-to-Dip top management created a new position. The company hired people to serve as missionary representatives who were responsible for helping the route people with the introduction of the new product line. They would approach the store managers and attempt to persuade them to adopt the Bakers' Choice line. If the store manager approved, the missionary reps would arrange the shelf displays and monitor cookie sales weekly and monthly. Basically they were to help the sales rep. The success of these people, who became known as "cookie reps," was not known due to the brief time period this approach had been in effect. Three cookie reps were assigned to Bartz's region and worked out of the distribution centers usually located in the metropolitan cities.

Jeff Bartz knew that his eight district sales managers had a serious problem on their hands. Although initial sales of Bakers' Choice had been strong, market enthusiasm over the new cookie line had dropped significantly over the past year. As a result, the sales force was less confident in the future of the cookie line. Serious discussions between certain salespeople about the value of their cookie sales efforts and the quality of the cookie product had erupted over the past four months. Afraid of morale problems which could potentially affect the entire regional sales force, Bartz decided to conduct an attitude survey of the salespeople in his region. A questionnaire was developed and mailed to the 72 route salespeople in Bartz's region. Questionnaires were completed and returned by 59 sales reps for a response rate of 81.9 percent. A copy of the questionnaire and frequencies follows:

CHIPS-TO-DIP ROUTE SALESPERSON
QUESTIONNAIRE

Instructions: Please fill out the following questionnaire
by placing an X on the appropriate line. (Please use numbers
where they apply.)

I. Bakers' Choice Cookies

1. How well do you feel the Bakers' Choice cookie line is selling
    compared to other brands in your market?

    much _4_ : _10_ : _15_ : _23_ : _7_ : _—_ : _—_ much
    worse   better

2. Please rate Bakers' Choice cookies against the competitors on
    the following attributes:

    PRICE

    much _6_ : _22_ : _19_ : _9_ : _2_ : _1_ : _—_ much
    higher   lower

    QUALITY

    much _18_ : _11_ : _11_ : _13_ : _4_ : _2_ : _—_ much
    better   worse

    PACKAGING

    more _4_ : _17_ : _16_ : _11_ : _3_ : _5_ : _3_ less
    appealing   appealing

    ADVERTISING SUPPORT

    greater _7_ : _15_ : _11_ : _11_ : _7_ : _6_ : _2_ less
    support   support

3. Do you feel that the fact that you have to promote two product
    lines is hurting your effectiveness on either or both lines?

    Check the appropriate box:

26		8		8		17
is not hurting		is hurting		is hurting		is hurting
either line		cookie line		salty line		both lines

4.   Please indicate the percentage of your selling time spent in:

Salty snacks ...*85*...%

Bakers' Choice cookies ...*15*..%

=   100%

5.   Please indicate the percentage of your selling time that should be spent in:

Salty snacks ...*75*.%

Bakers' Choice cookies ...*25*.%

=   100%

6. Do you currently use cookie displays?   *54*   *5*

Yes   No

7. What type of display equipment do you use most often?

...*26*. cookie   ...*16*. shelf   ...*4*... pole
    hutch   signs   bins

...*24*. stairstep   ...*11*. weekender   ...*10*. knockout
    display   units   displays

8. What effect do the cookie representatives have on your sales:

very ...*4*.. : *9*.. : *11*.. : *16* : *4*.. : *10*.. : *3*... very
helpful   harmful

9. In general, how cooperative are the store managers on your route toward the promotion of Bakers' Choice cookies?

very ...*2*.. : *3*.. : *6*.. : *11*.. : *14*.. : *15*.. : *8*.... very
coopera-   uncoop-
tive   erative

10. Please indicate the type of cookie which you feel tastes the best.

...*9*....   ...*18*...   ...*2*...   ...*4*...   ...*26*.
Sandwich   Twirl   Fruit   Ho-made   Old-tyme
Stacks   Filled

II. Chips-to-Dip versus the Competition

1. Please rate Chips-to-Dip salty snacks against all competitors' salty snacks on the following attributes:

PRICE

much higher _*24*_ _*25*_ _*10*_ _–_ _–_ _–_ _–_ much lower

much better _*29*_ _*24*_ _*4*_ _*1*_ _*1*_ _–_ _–_ much worse

more appealing _*35*_ _*16*_ _*7*_ _*1*_ _–_ _–_ _–_ less appealing

greater support _*32*_ _*16*_ _*7*_ _*3*_ _*1*_ _–_ _–_ less support

2. Please indicate your degree of agreement or disagreement with the following statements:

a. The lower priced salty snack brands are a threat to your sales.

....*12*.... ....*32*.... ....*6*.... ....*8*.... ....*1*....
strongly agree | agree | neither agree nor disagree | disagree | strongly disagree

b. The quality of the Chips-to-Dip product compensates for its higher price.

....*8*.... ....*30*.... ....*8*.... ....*12*.... ....*1*....
strongly agree | agree | neither agree nor disagree | disagree | strongly disagree

c. The lower priced competitors produce a product of equal quality to the Chips-to-Dip product.

....*3*.... ....*2*.... ....*12*.... ....*25*.... ....*17*....
strongly agree | agree | neither agree nor disagree | disagree | strongly disagree

3. Please indicate your perception of Chips-to-Dip's company
   image on the following attributes:

GROWTH

very _18_ : _25_ : _7_ : _5_ : _2_ : _1_ : _1_ very
satisfac-   unsatis-
tory   factory

QUALITY

very _23_ : _28_ : _5_ : _2_ : _—_ : _1_ : _—_ very
satisfac-   unsatis-
tory   factory

MARKET LEADERSHIP

very _22_ : _19_ : _12_ : _2_ : _1_ : _1_ : _1_ very
satisfac-   unsatis-
tory   factory

CUSTOMER LOYALTY

very _12_ : _17_ : _12_ : _9_ : _6_ : _3_ : _—_ very
satisfac-   unsatis-
tory   factory

4. Your overall perception of Chips-to-Dip as a company:

good _36_ : _16_ : _4_ : _3_ : _—_ bad

5. Do you feel that Chips-to-Dip's marketing activities are:

passive _1_ : _4_ : _8_ : _18_ : _28_ aggressive

6. Please rate Chips-to-Dip's performance on the following activities:

Scale of 1-5:   1 = poor, 5 = excellent

Product advertising   1 _1_ 2 _4_ 3 _6_ 4 _22_ 5 _26_
New product introduction 1 _4_ 2 _10_ 3 _11_ 4 _21_ 5 _13_
Sales support   1 _4_ 2 _4_ 3 _18_ 4 _19_ 5 _14_
Aggressive pricing   1 _7_ 2 _22_ 3 _21_ 4 _7_ 5 _2_
Discounts and coupons   1 _5_ 2 _5_ 3 _12_ 4 _19_ 5 _18_

Case 2–8
Denver Illini Genetics[*]

In September 1984, Denver Illini Genetics' marketing director, Mr. Robson noticed a trend toward fluctuating yearly sales volumes by some of the company's sales representatives. Certain representatives had good sales years followed by poor sales years every other year. Their sales growth, as a result, is flat and not anywhere close to DIG's objectives. Robson needed to determine the cause and extent of the problem.

The Company

Denver Illini Genetics (DIG), based in Denver, Colorado, is a young artificial insemination (AI) company with a small share of the total market. Although there are many small firms that provide AI services, such as Tri-State Breeders in Wisconsin, DIG's major competitors are American Breeders Service, also a Wisconsin firm, who is recognized as the world leader, and Select Sires from Ohio. The major market of both firms is dairy and only a small portion, estimated at less than 10 percent, is in the beef market. Artificial insemination is the artificial introduction of semen into the genital tract of the female animal. This procedure provides several advantages of economic importance to beef and dairy cattle breeders. Of prime benefit is that it allows the breeder the opportunity to take advantage of the superior genetics of certain sires. Second, cattle breeders have used artificial insemination to avoid and prevent recurrence of livestock diseases. With both beef and dairy cattle, artificial insemination has proven itself to be a major factor in improving herd productivity.

Mr. Robson started with the Western Beef Breeders Association when it was organized, eight years ago. A few years ago, Western merged with Illini Breeders, Inc. of Springfield, Illinois. Subsequently, the company was renamed Denver Illini Genetics. DIG "produces" and sells beef semen and sees sizable growth potential in the beef part of the market. DIG's management sees the company's niche in the beef market rather than the dairy cattle market because this is where DIG has technical expertise and the dairy market is dominated by ABS. DIG is aiming for leadership position in the U.S. beef AI industry.

---

[*]This case was prepared especially for this text by Regina Downey and Brett Kronholm, MBAs—Marketing, University of Wisconsin, Madison.

The Sales Force

DIG employs two regional sales managers and fourteen sales representatives. The sales representatives are self-employed, independent contractors. These representatives are responsible for providing:

1. insemination service, and
2. semen sales and refrigerator service to customers who breed their own herds in their designated, exclusive sales areas.

The list of customer services provided by DIG representatives includes the distribution of semen, equipment, and supplies. Utilizing DIG-owned equipment, they deliver semen, liquid nitrogen, refrigerators, and breeding supplies to their customers on regular, precise schedules.

The representatives promote their products and services through on-the-farm sales calls with the aid of DIG-prepared publications, promotional materials, and advertising. Promotional supplies that the representatives can purchase from DIG include car emblems, fabric decals, baseball caps, down vests, etc. In addition, DIG furnishes an annual cooperative advertising package that is designed to help the representatives get the attention of beef breeders. The ads use a theme similar to DIG's national advertising theme. The terms of the cooperative advertising package state:

1. DIG will reimburse you (the representative) for one half of your local advertising expense up to 2 percent of your 1984 semen purchases.
2. First-year representatives are eligible for reimbursement up to one half of $125 spent for advertising during that year.

The DIG cooperative advertising program is designed to help cover the cost of advertising in the print and radio media.

The main source and amount of the representatives' income varies considerably between areas and representatives. A major portion is derived through selling DIG products and services which are all individually commissionable. Payment by the herd owner for insemination service presents the second portion of the representatives' income. Most representatives, about 65 percent, work part time and have farms or part-time jobs elsewhere. A country veterinarian who sells DIG products and services "on the side" is an example of a part-time DIG representative.

DIG compensates its representatives using the commission/discount program shown in Exhibit 1. The company estimates that 65 percent of its total sales are made to the representatives at discounts determined using Plan D. The representatives buy DIG products for their own inventory and sell from this inventory to breeders. The representatives sell the products to the herd owners at suggested list prices. The remaining 35 percent of DIG's total sales are made directly to the herd owners. Direct sales to beef farmers occur primarily with new representatives who, due to financial limitations, are unable to carry enough inventory to

Exhibit 1
Plan D

DENVER ILLINI GENETICS
PRICES AND TERMS
Effective January 1, 1985

F.O.B. Denver, Colorado. Semen may be purchased at the representative discount by paying cash with order, C.O.D. DIG truck using the DIG price list for beef, or credit can be obtained with prior approval from the district sales manager.

Accelerated Commission Prediscount Program

The prediscounted amount and the commission schedule will be accelerated during the calendar year, based on semen dollar volume of business by the representative both from purchase F.O.B. Denver or DIG Truck and commissionable sales to DIG customers at prevailing DIG list prices. The commission/discount level will be escalated under the following schedule:

Semen Only			
$	0 to $ 8,000	at 23%
8,001 to	13,000	at 26%
13,001 to	20,000	at 30%
20,001 to	and up	at 34%

Commissions shall be paid to the representative during the DIG fiscal month following the date of billing of the sale. The representative discount will be applied to all purchases at the time of billing the representative account.

Sales discount on all cash purchases made at the truck will be calculated by the route serviceman at 23 percent from the list price. The amount of discount greater than 23 percent will be credited as additional discount to the representative's account at the time of billing because charge purchases will be calculated at the full discount level when billed.

Discount/Commission on Additional Items

A 12 percent commission will be paid on the following items:

Refrigeration Equipment
Breeding Certificates
Refrigerator Rental Charges (Based on $1.75 per day equals 21 cents per day)

7 percent commission will be paid on supplies sold in representative's area.

A 12 percent discount will be allowed on the purchase price of breeding supplies.

Cooperative Advertising Program Charges

There will be a charge each month to representative's account for the DIG cooperative advertising program based on the following schedule:

Representative Commission/Discount Level	Monthly Fee
23%	$12.00
26	17.00
30	22.00
34	27.00

The representative commission/discount level in effect at year-end (December 31) will be used for the following year for both the monthly fee and eligibility of benefits.

Commissions for Semen, Supplies, and Additional Items Sold on Credit by Representatives

Commission will be paid to representative the DIG fiscal month following the date of billing of the sale. A commission will be granted the representative under these terms even though a credit sale; however, DIG will charge back the commission to representative against current commissions if the account balance should reach or exceed *120* days past due.

Refrigerator Rental and Nitrogen Service Charge

Refrigerator(s) for representative's own use, $12.00 per month; $17.00 for some special models. All other refrigerators used in sales area are subject to a charge of $1.75 per day.

meet demand. The representatives receive commissions as stated in Plan D for their assistance in these sales. Average sales volumes are hard to compute due to the full-time/part-time split. For part-time people, annual average sales are $15,000. Full-time people average $65,000. Usually, 90 percent of sales are for semen and 10 percent for products and supplies. For example, Harry Turner, Southern region, had 1982 semen sales of $96,023 and $10,669 sales of products and supplies for a total of $106,692. Turner also provides breeding services and in a typical year, will breed 3000 cows at a charge of $5 each.

In addition, the company motivates its representatives with a sales growth incentive program entitled, "Beef Bonanza" which has been employed since 1980. Under the plan, an escalating commission (7 to 12 percent) is paid at year-end, based on unit volume growth over the previous year. In 1985, all representatives whose 1985 average dollar sales exceed 105 percent of their 1984 average dollar sales will be eligible for the Beef Bonanza bonus (Exhibit 2). According to Mr. Robson, "It's a dollars program and no growth still gets you dollars. You can get dollars for just a dollar's (not unit) increase."

The company's objective is to increase both the number of semen units sold,

---

Exhibit 2

February 9, 1985

TO: All DIG Representatives

FROM: Bob Robson, Marketing Director

RE: Beef Bonanza 1985

cc: Regional Sales Personnel
    Management Staff

With a tremendous finish for the month of December, 1984 will go into the record books as the best year ever for Denver Illini Genetics. As we review 1984 and look to 1985, we:

1. increased our market share,
2. refined our sales oriented distribution system,
3. have increased our number of beef bulls and programs to provide you with the tools for continued success,
4. have our total offering of beef bulls priced competitively to provide a very aggressive posture, and

Following are the details of the plan:

A. All representatives whose 1985 average dollar sales exceed 105 percent of 1984 average dollar sales will be eligible for Beef Bonanza bonus.

B. An escalating bonus of 7 to 12 percent will be paid at year-end based on unit volume growth over prior year as follows:

Unit Volume Growth over Prior Year	Beef Bonanza Bonus Multiplier
0%	7%
2	8
5	9
7	10
8	11
10 and over	12

Exhibit 2 *(concluded)*

Following are some examples of the bonus potential of this program:

EXAMPLES

	Year	Units	Average Price	Retail Sales	−	1984 Base 105%	+	Increased Sales
A.	1985	4,400	$11.55	$ 50,820		$ 46,200		+$4,620
	1984	4,000	11.00	44,000				
		+400						

Unit increase = 400 / 4,000 = 10%

Bonus at 12% (10% unit growth) of $4,620 = $554

Total Bonus = $554.00

	Year	Units	Average Price	Retail Sales	−	1984 Base 105%	+	Increased Sales
B.	1985	4,160	$11.55	$ 48,048		$ 46,200		+$1,848
	1984	4,000	11.00	44,000				
		+160						

Unit increase = 160 / 4,000 = 4%

Bonus at 8% (4% unit growth) of $1,848 = $148

Total Bonus = $148.00

	Year	Units	Average Price	Retail Sales	−	1984 Base 105%	+	Increased Sales
C.	1985	6,400	$13.20	$ 84,480		$ 72,072		+$12,408
	1984	5,200	13.20	68,640				
		+1,200						

Unit increase = 1,200 / 5,200 = 23%

Bonus at 12% (10% and over unit growth) of $12,408 = $1,489

Total Bonus = $1,489.00

	Year	Units	Average Price	Retail Sales	−	1984 Base 105%	+	Increased Sales
D.	1985	3,840	$13.20	$ 50,688		$ 46,200		+$4,488
	1984	4,000	11.00	44,000				
		−160						

Unit decrease = 160 / 4,000 = −4%

Bonus at 7% (0% unit growth) of $4,488 = $314

Total Bonus = $255.00

	Year	Units	Average Price	Retail Sales	−	1984 Base 105%	+	Increased Sales
E.	1985	9,600	$13.20	$126,720		$101,871		+$24,849
	1984	8,400	11.55	97,020				
		+1,200						

Unit increase = 1,200 / 8,400 = +14%

Bonus at 12% (+14% unit growth) of $24,849 = $2,982

Total Bonus = $2,982

	Year	Units	Average Price	Retail Sales	−	1984 Base 105%	+	Increased Sales
F.	1985	3,360	$ 9.90	$ 33,264		$ 36,960		−$3,696
	1984	3,200	11.00	35,200				
		+160						

Unit increase = 160 / 3,200 = +5%

Bonus at 9% (5% unit growth) of −$3,696 = −$333

Total Bonus = 0

In summary, the 1985 Beef Bonanza program revolves around total increased retail sales with an added incentive for increased unit sales but no penalty for decreased units.

and the average semen unit blend price. This price is the average price paid for all semen units sold. A representative, therefore, can increase his unit blend price by selling the more expensive units of semen. In 1984, semen prices ranged from $6 to $100, with most semen units sold in the $8 to $16 range.

The Problem

As stated, in late 1984, Mr. Robson noticed fluctuations in some representatives' yearly sales totals. "A growing concern is that the current program is being "worked" and we (DIG) pay for the same growth again and again with the good-year, bad-year syndrome, instead of paying real dollars for real growth. Robson felt that the problem existed in both the southern and northern regions (Exhibit 3). Robson suspected that the sales incentive program, Beef Bonanza, was the reason for the fluctuations. The incentive payments are based entirely on the increase over the previous year. This allows a sales representative to manipulate his or her bonus by having a poor sales year and thus establishing a very low unit sales base to improve on. After establishing a low base figure in 1983, for example, the sales representative would not have to increase his or her sales volume very much in 1984 to earn a sizable incentive payment at year's end. The percentage gain in unit volume determines the bonus paid. "With sales reps playing this numbers game," exclaimed Robson, "we don't grow!"

Mr. Robson wondered if the Beef Bonanza bonus program should be changed to deter the sales representatives from channeling their sales efforts in this fluctuating manner. The company's goal of steadily increasing growth could not be realized if this "numbers game-playing" continued. With this in mind, Robson requested suggestions from the regional sales managers on how to motivate the representatives to strive for consistent, yearly sales growth. An actual response memo that he received from Rick Stone, Northern regional sales manager, is shown in Exhibit 4. This program revision suggestion includes a change to:

1. Using a historical best year base both for units and total retail sales dollars, and
2. Awarding a quarterly, instead of yearly bonus payment.

Stone affirmed, "I support a quarterly bonus system that will allow the Beef Bonanza program to work the entire year rather than encouraging heavy buying to take advantage of accelerated commissions and Beef Bonanza bonuses." However, his suggestion was rejected by Robson, who concluded that it would just provide an incentive for the game-playing representatives to manipulate their sales on a quarterly instead of yearly basis. Also, "Stone's idea ignores the seasonal aspect of beef semen sales." It was typical for a DIG representative with annual beef semen sales of $50,000 to sell $35,000 of those sales in the second quarter, due to the inherent seasonality factor.

Exhibit 3
Total representative semen sales,
northern and southern regions,
1982–1984

Name/Region	Year	Units	Average Unit Price	Dollar Sales
Northern Region				
Al Dempsey	1982	3,978	10.13	$ 40,297
	1983	6,075	10.78	65,489
	1984	3,715	12.26	45,546
Harry Turner	1982	7,280	13.19	96,023
	1983	7,840	14.09	110,466
	1984	6,473	13.28	85,961
Bill McDowney	1982	4,188	9.68	40,540
	1983	3,763	10.02	37,705
	1984	3,842	10.52	40,418
Jack Rabin	1982	4,765	12.48	59,467
	1983	5,569	14.10	78,523
	1984	6,719	11.42	76,731
Dean Morgan	1982	5,043	11.51	58,045
	1983	6,670	10.26	68,434
	1984	8,787	12.24	107,553
Dan McLaren	1982	242	47.20	11,422
	1983	312	40.35	12,590
	1984	297	36.71	10,903
Jerry Martin	1982	583	13.14	7,661
	1983	515	9.18	4,728
	1984	228	17.09	3,896
Southern Region				
Walt Earl	1982	4,569	13.84	63,235
	1983	3,636	13.78	50,104
	1984	4,073	14.90	60,688
Gene Harms	1982	6,954	14.04	97,634
	1983	6,314	13.40	84,608
	1984	7,501	12.94	97,063
F. G. Brand	1982	4,437	9.88	43,838
	1983	4,146	11.81	48,964
	1984	7,242	12.63	91,466
Mitch Kramer	1982	2,518	12.52	31,525
	1983	2,099	12.66	26,573
	1984	1,683	11.40	19,186
H & M Arnold	1982	4,102	9.72	39,871
	1983	4,191	10.63	44,550
	1984	3,709	9.87	36,608
Don Larson	1982	5,555	11.36	63,105
	1983	6,485	11.03	71,530
	1984	6,798	11.70	79,537
Dave Ipson	1982	5,102	13.46	68,673
	1983	7,268	14.00	101,752
	1984	8,987	12.46	111,978

Source: DIG records.

Exhibit 4
Denver Illini Genetics
October 12, 1984

TO: Bob Robson

FROM: Rick Stone, Northern Regional Sales Manager

SUBJECT: Beef Bonanza Bonus Program

Bob, you asked that I put some of my thoughts on the Beef Bonanza Bonus Program together for you. My feeling on the matter is that we continue a bonus program that pays real dollars for real growth.

Rule 1: Best year for units and best year for retail sales dollars become the base year. They may be different years.

Rule 2: A 5% Beef Bonanza bonus will be paid quarterly on retail sales dollars above $ base with a 10% unit volume growth over unit base. This would apply to the first three quarters. Fourth quarter would apply to year-end.

Rule 3-A: Retail sales $ base is established as follows:

105% × best retail sales $ = Total Base $

Total Base $ / 4 = quarterly base $

(Quarterly base $ × 2 = Mid-year base $, etc.)

Rule 3-B: Total unit base = previous best year units. Previous best units / 4 = quarterly base units (Quarterly base units × 2 = mid-year base, etc.)

Rule 4: At year-end the final bonus will be calculated and any quarterly bonuses subtracted and the difference paid based on the following:

Unit Volume Growth over Base	Over $ Base Beef Bonanza Bonus Escalation
0%	5%
3%	6%
6%	7%
9%	8%
12%	9%
15% and over	10%

EXAMPLE:

		Units	$	Bonus
1st Quarter	Base	100	1,000	0% × 100 = $0 bonus
	Actual	105	1,100	
	Dev	5	100	5% = 0% bonus
2nd Quarter	Base	200	2,000	5% × $1,000 = $50 total
	Actual	240	3,000	
	Dev	40	1,000	20% = 5% bonus
3rd Quarter	Base	300	3,000	0% × 1,000 = $0 bonus
	Actual	300	4,000	
	Dev	0	1,000	0% = 0% bonus
4th Quarter	Base	400	4,000	No 4th quarter bonus pd but go to year-end.
	Actual	600	6,000	
	Dev	200	2,000	50% = year-end schedule
Year-end	Base	400	4,000	10% × 2,000 = $200
	Actual	600	6,000	200 − 50 = $150
	Dev	200	2,000	pay $150 bonus
				Total bonus = $200

Conclusion: This program would eliminate the good-year, bad-year problem and allow the truly progressive, growing representative to be recognized and paid for his efforts.

The effect of good quarters would be eliminated by dividing the base for units and dollars over the entire year.

Representatives who have been working the system will not like such a program.

A quarterly system will allow the program to work the entire year rather than encourage heavy buying to take advantage of accelerated commissions and Beef Bonanza bonuses.

Summary: My description may be rough, but I feel the idea is described.

In January 1985, Robson held a sales meeting with the company's managers to obtain their input on this problem. He explained that some of the representatives had experienced questionable yearly sales fluctuations that were possibly due to the Beef Bonanza bonus plan and asked for the sales managers' thoughts on this matter. The managers strongly opposed the idea that a serious problem existed. According to Dave Williams, Southern regional sales manager, "Some people perhaps have a good year and then a bad year, and are not purposely playing games. Maybe it's a little unrealistic to think that a person would grow every year for eight years in a row." Robson quickly interjected, "The long term man does not count on Beef Bonanza because he is not counting on overall growth increases as much as a solidification of his business and holding good value. The man that is starting is the one that we should aim Beef Bonanza at." When questioned about the extent of the problem, Robson admitted, "I don't know how large it is. All I have is a gut feeling. I do know that the representatives are very sensitive about this issue."

The discussion then turned to generation of possible solutions to this problem. Barry Norem, sales analyst, was not enthusiastic about changing the Beef Bonanza program. "Let's say that we do want to put a stop to the good-year, bad-year reps. What about the other reps that had a good year in 84? . . . You're almost damned if you do and damned if you don't." The managers were generally supportive in their comments about Beef Bonanza.

When queried about the program's effectiveness, Robson replied, "Beef Bonanza has served us well. Its been fairly motivational. We want to motivate the rep . . . even if he does play games."

At the meeting, the managers generated these additional ideas for adjusting the Beef Bonanza program:

1. Changing the unit base to the historical best year's base instead of the previous year's base. In opposition, one manager, stated, "If we look at 1985 and say its an unsettled one because of the economy, etc., then it may not be a good time to increase the unit base because it'll probably have a poor psychological effect on a lot of people. . . . A lot more people would be negatively affected psychologically than would be affected financially."

2. Determining the base by averaging the previous two years sales figures. This idea came from Kyle Dean, vice president of finance. Dean felt that this would make it more difficult to work the system.

3. Increasing the unit base increase needed to reach the highest bonus level to 15 percent instead of 10 percent. Andy Marien, research director, said: "This is easy to use and would help solve the problem."

4. Making the dollar base the highest of the last two years. "This would prevent the good year-bad year problem," claimed John Ruppert, Kyle Dean's assistant.

The managers also suggested:

5. Rewarding with gifts or travel instead of, or in addition to cash. "When you're talking about incentives, you can have monetary incentives, gift incentives,

or travel incentives. That's basically what you have to deal with," claimed Dave Williams.

6. Refunding a portion of the sales representatives' travel expenses.
7. Awarding national recognition for top performers. Rick Stone noted: "We could publish the sales results in the newsletter throughout the year. You'd be surprised at how much just having their name on a list excites them. They are motivated by this."
8. Attaching incentives to particular breed-specific sales 'rather than overall sales. For example, "Beef up Brahman in 85."

A frequently voiced concern of Bob Robson and his managers was the uncertain economic outlook of 1985. "It's very undecided what the economy is going to do to our business," Robson claimed. This uncertainty affected their decision when the roll call vote was taken on how to handle the sales fluctuation problem.

Case 2–9
Western Business Forms, Inc.

"These results are rather dismal," exclaimed M. Carter, who was reviewing a study of sales force job satisfaction conducted for Western Business Forms by an outside consulting agency. In particular, Carter was concerned with the sales force's attitude toward Western's compensation program as indicated by Exhibit 1. "I thought our system was really working, but it seems that our sales force is not satisfied with how they are paid," Carter said to Western's vice president of marketing, H. W. Thompson "You have a problem," Thompson indicated, "but any general increase in compensation without a corresponding increase in sales is just out of the question. Furthermore, we have an excess inventory problem that needs your immediate attention. Our vice president of finance wants to know why our sales force is not doing a better job of selling off the excess inventory." This last comment bothered Carter, who pointed out to Thompson, "the inventory problem was not created by the sales force. Our inventory problem is the result of poor sales forecasting." "That may be true," Thompson said, "but we still have to sell off the inventory and that's the job of the sales force."

Carter did not like this situation. "Pushing the sales force to solve an inventory problem which they did not create will be tough," Carter thought. "Now, we have a report that tells us that the compensation plan does not provide enough selling incentive to the sales force." Carter was also concerned about another finding which revealed that the sales force was not being adequately recognized for good

Exhibit 1
Pay component of job satisfaction*

	Western Mean	Mean Across All Companies
1. My pay is high in comparison with what others get for similar work in other companies	2.41	2.51
2. My pay doesn't give me much incentive to increase my sales	2.76	3.41
3. My pay is low in comparison with what others get for similar work in other companies	3.10	2.91
4. In my opinion the pay here is lower than in other companies	3.22	2.97
5. I am highly paid	2.44	2.40
6. My income provides for luxuries	2.66	2.91
7. My selling ability largely determines my earnings in this company	2.15	3.25
8. I'm paid fairly compared with other employees in this company	3.32	3.38
9. My income is adequate for normal expenses	3.78	3.49
10. I am very much underpaid for the work that I do	3.71	3.43
11. I can barely live on my income	4.12	3.78
Total	47.68	50.00

*The higher the score, the more the sales representatives are satisfied for both positive and negative items, since the negative items are reversed scored. The range is from 1 to 5.

Exhibit 2
Company policy and management
support component of job
satisfaction*

		Western Mean	Mean across All Companies
1.	Management keeps us in the dark about things we ought to know	2.78	2.79
2.	Management is progressive...................................	2.97	3.17
3.	Our sales goals are set by the higher-ups without considering market conditions	2.73	3.15
4.	Management really knows its job	3.34	2.88
5.	This company operates efficiently and smoothly......................	2.73	2.46
6.	Our home office isn't always cooperative in servicing our customers ..	3.22	2.65
7.	I'm satisfied with the way employee benefits here are handled	3.97	3.26
8.	We have a real competitive advantage in selling because of the quality of our products	3.66	3.21
9.	Sometimes when I learn of management's plans, I wonder if they knew the territory situation at all	2.66	2.57
10.	The company's sales training is not carried out in a well-planned program...	3.27	2.66
11.	Management is weak	3.49	3.07
12.	I have confidence in the fairness and honesty of management	3.10	3.29
13.	Management here is really interested in the welfare of employees	3.39	3.25
14.	The company has satisfactory profit sharing	3.71	2.02
15.	Compared with other companies, employee benefits here are good ...	3.95	2.96
16.	I feel that the company is highly aggressive in its sales promotion efforts	2.61	2.42
17.	Sales representatives in this company receive good support from the home office	2.63	3.09
18.	Management here sees to it that there is cooperation between departments	2.85	2.71
19.	There isn't enough training for sales representatives who have been on the job for awhile	2.90	2.65
20.	Management ignores our suggestions and complaints	3.12	3.07
21.	Management fails to give clear-cut orders and instructions...........	3.17	3.08
22.	Formal recognition programs compare favorably with those of other companies......................................	2.34	None
23.	There are not enough formal recognition programs in this company...	2.61	None
24.	I do not get enough formal recognition for the work I do.............	2.76	None
25.	Formal recognition programs in this company are attractive	2.12	None
26.	I am satisfied with the way our formal recognition programs are administered..	2.39	None
27.	Recognition awards are based on ability	2.44	None
28.	If a sales representative is dismissed, it is usually for good reason	4.17	None
29.	Sales representatives have been dismissed for inadequate reasons....	4.15	None
30.	Recognition awards are given in an arbitrary manner...............	2.97	None
31.	There are opportunities for additional training for experienced sales representatives	3.12	None
32.	This company provides me opportunity for released time for professional development......................................	2.76	None
	Total†	54.52	50.00

*The higher the score, the more the sales representatives are satisfied. This applies to both positive and negative items, since the negative items are reversed scored. The range is from 1 to 5.
†Total score is composed of the sum of scores for questions 1–21.

performance (see Exhibit 2). "What do they want," Carter wondered, "a pat on the back every time they make a sale?"

Western Business Forms, Inc., is a regional printer of a large line of business forms used by companies, institutions, and government agencies. Western, located in Denver, sells business forms throughout an area that includes Colorado, southern Wyoming, western Nebraska, western Kansas, the pan handle areas of Oklahoma and Texas, northern New Mexico, and northern Utah. Sales are made directly to users by 18 sales representatives who are paid on a salary plus commission basis. A sales representative's compensation consists of 85 percent salary plus 15 percent commission on gross margin for all sales. Most of the business forms are standard and have the customer's name imprinted if needed. In some situations, sales representatives help customers design business forms according to their particular needs. The average base salary in 1984 was $17,500 and the average commission was $3,500. Western's 1984 sales totaled $3,150,000, and cost of goods sold averaged 40 percent. Profit before taxes was $441,000.

The inventory problem is in the company's standard line of legal documents. These are preprinted forms that contain space for imprinting the customer's name and address. Based on 1983 sales of this product line, Western has enough inventory on hand to last well into 1985. Inventory carrying charges are substantial enough to cause concern among several Western executives. One said: "We have to get these forms unloaded before the laws change, or they will become candidates for recycling."

Carter reviewed several sales publications to gain some additional insight about sales force compensation. As a result of this literature search, the idea of having a sales contest seemed quite appealing. Moreover, a sales contest, in addition to providing financial rewards, would recognize contest winners. Carter's attention was directed to various publications and articles dealing specifically with contests. Eventually, Carter developed a sales contest proposal for Thompson to review and approve.

The proposed sales contest would involve all the sales force and their spouses as well. To increase spouse awareness and interest, contest details would be mailed directly to the sales representative's home. The contest would last three months, with cash prizes awarded monthly and a grand prize awarded at the end of the contest. Winners would be those three sales representatives who achieved the highest percentage increase in sales for each of the three months, compared with their sales for the same period last year. Monthly winners would receive $300, $200, or $100. The contest would start in April 1984, and sales would be compared with sales in April 1983. The grand prize of $500 would be awarded to the sales representative obtaining the highest percentage increase for all three months in 1984, compared with the same three-month period in 1983. In addition to the cash prizes, merchandise points would be awarded each month and mailed to the sales representatives' homes. A catalog would contain pictures of merchandise and the points needed to obtain the various articles. Carter proposed using a firm specializing in sales contests, Starr Enterprises, to handle the distribution of merchandise. Western would be billed for the retail price of the merchandise. Starr Enterprises considered the retail markup as their fee. Merchandise points would be awarded to sales representatives whose sales for any of the three months exceeded sales for the same month in 1983. Each percentage point would equal $3.00 worth of merchandise points. Each prize point was worth $0.50. Thus, if a sales representative's sales for April 1984 exceeded April 1979 sales by 18 percent, then 108 prize points worth $54 (18 percentage points × $3) would be mailed to his or her home. These prize points could be used immediately or saved in hopes of earning more. Each prize point earned a chance to win a grand prize at a drawing to be held at the end of the contest. The grand prize would be a stereo system with a retail value of $450. The drawing would take place at a dinner dance, at which time all cash prize winners would be recognized.

To help reduce the inventory problem, Carter proposed that four prize points be awarded for each case sold. Each case carried a suggested price of $20. Carter presented the contest proposal to Thompson for approval.

Case 2–10
Genner Security Systems, Inc.*

Genner Security Systems, Inc., of Chicago manufactures and installs a complete line of security alarms for both commercial and private use. The corporation was founded in 1938 by Dick Genner, who has been the president and chairman of the board for the past 45 years. Before this time, Genner was a pioneer in his development of security alarm systems for banking institutions that suffered frequent assaults by notorious Chicagoland gangsters in the early 1930s. At the present time, Genner Security is a nationally established business that holds nearly 60 percent of the market. Sales in 1983 totaled nearly $900 million, a 10-fold increase from 1958 sales of $90 million.

Present Situation

J. P. Genner, son of president and chairman of the board Dick Genner, was promoted to the position of central division sales manager in January 1983. At 35, J. P. is the youngest division manager by nearly ten years. His rapid advancement up the firm's marketing ladder (see Exhibit 1) was strictly an outcome of excellent

Exhibit 1
Organizational structure of the central sales division

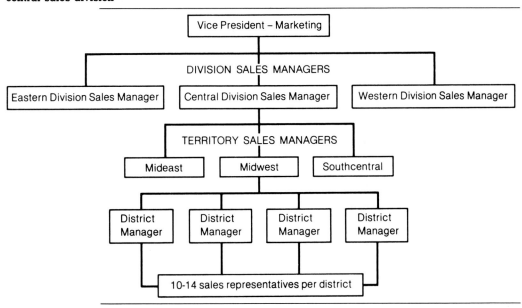

---

*This case was prepared especially for this text by J. Patrick Genn, MBA—Marketing, University of Wisconsin, Madison.

results in previous positions. In his new capacity, J. P. is primarily occupied with the following responsibilities:

1. To expand the level of sales within the division.
2. To analyze the competitive environment and make accurate sales forecasts.
3. To oversee the sales training and development program.
4. To select and develop district and territory sales managers.
5. To account for the total performance of the division.
6. To work with the vice president of marketing on executive level problems and decisions.

At the present time, J. P. is analyzing the division's historical and current year's sales performance in preparation for his year-end sales summary and forecast presentation. This being his first attempt at such an analysis, J. P. had obtained individual sales records for each salesperson in the division and proceeded to manipulate the data in several different ways, hoping to uncover any useful trends. One pronounced trend that puzzled J. P. a great deal involved the aggregate sales performance differences between salespeople who belonged to different seniority classes within the division. Exhibits 2 and 3 illustrate his findings. There was a definite trend for salespeople with between four and nine years of experience to produce the best sales results in terms of quota attainment and year-to-year growth. What concerned J. P. was the tendency for the senior salespeople to exhibit a decline in quota attainment and sales growth percentages when compared with the younger salespeople. He had previously been under the assumption that most of these "career" salespeople would fare much better when

Exhibit 2
Quota attainment by seniority—central division

Years as a Sales Rep	Combined Average Percent of Quota
1–3	122%
4–9	138
10 or more	104

Exhibit 3
Yearly growth in sales by seniority—central division

Years as a Sales Rep	Average Percent Growth, 1981–1982
1–3	65%
4–9	24
10 or more	6

compared with the less experienced ones. J. P. knew several 10-year veterans who were among the firm's very best, but he never realized the aggregate performance of all senior salespeople. In short, he felt that he had uncovered a potential weakness in the division's sales force. Furthermore, J. P. was not totally confident that he had enough experience with senior salespeople to determine how much could be expected of them or what it would take to get them to perform to their full potential. Knowing that his age may prove to be a handicap, he decided to seek the counsel of his fellow division sales managers and their superiors at the next monthly sales meeting.

The Sales Meeting

At the November 1, 1983, national sales meeting, J. P. produced the results depicted in Exhibits 2 and 3. He addressed three issues: (1) contributions of the senior salespeople, (2) why these people were never brought into management, and (3) why they showed a tendency to become stagnant in terms of sales performance as their length of service increased.

Howard Schultz, Genner's vice president in charge of marketing, first addressed the issue concerning why certain salespeople were not brought into management: "We're talking about two distinct professions, that of selling and that of managing. We should not mix, from a purpose point of view, these two separate professions. They are not interchangeable. I think it comes of no surprise that many sales reps prefer selling to managing and are not interested in the switch. There are others who would like to make the change, but because of age, administrative limitations, or the inability to lead people, just cannot be considered."

Dick Genner directed this comment to his son: "Occasionally, a top, younger salesman insists on trying his hand at management, even though we are completely convinced that he will not be happy in management or that he is neither keyed nor adapted for it. He may even say that he is going to leave us and go somewhere else if we don't give him the opportunity. So in some instances, we let him try. Almost inevitably, he does a fair-to-middling job at the start in the lower managerial rungs as an assistant district manager. But after a year or two of finding and training sales reps, he is perfectly content to go back to selling on his own. He simply does not like his taste of sales management, so he returns to the job where he does not have to take his satisfaction from the results of other people."

J. P. replied, "Okay, I guess I can understand why some people become career salesmen, but why do they seem to lose their drive after 10 or so years?"

Schultz interjected once again, "First of all, the older rep seems to prefer caring for his old garden, rather than planting the new seed. Second, because he has sold so many units and knows the product well, the veteran is inclined to assume that the customers know the product well. He often skims over the explanation of a feature that is really basic. Third, it is hard to interest the veteran in new sales techniques. Fourth, he is inclined to be spending more time on personal problems, on the administration of his own business, or on some supervision of the junior sales rep, and a lot less time, as he gets older, on actual selling. Of course, there are exceptions to this generalization. Many of our very best sales reps have been 15- to 20-year veterans. However, most of these people aren't with us anymore because they always seem to take a more attractive position with another firm or go into business for themselves."

This last comment seemed to arouse Dick Genner as he broke in with the following comment: "The lures of competition or of setting up their own business are not the real reasons why we lose these people. They are just the catalysts and the excuses. In nine out of 10 cases, the real reason behind the loss of a top veteran is that we in management have failed. We have not made it possible for the satisfactions of his job to keep pace with his growth, and in a sense, he has progressed faster than we have. He finds himself bumping his head on a ceiling that we never foresaw. These senior sales reps, like all people who are good at their job, need incentives—incentives that go beyond money alone. I think that J. P. has definitely struck upon a problem worthy of special attention—that of motivating the senior sales reps."

He then directed the following assignment at his son: "I'd like you to prepare a complete analysis of the situation as well as a set of recommendations on how we should go about motivating the senior sales reps to perform to their full potential while continuing with their careers at Genner. We'll plan on hearing your presentation at the year-end sales meeting, so you'd better get on it right away. We just received the results of our job satisfaction survey administered to the entire sales force, so be sure to pick up a copy of the findings before leaving today. I think you'll find it useful in working on this problem."

The next day J. P. sat in his office reviewing the notes he had taken at the sales meeting, as well as the job satisfaction survey results (see Exhibit 4). These data

Exhibit 4
Job satisfaction survey
(summary of results)

Component	Job Satisfaction*		
	I	II	III
1. Job	52.47	47.04	42.47
2. Fellow workers	48.84	46.07	46.75
3. Supervisor	64.51	66.93	60.11
4. Company policy and management support	74.96	71.03	68.06
5. Pay	34.84	34.90	34.28
6. Promotion and advancement	30.29	26.09	22.86
7. Customer	51.57	55.44	61.06

*I = 3 years or less, II = 4–9 years, III = 10 years or more. The higher the score, the higher is the degree of job satisfaction in that component.

showed significant differences among members of the sales force with different degrees of seniority. This was very consistent with the other information he had acquired. J. P. felt very confident that his success in designing strategies for motivating the senior sales representatives would have a very positive effect on the total performance of his division. He believed very strongly that these reps had a great deal to offer. It was just a matter of providing them with the motivation to give it.

Case 2–11
Heathcoate Pharmaceuticals[*]

Heathcoate Pharmaceuticals manufactures and distributes a wide range of prescription and over-the-counter medications worldwide. With sales in excess of $87 million during 1983, Heathcoate is one of the 10 largest firms in the industry. Corporate headquarters have been located in Rochester, Minnesota, since the company was founded in 1948. During the past 10 years, sales have doubled, and international operations have expanded to include Canada, Europe, and South America.

Heathcoate's national sales force is divided among three regions: eastern, southern, and western. Each region is divided into 7 to 12 districts of similar size. There are nearly 300 salespeople, working on a salary plus commission basis, calling on pharmacies, wholesale drug distributors, large retail drug chains, hospitals, and clinics. Due to the nature of the pharmaceutical industry, a large proportion of the salesperson's time is spent providing complete and accurate information to the medical community and subtly encouraging the use of the company's products.

Current Situation—Western Region

On January 3, 1984, Mike Grogan, Heathcoate Pharmaceuticals' national sales manager, announced two promotions within the western sales region. Ted Waldbillig was promoted from his position as the Los Angeles district manager to western region sales manager; John McLinden, who had previously held this post, had recently taken a position within the firm's European operations in Scandinavia.

The second promotion moved Tim McKenzie from his product development position at corporate headquarters to the San Francisco district manager's position. The need to fill this position arose when Dick Hansen, the former district manager, took early retirement in December.

Grogan had been concerned about the San Francisco district for the past four years, as it had not kept pace with the performance of the other western region districts. While the region as a whole had increased sales by more than 10 percent for each of the last five years, the San Francisco district had managed to increase sales less than 5 percent each year. In fact, the rate of growth had been declining each year to the point where district sales in 1983 amounted to only 5.2 percent of

---

[*] This case was prepared especially for this text by J. Patrick Genn, MBA—Marketing, University of Wisconsin, Madison.

national sales. In 1979, sales were 5.8 percent of national sales. Grogan estimated this district to be capable of contributing at least 6 percent of national sales.

During Waldbillig's first formal meeting with Grogan, he was advised to make a special effort to assist McKenzie in turning around the San Francisco district. Grogan commented on the reasons he gave for the district's poor performance. "Dick Hansen was 62 years old before he retired. Although he was a top company man for years, he was unable to stay abreast of the changes our industry has undergone during the past seven or eight years. McLinden often discussed the problem with me, but those two were very close, and I always had the feeling he was covering up for Hansen. However, we've got McKenzie in there now, and I think he's got what it takes to turn things around. He worked in that district under Hansen before working on special projects here at headquarters, so he has some familiarity with the district and the people selling there."

The rest of the meeting was spent going over the region in general, as well as outlining Ted's major responsibilities. As soon as Ted returned to his own office on the following day, he scheduled a meeting with McKenzie concerning the San Francisco district for January 28, 1984.

At this meeting, they worked out a target sales figure of $5 million to be reached by the district in 1984. This represented slightly more than 10 percent growth, which was consistent with the rest of the region. Ted suggested that Tim carefully review the information Hansen had maintained on each salesman in the district and then spend at least one full day making calls with each representative.

Ted indicated that Tim could take whatever steps he felt was necessary to bring sales up to the target level. The following comment illustrates Ted's opinion on the matter: "I don't care if you turn over your entire sales force there! Just make sure that the people you have can perform well enough to reach your sales goal, otherwise I'm going to have to answer a lot of questions from Grogan and you'll be answering to me. I want a complete rundown in two weeks of what your plans are as well as your summary of each salesman's potential. In February you'll be submitting salary change proposals, so this will give you a head start."

The San Francisco District

The San Francisco district was broken down into five territories as shown in Exhibit 1. McKenzie had obtained data from Hansen's files concerning each salesman's sales record, as well as salaries, commissions, and expenses in 1983, as shown in Exhibits 2 and 3.

Over the next days, McKenzie was able to travel with each salesman. He compiled the following summary of each one, using his own observations and the information passed on by Hansen.

Exhibit 1
San Francisco district

Exhibit 2

Salesperson	Territory	1982 Sales ($000)	Percent of District	1983 Sales ($000)	1983 Percent of Quota	Percent of District	1983 Active Accounts	1983 Calls
R. A. Tripp	A	$1,115	25.4%	$ 999	96%	22.1%	670	900
S. M. Smith ...	C	936	21.3	1,285	125	28.4	980	1,900
G. I. Roach....	D	865	19.7	507	86	11.2	300	500
T. R. Denson ..	E	847	19.3	1,257	130	27.8	1,100	1,700
M. L. Cribbs...	B	628	14.3	475	88	10.5	480	1,010
Total		$4,391	100.0%	$4,523	—	100.0%	3,530	6,010

Richard Tripp

At 42 years of age, Tripp had been married three times and is currently settling his third divorce. He has had his good years and his bad years as a salesman but is currently spending a great deal of time and energy with the legal problems of his divorce settlement. He seemed to be a very confident, professional salesman who was received warmly by his accounts. Hansen had at one time recommended that

Exhibit 3

Salesperson	Salary	Commissions	Total Compensations	Expenses	Percent Expenses of District	Total
R. A. Tripp	$21,000	$ 9,990	$ 30,990	$ 8,100	20.7%	$ 39,090
S. M. Smith	17,500	12,285	29,785	6,900	17.7	36,685
G. I. Roach.....	23,500	5,070	28,570	5,100	13.1	33,670
T. R. Denson ...	16,500	12,570	29,070	8,400	21.5	37,470
M. L. Cribbs....	18,000	4,750	22,750	10,500	26.9	33,250
Total	$96,500	$44,665	$141,165	$39,000	100.0%	$180,165

Tripp be promoted to a headquarters position, but Tripp showed little interest in moving from the Bay Area. In both 1972 and 1973, Tripp was the top salesman in the region.

Furthermore, he has been the top salesman in the district for five out of the last 10 years. However, he has not attained quota for the past two years.

Steve Smith

At 28, Steve was definitely aggressive. On the day we rode together, we made 14 calls, and I was exhausted. Steve has been selling for four years. Now, after receiving his M.S. degree in business (marketing) from Stanford in 1979, Smith was perhaps trying to reach management too fast. He frequently bucked for changes that he felt should be made within the district. He had a tendency for handling things his own way, often to the contradiction of district policy. However, Smith was the district's top salesman last year, so apparently his methods cannot be all wrong.

George Roach

Last year, George bought a piece of property in Lake Tahoe, where he has apparently been spending a great deal of time gambling and living the "life of Riley." At 56 years of age, George is slowing down quite a bit, even though he still seems to love his job. The main problem seems to be getting him to spend more time with it. As we called on accounts together, he spent more time talking to his clients about the real estate business than about our products. Some clients acted surprised to see George, as if it had been a long time since they last saw him. I don't think he is making as many calls on existing customers as he should. Furthermore, he has not shown much interest in reaching new prospects. However, Roach has maintained very strong relationships with a couple of the district's most lucrative wholesale distributor accounts.

Terry Denson

Terry is a really personable guy who is as aggressive as Smith. He attributes his recent increase in sales to the population explosion in Marin County. To me, Terry represents the ideal salesman.

Mike Cribbs

Mike recently turned 38, although he looks like he is 50. When we worked together here seven years ago, he had a drinking problem, and I think it has become worse. He complained that his territory was not growing as fast as the others and showed very little enthusiasm. Hansen had noted that Cribbs had missed several sales meetings during the past three years and showed up drunk for one meeting. In 1982, Cribbs was placed on probation for two months. Following this, he seemed to have shaped up considerably but then slipped back into his old form within a year. In addition to his drinking problem, I'm somewhat concerned about his willingness to work. His selling technique seems a bit lackadaisical, and he does not seem to know his territory like a veteran of nine years could be expected to.

In four days, McKenzie would once again be meeting with Waldbillig to discuss his plan for the forthcoming year. He knew that much of his success and ultimate rewards rested on the performance of his sales force. He also knew that Waldbillig would allow him a great deal of flexibility in his handling of salesmen who he felt were not performing as well as they should. Among his options were: using salary changes as an incentive or punishing force; firing and rehiring; probation; or adopting new rules and procedures that would be followed by all members of the sales force, such as a minimal number of calls per day. He also knew that his personal attention and advice could play an important role in producing better results. Since he was so new in his position, however, it was difficult for him to predict how effective he could be in changing and improving the performance of the district.

Case 2–12
Acme Machine Corporation

Bob Gaylord, marketing manager of Acme, was contemplating changes in the quota system used by Acme during the past few years. Prompting this change were several factors. First, inflationary price increases made the previous system unworkable. Second, the economic downturn that started in late 1983 was expected to continue into the fourth quarter of 1984. And, third, several sales engineers had complained that their quotas were unrealistic.

Acme Machine, located in Rockford, Illinois, is a manufacturer of machine tools such as vertical milling machines, broaching machines, turret lathes, boring machines, and grinding machines. These machines are sold to manufacturers of appliances, automobiles, farm equipment, trucks, railway equipment, engines, and other manufacturers of metal products.

Acme's sales force consists of 16 sales engineers and 16 manufacturer's agents. The average age of the sales engineers is 48, and they have been with Acme for an average of 12 years. Most sales engineers had prior sales experience in related industries before joining Acme. A few sales engineers moved into sales after spending time in Acme's production and engineering divisions.

The 16 sales engineers were assigned to territories that had been constructed using market potential estimates. Thus, the majority of the sales engineers were in states known as centers of heavy industrial activities such as Michigan, Ohio, Indiana, Illinois, New York, New Jersey, and Pennsylvania. In some cases, sales engineers had territories consisting of several states, although customers were concentrated only in the major metropolitan areas. In other cases, states were split, with a sales engineer assigned to each part. Finally, a few sales engineers were assigned to one customer if the size of the customer justified this approach. Henry Sherman had one customer, for example—an automobile manufacturer with headquarters in Detroit. Two other sales engineers were also assigned to the Detroit area. In the recent past, quotas were established by taking the company sales forecast increase and applying this to last year's sales for each sales engineer. Thus, if the sales forecast showed a 15 percent increase for next year, then each sales engineer's quota was set equal to his last year's sales plus 15 percent.

This quota-setting technique was to be revamped, and Bob Gaylord was in the process of reviewing the proposal that had been submitted by Acme's sales manager, Byran Barnes.

Barnes proposed a system of quota setting that would require input from the 16 sales engineers and the two regional managers. Sales engineers would be asked to make quarterly sales forecasts by product and by customer. These forecasts would be discussed with the regional managers, who would review the forecasts and suggest modifications. Both the sales engineer and the regional sales manager would agree to the modifications. Next, the two regional managers would go over the forecasts with Barnes. It would be Barnes's responsibility to discuss the forecasts with Gaylord, who would then discuss the forecasts with other Acme managers from such areas as production, finance, engineering, and personnel. The sales forecasts made by the sales engineers would eventually become their quotas after the necessary modifications had been made.

Barnes felt this system would be superior to the present system. Gaylord agreed but felt that the issue of windfall sales had not been adequately handled. In the past, windfall sales were not included in the sales forecast or quota. If a sales engineer obtained a windfall sale of $6 million, commission would be paid, but the $6 million would not be added to the sales engineer's sales and would not be used as a basis for determining quota for the next year. Thus, if a sales engineer had "normal" sales of $10 million, plus $6 million in windfall sales, then next year's quota would be based on $10 million plus Acme's forecasted increase, say 15 percent increase or $11.5 million.

Barnes's approach was different. He proposed that if a windfall sale occurred, 80 percent of the dollars would be added to the sales engineer's present quarterly quota and 100 percent would be added to the sales engineer's quarterly sales. To illustrate:

Quarterly Quota $3,000,000
Quarterly Sales   2,000,000
Windfall Sale   1,000,000
New Quarterly Quota   3,800,000
New Quarterly Sales   3,000,000

The sales compensation plan at Acme was easy to understand. Sales engineers were paid a salary plus commission, with the base salary used to calculate commission. On up to 70 percent of quota, no commission was paid. On from 70.1 to 100.0 percent of quota, 0.75 percent of base salary was paid for each 1 percent of sales. Thus, if a sales engineer achieved quota, 22.5 percent of base salary would be paid as commission ($100 - 70 = 30 \times 0.75 = 22.5$). Acme paid 0.5 percent of base salary for each 1 percent of sales over quota. No commission would be paid on sales over 200 percent of quota. If a sales engineer had sales over quota of 8 percent, then 4 percent of base salary would be paid in addition to the 22.5 percent ($108 - 100 = 8 \times 0.50 = 4.0$). Base salaries averaged $22,500. The sales force was paid every two weeks. Commissions were paid quarterly but not in full. Forty percent of the quarter's commissions was paid every quarter, and the remaining 60 percent was paid equally over the next three quarters.

Barnes's assistant sales manager, Don Ingersoll, suggested a different approach for determining quotas. He was not in favor of asking sales engineers to participate in sales forecasting or in setting their own quotas. Sales engineers were perceived by Ingersoll to be either too optimistic or too pessimistic to make accurate predictions. Don suspected that the sales engineers would make low forecasts in order to have low, easier-to-obtain quotas. Don urged Barnes to make quotas equal to the sales engineer's sales for the last five years plus a management-determined increase based on specific factors affecting each sales engineer. Different sales engineers could have different percentage increases. If windfall sales occurred, they would be added to the five-year total and become part of the average. Ingersoll wanted yearly quotas instead of quarterly quotas. Ingersoll agreed with Barnes with respect to the compensation scheme, in that he, too, felt that applying 80 percent of a windfall sale to current quota and 100 percent to current actual sales was reasonable.

Bob Gaylord was aware of the methods advocated by both Byran Barnes and Don Ingersoll and knew that he had to make a decision soon. Sales force morale and company sales were at stake.

Case 2–13
Agrisystem Farm Machines Inc. (B)*

Agrisystem Farm Machines, Inc., is a major manufacturer of farm structures (silos, motorized bottom unloaders) and agricultural equipment, such as automatic feeding machines and animal waste-handling systems. The company employs a sales force with responsibility to sell the wide range of Agrisystem products to a network of independent dealers across the nation.

Each sales representative (known as an area sales manager) is also expected to call on large farmers, promote Agrisystem products in his or her territory, recruit and develop new dealers, etc. At the present time, Agrisystem has three different groups of salespeople. One sells both equipment and structures and is the largest in absolute numbers; a second group sells only structures; and the third group is responsible for selling strictly equipment. This situation stems from the fact that at one time, both structures and equipment were divided into separate divisions and were therefore represented by their own individual sales forces. All area sales managers (ASMs) are paid the identical salary of $12,000 a year, plus a percentage of each sale they make.

In late 1984, Mr. Warren, general sales manager of Agrisystem, was sitting in his office, contemplating whether or not he should modify the compensation package currently used to reward the sales force and, if so, how to design the changes to make them most effective in achieving the company's goals. In the past several weeks, some of Warren's regional managers had contacted him regarding an apparent problem with the way the ASMs were performing their duties. Although the sales force was accomplishing its unit volume and sales objectives, the regional managers were finding it difficult to motivate their ASMs to devote sufficient energy toward some other necessary functions of their job. On this basis, Warren had come to the conclusion that the present compensation structure encouraged an ASM to focus his or her attention only on short-term results—thus neglecting other required activities. These additional job functions were such that they did not have a direct impact on short-term sales but were nonetheless vital to the continued strength and success of the firm.

To make an appropriate decision, Warren decided to analyze the present situation in depth and then, based on his findings, recommend a compensation plan to top management that would alleviate any current problems. To assess the problem accurately, it was initially necessary to thoroughly understand both the customer buying process and the requirements of the ASM position. Depending on the type of product being sold, a customer's buying decision will be influenced in varying degrees by the price of the product, the perceived quality of the product in relation to competitive offerings, the customer's awareness of the product, effec-

---

*This case was prepared especially for this text by Myron R. Lyskanycz, MBA—Marketing, University of Wisconsin, Madison.

Exhibit 1
Relative importance of predominant influences on the customer buying decision

Individual Influences on the Buying Decision	Equipment Sales	Structure Sales
1. Pricing strategy 20%		15%
2. Product quality............................. 25		20
3. Customer awareness 20		15
4. Advertising 10		20
5. Influence of the field sales rep 25		30

tiveness of advertising, and the extent to which a salesperson can convince the customer to purchase a specific item. After reviewing these and other relevant factors with his regional sales managers and several Agrisystem dealers, Warren constructed Exhibit 1.

This illustrates their perceptions of the influence that each predominant factor has on the customer's decision to buy farm structures or equipment. As can be seen from these data, the Agrisystem ASM is not merely an order taker, but rather plays an important role in influencing the purchase decision.

The next task was to look at what the ASMs were currently spending their time on, what the individual job functions of the ASMs really were, and to prioritize each function in relation to its role in the firm's statement of marketing and sales objectives.

Researching this point, Warren discovered that the typical ASM was spending the majority of time simply making sales calls on existing dealers, trying to sell them the greatest quantity of product in the shortest time. After reviewing the pertinent job descriptions, however, it became evident that the ASM was expected to utilize his or her time quite differently.

Six ASM functional tasks were identified as being of primary importance to the firm. These were:

1. Establishment of a specified number of new dealers in selected "target markets."
2. Upgrading of existing dealer(s) to the sales volume level of the top dealer in each area.
3. Achievement of quarterly unit sales objectives (MBO).
4. Accomplishment of territorial promotion plan.
5. Maintenance of acceptable current accounts receivable levels.
6. Attainment of individual performance objectives as established with each ASM's assigned regional sales manager.

Exhibit 2 details the activities in each job function and also the relative importance of each category to the other functions of the job.

Exhibit 2
Area sales manager job functions

Job Function	Importance of Function as a Percentage of Aggregate Activities

I. Dealer development 15–25%
    A. New dealers
        1. Market research
        2. Call agribusiness dealer prospects
            Meet with community leaders, bankers, etc.
            Call on dealers selling other competitive products
            Call on major area farmers
            Call on dealers who sell one of our products
       *3. Set up approved dealership
            Show him/her potential sales
            Credit regulations
            Company policies and procedures, etc.
       *4. First order taken
       *5. Announcement activities
            Ads
            Open house
            Sales assistance on retail selling
    B. Current dealer 15–25%
       *1. Present features and benefits workshops
       *2. Present and sell company-sponsored sales training programs
       *3. Install ongoing prospecting system
       *4. Promote and schedule technical training
       *5. Promote and schedule (and conduct) target and group meetings, tours,
            field days, prospect meetings, etc.
        6. Set up dealer MBO objectives
        7. Dealer inventory control
        8. Update company policies and procedures
    C. Retail sales 20–35%
        1. Proof selling—line up satisfactory customers for tours and testimonials
        2. Farm calls—follow up on prospects *with* dealer
       *3. Meet MBO objectives
        4. Coaching calls with dealer
            Servicing
            Installation
            Collections
        5. Systems design
       *6. Find financial arrangements for farmers—call on finished installation
    D. Advertising and promotion 10%
       *1. Coordinate placing ads in local publications
        2. Develop contacts with agribusiness associates
       *3. Supply appropriate literature to dealer
            Fliers
            Dealer identification
       *4. Assist with setting up and manning company-sponsored shows
    E. Collections/credit 10–20%
        1. Assist dealer with collections
       *2. Collect on overdue dealer accounts
        3. Conduct monthly inventory of floor plan (equipment in dealer inventory
            that has not yet been paid for)

Exhibit 2 *(concluded)*

F. Area management—discretionary 10–15%
    1. Complete weekly and monthly reports
    2. Set up and maintain parts depot
    *3. Attend training meetings
    4. Understand and follow company policies and procedures
    5. Communicate with all relevant personnel
    *6. Territory and time management
         Planning and scheduling, control book
    7. Personal housekeeping

*Represents activities that Mr. Warren considered to be of greatest importance in each job function category.

Adequate attention by the ASM to each job function was considered very important to the best interests of the company. And, indeed, if each category of performance was optimized, the firm's financial condition would improve substantially. For example, Agrisystem's credit manager, Harry Jolson, provided Warren with the data in Exhibit 3 indicating that the average equipment salesman had an accounts receivable delinquency that could be shortened by 42 days. Considering that the company was paying 15 percent annually on borrowed money, it became evident how much Agrisystem was wasting in interest costs (and lost working capital) per average salesman simply because inadequate attention was paid to proper collection procedures.

Exhibit 3
Average equipment salesman in three-month period

Accounts receivable average over the past three months	$71,030.19
Current accounts receivable average in last three months	$50,662.51
Sales in last three months...	$43,364.56
Days sales outstanding = 71,030.19 × 90/43,364.56......................	147
Best possible days sales outstanding = $\dfrac{50,662.51 \times 90}{43,364.56}$	105
Average cost of delinquency = DSO less best possible	42
Average daily sales per representative = $\dfrac{\text{three month sales}}{90}$	$481.82/day

By this time, Warren had a fairly good understanding of what the ASMs were doing and what they theoretically should be doing. His next step was to review the current earnings of the sales force and compare them with those of competitive firms whose salespeople had similar responsibilities. He found that other firms in the industry were apparently compensating their sales personnel more generously (see Exhibits 4 and 5). Warren felt that the average ASM at Agrisystem was probably equally aware of this and that perhaps this was a major factor in explaining why the ASMs were so concerned about maximizing their short-term earnings.

Exhibit 4
Projected 1984 earnings of
agrisystem area sales managers

Group Selling Equipment Only	Group Selling Both Structures and Equipment	Group Selling Structures Only
$27,160	$21,936	$30,059
38,940	26,475	27,910
33,268	23,862	27,608
21,886	23,538	22,300
17,400	19,690	21,551
22,584	17,302	21,397
22,094	20,013	16,451
23,254	19,890	15,783
$25,823 (average)	26,945	17,600
	20,168	33,542
	22,526	$23,420
	19,781	
	$21,843	

Note: All ASMs are also provided with a company automobile, and the company pays for all expenses.

Exhibit 5
Survey to determine competitive
compensation range for jobs similar
to AFM area sales manager, 1984

John Doe Co.
Marketing trainee (observes): $18,000–$19,800
Marketing representative (surveys, special promotions): $21,896–$28,904 plus 3.5 percent bonus (average) and automobile
Territory manager: $28,136–$37,196 plus 5 percent bonus (average) and automobile

Farm Man, Inc.
Blockman: $1,666/month, draw 3 percent on collections, automobile (pay $30/month)
Earnings range 1984: $27,000–$52,000

Oharenko Bros.
Territory representative: $12,000 plus 2 percent commission on shipments, car allowance, expenses
Earnings range 1984: $24,000–$40,800

Finally, Warren had also received reports from several of his regional sales managers that some of the company's highest paid ASMs were showing signs of dissatisfaction with their jobs. These were generally older, career ASMs who had been with the company for a relatively long time and were considered quite successful. Warren was wondering whether some change in the compensation structure could be enacted to appease this select group of salespeople.

After considering these aspects of the problem, Mr. Warren recommended the following compensation package that included a fixed salary and an incentive plan:

1. A base salary of $13,200 per year. This represented a 10 percent increase over the current salary and was intended to make the ASM's reward structure a bit more competitive with those of other firms in the industry.
2. A commission plan figured as a percentage of total sales. A two-tiered commission rate was proposed. One rate would apply until the ASM reached his/her targeted sales level. A second, higher rate would then become effective and apply to all sales exceeding quota (rates are detailed in Exhibit 6). This system would provide the ASM with added incentive to reach high levels of productivity.
3. A target-based bonus plan which allows the ASM to earn a maximum of $5,000 in additional income yearly. The bonus element was proposed as a means of tying in successful accomplishment of important peripheral activities with resultant direct monetary gains for the ASM.

Exhibit 6
Proposed commission structure for area managers

	Up to Target	After Target Is Met
Commissions on structure sales	.005	.007
Commissions on structure repair contracts		
Size of contract:		
$ 0 to $ 5,000	.01	.01
5,001 to 10,000	.015	.015
10,000 to Up	.02	.02
Commissions on equipment sales	.04	.06

Note: It was expected that the average area sales manager should be over target at least 2 months per year.

The target-based bonus plan was originally to be applied to all six job functions identified in the job analysis. The earned bonus was to be paid out quarterly and would be allocated among the job categories as illustrated in Exhibit 7.
The bonus, as allocated for each functional category, may be earned in the following manner:

New Dealer. The first step is a territory market analysis performed for each dealer in the particular sales territory. Then, the information is used to select a market within the area that has potential for volume improvement with new dealer representation. The ASM is then given the objective of installing a new dealer who will provide the dollar volume equal to the best present dealer in the sales territory. Up to 50 percent of the available points can be earned by such activities as: identifying qualified prospects; making a presentation specifying sales objectives to the dealer; installing the dealer, and providing initial training.

Exhibit 7
**Bonus fund application for 100
percent accomplishment of
objectives per individual ASM**

	Percent of Total	Annual Fund	Earned Quarterly
New dealer............................ (establishing set number of new dealers per area)	20%	$1,000	$ 250
Dealer development .... (getting targeted dealers up to level of the best dealer in that ASM's area)	20	1,000	250
100% fulfillment of MBO objective	20	1,000	250
Territory promotion....................... (accomplishment of area promotional goals)	10	500	125
Collections	20	1,000	250
Other .... (discretionary items selected by regional managers)	10	500	125
Total	100%	$5,000	$1,250

A proportionate share of the remaining 50 percent can be earned by selling the new dealer(s) the targeted volume of units.

Dealer Development. The objective here is to select a dealer from existing dealers and upgrade sales performance so that the chosen dealer's sales volume is equal to that of the top dealer in the sales area. Up to 50 percent of the points can be earned for: getting the dealer to expand his sales force, installing a new prospecting system, or conducting workshops. The balance of the points are earned by attaining projected sales volume.

Retail Sales. Bonus points can be earned each quarter by attaining order entries equal to the unit objective (MBO) for that quarter. The objective is to get forecasted volume as targeted in a product mix forecast.

Territory Promotion. Benchmarks of performance are established for each sales area. These include: promoting farm tours and getting minimum numbers of farmers to participate in them; number of farming magazines mailed with inserted dealer advertisements; tear sheets from dealer-sponsored ads promoting AFM programs; and tear sheets verifying the amount of dealer paid local advertising featuring AFM structures and/or equipment. The criteria for bonus points awarded would be the accomplishment of agreed-upon objectives as formulated by the ASM and his or her Region Manager.

Credit Management. The bonus plan will reward the ASM for managing the accounts receivable in his or her area and keeping them current. Thus, an Area Manager who allows accounts to become past due suffers a commission deduction while the ASM who keeps accounts current is rewarded. The basis for bonus is no past-due accounts for the quarter.

Exhibit 8
Nonmonetary reward programs

The Achiever's Club

Each quarter that an Area Sales Manager achieves 90 percent of the available bonus points he becomes a member of "The Achiever's Club" and is awarded a medallion.

The President's Club

Each Area Sales Manager who earns membership in "The Achiever's Club" all four quarters becomes a member of "The President's Club". Membership is signified by a specially designed AFM President's Club ring.

Wives of President's Club members will receive a special charm bracelet and charm and each member will receive special business cards.

During the month of January, President Club members and their wives will meet with AFM President and Vice-President of Marketing for a special award trip.

Publishing Accomplishment, Awarding Bonus, and Providing Recognition

Point standings will be published each quarter. In the New Dealer and Dealer Development categories, up to 50 percent of the total points for the category can be awarded for such activities as:

Qualifying Dealer Prospect
Touring Dealer Prospect
Signing Up New Dealer
Feature/Benefit Workshop
Expanding Dealer Sales Force
Dealer Participation in AFM Training
Installing and Maintaining AFM Prospect System

The balance of the points will be awarded for volume improvement. This volume improvement objective will be established in the market analysis.

The MBO Unit Accomplishment and No Credit Delinquency prize points would be based on 100 percent accomplishment each quarter. Goal relief would be provided in the event of some action beyond the control of the Area Sales manager (i.e., the customer ordered a white roof and chute but crew installed an aluminized roof).

The Area Sales Manager would know exactly how many points he has earned and how many more he has the opportunity to earn. Since the points directly relate to dollars, he will constantly be aware of the bonus he has earned.

The Achiever Medallions will be awarded at quarterly Regional Sales Meetings. The President's Club will meet during January.

Other. The Region Sales Manager and the ASM agree on personal development activities and establish an objective. Bonus points are awarded at the Regional Managers' discretion.

Each area of the proposed bonus plan was justified to top management by illustrating the amount of money that could be saved when the individual ASM achieved his or her objectives in relation to the cost of the bonus outlay. For example, in the area of collections, when the ASM achieved maximum targeted results, Agrisystem would pay a bonus of $1,000.

Aside from the monetary plan, Mr. Warren also recommended the implementation of the nonmonetary reward program designed to increase the internal satisfaction of the salespeople that either did not have the opportunity of ever moving up into sales management or simply needed more than money to keep them happy and challenged in their jobs. This proposal is outlined in Exhibit 8.

Part **3**

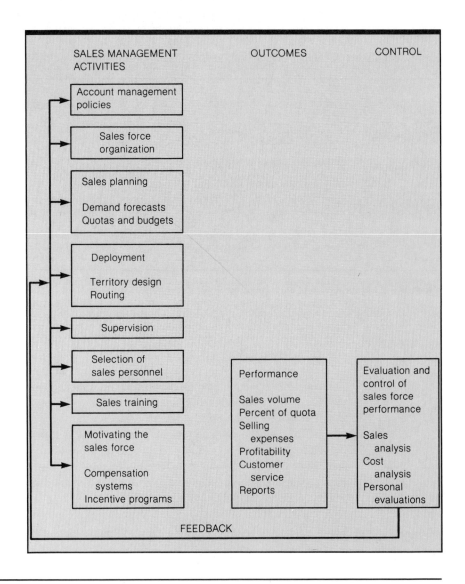

SALES MANAGEMENT ACTIVITIES

OUTCOMES

CONTROL

Account management policies

Sales force organization

Sales planning

Demand forecasts
Quotas and budgets

Deployment

Territory design
Routing

Supervision

Selection of sales personnel

Sales training

Motivating the sales force

Compensation systems
Incentive programs

Performance

Sales volume
Percent of quota
Selling expenses
Profitability
Customer service
Reports

Evaluation and control of sales force performance

Sales analysis
Cost analysis
Personal evaluations

FEEDBACK

Evaluation and Control of the Sales Program

Part 3 examines the issues involved in evaluating and controlling a firm's personal selling program. Chapter 15 examines the techniques of sales analysis, while Chapter 16 focuses on cost analysis. Finally, Chapter 17 discusses behavioral analysis and explores some corrective measures a sales manager might take when performance falls short of planned levels.

Chapter 15

Sales Analysis

The basic process by which managers operate consists of the three steps of (1) planning, (2) execution, and (3) evaluation and control. In sales management, planning involves such problems as organizational structure, territory design, and the establishment of sales quotas, whereas execution includes selecting, training, and motivating sales representatives. All these topics have been treated in this book. Now we turn to the issues of evaluation and control of the field selling effort.

Evaluation and control are vital parts of the management process. To operate most effectively, management needs feedback on the effectiveness of its plans and the quality of their execution; otherwise it is easy to lose sight of the firm's objectives and how to achieve them. A firm with no effective evaluation and control programs can easily end up under full power and no direction, consuming resources to no effective end, much like a ship that has lost its bearings because of a broken compass.

Nature of Control

The key role played by evaluation and control in the management process is depicted in the feedback-control loop of Figure 15–1. Company goals initiate the process by serving as the targets that guide the formulation of plans. Once designed, the plans need to be implemented to become part of the daily operations. The firm then needs to collect and organize information about its operations so that it can compare these data with its goals to determine how well it is doing. This evaluation and comparison provide the control for the enterprise. They allow the assessment of where the firm is now versus where it wants to go so that corrective action may be taken. The situation again parallels that of a ship at sea: by knowing where the ship is now compared with its target destination, the captain can adjust the course to arrive at the destination. It is not impossible for the ship to arrive there without such evaluation. By simply wandering about aim-

Figure 15–1
Basic management control process

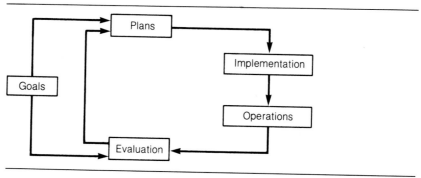

lessly, it may eventually get there by a stroke of good luck. Similarly, the firm may eventually get where it wants to go without proper evaluation and control procedures. On the other hand, it is certainly much more likely to get there faster and at less cost if it has the ability to assess where it is now and to compare that with where it wants to go so that the appropriate corrective action can be taken.

Marketing Audit

The most thorough mechanism for evaluating the marketing effort is a marketing audit. A marketing audit is a complete, systematic, objective evaluation of the total marketing effort of a firm. Marketing audits involve an examination of the firm's goals, policies, organization, methods and procedures, and personnel. They also include an assessment of the firm's current position and its strengths and weaknesses so that a new course can be plotted if necessary.

Marketing audits are of two basic types: vertical and horizontal.

The horizontal audit examines all of the elements that go into the marketing mix, with particular emphasis upon the relative importance of these elements and the "mix" between them. It is often referred to as a "marketing mix" audit. The vertical audit singles out certain functional elements of the marketing operation and subjects them to thorough, searching study and evaluation.[1]

The horizontal audit is thus a systems level audit in which the focus is more on the relationship among marketing activities than on any one activity. Certain activities may be isolated for more detailed investigation through the horizontal audit, but that is not its main purpose; that is the purpose of the vertical audit. The vertical audit is a complete, objective, systematic analysis of one part of the total marketing effort—for example, the personal selling effort. The term "*sales management audit* can be used to identify the vertical audit associated with the sales manager's responsibilities."[2]

Although this book emphasizes sales management audits, all functional audits within the firm must be coordinated so that their timing and scope coincide.

If a sales management audit reveals the sales force is encountering unusual difficulty in selling one major product line, it would be helpful if a parallel appraisal of the advertising function was available to show the effort and effectiveness of the advertising program for that product line. But if the advertising audit was an appraisal by geographic areas rather than by product line, sufficient information might not be available to diagnose the reason for the sales problem. A similar handicap might result if the two functional audits did not correspond in timing.[3]

---

[1] Richard D. Crisp, "Auditing the Functional Elements of a Marketing Operation," in *Analyzing and Improving Marketing Performance*, Report No. 32 (New York: American Management Association, 1959), pp. 42–44. Also see the article by Abe Shuchman, "The Marketing Audit: Its Nature, Purposes, and Problems," in the same volume.

[2] Thomas R. Wotruba, *Sales Management, Planning, Accomplishment, and Evaluation* (New York: Holt, Rinehart & Winston, 1971), pp. 466–67.

[3] Ibid., p. 467.

The relation between the vertical sales-management audit and the horizontal marketing audit can be discerned by looking at some of the issues addressed under each.

Objectives

The initial step in a horizontal marketing audit is to secure a clear statement of the company's goals and mission. This is often difficult to accomplish. The goals should be measurable. The goal "to achieve a high rate of sales" is too nebulous to be of value. One problem often uncovered with a marketing audit is that executives are operating with different goals and some of them have very imprecise targets.

The goals for the personal selling effort must be coordinated with those of the firm. The sales-management audit attempts to specify goals for the personal selling function and the role personal selling is to play in the total marketing effort of the firm. It also includes a statement of short-run objectives. Two examples are: increase the number of salespersons in the southeastern territory by two in the next two years and increase the frequency with which sales reps contact type A accounts by 10 percent within the next year.

Policies

The next audit step is to examine how well the firm's current policies coincide with its goals. Policies can grow obsolete in dynamic economies. J. C. Penney Company, with "its profits squeezed by competition from fancy department stores at the high end of the retailing scale and mass discounters on the low end," recently reappraised its policies and decided to drop paint, hardware, and lawn and garden-supply sections from its stores so as to move up the scale.[4] Timex decided to reduce its dependence on mechanical watches so as to shed its utilitarian image and hopefully reverse its declines in profits and market share.[5] Texas Instruments decided to get out of the increasingly price-competitive home computer industry, even though they were one of the early pioneers.[6] One primary function of the audit is to stimulate management to consider such questions.

Policies about personal selling might also need revision. Thus, if the firm's policy of promoting from within the sales force prevents it from filling an area manager's position with the type of person needed for that territory, the policy should be changed. Similarly, a policy of frequent assignment changes (even if to

---

[4] Claudia Ricci, "J. C. Penney Goes After Affluent Shoppers, But Store's New Image May Be Hard to Sell," *The Wall Street Journal*, February 15, 1983, p. 33.

[5] Jeffrey H. Birnbaum, "Falling Profit Prompts Timex to Shed Its Utilitarian Image," *The Wall Street Journal*, September 27, 1981, p. 27.

[6] "Texas Instruments Cleans Up Its Act," *Business Week*, September 19, 1983, pp. 56–64.

bigger and better territories) that produced excessive turnover in the sales force would be questioned. Any policy made obsolete by a changing external environment should be revised. Bliss and Laughlin Industries, Inc., a supplier of electronic and precision tools, construction materials, and other industrial products, found that it was better to switch from personal sales calls to mail-order catalogs to promote several products because of the rapidly increasing costs of a sales call and the small average customer purchase of these products.[7] Mannington Mills, Inc. installed computers in its retail outlets in an attempt to improve the productivity of its floor salespeople. Instead of the salesperson sorting through samples of vinyl floor covering with the customers, Mannington programmed some small computers to digest the answers to eight questions about the decor of a customer's room and then to display the style numbers of between three and 10 appropriate Mannington patterns.[8] The sales management audit similarly might suggest a change in salespeople's compensation scheme or the criteria used in hiring new representatives. The important thing is that the spectrum of sales management policies be systematically evaluated and those that need to be changed be identified. After such an analysis, for example, Xerox decided to sell off its retail stores in spite of the fact they were originally planned to complement its direct sales force.[9]

Organization

The marketing audit looks at the organization of the company as a whole and the marketing department in particular. It seeks to determine whether the organization is optimal in terms of the company's resources and talent. Perhaps an organization that is structured by function should be converted to a product-manager basis. Perhaps it should be revamped into strategic business units (SBUs), as has been done recently within General Electric and a number of other firms.[10]

The sales management audit focuses on the organization of the sales force. Is it optimal in the firm's current situation? Perhaps the increasing technical complexity of the firm's products warrants a shift from geographically defined sales territories to the use of product specialists. Perhaps a key national account sales force should be developed to supplement the firm's current area coverage. Or maybe recent growth in the southwestern region warrants the division of that region into two areas, each with its own regional manager. Then 7 salespeople would report to each manager, rather than the 14 now reporting to the one regional manager.

---

[7] "Marketing Observer," *Business Week*, August 3, 1974, p. 61.

[8] "Firms Start Using Computors to Take the Place of Salesmen," *The Wall Street Journal*, July 15, 1982, p. 29.

[9] Susan Chase, "Xerox Plans to Sell Most of Its Retail Stores to New Concern Headed by Texas Group," *The Wall Street Journal*, October 25, 1983, p. 60.

[10] William K. Hall, "SBUs: Hot, New Topic in the Management of Diversification," *Business Horizons*, February 1978, pp. 17–25.

Methods and Procedures

Methods and procedures are the tactical means by which the firm's policies are carried out. Perhaps the policies are good but their implementation is inadequate. The marketing audit would attempt to assess the quality of execution of each marketing activity. Have new products been properly test marketed? Have distribution channels evolved to reflect changing consumption patterns? Have pricing policies been adhered to?

The sales management audit attempts to assess how well those activities that directly influence the personal selling function have been carried out. It looks at such issues as how well recent recruits have been trained, how quickly customer orders have been processed, whether salespeople have been given accurate and prompt feedback on their sales and costs, and whether customer requests have been promptly satisfied.

Personnel

The marketing audit does not stop with a review of the goals, policies, organization, and procedures used to carry out the marketing function. It also examines the people involved to determine how well they are performing.

The sales management audit is similar. Most of its attention, however, is directed at individual salespeople and at branch, district, regional, and other area managers. In such audits, there is a heavy emphasis on determining where people are now versus where they should be if the personal selling effort were on target. Three of the more productive and partly overlapping programs for making such assessments are: (1) sales analysis, (2) cost and profitability analysis, and (3) individual performance evaluation. Not all firms use all three, though many are moving in that direction. Sales analysis is the most common, and cost analysis is the least used. The remainder of this chapter concentrates on sales analysis; Chapter 16 focuses on cost and profitability analysis; and Chapter 17 examines performance evaluation of individual salespeople using ratios and subjective supervisor ratings.

Sales Analysis

A sales analysis involves gathering, classifying, comparing, and studying company sales data. It may "simply involve the comparison of total company sales in two different time periods. Or it may entail subjecting thousands of component sales (or sales related) figures to a variety of comparisons-among themselves, with external data, and with like figures for earlier periods of time."[11]

---

[11] *Sales Analysis*, Studies in Business Policy, No 113 (New York: National Industrial Conference Board, 1965), p. 3.

Sales analysis in many companies evolved rather haphazardly, often starting with sporadic searches of company records to find sales information for a specific purpose. As the need was repeated, the searches became more routine: "certain reports, each one constant in the grouping and form of information it contained, were prepared at fixed intervals, and according to a fixed procedure, and distributed to a standard list of recipients."[12] As information needs changed, so did the reports. Often this was accompanied, and many times stimulated, by the change in information-processing capacity as computers replaced manual systems for generating reports. By and large, though, most changes in sales analyses were ad hoc, rather than planned. Companies reacted to this or that information need as the situations arose, rather than determining in advance what information would be needed and for what purposes and in what form. The benefits from even the most elementary sales analysis can be dramatic.

One manufacturer carried on extensive national advertising on the premise that the firm was, in fact, selling nationally. A simple sales analysis, however, revealed that the vast majority of its customers were within a 250-mile radius of the factory. Obviously, the firm was wasting most of the money spent on national advertising. Shortly after the analysis, the advertising manager was fired and the promotion blend readjusted, followed by significantly better sales results.[13]

As more and more firms have come to appreciate the benefits of sales analysis, its role in providing direction to many companies has been expanding. It is used not only in evaluating and controlling the sales effort, but also in contributing to: (1) the overall management of the company with respect to its orientation, expansion, and competitive effort; (2) the detection of marketing strengths and weaknesses and the formulation of marketing strategies; and (3) the administration of nonmarketing functions. These latter functions include production planning (when and at what plant to produce each product), inventory management (how great a stock of each product to have on hand and where to maintain it), cash management (how much money to provide for financing finished product inventories and when), and facilities planning (what additions to plant and equipment to make).

One real benefit of even the most elementary sales analysis is in highlighting those products, customers, orders, or territories in which the firm's sales are concentrated. A heavy concentration is so common that some have labeled the general phenomenon the "80:20 principle."[14] This means that it is not at all unusual to find 80 percent of the customers or products accounting for only 20 percent of total sales. Conversely, the remaining 20 percent of the customers or products account for 80 percent of the total sales volume. The same phenomenon applies to orders and territories; only a small percentage of the total number of

---

[12] Ibid., p. 64.

[13] E. Jerome McCarthy, *Basic Marketing: A Managerial Approach*, 3d ed. (Homewood, Ill.: Richard D. Irwin, 1968). p. 622.

[14] See, for example, Wotruba, *Sales Management*, p. 477; Charles H. Sevin, *Marketing Productivity Analysis* (New York: McGraw-Hill, 1965), pp. 7–8; and William J. Stanton and Richard H. Buskirk, *Management of the Sales Force*, 6th ed. (Homewood, Ill.: Richard D. Irwin, 1983), p. 502.

orders or a few of the firm's many territories account for the great percentage of its sales. The 80:20 principle describes the general situation, although the exact concentration ratio varies by company.

In one early study to assess the magnitude of the concentration ratio, 200 questionnaires were mailed to companies listed in the American Institute of Management's Manual of Excellent Managements. The companies were asked to rank their products, orders, customers, salespeople, and sales territories according to sales volume and to indicate the percentage of sales generated by the top third of each. Of those contacted, 80 responded. While the results did not yield an 80:20 ratio, they did suggest that there was a heavy concentration. For example, the percentages of sales accounted for by each of the top one-third items in each category were.[15]

Products	72 percent
Orders	73 percent
Customers	74 percent
Salespeople	59 percent
Sales territories	62 percent

To produce these overall percentages, some individual companies had to have concentration ratios much higher than these averages. There are some other interesting examples in this regard.

One manufacturer found that 78 percent of his customers produced only slightly more than 2 percent of his sales volume. In another business, 48 percent of the orders accounted for only 5 percent of the sales. In yet another case, 76 percent of the number of products manufactured accounted for only 3 percent of the sales volume. In another business, 59 percent of the salesmen's calls were made on accounts from which only 12 percent of the sales were obtained.

In a wholesale grocery firm, it was found that more than 50 percent of the total number of customers brought in less than 2 percent of the total sales volume. Similarly, 40 percent of the total number of items carried in stock accounted for less than 2 percent of the total sales volume.[16]

The most cursory sales analysis should reveal such concentrations, and for that reason alone, they are typically worthwhile. The Mosinee Paper Company, for example, almost dropped one of its products because of its dismal sales performance. Then an elementary sales analysis found that only a single salesman was selling the specific grade of industrial paper. Upon further investigation, Mosinee discovered how the buyers "were using the paper—an application that had been known only to the one salesman and his customers. This information enabled management to educate its other salespeople as to the potential market for the paper and sales rose substantially."[17]

---

[15] Harry D. Wolfe and Gerald Albaum, "Inequality in Products, Orders, Customers, Salesmen, and Sales Territories," *Journal of Business* 35 (July 1962), pp. 298–301.

[16] Sevin, *Marketing Productivity Analysis*, pp. 7–8.

[17] Jon G. Udell and Gene R. Laczniak, *Marketing in an Age of Change* (New York: John Wiley & Sons, 1981), p. 154.

Key Decisions

Those wishing to undertake a sales analysis must decide (1) the type of evaluation and control system, (2) the sources of information, and (3) the sales breakdowns that will be used. Figure 15–2 overviews the nature of these decisions.

Figure 15–2
Some key decisions when conducting a sales analysis

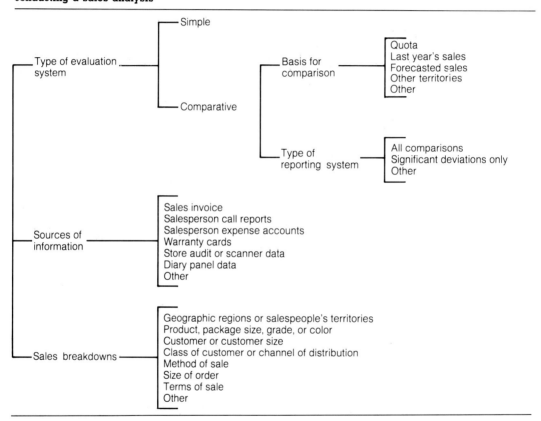

Type of Evaluation System

The type of evaluation system determines how the sales analysis will be conducted. Will it be a simple sales analysis or a comparative analysis?

When it is to be a comparative analysis, two additional questions arise: (1)

Table 15–1
Differences between simple sales
analysis and comparative analysis

Sales Representative	(1) 1985 Sales ($000)	(2) 1985 Quota ($000)	(3) Performance Index
Duane Barrington..............	$760.9	$700	108.7
John Bendt	793.5	690	115.0
James Dawson.................	859.2	895	96.0
George Richardson	837.0	775	108.0
Walter Keyes	780.3	765	102.0

What is to be the base for the comparison? (2) What type of reporting and control system is to be used?

In a simple sales analysis, the facts are merely listed, and there is no attempt to measure them against any standard. In a comparative analysis or, as it is sometimes called, a performance analysis, comparisons are made. Consider, for example, the data in Table 15–1. A simple sales analysis would be restricted to the facts in column (1). These figures suggest that Dawson was the best salesman in 1985 and Barrington was the worst, because Dawson sold the most and Barrington the least. A performance analysis would attempt to go beyond the mere listing of sales to determine where they are greatest and poorest; it would try to make comparisons against some "standard." In Table 15–1, the standard is the quota for each salesman, and column (3) provides a performance index for each. This performance index is calculated as the ratio of actual sales to sales quota ($PI = S/Q \times 100$). It suggests that Dawson was not the "best" in 1985, but rather Bendt was; and in fact, Dawson realized the smallest percentage of his total potential as judged by his quota.

Base for Comparison. The comparison with quota is only one type of comparison that can be made. It is one of the most common because it is very useful, particularly when quotas have been specified well. That is a big *if*, however. Quotas can be a real problem—as we saw in Chapter 7—when they are done poorly. Consequently, some firms resort to other bases of comparison when conducting a sales analysis. These include this year's sales versus last year's sales or the average of a number of prior years' sales; this year's sales versus forecasted sales; sales in one territory versus sales in another, either absolutely or in relation to the ratios in prior years; and the percentage change in sales from one territory to another, as compared with last year.

Such comparisons are certainly better than simply viewing raw sales figures, but they are not generally as productive as a "true" performance analysis. In the latter variations from planned performance are highlighted and the reasons for such exceptions are isolated.

Type of Reporting System. The other major question that arises in a comparative sales analysis is the type of reporting and control system to be used. At one extreme, all comparisons are provided. Thus, if one relevant comparison is to be sales as a percentage of quota, this statistic would be provided for each salesperson, branch, district, region, customer, product, and every other unit by which sales are to be analyzed. The problem with this type of "all comparisons" reporting scheme is that it can inundate the sales manager with information. He or she may be unable to process it effectively, and it becomes a useless pile of unused computer output.

At the other extreme, only "significant" deviations from the norm are highlighted—for example, all those that deviate by at least 10 percent from standard. According to this criterion, the only performance index in Table 15–1 that would be reported to management would be Bendt's. For many sales managers, this "extreme deviation" reporting does not provide the necessary detail for them to operate most effectively. Deviations just short of the significance cutoff go completely undetected and unnoticed.

Probably the most useful reporting system is one in which all comparisons are reported, or at least are available for inspection, while at the same time the significant deviations are highlighted. This can be done by a separate listing of those sales units beyond the predetermined boundaries or by simply highlighting on the all-comparisons report those deviations that are excessive, for example, by asterisking them. Sales managers can then concentrate on the exceptions while having the full profile of comparisons for assessing the significance of what happened.

Sources and Processing of Information

A second class of major decisions that must be made with respect to sales analysis is what information is to serve as input to the system and how the basic source documents are to be processed. To address this question, the firm first needs to determine the types of comparisons to be made. A comparison with sales in other territories will require fewer documents than a comparison against market potential or quota or against the average sales in the territory for the last five years. The firm also needs to decide the extent to which preparation of the sales report should be integrated with the preparation of other types of reports. These may include inventory or production reports or sales reports for other company units such as other divisions.

Generally, the one most productive source document is the sales invoice. From this, the following information can usually be extracted:

Customer name and location.
Product(s) or service(s) sold.
Volume and dollar amount of the transaction.
Salesperson (or agent) responsible for the sale.

End use of product sold.

Location of customer facility where product is to be shipped and/or used.

Customer's industry, class of trade, and/or channel of distribution.

Terms of sale and applicable discount.

Freight paid and/or to be collected.

Shipment point for the order.

Transportation used in shipment.[18]

Other documents provide more specialized input. Some of the more important of these are listed in Table 15–2. Most companies are likely to use only two or three of these sources of sales information in addition to the sales invoice. The particular ones depend on the company and the types of other analyses used to evaluate salespeople in addition to sales analysis.

Desired Breakdowns

The third major decision management must confront when designing a sales analysis is which variables will serve as points of aggregation. Without such categories, the firm would be forced to analyze every transaction in isolation or would need to look at sales in the aggregate. The latter is not particularly informative and the former is almost impossible for most companies.[19] By far the most common and instructive procedure is to assemble and tabulate sales by some appropriate groupings, such as:

1. Geographic regions such as states, counties, regions, or salespeople's territories.
2. Product, package size, grade, or color.
3. Customer or customer size.
4. Market including class of customer, end use, or channel of distribution.
5. Method of sale including mail, telephone, or direct salespeople.
6. Size of order.
7. Financial arrangement such as cash or charge.

The classes of information a company may use depends on such things as the diversity of its product line, the geographic extent of its sales area, the number of markets and customers it serves, and the level of management for which the information is to be supplied. The firm with a product management form of organization, for example, would be interested in sales by product groups. These managers, in turn, might focus on territory-by-territory sales of their respective products. The sales manager and regional managers might be much more interested

---

[18] Adopted from *Sales Analyses*, p 68.
[19] Some companies do analyze each sales transaction, such as the Hydraulics Products Division of Allis Chalmers; see *Sales Analysis*, p.50.

Table 15–2
Other sources of salespeople's evaluation information

Document	Information Provided
Cash register receipts	Type (cash or credit) and dollar amount of transaction by department by salesperson
Salesperson's call reports	Customers and prospects called on (company and individual seen; planned or unplanned calls)
	Products discussed
	Orders obtained
	Customers' product needs and usage
	Other significant information about customers
	Distribution of salespeople's time among customer calls, travel, and office work
	Sales-related activities: meetings, conventions, etc.
Salespeople's expense accounts	Expenses by day by item (hotel, meals, travel, etc.)
Individual customer (and prospect) records	Name and location and customer number
	Number of calls by company salesperson (agents)
	Sales by company (in dollars and/or units by product or service by location of customer facility)
	Customer's industry, class of trade, and/or trade channel
	Estimated total annual usage of each product or service sold by the company
	Estimated annual purchases from the company of each such product or service
	Location (in terms of company sales territory)
Financial records	Sales revenue (by products, geographic markets, customers, class of trade, unit of sales organization, etc.)
	Direct sales expenses (similarly classified)
	Overhead sales costs (similarly classified)
	Profits (similarly classified)
Credit memos	Returns and allowances
Warranty cards	Indirect measures of dealer sales
	Customer service
Summary reports from distributors and dealers	Sales by product, geographic area, class of customer, etc.
Store audits	Unit and dollar volume and market share of consumer purchases of the company's brands in selected retail outlets
Consumer diaries (as a rule they cover only packaged foods and personal care items)	Unit volume of purchases by package size of company's brand (and competing brands) made by selected families
	Details about prices, special deals, and types of outlets in which the purchases were made

Source: Adapted from *Sales Analysis*, Studies in Business Policy, No. 113 (New York: National Industrial Conference Board, 1965), p. 68.

in territory and customer analyses and only secondarily interested in the territory sales broken out by product.

These breakdowns are not necessarily mutually exclusive in the sense that the manager has to choose a breakdown by region or product or customer. Rather, sales analyses are most productive when they are done hierarchically, in the sense that one breakdown is carried out within another category. The categories are treated simultaneously instead of separately. For example, the analysis may end up showing that customer XYZ in the western region purchased so many units each of products A, B, C, and D; this illustrates a territory, customer, and product hierarchical breakdown. The advantage of hierarchical breakdowns is illustrated later. For now, you should know that the typical sales analysis results not in a single report but in a family of reports, each reflecting a different level of aggregation, tailored to the person receiving it. Table 15–3, for example, shows the family of reports generated in the Monsanto Company.

A Hierarchical Sales Analysis

To illustrate some relevant comparisons and the process used in conducting a sales analysis, consider the data in Table 15–4. The figures apply to a national manufacturer of small kitchen appliances, though the actual numbers, as well as the identity of the company, have been disguised. The Kitchenware Company previously determined that its sales are highly correlated with population, income, and the general level of retail sales. Thus, it has determined market potential by region using the corollary index method. More particularly, it has used the buying power index (BPI) published by *Sales and Marketing Management* to determine each region's market potential and has then multiplied these potentials by the company's expected market share to generate the regional quotas in Table 15–4.[20]

Note that, although the annual quota was $420 million, total sales in all regions were $421.23 million. Not only has the total company met quota, but so have most of the regions, for the performance index, the ratio of sales to quota, is greater than 100 for five regions. Four regions fell short of their targets, but three of those came very close. Only the east north-central region fell short by more than 2 percent, but it still had the highest absolute dollar value of sales of any of the major regions. Many sales managers might be tempted from this to assume that all is well. Perhaps at the very most, they might send a letter to the manager of the east north-central region, urging him to push the salespeople in the region to do better.

Fortunately, the sales manager for Kitchenware did neither. Rather he simply asked data processing for the sales breakdown for the east north central region, shown in Table 15–5. Note that the state quotas were determined by multiplying

---

[20] The BPI percentages in Tables 15–4 through 15–6 were taken from *Sales and Marketing Management's Survey of Buying Power,* which is published each July.

Table 15–3
Sales reports issued in the
Monsanto Company

Report Name	Purpose of Report	Frequency of Issue	Distribution
District	To provide sales information in units and dollars, by customer, within each territory and district, also a total for each territory and district	Monthly	Two copies of applicable portions to each district manager, one of which he sends to the salesmen in each territory
Summary— salesman	To provide summarized information regarding sales performance versus budget, by salesman and district; no customer or product detail is provided	Monthly	District managers and executive personnel
Product grade— customer	To provide statistical information regarding sales in units and dollars, by grade, for each customer; does not provide grade totals	Monthly	Product managers and their staffs
Summary— product grade	To provide information regarding total sales in units and dollars for each product grade; totals are also provided by product group	Monthly	Products managers and their supervisors
Product group	To provide statistical information regarding sales in units and dollars; by district, by product grade, by customer; totals for product grade in units and dollars; product group and district totals in dollars only	Quarterly	District managers and product managers
Summary— product district	To provide a summarized version of the product group run, eliminating grade and customer detail; totals are provided for each product group and each district	Monthly	District managers and management personnel responsible for executive accounts
Reverse summary— district product	To provide a summarized version of the product group run in reverse form in order to have available sales and budget data by product as related to the various districts; totals by product and product group	Monthly	Product managers, their supervisors, and executive personnel
Customer sales	To provide an alphabetical listing of all customers with grade detail of purchases in units and dollars; total dollars purchases are provided for customers buying more than one product or grade of product	Monthly	No general distribution; used for special sales analyses when needed

Source: *Sales Analysis*, Studies in Business Policy, No. 113 (New York: National Industrial Conference Board, 1965), p. 74.

Table 15–4
Sales and sales quotas for
Kitchenware Company

Region	BPI (percent of U.S.)	Sales Quota ($ millions)	Sales ($ millions)	Difference ($ millions)	Performance Index ($PI = S/Q \times 100$)
New England..............	5.8193%	$ 24.44	$ 25.03	$ 0.59	102.4
Middle Atlantic	18.3946	77.26	78.19	0.93	101.2
East north central..........	20.1329	84.56	79.48	−5.08	94.0
West north central	7.3982	31.07	30.51	−0.56	98.2
South Atlantic	14.7525	61.96	64.07	2.11	103.4
East south central..........	5.2571	22.08	23.20	1.12	105.1
West south central	9.2022	38.65	38.42	−0.23	99.4
Mountain..................	4.2819	17.98	17.73	−0.25	98.6
Pacific	14.7613	62.00	64.60	2.60	104.2
Total United States ...	100.0000%	$420.00	$421.23	$ 1.23	100.3

the BPI total U.S. percentages for each state by the $420 million total forecasted sales. In many cases, the firm might wish to convert each percentage to a percentage of the region, rather than of the United States as a whole. Thus, the percentage for Illinois would be $(6.0037 \div 20.1329) \times 100 = 29.8$; this percentage would then be applied to the $84.56 million quota for the region to get the quota for Illinois. Although the result is the same, this second alternative provides a clearer picture of the concentrations of demand in the region; the benefit holds particularly when one works with smaller and smaller units of analysis.

Table 15–5 shows that there is some problem with sales throughout the region. Only the sales representatives in Indiana exceeded quota, and then only slightly. Note that the deviations about quota are larger than they were in Table 15–4. This generally happens as one moves to smaller units of analysis. With larger aggregates—for example, regions versus states—the statistician's law of

Table 15–5
Sales breakdown for east north-central region

State	BPI (percent of U.S.)	Sales Quota ($ millions)	Sales ($ millions)	Difference ($ millions)	Performance Index ($PI = S/Q \times 100$)
Illinois	6.0037%	$25.22	$24.30	$−0.91	96.4
Indiana	2.4103	10.12	10.24	0.12	101.2
Michigan.........	4.6401	19.49	17.77	−1.71	91.2
Ohio	4.9764	20.90	20.43	−0.46	97.8
Wisconsin	2.1114	8.87	6.74	−2.12	76.1
Total region	20.1419%	$84.60	$79.48	$−5.08	94.0

large numbers seems to apply in that the pluses and minuses about quota tend to balance each other; thus, the performance indexes in the larger analysis tend to be closer to 100. It should therefore take a smaller deviation from quota to initiate further investigation when the analysis is based on large aggregates (regions) than on small ones (salespeople).

Although there is some negative deviation in actual sales from standard in Table 15–5 among four of the five states, the deviation in Wisconsin is most pronounced. Only 76 percent of the quota was realized there.

Again, it would be very easy for a sales manager to take impulsive action. Instead of getting on a plane to Wisconsin, having the east north-central regional manager call the Wisconsin district manager, or calling him himself, the Kitchenware general sales manager asked data processing for the tabulation of sales by sales representatives in the Wisconsin district. The eight areas into which the state is divided are shown in Figure 15–3, and the results of the tabulation are shown in Table 15–6. Sales are below quota in all sales areas in the state. This suggests there may be something fundamentally wrong. Perhaps economic conditions are poor and unemployment is high; perhaps competition is more intense than in other areas; or there may be a problem with sales force morale and motivation. Although there are many plausible explanations for the sales manager to check, the core problem seems to be Hutchins. If he had done as well as the other salesmen in the state, sales for the district would have been much closer to target. The problem is particularly acute because Hutchins has the prime Milwaukee market as his sales territory.

Before taking action about Hutchins, the sales manager wanted more information. Consequently, he requested the tabulation of Hutchins's sales by product, shown in Table 15–7. There is no question that Hutchins is below quota on the entire product line; however, he seems to be having the most problem with coffee makers and blenders/mixers/food processors.

Table 15–6
Sales by representative in the Wisconsin district

Area Representative	BPI (percent of U.S.)	Sales Quota ($000)	Sales ($000)	Difference ($000)	Performance Index ($PI = S/Q \times 100$)
1. T. Tate............	0.0953%	$ 400.2	$ 392.6	$ −7.6	98.1
2. T. Bir.............	0.1332	559.4	501.0	−58.4	89.6
3. C. Holzem	0.1325	556.5	512.4	−44.1	92.1
4. A. Elliott..........	0.2021	848.8	768.7	−80.1	90.6
5. P. Martin	0.2596	1,090.3	969.3	−121.0	88.9
6. J. Campbell.......	0.3384	1,421.3	1,340.3	−81.0	94.3
7. L. Hutchins	0.6975	2,929.5	1,285.0	−1,644.5	43.9
8. B. Lessner	0.2528	1,061.8	970.5	−91.3	91.4
Total Wisconsin ..	2.1114%	$8,867.8	$6,739.8	$−2,128.0	76.1

Figure 15–3
Sales territories in Wisconsin

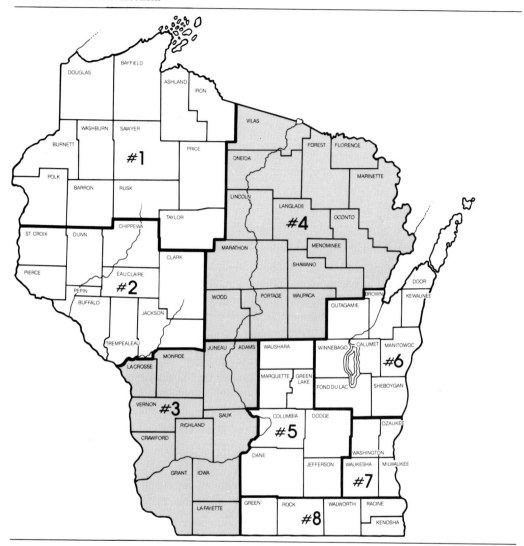

Is the problem Hutchins or these products? A further analysis of sales of these products by customer indicated that the problem was concentrated among large department store buyers. Furthermore, the problem was not unique to Hutchins but was common to all reps in the east and west north-central regions. It seemed that a major competitor had been attempting to improve its position in the north-central regions through a combination of heavy advertising and purchase rebate offers on these products. This problem had been obscured in other sales territo-

Table 15–7
Hutchins's sales by product

Product	Sales Quota	Sales	Difference	Performance Index (PI = S/Q × 100)
Can openers/knife sharpeners	$ 212,000	$ 168,000	$ −44,000	79.3
Toasters	468,000	357,000	−110,500	76.4
Coffee makers	627,000	201,000	−426,000	32.1
Blenders/mixers/ food processors	604,000	184,200	−419,800	30.5
Griddles/electric fry pans	573,000	460,000	−113,000	80.3
Other—electric carving knives/popcorn makers/hot trays, etc.	445,500	328,300	−117,200	73.7
Total	$2,929,500	$1,285,000	$−1,644,500	43.9

ries because sales of other products had compensated for lost sales in coffee makers and blenders/mixers/food processors. Hutchins was unfortunate in this regard because his sales of other products did not make up the deficit. His problem was compounded by the economic slowdown in the metal-working industry, a big employer in the Milwaukee area.

The problem then is not Hutchins. Rather, it is the special competitive situation in the north-central region. This situation, while of considerable impact to the competitive position of the company, would not have come to light without the sales analysis.

Iceberg Principle

One important principle illustrated by the preceding example is that aggregate figures can be deceiving and that small, visible problems are often symptoms of large, unseen problems. Several authors have likened this phenomenon to an iceberg.

Like the part of the iceberg that is below the water line, the part of the sales problem that you cannot see is often bigger than the visible portion.[21]

Icebergs, as everyone knows, show only about 10 percent of their mass above the water level, the other 90 percent being below the water level-and not directly below, either. The submerged portion always seems to be searching out ships that come too near.

The same is true of much business and marketing data. Since sales volumes may be large and overall company activities so varied, difficulties or problems in one area may be

---

[21] Richard D. Crisp, *Sales Planning and Control* (New York: McGraw-Hill, 1961), p. 59.

submerged below the surface. All may appear to be calm and peaceful, yet a more careful analysis may reveal jagged edges which can severely damage or even "sink the business. . . ." Averaging and summarizing data can be helpful to the business executive, but he had better be wary that his summaries do not hide more than they reveal.[22]

The iceberg principle is pervasive. The 80:20 rule or concentration ratio discussed earlier is one manifestation of it. Often, the concentration of sales within certain territories, products, or customers hides some specific weaknesses. More than one company has shown satisfactory total sales, but when the total was subdivided by territories, customers, and products, serious weaknesses were uncovered.

Simple versus Comparative Analysis

The preceding example also shows the difference between a simple sales analysis and a comparative sales analysis, as well as the advantages of the latter. The simple sales analysis would have focused on the sales data in Table 15–4; it would not have examined the differences from quota, but simply the raw figures. It is unlikely that it would have generated any detailed investigation of the east north-central region because sales there were higher than in any other region. The comparison with quota, however, emphasized that the potential in this region was also greater than in any other and that the firm was failing to get its share. The comparative analysis triggered the more intensive investigation and isolated the primary reason for the sales shortfall. Note that the execution of the process depended on having sales quotas available on a very small basis. They had to be available by customer, by product, and by salesperson, or the problem would never have come to light.

It is sometimes difficult to generate quotas on such a small basis. In the Kitchenware Company, it was possible because of the availability of detailed geographic statistics on the BPI. In situations where other data should be used, it is also important that they be available by small geographic area. That is one reason why the sales planning and sales evaluation questions are so inextricably intertwined. One must keep in mind the questions of evaluation and the comparisons needed when designing sales territories and sales quotas.

There have been many other instances where a comparative sales analysis uncovered problems that were not revealed at all by a simple sales analysis. The experience of the Hansen Manufacturing Company is interesting in this regard. The company manufactures quick connective couplings for air and fluid power transmission systems. It found that one distributor who had been a consistent winner of sales performance awards under its old system (no comparisons with potential but simply absolute dollar sales and yearly sales increases) ranked 31st out of the 31 distributors handling the products in a comparative sales analysis.

---

[22] McCarthy, *Basic Marketing*, p. 630.

"Subsequent investigation showed that the distributor did not know how to sell Hansen couplings to some important accounts. Recognition of the problem produced needed changes in the distributor's operations and performance improved."[23]

Isolate and Explode

Another concept the example illustrates is the principle of "isolate and explode,"[24] in which the most significant discrepancies between actual and standard are isolated and then exploded. The detail this explosion reveals is then analyzed, the most significant discrepancies are again isolated, and these in turn are exploded. The process continues until the "real" problems are isolated. Thus, in the Kitchenware example, the following were all isolated and exploded in turn: the east north-central region, the Wisconsin district, Hutchins's sales by product, and Hutchins's product sales by customer.

An alternative would have been to present masses of data to the sales manager. For example, he could have been given the detailed tabulation of sales by each salesman of each product to each customer initially. We can all appreciate what would happen with such a report. More than likely, it would go unused because of its size and the time it would take to decipher its contents. The isolate-and-explode principle makes the task manageable. The sales manager can quickly localize trouble spots by focusing on the most substantial exceptions from standard and then hone in more efficiently on the effective cure.

The principle can also be used to isolate exceptional performance areas for the clues they might provide to what the firm is doing especially right. An investigation of the fact that the east south-central region was 5.1 percent over quota when the entire company was only 0.3 percent over quota might suggest some effective competitive strategies.

Note that the isolate-and-explode principle rests on the assumption that the company's information system can provide sales data hierarchically. In Kitchenware, the sales manager could secure data broken out by customer, by product, by salesman, by district, and by region (see Figure 15–4). The breakdowns resemble a tree: total U.S. sales are the trunk, regions are the main limbs, districts the next branches, and so on. Further, all combinations of these branches are possible. For example, it is possible to do a study by product and territory, or by customer and product. These alternate types of analysis can also be productive, as can simple

---

[23] Sales potentials were determined by establishing the functional relationship between Hansen's sales and the number of employees in key SIC codes. It was found that the distributor, who had been increasing his sales of Hansen couplings for 20 years and, thus, had been recognized for good performance under the simple sales analysis scheme, was actually getting only 15.4 percent of the potential in the area. See William E. Cox, Jr., and George N. Havens, "Determination of Sales Potentials and Performance for an Industrial Goods Manufacturer," *Journal of Marketing Research* 14 (November 1977), p. 578.

[24] The term seems to have been coined by Simon, although the principle seems to have been applied by a number of authors working independently. See Sanford R. Simon, *Managing Marketing Profitability* (New York: American Management Association, 1969), p. 74.

Figure 15–4
Hierarchical sales analyses possible in Kitchenware Company

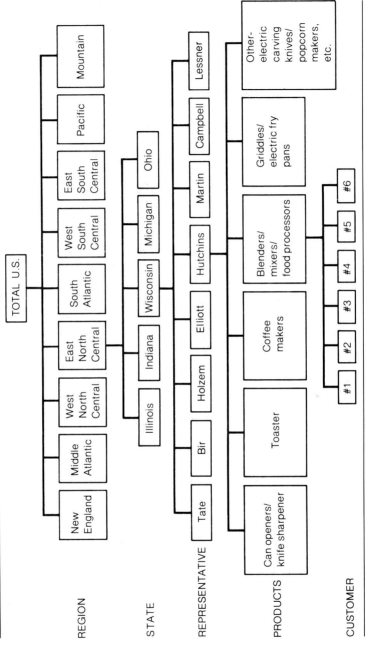

one-way categorizing of sales data. The simple tabulation of sales by product, for example, is very useful in showing a firm's product line strengths. Similarly, the simple tabulation of sales by major classes of customers is often informative about the company's market strengths.

Decision Support System (DSS)

The key to all these analyses, whether hierarchical or simple or whether produced interactively or via batched computer reports, is to have data in the files in a very disaggregated form. Instead of summing over products and customers to generate sales by representative and then entering that aggregate in the data processing system, a particular sale of a specific product to a particular customer is kept intact in the data files. In this way, the appropriate aggregations can be generated as needed.

An alternative strategy for producing "sales analysis" trees with different structures for different purposes that is rapidly gaining in popularity is a *Decision Support System* (DSS). Decision support systems represent the latest generation of management information systems (MIS), which first emerged in the 1960's and then experienced tremendous growth during the 1970's. As originally conceived, marketing information systems consisted of procedures and methods for the regular, planned collection, analyses, and presentation of information useful in marketing decision making. The development of an MIS relied on an accurate, objective assessment of each manager's decision-making responsibilities, capabilities, and decision-making style. Developers of MIS would typically seek answers to such questions as:

1. What type of decisions is each decision maker regularly called upon to make?
2. What types of information does he need to make these decisions?
3. What types of information does he regularly get?
4. What types of special studies does he periodically request?
5. What types of information would he like to get that he is not presently receiving?
6. What information would he like to receive daily, weekly, monthly, yearly?
7. What types of data analysis programs would he like to receive?
8. What improvements would he like to see made in the current information system?[25]

Given the answers to these questions, the developers would then attempt to develop reports that were issued at planned, regular intervals that satisfied the managers' needs.

Developers typically encountered several difficulties in attempting to carry out the design task. First, different managers often emphasized different things and,

---

[25] Philip Kotler, "A Design for the Firm's Marketing Nerve Center," *Business Horizons* 9 (Fall 1966), pp. 63–74.

consequently, had different data needs. There were very few report formats that were optimal for different users. Either the developers had to design "compromise" reports that were satisfactory for a number of users, although not ideal for any single user, or they had to engage in the laborious task of programming to meet each user's needs, one at a time. Second, regardless of how successful they were, their success was inherently temporary, in that it was unlikely that they could correctly anticipate future information needs. Business is dynamic. Not only are competitive positions constantly changing, but so are the firms themselves. New products are introduced, while others fade away. Organizations are restructured and sales territories are realigned. Managers are changed because of promotions, terminations, and new hiring. All such changes can affect the information that is needed and the way it needs to be presented. Depending on the change, this could involve only some minor reprogramming or major information system development work.

The emphases in a DSS are different. Instead of concentrating on the production of batch reports that satisfy multiple users, the emphases, as Figure 15–5 indicates, are on the design of data systems, model systems, and dialog systems.[26] The data system includes the processes used to capture and the methods used to store the transactions data coming from marketing, finance, and manufacturing, as well as information coming from any number of external or internal sources. The model system includes all the routines that allow the user to manipulate the data so as to conduct the kind of analysis the individual desires; thus the routines may run the gamut from summing a set of numbers, to conducting a complex statistical analysis, or to finding an optimization strategy using some kind of nonlinear programming routine. The dialog systems are the most important and clearly differentiate DSS from MIS. The dialog systems permit managers, who are not programmers themselves, to explore the data bases using the system models to produce reports that satisfy their own particular information needs. They allow a manager to ask a question, and on the basis of the answer, to ask a subsequent question, and then another, and another, and so on. In the Kitchenware example, for instance, the manager could have requested sales by product or by class of customer immediately after having seen the display of sales by major geographic area. Further, the manager could have conducted this analysis by keying in a set of commands at a terminal, instead of asking data processing for computer printouts showing the sales breakdowns.

In sum, DSS are heavily action-oriented. They allow manager's to use their own instincts when seeking answers to problems that arise. They are much more adaptable to changing environmental circumstances and different managerial styles than are MIS.

Decision support systems for evaluating the personal selling effort promise to be particularly important in the future as the microcomputer revolution contin-

---

[26] For an excellent discussion of the differences between traditional MIS and the newer DSS, see Ralph H. Sprague, Jr., and Eric D. Carlson, *Building Effective Decision Support Systems* (Englewood Cliffs, N.J.: Prentice-Hall, 1982), especially chapters 1 and 2. For a useful historical perspective on the status and promise of DSS in marketing, see John D. C. Little, "Decision Support Systems for Marketing Managers," *Journal of Marketing* 43 (Summer 1979), pp. 9–26.

**Figure 15–5
Components of a decision
support system**

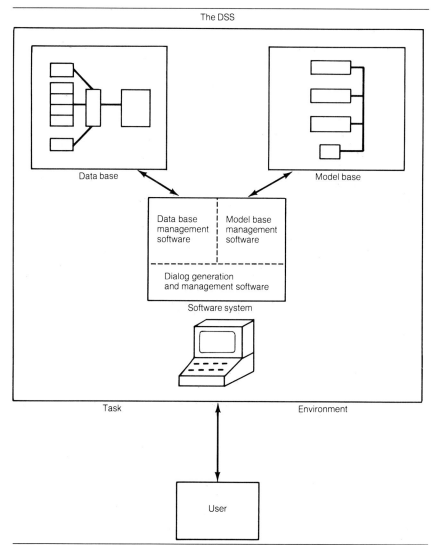

Source: Adapted from Ralph H. Sprague, Jr., and Eric D. Carlson, *Building Effective Decision Support Systems* (Englewood Cliffs, N.J.: Prentice-Hall, 1982), p. 29.

ues to unfold. Not only is it likely that branch, regional, and district managers will have microcomputers connected directly to the company's data bases at their desks, but many salespeople will probably have them as well. Further, with the explosion of user-friendly software, most sales managers should be able to use the micros to good advantage in the future. The readily available electronic spread sheets like VISICALC and SUPERCALC already permit the kinds of sales analyses discussed in this chapter for even the smallest of companies.[27]

Two of the main advantages of these electronic spread sheets are that they (1) are very easy to use, and (2) are very flexible in terms of the analysis they allow. Users can manipulate data simply by defining particular cell values to be some combination of other cell values. Suppose, for example, that cell D3 (the cell in column D or the fourth column and the third row on the worksheet) was defined as the difference between cells B3 and C3 (the cells in the second column, third row, and third column, third row, respectively). As the values in either cell B3 or cell C3 were changed, the value in D3 would be automatically changed, as would the value in any cells that were defined as other combinations of cells B3, C3, or D3. The spreadsheets thus allow managers to engage in a great deal of "what if" analysis.

Table 15–8 displays some electronic spread sheets that could be used to con-

Table 15–8
Electronic spreadsheet analysis of Kitchenware Company sales results

A	B	C	D	E	F
1]					Performance Index
2]	BPI	Sales			
3]	(Percent	Quota	Sales	Difference	$(PI =$
4]Entity	of U.S.)	($ mill.)	($ mill.)	($ mill.)	$S/Q^*100)$
5]					
6]Panel A—Regions					
7]New England	5.8193	C17*B7/100	25.03	DC-C7	D7/C7*100
8]Middle Atlantic	18.3946	C17*B8/100	78.19	D8-C8	D8/C8*100
9]East North Central	20.1329	C17*B9/100	79.48	D9-C9	D9/C9*100
10]West North Central	7.3982	C17*B10/100	30.51	D10-C10	D10/C10*100
11]South Atlantic	14.7526	C17*B11/100	64.07	D11-C11	D11/C11*100
12]East North Central	5.2570	C17*B12/100	23.20	D12-C12	D12/C12*100
13]West South Central	9.2022	C17*B13/100	38.42	D13-C13	D13/C13*100
14]Mountain	4.2819	C17*B14/100	17.73	D14-C14	D14/C14*100
15]Pacific	14.7613	C17*B15/100	64.60	D15-C15	D15/C15*100
16]	....	....	....	....	....
17] Total	Sum(B7:B15)	420	SUM(D7:D15)	D17-C17	D17/C17*100
18]					
19]Panel B—States					
20]Illinois	6.0037	C17*B20/100	24.30	D20-C20	D20/C20*100
21]Indiana	2.4103	C17*B21/100	10.24	D21-C21	D21/C21*100
22]Michigan	4.6401	C17*B22/100	17.77	D22-C22	D22/C22*100
23]Ohio	4.9764	C17*B23/100	20.43	D23-C23	D23/C23*100
24]Wisconsin	2.1114	C17*B24/100	6.74	D24-C24	D24/C24*100
25]	....	....	....	....	....
26] Total	SUM(B20:B24)	SUM(C20:C24)	SUM(D20:D24)	SUM(E20:E24)	D26/C26*100

This analysis was prepared using Super Calc which is the registered trademark of SORCIM Corporation of San Jose, California. Another very popular spreadsheet is VisiCalc, which is the registered trademark of Visi Corp., also of San Jose, California.

---

[27] For a discussion of how electronic spreadsheets can help sales managers make sales operations more efficient, see G. David Hughes, "Computerized Sales Management," *Harvard Business Review*, March-April 1983, pp. 102–12.

duct the Kitchenware Company analysis, for example. While only the region (Panel A) and state data (Panel B) are shown, the analysis could be easily expanded to include the salespeople serving Wisconsin and/or Hutchins' sales by product. One can see the essential notions at work in columns C, E and F and rows 17 and 26. The cells in column C are defined to be equal to the total national quota of $420 million found in cell C17 times the percentage of total potential in the area as defined by the BPI, values which are found in column B. The cells in column F are defined as the value in cell D divided by the value in cell C for the same row times 100. Except for cell C17 which is fixed by sales management, the entries in rows 17 and 26 are defined as the sum of the appropriate column entries.

If any of the cells in the spreadsheet were redefined, all of the cells that depended on that entry would be automatically recomputed. While perhaps not realistic, given how the other salespeople did, suppose for illustration purposes that the problems revealed in the analysis of Hutchins' performance led management to revise the national quota downward from $420 million to $400 million. Table 15–9 displays the results of such a change, which literally took seconds to

Table 15–9
Sales results if Kitchenware's national sales quota were $400 million rather than $420 million

A	B	C	D	E	F
1]					Performance
2]	BPI	Sales			Index
3]	(Percent	Quota	Sales	Difference	$(PI =$
4]Entity	of U.S.)	($ mill.)	($ mill.)	($ mill.)	$S/Q^*100)$
5]					
6]Panel A—Regions					
7]New England	5.8193	23.28	25.03	1.75	107.53
8]Middle Atlantic	18.3946	73.58	78.19	4.61	106.27
9]East North Central	20.1329	80.53	79.48	−1.05	98.69
10]West North Central	7.3982	29.59	30.51	.92	103.10
11]South Atlantic	14.7526	59.01	64.07	5.06	108.57
12]East North Central	5.2570	21.03	23.20	2.17	110.33
13]West South Central	9.2022	36.81	38.42	1.61	104.38
14]Mountain	4.2819	17.13	17.73	.60	103.52
15]Pacific	14.7613	59.05	64.60	5.55	109.41
16]	. . . .	. . . . .	. . . . .	. . . . .	. . . . .
17] Total	100.0000	400.00	421.23	21.23	105.31
18]					
19]Panel B—States					
20]Illinois	6.0037	24.01	24.30	.29	101.19
21]Indiana	2.4103	9.64	10.24	.60	106.21
22]Michigan	4.6401	18.56	17.77	−.79	95.74
23]Ohio	4.9764	19.91	20.43	.52	102.63
24]Wisconsin	2.1114	8.45	6.74	−1.71	79.80
25]	. . . .	. . . . .	. . . . .	. . . . .	. . . . .
26] Total	20.1419	80.57	79.48	−1.09	98.65

produce. It only involved changing the single number in cell C17 to $400 million. Similarly, any other number that resides in the company's data system or is controlled by managers could be changed and all of the appropriate entries would be adjusted.

Summary

This chapter is the first of three to discuss the important issue of management evaluation and control of the field selling effort. The most thorough mechanism by which evaluation is effected is through a marketing audit, which is a complete, systematic, objective evaluation of the total marketing effort of the firm. The sales management audit is an example of a vertical audit because it is the detailed analysis of one part of the total marketing effort. The sales management audit should include an examination of objectives, policies, organization, methods, and procedures used in managing the personal selling function, as well as an assessment of how individual personnel are performing.

A sales analysis can be one of the more revealing inputs in a performance appraisal. A sales analysis involves gathering, classifying, comparing, and studying company sales data. The study may simply involve the comparison of total company sales in two different time periods, or it may subject thousands of component sales figures to a variety of comparisons. One real benefit of a sales analysis is in highlighting the concentration ratio, or the 80:20 principle, for products, customers, and the like.

Those wishing to make a sales analysis must decide at least three things. First, the sales manager must decide the type of control system that is to be used. Will it involve simple or comparative sales analyses? Will it be one that provides all relevant comparisons, or one that reports only significant exceptions, or some combination of these schemes? Second, the source documents must be pinpointed or perhaps designed. The sales invoice is typically one of the most useful source documents, so great care must go into its design. Third, the sales manager must decide which variables are to serve as points of aggregation—for example, geographic regions, products, or salespeople. Most likely, the manager will want the input records to be maintained disaggregatively, so that hierarchical sales analyses can be conducted. A hierarchical sales analysis involves the investigation of sales by several components when the components are considered simultaneously.

One productive way of conducting a sales analysis is via the principle of isolate and explode, in which the most significant discrepancies between actual and standard are isolated and then exploded. The detail this explosion reveals is then analyzed, the most significant discrepancies are noted, and these are in turn exploded. A rather common output of an isolate and explode analysis is to find that small, barely visible problems are often underlying symptoms of large, invisible problems, much like an iceberg; thus, the phenomenon has been referred to as the iceberg principle.

Increasingly, the principle of isolate and explode is being implemented within companies using decision support systems (DSS). Decision support systems include data systems, model systems, and dialog systems. The dialog systems differentiate DSS from more traditional management information systems and are the most important in that they allow managers with limited understanding of computers to conduct their own analyses while sitting at a computer terminal that is connected to the companies data bases. DSS for evaluating the personal selling effort promise to be particularly important in the future, as microcomputers become more and more popular.

Discussion Questions

1. What are the differences between an MIS and a DSS? What developments led to the increase in popularity of DSSs?

2. Define marketing audit. How often should a firm conduct a marketing audit?

3. Distinguish among a horizontal marketing audit, a vertical marketing audit, and a sales management audit.

4. An effective sales analysis is a function of the quality of information, yet sales representatives, as a general rule, dislike completing various call reports and other reports requested by management. The quality of these reports suffers as a result. What suggestions can you offer to help alleviate problems associated with preparing call reports?

5. The Flambeau Corporation sells plastic moldings directly to automobile manufacturers. It also sells household products, reaching the retail market through manufacturer's agents. How would Flambeau's decision support systems vary in each situation?

6. One critic, commenting about sales analysis, said: "If you look long enough, and hard enough, you can find ratios that will make anybody look good and anybody look bad." What does this say about the sales analysis process?

7. Typically, management by exception concentrates on ratios that indicate substandard performance. What arguments can be advanced for analyzing ratios that reveal both substandard performance and exceptional performance?

8. The Amjoy Corporation has developed a series of ratios to evaluate regional, district, and individual performance. Upper and lower control limits permit quick identification of significant deviations. The accompanying chart shows the sales expense-to-sales ratio for Barbara Smith. What does this chart reveal? What action, if any, should Barbara's district sales manager take?

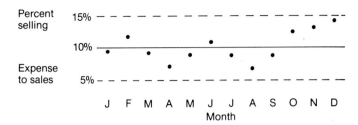

9. The use of personal computers by managers has been viewed as an invasion of privacy by some people. According to one critic: "Sales information is transmitted immediately, and I don't have a chance to explain any strange variations." Another commented: "This is like 'Big Brother' watching me. Before, my sales manager couldn't care less, now he's on my back constantly." Comment. Are these views justifiable?

10. The Recall Computer Co. has six sales territories each represented by one sales representative. After extensive planning, the company determines that each territory would be expected to achieve the following percentages of total company sales for 1985.

Territory 1	27%	Territory 4	12%
Territory 2	15%	Territory 5	20%
Territory 3	18%	Territory 6	8%

These figures are used as the standard for comparing each sales representatives' actual 1985 sales. The company projected sales for 1985 of $20,500,000. Determine which sales representatives' territory had the best performance, by using the performance index, if the actual sales for 1985 in each territory were $5,425,000, $3,205,000, $3,710,000, $2,400,000, $3,900,000, and $2,000,000, respectively.

11. How might the results of a sales analysis affect the following activities?
    a. Recruiting.
    b. Sales training.
    c. Compensation.
    d. Sales force motivation.
    e. Sales forecasting.
    f. Pricing.

12. In planning a sales analysis system, one must take into account that information needs vary from district sales manager to regional sales manager to national sales manager. Give specific examples of how information needs vary among individuals.

Chapter **16**

Cost Analysis

Cost analysis is complementary to sales analysis in the management of the personal selling effort. Whereas sales analysis focuses on the results achieved, cost analysis looks at the costs incurred in producing those results and whether the returns justify the expenditures. To do this, it is necessary to gather, classify, compare, and study marketing cost data, which is the essence of marketing cost analysis.

There is an important reason for sales management to conduct marketing cost analysis—it can help identify opportunities for increasing the effectiveness of marketing expenditures. Sales are achieved at some cost, and marketing productivity focuses on the sales or profit output per unit of marketing effort input. Unfortunately, it is often difficult for a firm to know what the output/input relationships are without some detailed analyses. Most firms today produce multiple products, which they sell in multiple markets. For each product and market, the mix of marketing elements differs. Only by analyzing specific relationships among these products and markets can the firm hope to identify situations where marketing input should be increased or altered, where it should remain at its historic levels, and where it should be decreased. These insights are simply not produced by the information that flows from normal accounting operations. Similarly, to deploy the firm's salespeople most effectively, the sales manager needs to appreciate the output/input relationships by territory, customer, channel of distribution, and so on. It is the purpose of marketing cost analysis to estimate these relationships.

Cost Analysis Development

Sales management has been somewhat slower to adopt cost (or as it is sometimes called, profitability) analysis than sales analysis for managing the sales function. One early study investigated whether manufacturing firms performed profitability analyses of their marketing operations. It found that, among the 273 companies surveyed, 97 percent performed profitability analyses for products. Only 67 percent of these companies did such analyses by territories, however—57 percent for salespeople and 54 percent for customers. Furthermore, only 19 percent of the large firms and 23 percent of the medium-sized ones analyzed profits by all four bases of products, territories, salespeople, and customers. Conversely, 43 percent of the large firms and 36 percent of the medium ones indicated they performed a profitability analysis for only one of these bases.[1] Other studies have confirmed the benign neglect accorded marketing cost and profitability analyses.[2]

One apparent reason for this neglect seems to be that most accounting systems are still not designed to meet the needs of marketing management. This is sur-

---

[1] Richard T. Hise, "Have Manufacturing Firms Adopted the Marketing Concept?" *Journal of Marketing* 29 (July 1975), pp. 9–12.

[2] "Report of the Committee on Cost and Profitability Analysis for Marketing," *The Accounting Review*, supplement to vol. 47 (1972), pp. 575–615; and L. Gayle Rayburn, "Accounting Tools in the Analysis and Control of Marketing Performance," *Industrial Marketing Management* 6 (1977), pp. 175–82.

prising, in view of the many advantages that the company can realize from carefully conducted cost and profit analyses.

Accounting systems were originally designed to report the aggregate effects of a firm's operations to its stockholders and creditors. In later years, accounting systems have been redesigned to meet the internal management needs within the production sector of the firm. The net result is an accounting system which is oriented towards both external reporting and production cost analysis.[3]

To understand the apparent gap between the need for accounting information to measure marketing performance and the supply of that information, it is necessary to appreciate the differences between normal accounting costs and marketing costs.

Accounting versus Marketing Costs

One has to recognize at the outset the different purposes that underlie accounting and marketing costs. Accounting costs are computed to provide a historical record of the company's operations. To an accountant, net income is essentially a historical record of the past. In computing net income, for example, the accountant attempts to allocate all the costs of the equipment used to produce the product during the time the equipment was used. This ensures that revenues equal to the original cost of the equipment are not distributed as dividends but are put back into assets, such as more equipment or cash. Whether this amount is enough to replace the asset is not part of the accounting problem.

The marketing perspective is much more like an economist's perspective because it is future-oriented. To an economist, net income is essentially a speculation about the future, not a historical record of the past. Thus, the economist looks to the future to determine the basic value of today's assets. The real costs of an asset are the opportunity costs foregone by putting the asset to one use versus another. To the businessperson, like the economist, the past is irrelevant except to forecast the future. Thus, although the accountant might classify costs on the basis of object (e.g., plant, equipment, materials) or process (e.g., finishing, assembly), a decision-making perspective requires that costs be classified in terms of those that will be affected by a proposed decision and those *that will not be affected.* Similarly, while the accountant looks at the original or outlay costs of an input factor to determine its value, the decision maker needs to look to *future value.* This value should include the full range of *opportunities foregone or sacrifice entailed.*

Note also that, although many other costs reflect the *result* of some particular activity—such as production—marketing costs are directed at *producing* some benefit. Thus, "in controlling production costs, management is concerned with

---

[3] Frank H. Mossman, Paul M. Fischer, and W. J. E. Crissy, "New Approaches to Analyzing Marketing Profitability," *Journal of Marketing* 38 (April 1974), p. 43

the effect of volume on costs. In the control of distribution costs, management's attention is directed toward the effect of costs on volume."[4] Further, "management is much less certain about the effects of marketing costs on volume than about the effects that volume changes have on production costs."[5]

Full Cost or Contribution Margin

Marketing cost analysis can take either a full-cost (or, as it is sometimes called, net profit) approach or a contribution margin approach. There is a good deal of controversy over which should be used.[6] To appreciate the controversy fully, it is helpful to understand the differences between direct and indirect costs and specific and general expenses.

Direct versus Indirect Costs

A *direct cost* is one that can be specifically identified with a product or a function.[7] It is a cost that is incurred because the product or function exists or is contemplated. If the product or function were to be eliminated,the cost would also disappear. An example is inventory carrying costs for a product.

An *indirect cost* is a shared cost because it is tied to several functions or products. Even if one of the products or functions were eliminated, the cost would not be. Rather, the share of the cost previously borne by the product or function that was eliminated would shift to the remaining products or functions. An example of an indirect cost is the travel expenses of a salesperson selling a multiple product line. Even if one product that the representative sells is eliminated, the salesperson's travel cost will not be.

Specific versus General Expense

The profit-and-loss or net income statement typically distinguishes between costs and expenses. More particularly, the term *costs* is often restricted to the materials, labor, power, rent, and so on that are used in making the product. The cost of goods sold on the following conceptual net income statement reflects these costs.

---

[4] William J. Stanton and Richard H. Buskirk, *Management of the Sales Force*, 6th ed. (Homewood, Ill.: Richard D. Irwin, 1983), p. 529.

[5] Ibid., p. 529.

[6] For a review of the controversy, as well as a historical perspective on why it exists, see John J. Wheatley, "The Allocation Controversy in Marketing Cost Analysis," *University of Washington Business Review*, Summer 1971, pp. 61–70.

[7] Sanford R. Simon, *Managing Marketing Profitability* (New York: American Management Association, 1969), p. 37. This is an excellent little book on profitability analysis, which all serious students of marketing cost analysis are urged to read. It illustrates the process that should be followed in carrying out a marketing cost analysis and the insights gained from doing so with detailed examples. Much of this and the following section rely heavily on this excellent book.

Sales
Less: Cost of goods sold
Gross margin
Less: General administrative and selling expenses
Profit or net income before taxes

The expenses reflect the other costs incurred in operating the business, such as the cost of advertising and of maintaining branches. Expenses cannot be tied nearly as well as costs to specific products, since they are general expenses associated with doing business. In marketing cost analysis, the distinction between costs and expenses is not nearly so clear and the terms are often used interchangeably.

A *specific expense* in that sense is just like a direct cost—it can be specifically identified with a product or function. The expense would be eliminated if the product or function were eliminated. If the product were eliminated, for example, the specific expense of the product manager's salary need not be incurred.

A *general expense* is like an indirect cost—it cannot be identified directly with a specific object of profit measurement such as a territory, salesperson, or product. Thus, the expense would not be eliminated if the specific object were eliminated. The sales manager's salary is an example when the object of measurement is a product in a multiple-product company. The elimination of the product would in no way eliminate this salary.

It is important to realize that a single cost may be direct for some measurement purposes and indirect for others. The object of the measurement determines how the cost should be treated.

If this is a product line, costs directly associated with the manufacture and sale of the product line are direct. All other costs in the business are indirect. If the object of measurement shifts to a sales territory, some of the costs of product-line measurement which were direct will remain direct costs now associated with the territory; some will become indirect; and others that were indirect will become direct. For example,[8]

	Object of Measurement	
Cost	Product	Territory
Sales promotion display	Direct	Direct
Salesman compensation	Indirect	Direct
Product line manager's salary	Direct	Indirect
Corporate president's salary	Indirect	Indirect

Which to Use

As mentioned, there is controversy about whether one should use a full-cost or contribution margin approach in marketing cost analysis. Proponents of the full-cost or net profit approach argue that all costs should be assigned and somehow

---

[8] Ibid., pp. 37–38.

accounted for in determining the profitability of any segment (e.g., territory, product, salesperson) of the business.

Under this approach, each unit bears not only its own direct costs which can be traced to it, but also a share of the company's cost of doing business, referred to as indirect costs. Full costing advocates argue that many of the indirect costs can be assigned to the unit being costed on the basis of a demonstrable cost relationship. If a strong relationship does not exist, *the cost must be prorated on as reasonable a basis as possible.* Under the full costing approach a net income for each marketing segment can be determined by matching the segment's revenue with its direct and *its share of indirect costs.* [Emphasis added.][9]

Contribution margin advocates argue, on the other hand, that it is misleading and confusing to allocate costs arbitrarily. They suggest that only those costs that can be specifically identified with the segment of the business should be deducted from the revenue produced by the segment to determine how well the segment is doing. Any excess of revenues over these costs contributes to the common costs of the business and thereby to profits. The contribution margin approach does not distinguish where the costs are incurred, but rather simply whether they are variable or fixed. Thus, the difference between sales and all variable costs, whether they originate in manufacturing, selling, or some administrative function, are subtracted from revenues or sales to produce the contribution margin of the segment. The net profit approach does attempt to determine where the costs were incurred. The difference in perspectives is highlighted in Figure 16–1.

Figure 16–1
Differences in perspective between net income and contribution margin approaches to marketing cost analysis

Full-cost approach
       Sales
  Less: Cost of goods sold

Equal: Gross margin
  Less: Operating expenses (including the segment's allocated
        share of company administration and general expenses)

Equal: Segment net income

Contribution margin approach
       Sales
  Less: Variable manufacturing costs
  Less: Other variable costs directly traceable to the segment

Equal: Contribution margin
  Less: Fixed costs directly traceable to products
        Fixed costs directly traceable to the market segment

Equal: Segment net income

Source: Adapted from Patrick M. Dunne and Harry I. Wolk. "Marketing Cost Analysis: A Modularized Contribution Approach," *Journal of Marketing* 41 (July 1977), p. 84.

---

[9] Rayburn, "Accounting Tools," p. 178.

The contribution margin advocates appear to be winning the battle. Although the early emphasis in accounting for distribution costs was on full-cost allocation,[10] all the recent emphasis is on the contribution margin approach.[11] The contribution margin approach does have unmistakable logic. If the costs associated with the segment are not removed with the elimination of the segment, why should they be arbitrarily allocated? That just confuses things and provides a blurred, distorted picture for management decision making. The costs still have to be borne after the segment is eliminated, but they must be borne by other segments of the business. This, in turn, can simply tax the ability of these other segments to remain profitable. Tables 16–1 and 16–2 illustrate this phenomenon.[12]

Table 16–1
Profit and loss statement by departments using a full-cost approach

	Totals	Depart-ment 1	Depart-ment 2	Depart-ment 3
Sales	$100,000	$50,000	$30,000	$20,000
Cost of goods sold	80,000	45,000	25,000	10,000
Gross margin..................	20,000	5,000	5,000	10,000
Other expenses				
Selling expenses.............	5,000	2,500	1,500	1,000
Administrative expenses......	6,000	3,000	1,800	1,200
Total other expenses	11,000	5,500	3,300	2,200
Net profit (loss)................	9,000	(500)	1,700	7,800

Source: Robert K. Jaedicke, "A Method for Making Product Combination Decisions," *Business News Notes* (Minneapolis: University of Minnesota, April 1958), pp. 1–2.

The example involves a department store with three main departments. The administrative expenses in Table 16–1 are all fixed costs; they were allocated to departments on the basis of the total percentage of sales accounted for by each department. This is a common allocation basis about which more will be said later. Some executives felt that Department 1 should be eliminated because of the net loss of $500 it was producing.

Note what would happen if this avenue were pursued. First, the sales of the department would be lost, but $2,500 of selling expenses would also be eliminated. However, it would also mean that the $3,000 of fixed costs must now be

[10] The early "classics" on marketing cost analysis emphasized the full-cost approach. See J. B. Heckert and R. B Miner. *Distribution Costs* (New York: Ronald Press, 1953); and D. R. Longman and M. Schiff, *Practical Distribution Cost Analysis* (Homewood, Ill.: Richard D. Irwin, 1955).

[11] See, for example. Simon, *Managing Marketing Profitability*; Sevin, *Marketing Productivity Analysis*; or L. Gayle Rayburn, *Financial Tools for Effective Marketing Administration* (New York: American Management Association, 1976).

[12] The example is taken from Robert K. Jaedicke, "A Method for Making Product Combination Decisions," *Business News Notes* (Minneapolis: University of Minnesota, April 1958), pp. 1–2.

Table 16–2
Profit and loss statement if
Department 1 were eliminated

	Totals	Depart- ment 1	Depart- ment 2
Sales	$50,000	$30,000	$20,000
Cost of goods sold	35,000	25,000	10,000
Gross margin......................	15,000	5,000	10,000
Other expenses			
Selling expenses..................	2,500	1,500	1,000
Administrative expenses..........	6,000	3,600	2,400
Total other expenses	8,500	5,100	3,400
Net profit (loss).....................	6,500	(100)	6,600

Source: Robert K. Jaedicke, "A Method for Making Product Combination Decisions," *Business News Notes* (Minneapolis: University of Minnesota, April 1958), pp. 1–2.

borne by the other departments. Now, allocating these costs on the basis of percentage of sales suggests that Department 2 is unprofitable (see Table 16–2). If one used the same argument as before, it too should be considered for elimination. The upshot would be that $6,000 of administrative expenses must now be borne entirely by Department 3. Fortunately, Department 3 would still be profitable, so management would not close a profitable store simply because one department displayed a small dollar loss—a loss that could be attributed to an arbitrary allocation of fixed costs. Department 1, in fact, makes a positive contribution to profits, as the contribution margin statement in Table 16–3 shows.

Another argument that supports a contribution margin versus a full-cost profitability analysis is the recognition that most marketing phenomena are highly interrelated.

Table 16–3
Contribution margin by departments

Sales	Totals	Depart- ment 1	Depart- ment 2	Depart- ment 3
Variable costs	$100,000	$50,000	$30,000	$20,000
Cost of goods sold	80,000	45,000	25,000	10,000
Selling expenses............	5,000	2,500	1,500	1,000
Total variable costs	85,000	47,500	26,500	11,000
Contribution margin	15,000	2,500	3,500	9,000
Fixed costs				
Administrative expenses......	6,000			
Net profit......................	9,000			

Source: Robert K. Jaedicke, "A Method for Making Product Combination Decisions," *Business News Notes* (Minneapolis: Univesity of Minnesota, April 1958), pp. 1–2.

The demand for a particular product in a multiproduct offering should . . . be viewed as being interrelated with the demand for all of the products in the line. One product frequently helps to sell another, and the absence of a product may cause the sale of another product to decline. In other words, the whole product line may often be greater than the sum of its parts in terms of sales and profits.[13]

The same is true for the other elements of the marketing mix. They provide complementary and substitute roles for one another. The contribution margin approach implicitly recognizes the synergistic effect that the whole may be greater than the sum of its parts through its emphasis on the contribution of each part or segment. "The contribution margin approach is considered to be more valid [than the full-cost approach] since contribution reporting places more emphasis on cost responsibility."[14]

Procedure

The general procedure followed in conducting a cost or profitability analysis first involves specifying the purpose for which the cost study is being done. This helps to determine the functional cost centers. The next step is to spread the natural account costs to these functional costs centers. Then the functional costs are allocated to appropriate segments using some reasonable basis. Finally, the allocated costs are summed, and the contribution of the segment is determined. Incidentally, *segment* is used here to mean a portion of the business, not in the normal sense of market segment.

The essential process is shown in Figure 16–2. Although the diagram is simple, its execution is difficult. It often involves some hard decisions about what costs or expenses are to be treated as fixed, semifixed, or variable, and how various costs should be allocated to segments.

Purpose

As mentioned, the first step in a profitability analysis is to determine the purpose for which it is being done. Is it designed to investigate the profitability of the various products in the line? Or is it designed to determine the profitability of sales branches, customers, or individual salespersons? The decision is essential because the treatment of the various costs and expenses depends on the purpose.

Ideally, the firm would want to break all its costs or revenues into small building blocks or modules. These elements would be as small as possible and yet still

---

[13] Wheatley, "Allocation Controversy," p. 66.
[14] Rayburn, "Accounting Tools," p. 179.

Figure 16–2
Steps in conducting a profitability
analysis

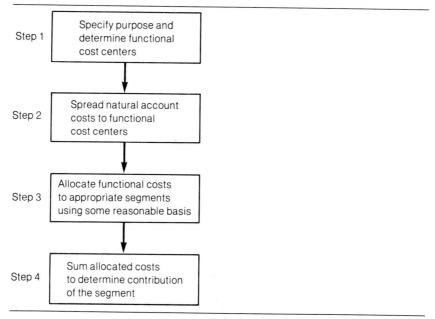

be meaningful.[15] This allows the firm to aggregate these building blocks as needed to produce profitability analyses for various segments of the business. An example of a basic building block or module of cost is a regional sales manager's salary. This is a general expense when the profitability of various product lines is at issue. It is a specific expense and needs to be taken into account when determining the contribution to profit of the region.

Thus, good profitability analyses require that the various costs be partitioned into direct and indirect expenses so that the proper aggregations can be made. What is properly treated as direct and what should be treated as indirect or general depend on the study's purpose. Sales managers typically are most concerned with the profitability of various regions, branches, salespeople, and customers; they are only remotely concerned with the profitability of various products. Thus, an individual salesperson's salary is more likely to be treated as a direct than an indirect expense, whereas a product manager's salary is likely indirect. Investigation of the profitability of the product line requires just the opposite treatment, which again illustrates the importance of specifying exactly the purpose for which the study is being conducted.

[15] Simon, *Managing Marketing Profitability*, p. 38. See also Donald W. Jackson and Lonne L. Ostrom, "Grouping Segments for Profitability Analysis," *MSU Business Topics* 28 (1980), pp. 39–44, for a discussion of the segments that are typically used in a marketing cost analysis.

Natural Accounts versus Functional Accounts

In the second step of the process, natural account costs need to be spread to the functional cost centers. This raises the question of the difference between a natural account and a functional account.

Natural accounts are the categories of cost used in the normal accounting cycle. These costs include such things as salaries, wages, rent, heat, light, taxes, auto expenses, raw materials, and office supplies. They are called *natural accounts* because they bear the name of their expense categories.

This is not the only way of classifying costs. In manufacturing cost accounting, for example, costs are often reclassified according to the *purpose* for which they were incurred. Thus, the cost of wages might be broken into the categories forging, turning, grinding, milling, polishing, and assembling. These categories are *functional* account categories because they recognize the function performed, which is the purpose for incurring the cost.

Marketing cost analysis has a similar orientation. It recognizes that marketing costs are incurred for some purpose, and it reorganizes general selling and administrative expenses according to their purposes or functions. As Edmund D. McCarry stated so elegantly, "The term function should be defined so as to meet the purpose for which it is used. The function of the heart is not simply to beat, which is its activity, but rather to supply the body with a continuous flow of blood."[16]

The salaries paid in a branch office, for example, could go to perform such functions as direct selling, advertising, order processing, and extending credit. A functional cost analysis would involve spreading the total salaries paid in the office to these various functions. Table 16–4 lists the major functional accounts that are useful in marketing cost analyses.

Allocate Functional Costs

As Figure 16–2 indicates, the third step in the process is to allocate the functional costs to the various segments of the business. One needs to recognize immediately that the bases for allocation are not fixed. Rather, they depend on the discretion of the decision maker and what he or she feels are "reasonable" bases.

One basis often used is to divide the expenses according to volume attained. Thus, if a regional sales manager was responsible for six branch offices, and one office produced 25 percent of the sales in the region, it would be charged with one fourth of the sales manager's salary and expenses. This method is often used

---

[16] Edmund D. McGarry, "Some Functions of Marketing Reconsidered," in *Theory in Marketing*, ed. Reavis Cox and Wroe Anderson (Homewood, Ill.: Richard D. Irwin, 1950), p. 267.

Table 16–4
Major functional accounts useful in marketing cost analysis

1. Direct selling
2. Advertising and sales promotion
3. Product and package design
4. Technical product services
5. Sales discounts and allowances
6. Credit extension
7. Warranty costs
8. Marketing research
9. Warehousing and handling
10. Inventory
11. Packaging, shipping, and delivery
12. Order processing
13. Customer service
14. Billing and recording of accounts receivable
15. Returned merchandise

Source: Adapted from Sanford R. Simon, *Managing Marketing Profitability* (New York: American Management Association, 1969), pp. 30–31, which also lists some of the main costs incurred in performing each function.

because of its simplicity. It is completely erroneous, however, in that it fails to recognize the purpose for which the regional sales manager's costs were incurred, which is the reason for a functional cost analysis. It may be that the branch proved troublesome to manage and consumed 50 percent of the manager's time. In this case, it should bear half his salary. Alternatively, it may have run extremely smoothly. The manager rarely had to get involved with the branch activities, so on net at the end of the year, it consumed only 10 percent of his time and effort. In this case, only one tenth of the regional sales manager's salary should be charged against the branch in determining its profit contribution. As Horngren, the eminent cost accountant, stated years ago, "The costs of efforts are independent of the results actually obtained, in the sense that the costs are programmed by management, not determined by sales. Moreover, the allocation of costs on the basis of dollar sales entails circular reasoning."[17]

If one should not use sales to allocate costs, what should one use? Although there are no unequivocal allocation bases, one generally searches for bases that "control" the functional cost in the sense that as the control factor changes, the functional costs tend to increase or decrease. In other words, one searches for factors that are measurable and for which there is a cause-and-effect relationship between the factor used as a basis of allocation and the dollar expenditure in the corresponding functional cost group.[18]

The causal relationships used can, and most likely will, be different for different questions. Table 16–5 shows some common bases for allocating functional costs to product groups, account size classes, and sales territories.

---

[17] Charles R. Horngren, *Cost Accounting: A Managerial Emphasis*, 2d ed. (Englewood Cliffs, N.J.: Prentice-Hall, 1967), p. 381.
[18] Simon, *Managing Marketing Profitability*, p. 18.

Table 16–5
Functional cost groups and bases of allocation

Functional Cost Group	Basis of Allocation		
	To Product Groups	To Account Size Classes	To Sales Territories
1. Selling—direct costs: Personal calls by salesmen and supervisors on accounts and prospects. Sales salaries, incentive compensation, travel, and other expenses	Selling time devoted to each product, as shown by special sales call reports or other special studies	Number of sales calls times average time per call, as shown by special sales call reports or other special studies	Direct
2. Selling—indirect costs: Field supervision, field sales-office expense, sales-administration expenses, sales-personnel training, sales management. Market research, new product development, sales statistics, tabulating services, sales accounting	In proportion to direct selling time, or time records by projects	In proportion to direct selling time, or time records by project	Equal charge for each salesman
3. Advertising: Media costs such as TV, radio, billboards, newspaper, magazine, etc. Advertising production costs; advertising department salaries	Direct; or analysis of space and time by media; other costs in proportion to media costs	Equal charge to each account; or number of ultimate consumers and prospects in each account's trading area	Direct; or analysis of media circulation records
4. Sales promotion: Consumer promotions such as coupons, patches, premiums, etc. Trade promotions such as price allowances, point-of-purchase displays, cooperative advertising, etc.	Direct; or analysis of source records	Direct; or analysis of source records	Direct; or analysis of source records

Cost item			
5. Transportation: Railroad, truck, barge, etc., payments to carriers for delivery of finished goods from plants to warehouses and from warehouses to customers. Traffic department costs	Applicable rates times tonnages	Analysis of sampling of bills of lading	Applicable rates times tonnages
6. Storage and shipping: Storage of finished goods inventories in warehouses. Rent (or equivalent costs), public warehouse charges, fire insurance and taxes on finished goods inventories, etc. Physical handling, assembling, and loading out of rail cars, trucks, barges for shipping finished products from warehouses and mills to customers. Labor, equipment, space, and material costs.	Warehouse space occupied by average inventory. Number of shipping units	Number of shipping units	Number of shipping units
7. Order processing: Checking and processing of orders from customers to mills for prices, weights and carload accumulation, shipping dates, coordination with production planning, transmittal to mills, etc. Pricing department. Preparation of customer invoices. Freight accounting. Credit and collection. Handling cash receipts. Provision for bad debts. Salary, supplies, space and equipment costs (teletypes, flexowriters, etc.)	Number of order lines	Number of order lines	Number of order lines

Source: Charles H. Sevin, *Marketing Productivity Analysis* (New York: McGraw-Hill, 1965), pp. 13–15. Used with permission.

Sum Allocated Costs

The fourth step in the process is to sum the costs allocated to the segment. Costs for which there is no direct causal relationship remain unallocated in determining the contribution of the segment. A comparison of the contributions of like segments then indicates the remedial action that might be taken, if any.

The Process Illustrated

To illustrate the process, consider the situation encountered by the Baitinger Bicycle Company, which was faced with a loss in its St. Louis branch of more than $80,000.[19]

BAITINGER BICYCLE COMPANY
St. Louis Office
Profit and Loss Statement

Sales		$2,481,750
Cost of goods sold		2,030,500
Gross margin		451,250
Selling and administrative expenses:		
Salaries.......................................	$154,500	
Commissions...................................	24,818	
Advertising	127,000	
Postage and office supplies	490	
Packaging materials	30,420	
Transportation charges	91,260	
Travel expenses	38,000	
Rent	65,000	
Total selling and administrative expenses		531,488
Net profit (loss)		(80,238)

Suppose the sales manager is interested in further analyzing the branch to see whether the loss can be traced to particular sales representatives or customers, much as the discrepancy between sales and quota was localized in Chapter 15.

---

[19] The example is purposely hypothetical so as to throw the basic process into more bold relief, while at the same time illustrating some common features of such situations. For actual examples, which at times can get quite complex, see Simon, *Managing Marketing Profitability*; Charles H. Sevin, *Marketing Productivity Analysis* (New York: McGraw Hill, 1965); Patrick M. Dunne and Harry I. Wolk, "Marketing Cost Analysis: A Modularized Contribution Approach," *Journal of Marketing* 41 (July 1977), pp. 83–94; and Merrett J. Davoust, "Analyzing a Client's Customer Profitability Picture," *Management Adviser*, May-June 1974, pp. 15–19.

Apportion Natural Account Costs to Functional Accounts

The sales manager has completed the first step in a cost analysis—the manager has decided that the purpose of the analysis is to isolate the profit contributions of the various sales representatives in the branch. The next thing he must do is to spread the general selling and administrative expenses incurred by the branch in the profit-and-loss statement to the various functional accounts. To keep the example simple, the fixed and variable costs incurred in manufacturing will not be separated, although a more sophisticated contribution margin analysis would reflect such differences. Rather, the cost of goods sold is assumed to be a fixed charge to the St. Louis branch. The manager concentrates on spreading only the selling and administrative expenses to functional cost groups.

Table 16–6 lists the functional cost categories across the top and the natural account categories along the side. The individual entries indicate how a total natural cost is apportioned according to purpose. Note that the sum of all the functional costs in a row equals the natural cost for that row; that is, all natural costs are accounted for in the spread.

Table 16–6
Allocation of natural accounts to functional accounts

Natural Accounts		Direct Selling	Advertising	Warehousing and Shipping	Order Processing and Billing	Transportation
Salaries	$154,500	$128,500		$12,000	$14,000	
Commissions	24,818	24,818				
Advertising...........	127,000		$127,000			
Postage and supplies ..	490				490	
Packaging materials ...	30,420			30,420		
Transportation charges .	91,260					$91,260
Travel expenses	38,000	38,000				
Rent	65,000	14,000		47,500	3,500	
	$531,488	$205,318	$127,000	$89,920	$17,990	$91,260

The details in the division of costs depend directly on the operation of the branch. In this case, the branch in the previous year paid $154,500 in salaries. They were distributed in the following way: branch manager —$39,000; four salespeople—$89,500; warehouse clerk—$12,000; and a clerical person handling order processing and billing—$14,000. The salaries of the branch manager and salespeople are charged against direct selling expenses because that is the purpose for which they were incurred. Similarly, the office and warehouse clerk salaries are charged against their main functions. Note that the functional account direct selling is also charged with the commissions earned by the four representatives; in addition to their base salaries, all salespersons were paid a commission equal to 1 percent of sales.

Advertising charges reflect both a natural account cost and a functional account cost. Advertising charges are typically maintained in a separate category in the normal accounting cycle, and their name speaks to their purpose. The same is true of transportation charges.

The postage and supplies the office consumed were used to support the order-processing and billing functions, and thus they are assigned to this category. Similarly, packaging material costs are assigned to warehousing and shipping because that is the function for which they are used. Travel expenses reflect the food, lodging, and other expenses incurred by the sales representatives in carrying out their main function of selling; thus, these costs are so assigned.

Perhaps the one natural account cost that requires the most explanation is rent. The company was paying $35 per square foot for office space and $10 per square foot for warehouse space. These costs are spread to the functional accounts in proportion to the space used by each activity. More particularly, the order-processing and selling functions used 100 of the 500 square feet of office space the company rented; the salespeople and sales manager used the remainder. The $47,500 assignment of rent to warehousing and shipping costs reflects the 4,750 square feet of warehouse space the company rented at $10 per square foot.

Allocate Functional Costs to Segments

To assess the profit contribution of each salesperson, it is necessary to allocate all "relevant" functional costs to salesmen. More particularly, costs that bear some causal relationship to the level of activity should be allocated; these include salaries, commissions, and travel expenses. Conversely, costs that are not affected by the level of activity are not allocated. Office rent is an example. Even if one salesperson were fired, this cost would not change; thus, it should not be allocated because this only confuses things.

Table 16–7 provides much of the data on which the allocations to generate the profitability analysis by salesperson in Table 16–8 are based. Table 16–8 lists the gross margin by salesperson. From this, all direct expenses are subtracted to derive the contribution to profit by salesperson. Let us consider each expense category.

Direct selling. The salary and commission items need little explanation; they reflect what each representative is paid and the 1 percent commission each earned on what he sold. Travel expenses per sales representative were determined by dividing total travel expenses by the number of calls to generate the cost per call. This turned out to be $95, which was then multiplied by the number of calls each salesperson made. If the branch accounting records allowed the identi-

Table 16–7
Basic data used for allocations

Products	Selling Price per Unit	Cost per Unit	Gross Margin per Unit	Number Sold in Period	Sales in Period	Advertising Expenditures
A $115	$90	$25	6,450	$ 741,750	$ 60,000
B 90	75	15	10,060	905,400	40,000
C 60	50	10	13,910·	834,600	27,000
				30,420	$2,481,750	$127,000

Salesperson	Number of Sales Calls	Number of Orders	Number of Units Sold			Total
			A	B	C	
Steve Nicholls 75		50	1,400	2,210	3,410	7,020
Sharon Pogue 125		65	1,725	2,725	3,515	7,965
Paul Vilwock 100		50	1,711	2,609	3,506	7,826
Stan Tucker 100		80	1,614	2,516	3,479	7,609
	400	245	6,450	10,060	13,910	30,420

fication of travel expenses by sales representative, these numbers would be used directly. If the office records also specified the amount of time the sales manager spent with each representative, one could allocate a portion of the sales manager's salary to each salesperson. This cost is not allocated in the example because this information was not available, and in its absence, there is no reasonable cause-and-effect basis for making the allocation.

Advertising. Table 16–7 lists the amount spent on advertising for each product. When these amounts are divided by the number of units sold of each, the following advertising charges per unit are generated:

$$A—\$60,000 \div \ 6,450 \text{ units} = \$9.30/\text{unit}$$
$$B—\$40,000 \div 10,060 \text{ units} = \$3.98/\text{unit}$$
$$C—\$27,000 \div 13,910 \text{ units} = \$1.94/\text{unit}$$

The advertising expenses borne by each salesperson are determined by multiplying these per-unit advertising charges by the number of bicycles of each model that each representative sold.

The number of units of the product that are sold is a very common basis for allocating advertising expenses. Two other common bases are the number of prospects secured and the number of sales transactions.[20] The decision to allocate advertising expenses on the basis of the number of units sold illustrates the point made earlier that there can be a good deal of controversy associated with any of the allocation decisions. While the per-unit-of-product-sold approach is popular, it is not hard to develop an argument against it. One could argue, for example, that advertising expenses are fixed for a period and, since they are fixed costs,

---

[20] L. Gayle Rayburn, *Principles of Cost Accounting and Managerial Implications* (Homewood, Ill.: Richard D. Irwin, 1979), especially pp. 812–14.

Table 16–8
Profitability analysis by salesperson

	Total	Nicholls	Pogue	Vilwock	Tucker
Sales					
A	$741,750	$161,000	$198,375	$196,765	$185,610
B	905,400	198,900	245,250	234,810	226,440
C	834,600	204,600	210,900	210,360	208,740
Total sales	2,481,750	564,500	654,525	641,935	620,790
Cost of goods sold					
A	580,500	126,000	155,250	153,990	145,260
B	754,500	165,750	204,375	195,675	188,700
C	695,500	170,500	175,750	175,300	173,950
Total cost of goods sold	2,030,500	462,250	535,375	524,965	507,910
Gross margin	451,250	102,250	119,150	116,970	112,880
Expenses					
Direct selling					
Salary	89,500	20,000	22,500	23,000	24,000
Commissions	24,818	5,654	6,545	6,419	6,208
Travel	38,000	7,125	11,875	9,500	9,500
Advertising					
A	59,985	13,020	16,043	15,912	15,011
B	40,039	8,796	10,846	10,384	10,013
C	26,985	6,615	6,819	6,802	6,749
Warehousing and shipping	30,420	7,020	7,965	7,826	7,609
Order processing	490	100	130	100	160
Transportation	91,260	21,060	23,895	23,478	22,827
Total expenses	401,497	89,381	106,618	103,421	102,077
Contribution to profit (loss)	49,753	12,869	12,532	13,549	10,803

productive salespeople should not be obliged to assume a larger advertising burden than unproductive salespeople. One could also argue that the per unit approach treats advertising as a consequence of sales, rather than as a cause, and therefore the scheme violates the control principle alluded to earlier that one should search for factors that control the functional cost. While both of these arguments have merit, we will use the per-unit-of-product basis for allocating advertising expenses below for three reasons: (1) the per unit approach is one of the most popular; (2) there is no clearly preferred alternative in the literature; (3) the example is designed to illustrate the cost analysis process, not to provide the last word on all possible nuances. Yet, you should be aware that the decision one makes as to how to allocate advertising expenses or any of the expense categories can change the fundamental conclusions that one draws about the profitability of a particular segment of the business.

Warehousing and Shipping.   The profitability analysis by sales representative does not include an allocation for the warehouseman's salary because his salary would continue regardless of what any sales representative sold. Rather, all that is allocated to the salespeople are the packaging costs per unit, which amounted to $1 per bicycle.

Order Processing.   The office clerk's salary is not allocated to salespeople because there is no causal link between an individual representative's sales and that salary. The office rent charged to this activity is similarly not allocated. The order-processing costs that are allocated are the direct expenses for postage and supplies. This is most directly linked to the number of orders, which produces an allocation of $2 per order.

Transportation.   Transportation charges amounted to $3 per bike. These are charged against the individual sales representatives according to the number of bicycles each sold.

When all these expenses are aggregated and subtracted from gross margin, it is found that each representative is making a contribution to profits. This poses a real dilemma for the company sales manager. On the one hand, the branch is not profitable, but on the other, each salesperson in the branch is contributing to profits. Admittedly, the sales representatives may not be making a large enough contribution. If there were a profit standard for each salesperson, this could be assessed. This demonstrates the difference between a performance analysis in which a standard of comparison is established beforehand and a straight cost and profitability analysis.

The company sales manager could compare the contributions to profit of the representatives in the St. Louis branch with those of other sales representatives by doing a similar analysis for other branches. If the St. Louis salespeople were found to be low, it might indicate that the payroll in the St. Louis branch was too high for the number of bicycles sold. The sales manager might then consider removing one or more representatives from the territory. Alternatively, he might consider increasing the number of calls or changing the salary/commission mixture in the salespeople's compensation package. Still other strategies would be to close the warehouse associated with the branch or to close the branch altogether.

The profit implications of each strategy would be different. They could be calculated, however, if the company maintains sales and cost records by small units. Conversely, when basic records are aggregated into larger totals and are stored that way in the company's accounting system, such isolate and explode analyses are precluded.

Profitability of Stan Tucker by Customer

Suppose the sales manager felt that for strategic reasons, he did not wish to close the branch or the warehouse. Rather, he wished to consider reassigning one representative in the branch to another office and territory. Since there are typically significant company costs and personal disruptions to the representative and his or her family in such a switch, the sales manager did not take these reassignments lightly. Suppose, therefore, that he wanted to ascertain the profitability of each account to the salesperson and the company.

Table 16–9 and Table 16–10 contain, respectively, the activity levels of Stan Tucker, the "worst"-performing representative, broken down by account and the resulting profit contribution of each account. The analysis illustrates the operation of the iceberg principle. Although Tucker overall makes a contribution to profit, one of his accounts is generating a loss. The loss can be traced to the number of bicycles ordered by Cooper. While Cooper orders every time Tucker calls, his average order size is very low. Less frequent calls might be the answer; this might produce the same net sales, but reduce Stan's travel expenses charged to Cooper. The analysis also reveals that, although Allen purchased the most bikes, Brown was the most profitable account Tucker had. Again these types of insights would be impossible to generate if Baitinger Bicycle Company did not use modularized marketing cost analyses.

The profitability analyses by marketing segment do not tell the sales manager of Baitinger Bicycle Company what he should do. They do, however, provide him with the basic information for making intelligent choices.

Table 16–9
Activities of Stan Tucker broken down by account

Customers of Stan Tucker	Number of Sales Calls	Number of Orders	Number of Units Purchased			
			A	B	C	Total
Allen	50	35	807	1,258	1,567	3,632
Brown	25	20	645	880	1,043	2,568
Cooper..........	25	25	162	378	869	1,409
Total	100	80	1,614	2,516	3,479	7,609

Table 16–10
Profitability analysis for Stan Tucker broken down by customer

	Total	Allen	Brown	Cooper
Sales				
A	$185,610	$ 92,805	$74,175	$18,630
B	226,440	113,220	79,200	34,020
C	208,740	94,020	62,580	52,140
Total sales	620,790	300,045	215,955	104,790
Cost of goods sold				
A	145,260	72,630	58,050	14,580
B	188,700	94,350	66,000	28,350
C	173,950	78,350	52,150	43,450
Total cost of goods sold	507,910	245,330	176,200	86,360
Gross margin	112,880	54,715	39,755	18,410
Expenses				
Direct selling				
Salary	24,000	12,000	6,000	6,000
Commissions	6,208	3,000	2,160	1,048
Travel	9,500	4,750	2,375	2,375
Advertising				
A	15,011	7,505	5,999	1,507
B	10,013	5,007	3,502	1,504
C	6,749	3,040	2,023	1,686
Warehousing and shipping	7,609	3,632	2,568	1,409
Order processing	160	70	40	50
Transportation	22,827	10,896	7,704	4,227
Total expenses	102,077	49,900	32,371	19,806
Contribution to profit (loss)	10,803	4,815	7,384	(1,396)

Prospects and Problems

The preceding example, while basic, reveals both the promise and some of the problems associated with marketing cost analysis. The real benefit is the opportunity it provides managers to isolate segments of the business that are most profitable as well as those that generate losses. This information allows those involved to improve their planning and control of the firm's activities. When combined with proper sales analysis techniques discussed in Chapter 15, it provides sales managers with a formidable analytical weapon for managing the personal selling function.

The example also illustrates the problems associated with the technique. It requires that data be available in the proper detail. Some data can be costly to generate and expensive to maintain. Furthermore, the technique requires a good deal of sophistication from the company's information system. The system must be able to select and aggregate only those inputs appropriate to the particular segment of the business being analyzed. As the example indicates, there is often a question as to which costs should be allocated and what bases should be used to allocate these costs. The most appropriate allocation bases can generate some spirited discussion among those involved. Allocations cannot be taken lightly because they ultimately affect the profitability of a segment; at the same time, however, there are usually no perfect answers as to how costs should be allocated. Thus, setting up a good marketing cost system can take a good deal of expensive executive time.

The benefits increasingly seem to be higher than the costs, if the literature on the subject is a reliable barometer. Not only has more been written on the subject of late, but the literature describes an increasing number of companies that have profited from implementing marketing cost analysis.[21]

Return on Assets Managed

Sales and cost analyses provide the sales manager with two important financial techniques for controlling the personal selling function. The first measures the results achieved and the second the cost of producing those results. The important financial ingredient that is left out of those analyses is the assets that need to be committed to produce those results. At a minimum, the company will be committing working capital in the form of accounts receivable and inventories to support the sales function. The return produced on the assets used in each segment of the business provides sales managers with a useful variation of more traditional cost analysis procedures for evaluating and controlling various elements of the personal selling function.

The formula for return on assets managed (ROAM) reflects both the contribution margin associated with a given level of sales and asset turnover.[22] More particularly, it is:

$$\text{ROAM} = \frac{\text{Contribution as a}}{\text{percentage of sales}} \times \frac{\text{Asset turnover}}{\text{rate}}$$

The formula indicates that the return to a segment of the business can be increased either by increasing the profit margin on sales or by maintaining the same profit margin and increasing the asset turnover rate. The formula can then be used to evaluate segments or to select the best alternative from a set of strategies under consideration.

---

[21] In addition to the references previously cited, see also: C. Davis Fogg and Josef W. Rokus, "A Quantitative Method for Structuring a Profitable Sales Force," *Journal of Marketing* 37 (July 1973), pp. 8–17; Leland L. Beik and Stephen L. Buzby, "Profitability Analysis by Market Segments," *Journal of Marketing* 37 (July 1973), pp. 48–53; Vishnu H. Kirpalani and Stanley S. Shapiro, "Financial Dimensions of Marketing Management," *Journal of Marketing* 37 (July 1973), pp. 40–47; B. M. Smackey, "A Profit Emphasis for Improving Sales Force Productivity," *Industrial Marketing Management* 6 (1977), pp. 135–40; and Jeffrey H. Wecker, "An Approach to Higher Profits with Reduced Selling Costs," *Industrial Marketing Management* 6 (1977) pp. 57–58

[22] J. S. Schiff and Michael Schiff, "New Sales Management Tool: ROAM," *Harvard Business Review* 45 (July-August 1967), pp. 59–66.

Consider, for example, the use of the concept to evaluate the performance of two sales branches. Table 16–11 contains the basic financial data. Note that Branch A sold more than Branch B and that the gross margin on these sales was higher, both in total and as a percentage of sales, because of the mix of products. Furthermore, the contribution of total company profits was higher for Branch A than for Branch B, and earnings as a percentage of sales were 10.0 percent in Branch A and only 6.3 percent in Branch B. By all these standards, Branch A performed better.

Table 16–11
Analysis of return on assets managed

	Branch A	Branch B
Sales	$2,500,000	$1,500,000
Cost of goods sold	2,000,000	1,275,000
Gross margin	500,000 (20%)	225,000 (15%)
Less variable branch expenses		
Salaries	155,000	80,000
Commissions	25,000	10,000
Office expenses	30,000	20,000
Travel and entertainment	40,000	20,000
	250,000	130,000
Branch contribution to profit	250,000	95,000
Branch investments		
Accounts receivable	500,000	150,000
Inventories	750,000	225,000
	1,250,000	375,000
Earnings as a percent of sales	10.0%	6.3%
Turnover	2.0	4.0
Branch percent return on assets managed	20.0%	25.2%

These criteria, however, ignore the assets that were needed to produce these results. When the investment in assets, which in the example consists of accounts receivable and inventories for each branch, is also taken into account, the picture changes. Branch B required a smaller commitment of the firm's capital. Consequently, Branch B was able to effect an asset turnover twice as large as Branch A with the result that the return on investment was higher in Branch B than in Branch A.

While the basic ROAM formula can be used to provide some useful management information, the managerial insights it affords can be magnified by breaking the basic formula down by its components. The first component—contribution as a percent of sales—equals the ratio of net contribution divided by sales. The second component—the asset turnover rate—equals sales divided by the assets needed to produce those sales. Each of these second level components could, in turn, be expanded. One could, for example, break down the sales component by product or salesperson and could similarly break down the assets to assess the impact of each product or salesperson on profitability. Alternatively, one might choose to explode into its detailed elements only one of the second level components of net contribution, sales, and assets. Exploding one or more of the components of the equation allows management to trace the impact of a number of "what if" scenarios.

Figure 16–3, for example, diagrams the return-on-assets model, with the asset component exploded. Each of the boxes applies to the segment of the business being analyzed. Previously, we saw, for example, that Branch B produced a higher ROAM than Branch A. With the exploded model, management can quickly explore what might be done to bring the returns into line. Table 16–11 indicates, for example, that the amount invested in receivables and inventories as a percentage of sales varies across the two branches and that, in particular:

Figure 16–3
Expended return on assets managed
(ROAM) model

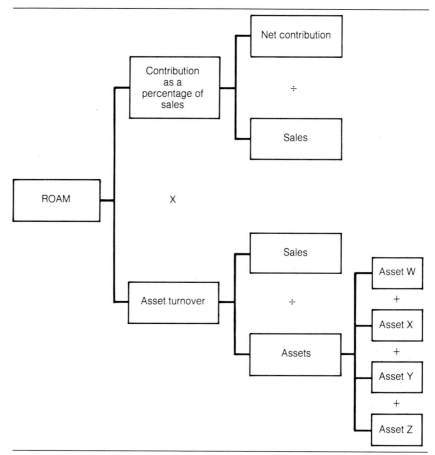

Figure 16–4
Impact of a reduction in accounts
receivable to $250,000 in Branch A

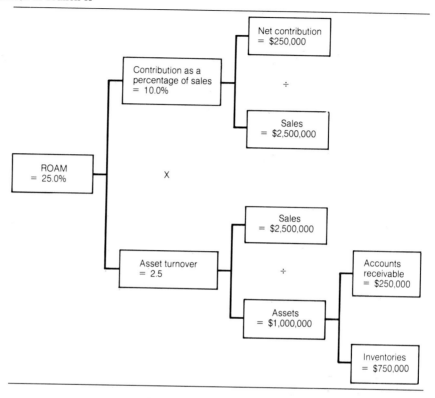

	Branch A		Branch B	
Receivables as a percentage of sales	$\dfrac{500,000}{2,500,000}$	$= 20\%$	$\dfrac{50,000}{1,500,000}$	$= 10\%$
Inventories as a percentage of sales	$\dfrac{750,000}{2,500,000}$	$= 30\%$	$\dfrac{225,000}{1,500,000}$	$= 15\%$

Management might logically ask the question: What would happen to ROAM in Branch A if receivables or inventories as a percentage of sales or both were reduced to the levels existing in Branch B? Figure 16–4 traces the implication of what a reduction in accounts receivables to 10 percent of sales or $250,000 in Branch A through better billing and follow-up procedures might do for its profitability. The example, which assumes no lost sales because of these billing efforts, demonstrates the returns could be brought directly in line with this one change. Management could just as easily assess the profit implications of, say, 5, 10, and 15 percent declines in sales to determine how sensitive the branch returns might be to a change in the billing procedures.

In sum, the assets managed has added another important dimension to the financial control picture. The investment required for a venture needs to be recognized because long-run profits can be maximized only if the optimal level of investment in each asset is achieved.[23] As Alfred P. Sloan, who was chief executive officer for 23 years at General Motors, comments in his book *My Years with General Motors,* "No other financial principle with which I am acquainted serves better than rate of return as an objective aid to business judgment."[24]

The point was made earlier that marketers have been slower to embrace cost analysis than sales analysis. The evidence indicates that they have been even slower to adopt ROAM. Table 16–12, for example, summarizes the results of a survey among 146 industrial manufacturers in SIC codes 20–39 regarding their use of sales, cost, and ROAM analysis in managing the marketing function in general, and the personal selling function in particular. While most of these firms engaged in sales analysis by customer, salesperson, or geographic area, only about one third of them engaged in some sort of profitability analysis by these segments, and only one tenth investigated the returns they realized on the assets devoted to these segments. Clearly, in spite of their compelling intuitive appeal, cost or profitability analysis and asset return analysis have a way to go before they match the popularity of sales analysis in managing the personal selling function.

Table 16–12
Popularity of sales, cost, and asset
return analysis by segment

Description	Segment			
	Product	Customer	Salesperson	Geographic Area
Sales analysis:				
Sales volume (units or dollars) 92		91	87	92
Sales volume (versus quota or objective) 54		48	75	70
Cost analysis:				
Expenses 40		18	53	38
Contribution to profit				
(sales less direct costs) 75		41	32	26
Net profit (sales less direct				
costs less allocated indirect costs) 57		24	19	12
Return on assets 29		10	10	7

Source: Developed from information provided in Donald W. Jackson, Jr., Lonnie L. Ostrom, and Kenneth R. Evans, "Measures Used to Evaluate Industrial Marketing Activities," *Industrial Marketing Management* 11 (1982), pp. 269–74.

---

[23] Rayburn, *Financial Tools for Effective Marketing Administration,* p. 91. This book also contains a useful discussion of the problems involved in using return on assets managed as an evaluation criterion in marketing. See particularly pages 90–92.

[24] Alfred P. Sloan, *My Years with General Motors* (Garden City, N.Y.: Doubleday, 1964), p. 140.

Summary

Marketing cost analysis attempts to isolate the costs incurred in producing various levels of sales to determine the profitability of sales by segment of the business. Marketing cost analysis can be used to advantage by sales managers to investigate the profitability of regions, branches, territories, customers, or various channels of distribution.

Most firms have been slower to embrace cost analysis than sales analysis for studying their marketing activities. Part of this lag can be explained by the fact that many costs associated with doing business are not entered in the firm's accounting system in their most useful form for decision making. Thus, it becomes necessary to rework these costs so that they are more useful.

A marketing cost analysis can be conducted using either a full-cost or a contribution margin approach. The full-cost approach entails allocating all the costs of doing business, even fixed costs, to one of the operating segments. The contribution margin approach charges only those costs that can be specifically traced to the operating segment to determine the profitability of the segment. The contribution margin approach is more logically defensible from a decision-making perspective, although there is controversy as to which is better.

There are four steps in conducting a marketing cost analysis. First, the purpose of the study must be specified. Second, the natural account costs must be spread to functional cost centers. Next, the functional costs must be allocated to appropriate operating segments using some reasonable bases. Here one looks for those factors that bear a cause-and-effect relationship with the cost, in the sense that, as the level of the factor is altered, the cost also changes. Finally, the allocated costs are summed so that the contribution of the segment can be determined.

Return on assets managed provides the sales manager with still another financial tool for controlling the personal selling function. Return on assets managed is the product of contribution to profit as a percentage of sales multiplied by asset turnover. Asset turnover, in turn, is found by dividing sales by the assets needed to produce those sales. The formula recognizes that the sales manager has only limited assets with which to work. He or she can maximize the profits produced by the personal selling function only if each asset is put to its highest and best use. Return on assets managed is currently less popular than either sales or cost analysis in managing the personal selling function.

Discussion Questions

1. What is the relationship between cost analysis and sales analysis? Which comes first?
2. The Boston territory sales manager was unhappy with the recent report

which revealed that, although the Boston territory exceeded its sales goals by 20 percent, its contribution to profits was below expectations. In analyzing territorial profitability, the Jamieson Corporation includes rent and utilities as part of each territory's overhead. The Boston sales manager contends that this is unfair: "Energy costs are higher here than in any other territory. Besides, the building is old and not insulated and, furthermore, where we are located in Boston is not my decision, its made by top management." Top management's response has been: "The location of the Boston office provides us with the most efficient location in terms of distribution costs. Our shipping costs would be too high if we relocated to one of the suburban areas where we could rent an energy efficient building." Whose view is right? What should be done?

3. Advertising has a synergistic effect. For example, in the Baitinger Bicycle Company case, the $60,000 advertising expenditure for product A had a positive impact on products B and C and on the company as well. Besides, dollars spent in one period have a carry-over effect to future periods. What recommendations would you make to handle these situations?

4. There is widespread agreement among sales managers as to how functional costs should be allocated to the various segments of a business. Do you agree?

5. "We have too many unprofitable products, unprofitable customers, and unprofitable sales representatives. If we are going to survive, now is the time to get rid of these problems." Do you agree with this statement?

6. What does ROAM tell us? Why not reduce the equation to dividing contribution to profit by assets employed? Why have marketers been slow to adopt ROAM?

7. The Rite-Way Corporation, a manufacturer of a line of writing instruments, has completed a ROAM analysis for all products. The deluxe model in their line of fountain pens sells for $145.50 but produces a ROAM of 8.3 percent, well below the 23.5 percent average for the other products. Management feels that rising raw material costs, such as gold and silver prices, are beyond Rite-Way's control. Should Rite-Way drop its deluxe product? Should Rite-Way eliminate commissions paid to sales representatives for deluxe sales?

8. The midwestern territory manager of the Knickerbocker Corporation disagrees with the allocation of advertising costs. The manager contends that it is the efforts of the sales force that produces sales, not advertising. In any case, according to the manager, "The advertising is wasted and stresses the wrong product features. My profitability suffers when you allocate advertising costs to my territory." What do you think should be done in this situation? What would you tell the midwestern manager?

9. The sales manager of Branch A (Table 16–11) was dismayed with the results. The 20 percent ROAM for the branch were below expectations. The sales manager's response was "OK, they want better results, then we'll in-

crease sales by at least 10 percent. But, we'll have to cut prices by 5 percent to do this." Will this benefit Branch A?

10. The accounting manager was adamant: "Those small accounts are unprofitable. I say that we stop selling to them and, instead, allocate our resources to the medium and larger accounts." "It's not that simple," exclaimed the sales manager. "Besides, most of our medium and large accounts were once small accounts." What recommendations would you make to solve this problem? Under what possible conditions should a company accept unprofitable business?

11. Accounts receivables are too high for Branch A, Table 16–11. One sales analyst recommends giving credit and collection responsibilities to the sales force. Sales reps would be provided with delinquency objectives aimed at reducing accounts receivables by 20 percent. Those meeting their objectives would earn an additional 1 percent of sales for commission. Will this work? Another analyst contends that, since the sales force has no training in credits and collections, accounts receivables should be excluded from ROAM calculations. Do you agree? What would happen to Branch A's ROAM if accounts receivable were excluded?

12. You are given the following information on two salespeople:

Salesperson	Number of Calls	Number of Orders	Units Sold	Total Sales	Total Cost of Sales
A	200	250	15,000	$750,000	$600,000
B	295	230	18,000	$900,000	$720,000

Salesperson A earns a $22,000 salary compared to $23,000 for salesperson B. Both earn 1 percent commission. Advertising costs $3 per unit. Shipping expenses are $2 per unit. Order processing costs total $1 per unit. Travel expenses amount to $.50 per call. Your task is to calculate the contribution to profit (loss) made by each salesperson.

13. Given the following profit and loss statement for the XYZ Company, allocate the natural accounts to the functional accounts:

XYZ COMPANY
Profit and Loss Statement
1984

Sales		$1,676,000
Cost of goods sold		1,003,000
Gross margin		$ 673,000

Selling and administrative expenses:
Salaries

Salespeople	120,000	
Sales manager	30,000	
Office personnel	38,000	
Warehouse personnel	30,000	
Commissions	16,760	

Advertising...............................	93,800
Postage	450
Supplies	
Office	200
Warehouse	500
Packaging................................	30,000
Transportation..........................	80,290
Travel expenses	40,000
Rent	
Sales	15,000
Warehouse	35,000
Order processing	10,000
Heat and electricity	
Sales	7,000
Warehouse	18,000
Order processing	5,000
Total selling and administrative expenses ...	570,000

Net profit (loss) $103,000

14. As the sales manager of the M.N.O. Company, you are trying to evaluate the performance of two districts. You have decided to look at how each district has managed its assets employed in the selling function. From the following information, determine each district's ROAM.

		District 1	District 2
Sales		$800,000	$500,000
Cost of goods sold		624,000	390,000
Gross margin.................		176,000	110,000
Variable district expenses			
Salaries	$49,600		$31,000
Commissions	8,000		5,000
Office expenses	9,600		6,000
Travel	12,800		8,000
Total expenses		80,000	50,000
Net profit (loss)		96,000	60,000
District investment in assets:			
Accounts receivable		120,000	45,000
Inventories.................		200,000	80,000
Earnings as a percent of sales .		.12	.12
Turnover....................		2.5	4.0

Chapter 17

Behavior and Other Performance Analyses

Sales and cost analysis are two very important techniques sales managers can use to assess the overall personal selling effort. They help to measure whether the selling effort is on target with respect to the goals established for this portion of the marketing mix and also provide strong clues of where and how it can be improved. Although these techniques also provide valuable input for salespeople's evaluation, an exclusive reliance on them can produce a distorted picture of what an individual sales representative accomplished. "A measure of unit sales (or even current contribution to profit) ignores the contributions of information that a salesperson may have brought back to the firm from the field, the goodwill that the salesperson has generated, efforts to develop new accounts which offer long-term profit potential, and the like."[1] Recognizing this, most firms supplement sales and cost analyses with other evaluations of how individual salespeople are doing.

This chapter reviews some other evaluation measures. Particularly, the chapter first highlights why they are necessary. It discusses some supplemental objective measures for evaluation and then some subjective or qualitative measures. The chapter concludes with a brief discussion of the corrective action that might be warranted if the evaluations isolate a problem.

Performance versus Effectiveness

Part 2 of this book was concerned with understanding the individual salesperson. The model used to structure that discussion suggested that a sales representative's performance was a function of five factors: the individual's (1) motivation, (2) skill level, (3) aptitude, (4) role perceptions, and (5) personal, organizational, and environmental variables that influence his performance. Figure 17–1 depicts a slightly modified form of that model. The main change is the distinction among behavior, performance, and effectiveness.[2] While motivation, aptitude, skill level, and role perceptions were previously pictured as being directly linked to performance, now they are directly linked to behavior. The modified form of the model is useful for understanding the role of sales and cost analyses in salespeople's evaluation as well as why other measures for evaluating representatives are necessary.

Behavior refers to what representatives do—that is, the tasks they expend effort on while working. These tasks might include calling on customers, writing orders, preparing sales presentations, developing formal equipment proposals, and the like. *Performance* is behavior evaluated in terms of its contributions to the

---

[1] Douglas N. Behrman and William D. Perreault, Jr., "Measuring the Performance of Industrial Salespersons," unpublished manuscript, p. 4.

[2] This section borrows heavily from the paper by Orville C. Walker, Jr., Gilbert A. Churchill, Jr., and Neil M. Ford, "Where Do We Go From Here? Selected Conceptual and Empirical Issues Concerning the Motivation and Performance of the Industrial Salesforce," in *Critical Issues in Sales Management: State-of-the Art and Future Research Needs*, ed. Gerald Albaum and Gilbert A. Churchill, Jr. (Eugene: College of Business Administration, University of Oregon, 1979), pp. 10–75.

Figure 17–1
Sales behavior, performance, and
effectiveness

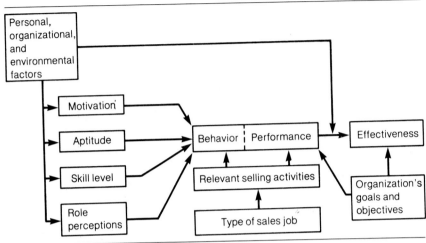

Source: Orville C. Walker, Jr., Gilbert A. Churchill, Jr., and Neil M. Ford, "Where Do We Go From Here? Selected Conceptual and Empirical Issues Concerning the Motivation and Performance of the Industrial Salesforce,"
in *Critical Issues in Sales Management: State-of-the-Art and Future Research Needs*, ed. Gerald Albaum and
Gilbert A. Churchill, Jr., (Eugene: College of Business Administration, University of Oregon, 1979), p. 36.

goals of the organization. Performance, in other words, has a normative element
reflecting whether a salesperson's behavior is "good" or "bad" in light of the organization's goals and objectives. Note that behavior and performance are both influenced by the sales activities that are relevant to the job at hand. These in turn
depend on the types of sales jobs in question.

There is also a distinction in Figure 17–1 between performance and effectiveness. By definition, *effectiveness* refers to some summary index of organizational
outcomes for which an individual is at least partly responsible, such as sales
volume, market share, or profitability of sales.[3] The crucial distinction between
performance and effectiveness is that the latter does not refer to behavior directly;
rather it is a function of additional factors not under the individual salesperson's
control. These include top management policies, the sales potential of a territory,
and the actions of competitors.

In terms of Figure 17–1, sales and cost analyses produce effectiveness measures; that is, the results are partially determined by the performance of the sales
representatives. However, differences between two salespersons' "performances"
are not solely determined in this way. Rather there may be differences in the
potential in their territories, or in the physical makeup of the territories and consequently in what it takes to service them. There may be differences in the level
of company support by territory or the competitive conditions within each. When

---

[3] John P. Campbell et al., *Managerial Behavior, Performance, and Effectiveness* (New York: McGraw-Hill, 1970).

such differences exist, is it reasonable to say that one salesperson did better than another because his or her sales, market share, or contribution to profit was higher?

It is generally agreed that salesmen should be judged solely on those phases of sales performance over which they exercise control, and should not be held responsible for results beyond their control. If a company's method of measuring salesmen's performance is to result in valid comparisons, serious consideration must be given to such factors in developing yardsticks for objective or subjective evaluation.[4]

One could argue that a careful specification of performance standards by territory should eliminate inequities across territories. For example, percentage of quota attained should be an acceptable measure of performance because quotas supposedly take into account variations in environmental factors across territories. Admittedly, a comparison of salespeople with respect to percentage of quota attained is a better measure of their performance than is a comparison that simply looks at each representative's level of absolute sales or market share, *assuming* the quotas were done well. This is a big *if* however; sometimes they are not. In some instances, they are arbitrary and are not necessarily based on an objective assessment of all the factors that facilitate or constrain a salesperson's ability to make a sale.

Even when quotas are done well, the measure "percentage of quota attained" still omits much with respect to a salesperson's performance. For one thing, it ignores the profitability of sales. Sales representatives can be compared with respect to profitability, or the return they produce on the assets under their control, as shown in Chapter 16. Nevertheless, determining the appropriate standards of profitability for each territory is even more difficult than establishing quotas that accurately take into account the many factors that affect the level of sales a representative should be able to produce in a territory.

Even if good standards could be developed, the problem of salespeople's evaluation would not be solved because neither measure incorporates activities that may have no short-term payout but still have substantial consequences to the firm. These include the time devoted to developing a potential large account, to building long-term territorial goodwill for the company, or to developing detailed understanding of the capabilities of the firm's products. That is why many firms supplement sales and cost analyses with other measures that more directly reflect each sales representative's performance.

The other measures firms use to evaluate salespeople fall into two broad categories, (1) objective measures and (2) subjective measures. The objective measures reflect other statistics the manager can gather from the firm's internal data. The subjective measures rely on personal evaluations by someone in the organization, typically the salesperson's immediate supervisor, of how individual salespeople are doing.

---

[4] *Measuring Salesmen's Performance,* Business Policy Study, No. 114 (New York: National Industrial Conference Board, 1965), p. 8.

Objective Measures

The objective measures that firms use to supplement traditional sales and cost analyses fall into the three subcategories of (1) output measures, (2) input measures, and (3) ratios of output and/or input measures. Table 17–1 summarizes some of the more common output and input measures and Table 17–2 displays some of the more commonly used ratios.

Table 17–1
Common output and input factors used to evaluate salespeople

I. Output factors
   A. Orders
      1. Number of orders
      2. Average size of orders
      3. Number of cancelled orders
   B. Accounts
      1. Number of active accounts
      2. Number of new accounts
      3. Number of lost accounts
      4. Number of overdue accounts
      5. Number of prospective accounts

II. Input factors
   A. Calls
      1. Number of calls
      2. Number of planned calls
      3. Number of unplanned calls
   B. Time and time utilization
      1. Days worked
      2. Calls per day (call rate)
      3. Selling time versus nonselling time
   C. Expenses
      1. Total
      2. By type
      3. As a percentage of sales
      4. As a percentage of quota
   D. Nonselling activities
      1. Letters written to prospects
      2. Telephone calls made to prospects
      3. Number of formal proposals developed
      4. Advertising displays set up
      5. Number of meetings held with distributors/dealers
      6. Number of training sessions for distributor/dealer personnel
      7. Number of calls on distributor/dealer customers
      8. Number of service calls made
      9. Number of customer complaints received
      10. Number of overdue accounts collected

Table 17–2
Common ratios used to evaluate salespeople

I. **Expense ratios**

A. Sales expense ratio $= \dfrac{\text{Expenses}}{\text{Sales}}$

B. Cost per call ratio $= \dfrac{\text{Total costs}}{\text{Number of calls}}$

II. **Account development and servicing ratios**

A. Account penetration ratio $= \dfrac{\text{Accounts sold}}{\text{Total accounts available}}$

B. New account conversion ratio $= \dfrac{\text{Number of new accounts}}{\text{Total number of accounts}}$

C. Lost account ratio $= \dfrac{\text{Prior accounts not sold}}{\text{Total number of accounts}}$

D. Sales per account ratio $= \dfrac{\text{Sales dollar volume}}{\text{Total number of accounts}}$

E. Average order size ratio $= \dfrac{\text{Sales dollar volume}}{\text{Total number of orders}}$

F. Order cancellation ratio $= \dfrac{\text{Number of cancelled orders}}{\text{Total number of orders}}$

III. **Call activity and/or productivity**

A. Calls per day ratio $= \dfrac{\text{Number of calls}}{\text{Number of days worked}}$

B. Calls per account ratio $= \dfrac{\text{Number of calls}}{\text{Number of accounts}}$

C. Planned call ratio $= \dfrac{\text{Number of planned calls}}{\text{Total number of calls}}$

D. Orders per call (hit) ratio $= \dfrac{\text{Number of orders}}{\text{Total number of calls}}$

Output Measures

Certainly, the most used output measures for evaluating salespeople are sales statistics. More than eight of 10 firms evaluate salespeople with respect to their absolute level of sales and three of four assess how closely salespeople come to the quota assigned them.[5] At the same time a number of firms look beyond dollar or unit sales data and focus instead on order and account data.

Orders. The number of orders each salesperson secures is often used to assess the representative's ability to make sales presentations since it reflects the individual's ability to "close." Not only must the timing with respect to the close

---

[5] Donald W. Jackson, Jr., Lonnie L. Ostrom, and Kenneth R. Evans, "Measures Used to Evaluate Industrial Marketing Activities," *Industrial Marketing Management* 11 (1982), pp. 269–74.

be right, but the salesperson must have done an adequate job of moving the buyer through the prior stages of the buying process via the sales presentation if the close is going to be successful.[6]

While the number of orders a salesperson secures is important, the average size of those orders is equally so. A great many orders may mean the orders are small and may indicate that the salesperson is spending too much time calling on small type C accounts, and not enough time calling on large type A accounts.

Still another measure of a salesperson's presentation effectiveness is the number of canceled orders. A salesperson who loses a large proportion of his total orders to subsequent cancellation may be using excessive high pressure tactics in his sales presentations.

Accounts. The various account measures provide a perspective on the equity of territorial assignments and also on how the salesperson is handling the territory. One popular measure focuses on the number of active accounts in the salesperson's customer portfolio. Various definitions of active accounts are used. It may be any customer who has placed an order in the past six months or in the past year. A salesperson's performance in one year may be compared to performance in past years by contrasting the number of active accounts. Hopefully, this number will be increasing rather than declining or remaining stable. Closely related to this yardstick is a measure that tracks the number of new accounts a salesperson develops in a given time. Some companies even establish new prospect quotas by salespeople that allow a ready comparison of performance to standard.

While not as popular as the number of new accounts, the number of lost accounts can be a revealing statistic, since it indicates how successfully the salesperson is satisfying the ongoing needs of the established accounts in the territory. Still other accounts measures by which salespeople can be compared are (1) the number of overdue accounts which might indicate the salesperson is not following company procedures in screening accounts for their creditworthiness, and (2) the number of prospective accounts which assesses the salesperson's abilities in identifying potential target customers.

Input Measures

Many objective measures of performance evaluation that companies use to supplement sales and cost analyses focus on the efforts sales representatives expend rather than the results of those efforts. There are at least two good reasons for this. First, efforts or desirable behaviors are much more controllable than results. If a representative's sales fall short of quota, the problem may lie with the person, the quota, or perhaps a change in the environment. If the number of calls

[6] For a discussion of the steps in the selling process, see Carlton A. Pederson, Milburn D. Wright, and Barton D. Weitz, *Selling: Principles and Methods*, 8th ed. (Homewood, Ill.: Richard D. Irwin, 1984) or Charles Futrell, *Fundamentals of Selling* (Homewood, Ill.: Richard D. Irwin, 1984).

a salesperson makes falls short of the target, however, the problem lies much more directly with the individual.[7] Second, in many selling situations, there is a time lag between inputs and outputs. A particularly large sale may be the result of several years of efforts.

> At the age of 29, Kim Kelley is already something of a legend around Honeywell, Inc. "He's the one who cried when he made his sale, isn't he?" a fellow Honeywell salesman asks with a chuckle.
>
> Indeed, he is. Kim stood there in his customer's office last June and bawled like a baby. And for good reason. Kim had just shaken hands on an $8.1 million computer sale to the state of Illinois. He had gambled his whole career on making that sale. He had spent three years laying the groundwork for it, and for three solid months he had been working six days a week, often 14 hours a day, competing against salesmen from four other computer companies.
>
> It was a make-or-break situation for Kim Kelley, and, standing there with tears of joy and relief streaming down his cheeks, he knew he had it made. A bright future with Honeywell was assured, and he had made an $80,000 commission—more money than he had earned in all four of his previous years with the company. . . .
>
> For three years, he patiently made daily rounds of key state offices, pausing a few minutes in each one to drop off technical documents or just to chat.[8]

In such situations, it seems more reasonable to conclude that performance was good during all three years, rather than that it was bad in all years except the one in which the order was finally placed.

Calls. The number of current customer and/or prospect calls is often used to decide whether a salesperson is covering his or her territory in accord with the company's plan. As discussed previously, the number of calls on each of the various classes of accounts is an important factor in the design of territories. Thus, it stands to reason that such information should also be used to evaluate the salesperson assigned to the territory. The number of calls typically can be determined from a salesperson's call reports.

Many companies further distinguish between the number of planned and unplanned calls. They would like salespeople to make a lot of calls and also prefer that these are planned. Unplanned calls typically reflect some emergency or breakdown in customer service. While these will always occur, they create inefficiencies in covering the territory; it is a mark of good territory management when they are low relative to the number of planned calls.

Time and Time Utilization. The number of days worked and the calls per day or call rate are routinely used by many companies to assess salespeople's efforts since the product of the two quantities provides a direct measure of the extent of customer contact. If the amount of customer contact by a particular salesperson is low, one can look separately at the components to see where the

---

[7] The distinction between outcomes and desirable behaviors is an important one. Most performance appraisal systems emphasize the former rather than the latter—a condition one of the leading writers in personnel has labeled the "Achilles heel of our profession." See Herbert Heneman III, "Research Roundup," *The Personnel Administrator*, June 1975, p. 91.

[8] "To Computer Salesmen, the 'Big-Ticket' Deal Is the One to Look for," *The Wall Street Journal*, January 22, 1974, p. 1+.

problem lies. Perhaps the salesperson has not been working enough because of sickness, extenuating circumstances, or just plain laziness, a situation that would show up in the number of days worked. Alternatively, perhaps the salesperson's total time input was satisfactory, but the salesperson was not using that time wisely and, consequently, had a low call rate.

A useful perspective about the efficiency with which salespeople are covering their territories can be gained by comparing their division of time between sales calls, traveling, and office work. For the most part the firm would want salespeople to maximize the time in face-to-face customer contact at the expense of the other two factors. The company would want representatives, particularly to minimize unproductive travel time. The problem with such analyses is that they require detailed input on how each person is, in fact, spending his or her time. Conducting such a time and duty analysis can be expensive. There are companies, however, who routinely conduct such analyses because the benefits are deemed to outweigh the costs.[9]

Expenses. The objective inputs discussed so far for evaluating salespeople focus mainly on the extent of the salespeople's effort. Another key emphasis when evaluating them is the cost of those efforts. Thus many firms will keep records detailing the total expenses incurred by each salesperson. Some will break these expenses down by type, such as automobile expenses, lodging expenses, entertainment expenses, and so on. They might look at these expenses in total and/or as a percentage of sales or quotas by salesperson.

Nonselling Activities. In addition to assessing the direct contact of salespeople with customers, some firms monitor indirect contact. They use indexes such as the number of letters written, the number of telephone calls made, and the number of formal proposals developed.

In many industries, the sales representative has duties servicing accounts that go beyond what might be considered a normal selling emphasis. In such instances, firms often try to monitor the extent of these duties, using such indexes as the number of promotion or advertising displays set up, the number of dealer meetings and the number of training sessions for distributor personnel that were held, the number of calls the salesperson made on dealer customers, the number of service calls made, the number of customer complaints received, and the number of overdue accounts collected. Some of this information can be gathered from sales-call reports. The rest of it, such as the number of customer complaints, requires a systematic monitoring of other correspondence coming into the firm.

There are also other ways to secure feedback. Consider, for example, the lengths to which one company went to assess sales-force feedback. The company had always emphasized to its sales force the importance of feedback and prided itself on the amount it secured. Nevertheless, to quantify the amount of information it actually did get, the firm decided to conduct an experiment. Two other firms agreed to supply new products that were strategically placed with custom-

---

[9] Robert F. Vizza and Thomas E. Chambers, *Time and Territorial Management for Salesmen* (New York: The Sales Executive's Club, 1971).

ers who would mention to the firm's salespeople that these were superior competitive products. The salespeople's feedback about the new competitive products was then carefully monitored. You can appreciate the firm's dismay when it found that this information was transmitted back to management less than 20 percent of the time.[10]

Ratios

The focus on outputs other than sales volume itself can be revealing of how salespeople are performing. So can an analysis of their efforts. Additional insights can also be gathered by combining the various outputs and/or inputs in selected ways, typically in the form of ratios. Table 17–2, for example, lists some of the ratios that are commonly used to evaluate salespeople.

Expense Ratios.   The sales-expense ratio possesses the attractive feature of combining both salespeople's inputs and the results produced by those inputs in a single number. Salespeople can affect this ratio either by making sales or by controlling expenses. The ratio can also be used to analyze salesperson expenses by type. Thus, a sales/transportation-expense ratio that is much higher for one salesperson than others might indicate that the salesperson is covering his or her territory inefficiently. One does need to recognize territorial differences when comparing these ratios, though; the salesperson who has the out-of-line ratio may simply have a larger, more geographically dispersed sales territory to cover.

The cost-per-call ratio expresses the costs of supporting each salesperson in the field as a function of the number of calls the salesperson makes. The ratio can be evaluated using total costs or the costs can be broken down by elements and ratios such as expenses per call and travel costs per call can be computed. Not only are these ratios useful for comparing salespeople from the same firm but they can also be compared to those of other companies in the same industry to assess how efficient the firm's personal selling effort is since industry average figures are readily available.

Account Development and Servicing Ratios.   There are a number of ratios having to do with accounts and orders that reflect on how well salespeople are capturing the potential business that exists in their territories. The account penetration ratio, for example, measures the percentage of accounts in the territory from which the salesperson secures orders. It provides a direct measure of whether the salesperson is simply skimming the cream of the business or is working the territory systematically and hard. The new account-conversion ratio similarly measures the salesperson's ability to convert prospects to customers. The lost account ratio measures how well the salesperson is able to keep prior accounts as active customers and reflects on how well the representative is serving the established accounts in the territory.

---

[10] Dan H. Robertson, "Sales Force Feedback on Competitive Activities," *Journal of Marketing* 38 (April 1974), pp. 69–72.

The sales-per-account ratio provides an indication of the salesperson's success per account on average. A low ratio could indicate the salesperson is spending too much time calling on small, nonprofitable accounts and not enough time calling on larger ones. One could also look at the sales per account ratios by class of account, which can reveal the strengths and weaknesses of each salesperson. A salesperson who has a low sales per account ratio for class A accounts might need help in learning how to sell when there are multiple buying influences, for example. The average order size can also reveal the salesperson's call patterns. A very low average size might suggest the calls are too frequent and the salesperson's productivity could be improved by spacing them more. The order-cancellation ratio reflects on the salesperson's method of selling; a very high ratio could mean the salesperson is using high pressure tactics to secure orders, rather than satisfactorily handling customer concerns.

Call Activity and/or Productivity Ratios. The call-activity ratios measure the effort and planning salespeople put into their customer call activities and the successes they derive from it. The measures might be used to compare salesperson activities in total—such as when using calls per day or when using calls per total number of accounts, or by type of account. The planned call ratio could in turn be used to assess if the salesperson is systematically planning the coverage of his or her territory or whether the representative is working the territory without much of an overall game plan. The orders-per-call ratio bears directly on the question of whether the salesperson's calls on average are productive. This ratio is sometimes called the hit ratio or batting average, since it captures the number of successes (hits or orders) in relation to the number of at-bats (calls).

Caution Is in Order

As Tables 17–1, 17–2, and the above discussion indicate, there are many objective outputs, inputs, and ratios by which salespeople can be compared. As you probably sense, many of the measures are somewhat redundant, in that they provide overlapping information on salespeople's behavior and successes. As you also probably sense, a number of other ratios could be developed by combining the various outputs, inputs, or ratios in various ways. One combination that is often used to evaluate salespeople, for example, is the equation:

$$\text{Sales} = \text{Days worked} \times \frac{\text{Calls}}{\text{Days Worked}} \times \frac{\text{Orders}}{\text{Calls}} \times \frac{\text{Sales}}{\text{Orders}}$$

or

$$\text{Sales} = \text{Days worked} \times \text{Call rate} \times \text{Batting average} \times \text{Average order size}$$

The equation highlights nicely what the salesperson can do to increase his or her sales. The representative has the option of (1) increasing the number of days he or she works, (2) the calls he or she makes per day, (3) his or her success in securing an order on a given call, and (4) the size of those orders. Thus, the equation can be used to isolate how an individual salesperson's performance could be improved. Such an equation, though, focuses on the results of the salesperson's efforts and ignores the cost of these efforts. Similarly, many of the other measures that have been reviewed and which could be combined via similar equations would probably ignore one or more elements of salesperson success.

There are two essential points to this discussion. First, just as sales and cost analyses have advantages and disadvantages, so do all of these other objective measures of performance. Rather than relying on only one or two of the measures to assess performance, the methods are most productively used in combination. Second, and more important, all of the indices are an aid to judgment, not a substitute for it. The comparisons which the indices allow *should be the beginning, not the conclusion,* of any analysis aimed at assessing how well individual salespeople are doing.

Subjective Measures

One author has distinguished between the objective measures of effort and performance discussed in the preceding section and the subjective measures discussed here. "Quantitative measures of effort relate to the salesperson's notions, whereas qualitative measures reflect how well he carries out those notions."[11] This subtle difference in what is being measured creates some marked differences in the way the measurements are effected.

In many ways, it is more difficult to assess the quality than the quantity of a salesperson's efforts. The quantity measures do indeed create some problems. They can require a detailed analysis of salespeople's call reports, an extensive time and duty analysis, or even perhaps some experimentation. Once the process is set up, though, it can be conducted with little bias and inconsistency in application. Not so with quality assessments. Even with a well-designed process that is firmly in place, there is substantial room for bias. Such schemes must invariably rely on the personal judgment of the individual or individuals charged with evaluation. Typically, these judgments are secured by having the appraiser rate the salesperson on each of a number of attributes using some kind of rating scale.

The attributes most commonly evaluated using merit rating forms are:

1. Sales results—volume performance, sales to new accounts, selling the full product line.
2. Job knowledge—knowledge of company policies, prices, products.
3. Management of territory—planning of activities and calls, controlling expenses, handling reports and records.

---

[11] Thomas R. Wotruba, *Sales Management: Planning, Accomplishment, and Evaluation* (New York: Holt, Rinehart & Winston, 1971) p. 525.

Figure 17–2
Sales Personnel Inventory, used by the Testor Corporation

SALES PERSONNEL INVENTORY

Employee's Name _____

Position Title _____

Territory _____

Date _____

INSTRUCTIONS

Read Carefully

1. Base your judgment on the previous six month period and not upon isolated incidents alone.
2. Place a check in the block which most nearly expresses your judgment on each factor.
3. For those employees who are rated at either extreme of the scale on any factor, for example, outstanding, deficient, limited, etc., please enter a brief explanation for the rating in the appropriate space below the factor.
4. Make your rating an accurate description of the man rated.

FACTORS TO BE CONSIDERED AND RATED:

1. KNOWLEDGE OF WORK (Includes knowledge of product, knowledge of customer's business)

☐ Does not have sufficient knowledge of products and application to represent Company effectively.

☐ Has mastered minimum knowledge. Needs further training.

☐ Has average amount of knowledge needed to handle job satisfactorily.

☐ Is above average in knowledge needed to handle job satisfactorily.

☐ Is thoroughly acquainted with our products and technical problems involved in this application.

Comments _____

2. DEGREE OF ACCEPTANCE BY CUSTOMERS

☐ Not acceptable to most customers. Cannot gain entry to their offices.

☐ Manages to see customers but not generally liked.

☐ Has satisfactory relationship with most customers.

☐ Is on very good terms and is accepted by virtually all customers.

☐ Enjoys excellent personal relationship with virtually all customers.

Comments _____

3. AMOUNT OF EFFORT DEVOTED TO ACQUIRING BUSINESS

☐ Exceptional in the amount of time and effort put forth in selling.

☐ Devotes constant effort in developing business.

☐ Devotes intermittent effort in acquiring moderate amount of business.

☐ Exerts only minimum amount of time and effort.

☐ Unsatisfactory. Does not put forth sufficient effort to produce business.

Comments _____

4. ABILITY TO ACQUIRE BUSINESS

☐ Is able to acquire business under the most difficult situations.

☐ Does a good job under most circumstances.

☐ Manages to acquire good percentage of customer's business if initial resistance is not too strong.

☐ Able to acquire enough business to maintain only a minimum sales average.

☐ Rarely able to acquire business except in a seller's market.

Comments _____

5. AMOUNT OF SERVICE GIVEN TO CUSTOMERS:

☐ Rarely services his accounts once a sale is made.

☐ Gives only minimum service at all times.

☐ Services accounts with regularity but does not do any more than he is called upon to do.

☐ Gives very good service to all customers.

☐ Goes out of his way to give outstanding service within scope of Company policy.

Comments _____

Figure 17–2 (continued)

6. DEPENDABILITY AMOUNT OF SUPERVISION NEEDED				
☐ Always thoroughly abreast of problems in his territory, even under most difficult circumstances. Rises to emergencies and assumes leadership without being requested to do so.	☐ Consistently reliable under normal conditions. Does special as well as regular assignments promptly. Little or no supervision required.	☐ Performs with reasonable promptness under normal supervision.	☐ Effort occasionally lags. Requires more than normal supervision.	☐ Requires close supervision in all phases of job.

Comments _____

7. ATTITUDE TOWARD COMPANY—SUPPORT GIVEN TO COMPANY POLICIES				
☐ Does not support Company policy—blames Company for factors which affect his customers unfavorably.	☐ Gives only passive support to Company policy—does not act as member of a team.	☐ Goes along with Company policies on most occasions.	☐ Adopts and supports Company viewpoint in all transactions.	☐ Gives unwavering support to Company and Company policies to customers even though he personally may not agree with them.

Comments _____

8. JUDGMENT				
☐ Analyses and conclusions subject to frequent error and are often based on bias. Decisions require careful review by supervisor.	☐ Judgments usually sound on routine, simple matters but cannot be relied upon when any degree of complexity is involved.	☐ Capable of careful analyzing day-to-day problems involving some complexity and rendering sound decisions. Decisions rarely influenced by prejudice or personal bias.	☐ Decisions can be accepted without question except when problems of extreme complexity are involved. Little or no personal bias enters into judgment.	☐ Possesses unusual comprehension and analytical ability. Complete reliance may be placed on all judgments irrespective of degree of complexity. Decisions and judgments are completely free of personal bias or prejudice.

Comments _____

9. RESOURCEFULNESS

☐ Work is consistently characterized by marked originality, alertness, initiative and imagination. Can be relied on to develop new ideas and techniques in solving the most difficult problems.

☐ Frequently develops new ideas of merit. Handling of emergencies is generally characterized by sound decisive action.

☐ Meets new situations in satisfactory manner. Occasionally develops original ideas, methods, and techniques.

☐ Follows closely previously learned methods, and procedures. Slow to adapt to changes. Tends to become confused in new situations.

☐ Requires frequent reinstruction. Has failed to demonstrate initiative or imagination in solving problems.

Comments _____

TO BE MORE EFFECTIVE ON PRESENT JOB, THIS MAN SHOULD:

1. Be given additional instruction on _____

2. Be given additional experience such as _____

3. Study such subjects as _____

4. Change his attitude as follows: _____

5. There is nothing more that I can do for him because _____

6. Remarks _____

Figure 17–2 (concluded)

Date Hired	Base Salary When Hired	Present Base Salary	Date of Last Increase	Amount	Hired by	Trained by

SALES RECORD

% Objective _____ %

	Last Year Total Sales	This Year To Date
Total Sales		
Pla Spray		
Pla		
Adhesives		
Gliders		
Oil Paint Kits		

EARNINGS RECORD

	Last Year Total Earnings	Last Year To Date	This Year To Date
Salary			
Bonus			
Total			
Expenses			
Total			
% Sales			

This review was / was not discussed with employee on _____

His reactions were _____

Salary change recommendation: _____

Signature _____ Date _____

Approved _____ Date _____ Sales Mgr.

Approved _____ Date _____ V. P. Sales

Approved _____ Date _____ President

4. Customer and company relations—standing with customers, associates, and company.
5. Personal characteristics—initiative, personal appearance, personality, resourcefulness, and so on.[12]

The particular emphasis given to each varies by company.

Figure 17–2 shows the rating scale used by the Testor Corporation. This sales personnel inventory is completed for every Testor salesperson every six months. These evaluations supplement the computer-generated reports of sales of each product to each customer to provide an overall evaluation of a salesperson's performance. The Testor inventory form is better than many of those in use because it contains anchors or verbal descriptors for the various points on the scale. Furthermore, it provides room for verbal comments, which enhance understanding of the ratings supplied. The form contains a section where needed improvements and corrective action can be detailed. All in all, the form should help a salesperson understand his or her weaknesses and improve performance.

The worst type of merit rating forms simply list the attributes of interest along one side of the form and the evaluation adjectives along the other. Figure 17–3, which is a recast version of the Testor inventory, illustrates such a form. The form can be completed very easily; the evaluator simply checks the adjective that most clearly describes the salesperson's performance on that attribute. While such forms are common, they work very poorly in practice.

Figure 17–3
Modified version of Testor Personnel Inventory

	Poor	Fair	Satisfactory	Good	Outstanding
Knowledge of work	☐	☐	☐	☐	☐
Degree of acceptance by customers	☐	☐	☐	☐	☐
Amount of effort devoted to acquiring business	☐	☐	☐	☐	☐
Ability to acquire business	☐	☐	☐	☐	☐
Amount of service given to customers	☐	☐	☐	☐	☐
Dependability—amount of supervision needed	☐	☐	☐	☐	☐
Attitude toward company—support given to company policies	☐	☐	☐	☐	☐
Judgment	☐	☐	☐	☐	☐
Resourcefulness	☐	☐	☐	☐	☐

[12] *Measuring Salesmen's Performance*, p. 33. For examples of forms used by organizations for sales control purposes, see this NICB publication.

Problems in Use

Some common problems with performance appraisal systems that rely on merit rating forms, particularly those using the simple checklist type, include the following.[13]

1. Lack of an outcome focus. The most useful type of performance appraisal highlights areas of improvement and the actions that must be taken to effect such improvements. For this to occur, the key behaviors in accomplishing the tasks assigned must be identified. Unfortunately, many companies have not taken this step. Rather, they have simply identified attributes thought to be related to performance, but they have not attempted to assess systematically whether the attributes are key. A recent emphasis in performance appraisal called BARS ("behavioral anchored rating scale") overcomes this weakness. More particularly, a BARS system attempts to identify behaviors that are more or less effective with respect to the goals established for the person. It then secures superior ratings on these behaviors.

2. Ill-defined personality traits. Many merit rating forms contain personality factors as attributes. In the case of salespeople, these attributes might include such things as initiative, personal appearance, and resourcefulness. Although these attributes are intuitively appealing, their actual relationship to performance is open to question.[14]

3. Halo effect. A halo effect is a common phenomenon in the use of any rating form. It refers to the fact that the rating assigned to one characteristic significantly influences the ratings assigned to all others. In one experiment that investigated the phenomenon among sales managers, it was found that their overall evaluations could be predicted quite well from their rating of the salesperson on the single performance dimension they felt to be the most important.[15] When one considers that different branch or regional managers might have different feelings about what is most important, the problem is compounded.

4. Leniency or harshness. Some sales managers rate at the extremes. Some are very lenient and rate every salesperson as good or outstanding on every attribute, whereas others do just the opposite. This behavior is often a function of their own personalities and their perceptions of what is outstanding performance. There may be no fundamental differences in the way the salespeople under them

---

[13] The list of weaknesses is taken from A. Benton Cocanougher and John M. Ivancevich, "'BARS' Performance Rating for Sales Force Personnel," *Journal of Marketing* 42 (July 1978), pp. 87–95. See also Campbell et al., *Managerial Behavior*, pp. 119–23.

[14] A number of studies have attempted to assess the relationship between personality factors and salespeople's performance. The results have generally been disappointing. For a summary of the results of these studies, see Gilbert A. Churchill, Jr., Neil M. Ford, Stephen W. Hartley, and Orville C. Walker, Jr., "The Determinants of Salesperson Performances: A Meta Analysis," unpublished manuscript, 1984. For an example, see Lawrence M. Lamont and William J. Lundstrom, "Identifying Successful Industrial Salesmen by Personality and Personal Characteristics," *Journal of Marketing Research* 14 (November 1977), pp. 517–29.

[15] William D. Perreault, Jr., and Frederick A. Russell, "Comparing Multiattribute Evaluation Process Models," *Behavioral Science* 22 (November 1977), pp. 423–31.

are performing. The use of different definitions of performance can seriously undermine the whole performance appraisal system.

5. Central tendency. Some managers err in the opposite direction in that they never, or very rarely, rate people at the ends of the scale. Rather, they use middle-of-the-road or play-it-safe ratings. One learns very little from such ratings about differences in performance.

6. Interpersonal bias. Interpersonal bias refers to the fact that our perceptions of others and the social acceptability of their behaviors are influenced by how much we like or dislike them personally. Many sales managers' evaluations of the performance of the sales representatives working under them are similarly affected. Furthermore, research evidence suggests that a salesperson can use personal influence strategies on the manager to bias his evaluations upward.

7. Organizational uses influence. Performance ratings are often affected by the use to which they will be put. "If promotions and monetary payments hinge on the ratings, there is often a tendency for leniency on the part of the manager who values the friendship and support of subordinates who press for higher ratings. It is not difficult to imagine the dilemma of a district sales manager if other district sales teams received consistently higher compensation increments and more promotions than his or her sales group. On the other hand, when appraisals are used for the development of subordinates, managers tend to more freely pinpoint weaknesses, and focus on what is wrong and how it can be improved."[16]

To guard against the distortions introduced in the performance appraisal system by such occurrences, many firms issue admonitions to those completing the forms. Some common instructions issued with such forms are:

1. Read the definitions of each trait thoroughly or carefully before rating.
2. Guard against the common tendency to overrate.
3. Do not let personal like or dislike influence your rating. Be as objective as possible.
4. Do not permit your evaluation of one factor to influence your evaluation of another.
5. Base your rating on the observed performance of the salesman, not his potential abilities.
6. Never rate an employee on several instances of good or poor work, but rather on his general success or failure over the whole period.
7. Have sound reasons for your ratings.[17]

Behaviorally Anchored Rating Scales

These admonitions probably help some, particularly when the evaluator must supply the reasons for his or her ratings. They do not resolve the question of attributes used for the evaluation in the first place, however. A recent emphasis

---

[16] Cocanougher and Ivancevich, "BARS" Performance Rating, pp. 89.
[17] *Measuring Salesmen's Performance*, p. 34.

in performance appraisal directed at this question is BARS, which stands for "behaviorally anchored rating scale." A BARS system attempts to concentrate on behaviors and performance criteria that can be controlled by the individual. A BARS system reflects the condition that there are a number of factors that affect any employee's performance. Some of these factors are more critical to job success than are others, and the key to evaluating people is to focus on these "critical success factors" (CSFs).[18] The implementation of a BARS system for evaluating salespeople requires that the behaviors that are key to their performance be identified. Also, the subsequent evaluation of a salesperson's performance must be conducted by rating these key behaviors using the appropriate descriptions.

The whole process is implemented in the following way.[19] First, the key behaviors with respect to performance are identified using critical incidents. Critical incidents, as the name suggests, are occurrences that are critical or vital to performance. To use the critical incident technique, those involved could be asked to identify some particularly outstanding examples of good or bad performance and to detail the reasons why.[20] The performances identified are then reduced to a smaller number of performance dimensions by those working on the BARS development. Next, the group of critical incidents is presented to a group of sales personnel who are asked to assign each critical incident to an appropriate dimension. An incident is typically kept in if 60 percent or more of the group assigns it to the same dimension, as did the instrument development group. The sales personnel group is also asked to rate the behavior described in the critical incident on a 7- or 10-point scale with respect to how effectively or ineffectively it represents performance on the dimension. Incidents that generate good agreement in ratings, typically measured by the standard deviation, are considered for the final scale. The particular incidents chosen are determined by their location along the scale, as measured by the means. Typically, the final scale has six to eight anchors. An example of a BARS scale that resulted from such a process for the attribute "promptness in meeting deadlines" is shown in Figure 17–4.

The advantage of a BARS system over the "normal" performance appraisal system using merit rating forms is that it requires appropriate personnel to consider in detail the components of a salesperson's job performance. They must also define anchors for those performance criteria in specific behavioral terms. In terms of the model of Figure 17–1, a BARS system tends to emphasize behavior and performance rather than effectiveness. Perhaps that is what a system appraising the performance of salespeople should emphasize, particularly when effectiveness is already assessed through sales and cost analyses.

---

[18] The notion of critical success factors also plays a role in design of modern decision support systems. See, for example, John F. Rockart, "Chief Executives Define Their Own Data Needs," *Harvard Business Review*, March-April 1979, pp. 81–93.

[19] Cocanougher and Ivancevich "BARS" Performance Rating, pp. 90–99. For a review of the research literature on BARS, see Donald P. Schwab, Herbert G. Heneman III, and Thomas A. DeCotiss, "Behavioral Anchored Rating Scales: A Review of the Literature," *Personnel Psychology* 28 (1975), pp. 549–62. For a discussion of the use of BARS in ongoing performance appraisal systems, see H. John Bernardin and Richard W. Beatty, *Performance Appraisal: Assessing Human Behavior at Work* (Boston, Mass.: Kent Publishing, 1984).

[20] For a general discuss on of critical incidents, see J. Flanagan, "The Critical Incident Technique," *Psychological Bulletin* 51, (1954), pp. 327–58. For a sales application, see Wayne K. Kirchner and Marvin D. Dunnette, "Identifying the Critical Factors in Successful Salesmanship," *Personnel* 34 (1957), pp. 54–59. For some general examples, see Bernadin and Beatty, *Performance Appraisal*.

Figure 17–4
A BARS scale with behavioral
anchors for the attribute
"promptness in meeting deadlines"

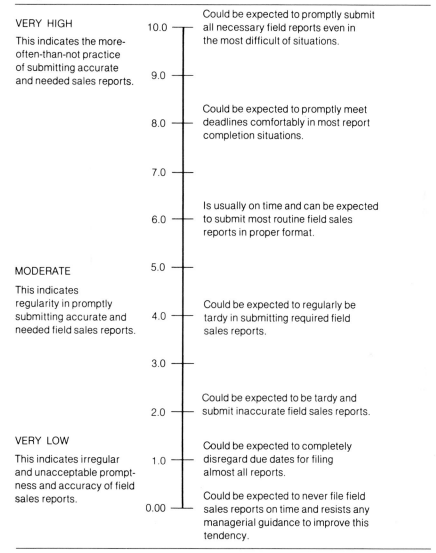

VERY HIGH

This indicates the more-often-than-not practice of submitting accurate and needed sales reports.

MODERATE

This indicates regularity in promptly submitting accurate and needed field sales reports.

VERY LOW

This indicates irregular and unacceptable prompt-ness and accuracy of field sales reports.

10.0 — Could be expected to promptly submit all necessary field reports even in the most difficult of situations.

9.0

8.0 — Could be expected to promptly meet deadlines comfortably in most report completion situations.

7.0

6.0 — Is usually on time and can be expected to submit most routine field sales reports in proper format.

5.0

4.0 — Could be expected to regularly be tardy in submitting required field sales reports.

3.0

2.0 — Could be expected to be tardy and submit inaccurate field sales reports.

1.0 — Could be expected to completely disregard due dates for filing almost all reports.

0.00 — Could be expected to never file field sales reports on time and resists any managerial guidance to improve this tendency.

Source: A. Benton Cocanougher and John M. Ivancevich, "'BARS' Performance Rating for Sales Personnel," *Journal of Marketing* 42 (July 1978), p. 92.

Decision Support Systems and Use of Microcomputers

Firms are increasingly using the methods discussed in this chapter to evaluate salespeople, not in lieu of their traditional emphases on sales analysis and to a lesser extent on cost and ROAM analysis, but as a supplement to them. There seem to be several factors underlying their adoption. For one thing, their value is being more explicitly recognized. Sales, cost, and ROAM analyses are basically effectiveness measures. Whether a salesperson does well with respect to most of these measures is certainly a function of the salesperson's efforts or behaviors and the quality of those efforts. At the same time, whether the individual does well with respect to these measures is partly a function of what the company does on the representative's behalf in the territory. As stated earlier, one could reasonably question whether individual salespeople should be rewarded or punished because of company territorial differences. An emphasis on these other objective and subjective input and output factors provides a more holistic perspective on how individual salespeople are doing.

Probably the most important prime mover for the adoption of these methods of evaluation, though, is the development of decision support systems for managing the personal selling function, particularly via microcomputers. The general notions underlying decision support systems were discussed earlier and there is no need to repeat that discussion. It is worthwhile to mention, though, that more decision support systems have been developed to assist in managing the personal selling effort than with respect to any of the other elements captured in the marketing function. This is partly because the personal selling function is the most important element in the marketing effort of most firms as we saw in Chapter 1, and the payoffs to improvement in the function can be substantial. The Computer Instrumentation Division of Westinghouse Corporation, for example, installed a decision support system for the personal selling effort that frees salespeople from paperwork and gives management information about the status of marketing plans. The decision credits the system with a member of productivity gains—including a 27-percent increase in sales contracts, a 300-percent increase in new customer contracts per salesperson, and a decrease of 25-percent in the cost per sales call.[21] Similarly, a decision support system focusing on sales leads resulted in a 70-percent documented lead follow-up by the Stanley Vedmar division of the Stanley Works with substantially increased sales and reduced costs, whereas previously lead follow-ups were below industry norms.[22] Their adoption, though, is also attributable to the fact that the personal selling effort lends itself to the development of decision support systems, since it is a reasonably structured function

---

[21] T. C. Taylor, "Talk About Sales Productivity!" *Sales & Marketing Management*, July 6, 1981, pp. 38–39.

[22] Ernest J. Krepelka, "Computerize Lead-Fulfillment to Reduce Marketing Costs," *Marketing News*, November 25, 1983, p. 10.

in which the required inputs and needed outputs are known with some degree of certainty.

Decision support systems for managing the personal selling function would probably not have come as far as they have if it were not for microcomputers. The steadily decreasing cost of these machines combined with their steadily increasing capabilities have produced a situation where companies can afford to make them available to all sales managers, regardless of level, and even to salespeople in some cases. Further, the uses to which these machines can be put—such as assessing sales potential, improving an account's product mix, reducing the costs of servicing an account, or restructuring the account mix—are well known.[23] In addition, there is a great deal of microcomputer software currently available, and more material is being published every day that is specifically devoted to managing the personal selling effort.[24]

Corrective Action

Performance and effectiveness evaluations have brought us full circle with respect to the personal selling program. As described in Chapter 1, the three essential sales management activities are:

1. The formulation of a strategic sales program.
2. The implementation of the sales program.
3. The evaluation and control of sales force performance.

The formulation of the strategic sales program involves the organization and planning of the company's overall personal selling efforts and the integration of these efforts with other elements of the firm's marketing strategy. It includes such considerations as how the sales force should be organized, the appropriate design of sales territories, and the proper types and levels of quotas.

The implementation phase involves selecting appropriate sales personnel and designing and implementing policies and procedures that will direct their efforts toward the desired objectives. It includes all the issues surrounding the selection, training, and motivation of the individual representatives.

All these activities are undertaken to produce the results targeted in the sales and marketing plans, which in turn must be consistent with overall corporate goals. In the evaluation and control phase, the sales manager needs to find out what happened, and why it happened, and then needs to decide what to do about it. There are no automatic answers to these questions or decisions though, although the analysis techniques discussed in these last three chapters should provide a number of clues.

---

[23] For specific examples of how electronic spreadsheets on microcomputers can be used to accomplish these functions see G. David Hughes, "Computerized Sales Management," *Harvard Business Review*, March-April 1983, pp. 102–12.

[24] For a list of the packages broken out by the type of microcomputer for which they are available, see "Software Package for Sales/Marketing," *Industrial Marketing*, July 1982, pp. 50–56.

A serious discrepancy between goals and results in any area might suggest a revision of goals, a change in plans, or some alteration of how the plans are implemented. The particular corrective action called for depends on what the analysis highlights as the fundamental problem or problems. There may have been a serious erosion in economic conditions since the marketing and sales plans were first formulated. In this case, all that may be warranted is a lowering of the sales goals to a more realistic level. Alternatively, the goals may be diagnosed as still realistic and the fault traced to the plans and their implementation. Then these need to be changed.

With respect to the job of the sales manager, discrepancies between goals and results might call for restructuring of sales territories, reassignment of salespeople to territories, or respecification of the frequency with which representatives are to call on different types of accounts. These actions would deserve consideration if there seemed to be some general problems in most or the entire personal selling effort.

Alternatively, the problems might be traced to an individual representative or perhaps several salespeople. The problem would then be to determine why they did not do as well as they should. Again, there could be a number of reasons. Perhaps the quota assigned them was unrealistic, in that it did not accurately reflect the economic and competitive conditions in their territory. On the other hand, the analysis might reveal that the individual sales representative is personally at fault. The task is then to determine why. Does the representative truly possess the necessary aptitude for a personal selling career with the company? Has the person acquired all the necessary skills for success through training? Does the person find the rewards available within the company attractive? Do they serve to motivate him or her? The model used to organize our understanding of the behavior of individual salespeople can be used to highlight the questions one might pose to get at the root cause of why a particular salesperson's performance was poor. It can also be used to formulate corrective action.

Summary

Although sales and cost analyses are two important tools in sales management control and evaluation of individual representatives, they are not without their problems. A main difficulty in using them is that they measure effectiveness rather than performance. The distinction between these notions is important. Performance is directly related to salesperson behavior. More specifically, behavior refers to what the representatives do or the tasks on which they expend effort. Performance is behavior evaluated in terms of its contributions to the organization. It focuses on such questions of whether the number of calls a salesperson made or the number of proposals the representative developed are good or bad, above expectations or below. Effectiveness includes additional factors not under the individual salesperson's control, such as the potential within the territory and the actions of competitors. Many firms consequently supplement their sales and cost analyses with other measures that assess salesperson performance more directly.

These other measures can be either objective or subjective, and either group can be used to assess inputs or outputs. The objective measures reflect other statistics the manager can gather from the firm's internal data. Some of the most common objective output measures focus on orders or accounts such as the number of orders, the number of canceled orders, the number of active accounts, the number of new accounts, the number of lost accounts, and so on. The more common objective input measures emphasize calls, time and time utilization, expenses, and nonselling activities. Typical ones from each category would be the number of calls, the number of days worked, the salesperson's total expenses, and the number of service calls made. The input for these objective measures often comes from salespeople's call reports or from time and duty analyses. The data can also be secured from other operating systems within the firm or from special research investigations.

Many firms combine the various outputs and/or inputs to form ratios. The three most common types are expense ratios, account development and servicing ratios, and call activity and/or productivity ratios.

The various measures are most productively used in combination. They are an aid to judgment, not a substitute for it. The comparisons which the indices allow should be the beginning and not the end of any analysis aimed at assessing how well the personal selling effort is going and how individual salespeople are doing.

Some common performance attributes assessed using subjective measures are job knowledge, management of the territory, customer and company relations, and personal characteristics. Also included are other aspects of sales such as whether the person sold the full product line. The subjective assessments are typically made using some type of merit rating form in which the evaluator checks the amount of each of a number of predetermined attributes of the salesperson. Among the problems associated with using merit rating forms, one of the most severe is their lack of an outcome focus; that is, they often contain many attributes not critical or vital to performance. To get at the more essential attributes, a number of firms are turning to BARS ("behaviorally anchored rating scales") The BARS procedure emphasizes the isolation of behaviors most critical to performing the duties assigned. Subsequent evaluations are carried out with respect to these critical behaviors.

The growth of decision support systems in conjunction with the proliferation of microcomputers have combined to produce an environment in which a firm must systematically evaluate its personal selling effort if it is to compete successfully. The evaluation and control phase of the sales management process requires managers to (1) find out what happened, (2) find out why it happened, and (3) decide on what steps need to be taken to correct the situation. The last step can bring the manager full circle with respect to his or her major activities. The manager may need to revise the strategy for the sales program and/or may need to correct some implementation deficiencies. There are no pat answers to what should be done; it all depends on what the various analyses reveal as to what the major deficiencies are.

Discussion Questions

1. What role will the extensive adoption of microcomputers play in the evaluation of sales performance? Do you expect sales performance activities to be more effective?

2. What is a decision support system? How can sales managers use such a system? Assume that you have been hired by Arthur Andersen, a public accounting firm, to help their clients develop decision support systems. How would you proceed?

3. Many companies include the sales representative in the performance evaluation process. Thus, the sales representative and the immediate supervisor discuss the representative's performance. With this process, is there a danger of giving the sales representative too much information?

4. "Our new performance evaluation procedure is so precise—all terms have been defined and all scales have been tested—that we will no longer have to train our district sales managers on how to conduct a performance evaluation." Do you agree with this statement?

5. "I'm sorry, Gregg," said Gregg's sales manager, "your performance evaluation is being downgraded. Who you live with is your business, but when you and your lady friend showed up at the recent three-day convention together, it was a source of embarrassment for many of the wives present." "But I'm the district's top producer," argued Gregg, "and that's what's important." Comment.

6. "What can I do to get a rating higher than just 'satisfactory'?" pleaded Helen Graham. Her sales manager said, "Why don't you go talk to Sarah Carlin? She got a 'superior' rating and maybe she'll give you a few pointers." What should Helen do?

7. "In this company, you had better make quota four out of five years or you can start looking for another job. I don't care if you are doing the right things—its the results that count." Do you agree with this position?

8. A large corporation notices an irregular decrease in the sales of a particular representative. The sales representative, normally in very high standing among other salesmen and quotas, has of failed lately to achieve his own quota. What can be done by the corporation to determine whether the slump in the sales curve is the responsibility of the representative or due to things beyond his control?

9. Given the following information from evaluations of the performance of different sales representatives, what possible deductions could be made about the sales representatives *not achieving quota?*

    a. Representative 1: Achieved target goals for sales calls, telephone calls and new accounts; customer relations good, no noticeable deficiencies in any areas.

    b. Representative 2: Completed substantially fewer sales calls than target;

telephone calls high in number, but primarily with one firm. Time management analysis shows the sales representative to be spending a disproportionately large amount of time with one firm. New accounts are low; all other areas very good to outstanding.

c. Representative 3: Number of sales calls low, below target; telephone calls, letters, proposals all very low and below target; evaluation shows poor time utilization, very high amount of service-related activities in sales representative's log; customer relations extremely positive, high amount of feedback on product function produced lately.

10. "We have spent many hours establishing our quotas using sophisticated statistical techniques. Thus, we are very confident that these can be used as valid measures of performance for our salespeople." Evaluate this statement in light of the possible problems that this type of policy may cause.

11. Bill Smith has just finished performing a cost analysis on his district. The results show that while two salespeople have reached their planned sales goal, two other salespeople have missed their planned sales goals (see Table 1). To gain insight into what is happening in his district, Bill has decided to do a ratio analysis. He used the information shown in Table 2 to complete the ratio analysis. Compute the following ratios for each salesperson:
   a. Sales expense ratio.
   b. Account penetration ratio.
   c. New account conversion ratio.
   d. Average order size ratio.
   e. Calls per day ratio.
   f. Orders per call ratio.

Table 1

	Sales Representative			
	1	2	3	4
Planned sales	$575,000	$650,000	$640,000	$650,000
Actual sales	550,000	650,000	640,000	620,000
Cost of sales	445,000	530,000	520,000	500,000
Gross margin	105,000	120,000	120,000	120,000
Expenses:				
Salaries	20,000	22,000	21,000	23,000
Commissions	5,500	6,500	6,400	6,200
Travel	7,000	10,000	9,500	9,500
Advertising	27,000	28,000	31,000	31,000
Warehouse	7,000	8,000	8,000	7,600
Order processing	100	140	100	160
Transportation	21,000	24,000	24,000	23,000
Total expenses	87,600	98,640	100,000	100,460
Net profit (loss)	$ 17,400	$ 21,360	$ 20,000	$ 19,540

Table 2

	Sales Representative			
	1	2	3	4
Number of calls....................	90	125	100	100
Number of orders	50	70	50	80
Number of accounts in territory......................	250	260	240	275
Number of accounts sold	40	70	70	75
Number of new accounts	3	7	6	7
Number of days worked	20	20	20	20

Cases for Part 3

Case 3-1
Susan Kay Greenhouses[*]

Jennifer Hogue, sales manager for District 2 of Susan Kay Greenhouses, hung up the phone after a conversation with the president of the company and thought about what he had just said:

"Jennifer, your district has continued to be the leader in sales among our five districts, of which we are extremely proud. However, your district is low in its contribution to our profit goals. Since it is the sales leader, we anticipated a greater contribution than what we are receiving. We are having a company sales meeting in two weeks. I would like you to see if you can come up with some reasons for the low profitability and some ideas on how we can increase this profitability."

Susan Kay Greenhouses is a wholesale greenhouse that supplies fresh cut flowers and plants to floral shops and businesses in the Dallas-Ft. Worth area. Each district's staff is comprised of a sales manager and five salespeople. Three secretaries provide the necessary district office support. All districts share the same warehouse and shipping location. The company also owns its own fleet of trucks, which are operated by company drivers who deliver all flowers and plants daily.

Jennifer's district is divided between five salespeople. Table 1 gives the breakdown of the salespeople's years with the company.

Table 1
District 2 sales force

Salesperson	Section of the District	Number of Years with the Company
Kathryn Johnston	A	3
Jeff Wick	B	2.5
Dennis Thompson	C	5
Charles Stevens	D	4.5
Ed Wilms	E	3

---

[*]This case was prepared especially for this text by Larry Hogue, BBA—Accounting, University of Wisconsin, Madison.

Susan Kay Greenhouses markets four basic product groups. The first group consists of plants for businesses and office decorations which are sold by the dozen. The second group includes house plants. These are also sold by the dozen. The third group consists of fresh cut flowers. These are either used in arrangements or sold individually. They are sold in groups of six dozen per type of flower. The fourth group differs from the third in that the flowers are sold in groups of six dozen in assorted types.

The company has grown steadily from year to year due to their marketing innovativeness and their willingness to keep up with the latest business analysis computer techniques. The company feels so strongly about the importance of the computer analysis that it supplies each district manager with a microcomputer so that the managers can conduct in-depth business analyses on their own.

Table 2
Profit and loss statement

Sales		$1,630,950
Cost of goods sold		1,188,700
Gross margin		442,250
Selling and administrative expenses:		
Salaries	$ 15,470	
Commissions	4,893	
Advertising	104,750	
Supplies (postage)	570	
Packaging material	44,400	
Transportation charges	148,000	
Travel expenses	25,000	
Rent	14,500	
Total		357,583
Net profit (loss)		$ 84,667

Jennifer decided that she should perform a cost analysis for her district for the last month to help isolate the causes of the district's low profitability. She was glad that she could use her microcomputer to access the necessary information. The first set of information that she "pulled up on her screen" allowed her to complete a profit-and-loss statement for the last period (Table 2). The next set of data she obtained was the sales for each product group and for each salesman according to the product group (Table 3). She also accessed the total cost of sales for each product group, and the cost of sales for each salesperson according to the product groups (Table 4). Table 5 shows the number of calls and orders that each salesperson made last month, and the person's annual salary. The other information that Jennifer accessed to help her complete the cost analysis appears below.

Table 3
Sales data

Product:	Sales in Units	Selling Price	Sales in Dollars
Business plants	6,600	$50	$ 330,000
House plants	6,250	48	300,000
Cut flowers group 1	11,650	43	500,950
Cut flowers group 2	12,500	40	500,000
Totals	37,000		$1,630,950

	Wick		Wilms		Thompson		Stevens		Johnston	
Product:	Units	$	Units	$	Units	$	Units	$	Units	$
Business plants	1,500	75,000	1,200	60,000	1,500	75,000	500	25,000	1,900	95,000
House plants	1,400	67,200	900	43,200	1,450	69,600	800	38,400	1,700	81,600
Cut flowers group 1	2,450	105,350	1,900	81,700	2,350	101,050	2,400	103,200	2,550	109,650
Cut flowers group 2	3,000	120,000	2,200	88,000	2,600	104,000	1,900	76,000	2,800	112,000
Totals	8,350	$367,550	6,200	$272,900	7,900	$349,650	5,600	$242,600	8,950	$398,250

Table 4
Cost of sales data

	Wick	Wilms	Thompson	Stevens	Johnston	Totals
Product:						
Business plants	$ 45,000	$ 36,000	$ 45,000	$ 15,000	$57,000	$ 198,000
House plants	43,400	27,900	44,950	24,800	52,700	193,750
Cut flowers group 1....	80,850	62,700	77,550	79,200	84,150	384,450
Cut flowers group 2....	99,000	72,600	85,800	62,700	92,000	412,500
Total	$268,250	$199,200	$253,300	$181,700	$286,250	$1,188,700

Table 5
General data

	Number of Calls	Number of Orders	Annual Salary
Wick	75	50	$ 21,000
Wilms..................	100	60	20,400
Thompson	95	50	23,040
Stevens	125	50	25,200
Johnston...............	105	90	21,000
Total	500	300	$110,640

Advertising expenditures per product

Business plants	$ 19,800
House plants...	25,000
Cut flowers group 1	34,950
Cut flowers group 2	25,000
Total	$104,750

Other salaries   **Annual Salary**

Jennifer Hogue.......................................	$39,000
Office personnel......................................	36,000

Time spent with each
salesperson by Hogue:

Wick	20%
Wilms...	20
Thompson	20
Stevens...	24
Johnston	16

Rent

Rental space was $25 per sq. ft. for office space and $10 per sq. ft. for warehouse space. Of the 1,000 sq. ft. total of space use, 300 sq. ft. was in office space and 700 sq. ft. was in warehouse space. The sales department used 250 sq. ft.

Other Costs
1. $50 for each sales call.
2. $1.90 for each order processed.
3. $1.20 packaging costs for each unit sold and shipped.
4. $4.00 transportation costs for each unit sold and shipped.
5. Salespeople earned 0.3 percent commission on their sales.

Feeling confident that she could now perform the cost analysis, she inserted a VisiCalc[1] program into the disk drive and began entering the necessary information.

---

[1] VisiCalc is the registered trademark of VisiCorp, San Jose, California.

Case 3–2
Pure Drug Company[*]

David Thomas had been transferred to the Syracuse, New York, Division of Pure Drug Company in the first week of May 1970. At this time he was appointed sales manager of the Syracuse wholesale drug division. Formerly he had been an assistant to the vice president in charge of sales at the company's headquarters in New York.

At the month-end sales meeting on the first Friday of June 1970, Harvey Brooks, a salesman in one of the division's rural territories, informed Thomas that he wished to retire at the end of July when he reached his 65th birthday. Thomas was surprised by Brooks's announcement because he had been informed by the division manager, Robert Jackson, that Brooks had requested and received a deferment of retirement until he reached his 66th birthday in July 1971. The only explanation offered by Brooks was that he had "changed his mind."

The retirement of Brooks posed a problem for Thomas, in that he had to decide what to do with Brooks's territory.

Background of the Syracuse Division

When Thomas became the divisional sales manager, he was 29 years old. He had joined Pure Drug (as the firm was known in trade circles) as a sales trainee after his graduation from Stanford University in 1964. During the next two years he worked as a salesman. In the fall of 1966, the sales manager of the company made Thomas one of his assistants. In this capacity, Thomas helped the sales manager to arrange special sales promotions of the lines of different manufacturers.

Thomas's predecessor, Harry L. Schultz, had served as divisional sales manager for 15 years before his death in April. "H. L.," as Schultz had been known, worked as a salesman for the drug wholesale house that had been merged with Pure Drug to become its Syracuse division. Although Thomas had made Schultz's acquaintance in the course of business, he did not know Schultz well. The salesmen often expressed their admiration and affection for Schultz to the new sales manager. Several salesmen, in fact, made a point of telling Thomas that "old H. L." knew every druggist in 12 counties by his first name. Schultz had died of a heart attack while trout fishing with the president of the Syracuse Pharmacists' Association. The Syracuse division manager said that most of the druggists in town attended Schultz's funeral.

The Syracuse division of Pure Drug was one of 74 wholesale drug houses in

* This case was prepared as the basis for class discussion rather than to illustrate either effective or ineffective handling of an administrative situation. Copyright 1972 by the President and Fellows of Harvard College. Harvard Business School case 9–573–002. Reproduced by permission. This case was prepared by Ralph Sorenson

the United States owned by the firm. Each division acted as a functionally autonomous unit, having its own warehouse, sales department, buying department, and accounting department. The divisional manager was responsible for the performance of the unit he managed. There were, however, line functions performed by the regional and national offices that pertained directly to the individual departments. A district sales manager, for instance, was associated with a regional office in Albany for the purpose of implementing marketing policies established by the central office in New York.

As a service wholesaler, the Syracuse division sold to the retail drug trade a broad line of approximately 18,000 items. The line might be described most conveniently as consisting of everything sold through drug stores except fresh food, tobacco products, newspapers, and magazines. In the trading area of Syracuse, Pure Drug competed with two other wholesalers; one of these carried substantially the same line of products; the other, a limited line of drug products.

The history of the Syracuse division had been a profitable family-owned wholesale drug house before its merger with Pure Drug in 1950. The division had operated profitably since that date, although it had not shown a profit on sales equal to the average for the other wholesale drug divisions of Pure Drug. Since 1961, the annual net sales of the division had risen each year. Because the competitors did not announce their sales figures, it was impossible to ascertain, however, whether this increase in sales represented a change in the competitive situation or merely a general trend of business volume in the Syracuse area. Schultz felt that the increase had been at the expense of competitors. The district drug manager, however, maintained that, since the trend of increase was less than that of other divisions in the northern New York region, the Syracuse division may have actually lost ground competitively. A new measuring technique of calculating the potential wholesale purchasing power of retail drugstores, which had been adopted shortly before Thomas's transfer, indicated that the share of the wholesale drug market controlled by the Syracuse division was below the median and below the mean for Pure Drug divisions.

Only a few of the present employees working in 1970 for the Syracuse division had also been employed by the predecessor company. Schultz was one remaining man of the executive echelon whose employment in the Syracuse division antedated the merger. Most of the executives and salesmen currently active in the organization had been employed as executives or salesmen in the organization during the 1950s and 1960s. Two salesmen, however, Mr. Brooks and Mr. Clifford Nelson, had sold for the predecessor company before the merger.

Of the men who were employed as executives or salesmen before the 1960s, only Robert Jackson, the division manager, had a college degree, which he had earned at a local YMCA night school. All the more recently employed young men were university or pharmacy college graduates. None of the younger men had been promoted when vacancies had occurred for the job of operations manager (who was in charge of the warehouse) and merchandise manager (who supervised buying) in the Syracuse division; however, two of the younger men had been promoted to similar positions in other divisions when vacancies had occurred.

The Syracuse Division Sales Force

From the time when Thomas took over Schultz's duties, he had devoted four days a week to the task of traveling through each sales territory with the salesmen who covered it. He had, however, made no changes in the practices or procedures of the sales force. The first occasion on which Thomas was required to make a decision of other than routine nature was when Brooks asked to be retired.

When Thomas took charge of the Syracuse division sales force, it consisted of nine salesmen and four trainees. Four of the salesmen, Frederick Taylor, Edward Harrington, George Howard, and Larry Donnelly, had joined the company under the sales training program for college graduates initiated early in the 1960s. The other five salesmen had been with the company many years. Harvey Brooks and Clifford Nelson had seniority status. William Murray joined the company as a warehouse employee in 1946 when he was 19. He became a salesman in 1951. Walter Miller was employed as a salesman in 1951, when the wholesale drug firm that he had previously sold for went out of business. Miller, who was 48 years old, had been a wholesale drug salesman since he was 20. Albert Simpson came to Pure Drug after working as a missionary salesman for a manufacturer. Simpson, who was 26 when he joined the company in 1954, had served as an officer in the Army Medical Corps during the Korean War. He was discharged as a captain in hospital administration in 1958.

The four trainees were men who had graduated from college the preceding June. When Thomas arrived in Syracuse, these men were in the last phase of their 12-month training program. The trainees were spending much of their time traveling with the salesmen. Thomas, who now had the full responsibility for training these men, believed that Schultz had hired four trainees to cover anticipated turnover of salesmen, to cover anticipated turnover among the trainees themselves, and to implement the New York office's policy of getting more intensive coverage of each market area. The trainees, he understood, expected to receive territory assignments either in the Syracuse division or elsewhere on the completion of their training period.

Thomas had not seen very much of the salesmen. His acquaintance with them had been formed at the sales meetings and while traveling with them through their territories.

Mr. Thomas was of the opinion that Walter Miller was a very easy-going, even-tempered person. He seemed to be very popular with the other salesmen and with his customers. Miller was very proud of his two sons, the younger one of whom was in high school while the other was the father of a grandson named after Mr. Miller. Thomas thought that the salesman liked him because Miller had commented to him several times that the suggestions offered by Thomas had been very helpful to him.

Harvey Brooks had not, in Thomas's opinion, been particularly friendly. Thomas had observed that Brooks was well liked because of his good humor and friendly manner with everyone; however, Thomas had noticed that on a number of occasions Brooks had intimated that his age and experience should cause the sales manager to defer to his judgment. Brooks and his wife lived in the town of Oswego.

On June 4, 1970, Thomas had traveled with Brooks, and they had visited five of Brooks's accounts. On a routine form for sales managers reports on field work with salesmen, which was filed with the district sales manager and New York sales manager, Thomas made the following comments about Brooks:

Points requiring attention: Not using merchandising equipment; not following weekly sales plan. Pharmaceutical business going to competitors because of lack of interest. Too much time spent on idle chatter. Only shows druggist what "he thinks they will buy." Tends to sell easy items instead of profitable ones.

Steps taken for correction: Explained shortcomings and demonstrated how larger, more profitable orders could be obtained by following sales plan—did just that by getting the biggest order ever written for Carthage account. Remarks: Old-time "personality." Should do terrific volume if trained on new merchandising techniques.

On a similar form made out by Harry L. Schultz on the basis of working with Brooks on March 3, 1970, the following comments were made:

Points requiring attention: Not getting pharmaceutical business. Not following promotion plans.

Steps taken for correction: Told him about these things.

Remarks: Brooks made this territory—can sell anything he sets his mind to—a real drummer—very popular with his customers.

George Howard, 29 years old, was the oldest of the group of salesmen who had passed through the formal sales-training program. Thomas considered him earnest and conscientious. He had increased his sales each year. Although Thomas did not consider Howard to be the "salesman type," he noted that Howard had been quite successful in the use of the merchandising techniques which Thomas was seeking to implement.

William Murray handled a number of the big accounts in downtown Syracuse. Thomas believed that Murray was an excellent salesman who considered himself "very smooth." Thomas had been surprised at the affront Murray had taken when the sales manager had offered a few suggestions about the improvement of his selling technique. Mr. and Mrs. Murray were good friends of the Jacksons. The Murrays were social friends of the merchandise and operations managers and their wives. Thomas suspected that Murray had expected to be Schultz's successor.

Clifford Nelson seemed to Thomas to be an earnest and conscientious salesman. He had been amiable, though not cordial, toward Thomas. Thomas's report on calls on 10 accounts on June 5, 1970, with Nelson contained the following statements:

Points requiring attention: Rushing calls. Gets want book and tries to sell case lots on wanted items. Carries all merchandising equipment but doesn't use it.

Steps taken for correction: Suggested change in routing; longer, better planned calls; conducted presentation demonstration.

Remarks: Hardworking, conscientious, good salesman, but needs to be brought up to date on merchandising methods.

Schultz's comments on observations of Nelson on March 4, 1970, reported on the same form, were as follows:

Points requiring attention: Uses the want book on the basis of most sales. Not pushing promotions.

Steps taken for correction: Discussed shortcomings.

Remarks: Nelson really knows how to sell—visits every customer each week. Hard worker—very loyal—even pushes goods with very low commissions.

On the day Thomas had traveled with Nelson, the salesman suggested that Thomas have dinner at the Nelson's home. Thomas accepted the invitation, but at the end of the day Nelson took him to a restaurant in Watertown, explaining that he did not want to inconvenience his wife because his two daughters were home from college on vacation.

Albert Simpson had caused Thomas considerable concern. Simpson complained about sales management procedures, commission rates, the "lousy service of the warehouse people," and other such matters at sales meetings. Thomas believed that most of the complaints were founded in fact, but that the matters were usually trivial in that the other salesmen did not complain of these matters. Thomas mentioned his difficulties with Simpson to Jackson. Jackson's comment was that Simpson had been very friendly with Schultz. Simpson seemed to be quite popular with his customers.

Frederick Taylor was, in Thomas's opinion, the most ambitious, aggressive, and argumentative salesman in the Syracuse division. He had been employed by the company since his graduation from the University of Rochester in 1966, first as a trainee and then as a salesman. Taylor had substantially increased the sales volume of the territory assigned to him. He had persuaded Schultz to assign him six inactive hospital accounts in July of 1968. In six months, Taylor made sales to those accounts in excess of $50,000. The other salesmen considered him "cocky" and a "big spender." Thomas thought his attitude was one of independence. If Taylor agreed with a sales plan, he worked hard to achieve its objectives, but if he did not agree, he did not cooperate at all. Thomas thought that he had been very successful in working with Taylor.

Larry Donnelly impressed Thomas as being unsure of himself. Donnelly seemed to be confused and overworked. Thomas attributed this difficulty to Donnelly's trying to serve too many accounts in too large an area. Donnelly was very solicitous about Thomas's suggestions on improvement of his work. Donnelly was 24 years old. Thomas believed that he would improve in time with proper help. Donnelly had raised his sales to the point where he was on commission instead of salary in March of 1970.

Edward Harrington was the only salesman who worked on a salary. His sales volume was not sufficient to sustain an income of $600 a month, which was the company minimum for salesmen with more than one year's experience. Harrington was very apologetic about being on a salary. Thomas believed that Harrington's determination to "make good" would be realized because of the latter's conscientiousness. The salesman was 25. When he had been assigned the territory two years before, it had consisted largely of uncontacted accounts. The vol-

ume of sales had tripled in the meantime. Thomas felt that Harrington appreciated all the help he was given and that in time Harrington would be an excellent
salesman.

Sales commission rates were as follows:[1]

Brooks and Nelson	2⅜ percent
Miller and Donnelly	2¼ percent
Murray and Simpson	2⅛ percent
Howard and Taylor	2 percent

Thomas said that expense accounts amounted to about 0.75 percent of sales
for both city and country salesmen. The differences in percentage rates of commission were explained by Thomas in terms of the differential commissions set
by the company. Higher commission rates were given on items the company
wished to "push," such as pharmaceuticals and calendar promotion items.

The trainees were something of an unknown quantity to Thomas. He had
training conferences with them in which he had thought they had performed
rather poorly. He believed that Schultz had neglected the training of the new
men. All four of them seemed to be good prospects. They were eager to be assigned territories, and they conveyed their eagerness to Thomas often.

The turnover of the Syracuse division sales force has been very low among the
senior salesmen. Six of the sales training program men had left the division since
1956. Two had been promoted to department heads in other divisions. Four had
left to work for manufacturers. Because manufacturers valued salesmen with
wholesaling experience and competing wholesalers did not have training programs for young men, there were many opportunities for a salesman who desired
to leave.

Sales Management

Since Thomas had replaced Schultz, he had devoted considerable thought to
the problem of improving the sales performance of the Syracuse division. He had
accepted a transfer to the new job at the urging of Mr. Richard Topping, the vice
president in charge of sales. Thomas was one of a dozen young men whom Topping had brought into the New York office to work as assistants to the top sales
executives. None of the young assistants had remained in the New York office for
more than three years, for Topping made a policy of offering the young men field
assignments so that they could "show their stuff." Thomas believed that the sales
performance of the Syracuse division could be bettered by an improved plan of
sales management. He knew that the share of the Syracuse market for wholesale

---

[1] Using commission rates as given, earnings are: Miller, $12,270; Brooks, $14,290; Murray, $16,080; Nelson,
$15,400; Simpson, $15,600; Howard, $13,020; Taylor, $12,760; Donnelly, $10,620; Harrington, $7,200.

purchases of retail drugstores held by Pure Drug was only 20.05 percent versus a 48 percent share for some of the other divisions.[2]

Topping, for whom Thomas worked immediately before his transfer, had focused his staff's attention upon the qualitative aspects of sales policy. Thomas had assisted Topping in implementing merchandising plans intended to utilize the salesmen's selling efforts in such a way as to minimize the handling cost of sales and maximize the gross margin.

The company encouraged the salesmen to use a threefold plan for increasing profitability:

1. Sales of larger average value per line of the order were encouraged because the cost of processing and filling each line of an order was practically constant.
2. Sales of larger total value were encouraged because the delivery cost for orders having a total weight between 20 and 100 pounds was practically constant.
3. Because some manufacturers offered margins considerably larger than others, sales of products carrying higher margins were encouraged. Salesmen's commissions varied with the margins available to Pure Drug on the products they sold.

The executives of the company also sought to increase the effectiveness of Pure Drug promotions by setting up a sales calendar. The sales calendar coordinated the activities of all Pure Drug divisions so that during a given calendar period every account would be solicited for the sale of particular items yielding satisfactory profits. The type of activity represented by the sales calendar required that the salesmen in each division follow a pattern in selling to every individual account. The sales manager was responsible for coordinating the activities of his salesmen.

The matter of selling patterns was largely the responsibility of the division sales manager. Thomas believed that his predecessor had never really accepted the changes that had taken place in the merchandising policy of the New York office.

Thomas had inherited from his predecessor a system of sales department records which had been carefully maintained. The national offices required each division to keep uniform sales and market analysis records. During the period of Thomas's work in the New York office, he had developed a familiarity with the use of these records.

The basis of the sales and market analysis record was the division trading area. The limits of the trading area were determined by the economics of selling costs, and the factors on which the costs were based were transportation costs of delivery and salesmen's traveling expenses. Thomas knew from his own experience that delineation of trading areas was influenced by tradition, geographic condi-

---

[2] The potential wholesale sales for retail drugstores were calculated by the New York office market analysis section. This market estimate, called the PWPP (potential wholesale purchasing power), was calculated for each county by adjusting retail drugstores' sales to an estimate of the purchases of goods from wholesalers.

Exhibit 1
Syracuse division trading area

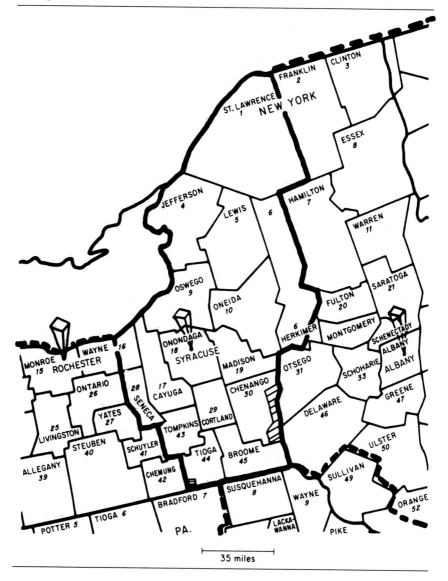

35 miles

tions, the number of salesmen, the number of calls a salesman could make, the estimated market potential, competition, and agreements with adjacent Pure Drug divisions. The Syracuse division was bordered by the trading areas of Pure Drug divisions located in Rochester and Albany on the east, south, and west; to the north was the Canadian border. A map of this division is included here in Exhibit 1.

Exhibit 2
Selected data on sales and sales potentials, by counties

County	Code	Population (000s)	Per cent	Retailers Sold	Inactive Accounts	Accounts Not Sold	Total	Potential Wholesale Purchasing Power* (000s)	Per-cent Area PWPP	Sales (000s)†	Sales per cent PWPP	Hospitals Sold	Not Sold	Sales (000s)	Miscellaneous Sales (000s)
St. Lawrence	1	117.2	6.3%	23	1	2	26	$ 1,090	4.4%	$ 408	37.4%	2	4	$ 8	$ 6
Jefferson	4	90.2	4.9	34	—	—	34	1,306	5.3	367	28.2	2	2	4	—
Lewis	5	24.8	1.3	8	—	—	8	261	1.0	86	32.2	—	1	—	3
Herkimer	6	69.3	3.7	10	6	1	17	624	2.5	98	15.7	1	2	—	—
Oswego	9	97.8	5.3	25	1	—	26	1,340	5.5	373	27.1	—	2	—	10
Oneida	10	285.4	15.5	46	14	12	72	3,480	14.2	375	10.5	—	13	—	7
Wayne	16	76.6	4.1	4	—	1	5	247	1.0	55	22.3	—	—	—	—
Cayuga	17	75.6	4.1	12	4	—	16	561	2.3	101	18.0	2	—	4	27
Onondaga	18	474.8	25.8	98	9	13	120	7,647	31.2	2,166	28.7	6	9	108	192
Madison	19	59.7	3.2	12	2	3	17	1,250	5.1	261	20.9	—	2	—	—
Seneca	28	34.4	1.9	6	1	3	10	558	2.3	84	15.0	2	1	6	24
Cortland	29	45.4	2.5	6	2	1	9	510	2.1	161	31.5	—	2	—	—
Chenango	30	48.2	2.6	4	2	6	12	568	2.3	63	11.1	—	3	—	—
Thompkins	43	75.7	4.1	9	1	4	14	815	3.3	132	16.2	—	5	—	—
Tioga	44	46.2	2.5	4	—	7	11	322	1.3	80	24.8	—	—	—	—
Broome	45	225.3	12.2	22	2	13	37	3,970	16.2	253	6.4	—	8	—	18
Total		1,846.6	100.0%	323	45	66	434	$24,549	100.0%	$5,041	20.5%	15	54	$130	$287

*Includes miscellaneous but not hospital or house sales.

†Excludes miscellaneous sales, sales to hospitals, and house sales.

Exhibit 3
Selected data on salesmen's
territory assignments by county

Salesman	County	Sales 1969*	Active Accounts‡	Estimated Potential† (in 000)	Assigned Accounts‡
Miller	Chenango	$ 61,902	4	$ 567	15
	Tompkins	132,900	9	815	19
	Tioga	79,678	4	322	11
	Broome	270,300	22	3,971	45
	Total	544,780	39	5,675	90
Brooks	Jefferson	146,034	16	906	18
	Lewis	86,394	8	261	9
	Oswego	369,860	25	1,070	28
	Total	602,288	49	2,237	55
Howard	Onondaga	229,017	14	910	14
	Madison	260,850	12	1,250	19
	Cortland	161,000	6	510	11
	Total	650,867	32	2,670	44
Murray.......	Onondaga	756,153	33	2,225	44
	Total	756,153	33	2,225	44
Nelson	St. Lawrence	408,176	25	1,090	32
	Jefferson	222,159	20	400	20
	Oswego	2,780	1	270	1
	Total	633,425	46	1,760	53
Simpson	Onondaga	733,926	29	3,008	48
	Total	733,926	29	3,008	48
Taylor........	Onondaga	638,073	29	1,504	29
	Total	638,073	28	1,504	29
Donnelly	Herkimer	97,060	10	624	19
	Oneida	375,000	46	3,480	85
	Total	472,060	56	4,104	104
Harrington ...	Wayne	54,400	4	247	5
	Cayuga	127,000	14	561	18
	Seneca	108,780	8	558	13
	Total	290,180	26	1,366	36
Hospitals	Taylor—Syracuse	108,000	House accounts: $529,012		
	All others	22,000	Total division sales: $5,980,764		

*The figures by salesman include sales to chain and independent drugstores and to miscellaneous accounts, but do not include sales to hospitals or house accounts indicated at the bottom of the table.
†No potential is calculated for hospitals or miscellaneous sales. However, where a county is divided among several salesmen, the potential sales figure for each salesman is obtained by allocating the county potential in proportion to the total *number* of potential drugstore and miscellaneous accounts in that county assigned to that salesman.
‡Includes hospitals and other recognized drug outlets in the territory.

Exhibit 4
Summary data on salesmen's performance

	1969 Sales (000s)	Per-cent	1969 Potential (000s)†	Per-cent	Sales Percent of Potential	1969 Active Accounts‡ No.	Percent	1969 Assigned Accounts‡ No.	Percent	Active Accounts Percent of Assigned	1969 Sales per Account	Potential per Assigned Account#
I												
Miller	$ 545	10.2%	5,675	23.2%	9.6%	39	11.5%	90	17.9%	43.4%	$14,000	$63,100
Brooks	602	11.3	2,237	9.1	27.0	49	14.5	55	10.9	89.0	12,300	40,600
Murray	756	14.2	2,225	9.1	34.0	33	9.8	44	8.8	75.0	22,900	50,500
Nelson	634*	11.9	1,760	7.2	36.0	46	13.6	53	10.5	85.0	13,800	33,200
Simpson	734	13.8	3,008	12.2	24.5	29	8.6	48	9.5	60.5	25,350	62,700
Subtotal	$3,271	61.4%	14,905	60.8%	22.0	196	58.0%	290	57.6%	67.2	16,700	51,400
II												
Howard	$ 651	12.2%	2,670	10.9%	24.4	32	9.5%	44	8.7%	72.7	20,360	60,600
Taylor	638*	12.0	1,504	6.1	42.4	28	8.3	29	5.8	96.5	26,700	51,800
Donnelly	472	8.9	4,104	16.7	11.5	56	16.5	104	20.7	53.8	8,420	39,500
Harrington	290*	5.5	1,366	5.5	21.3	26	7.7	36	7.2	72.3	11,150	38,000
Subtotal	$2,051	38.6%	9,644	39.2%	21.3	142	42.0%	213	42.4%	66.7	14,470	45,300
Total	$5,322*	100.0%	24,549	100.0%	21.7%	338	100.0%	503	100.0%	67.0%	15,730	$48,800

Hospital sales by:
Taylor 108
Nelson 12
Harrington 10
House sales: 529
Grand total: $5,981

*Excluding hospital sales.
†No potential is calculated for hospital or miscellaneous sales. However, where a county is divided among several salesmen, the potential sales figure for each salesman is obtained by allocating the county potential in proportion to the total number of potential drugstore and miscellaneous accounts in that county assigned to that salesman.
‡Includes hospitals and other recognized drug outlets in the territory.
Understated since hospitals and miscellaneous accounts are included in the assigned accounts listed but not in the potential.

Exhibit 2 gives information on sales and sales potential by county. Exhibits 3 and 4 show selected data on salesmen's territory assignments and performance. During the time since his arrival, Thomas had formed the opinion that the present salesmen's territories had been established without careful regard for the number of stores in the area, the sales potential, or the amount of traveling involved. Although Thomas had not yet studied any one territory carefully, he suspected all his salesmen of skimming the cream from many of their accounts because they did not have adequate time to do a thorough selling job in each store.

Thomas had been able to observe the performance records of other divisional sales managers while he worked in New York. He knew that some sales managers had achieved substantial improvements on the past performances of their divisions.

Sales Territories of Brooks and Nelson

The territory that Brooks covered included accounts scattered through small towns in four counties of the rural area northeast of Syracuse (see Exhibit 5). Brooks had originally developed the accounts in the four-county area for the predecessor company. At the time he undertook this task, the competing service wholesaler already had established a mail-order business with the rural druggists in this area. Brooks had taken to the road in 1940 to build up the sales in all four counties. He had been hired specifically for this job because he was a native of the area and an experienced "drummer."

Five years later Clifford Nelson, a friend of Brooks, became a division salesman, and, at the suggestion of Brooks, covered other accounts in the same four-county area. Nelson had been a salesman for a proprietary medicine firm before he joined the wholesale drug house. He was seven years younger than Brooks. Since that time, Brooks had serviced a number of accounts in the four-county area. The list of accounts that each of these men handled appears in Exhibits 6 and 7. Thomas noticed that the incomes which Brooks and Nelson had received from commissions were very stable over the years.

A Visit from Mr. Nelson

On the Wednesday morning following the June sales meeting, Thomas saw Nelson come in the front door of the Syracuse division offices. Although the salesman passed within 30 feet of Thomas's desk, he did not appear to notice the sales manager. Nelson walked through the office area to the partitioned space where Jackson's private office was located. Twenty minutes later Nelson emerged from the division manager's office and made his way to Thomas's desk.

"Hi there, young fellah!" he shouted as he approached.

Exhibit 5
Counties sold by Brooks and Nelson

"Howdy, Cliff. Sit down and chat awhile," Thomas replied.

"What got you out of bed so early?" he asked, knowing that the salesman must have risen at 6 o'clock to make the drive to Syracuse from his home in Watertown.

Nelson squeezed his bulky frame into the armchair next to the desk. "It's a shame Harvey is retiring," he said. "I never thought he could give it up. I never knew anyone who enjoyed selling as much as Harvey—'cept, maybe me." Nelson continued praising Brooks and telling anecdotes which illustrated his point until

Exhibit 6
Accounts sold by Harvey Brooks, by counties, with 1969 purchases*

Jefferson County			Oswego County		
Adams Center	D	$ 3,570	Calosse	D	$ 1,709
(Alexandria Bay	D	18,300)	Central Square	D	1,857
(Alexandria Bay	D	15,790)	Constantia	M	72
Bellville	D	2,100	Cleveland	M	390
(Carthage	D	61,000)	(Fulton	D	15,120)
Chaumont	D	604	(Fulton	D	24,510)
(Clayton	D	10,630)	(Fulton	D	27,800)
(Clayton	D	16,400)	(Fulton	D	38,400)
Deferiet	D	369	Hannibal	D	3,890
Dexter	D	11,670	Hastings	M	3,840
Ellisburg	D	236	Lacona	M	462
LaFargeville	D	522	Mexico	D	15,900
Plessis	D	880	Oswego	D	12,075
Redwood	M	108	(Oswego	D	20,760)
Rodman	D	3,210	(Oswego	D	24,100)
Sackets Harbor	D	645	(Oswego	D	41,000)
County total		$146,034	(Oswego	D	43,900)
Lewis County					
Beaver Falls	D	$ 3,810	(Oswego	D	22,430)
Croghan	D	24,597	Oswego	H	15
Harrisville	D	18,516	Parish	M	5,160
Lowville	D	23,688	Phoenix	D	9,730
Lowville	D	4,314	(Pulaski	D	8,750)
Lyon Falls	D	6,024	(Pulaski	D	29,080)
Port Leydon	D	2,325	Sandy Creek	D	14,130
Turin	M	3,120	West Monroe	D	4,780
County total		$ 86,394	County total		$369,860
		Territory total:	$602,288		

*Codes: D = independent drugstore, M = miscellaneous account, H = hospital.
Note: Accounts in parentheses are those indicated by Nelson as the ones he wanted.

Thomas began to wonder whether Nelson thought that the sales manager was biased in some way against the retiring salesman. Thomas recalled that he had made some critical remarks about Brooks to Jackson, but he could not recall any discussion of Brooks's shortcomings with the man himself or any of the other salesmen. Nelson ended his remarks by saying "Old 'H. L.,' God rest his soul, always said that Harvey was the best damn wholesale drug salesman we'd ever known."

There was a brief silence as Thomas did not realize that Nelson was finished. Finally Thomas said, "You know, Cliff, I think we ought to have a testimonial dinner for Harvey at the July sales meeting."

Nelson made no comment on Thomas's suggestion; instead, he went on to say, "None of these green trainees will ever be able to take Harvey's place. Those

Exhibit 7
Accounts sold by Clifford Nelson, by counties, with 1969 purchases*

St. Lawrence County			Jefferson County		
Canton............... D	$ 39,240		Adams........... C	$ 1,885	
Edwards .... D	2,016		Carthage C	2,130	
Edwards .... M	5,655		Evans Mills ...... D	2,210	
Gouverneur .... D	678		Philadelphia ..... D	3,780	
Gouverneur .... D	28,149		Watertown....... D	30,200	
Gouverneur .... D	49,559		Watertown....... D	4,740	
Heuvelton .... D	324		Watertown....... D	8,800	
Messena .... D	33,777		Watertown....... D	30,680	
Messena .... D	10,191		Watertown....... D	18,440	
Messena C	7,344		Watertown....... D	26,300	
Messena C	6,675		Watertown....... D	38,200	
Messena .... H	114		Watertown....... D	23,000	
Madrid............... D	4,296		Watertown ....D	9,700	
Morristown .... D	8,193		Watertown....... D	854	
Norfolk............... D	8,985		Watertown ...... D	11,320	
Norwood .... D	9,417		Watertown....... C	3,630	
Ogdensburg.......... D	24,270		Watertown C	5,970	
Ogdensburg.......... D	67,665		Watertown ....M	680	
Ogdensburg.......... D	21,609		Watertown ....H	126	
Ogdensburg.......... D	10,140		Watertown ....H	3,600	
Ogdensburg.......... M	447		County total	$226,245	
Ogdensburg.......... H	7,959				
Potsdam .... D	46,332		Oswego County		
Potsdam C	22,113		Pulaski C	$ 2,730	
Potsdam Falls .... D	1,101				
County total	$416,249				
	Territory total:	$645,224			

*Codes: D = independent drugstore, M = miscellaneous account, C = chain drugstore, H = hospital.

druggists up there are old-timers. They would resent being high-pressured by some kid blown up to twice his size with college degrees. No, sir! You've got to sell 'em right in those country stores."

Thomas did not believe that Nelson's opinion about the adaptability of the younger, college-educated salesmen was justified by the evidence available. He recalled that several of these men in country territories had done better on their May sales quotas than either Brooks or Nelson. He was proud of his self-restraint when he commented, "Selling in a country territory is certainly different."

"That's right, Dave, I wanted to make sure you understood these things before I told you." Nelson was nervously massaging his double chin between his thumb and forefinger.

Thomas looked at him with a quizzical expression. "Told me what."

"I have just been talking to Mr. Jackson. Well, I was talking to him about an understanding between Harvey and me. We always agreed that if anything should happen to the other, or he should retire, or something—well, we agreed that the one who remained should get to take over his choice of the other's accounts. We told "H. L." about this and he said, "Boys, what's O.K. by you is O.K. by me. You two developed that territory and you deserve to be rewarded for it." Well, yes sir, that's the way it was."

Without pausing, Nelson went on, "I just told Mr. Jackson about it. He said that he remembered talking about the whole thing with 'H. L.' 'Yes,' he said, 'Tell Thomas about it,' he said, 'Tell Thomas about it.' Harvey and I went over his accounts on Sunday. I went over his list of accounts with him and checked the ones that I want. Here is the list with the accounts all checked off.[3] I already know nearly all the proprietors. You'll see that—"

"Wait a minute, Cliff! Wait a minute!" Thomas interrupted. "You've lost me completely. In the first place, if there is any assignment of accounts to be made, I'll do it. It will be done on a basis that is fair to the salesmen concerned and profitable to the company. You know that."

"Dave, I'm only asking for what is fair," Nelson's face was flushed. Thomas noticed that the man he had always believed to be deliberately confident and self-possessed was now so agitated that it was difficult for him to speak. "I don't want my territory chopped up and handed to some green kid."

Thomas noticed that everybody in the office was now watching Nelson. "Calm down, Cliff," he whispered to the salesman, indicating with a nod of his head that others were watching.

"Don't talk to me that way, you young squirt!" replied Nelson. "I don't care. A man with 25 years' service deserves some consideration!"

"You're absolutely right, Cliff. You're absolutely right." As Thomas repeated his words, Nelson settled back in his chair. The typewriters started clattering again.

"Now, first of all, Cliff," queried Thomas, as he tried to return the conversation to a friendly basis, "where did you get the idea that your territory was going to be 'chopped up'?"

"You said so yourself. You said it at the very first sales meeting when you made that speech about how you were going to boost sales in Syracuse." Nelson emphasized his words by pounding on the side of the desk with his masonic ring.

Thomas reflected for a moment. He recalled giving a talk at his first sales meeting at the end of May called, "How we can do a better job for Pure Drug." The speech was a restatement of the merchandising policy of the New York office. He had mentioned that getting more profitable business would require that a larger percentage of the purchases of each account would have to come to Pure Drug; that receiving a larger share of the business from each store would require more selling time in each store; and that greater concentration on each account would require reorganization of the sales territories. He realized that his future plans did

---

[3] Nelson's selected accounts are the accounts in parentheses in Exhibit 6. Brooks's accounts that Nelson wants total $417,985 (87.7 percent of Brooks's sales in Jefferson County, 80 percent in Oswego County, or 69.4 percent of the territory total). Added to Nelson's 1969 sales, would increase his volume 65 percent to $1,063,207. Brooks's old territory would be left with $184,303 in sales.

entail reorganization of the territories; he had not anticipated, however, any such reaction as Nelson's.

Finally, Thomas said, "I do plan to make some territorial changes—not right away—at least not until I have looked things over pretty darn carefully. Of course, you understand that our first duty is to make greater profits for the company. Some of our territories would be a great deal more profitable if they were organized and handled in a different manner."

"What are you going to do about Harvey's territory?" asked Nelson.

"Well, I just haven't had a chance to study the situation yet," he replied. "If I could make the territory more profitable by reorganizing it, I guess that is what they would expect me to do." Since Thomas had not yet looked over the information about the territory, he was anxious not to commit himself to any course of action relating to it.

"What about the promises the company made to me about letting me choose the accounts I want?" the salesman asked.

"You don't mean the company's promise; you mean Mr. Schultz's promise," Thomas corrected him.

"Well, if Mr. Schultz wasn't 'the company,' I don't see how you figure that you are!" Nelson's face resumed its flush.

"O.K., Cliff. How about giving me a chance to look over the situation. You know that I want to do the right thing. Let me go over your list of the accounts you want. In a few days I can talk intelligently about the matter." Thomas felt that there was no point in carrying on the discussion.

"All right, Dave," said Nelson, rising. The two men walked toward the front entrance of the office. As they reached the top of the steps leading to the front door, Nelson turned to the sales manager and offered his hand. "Look, Dave. I'm sorry I got so mad. You just can't imagine what this means to me. I know you'll see it my way when you know the whole story." Nelson's voice sounded strained.

Thomas watched the older man leave. He felt embarrassed at the realization that Nelson's parting words had been overheard by several manufacturers' representatives standing nearby.

A Conversation with the Division Manager

Thomas decided to talk at once to Jackson about his conversation with Nelson. He walked over to Jackson's office. He hesitated in the doorway; Jackson looked up and then indicated with a gesture that Thomas was to take a seat.

The sales manager sat down. He waited for Jackson to speak. Jackson was occupied for the moment with the problem of unwrapping a cigar. Thomas opened the conversation by saying, "Clifford Nelson just stopped by to speak to me."

"Yeah?" said Jackson, removing bitten flakes of tobacco from the end of his tongue.

"He said something about getting some of Harvey Brooks's accounts when Harvey retired," Thomas said in a deliberately questioning manner.

"Yeah."

The sales manager continued, "Well, this idea of his was based on a promise that he said 'H.L.' had made."

"Yeah. He told me that, too."

"Did Schultz make such a promise?" Thomas inquired.

"Hell, I don't know. It sounds like him." He tilted back in his swivel chair.

"What shall I do about it?"

"Don't ask me; you're the sales manager." Jackson paused, holding his cigar away from his lips as if he were about to speak. Just as Thomas was about to say something, Jackson lurched forward to flick the ashes from his cigar into his ash tray. "Look here, Dave. I don't want any morale problems around here. You're the first of the 'wonder boys' to be put in charge of a department in this division. I don't want you to do anything to mess up the morale. We never had any morale problems when Schultz was alive. We don't want anything like that in this division."

Thomas was momentarily bewildered. He knew by the way that Jackson used the phrase "wonder boys" that he was referring to the college men who had been brought into the organization by Topping, the vice president in charge of sales.

Jackson went on, "Why the devil did you tell the men that you were going to reassign the sales territories without even telling me?"

"But you were there when I said it."

"Said what?"

"Well, at my first sales meeting, that one of the ways we were going to get more business was to reorganize the sales territory," Thomas replied.

"I certainly don't remember anything like that. Dave, you gave a good inspirational talk; but I sure can't remember anything about reassigning territories."

"Actually, I just mentioned the reorganization of territories in passing," the sales manager smiled.

"I'll be damned. That sort of thing is always happening. Here everybody is frothing at the mouth about something that they think we are going to do and we haven't the slightest idea why they think we're going to do it. You know, the real reason Harvey Brooks asked to be retired instead of staying on as he planned was probably this fear of having his territory reorganized. Both he and Nelson know that their pension on retirement is based on their earnings in the last five years of active employment. Now that I think of it, three or four of the other salesmen have stopped in during the last couple of weeks to tell me what a fine job they were doing. They probably had this territory reassignment bogey on their minds."

Jackson's cigar was no longer burning. He began groping under the papers on his desk for a match.

Thomas took advantage of this pause in the conversation. "Mr. Jackson, I think there are some real advantages to be won by an adjustment of the sales territories. I think . . .”

“You still think that after today?” the division manager asked in a sarcastic tone.

“Why, yes! The profit we make on sales to an individual account is related closely to delivery expense. The larger the total proportion of the account’s business we get, the more profit we make because the delivery expense remains more or less constant.”

“Look, Dave. You college men always have everything all figured out with slide rules, but sometimes that doesn’t count. Morale is the important thing. The salesmen won’t stand for having their territories changed. I know that you have four trainees that you’d like to put out on parts of territories belonging to some of the more experienced men—bam! God knows, maybe we could get 40 percent of the business. That is what the New York office watches for. The sales manager who increases his division’s share of the market gets the promotions when they come along. I know Mr. Topping transferred my men—bam! God knows how many of our good salesmen would be left. Now, I’ve never had any trouble with sales force morale since I’ve been manager of this division. Old Schultz, bless his soul, never let me down. He wasn’t any damn Ph.D., but, by golly, he could handle men. Don’t get off on the wrong foot with the boys, Dave. With the labor situation in the warehouse being what it is, I’ve just got too much on my mind. I don’t want you to be creating more problems than I can handle. How ’bout it, boy!” Jackson ground out his half-smoked cigar, looking steadily at Thomas.

Thomas was upset because the division manager had imputed to him a lack of concern for morale problems. He had always thought of himself as being very considerate of the thoughts and feelings of others. He realized that at the moment his foremost desire was to get away from Jackson.

Thomas rose from his chair saying, “Mr. Jackson, you can count on me. I know you are right about this morale business.”

“Atta boy,” said the division manager. “It does us a lot of good to talk like this once in a while. Now, you see if you can make peace with the salesmen. I want you to handle everything yourself.”

“Well, thanks a lot,” said the sales manager, as he backed out of the office door.

As he walked through the office after talking with Jackson, he saw two manufacturers’ representatives with whom he had appointments already seated near the receptionist’s desk. His schedule of appointments that day did not permit him to do more than gather the material pertaining to the Nelson and Brooks territories.

Mr. Thomas Goes Home

Thomas left the office shortly after 5 o’clock to drive to his home in a suburb of Syracuse. It was a particularly hot and humid day. Pre-fourth-of-July traffic lengthened the drive by nearly 20 minutes. When he finally turned into his own driveway, he felt as though his skin were caked with grime and perspiration. He got out of the car and walked around the house to the terrace in the rear. Betsy, his wife, was sewing in a deck chair under the awning.

"Hello, Dave. You're late," she said, looking up with a smile.

"I know it. Even the traffic was bad today." He dropped his coat on a glass-topped table and sprawled out full length on the glider. "Honestly, I'm so exhausted and dirty that I am disgusted with myself."

"Bad day?"

"Awful. You just can't imagine how discouraging it is trying to get this job organized. You would think that it would be obvious to everybody that what ails the Syracuse division is the organization of the sales force," said Thomas, arranging a pillow under his head.

"I didn't realize that you thought anything was wrong with the Syracuse division."

"Well, what I mean is that we get only 20 percent of the potential wholesale business. If I could organize the sales force my way—well, God knows, maybe we could get 40 percent of the business. That is what the New York office watches for. The sales manager who increases his division's share of the market gets the promotions when they come along. I know Mr. Topping transferred me to this division because he knew these possibilities existed."

"I don't understand. Is Mr. Topping still your boss, or is Mr. Jackson?" asked his wife.

"Betsy, it's terribly discouraging. Mr. Jackson is my boss, but I'll never get anywhere with Pure Drug unless Mr. Topping and the other people in New York promote me."

"Don't you like Mr. Jackson?"

"I had a run-in with him today."

"You didn't!" she said crossly as she laid her sewing aside.

Thomas had not anticipated this reaction. He gazed up at the awning as if he did not notice his wife's intent expression. "We didn't argue particularly. He just—well, he doesn't know too much about sales management. He put his foot down on my plans to reorganize the territories."

"I can't understand why you would go and get yourself into a fight with your boss when you haven't been here even two months. We should never have bought this house."

"Honestly, honey, I didn't have any fight. Everything is O.K. He just—well, do you want me to be a divisional manager all my life?"

She smiled and said nothing.

He continued, "I'm sorry you married such a grouch, but I just get plain mad when somebody called me a wonder boy."

"You're tired," she said sympathetically. "Why don't you go up and take a shower while I feed the children. We can have a drink and then eat our dinner whenever we feel like it. It's only meat loaf, anyway."

"That sounds wonderful," he said, raising himself from his prone position.

An Unexpected Caller

Thomas had just stepped out of the shower when he heard his wife calling to him. "Dave, Fred Taylor is here to see you."

"Tell him I'll be down in just a minute. Give him a drink, Betsy."

As he dressed, Thomas wondered why the salesman had chosen the dinner hour to call. During the month since he had moved into his new home, no salesman had ever dropped in uninvited.

When Thomas came downstairs, he found Taylor on the living room couch with a gin and tonic in his hand.

"Hello, Fred," said Thomas crossing the room with his right hand extended. "You look as if you had a hot day. Why don't you take off your coat? If we go out to the terrace, you may get a chance to cool off."

"Thanks, Dave," the visitor said as he moved out to the terrace. "I'm sorry to come barging in this way, but I thought it was important."

"Well, what's on your mind?" said Thomas as he sat down.

Taylor started to speak but hesitated as Mrs. Thomas came out of the door with two glasses in her hand. She handed one glass to Mr. Thomas, then excused herself, saying, "I think I better see if the children are all right."

After she had disappeared into the house, Taylor said, "I heard about what happened at the office today, so I thought I'd come over to tell you that we stand 100 percent behind you."

Thomas was perplexed by Taylor's words. He realized that the incident to which the salesman referred was probably his meeting with Nelson. Thomas said, "I'm not sure what you mean, Fred."

"I heard that you and Nelson had it out this morning about changing the sales territories," Taylor replied.

Thomas smiled. Two thoughts entered his mind. He was amused at the proportions that the brief conversation of that morning had assumed in the minds of so many people; but, at the same time, he was curious as to how Taylor, who had presumably been in the field selling, had heard about the incident so soon. Without hesitation he asked, "Where did you hear about this, Fred?"

"Bill Murray told me! He was down at the warehouse with Walter Miller when I stopped off to pick up a special narcotics order for a customer. They are all excited about this territory business. Murray said Nelson came out to his house at lunch time and told him about it. Everybody figured that you were going to change the territories when you started traveling around with each of the boys, especially after what you said at your first sales meeting."

"Well, the reason I went on the road with each of the men, Fred," said Thomas, "was so that I could learn more about their selling problems and, at the same time, meet the customers."

Taylor smiled, "Sure, but when you started filling out a rating sheet on each account, I couldn't help thinking you had some reason for it."

Thomas realized that the salesmen had spoken with irony in his voice, but he thought it was better to let the matter pass as if he had not noticed it. Since he was planning to use the information that he gathered for reorganization of the sales territories, he decided that he would be frank with Taylor in order to find out what the young salesman's reaction might be on the question of territorial changes. He said, "Fred, I've thought a lot about making some changes in the territories—"

Taylor interrupted him. "That's terrific. I'm sure glad to hear that. I don't like to speak ill of the dead, but old Schultz really gave the trainees the short end of the stick when he put us on territories. He either gave a man a territory of uncontacted accounts so he beat his head against a stone wall until he finally quit, and that is just what happened to two guys who trained with me, or else he gave him a territory where somebody had to be replaced and where some of the best accounts had been handed over to one of the older salesmen. Well, I know for a fact that when I took over my territory from Mike Green, Bill Murray and Albert Simpson got 12 of Green's best accounts. And, damn it, I got more sales out of what was left than Green ever did, but Murray and Simpson's total sales didn't go up at all. It took me a while, but, by golly, I had the laugh at every sales meeting when our monthly sales figures were announced."

"Is that right?" said Thomas.

"Damn right! And I wasn't the only one. That's why those old duffers are so down on the four of us that have come with the division since the mid-1960s. We've beaten them at their own game."

"Do you think that Harrington and Howard and Donnelly feel the same way?" asked Thomas.

"Think, hell! I know it! That's all we ever talk about. If you reorganize those territories and give us back the accounts that Schultz took away, you'll see some real sales records. Take, for example, the Medical Arts Pharmacy out by Mercy Hospital. Bill Murray got that one away from my territory and he calls there only once a week. If I could get that one back, I'd get in there three times a week and get five times as much business."

Thomas had to raise his hands in a gesture of protest. "Don't you have enough accounts already, Fred, to keep you busy?"

"Dave, I spend 50 hours a week on the road and I love it; but I know damn well that if I put some of the time I spend in 'two-by-four' stores into some of those big juicy accounts like Medical Arts Pharmacy, I'd do even more business."

Thomas commented, "I'm not particularly anxious to argue the point now, but if you start putting your time into Medical Arts Pharmacy, what's going to happen to your sales to the 'two-by-four' stores?"

The salesman replied, "Those druggists all know me. They'd go right on buying."

Thomas did not agree with Taylor, and he thought that the salesman realized this.

After a moment of silence, Taylor rose from his chair saying, "I'd better scoot home. My wife will be waiting for me with a rolling pin for being late so I'd better get out before your wife gets at me with a skillet." Taylor laughed heartily at his own joke.

The two men walked around the house to Taylor's car. As the salesman climbed into the car, he said, "Dave, don't forget what I said, Harrington, Howard, Donnelly, and I stand 100 percent behind you. You won't ever hear us talk about going over to a competitor!"

"Who's talking about that?" asked Thomas.

"Well," said Taylor as he started the motor and shifted into gear, "I don't want to tell tales out of school."

"Sure," Thomas said quickly. "I'm sorry I asked. So long, Fred. I'll see you soon."

Thomas watched the salesman back out of the driveway and drive away.

Case 3–3
Sierra Chemical Company (A)[*]

Jay Rossi, newly appointed marketing vice president for the Sierra Chemical Company, was troubled about his firm's ability to execute an effective sales program. Although Sierra seemed to be recovering from a leveling off of sales in late 1974 and early 1975, it was not at all obvious that sales performance was up to potential. Unfortunately, Jay had inherited a primitive (at best) sales information system and was not particularly experienced in the chemical fertilizer industry; hence, he wasn't sure what were appropriate performance standards. He was concerned, therefore, about how to take hold of the sales operation: what performance to expect; what reports to institute; what compensation and evaluation systems to install; what standards to impose.

Sierra Products and Markets

Sierra produced and sold slow-release fertilizers, Osmocote® and Agriform™ by name.[1] Small pellets in form, almost like BBs, the products were coated with a patented rosin material. This coating had tiny pores which allowed small amounts of water to seep into the fertilizer ingredients, which were then released at a predictable rate (i.e., over two months, four months, six months, etc.). Sierra product uniqueness was in the coating (the manufacturing process) and product form, not in the fertilizer. Fertilizer is primarily a standard commodity, consisting of varying proportions of nitrates, phosphates, and potassium. Growers buy different combinations, depending upon individual needs.

Growers could apply fertilizer three ways: by liquid feeding systems, by dry application to the soil, or by slow release. The greatest tonnage of fertilizer was sold in dry form to agricultural markets and consisted of the three essential ingredients named above. Prices per ton were in the $100 to $150 range.

Slow-release products were designed for specialty markets not the huge field crops such as corn, wheat etc. There were three important specialty markets: (1) commercial growers (nurseries and greenhouses), (2) landscape specialists, and (3) row crops (strawberries, tomatoes, etc.). It was estimated that slow-release fertilizers were distributed in these three markets in the proportions 60 percent, 10 percent, and 30 percent.

Slow-release fertilizers, however, were not without competition in the specialty markets. Growers also used dry and liquid alternatives, often in combina-

---

[*] Copyright 1977 by the Board of Trustees of the Leland Stanford Junior University. Used with permission.

[1] Agriform represented 10 percent of Sierra sales and was sold only as a landscape product—that is, it was bought by commercial landscapers. The same distributors handled this product as Osmocote®, and it was sold by the same Sierra representatives. Hence, for the rest of this case, Agriform™ remains unmentioned but can be assumed to run parallel to Osmocote®.

tion. Whether a grower used dry, liquid, or slow-release fertilizers was a function of his particular plants, prejudices, soil and weather conditions, and timing problems (i.e., Did he want to "force bloom" roses for Mother's Day?). It was not unusual, therefore, to find use of all three application techniques within a single establishment. Most growers were convinced, needless to say, that they were experts at growing their particular product(s).

Liquid systems typically made use of locally supplied fertilizer ingredients. The problem with liquid systems was that they were continuous and many of the nutrients were washed or leached away. Dry fertilizers were limited by the fact that release was not controlled, and application might be required several times during the season.

There were a number of large (as well as small) competitors in dry, liquid, and slow-release fertilizers. For example, firms like International Chemical, Scott, Swift, Dupont, and Hercules were important competitors. Urea formaldehyde was a controlled-release product, as were some of Scott's items. Osmocote was the only product, however, which controlled the release of all three fertilizer ingredients.

It was estimated by Sierra management that slow-release products were gaining share in the total specialty markets and accounted for almost 35 percent of the market in 1976. One out of four nursery plants was grown on Osmocote®, and it was the only national label in its segment.

There were many reasons, of course, why growers accepted or rejected Osmocote®. On the positive side:

1. It produced better plants—greener, healthier, faster, more consistently.
2. It was safer—reduced the chance of error (human or environmental).
3. It saved money—primarily in labor savings versus other dry types; in less raw material waste versus liquid feeds.

And on the negative side:

1. Its initial price was high—four times normal fertilizers and two times most slow-release types.
2. It was inflexible—once applied it went! There was no way to slow it down, speed it up, or stop it.

Growers tended to be concentrated—in southern California, northern California, and the Seattle-Portland belt; Florida, North Carolina, and Connecticut; Texas, Wisconsin, and Ohio. Growers were reached through distributors, who carried thousands of items and regularly serviced their accounts. Manufacturer salesmen, such as Sierra's, were supposed to establish and maintain distribution and do missionary selling among nurserymen. For instance, in creating a new grower-user, it was essential that the grower set up some test plantings, measure the results, and compare these results with alternative fertilizing techniques. Distributor salesmen were not effective in this kind of selling; they were primarily sources of supply for already established users. Moreover, test plantings took time.

The nursery business was heavily populated (1976) with "cottage type" operations. Large 100-plus acre nurseries were important, but Sierra's real expansion had been among "start-ups" with one to five acres under shade but planning to add more each year. As a rule of thumb, each new acre was a potential one-ton sale for Sierra. There were several thousand such small operators.

Osmocote®, by 1976, was the single most important specialty fertilizer on the market and was well known and regarded among commercial growers and state extension agents. The agents were important product endorsers, since they were the acknowledged experts. Their "stamp of approval" was virtually mandatory, though approval by no means guaranteed purchase. A summary of the product lines and markets is contained in Exhibit 1 (company brochure).

Sales, by 1976, had reached 247,494 units or $4 million. The following table summarizes the company's unit sales during the past six years, with 1977 forecasted.

Sales in units 150-pound bags

	1971	1972	1973	1974	1975	1976 est.	1977 est.
Domestic	111,290	147,639	214,043	233,666	211,315	247,494	305,956
Foreign ..	6,932	6,659	22,900	47,834	36,028	82,600	104,000

The company traced its history to Agriform of Woodland, which was later acquired by Leslie Salt. In 1967, a new venture capital team purchased the company from Leslie and established it as the Sierra Chemical Company in Newark, California, after combining its Agriform technology with a fertilizer rosin coating process developed by Archer Daniel Midland (Osmocote®). A final series of transactions resulted in a new management takeover in 1971 under Robert Severns as president.

By the middle of 1976, Sierra was beginning to generate a healthier cash position, although funds were not plentiful by any means. Jay Rossi estimated that the company could probably borrow $500,000 from banks if it had to. Current assets exceeded current liabilities in the ratio of 1.3 to 1.0. The company had moved to a new plant in Milpitas, California, during 1973, and in 1976, the plant was operating at 50 percent of capacity.

Rossi Hired

By 1975, Sierra had experienced a slow but reasonable growth. Dollar sales were steadily rising and business was beginning to develop in Europe. In the United States, penetration of particular markets was encouraging, such as tomatoes and strawberries, but the overall situation was deceptive. Between 1973 and 1975, the potential market grew an estimated 30 percent, but Sierra's unit sales were fairly flat. Inflation and European dollar sales had disguised the domestic unit sales problem.

Exhibit 1

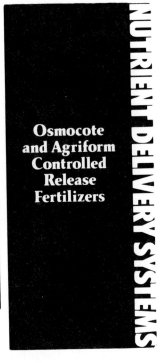

Agriform controlled release fertilizer provides safe, efficient nutrients for all landscaping applications.
Agriform is an advanced controlled release fertilizer specially developed for a variety of landscaping projects. Agriform is available in two formulations: 20-6-10 for a 3 to 4 month term, and 16-7-12 + Iron for a 5 to 6 month term.

Agriform Planting Tablets provide safe, economical feeding for a full two years.
Agriform 20-10-5 Planting Tablets are a non-burning, long lasting complete fertilizer for root zone feeding of trees, shrubs and ground covers. Used for new plantings or the feeding of established stock, Agriform is superior to granular products or nutrient spikes. Agriform Planting Tablets feed fully for 2 years from a single application.

Agriform Container Tablets provide plants a complete diet of essential nutrients.
Agriform 14-4-6 Container Tablets have been designed for surface application on pot plants or container grown nursery stock. The gradual release of nutrients virtually eliminates the danger of salt injury when tablets are used as directed.

Agriform Starter Tablets for specific crops.
Agriform Starter Tablets have been designed with specific formulas for particular crop needs. Starter tablets are available for new or young established forest, orchard, and vineyard plantings. All Starter Tablets provide nutrients for a full 2 years as well as offering a safe alternative to the hazards of short-lived soluble fertilizers.

Sierra Chemical Company
1001 Yosemite Drive
Milpitas, California 95035
Telephone (408) 263-8080
TWX 910-338-0565

Distributed by:

Osmocote

Product	Longevity	General Use	Specific Use
Osmocote 14-14-14	3-4 mo	Greenhouse Nursery	Pot plants, bedding plants, foliage plants, nursery stock. For use in growing media containing no soil.
Osmocote 19-6-12	3-4 mo	Greenhouse Nursery	For plants requiring high nitrogen. For use in growing media containing 25% soil or more.
Osmocote 18-6-12 Regular	8-9 mo	Nursery	For all nursery stock. For propagation and establishment of young transplants. Spring, summer or fall application.
Osmocote 18-6-12 Fast Start	8-9 mo	Nursery	For use only with established, rapidly growing plants that require nutrients immediately. Spring, summer or fall application.
Osmocote 18-5-11	12-14 mo	Greenhouse Nursery	For mild climate, long season areas; spring and summer use on long term crops. Not generally used for fall feeding. For long term greenhouse crops, roses, carnations.
Osmocote 14-14-14 Retail Pack	3-4 mo	Home & Garden	House plants, flowers, and vegetables.
Osmocote 18-6-12 Retail Pack	8-9 mo	Home & Garden	House plants, flowers, and vegetables.

Agriform

Product	Longevity	General Use	Specific Use
Agriform 16-7-12 + Iron	5-6 mo	Landscaping	Turf, hydroseeding, flowers and ground covers, trees and shrubs
Agriform 21-6-8	3-6 mo	Landscaping	Maintenance of turf, ground cover and landscape plants
Agriform 18-18-6	3-6 mo	Landscaping	Establishment of turf, ground cover and landscape plants
Agriform Planting Tablets			
Planting Tablets 20-10-5	24 mo	Landscaping	New tree and shrub plantings, established trees and shrubs, liners, ground covers, perennials
Agriform retail pack 20-10-5	24 mo	Home Landscaping	New tree and shrub plantings, established trees and shrubs, ground covers, perennials
Container Tablets 14-4-6	3-4 mo	Nursery Greenhouse	Pot plants, retail nursery stock
Orchard Starter Tablet 26-8-4	24 mo	Orchards	New plantings on young established trees
Grape Starter Tablet 28-8-4	24 mo	Vineyard	New plantings or young established vines
Forest Starter Tablet 22-8-2	24 mo	Tree farms	Xmas trees, reforestation, land reclamation
Forest Starter Tablet 18-8-4	24 mo	Tree farms	Xmas trees, reforestation, land reclamation. This formulation used in magnesium deficient areas as in N.E. U.S.

Osmocote is the most economical, efficient controlled release fertilizer available.
Osmocote provides a steady, continuous metering of N-P-K nutrients corresponding closely to the requirements of all nursery stock. This prolonged, constant feeding helps ensure an ideal level of nutrients for optimum plant growth.

One application of Osmocote lasts for an entire crop cycle.
Osmocote is available in a variety of formulations: 3 to 4 months, 8 to 9 months and 12 to 14 months. This offers the grower a nutrient release rate based on individual crop cycles.

Osmocote is safe and efficient.
There is virtually no risk of burning plants with Osmocote when used at recommended rates. Nutrients are released approximately 1% per day with the 3 to 4 month formulations, 0.4% per day with the 8 to 9 month formulations, and 0.25% per day with the 12 to 14 month formulation.

Osmocote is economical.
There is less labor cost and management concerns involved with the use of Osmocote because one application is sufficient for an entire crop cycle. And, since Osmocote is resistant to leaching loss, the grower also saves on materials.

Osmocote releases nutrients as plants need them.
The rate of nutrient release from Osmocote is *not* significantly affected by:
· soil moisture levels
· total volume of water applied
· External salt concentration of the soil
· Soil pH
· Soil bacteria
   Nutrient release from Osmocote is *only* affected by changes in soil temperature. The release rate increases as the soil warms, and decreases as the soil cools, therefore corresponding to plant needs.

Then suddenly, in October of 1974, Sierra sales growth ground to a halt for six to eight months. The economy was bad, but that didn't seem to be the entire explanation. Growers were still in business; they just appeared to be turning away from Osmocote® and its higher prices, and substituting alternative fertilizers. In an attempt to better understand the real problem, the president made a number of field visits. He was appalled at the level of sales performance. The salesmen were not aggressive, appeared to consider themselves as advisors and horticultural experts to the growers, and blamed the distributors for all their selling problems. While it had been true that this type of advisory selling was desirable in the early introduction of the controlled-release fertilizer, this innovation stage of the selling cycle had been over by 1970.

Some indication of the firm's lack of sales aggressiveness could be inferred from the then-existing job description of regional managers, i.e., salesmen (Exhibit 2), and one typical salesman's call report (Exhibit 3). The decision was made, therefore, to bring in an experienced and professional marketing executive. Continued success, it seemed, would require a new look in both sales and marketing.

Jay Rossi was offered the job. Not only had he enjoyed a successful career in marketing, but he had been a consultant to Sierra. Bob Severns and his management team knew and respected Jay. And Jay knew enough about the Sierra products and markets to be optimistic about the future. There were, to be sure, some short-term problems. For half of the previous six quarters, for example, Sierra experienced losses in operations. Cash itself was tight. Not only were all sales factored, but projections for 1975 indicated that cash flow would be barely enough to cover a bank repayment due in January.

Jay Rossi had graduated from Stanford University and its Business School and spent four years at Maxwell House in product management; seven years at Basic Vegetable Products Company (San Francisco) as marketing manager; 18 months as an independent consultant; and six months as vice president of marketing for Saga Corporation. He left Saga with no ill feelings, since Saga management recognized that the Sierra offer was "one in a lifetime."

Jay arrived at Sierra in May 1975 and took immediate stock of his situation in terms of people, he inherited the following:

1. *David Martin (sales manager)*—age 62; highly competent and experienced, a slow release fertilizer salesman since 1957 (in the predecessor company) and sales manager since 1973. Dave had earlier owned a range of greenhouses and three retail outlets in Wisconsin and was a well-known and respected member of the industry. He was an active member, for example, of many important industry committees.

2. *William K. McFarland (marketing manager)*—age 53; very strong in advertising and publicity. A frequent contributor of articles to trade magazines and the "book editor" of *Nursery Business* magazine. He admittedly had no interest in profit and loss statements, nor did he enjoy his management responsibilities.

3. *Tom James (regional manager or salesman)*—age 32; a horticultural graduate

Exhibit 2
Job description—regional manager
(i.e., salesman)

The regional manager is responsible for the representation of the company, its products, and policies to customers, distributors, dealers, and the general public within his area. The manager is responsible for maintaining contact with universities, experiment stations, corporate research facilities, and other areas where technical interest may be expressed in controlled-release fertilizers. He strives to maintain a favorable public relations image for the company in his territory and works in conjunction with the advertising and sales promotion manager as required.

He is responsible for the securing, training, and supervision of distributors for Sierra products within his territory. The following specific responsibilities apply:

1. Selection and evaluation of candidate distributors.
2. Recommendation of distributor appointments to home office.
3. Training of distributor salesmen to acceptable levels of product knowledge and proficiency.
4. Establishment of goals and programs with the distributor to provide acceptable sales levels for our products.
5. Maintain overview of distributor's operations to be certain that they are conducted on a businesslike and creditworthy basis.
6. Maintain distributor interest in our programs, products, and activities so that vigorous representation of our products to the trade is maintained.

The manager will be responsible for a knowledge of the market within his territory. This knowledge shall include:

1. The major users and customers within the area.
2. The size, location, and trends of the various markets within the region.
3. Advice to the home office on business opportunities requiring development of new products or adaptation of existing products to new opportunities.
4. Investigation of new crops or uses or industries as may be requested and directed by the main office.

The manager is responsible for securing and maintaining an acceptable sales level within his region.

1. An annual sales plan will be prepared and presented to management for acceptance.
2. Quotas for distributors will be assigned and discussed with the responsible distributor personnel.
3. Adequate representation of our products to meet sales plan throughout the region by dealers or distributors is required.
4. Performance of distributors and dealers in compliance with the distributor agreements is the responsibility of the regional manager.
5. Development of sales programs specifically tailored to an area or region as may be required to develop and maintain sales.
6. Giving advice to dealers and distributors on the most profitable ways for them to handle Sierra Chemical Company's product line is also within the regional manager area.

The regional manager is responsible for the investigation and evaluation of complaints registered by customers.

1. A report of the situation as determined by personal investigation will be made to the home office, attention technical director.
2. A recommendation on the disposition of the complaint will be made by the regional manager to the operating vice president.
3. A complaint settlement up to $200 invoiced cost may be made by the regional manager at his own discretion.

The regional manager is further responsible for the following activities.

1. Preparation of an expense budget for the operation of the region each year, and operation within the accepted budget level.
2. Recommendations for attendance at regional trade shows.
3. Maintaining office complete with necessary records for distributor followup, correspondence with customers, and activity reports to sales management.

Exhibit 3

To: David Martin
From: George Parker
Subject: Call Report for the week of May 25, 1975

Harvey Blake Poinsettia Ranch, Sonoma, California

We were able to confirm this morning that the problem in the stock bench area at the ranch was twofold, as Harvey and I suspected but previously were unable to confirm:

1. The rooted cuttings were slightly infected with pythium when they were set out in the stock benches. Mr. Metkin at Soil & Plant Laboratory had earlier confirmed this point and further indicated that poinsettia plants could, in fact, recover from a slight infection of pythium.
2. The workers assigned to apply Osmocote to the surface of the test benches were using a drop-type spreader, the result being that several of the particles of the Osmocote were crushed. Sally Jones, their in-house technical advisor, further stated that when the Osmocote granules would clog up the applicator, the workers merely lifted the spreader and forced the wheels around until they again moved freely. The Osmocote was substantially worked into the top six inches of planting bed with a rototiller, which would tend to erase any severely turned areas across the bench.

Dave, we understand that all of the principals of the Blake organization are away on their annual selling trip, but when they return, I will make sure that they are aware of the cause of the earlier damage.

B & D Wholesale Nursery

I left a sample of our Osmocote 18-5-11 with Mr. Bill Ramsey, who is the head grower for their container division. We outlined a trial for Bill similar to the one we have set out earlier at Valborg's Nursery, and I'll be checking back with Bill in 3–4 weeks to make sure that the trial was set out in a proper manner.

John Liddicoat, who is in charge of their rose breeding program, is also the man we'll have to talk to about setting up Osmocote trials in their field-grown roses. John is already aware, as previously reported, of the benefits derived from using Osmocote, and there is a good chance we can get him to begin using the product in certain sandy fields this next February.

Our first meeting with John was rather brief, due to a previous commitment on his part, and John is now away on a six-week business trip through Europe. I plan to see him as soon as he returns from his trip and will keep you posted as to the progress we make.

Willamette Chemical, Eugene

The recent ten-ton (approximately) order from this company should have been a full truckload and reflects a continuing desire on the part of our major distributor to carry a reduced inventory in the hope that prices on all fertilizer products will eventually come down.

I'm having a meeting the week of June 16th with Steve Lookabill, who is in charge of specialty sales programs through the various branch offices. I told Steve that we would shortly be selling some of the major accounts on a direct basis in the Salem basin, but there was still a huge potential in that area that was not being tapped by any of our present distributors.

I feel this company has a place in our chain of distributors, even though they did not sell their initial truckload as quickly as we would have liked. I feel that Steve in his new position will certainly enhance our total sales program.

Eureka Plant Growers

I reported earlier that Eureka had placed a small initial order for Osmocote through Willamette Chemical, and I was supposed to meet him at the Summit growing grounds this morning to instruct the workers on the proper amount of Osmocote to apply to each can. Little did we know that the Immigration Department was going to raid their field yesterday, so they are without help for two or three weeks until workers can get back up and begin working again.

I reported earlier that George is having middle management problems and has a new grower in charge of the Summit growing grounds, so it may be a while until we really get the program started here, even though we have sold the merchandise and made the initial delivery.

Exhibit 3 *(concluded)*

Butler's Mill, Crescent City

Open house was a tremendous success, both in terms of general interest in our product line and the number of people who attended. Between 200 and 300 people came to the exhibit area (outside) between 10:00 A.M. and 2:00 P.M., and it seemed that most of them either knew about Osmocote or were using one of our products, and I was extremely grateful for Dick Spray's assistance during this time.

We picked up several good leads of people who deserve a follow-up call, and we'll certainly sell a lot more merchandise as a result of being at this meeting.

The dealers-only portion of the open house was held in the evening between 5:00 and 7:00 P.M. Approximately 36 dealers showed up, and although many of them were from the various chain store garden departments, we did sell three new Green Green accounts. In addition, there was a great deal of interest in Green Green on the part of both Sears & Roebuck and Handyman, so we should begin to see real movement of this product in the Del Norte County area. Dick Spray was going to spend all day Friday, the 30th, detailing some of the region accounts in the Crescent City area and will be anxious to hear how well he is able to do.

---

from Ohio. Work experience with Procter & Gamble, Horticultural Division. He was an excellent salesman but weak on administration, i.e., paper work, reports.

4. *George Parker (salesman)*—age 45; one of Martin's first hires in the predecessor company (early 1960s). He had an excellent understanding of horticulture matters.

5. *Dick Smith (salesman)*—age 45; with Sierra since 1972. Smith previously sold insurance and fertilizer on the East Coast. An "old time, stand up and tell you what you have to do" salesman.

6. *James Van Horn (salesman)*—age 26; an ex-plant superintendent who asked for a field selling assignment and seemed to be floundering.

7. *George Schwartz (technical director)*—age 52; the "dean" of slow-release fertilizer technology and the company's best asset "as a spokesman." A sought-after speaker, careful scientist, well acquainted with major growers, Schwartz had a master's degree in horticulture.

A complete organization chart follows:

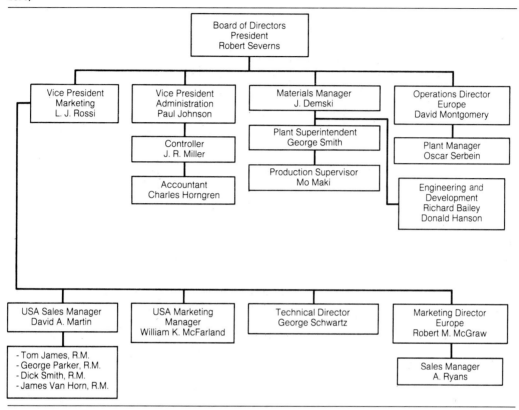

What Rossi Found

It didn't take Jay Rossi long to discover that David Martin was right in his diagnosis of the problem: Here was a department with little direction, strategy, controls, or leadership. For example, there were no records that indicated how the company was doing with its various lines in different markets. Field reports were filled in sporadically, and forecasting was naive. Weekly reports were sometimes backed up in the system for two weeks by the two typists. Phone calls were used to get things accomplished, since reports were useless. Penetration rates were rarely known, potentials were guesses at best, and most sales efforts seemed to be reactive. There was no professional selling. Servicing old accounts and distributors was the philosophy—prospecting was given little priority. In short, the management mode was reactionary. All information was after the fact. "We were always putting out fires." Quotas were ignored, and compensation was by salary.

An extended field trip confirmed Jay Rossi's fears about the sales force. The first man he contacted, for example, criticized his "dumb distributors," complained about the tough market situation, and never even talked about Osmocote's® advantages to a new customer because "he didn't ask." The second salesman evidenced reasonable activity but had neither a sense of urgency nor any apparent professional selling skills. The third man was a great salesman but terrible in managing his time. He would spend hours driving between calls and averaged only 2.9 calls per day (which was also the company average).

All of them seemed to blame their problems on the distributors. Their calls to users were courtesy calls; the men didn't feel that they were supposed to "sell." It was apparent, furthermore, that the group believed strongly in a number of "principles":

1. You can't do much about sales in the short run. After all, growers were reluctant to try a new technique until they had been conditioned, educated, and made confident that the new supplier was reliable. And this took time.
2. Salesmen had to be horticulturists. Because controlled-release fertilizers were a technical innovation and commercial growing a scientific endeavor, it was obvious that horticultural skill was the most important prerequisite for a field salesman. His advice and counsel were crucial if he was to successfully convert growers into Osmocote® users.
3. The product was expensive and therefore hard to sell (a typical price was $650 per ton).
4. Quality was irregular and a problem to the salesmen in the field.
5. Comparison between salesmen and regions was not possible because of the great differences between various parts of the market.
6. Distributors are not on "our team" but rather are "our customers." And you can't ask your customers to do things for you!

Rossi's Challenge

As Jay Rossi and sales manager David Martin saw their problem, it was to:

1. Change the attitude of the sales force from horticultural specialists to aggressive salesmen.
2. Introduce controls that would direct the salesmen toward a more productive use of their time.
3. Establish new incentive systems that would redirect the selling effort.
4. Give the organization a sense of mission and direction.

Case 3–4
Supersonic Stereo, Inc.

"At this rate, I'll be looking for a new job," thought Bob Basler, sales manager of Supersonic's Atlanta district. "Our sales are stagnant, and what's worse, our profits are down." Sales and profit results for the last five years did not measure up to objectives established for the Atlanta district (see Exhibit 1). Basler knew that very shortly he would be hearing from Pete Lockhart, Supersonic's national sales manager, and that the same question would be asked: "When are you going to turn the Atlanta district around?"

Exhibit 1
Total sales and profit for the Atlanta district, 1980–1984

	1980	1981	1982	1983	1984
Total sales....	$2,641,081	$2,445,120	$2,610,029	$2,514,113	$2,638,340
Net profit.....	13,873	14,050	15,381	16,511	14,383

Bob was faced with another problem that added to his worries. One of his sales representatives, Charlie Lyons, was very upset and was threatening to quit unless he received a substantial salary increase. Lyons felt that since he led the district in sales volume, he should be amply rewarded. "I have to find out what's happening in the Atlanta district before I go and make recommendations for salary increases," Basler thought. "Besides, if I make such a recommendation, Pete will think that I have taken leave of my senses. He will not approve any salary increases for anybody as long as the Atlanta district's performance is so weak."

Supersonic Stereo is one of the country's leading manufacturers of stereo equipment. Since its formation in 1962, Supersonic has experienced rapid growth, based largely on its reputation for high-quality stereo products. Prices were competitive, although some dealers engaged in discounting. Supersonic distributed its stereo equipment on a selective basis. Only those dealers who could provide strong marketing support and reliable servicing were selected by Supersonic. Dealers were supported by Supersonic's national advertising campaign. Advertising averaged 5 percent of sales, somewhat more than what other stereo manufacturers spent for this item.

Supersonic's sales force was compensated with salary plus commission of 6 percent based on gross margin. Gross margin was used to discourage sales representatives from cutting prices. Accounts were assigned to sales representatives based on size. New sales representatives were usually assigned a number of small accounts at first. As they progressed, they were assigned larger accounts. The more experienced sales representatives were assigned the larger, more desirable accounts. In some cases, a sales representative would have only three or four accounts, each averaging $250,000 a year.

The average base salary for the sales force reached $26,500 in 1984. Commissions averaged $9,500 in 1984. Total average sales force compensation was $36,000 in 1984. Travel expenses were paid by Supersonic. The total package was considered by one executive to be too plush. This executive, Stella Jordan, felt that not enough was expected from the sales force. "I know of one sales representative who calls on three accounts and in 1983 earned $38,563," she stated at a recent meeting. "If we want to improve our profits, then we need to either reduce our base salaries or cut back our commission rate."

Jordan's suggestion was not favorably received by Basler, who felt that such a move would have a disastrous effect on sales force motivation. Stella countered by pointing out that motivation must be lacking since the Atlanta district's performance is so poor. "If salaries or commissions cannot be reduced, at least let's not raise them," she suggested. "Maybe we should consider raising quotas and not pay commissions until sales representatives exceed their quotas. Or," she continued, "maybe a management by objectives approach should be developed."

Basler knew that Jordan's comments demanded a response. He also knew that she was talking about Charlie Lyons when she mentioned a sales representative with three accounts earning $38,563. Basler suggested that he should be allowed time to do a complete cost analysis by sales representative before adopting any corrective action. Jordan agreed and offered her assistance. Salaries for the others were: Sand $24,500, Gallo $27,500, and Parks $26,000.

Basler's first activity was to identify available information for his district. He was able to secure a profit and loss statement for the Atlanta district (see Exhibit 2). Jordan suggested that since Basler was interested in sales force profitability,

Exhibit 2
Profit and loss statement, Atlanta district, 1984

Sales		$2,638,340
Cost of goods sold		2,014,485
Gross margin		$ 623,855
Expenses:		
Salaries	$177,000	
Commissions	37,431	
Advertising	131,915	
Packaging	43,642	
Warehousing and transportation	76,374	
Travel expenses	59,340	
Order processing	770	
Rent	83,000	
Total expenses		609,472
Net profit (before taxes)		$ 14,383

Exhibit 3
Allocation of natural accounts to functional accounts, Atlanta district

Natural Accounts	Functional Accounts					
	Selling Direct Costs	Selling Indirect Costs	Advertising	Order Processing	Warehouse and Transportation	Packaging
Salaries	$177,000	$106,500	$47,500		$12,000		$11,000
Commissions	37,431	37,431					
Advertising	131,915			$131,915			
Packaging	43,642						43,642
Warehousing and transportation	76,374					$76,374	
Travel expenses	59,340	57,340	2,000				
Order processing	770				770		
Rent	83,000		18,500		4,500	40,000	20,000
Total expenses	$609,472	$201,271	$68,000	$131,915	$17,270	$116,374	$74,642

Exhibit 4
Product line sales and costs

Product	Selling Price per Unit	Cost per Unit	Gross Margin per Unit	Number Sold in Period	Sales in Period	Advertising Expenditures	Packaging
Receivers	$250	$212	$38	3,151	$ 787,750	$ 40,000	$ 6,302
Turntables	85	64	21	12,079	1,026,715	50,000	24,158
Speakers	125	87	38	6,591	823,875	40,000	13,182
				21,821	$2,638,340	$130,000	$43,642

his next step should be to allocate the natural accounts in Exhibit 2 to their appropriate functional accounts. Exhibit 3 shows the results of this step.

"If we are going to do an analysis by sales representative, we need much more information," Stella indicated. To help in this regard, she compiled product sales data (see Exhibit 4).

Basler provided data for each sales representative, showing number of sales calls, number of orders, and unit sales by product line (see Exhibit 5). The next step would be to compile the data to develop a profitability analysis by sales representative.

Exhibit 5
Sales calls, orders, and units sold
by salesperson

Salesperson	Number of Sales Calls	Number of Orders	Number of Units Sold			
			Receivers	Turntables	Speakers	Total
Paul Sand........	85	60	668	2,652	1,534	4,854
Diane Gallo	105	85	823	3,270	1,582	5,675
Kathy Parks	110	60	816	3,131	1,578	5,525
Charlie Lyons	170	75	844	3,026	1,897	5,767
	470	280	3,151	12,079	6,591	21,821

The problem with Charlie Lyons is still there, mused Basler. He wants more money and Stella Jordan thinks he is overpaid and underworked. Since Charlie Lyons is something of a focal point, we ought to do a profitability analysis for each of his customers. Basler's next step was to compile data by customer. Exhibit 6 presents customer data for each of Lyon's three accounts.

Preparing guidelines for allocating costs to sales representatives and customers was Basler's next task. Based on his review of several distribution cost and analysis textbooks and further conversations with Stella Jordan, Basler developed the following guidelines:

Functional Cost Item	Basis of Allocation
Direct selling	Number of calls × average time spent with each customer
Commissions	6 percent of gross margin
Travel............................	Total travel costs divided by number of calls; this figure is then multiplied by individual salesperson calls or customer calls
Advertising.......................	5 percent of sales dollars
Packaging........................	Number of units × $2
Warehousing and transportation	Number of units × $3.50
Order processing	Number of orders × $2.75

Exhibit 6

Customer activity analysis for Charlie Lyons

Customers of Charlie Lyons	Number of Sales Calls	Average Time Spent on Each Call (minutes)	Number of Orders	Number of Units Purchased			
				Receivers	Turntables	Speakers	Total
American TV	65	55	40	422	1,513	854	2,789
Appliance Mart	55	45	15	337	1,058	569	1,964
Audio Emporium	50	45	20	85	455	474	1,014
	170	50	75	844	3,026	1,897	5,767

Basler's next step is the development of the necessary accounting statement, which will permit a detailed analysis of each sales representative's profitability. From there he will proceed to a customer profitability analysis for Charlie Lyons's customers.

Case 3–5
Christopher Industries

Mark Parrett, who had just returned from a meeting with Joan Emerson, was contemplating what his first move should be. After a very successful sales career, Mark had been recently promoted to sales manager of the midwest region for Christopher Industries by Emerson, the general sales manager.

The meeting had taken place on Monday, February 25, 1984, Mark's first full day in the new position. Joan had reviewed the kind of working relationships she liked to maintain with her regional managers. She also reviewed the lines of authority and territorial boundaries within the sales organization and some problems in the midwest region. The meeting ended on the note that Joan and Mark were to meet again two weeks later to discuss Mark's preliminary thoughts about what should be done to improve the midwest region's performance.

Mark was aware that the previous manager of the region had resigned after 15 years with the company; the resignation came less than 2 years after the new sales force management information system became effective. The system had been one of Emerson's first priorities when she was hired as general sales manager. Mark also understood that the primary reason the previous manager had resigned was that he did not agree with Emerson's contention that performance in the region was below par. Parrett had been supplied a good deal of data by Emerson in their meeting, and he was flipping through it casually now as he contemplated what he should do and how he should prepare for the next meeting.

Joan Emerson

Joan Emerson was 40 years old and had been with Christopher Industries for three years. She had an undergraduate degree in home economics from Purdue University, which she received in 1965, and an MBA degree from Indiana University, which she received two years later. Upon graduation, she had gone to work for Ethan Allen as a field salesperson but was quickly moved to the headquarters office as sales analyst reporting to the general sales manager. She served in that capacity for 10 years, until the opportunity to be general sales manager at Christopher Industries presented itself.

Mark Parrett

Mark Parrett was 32 years old. He had been with Christopher Industries since he graduated from the University of Iowa with an undergraduate degree in business administration in 1970. As was customary at the time, he started in sales with a large territory geographically, but one that was low in potential. He quickly proved himself to be a top-flight salesman. He consistently registered some of the largest year-to-year percentage increases in sales within Christopher Industries. Because of that, he had been "promoted" three times within the 10 years to better territories. In each instance, he was able to generate large year-to-year sales increases. Mark liked to attribute that performance to his organizational capabilities; he felt he always covered his territory most efficiently. As a salesperson, he spent a good deal of time analyzing his accounts, their needs, and potential. He then planned his calls, both their number and duration, on the basis of these account analyses.

Christopher Industries

Christopher Industries had been founded by Janet Christopher in the immediate post-Korean War era as an interior decorating service. When she experienced continual difficulty in securing drapery rods that suited the motif she was trying to create, she began to design some herself and subcontract their manufacture. Her designs proved to have great appeal to homeowners. When she found herself spending the majority of her time coordinating the production of her special designs, she decided to manufacture them herself. From this small beginning, Christopher Industries had grown until, in 1984, it was one of the five largest companies in the industry.

Christopher Industries produces four basic classes of products: drapery rods in both metal and wood; drapery rod accessories that include such things as rope, rod holders, hooks, and pulleys; woven wood draperies that roll up; and designer items like gold rope, chains, and other forms of tiebacks that mount on the wall.

Total sales in 1983 were $76,597,800. Management estimated that it has an approximate share of 12 percent in the product categories in which it competed.

Sales Organization

Christopher Industries serves two basic types of accounts: home decorating stores and furniture stores. In contrast to its competitors, Christopher Industries does not attempt to sell through discount stores or department stores.

Decorating and furniture stores are called on directly by salespeople. Each salesperson is responsible for all stores of either type in his or her assigned sales territory. A salesperson's primary responsibility is to assist the store personnel in selling more Christopher products. This means not only educating store personnel in Christopher's new designs and new product features, but also setting up displays in the store, supplying home furnishing books, and assisting store personnel in preparing bids on large commercial and industrial installations. Another major activity of salespeople is to get Christopher products featured in store advertisements. Most typically, this involves some sort of cooperative advertising arrangement in which Christopher Industries shares in the cost of the ad. The salesperson serves as a factory representative within the store during one or two days of the special promotion. All such arrangements are the responsibility of the salesperson but have to be approved by his or her district manager.

All salespeople are paid a base salary plus 0.5 percent commission on all they sell. In addition, each salesperson is supplied with an automobile.

Exhibit 1 shows the organization of the sales force for Christopher Industries. The United States is divided into four regions, each with its own regional manager. Each region in turn is divided into two districts. There are typically six to eight salespeople reporting to a district manager, who in turn reports to the regional manager. Exhibits 2–21 provide the background data supplied to Mark Parrett during his meeting with Joan Emerson.

Exhibit 1
Sales organization chart for Christopher Industries

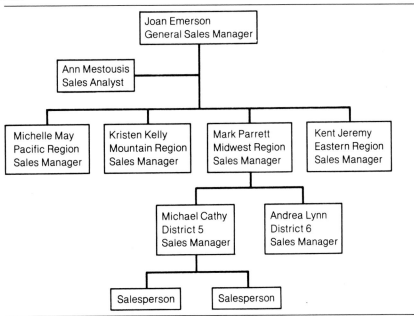

Exhibit 2
Sales performance, 1983 versus 1982

Region	1983 ($000)	1982 ($000)	Difference	Percentage Change
Pacific	$19,016.4	$17,130	$1,886.4	11.0%
Mountain	21,738.9	20,133	1,605.9	8.0
Midwest	19,138.5	16,686	2,452.5	14.7
Eastern	16,704.0	15,417	1,287.0	8.3
Total	$76,597.8	$69,366	$7,231.8	10.4%

Exhibit 3
Sales by type of account by region
(in $000)

Region	Home Decorating Stores		Furniture Stores		Total	
	Quota	Sales	Quota	Sales	Quota	Sales
Pacific	$15,375	$15,505.2	$ 3,133	$ 3,511.2	$18,508	$19,016.4
Mountain....	17,466	17,242.8	3,519	4,496.1	20,985	21,738.9
Midwest.....	16,627	16,443.0	3,736	2,695.5	20,363	19,138.5
Eastern	10,814	11,240.1	5,718	5,463.9	16,532	16,704.0
Total	$60,283	$60,431.1	$16,106	$16,166.7	$76,389	$76,597.8

Exhibit 4
Sales by product line, 1983 (in $000)

Region	Drapery Rods	Accessories	Woven Woods	Designer Items	Total
Pacific	$15,114.9	$ 2,160.9	$1,643.4	$ 97.2	$19,016.4
Mountain.....	16,546.8	3,057.3	1,963.2	171.6	21,738.9
Midwest......	14,853.3	2,709.6	1,436.1	139.5	19,138.5
Eastern	13,118.4	2,181.3	1,287.3	117.0	16,704.0
Total	$59,633.4	$10,109.1	$6,330.0	$525.3	$76,597.8

Exhibit 5
Sales by product type by type of outlet by region (in $000)

Region	Drapery Rods*		Accessories*		Woven Woods*		Designer Items*		Total*	
	HDS	FS	HDS	FS	HDS	FS	HDS	FS	HDS	FS
Pacific										
District 1	$ 5,550.6	$ 1,409.4	$ 772.2	$ 117.0	$ 596.5	$ 82.2	$ 33.3	$ 3.9	$ 6,952.8	$ 1,612.5
District 2	6,529.8	1,625.1	1,193.1	78.6	787.8	176.7	41.7	18.3	8,552.4	1,898.7
Total	12,080.4	3,034.5	1,965.3	195.6	1,384.5	258.9	75.0	22.2	15,505.2	3,511.2
Mountain										
District 3	6,060.3	1,669.2	1,258.2	279.0	755.1	123.0	29.7	13.5	8,103.3	2,084.7
District 4	6,708.0	2,109.3	1,332.3	187.8	993.3	91.8	105.9	22.5	9,139.5	2,411.4
Total	12,768.3	3,778.5	2,590.5	466.8	1,748.4	214.8	135.6	36.0	17,242.8	4,496.1
Midwest										
District 5	5,442.3	1,058.4	1,389.6	67.2	471.0	60.6	65.1	7.5	7,368.0	1,193.7
District 6	7,026.0	1,326.6	1,155.6	97.2	838.5	66.0	54.9	12.0	9,075.0	1,501.8
Total	12,468.3	2,385.0	2,545.2	164.4	1,309.5	126.6	120.0	19.5	16,443.0	2,695.5
Eastern										
District 7	3,562.8	1,983.0	812.4	206.4	451.5	73.8	39.0	21.9	4,865.7	2,285.1
District 8	4,775.1	2,797.5	942.3	220.2	622.5	139.5	34.5	21.6	6,374.4	3,178.8
Total	8,337.9	4,780.5	1,754.7	426.6	1,074.0	213.3	73.5	43.5	11,240.1	5,463.9
Total	$45,654.9	$13,978.5	$8,855.7	$1,253.4	$5,516.4	$813.6	$404.1	$121.2	$60,431.1	$16,166.7

*HDS—home decorating stores; FS—furniture stores.

Exhibit 6
Advertising expenditures by product type by region

Region	Drapery Rods	Accessories	Woven Woods	Designer Items	Total
Pacific	$ 392,544	$ 94,113	$ 47,592	$ 24,030	$ 558,279
Mountain.....	352,647	105,921	53,514	33,768	545,850
Midwest......	311,094	106,569	41,841	21,654	481,158
Eastern	294,354	93,456	38,826	28,728	455,364
Total	$1,350,639	$400,059	$181,773	$108,180	$2,040,651

Exhibit 7
Advertising expenditures by type of account by region

Region	Home Decorating Stores	Furniture Stores	Total
Pacific	$ 451,161	$107,118	$ 558,279
Mountain...........	431,928	113,922	545,850
Midwest............	392,211	88,947	481,158
Eastern	312,363	143,001	455,364
Total	$1,587,663	$452,988	$2,040,651

Exhibit 8
Gross margin by region by product*

Region	Drapery Rods	Accessories	Woven Woods	Designer Items	Total
Pacific	$2,418,384	$ 388,962	$ 377,982	$ 24,300	$ 3,209,628
Mountain....	2,647,488	550,314	451,536	42,900	3,692,238
Midwest.....	2,376,528	487,728	330,303	34,875	3,229,434
Eastern	2,098,944	392,634	296,079	29,250	2,816,907
Total	$9,541,344	$1,819,638	$1,455,900	$131,325	$12,948,207

*Based on Christopher Industries earning the following gross margins on each of the products it sells: drapery rods—16 percent; accessories—18 percent; woven woods—23 percent; designer items—25 percent.

Exhibit 9
Total market potential by type of outlet by region (in $000)

Region	Home Decorating Stores	Furniture Stores	Total
Pacific	$123,002	$ 25,064	$148,066
Mountain...........	139,727	28,153	167,880
Midwest............	162,113	29,826	191,939
Eastern	86,514	45,741	132,255
Total	$511,356	$128,784	$640,140

Exhibit 10
Account analysis by region

Region	Total Stores	Number of HDS*	Number of FS*	Active HDS*	Active FS*	Sales calls* HDS	Sales calls* FS
Pacific	1,623	978	645	579	369	1,457	685
Mountain	1,935	963	972	645	504	1,762	908
Midwest	1,938	1,149	787	600	297	1,723	632
Eastern	1,323	588	735	345	447	1,238	667
Total	6,819	3,678	3,141	2,169	1,617	6,180	2,892

*HDS—home decorating stores; FS—furniture stores.

Exhibit 11
Compensation and expenses

Region	Salary	Commissions	Total Compensation	Expenses	Total
Pacific	$ 249,163	$ 63,388	$ 312,551	$ 79,851	$ 392,402
Mountain	297,094	72,462	369,556	122,207	491,763
Midwest	291,900	95,697	387,597	110,649	498,246
Eastern	233,843	55,677	289,520	106,227	395,747
Total	$1,072,000	$287,224	$1,359,224	$418,934	$1,778,158

Exhibit 12
Sales by salesperson in midwest region, 1983 versus 1982

District/ Salesperson	1983 ($000)	1982 ($000)	Difference	Percentage Change
District 5				
Amy Hathaway	$1,379.7	$1,362	$ 17.7	1.3%
Marc Anthony	1,412.1	1,230	182.1	14.8
Ann Marie	1,272.6	1,260	12.6	1.0
Kurt Stromberg	1,847.7	1,359	488.7	36.0
Kassandra Lynn	1,039.5	873	166.5	19.0
Lisa Crosby	1,610.1	1,260	350.1	27.8
Total	$8,561.7	$7,344	$1,217.7	16.6%
District 6				
Carol Crescentia	$ 1,251.9	$1,197	$ 54.9	4.6%
Elizabeth Ann	1,404.6	1,383	21.6	1.6
Dave Michael	979.5	930	49.5	5.3
John Church	1,412.4	1,224	188.4	15.4
Thomas Stein	256.5	180	76.5	42.5
Betty Lane	1,685.1	1,251	434.1	34.7
Ruth Dresen	676.8	486	190.8	39.3
Dorothy Peterson	1,116.6	1,143	−26.4	−2.3
Susan Rowe	1,793.4	1,548	245.4	15.9
Total	$10,576.8	$9,342	$1,234.8	13.2%

Exhibit 13
Sales by salesperson in midwest region by type of account, 1983 (in $000)

District/Salesperson	HDS*		FS*		Total Quota	Total Sales
	Quota	Sales	Quota	Sales		
District 5						
Amy Hathaway....	$1,246	$1,241.7	$ 240	$ 138.0	$ 1,486	$ 1,379.7
Marc Anthony	1,367	1,226.1	291	186.0	1,658	1,412.1
Ann Marie	1,270	1,000.2	174	272.4	1,444	1,272.6
Kurt Stromberg	1,385	1,535.4	450	312.3	1,835	1,847.7
Kassandra Lynn ...	574	872.7	174	166.8	748	1,039.5
Lisa Crosby	1,495	1,491.9	126	118.2	1,621	1,610.1
Total	$7,337	$7,368.0	$1,455	$1,193.7	$ 8,792	$ 8,561.7
District 6						
Carol Crescentia...	$1,277	$1,172.4	$ 291	$ 79.5	$ 1,568	$ 1,251.9
Elizabeth Ann	1,121	1,147.8	333	256.8	1,454	1,404.6
Dave Michael	1,246	873.3	294	106.2	1,540	979.5
John Church.......	730	1,122.9	516	289.5	1,246	1,412.4
Thomas Stein......	245	245.1	30	11.4	275	256.5
Betty Lane.........	1,320	1,477.8	147	207.3	1,467	1,685.1
Ruth Dresen	888	605.7	162	71.1	1,050	676.8
Dorothy Peterson ..	1,090	1,036.8	189	79.8	1,279	1,116.6
Susan Rowe.......	1,373	1,393.2	303	400.2	1,676	1,793.4
Total	$9,290	$9,075.0	$2,265	$1,501.8	$11,555	$10,576.8

*HDS—home decorating stores; FS—furniture stores.

Exhibit 14
Sales by salesperson in midwest region by product line, 1983 (in $000)

District/Salesperson	Drapery Rods	Accessories	Woven Woods	Designer Items	Total
District 5					
Amy Hathaway.....	$1,097.4	$ 200.7	$ 75.6	$ 6.0	$ 1,379.7
Marc Anthony	1,025.4	294.3	87.9	4.5	1,412.1
Ann Marie	954.9	207.9	90.0	19.8	1,272.6
Kurt Stromberg	1,335.0	300.3	184.5	27.9	1,847.7
Kassandra Lynn	753.0	253.5	24.6	8.4	1,039.5
Lisa Crosby	1,335.0	200.1	69.0	6.0	1,610.1
Total	$6,500.7	$1,456.8	$531.6	$72.6	$ 8,561.7
District 6					
Carol Crescentia....	$ 945.6	$ 193.2	$ 99.6	$13.5	$ 1,251.9
Elizabeth Ann	1,134.0	157.2	106.5	6.9	1,404.6
Dave Michael	708.6	114.0	149.7	7.2	979.5
John Church........	1,186.2	142.8	72.0	11.4	1,412.4
Thomas Stein.......	224.4	22.5	6.3	3.3	256.5
Betty Lane..........	1,400.4	193.5	85.8	5.4	1,685.1
Ruth Dresen	460.8	121.5	93.0	1.5	676.8
Dorothy Peterson ...	939.3	86.7	79.5	11.1	1,116.6
Susan Rowe........	1,353.3	221.4	212.1	6.6	1,793.4
Total	$8,352.6	$1,252.8	$904.5	$66.9	$10,576.8

Exhibit 15
Sales by salesperson in midwest region by product type by type of account

District/Salesperson	Drapery Rods*		Accessories*		Woven Woods*		Designer Items*		Total*	
	HDS	FS	HDS	FS	HDS	FS	HDS	FS	HDS	FS
District 5										
Amy Hathaway	$ 965.7	$ 131.7	$ 198.6	$ 2.1	$ 72.3	$ 3.3	$ 5.1	$ 0.9	$1,241.7	$ 138.0
Marc Anthony	860.7	164.7	281.7	12.6	79.8	8.1	3.9	0.6	1,226.1	186.0
Ann Marie	696.6	258.3	199.5	8.4	88.5	1.5	15.6	4.2	1,000.2	272.4
Kurt Stromberg	1,091.4	243.6	273.3	27.0	143.4	41.1	27.3	0.6	1,535.4	312.3
Kassandra Lynn	609.0	144.0	237.6	15.9	18.9	5.7	7.2	1.2	872.7	166.8
Lisa Crosby	1,218.9	116.1	198.9	1.2	68.1	0.9	6.0	0.0	1,491.9	118.2
Total	$5,442.3	$1,058.4	$1,389.6	$67.2	$471.0	$60.6	$65.1	$ 7.5	$7,368.0	$1,193.7
District 6										
Carol Crescentia	$ 880.8	$ 64.8	$ 187.8	$ 5.4	$ 91.2	$ 8.4	$12.6	$ 0.9	$1,172.4	$ 79.5
Elizabeth Ann	886.2	247.8	153.6	3.6	102.0	4.5	6.0	0.9	1,147.8	256.8
Dave Michael	618.3	90.3	109.8	4.2	140.7	9.0	4.5	2.7	873.3	106.2
John Church	915.3	270.9	134.7	8.1	65.1	6.9	7.8	3.6	1,122.9	289.5
Thomas Stein	213.6	10.8	22.5	0.0	5.7	0.6	3.3	0.0	245.1	11.4
Betty Lane	1,228.5	171.9	163.5	30.0	81.6	4.2	4.2	1.2	1,477.8	207.3
Ruth Dresen	406.5	54.3	111.9	9.6	85.8	7.2	1.5	0.0	605.7	71.1
Dorothy Peterson	870.9	68.4	84.6	2.1	70.8	8.7	10.5	0.6	1,036.8	79.8
Susan Rowe	1,005.9	347.4	187.2	34.2	195.6	16.5	4.5	2.1	1,393.2	400.2
Total	$7,026.0	$1,326.6	$1,155.6	$97.2	$838.5	$66.0	$54.9	$12.0	$9,075.0	$1,501.8

*HDS—home decorating stores; FS—furniture stores.

Exhibit 16
Advertising expenses by salesperson
in the midwest district by product
type

District/ Salesperson	Drapery Rods	Accessories	Woven Woods	Designer Items	Total
District 5					
Amy Hathaway.....	$ 25,812	$ 7,911	$ 4,185	$ 2,070	$ 39,978
Marc Anthony	24,570	9,522	3,447	990	38,529
Ann Marie	17,712	7,389	2,466	1,143	28,710
Kurt Stromberg	28,458	9,999	4,518	2,358	45,333
Kassandra Lynn	9,468	4,734	828	441	15,471
Lisa Crosby	23,841	10,638	2,565	630	37,674
Total	$129,861	$50,193	$18,009	$ 7,632	$205,695
District 6					
Carol Crescentia....	$ 26,280	$ 8,919	$ 2,448	$ 1,242	$ 38,889
Elizabeth Ann	19,881	6,885	1,962	1,161	29,889
Dave Michael	18,603	6,948	2,907	2,871	31,329
John Church........	19,917	5,058	1,989	2,277	29,241
Thomas Stein	5,220	1,431	369	162	7,182
Betty Lane..........	25,884	8,190	3,744	1,359	39,177
Ruth Dresen	13,743	3,969	2,322	2,088	22,122
Dorothy Peterson ...	17,820	4,923	3,483	621	26,847
Susan Rowe........	33,885	10,053	4,608	2,007	50,553
Total	$181,233	$56,376	$23,832	$13,788	$275,229

Exhibit 17
Advertising expenses by salesperson
in the midwest district by type of
account

District/ Salesperson	Home Decorating Stores	Furniture Stores	Total
District 5			
Amy Hathaway...........	$ 35,343	$ 4,662	$ 40,005
Marc Anthony	32,085	6,453	38,538
Ann Marie	24,561	4,167	28,728
Kurt Stromberg	36,027	9,333	45,360
Kassandra Lynn	8,874	6,597	15,471
Lisa Crosby	34,218	3,474	37,692
Total	$171,108	$34,686	$205,794
District 6			
Carol Crescentia..........	$ 34,758	$ 4,158	$ 38,916
Elizabeth Ann	23,022	6,876	29,898
Dave Michael	25,686	5,662	31,348
John Church..............	19,917	9,342	29,259
Thomas Stein	6,318	864	7,182
Betty Lane................	32,247	6,984	39,231
Ruth Dresen	16,920	5,211	22,131
Dorothy Peterson	23,121	3,735	26,856
Susan Rowe..............	39,114	11,439	50,553
Total	$221,103	$54,271	$275,374

Exhibit 18
Gross margin by account (in $000)*

District/Salesperson	Drapery Rods†		Accessories†		Woven Woods†		Designer Items†		Total†	
	HDS	FS	HDS	FS	HDS	FS	HDS	FS	HDS	FS
District 5										
Amy Hathaway	$ 154.51	$ 21.07	$ 35.75	$ 0.38	$ 16.63	$ 0.76	$ 1.28	$0.23	$ 208.17	$ 22.44
Marc Anthony	137.70	26.35	50.71	2.27	18.35	1.86	0.98	0.15	207.74	30.63
Ann Marie	111.46	41.33	35.91	1.51	20.36	0.35	3.90	1.05	171.63	44.24
Kurt Stromberg	174.62	38.97	49.19	4.86	32.98	9.45	6.83	0.15	263.62	53.43
Kassandra Lynn	97.44	23.04	42.77	2.86	4.35	1.31	1.80	0.30	146.36	27.51
Lisa Crosby	195.02	18.58	35.80	0.22	15.66	0.21	1.50	0.00	247.98	19.01
Total	$ 870.75	$169.34	$250.13	$12.10	$108.33	$13.94	$16.29	$1.88	$1,245.50	$197.26
District 6										
Carol Crescentia	$ 140.93	$ 10.37	$ 33.80	$ 0.97	$ 20.98	$ 1.93	$ 3.15	$0.23	$ 198.86	$ 13.50
Elizabeth Ann	141.79	39.65	27.65	0.65	23.46	1.04	1.50	0.23	194.40	41.57
Dave Michael	98.93	14.45	19.76	0.76	32.36	2.07	1.13	0.68	152.18	17.96
John Church	146.45	43.34	24.25	1.46	14.97	1.59	1.95	0.90	187.62	47.29
Thomas Stein	34.18	1.73	4.05	0.00	1.31	0.14	0.83	0.00	40.37	1.87
Betty Lane	196.56	27.50	29.43	5.40	18.77	0.97	1.05	0.30	245.81	34.17
Ruth Dresen	65.04	8.69	20.14	1.73	19.73	1.66	0.38	0.00	105.29	12.08
Dorothy Peterson	139.34	10.94	15.23	0.38	16.28	2.00	2.63	0.15	173.48	13.47
Susan Rowe	160.94	55.58	33.70	6.16	44.99	3.80	1.13	0.53	240.76	66.07
Total	$1,124.16	$212.25	$208.01	$17.51	$192.85	$15.20	$13.75	$3.02	$1,538.77	$247.98

*Based on Christopher Industries earning the following gross margins on each of the products it sells: drapery rods—16 percent; accessories—18 percent; woven woods—23 percent; designer items—25 percent.

†HDS—home decorating stores; FS—furniture stores.

Exhibit 19
Total market potential by type of outlet by salesperson in the midwest region (in $000)

District/ Salesperson	Home Decorating Stores	Furniture Stores	Total
District 5			
Amy Hathaway...........$10,514	$ 1,928	$ 12,442
Marc Anthony 13,756	2,351	16,107
Ann Marie 12,807	1,387	14,194
Kurt Stromberg 12,648	3,543	16,191
Kassandra Lynn 4,787	1,405	6,192
Lisa Crosby 14,976	1,024	16,000
Total $69,488	$11,638	$ 81,126
District 6			
Carol Crescentia..........$11,568	$ 2,339	$ 13,907
Elizabeth Ann 9,750	2,672	12,422
Dave Michael 11,735	2,357	14,092
John Church.............. 13,360	4,143	17,503
Thomas Stein............. 1,835	232	2,067
Betty Lane............... 14,054	1,178	15,232
Ruth Dresen.............. 7,238	1,309	8,547
Dorothy Peterson 11,235	1,518	12,753
Susan Rowe.............. 11,850	2,440	14,290
Total $92,625	$18,188	$110,813

Exhibit 20
Account analysis by salesperson in midwest region

District/ Salesperson	Total Accounts	Home Decorating Stores	Furniture Stores	Active HDS	Active FS	Sales Calls HDS	Sales Calls FS
District 5							
Amy Hathaway...	141	96	45	54	21	122	56
Marc Anthony	156	87	69	54	18	104.5	53
Ann Marie	114	81	33	42	21	130	36
Kurt Stromberg ...	120	66	54	54	27	106	63
Kassandra Lynn ..	39	15	24	12	21	112	5
Lisa Crosby	126	84	42	54	21	151	20
Total	696	429	267	270	129	725.5	233
District 6							
Carol Crescentia..	141	84	57	51	6	167	8
Elizabeth Ann	147	72	75	39	24	118	52
Dave Michael	192	111	81	42	21	112	63
John Church......	123	63	60	36	33	129	44.5
Thomas Stein.....	42	33	9	15	3	47	29
Betty Lane........	120	78	42	42	21	136	34
Ruth Dresen......	105	54	51	21	6	80	34
Dorothy Peterson .	150	96	54	30	18	89	83
Susan Rowe......	222	129	93	54	36	119	51
Total 1,242	1,242	720	522	330	168	997	398.5

Exhibit 21
Compensation and expenses

District/ Salesperson	Salary	Commissions	Total Compensation	Expenses	Total
District 5					
Amy Hathaway.......$ 19,500		$ 6,899	$ 26,399	$ 9,384	$ 35,783
Marc Anthony	20,700	7,061	27,761	7,975	35,726
Ann Marie	18,000	6,363	24,363	9,236	33,599
Kurt Stromberg	23,500	9,239	32,739	1,439	34,178
Kassandra Lynn	15,400	5,198	20,598	12,970	33,568
Lisa Crosby	22,100	8,051	30,151	6,234	36,385
Total $119,200		$42,811	$162,011	$47,228	$209,239
District 6					
Carol Crescentia......$ 19,000		$ 6,260	$ 25,260	$ 8,753	$ 34,013
Elizabeth Ann	22,800	7,023	29,823	2,163	31,986
Dave Michael	15,700	4,898	20,598	4,862	25,460
John Church..........	18,300	7,062	25,362	8,617	33,979
Thomas Stein	14,600	1,283	15,883	10,125	26,008
Betty Lane............	23,300	8,426	31,726	8,713	40,439
Ruth Dresen	17,300	3,384	20,684	5,059	25,743
Dorothy Peterson	18,900	5,583	24,483	6,660	31,143
Susan Rowe..........	22,800	8,967	31,767	8,469	40,236
Total $172,700		$52,886	$225,586	$63,421	$289,007

Case 3–6
Anderson Distributors, Inc.*

Anderson Distributors, Inc. was a Phoenix Corporation which wholesaled a full line of dry groceries. The line included 12,000 items and was sold primarily to independent food retailers in Arizona and parts of Southern California. Stocks were held in three warehouses scattered throughout the territory. The company had prospered since it was formed 30 years earlier by three brothers who, before that, had managed a successful small chain of three retail stores. Sales were made by 45 salespeople who operated out of eight district offices. In brief, the sales organization consisted of the following:

45 Salespeople

8 District Managers

2 Regional Managers

1 Sales Vice President

Salesperson compensation ranged from $280 to $370 a week, district managers from $380 to $450. Anderson operated as a voluntary cooperative. That is, the member retailers agreed to concentrate the bulk of their purchases with Anderson in return for quality discounts, a standard, simplified ordering system, special merchandising and promotional programs, and a convenient delivery system by Anderson trucks. All retailers in the system were allowed to use the co-op logo "Best Stores." In 1980, Anderson had over 3,000 affiliated retailers, most of whom did concentrate their dry grocery purchases.

As was true with any extensive field sales organization, Anderson experienced most of the routine field management problems concerning salesperson evaluation, compensation, and supervision. A handful of these problems has been summarized on the following pages.

Evaluating Salesmen

District managers were required to make quarterly and annual evaluations of their salespeople. Clark Philbin had been a district manager for one month when he received a memo from Dan Pace, his regional manager, stating that all current quarterly evaluations were due in three weeks. The memo concerned Clark because he felt that he could not honestly evaluate his sales force after such a short time in his new position. He had had no management training or experience in evaluating people, except for the infrequent occasions when his previous boss had asked him to take over a sales meeting.

---

* This case was prepared by Professor Robert T. Davis, Stanford University, Graduate School of Business. Reprinted from *Stanford Business Cases 1980* with permission of the publisher, Stanford University Graduate School of Business, © 1980 by the Board of Trustees of the Leland Stanford Junior University.

Clark knew that he could accept the recommendations of the former district manager in writing his first quarterly evaluations, but there were several which he considered questionable. He could not easily identify specific reasons for his disagreement, but felt strongly nonetheless. Not wanting to make any serious mistakes, he decided to talk with his regional manager about evaluation techniques and standards before making any recommendations:

Pace: Well, Clark what's on your mind?

Philbin: Dan, I'm worried about this rating business. I've never evaluated anyone for anything before, and rather than make some real blunder, I wanted to ask you if you could offer me any guides or ground rules to follow.

Pace: Well, you've really picked a good question. What's bothering you now has been, and still is, a problem for most managers. As far as I know, there is no effective form or rating chart for evaluating people. This is something you just have to pick up from experience.

Philbin: Yes, Dan, but this is quite a responsibility and I'm afraid of making some big mistakes during the learning process.

Pace: True, Clark, but it's hard for me to be specific. It's something all managers go through. You learn by doing, and basically have to develop your own standards. What I find acceptable performance, you might question. There's a lot of "feel" to it.

Philbin: O.K., Dan. I'll do the best I can. I have one question, though—this business of looking for people with management potential rather than sales potential. I don't understand why there should be so much emphasis on management. Aren't good salespersons just as important to the company as potential managers? After all, the business is becoming so competitive that we have to have top caliber salespeople. Today most of the buyers are pretty sophisticated and the old-fashioned drummer has no place anymore. We need people who can read income statements and talk in terms of profits and other customer benefits.

Pace: I agree with you on the last part, Clark, and I guess the argument can be made that the best salespeople under these new conditions have to be more like managers. And if we continue to grow there will always be room for the best young managers. Good luck with your evaluations!

After returning to his office, Clark began to think over the interview. He realized that experience was undoubtedly a good, if not the best, teacher but he still felt that some effective evaluation technique would be helpful. He decided to try one other approach. He called an old boss, Kelly O'Brien, and asked him for his opinion on the problem. Kelly indicated that he would be glad to help. He said that the same problem had bothered him when he first became a district manager. Consequently, he had attempted to quantify some of the criteria commonly used in determining a person's management and sales potential. He had drawn up a rough chart which was divided into two separate areas of recognition: one for people with management potential and one for those with sales potential. The chart had proven useful to him and he offered it to Clark to use in making his evaluation (see Exhibit 1). Clark, of course, wasn't sure if he could separate the requirements for selling and management, nor was he even sure if an "attribute" approach was reasonable.

Exhibit 1
Evaluation of sales and
management potential

Management		Points	Sales		Points
1.	Judgment	25–35	1.	Aggressiveness	20–25
2.	Maturity	15–25	2.	Enthusiasm	25–30
3.	Aggressiveness	15–20	3.	Adaptability	25–35
4.	Enthusiasm	20–30	4.	Planning (sales calls)	30–40
5.	Adaptability	20–30	5.	Initiative	20–25
6.	Planning		6.	Dependability	25–30
	(organizing ability)	20–25	7.	Promptness	15–18
7.	Creativity	15–25			160–203
8.	Dependability	10–15			
9.	Report Writing	10–15	1.	Making quota	48–62
10.	Motivating	10–15	2.	Reports (clean,	
11.	Controlling	10–15		concise and factual)	8–12
		170–250	3.	Servicing accounts	14–18
			4.	New account generation	15–25
			5.	Calls/day (quarter beds)	6–10
			6.	Appearance	12–14
			7.	Care of company property	10–12
					113–153

Rating scale:	7	80	90	100
	poor	fair	good	excellent

Recommending Salary Increases

After Clark had finished making his evaluations, he reviewed the salary levels of the salespeople in his territory. He noticed that one man, Larry Gilbert, had been recommended for an increase six weeks earlier by the former manager. Since Clark had just completed his own evaluation of this man, he was interested in seeing how Gilbert had been rated over the years. Gilbert's file showed that he had been with Anderson as a salesman for 12 years but had only progressed to the middle of the current salary range. He had not been granted a salary increase for 22 months, although most salesmen received increases every ten to twelve months. The recommendation written by the former district manager stated, "Larry is continually trying to improve, and some progress is noted every so often. He hasn't had an increase for over a year and a half and should be considered for one soon."

In his own evaluation Clark had ranked Gilbert as one of his poorest salespersons—one who had little or no probability of improving and who should possibly be terminated. Clark realized that he had only worked with Larry for a short time and felt he should take a second look at him. However, he felt strongly about his own evaluation in this case and was absolutely against recommending a raise. Although the increase had already been submitted by the former district manager, Clark did not know whether it had been reviewed by the regional manager yet. Clark thought to himself how difficult it would be to give someone an increase and then fire him a month later.

Awarding Salary Increases

The regional manager approved the salary increases that Clark had recommended for his sales staff. Awarding an increase was generally considered fairly routine, but Clark could remember well how, as a young salesman, he had reacted to the way his supervisors had awarded increases to him. Once, his local manager called him long distance and said, "Next week your pay check will be $10 larger . . ." Before Clark had a chance to say a word his manager had hung up. On another occasion with a different manager, both he and his wife were taken out to dinner by the district manager on the day he had received his raise.

Clark felt that the way in which increases were awarded could make a significant difference in a person's future performance. Moreover, he believed that one should be told why he/she was receiving the raise. However, he was undecided about two things: whether it was a good idea to involve the family in company business by including the spouse; and whether one would be motivated to a greater degree if salary increases were constantly promised.

Compensation Policy

Anderson's policy was to give fairly quick salary increases (perhaps six to nine months apart) up to the median of the salary range. It was more difficult to earn a salary increase over the median; generally, a person did not receive a raise for 10 months or more, depending on his/her efficiency and potential for promotion.

In April, Clark Philbin recommended a salary increase for one of his salesmen, Al Peters. Peters was making $325 per week and had not had a raise in three years. He had been a salesman with the company for about fourteen years. Clark wrote the following as a basis for the salary increase: "Peters has demonstrated consistent up-grading of accounts and increased sales to key accounts and has shown marked improvement in establishing better relations with his customers." Philbin indicated that, after working closely with Peters, he was convinced an increase was warranted. He believed that salary administration was a serious responsibility and that increases should be recommended only when merited by performance.

The regional manager, Dan Pace, thought that Peters was about average. Due to the lapse of time since the last salary increase, however, he approved the recommendation and passed it along to the sales vice president for final approval.

The vice president knew that Al Peters had not had an increase for over 18 months, but from past experience he had also considered Peters an average performer. He believed, however, that Clark Philbin was very conscientious about awarding salary increases solely on a merit basis rather than time elapsed since the last raise.

The incident brought a matter to the vice president's mind which he had been pondering for some time. He wondered whether senior salespeople should be given automatic salary increases (other than cost of living increases) or whether (in line with company policy) increases should be awarded strictly on a merit basis. In the case of Philbin's recommendation on behalf of Al Peters, the vice president was not convinced that Peters deserved a merit increase. Possibly this was a case in which a salesperson should be considered for an automatic annual increase. In either event, Ken was reluctant to turn down the application since it had been passed by the regional manager and district manager, both of whom he considered very capable. Moreover, these people knew Peters and his capabilities far better than he did because of their closer association with him.

Bonus Incentive Plan

Clark Philbin was concerned about unrest exhibited by his sales force. He attributed it to the company's newly-instituted bonus incentive plan.

Formerly, Anderson had an individual incentive plan based on each man or woman's sales volume over and above his or her quota. Each person was directly responsible for attaining the individual quota assigned. The percentage by which a salesperson surpassed that quota was applied to his or her base salary for that period, as a bonus.

The new bonus incentive plan was based on the performance of the group rather than the individual. Each district was a team which consisted of the district manager and the salespeople. At the end of a quarter, the district bonus was computed on the basis of combined sales over quotas, and the quota was set so that it would be almost impossible to meet the total requirements unless each team member contributed his/her share. Consequently, if one territory fell short due to a weak salesperson, the whole district could lose its chance for a bonus. It was expected that any staff member would be willing to help out those who were falling behind.

Each individual's share under the new system was based on a "stated percentage" of his/her salary for the preceding quarter (see Exhibit 2). This percentage was determined by the amount by which the district exceeded its budget.

Philbin questioned whether the new plan was better or worse than the old one, and in order to evaluate the two plans he wondered how he could get honest

Exhibit 2
Computation table—quarterly incentive

Quarterly Invoiced Sales versus Total Budget	Percent Gross Salary* at End of Quarter
I. 100.0 to 105	7%
II. 106 to 110	8
III. 110 to 115	9
IV. 115 to beyond	10

*Weekly salary rate × 13.

opinions from the sales force. Clark decided that a good way to find out what was troubling everyone was to have a post-sales meeting "gripe" session. He had tried this once before and it had yielded favorable results. The salespeople were asked to participate by writing down any complaints they might have and by bringing them to the "gripe" session. At a previous session Clark had assured them that anything they said would be confidential, and that the point of the meeting was to improve understanding between management and the sales force. Because confidences had been maintained in the past, Clark hoped that the meeting might be beneficial.

At the meeting the following opinions were expressed:

Salesperson 1: Clark, this new incentive plan has killed individual effort. Not only is the weakest person boosted up in each territory, but also one weak territory is helped by stronger or harder working ones . . .

Salesperson 2: Yes, and that brings up something else. I don't mean to offend you (turning to a new man), but under this system you guys get the same share of the bonus as we old timers do. I know that we all had to start from scratch, and I'm not objecting to that. But, and I think everyone will agree, a new man just isn't worth as much to the company as an older man in terms of actual sales volume. Under the old system a guy really got paid for what he was worth. Any extra effort was rewarded by extra pay.

Salesperson 3: You bet. This place is becoming a loafer's paradise!

Salesperson 4: You guys have a point on this "individual effort business," but I still think the team effort idea is good. Everyone works together for the benefit of all. We're all interested in how we do as a district.

Salesperson 2: Sure, that's fine if everyone works together but how do we know that some guy can't improve his performance?

Salesperson 4: Well, I'm sure we all want the extra cash flow, as much as we did before under the old system, so I think everyone will work just as hard if not harder.

(Clark Philbin began to wonder if the new system really was better than the old one. Just as the meeting was breaking up one of the men approached Clark.)

Salesperson 5: Clark, one of our men puts in about a four day week but still makes quota. There's something strange about this system if things like that can go on.

Philbin: Well, I think we all know that these things can happen in any territory—even in this one—but they happened under the old incentive plan, too. Suppose we have two salesmen. One is a plugger, putting in a 10- to 12-hour day and barely making quota each time. The other is a whiz-kid. Works six to seven hours a day, four days a week, but is way over quota each time. Now, under these conditions, is the second person getting away with anything if the quotas are fairly set? Under the new system that person is really helping the other.

Salesperson 5: Well, I just can't see a guy or gal working only four days a week when everyone else is working five. Somehow, it's different when someone overworks—sort of makes a healthy competitive environment.

Philbin: Yes, but don't you resent someone who is *always* putting in extra time trying to get ahead, especially if he or she is barely making quota?

Salesperson 5: No, as I said, I think it makes a healthier working environment.

Clark Philbin was very interested in this discussion because he felt that the issues were causing the unrest in the sales force. There was not much he could do about the new incentive plan, but he felt he should do something to correct the situation concerning the short work week.

Compensating Managers

The Sales Training department of Anderson was reviewing its current hiring policy for college graduates and MBA's. In the past few years the company had been hiring more and more well-educated people. There was, however, a problem which involved paying these people the salary required to attract them to Anderson. For example, those hired for the product management group were first sent to the field as sales trainees, and in order to get top caliber people, it was necessary to pay them more than the salesperson scale.

One MBA, for example, was hired recently by the Product and Research department and was assigned to the field as a salesman for five months as the first phase of his training. His initial salary was well above the maximum that could be earned by a salesperson. Thus, he had been told by the head office not to discuss his salary with anyone, not even his district manager. All went well for about three weeks until, through the grapevine, the others found out that the new hire was earning more than any of them.

The Sales Training department was stumped as far as future hiring and salary ranges were concerned. They realized that they had to continue to pay high salaries in order to get top caliber people, but on the other hand, it was risky to continue to antagonize the sales force.

Internal Corporate Politics

The sales vice president was due to visit Clark Philbin after spending a few days with Dan Pace at the regional office. Clark was uneasy about the forthcoming visit because he had heard a number of unpleasant rumors about the vice president from his regional manager. Clark thought highly of Dan, but he felt that it had been poor practice on Dan's part to have passed the rumors down. Clark believed that no matter how well deserved, remarks such as these should not be transmitted to lower levels in the organization.

The vice president's visit went smoothly except for two incidents. The first concerned Andy Smith, a salesman whom Clark considered an "average to good" performer. The salesman had recently grown a long handlebar mustache and the vice president commented to Philbin, "Clark, why don't you tell Andy to shave off that damn thing, or at least bring it back to normal size. It's so out of keeping with what our customers are used to."

The second incident concerned a saleswoman, Lee Beckwith. The vice president had previously met Lee at a sales meeting shortly after Lee was hired and had been very impressed with her after this brief contact. Now, after spending a few more hours with Lee, he commented to Clark, "That certainly is an outstanding girl; if she receives the proper training, she'll make a good manager."

After the vice president had left, Clark pondered what had been said. In recalling the mustache situation he remembered that his regional manager had expressed a concern about the vice president interfering in the evaluation of his staff. The promotion record showed that, over the years, many of the vice president's favorites had followed him up the corporate ladder.

With these points in mind, Clark wondered what he should do about Andy and Lee. In the recent evaluations he had recommended Andy both for a salary increase and for a possible promotion. On the other hand, he had characterized Lee as an opportunist with not too much potential for sales or management. Clark felt that Pace was a "fair-shooter" and would back him up, but the fact that the vice president had the final say in approving all recommendations could negate Dan's influence.

Characteristics of a Good
Sales Manager

After attending a management training seminar at a nearby university, Dan Pace returned to his office with several ideas in mind for improving the performance of his districts. First, he decided to examine the characteristics of his managers in order to determine what qualities were important.

He summarized his conclusions as follows:

Clark Philbin: Clark is very systematic in his approach to evaluating his staff. He carefully weighs all the important factors which contribute to a person's potential and actual sales ability. So far Clark's recommendations for promotions and increases have been granted exactly as requested. He is neither consistently high nor low in his praise pattern: rather he awards increases as he feels they are due. If someone is worth $40/week raise, then it is requested; similarly for a $10/week raise. Clark keeps running files on all of his people, so there are few, if any, last minute or "impulse" decisions on a man's or woman's value. Clark once commented, "After a framework is outlined, a manager should be permitted to operate autonomously within it." He motivates his staff largely through recognition of jobs well done. On a person's anniversary with the company or on a birthday, he always sends out a card. Also, if someone makes a single outstanding contribution, such as getting a large new account, then in addition to counting it toward a raise or promotion, Clark may take that person out to dinner, give a "pat on the back," or send a letter of commendation.

Jack Steelman: It seems that Jack is always sending in a raise request for one of his staff. He seldom changes the amount; it is always a minimum amount. A number of Jack's raise requests have been turned down because they seem like automatic increases. In many cases the people haven't actually earned them. Jack, however, is a very aggressive guy and an excellent salesman, as well as a good manager. He was once asked whether there was much variance in the quality of his sales force and he commented: "No, they are all great guys and gals who work hard and deserve to be paid well." Jack is sometimes referred to as the "Little King." He tries to maintain self respect and to motivate salespeople by always doing things for them, such as recommending raises. On the other hand, he usually keeps all but the most general information quite private. This makes his position appear to have a little more prestige.

Ozzie Davidson: Ozzie is sort of impulsive in the way he awards increases and promotions. On several occasions good salespeople have gone without raises for over a year, even though their quality evaluation forms showed excellent progress. In each case, however, when Ozzie worked with someone just before an evaluation, something happened which, in Ozzie's eyes, ruined the person's chances for an increase. He apparently is fairly well-liked by his staff and is always promising one of them a raise or promotion. This was often done before the increase was sent in for approval. In several instances this method of motivation caused difficulties when raises were not sanctioned by senior supervisors.

Jerry Hatch: Jerry does not believe in using pats on the back for jobs well done or any other type of non-financial recognition. He thinks that the dollar reward is sufficient, and if his people produce, they get paid for it; if they don't, they get fired. Jerry has always worked hard himself and is very fond of a dollar. He also feels that actual performance is the best measure of whether or not a person deserves an increase or promotion.

In reviewing his findings, Dan Pace found it difficult to decide which techniques or characteristics peculiar to each manager contributed the most to success in the job. He was not thinking solely in terms of an Anderson manager but more of a sales manager in general.

Case 3–7
Wentworth Industrial Cleaning Supplies[*]

Wentworth Industrial Cleaning Supplies (WICS), located in Lincoln, Nebraska, is currently experiencing a slowdown in growth; sales of all WICS products have leveled off far below the volume expected by management. Although total sales volume has increased for the industry, WICS's share of this growth has not kept pace. J. Randall Griffith, Vice-President of Marketing has been directed to determine what factors are presently stunting growth and to institute a program that will facilitate further expansion.

Company and Industry Background

WICS is a division of Wentworth International, competing in the janitorial maintenance chemical market. According to trade association estimates, the total market is roughly $5.8 billion in 1984. Exhibit 1 shows the nature of this market. Four segments comprise the institutional maintenance chemical market, which consists of approximately 2,000 manufacturers providing both national and private labels.

Total industry sales volume in dollars of janitorial supplies is approximately $2.5 billion. Exhibit 2 shows the breakdown by product type for the janitorial market. WICS addresses 80 percent of the market's product needs with a line of high quality products. The composition of WICS's product line is as follows:

Special purpose cleaners	46%
Air fresheners	9
General purpose cleaners	16
Disinfectants	15
Other	14

The janitorial maintenance chemical market is highly fragmented; no one firm, including WICS, has more than 10 percent market share. Agate and Marshfield Chemical sell directly to the end-user, while Lynx, Lexington Labs and WICS utilize a distributor network. Most of WICS's competitors utilize only one channel of distribution: only Organic Labs and Swanson sell both ways. Most private label products move through distributors. Sanitary Supply Distributors (SSDs) deliver 80 percent of end-user dollars, while direct-to-end-user dollar sales

---

[*] The assistance of Joan Russler and Jeffrey Forbes, MBAs—Marketing, University of Wisconsin, Madison, in the preparation of this case is greatly appreciated.

Exhibit 1
Institutional maintenance chemical market

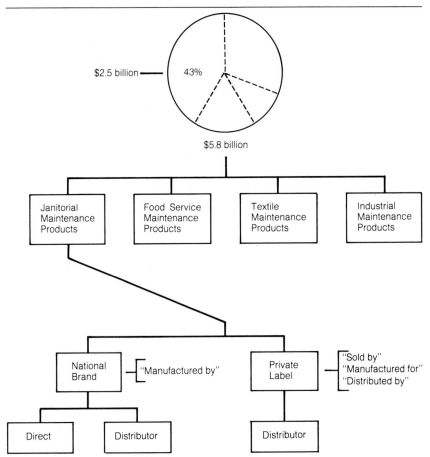

are 20 percent (Exhibit 3).[1] The following shows the sales breakdown by target market by type of distribution:

Distributor sales

Retail 20%
Industrial 18
Health Care 18

---

[1] Includes paper supply distributors that carry janitorial supplies.

Exhibit 2
WICS "served" portion of the
janitorial maintenance chemical
market

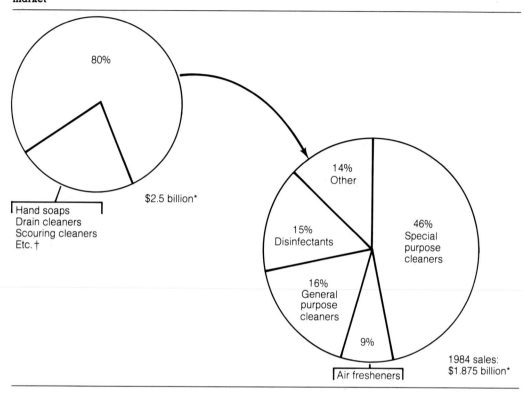

80%

$2.5 billion*

Hand soaps
Drain cleaners
Scouring cleaners
Etc. †

14%
Other

15%
Disinfectants

16%
General
purpose
cleaners

46%
Special
purpose
cleaners

9%

Air fresheners

1984 sales:
$1.875 billion*

*End user dollars.
**Includes some general purpose cleaners and air fresheners that WICS does not manufacture.

Exhibit 3
Janitorial maintenance chemical
market (end user dollars)

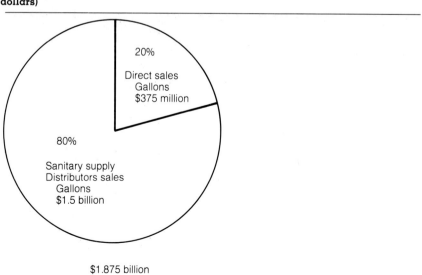

20%

Direct sales
Gallons
$375 million

80%

Sanitary supply
Distributors sales
Gallons
$1.5 billion

$1.875 billion

Schools 11
Building Supply Contractors 10
Restaurants 3
Hotels 3
Other 17

Direct sales

Retail 47%
Building Supply Contractors 35
Health Care 15
Hotels 2
Restaurants 1

Trade association data plus information from other sources estimate the number of SSDs to be between 5,000 and 6,000. The following shows the sales volume breakdown for the SSDs based on an average of 5,500:

Size in Sales Volume	Number
Less than $100,000	1,210
$100,000–$500,000	2,475
$500,000–$1,000,000	1,375
More than $1,000,000	440
Total	5,500

According to a recent analysis of end-users, WICS provides cleaning supplies for approximately 20,000 customers. WICS's sales force is expected to call on these accounts as well as prospect for new business. These 20,000 end-users receive product from the SSDs who supply cleaning supplies manufactured by WICS and others as well. About one third of the average SSDs total sales is accounted for by WICS's products. An exception is the paper supply distributor, where WICS's products account for an average of 10 percent of sales.

The typical SSD carries other related items. In fact, according to a survey conducted by an independent firm, SSDs almost always carry a private label line of cleaning supplies plus one to two additional branded products besides the WICS' line. This survey revealed that 60 percent of the SSDs carry a private label line along with WICS and one other national brand. Forty percent carry two national labels and WICS and a private label. The private label may be a regional label or the SSDs own label.

WICS places almost total reliance on selling through the SSDs, although a small amount of sales (less than 10 percent) are made direct. At the present time, WICS sells its janitorial maintenance products through roughly 400 distributors, who in turn "see" 65 percent of the end-user dollar market. Thus, 80 percent of sales in the total janitorial maintenance market are made through SSDs (20 percent are direct sales); and the 400 SSDs used by WICS provided 65 percent coverage. The market seen by each distributor, referred to as his or her "window" on the market, is a function of:

Exhibit 4
WICS's access to the market

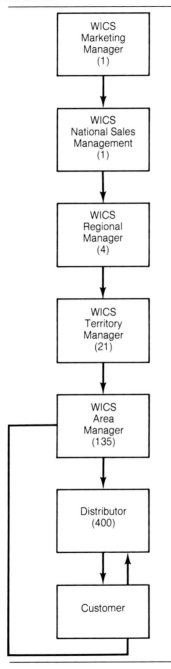

Product lines carried (paper versus chemical).

Customer base (type and size).

Nature of business (specialization by market versus specialization by sales function).

The combination of these factors produces end-user market coverage of 52 percent (80 percent distributor sales × 65 percent coverage). WICS has very limited direct sales.

To reach their market, WICS uses a sales force of 135 area managers, 21 territory managers, and four regional managers (Exhibit 4). Regional managers are located in San Francisco, Denver, Chicago, and Boston.

Although WICS is viewed as a giant in the industry, it does not produce a complete line of janitorial chemicals. Janitorial chemicals are rated based on their performance. At the present time, WICS produces products that have average to premium performance ratings; WICS has no products in the economy class. Moreover, due to various factors, WICS's coverage in the average and premium classes is not complete. Their emphasis on premium and average products results in providing only 80 percent of the market's product needs.

In order to provide high distributor margins and extensive sales support, WICS charges premium prices. Recent estimates reveal that only 60 percent of the served market is willing to pay these premium prices. The impact of WICS's limited product line coupled with their premium prices is evident in Exhibit 5.

Exhibit 5
End user product coverage

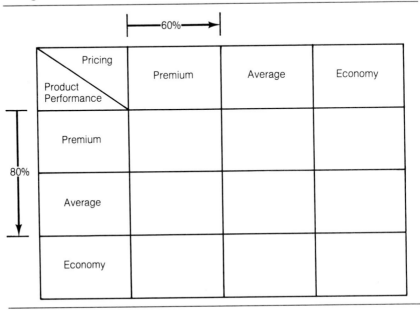

An overall description of WICS's marketing program shows that their focus has been on market development. Distributors receive high margins (30–40 percent) and sales costs are high (10–15 percent) due to emphasis on selling technical benefits, emphasis on demonstrations and emphasis on cold calls. Area managers call on prospective end users to develop the market for the SSD. By comparison, WICS's competitors offer SSDs low margins (15–20 percent) and incur low sales costs (5–8 percent).

Griffith recently received a memo from Steve Shenken, WICS's national sales manager, reporting on a study of the effectiveness of SSDs. Territory managers evaluated each SSD in their respective regions on a basis of reach (advertising and promotional programs) and frequency of sales calls. The composite report indicated that distributors as a whole were doing an excellent job in servicing present accounts. In other words, 400 SSDs provide WICS with a sizable share of the market, which has the potential to use janitorial supplies manufactured by WICS.

Exhibit 6
Allocation of area manager duties*

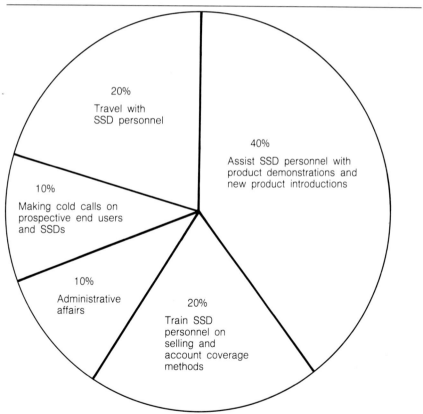

*Based on an analysis of call reports.

Area managers (AMs) represent WICS in distributor relations. The AMs "prime focus is to sell and service existing key end-user accounts and selected new target accounts in their assigned territories." According to a recent study, maintenance of current accounts comprises approximately 80 percent of the AMs time (Exhibit 6). In addition to handling old accounts, the AM makes "cold calls" on prospective distributors as directed by the territory manager. However, the number of cold calls made monthly has decreased substantially in the past year since the major SSDs now carry WICS products. A study of AM and SSD attitudes, conducted by MGH Associates, management consultants, is presented in Appendices A and B. Some of the sales management staff question the use of AM time; however, there has been no indication that formal changes will be made in the future regarding sales force organization and directives. The AM job description has seen few revisions, if any, during the firm's past 10 years of rapid growth (Exhibit 7).

Exhibit 7
Wentworth industrial cleaning
supplies position description

Date: January 1, 1978	Position:	Area Manager, Maint. Prods.
Approved by: (1)_____	Incumbent:	135 Positions Nationally
(2)_____		
(3)_____	Division:	Janitorial Maintenance Products Division
		Reports to: Territory Manager, Janitorial Maintenance Products Division

POSITION PURPOSE:

To sell and service user accounts and authorized distributors in an assigned territory to assure that territory sales objectives are attained or exceeded.

DIMENSIONS:

Annual sales:	$860 M (average)
Number of distributors:	4 (average)
Number of distributor salesmen:	12 (average)
Annual expense budget:	$12.3 M (average)
Company assets controlled or affected	$8 M (average)

Area managers are compensated with a straight salary, enhanced periodically by various incentive programs and performance bonuses. Incentive programs generally require that AMs attain a certain sales level by a specified date. For example, the "Christmas Program" necessitated that AMs achieve fourth quarter quotas by November 15; upon completion of this objective, the AM received a gift of his or her choice, such as a color television. To date, management considers the Zone Glory Cup the most effective incentive program. The Glory Cup is an annual competition between areas within territories which entails meeting or exceeding sales objectives by a specified date. An all-expense paid vacation at a plush resort for area, territory and region managers and their "legal" spouses is the prize for the winning team. However, management at WICS believes that prestige is the prime motivator in this competition and the underlying reason for the program's success.

In a recent meeting, Terry Luther, executive vice president of the WICS division of Wentworth International, expressed his concern to Griffith about WICS's mediocre performance. Luther indicated that corporate cash flow expectations from WICS were not being met and that a plan of action was needed from Griffith concerning how WICS could improve its overall operating performance. Griffith was quite aware that Wentworth International would make personnel changes to meet corporate objectives and that selling off divisions not able to meet corporate expectations was not unlikely. Griffith informed Luther that an action plan would be developed and be on his desk within 30 days.

Griffith's first step was to approve an earlier request made by Mike Toner, sales and distributor relations manager, for a study of sales force and distributor attitudes and opinions (Appendices A and B). Next, the following memo was sent, discussing Griffith's assignment from Luther:

Intra-Office Memorandum

To: Steve Shenken, national sales manager
   Caitlin Smith, manager—sales analysis
   Ryan Michaels, manager—sales training
   Calla Hart, manager—special sales program
   Charlotte Webber, senior product manager
   Mike Toner, sales and distributor relations manager

From: Randall Griffith, vice president—marketing

Subject: WICS Performance Review

As you all know, our performance has not met corporate expectations. To rectify this situation, before we all lose our jobs, we need to meet to discuss ways for improving our market performance.

At our next meeting, I want each of you to develop proposals for your areas of responsibility. These proposals need not be detailed at this time. For the moment, I am seeking ideas, not final solutions.

Staff reaction to Griffith's memo was one of frustration and anger. Several managers felt that they had already complied with Griffith's request. One person commented, "I've told Randy numerous times what we need to do to turn the division around, and all he does is nod his head. Why go through this 'wheel-spinning' exercise again?" Another said, "The only time old J.R. listens to us is when the top brass leans on him for results." Despite staff reaction, the meeting would be held and everybody will have suggestions for consideration.

To provide adequate time, Griffith scheduled an all-day meeting to be held at Wentworth's nearby lodge, located on Lake Woebegone. Griffith started the meeting by reviewing past performance. Next, he asked each manager to outline their proposal. First to speak was Steve Shenken, who indicated that Mike Toner would present a proposal combining both of their ideas. Shenken also said that he would listen to all sales force proposals and try to combine the best parts into an overall plan.

Mike Toner's Proposal.   Toner's proposal was rather basic. If improving market is WICS's objective, then more SSDs are needed in all territories. According to Toner:

> Each area manager serves, on the average, four SSDs. Since we can only get so much business out of a SSD, then to increase sales we need more SSDs. I suggest that each area manager add two more distributors. Of course, this move will require that we either add more area managers or that we hire and train a special group to call on new end users and new distributors. It's difficult to attract new SSDs unless we show them a group of prospective end users who are ready to buy WICS's products. Now, I have not made any estimates of how many more people are needed, but we do know that present AMs do not have enough time to adequately seek new business.

After Toner presented his proposal, Griffith asked if the existing AMs could not be motivated to apply more effort toward securing new business. Calla Hart thought the AMs could do more and that her proposal, if adopted, would alleviate the need for expansion of the AMs and SSDs.

Calla Hart's Proposal.   As expected, Hart's proposal revolved around her extensive experience with WICS's incentive programs. This satisfactory experience led Calla to suggest the following:

> If I thought that the AMs and the SSDs were working at full capacity, I would not propose more incentive programs. But they are not! We can motivate the AMs to secure more new business, and we can get more new business from our distributors. We all know that the SSDs are content to sit back and wait for the AMs to hand them new business. Well, let's make it worthwhile to the SSDs by including them in our incentive programs. For the AMs I suggest that we provide quarterly incentives much like our Christmas Program. AMs who achieve their quotas by the fifteenth of the second month of the quarter would receive a gift.
>
> In addition, we need to develop a program for recognizing new end user sales. Paying bonuses for obtaining new end user accounts would be one approach. For example, let's reward the AM from each territory who secures the highest percentage increase in new end user accounts. At the same time, we need to reward the distributor from each territory who achieves the highest percentage increase in new end user sales dollars. And, let's recognize these top producers each quarter and at year end as well. Our incentive programs work. We know that, so let's expand their application to new sales.
>
> Finally, on a different note, I support establishing quotas for our distributors. We have quotas for our sales force, and we enforce them. AMs who do not make quotas do not stay around very long. Why not the same procedures for some of our SSDs? We all know that there are some distributors who need to be replaced. Likewise, I have not made any cost estimates but feel that we are just searching for new ideas.

Griffith thanked Hart for her comments. He wondered whether applying more pressure to the distributors was the most suitable approach. He agreed with Hart that WICS's incentive programs seemed to be very popular but questioned if other techniques might not work. Griffith then asked Ryan Michaels for his comments.

Ryan Michael's Proposal.   During his short period of time with WICS, Michaels has gained the respect as being very thorough and analytical. He is not willing to accept as evidence such comments as, "we know it works," as a reason for doing something. Determining the value of sales training, Michael's area of assignment, has caused him considerable concern. He knows it is useful, but how useful is the question he is trying to answer. According to Michaels, WICS needs to examine the basic selling duties of the area managers:

> Before we recruit more AMs and SSDs, or try to motivate them to obtain more new business with incentive programs, we need to examine their job activities. I favor doing a job analysis of the area manager. Some evidence that I have seen indicates that job descriptions are outmoded. AMs do not perform the activities detailed in the job descriptions. For example, most AMs spend very little time calling on prospective end users. Accompanying distributor sales reps on daily calls does not lead to new end user business. Possibly the AMs could better spend their time doing new account development work. But before we make any decisions concerning time allocation we need to conduct a job analysis. And, while we are collecting data, let's ask the AMs what rewards are important to them. How do they value promotions, pay increases, recognition, et cetera? Maybe the AMs do not want more contests.

Griffith agreed that the job descriptions were out of date. He also contended that this is a typical situation and nothing to be concerned about in the short run. The idea of finding out what rewards AMs value intrigued Griffith. Next, Griffith asked Charlotte Webber for her reactions to WICS's market share problem.

Charlotte Webber's Proposal.   Ms. Webber's proposal was more strategic in nature than the previous suggestions. Her experience as a product manager led her to consider product oriented solutions and to suggest the following:

> I think we can increase market share and sales volume through the expansion of current lines and the addition of a full line of economy based products. We can expand our present premium and average lines to cover 100 percent of the product class by adding air fresheners and general purpose cleaners. In addition we must introduce the economy based products to counter competition.
>
> The proposed plan would not be costly because we could use our existing distributor network. If additional SSDs are necessary we can select those in the $500,000 to $1,000,000 sales volume range. I feel that through these extensions and an increased number of SSDs we can address 75 percent of the SSD end user dollars.

Griffith agreed that line extensions were indeed a viable means of achieving some corporate goals. He expressed concern over entry into the low quality segment of the market due to WICS's present customer perceptions of the company as a high quality producer. Griffith turned to Caitlin Smith for additional suggestions on how to increase market share.

Caitlin Smith's Proposal.   Smith's proposal came as no surprise to those attending the meeting. Her position in sales analysis made her critically aware of WICS's high cost of sales. It was only recently, however, that she developed a plan incorporating market share and cost of sales. Her views were accurate, but often given little weight due to her inexperience. According to Smith:

> Our cost of sales are currently running at (10–15 percent), while our competitors costs average (5–8 percent). As many of you know I am in favor of changing the job description of the area manager and the sales presentation. These changes are necessary due to our products' stage in the life cycle and customer service level preferences. Recently I have become convinced that there is another means of reducing sales costs. By reducing prices we could increase sales volume and reduce the cost of sales. This strategy would also increase penetration and market share.

Griffith conceded that price reductions were a possibility but expressed concern over the possibility of weakening consumer perceptions of WICS as a high quality manufacturer. He also questioned Smith's assumption that the industrial cleaning supplies industry was presently in the mature stage of the product life cycle.

Following these comments, Griffith thanked the participants for their input and adjourned the meeting. Upon retiring to his room he reflected upon the suggestions presented during the course of the meeting and his own beliefs. He knew that he must begin to formulate an action plan immediately since the 30-day deadline was drawing near.

Nature and Scope

This position reports to a territory manager, janitorial maintenance products. Each district is subdivided into sales territories that are either assigned to an individual member of the district or to a team effort, based upon market and/or manpower requirements.

The janitorial maintenance products division is responsible for developing and marketing a broad line of chemical products for building maintenance purposes.

The incumbent's prime focus is to sell and service existing key user accounts and selected new target accounts in his assigned territory. He multiplies his personal sales results by spending a major portion of his time working with distributor sales personnel, selling WICS maintenance products and systems to key accounts such as commercial, industrial, institutional, governmental accounts, and contract cleaners. When working alone he sells key user accounts through an authorized distributor as specified by the user customer.

The incumbent plans, schedules and manages his selling time for maximum sales productivity. He interviews decision makers and/or people who influence the buying decision. He identifies and evaluates customer needs through careful observation, listening and questioning techniques to assure proper recommendations. He plans sales strategy to include long-term/quick-sell objectives and develops personalized user presentations to meet individual sales situations, utilizing product literature, manuals, spot demonstrations, and sales aids to reinforce presentations. This position sells systems of maintenance to major volume user accounts through the use of surveys and proposals, test programs and other advanced sales techniques. He develops effective closing techniques for maximum sales effectiveness. This position trains custodial personnel in product usage techniques through the use of product demonstrations and/or audio visual training to assure customer satisfaction. He follows up promptly on customer leads and inquiries. He services customer and distributor complaints or problems and provides technical support as required. On a predetermined frequency basis, he surveys and sells assigned local accounts currently being sold on national contract. He represents the division in local custodial clinics and trade shows as required. He maintains an adequate current supply of literature, forms and samples, and maintains assigned equipment and sales tools in a business-like condition.

The incumbent is responsible for training, developing and motivating distributor sales personnel. This is accomplished by frequent on-the-job training in areas of product knowledge, selling skills and demonstration techniques. He sells distributor management and assists distributor to maintain an adequate and balanced inventory of the full product line. He introduces marketing plans and sells new products and sales promotions to distributor management. He participates in distributor sales meetings to launch new products or sales promotions, or for training and motivational purposes. He keeps abreast of pertinent competitive activities, product performance, new maintenance techniques, and other problems and opportunities in the territory. Periodically, he communicates Wentworth growth objectives versus distributor progress to distributor management; i.e., sales coverage, volume and product sales, etc. He assists the distributor to maintain a current and adequate supply of product literature, price lists and sales aids.

The incumbent prepares daily sales reports, weekly reports, travel schedules, weekly expense reports, etc., and maintains territory and customer records. He maintains close communication with his immediate supervisor concerning products, sales, distributor and shipping problems.

He controls travel and business expenses with economy and sound judgment. He handles and maintains assigned company equipment and territory records in a business-like manner.

Major challenges to this position include maintaining established major users, selling prospective new target accounts, and strengthening distribution and sales coverage to attain or exceed sales objectives.

The incumbent operates within divisional policies, procedures and objectives. He consults with his immediate supervisor for recommendations and/or approval concerning distributor additions or terminations, exceptions to approved selling procedures, and selling the headquarters level of national or regional accounts.

Internally, he consults with the editing office concerning distributor shipments, credit, etc. Externally, he works closely with distributor personnel to increase sales and sales coverage and with user accounts to sell new or additional products.

The effectiveness of this position is measured by the ability of the incumbent to attain or exceed territory sales objectives.

This position requires an incumbent with an in-depth and professional knowledge of user account selling techniques, product line and janitorial maintenance products distributors, and requires a minimum of supervision.

Principal Accountabilities

1. Sell and service key user accounts to assure attainment of territory sales objectives.
2. Sell, train, develop, and motivate assigned distributors to assure attainment of product sales, distribution and sales coverage objectives.
3. Plan, schedule and manage personal selling efforts to assure maximum sales productivity.
4. Plan and develop professional sales techniques to assure maximum effectiveness.
5. Train custodial personnel in the use of Wentworth products and systems to assure customer satisfaction.
6. Maintain a close awareness of territory and market activities to keep the immediate supervisor abreast of problems and opportunities.
7. Perform administrative responsibilities to conduct an efficient territory operation.
8. Control travel and selling expenses to contribute toward profitable territory operation.

Appendix A: Conclusions of Study of Area Manager Attitudes

MGH Associates, management consultants, was retained by WICS to investigate attitudes and opinions of field personnel and sanitary supply distributors. Initially, MGH conducted lengthy interviews with selected individuals, followed by the administration of a comprehensive questionnaire. The results below identify role expectations and attitudes toward their reasonableness.

Territory Manager's Role Expectations

MGH Associates interviews included territory managers because the territory manager is really the only management level contact the distributor has.

The territory manager interprets his or her role to be that of an overseer, to assure that WICS objectives are achieved that quotas are met.

The territory manager interprets his or her role to include:

Training the area managers.
  To sell WICS products.
  To train and motivate the distributor salesforce.
Coordinating area manager activities with Lincoln.
Hiring and firing area managers.
Striving for new product commitments from the distributors.
Acting as "referee" for competition between distributors.
"Building the book" for the adding or deleting of distributors.
The "study" is submitted to the regional manager, who writes a proposal based on the territory manager's "study" and it is submitted to corporate management where the final decision is made.

Area Manager's Role Expectations

The following is the area manager's view of the role he or she feels WICS management expects to be performed.

Multiply sales effort through distributor's sales force.
  Listed first because it was consistently mentioned first.
Teach and motivate the distributor's salesforce to sell WICS products.
Introduce new products to the market.
  Through direct calls on end users.
  Through distributors.
Keep margins high to keep distributors happy.
  If they are happy, they will push WICS.
Follow through on direct sales responsibilities.
Collect information for management.
Fulfill responsibilities relating to incentives.
  New gallon sales.
  Repeat gallon sales.
  Demonstrations.
  30, 35, 40 ? calls/week.
  Major account calls.
  Cold calls—"to develop business the distributor is reluctant to go after."

Area Manager's Role Problems

The area manager's perception of what management expects does not imply that the area manager feels that management's approach is working.

In general, the sales force appears frustrated by a sales role they see as ineffec-
tive.
A sales role stressing
New gallon sales.
Cold calls on end users.
Product demonstrations.
New product introduction.
"Checking the boxes" rather than being "creatively productive."
15 demos.
10 cold calls.
5 distributor training sessions.
Incentives stress selling techniques that may not be the most productive ways
to sell.
Emphasis is on new gallon sales over repeat gallon sales.
Incentives weight new gallons over repeat gallons (two to one).
Emphasis to "demonstrate as often as possible" for the points.
Demonstrate to show you are a regular "guy" that gets his hands dirty, not
necessarily to show product benefits.
Bonus incentives appear to be a "carrot" only for those who don't regularly
make bonus.
That is, "hit 106 for maximum bonus and minimum quota increase."
The sales role gives the area manager little ability to impact his or her own
success.
To change distribution.
To move distributor outside his window.
The area manager describes his or her role as:
Being a "lackey."
Serving as a "chauffeur."
As a "caretaker of old business."

Area Manager's Role: Making Cold Calls

One of the causes of area manager frustration is the general ineffectiveness of
their cold calls sales role.

The area manager makes cold calls on end users not presently sold by the
WICS distributor.
With the difficult objective of moving these accounts to the WICS distribu-
tor.
If the area manager succeeds in moving this account over to WICS products,
chances are small that the distributor will keep the business.

Without a major portion of the account's total purchases the distributor cannot afford to continue to call on the account.

Distributor sales rep is on commission.

After five calls will stop calling if purchases have not begun to increase.

The distributor that lost the account will try extremely hard to get back the business.

This may mean giving the product away to keep control of the account—maintain majority of the account's purchases.

Past experience indicates that it is very difficult to move distributors outside their "window."

Appendix B: Conclusions of Study of WICS Sanitary Supply Distributor Attitudes

WICS Distributor's Role Expectations

The following is the WICS distributor's role as outlined by WICS management and sales force.

Act as an extension of the WICS sales force.

Push and promote WICS product line in a *specified area*

Sell WICS over other brands.

Always sell the premium benefits of WICS products to the end user, instead of distributor's private label.

Be aware that the WICS line could be lost if private label sales grow too large

Actively market new WICS products.

Distributor's Role Problems

Distributors have been angered by WICS's attempt to run their businesses ("WICS is trying to tell me what to do").

WICS makes demands—"uses pressure tactics."

Distributors say they are told "our way or no way."

Distributors feel they are forced to carry products they don't want.

High minimum buy-ins.

"Won't see area manager if we don't carry the new product."

Distributors say WICS management doesn't "realize we make our living selling all our products—not just WICS."

Communication is poor with WICS management.

One way—"our opinions never reach Lincoln."

"WICS uses the distributor as a testing ground for new products."

Distributor is not told what to expect.

After 14-week blitz, "you never hear about the product again."

The distributor sales force is not trained to sell to, and cannot afford to call on, certain segments of the market.

Growth takes the distributor into new geographical market areas, and WICS may elect not to go/grow with him.

New branch in different city.

Growth may take distributor sales personnel out of area manager's district. Receives no support from WICS.

Worst case—distributor sales rep's territory is completely outside district.

No WICS representative at any accounts.

Prefer to sell other than WICS.

WICS does not realize that a distributor's total business extends beyond "his own backyard" in many markets.

Distributor's Role Selling Costs

Distributors have shown concern over the high cost of selling WICS products. Sales costs are approximately 45 percent of the total operating costs.

"WICS products are basically no better than anyone else's."

Yet WICS asks distributors to switch their competitor's accounts over to WICS products.

Price advantage is very rare.

A problem must exist.

A demonstration is required.

All these making the "problem-solving" sale time-consuming and costly.

Result: When WICS product is sold, it is easy for competitive WICS distributors to cut price to try to get the business.

They have very low sales costs.

Required Action: Original distributor must cut margin to keep the business.

This frustrates distributor sales people.

Causes them to sell private label.

Case 3–8
Twin City Electric Motor Company

The Twin City Electric Motor Company manufactures and sells electric motors of all types and sizes. Customers range from manufacturers of model railroads to manufacturers of computers and machine tools. The company has organized its sales force by product line and by customer type. Although sales have been increasing steadily in recent years, Twin City's market share has dropped slightly. In an attempt to reverse this trend, Twin City surveyed its sales force of 185 people to see whether they had any insights into the problem. Questions were directed at such things as product quality, company support, and overall satisfaction with various aspects of the job. Several salespeople commented that the process of performance evaluation was unrealistic and did little to motivate salespeople toward better performance. Satisfaction with performance evaluation based on answers to several questions substantiated the written comments.

After reviewing the results, Harvey Hoover was dismayed. The whole performance evaluation process had always been a serious problem. Harvey thought that after the latest revision the problem had been solved, but the survey suggested otherwise.

Several years ago, the main indicator of sales performance was based on quota. The sales force was paid a combination salary plus commission. Quota performance was used to make merit adjustments to the salary base.

At first the sales force responded favorably to this plan, but the satisfaction was short-lived. A sales position at Twin City involved much more than dollar or unit sales; many qualitative factors were not being considered. Hoover argued that good performance on the qualitative factors would lead to greater sales. To evaluate the sales force on both qualitative and quantitative factors was the same as double counting. Twin City's marketing manager felt otherwise and insisted that evaluation of sales performance be based on both factors. A new system was developed by Hoover that gave equal weight to quota performance and a series of qualitative factors. Exhibit 1 is the form developed to be used by Twin City's 15 district sales managers, three regional sales managers, and the general sales manager, Hoover. Performance reviews were to take place each year before January 31 and were to be initiated by the district sales manager.

At first the new procedure was well received. Problems developed, however, when it became known that most sales representatives were receiving above average or better performance evaluations from their district sales managers. Typically, these evaluations were approved by the regional sales managers. Harvey Hoover, since he developed the system, usually went along with the district manager's evaluation. Even before the survey results became known, Hoover was getting complaints from the head of personnel about salary costs and equity problems. One sales representative complained that mediocre salespeople were being rewarded the same as better performers.

Exhibit 1

Sales Force Evaluation Report

Date————————

Sales representative————————————————
District sales manager————————————————
Regional sales manager————————————————
General sales manager————————————————

Quota performace

	Sales quota	Actual sales	Actual sales sales quota
Last year	————	————	————
Current year	————	————	————

Work habits

	Below average	Average	Above average	Exceptional
Sales presentations	————	————	————	————
Product knowledge	————	————	————	————
Time and territory management	————	————	————	————
Written reports	————	————	————	————

Customer relations

	Below average	Average	Above average	Exceptional
Tact	————	————	————	————
Aggressiveness	————	————	————	————
Initiative	————	————	————	————
Prestige	————	————	————	————
Customer complaints	————	————	————	————
Customer development	————	————	————	————

Personal qualities

	Below average	Average	Above average	Exceptional
Attitude	————	————	————	————
Appearance	————	————	————	————
Judgment	————	————	————	————
Personality	————	————	————	————
Enthusiasm	————	————	————	————

Evaluation Summary

Overall performance
Exceptional————————————
Superior————————————
Above average————————————
Average————————————
Below average————————————
Unsatisfactory————————————

Exhibit 1 *(concluded)*

Promotion opportunities
Ready now_____
Next year_____
Developing_____
Needs help_____
Not likely_____
Never_____

Reviewed by _____ District Sales Manager

and _____ Sales Representative

Hoover discussed the problem with a sales manager friend from another company who recommended that a forced distribution would eliminate the "halo effect." Hoover's associate also suggested having only five categories: exceptional, above average, average, below average, and unsatisfactory. With a forced distribution and assuming an average of 12 sales representatives for each district sales manager, the results would appear as:

1	2	4	3	2
Unsatisfactory	Below Average	Average	Above Average	Exceptional

The simplicity of this approach appealed to Hoover. He wanted to recommend its adoption to Twin City's marketing manager.

Index

A

ABC Rule of Account Classification, 181, 197, 202
A. B. Dick Company, 116
Account-conversion ratio, 631
Account development and servicing ratios, 631–32
Account management
  classification of accounts, 74
  customer's representatives, 91
  major accounts, 90–92
  national and key accounts, 117–21
  policies, 22–23, 72–75
  systems selling, 91
  telemarketing, 115–17
Account penetration ratio, 631
Accounting costs, 592–93
Accounts
  classification of, 181–82
  frequency of calls, 182
  major, 90–92
  national and key, 117–21
  natural and functional, 600
  optimal number of calls, 200–201
  servicing, 89–90
Achenbaum, Alvin R., 147 n, 149 n
Ackoff, Russell L., 182 n, 212 n
Acme Machine Company, 547–49
Acorn Computers, Ltd., 243
Activity quotas, 217–18
  in practice, 226
Activity reports, 218
Adam computer, 242–43
Advertising
  for brand awareness, 15
  for job applicants, 373–75

AES Data, Ltd., 15
Agrisystem Farm Machines, Inc., 491–96, 550–57
AIDA theory of persuasion, 96
Alderfer, Clayton P., 442
Albaum, Gerald, 297 n, 342 n, 343 n, 567 n, 623 n, 624 n
American Hoist and Derrick Company, 147
American Hospital Supply Corporation, 82–83
American Institute of CPAs, 424
American Institute of Management, *Manual of Excellent Management,* 567
Ames, B. Charles, 66 n
Ammons, Benjamin G., 214 n
Amway Distributors, 241
Anderson (Arthur) and Company; *see* Arthur Anderson and Company
Anderson, Eric M., 109 n
Anderson, Richard, 312 n, 313 n, 314 n
Anderson Distributors, Inc., 708–16
Anesthesia sales organization, 258
Ansul Company, 101–3
Antitrust laws, 52
Application blanks, 376–78
  equal opportunity requirements, 386
Aptitude, sales; *see* Sales aptitude
Aptitude component, of sales personnel, 300–301
Aptitude tests, 383
Armstrong, Gary M., 202 n
Arnoff, E. Leonard, 222 n
Arnold, Roy, 275–82

Arthur Andersen and Company, 115
Associated Merchandising Corporation, 35
Atari computers, 242
AT&T (American Telephone and Telegraph Company), 183
Atkinson, John W., 444 n
Atlanta, Ga., 167

B

Back-to-basics approach, in sales training, 396–400
Backes, Karl, 270, 274
Baehr, Melany E., 342, 343 n
Bagozzi, Richard P., 57 n, 59 n, 91 n, 118 n, 179 n, 203 n, 321 n, 322 n, 342, 343 n, 440 n
Baier, Donald E., 342, 343 n
Bailey, Earl L., 138 n, 140 n, 160 n, 161 n
Baily, John, 497
Baitinger Bicycle Company, 604–11
Banville, Guy R., 81 n
Barns, Jesse, 491, 494–95
Barr, Jay, 512
Barry, Thomas E., 377 n, 401 n, 471 n, 474 n
BARS; *see* Behaviorally anchored rating scales
Basic control unit, of sales territories, 187–95
Basu, Shanker, 147 n
Beach, Frank H., 86 n
Beatty, Richard W., 642 n
Beck, Leland L., 612 n
Behavior
  definition, 623

Behavior—*Cont.*
three tiers of, 397–98
Behavior modeling, 396–400
Behavioral analysis, 28
Behavioral skills, 398–400
Behavioral strategies, 398–400
Behavioral tactics, 398–400
Behaviorally anchored rating
scales (BARS), 641–43
Behrman, Douglas N., 623 n
Belasco, James A., 311 n
Bellizzi, Joseph A., 78 n
Benet, Terry, 491
Berkowitz, Eric N., 49 n, 51 n,
302 n, 321 n
Berky, Edwin, 148
Bernardin, H. John, 642 n
Berne, Eric, 410
Bernhardt, Kenneth L., 321 n,
402 n
Best, Roger J., 145 n
Beswick, Charles A., 57 n,
179 n, 203 n
Bianchi, Suzanne M., 346 n
Bids, acquisition of, 80
Billings, Gus, 290
Birnbaum, Jeffrey H., 563 n
Black Americans, sales aptitude,
345–50
Bliss and Laughlin Industries,
Inc., 564
BMW company (Bavarian Motor
Works), 57
Boatwright, Bob, 505
Bonheim, Frank W., 392 n
Bonjean, Charles M., 321 n
Bon-Quer Industries, 231–33
Bonus plan, 211, 467, 528, 712–
14; *see also* Compensation
programs *and* Incentive pro-
grams
Boundary position, of sales per-
sonnel, 311–12
Box, G. E., 153 n
Box-Jenkins methods of fore-
casting, 153 n
Boyd, Joseph, 19
BPI; *see* Buying Power Index
Bragg, Arthur J., 91 n, 118 n
Brand awareness, 15
Breakdown method, of deter-
mining sales force size,
180–81

Brice, M. A., 176 n, 183 n
Brock, Timothy C., 351 n
Brown, Arthur A., 182 n
Bruce, Grady D., 321 n
Bryden, Thomas, 203 n
Bucholz, Rogene A., 52 n
Burgoyne, David, 326 n
Busch, Paul, 323 n, 351 n
Business
acquisition, 36
unit plans, 41
Buskirk, Richard H., 8 n, 86 n,
137 n, 187 n, 210 n, 322 n,
414 n, 566 n, 593 n
Buyers, role in organizational
buying, 76
Buying center; *see* Organiza-
tional buying
Buying Power Index (BPI),
164 n, 167–68, 573–75,
579
Buzby, Stephen L., 612 n

C

Call activity ratio, 632
Callahan, Earl, 253–55, 257,
259
CALLPLAN program, 200–202
Calls, by sales personnel, 629;
see also Customers
Campbell, John C., 299 n
Campbell, John P., 418 n, 434 n,
440 n
Canned sales presentation, 95–
96
Canvassing for customers, 86
Career path incentives, 480–81
Carey, James F., 394 n
Carlson, Eric D., 583 n
Carlson, Rodney L., 157
Carroll, John, 512–15
Case analysis, 231–92, 418–19,
487–557, 651–737
Catalanello, Ralph H., 426 n
Celanese Corporation, 183, 202
Central tendency, in perform-
ance ratings, 641
Chambers, John C., 160 n
Chambers, Thomas E., 201 n,
630 n
Chase, Marilyn, 213 n
Chase, Susan, 564 n

Chatfield, C., 150 n
Chips-to-Dip, Inc., 516–22
Chonko, Laurence B., 323 n
Christopher Industries, 695–707
Churchill, Gilbert A., Jr., 7 n,
8 n, 9 n, 10 n, 141 n, 149 n,
166 n, 297 n, 302 n, 303 n,
309 n, 311 n, 314 n, 321 n,
323 n, 327 n, 336 n, 338 n,
341 n, 343 n, 347 n, 352 n,
402 n, 439 n, 440 n, 443 n,
448 n, 480 n, 623 n, 624 n,
640 n
Churchman, C. West, 222 n
Cities, as sales territories, 190–
93
Civil Rights Act of 1964, 346,
385
Clark, Donald F., 182 n
Clark, Russell A., 444 n
Clarke, Darrel G., 162 n
Clarke, Walter V., 342, 343 n
Classroom training, 415, 418–19
Closing a sale, 89
Clowes, Kenneth W., 57 n,
187 n, 202 n
Cocanougher, A. Benton, 640 n,
641 n, 642 n, 643 n
Cohen, Gary, 512 n
Coleco computers, 238, 242–43
Collins, Robert H., 347 n, 352 n
Comer, James M., 427 n
Combination plans, of compen-
sation, 467–70
Commissions
plan, 211
straight, 466–67
Commodore computers, 237,
240–41
Companies
goals and mission, 42–43
needs, 79
organizational environment,
55–57
participants in buying decisions, 76
resources and objectives, 69
Company dealer organization,
263–65
Company orientation, in sales
training, 408–9
Company sales force, 106–9; *see
also* Sales force

Compensation programs, 455–77, 533–36
  Agrisystem Farm Machines, Inc., 550–57
  appropriate level of compensation, 461–63
  bonus incentives, 712–14
  bonuses, 467
  choosing an effective form, 463–71
  combination plans, 467–70
  and company objectives, 457–60
  drawing account, 466–67
  earnings opportunity ratio, 449
  incentive pay, 469–70
  and motivation, 449–50; *see also* Motivation
  procedures for designing, 457
  reimbursement of selling expenses, 471–77
  salary increases, 710–12
  straight commission, 466–67
  straight salary, 464–65
  too much or too little, 462–63
  variety of rewards, 460–61
  windfalls, 470
Competition, variations of intensity, 59–60
Competitive analysis, 240–43
Competitors, recruiting from, 372
Computers
  sales information on, 177
  use in
    cost analysis, 642–44
    decision support systems, 582–87
    performance appraisal, 644–45
    sales analysis, 582–87
Concept of sales ability, 300
Conference Board, 160–62, 212–13, 411
Conference-discussion method of training, 418
Consumer goods, territory demand estimates, 167–68
Consumer protection laws, 52
Contribution margin approach in cost analysis, 593–98
Control Data Corporation, 410

Cook, Michael, 392
Cook County, Ill., 190
Coors Brewing Company, 57
Corning Glass Works, 147
Corporate culture, 56
Corporate strategic plan, 41
Cost analysis, 28, 591–617, 652–55
  accounting versus marketing costs, 592–93
  advertising, 607–9
  allocation of functional costs, 600–603
  Baitinger Bicycle Company, 605–11
  development, 591–92
  direct and indirect costs, 593
  direct selling, 606–7
  full cost or contribution margin, 593–98
  functional cost centers, 598
  natural and functional accounts, 600
  order processing, 609
  procedure, 598–611
  prospects and problems, 611–12
  return on assets managed, 612–16
  and sales analysis, 591
  specific versus general expense, 593–94
  summing allocated costs, 604
  transportation, 609–10
  warehousing and shipping, 609
Cost-control, in sales territories, 178–79
Cost-per-call ratio, 631
Costs
  accounting versus marketing, 592–93
  direct and indirect, 593
  functional, 600–603
Costello, John, 346 n
Cotham, James C., III, 342, 343 n, 378 n
Counties, as sales territories, 189–91
County and City Data Book, 190, 279
Cox, James E., Jr., 160 n
Cox, William E., Jr., 163 n, 580 n

Crask, Melvin R., 71 n
Cravens, David W., 42 n, 57 n, 179 n, 187 n, 197 n, 199 n, 203 n
Credibility, in sales training, 393–95
Cribbs, Mike, 546
Crisp, Richard D., 562 n, 578 n
Crissy, W. J. E., 86 n, 592 n
Critical success factors, 642
Cron, William L., 219 n, 329 n
Crosby, Helen Jane, 487
Crosby Flour Mills, Ltd., 487–89
Culture, organizational, 56
Cummings, Larry L., 322 n, 401 n
Cundiff, Edward W., 134 n, 181 n, 183 n, 204 n, 217 n
Cunningham, Isabelle C. M., 86 n
Cunningham, William H., 86 n
Curham, R. C., 314 n
Customer-oriented strategy, 14–15
Customer relations, 402
Customer service, 177
Customer type sales force, 112–14
Customers
  advantages of telemarketing, 86–87, 115
  canvassing for, 86
  characteristics, 350–53
  classification of, 181–82
  closing a sale, 89
  direct and indirect, 354–55
  frequency of calls, 182
  initial approach to, 87–88
  market forecasting, 133–69
  market motivations, 138
  missionary selling, 354–55
  modified rebuy, 83
  new business selling, 356
  optimal number of calls on, 200–201
  organizational buying process, 75–83
  prospecting for, 86–87
  qualifying prospects, 88
  repeat purchase behavior, 82–83

Customers—*Cont.*
    sales presentation to, 88–89
    servicing accounts, 89–90
    straight rebuy, 82–83
    in technical selling, 355
    in trade selling, 353–54
Customer's representative, 91
Cyclical factor, of time series
    analysis, 154

D

Dachler, H. Peter, 442 n
Dalkey, Norman C., 145 n
Dallas Cowboys, 335
Dalrymple, Douglas J., 134 n,
    161 n, 162 n, 219 n
Darden, Bill R., 303 n
Darmon, Rene Y., 370 n, 461 n,
    463 n
Data system, in decision support
    system, 583
Davenport, William J., 351 n
Davey, Jim, 292
Davis, Robert T., 286 n, 503 n,
    708 n
Davoust, Merrett J., 604 n
Day, Ralph L., 203 n
Deal, Terrence E., 56 n
Dealers, 263–65
Death of a Salesman (Miller), 3,
    422
Deciders, role in buying deci-
    sions, 76
Decision support systems (DSS)
    data/model/and dialog sys-
        tems, 583
    electronic spread sheets, 585–
        87
    in performance appraisal,
        644–45
    in sales analysis, 582–87
Decomposition method of fore-
    casting, 153–56
DeCotiss, Thomas A., 642 n
Decreasing returns principle of
    sales force size, 184
Delaware Paint and Plate Glass
    Industries, Inc., 270–74
Delphi technique of forecasting,
    145–47
Demand estimation, 136–38

Demographic characteristics of
    sales personnel, 443
Denson, Terry, 546
Denver Illini Genetics, 523–32
Deutscher, Terry, 326 n
Developmental sales people,
    114
Dialog systems, in data support
    systems, 583
Dick, (A. B.) Company; *see* A. B.
    Dick Company
Direct cost, 593
Direct reimbursement plans,
    475
Direct selling
    characteristics, 244
    research results, 244–45
Direct Selling Association, 239,
    244–45
Discrimination in employment,
    346; *see also* Equal employ-
    ment opportunity
Distribution policies, 71–72
Division of labor, 104
Dixon, Richard, 177
DMI; *see* Dun's Market Identi-
    fiers
Dollar volume quotas, 216
Donnelly, James H., Jr., 321 n
Doreen, Dale, 351 n
Dornoff, Ronald J., 81 n
Downey, Regina, 261 n, 533 n
Drawing account, 466–67
Drew, Linda, 261 n
DSA; *see* Direct Selling Associa-
    tion
DSS; *see* Decision support sys-
    tems
Dubinsky, Alan J., 3 n, 4 n, 5 n,
    6 n, 49 n, 50 n, 51 n, 377 n,
    401 n, 471 n, 474 n
Duggan, Robert D., 342, 343 n
Dumesic, Ruth J., 424 n
Dunne, Patrick M., 595 n, 604 n
Dunnette, Marvin D., 299 n,
    343, 418 n, 642 n
Dunning, Harrison F., 148
Dun's Market Identifiers, 193,
    195
Dutton, John M., 312 n
Dynasty Corporation, 238–40,
    245–52
Dynasty sales plan, 245–52

E

Earnings opportunity ratio, 449
Easton, Allan, 220 n, 222 n
Eby, Frank H., Jr., 139 n
Economic environment, 49
Edwards Personnel Preference
    Schedule, 344, 383
Effectiveness, definition, 624
Elaine Powers salons, 137
El-Ansary, Adel I., 107 n
Electronic spread sheets, 585–
    87
Emery, Donald R., 351 n
Emery, John C., Jr., 209
Employment agencies, recruit-
    ment through, 375–76
Enis, Ben, 8 n, 75 n
Environment
    changing, 40–41
    constraints on sales force, 57–
        58
    economic, 49
    external, 49–55, 59–60
    impact on marketing plan-
        ning, 48–57
    impact on motivation, 445–47
    legal, 52
    marketing failures, 54–55
    natural, 52–54
    organizational, 55–59
    political, 52
    and sales program, 38–39
    scanning and forecasting, 54–
        55
    social, 49
    social and ethical dilemmas,
        49–52
    technical, 54
Environmental analysis, 54–55
Environmental variable compo-
    nent, sales personnel, 302
Equal employment opportunity
    legal requirements, 346
    recruitment requirements,
        385–87
Equal Employment Opportunity
    Commission, 346, 385 n
Equal opportunity laws, 52
Ericson, Bob, 290
Ethical dilemmas, 49–52
Evan-Picone, 35–41, 44, 54, 56
Evans, Charles, 36

Evans, Franklin, 345 n, 350–51
Evans, Kenneth R., 616 n, 626 n
Ex-Cell-O Corporation, 142
Expectancies
  accuracy of, 327–29
  magnitude of, 329
  of motivation, 299, 435–37
Expense quotas, 219
Expense ratios, 631
Expenses
  of sales personnel, 630
  specific and general, 593–94
Experienced personnel, training
  for, 420–21
Expert opinion method of fore-
  casting, 144–45
Exponential smoothing method
  of forecasting, 152–53
External environment, effect on
  sales productivity, 59–60
Extrinsic rewards, 303

F

Face-to-face contact, in personal
  selling, 67–68
Fahey, Liam, 55 n
Falvey, John J., 393 n, 400,
  410 n, 417 n, 419 n
Family situation, and sales apti-
  tude, 340
Faris, Charles W., 79 n, 82 n
Feedback, on purchases, 82
Feldman, Ted, 491, 493–94
Ferber, Robert, 147 n
Festinger, Leon, 352 n
Field sales force, 115–17
Field selling expenses
  controlling, 219
  quota, 227
Fildes, Robert, 139 n
Financial quotas, 218–20
  levels of, 226–27
Financial resources, corporate,
  56–57
Fiocca, Renato, 197 n, 199 n
Fireman Protection Group, 101
Fischer, Paul M., 592 n
Fitch, H. G., 312 n
Fitwell Fashion Shop, 433–34,
  455
Flanagan, J., 642 n
Forbes, Jeffrey, 717 n

Fogg, C. Davis, 187 n, 612 n
Ford, Neil M., 7 n, 8 n, 9 n,
  109 n, 297 n, 302 n, 303 n,
  309 n, 311 n, 314 n, 321 n,
  323 n, 327 n, 402 n, 424 n,
  439 n, 440 n, 443 n, 448 n,
  480 n, 623 n, 624 n, 640 n
Formal education, and sales ap-
  titude, 340
Frazier, Gary L., 329 n
French, Cecil L., 342, 343 n
French, Warren, 303 n
Fudge, William K., 201 n
Full-cost approach, in cost anal-
  ysis, 593–98
Functional accounts, 600
Functional costs
  allocation of, 600–603
  centers, 598
Furstenberg, Diane von, 35
Futrell, Charles M., 7 n, 347 n,
  628 n

G

Gadel, M. S., 351 n
Games People Play (Berne), 410
Gatekeepers, role in buying de-
  cisions, 76
General Electric, 226, 564
General expenses, 594
General Foods, 347
General lines sales organization,
  258–60
General Mills, 347
General role inaccuracy, 324
General Typewriter Company,
  510–11
Genn, J. Patrick, 537 n, 542 n
Genner Security Systems, Inc.,
  537–41
Geographical sales organization,
  109–11
Geographical territory; *see* Sales
  territory
Ghiselli, Edwin E., 300 n, 342,
  343 n
Gifts, to customers, 50
Gildersleeve Furniture Enter-
  prises, 231–33
Goals
  organizational, 56
  in planning, 42–43

Golden Bear Distributors, 503–9
Goldman Chemical Company,
  286–92
Gonik, Jacob, 224 n
Gopel, R. A., 427
Gordon, Joe, 290–92
Govoni, Norman A. P., 134 n,
  181 n, 183 n, 204 n, 217 n
Gray, John, 503–4, 509
Green Giant Company, 112
Greenberg, Herbert, 343
Greene, Charles N., 311 n,
  322 n, 401 n
Griese, Bill, 257
Grocery Trading Area Map, 189
Gross, Neil C., 311 n
Gross margin quotas, 219
Grossman, Elliott S., 140 n
Grothman, Pamella, 234 n
Grover, Robert, 512
Gultman, Joseph P., 46 n
Gwin, John M., 73 n, 75 n
Gwinner, R., 95 n, 97 n, 226 n

H

Haberstroh, Chadwick J., 312 n
Hackett, Donald W., 347 n
Hahne, Gene, 393 n, 395
Hall, William K., 564 n
Hall, William P., 202 n, 219 n
Hallmark Cards, 347
Halo effect, in performance ap-
  praisal, 640
Hancock Industries, 497
Hannan, Mack, 113 n
Hansen Manufacturing Com-
  pany, 579–80
Hardy, Jeff, 257
Haring, Albert, 438 n, 478 n
Harper, Irv, 513–15
Harrell, Thomas W., 342–43
Harris, Clyde E., Jr., 71 n
Harris, Thomas A., 410
Harris Corporation, 18–19
Harris Intertype Corporation,
  141–42
Hartley, Steven W., 338 n,
  640 n
Havens, George N., 580
Heathcoate Pharmaceuticals,
  542–46
Heckert, J. B., 596 n

Helmer, Olaf, 146 n
Helmer, Richard M., 153 n
Heneman, Herbert G., III,
    629 n, 642 n
Henry, Porter, 181 n
Herzberg, Frederick, 442
Hess, Sidney W., 203 n
Hibon, Michele, 163 n
Hierarchy sales analysis, 573–
    82
Hise, Richard T., 591 n
Hofer, Charles W., 42 n
Hogue, Larry, 651 n
HOMAP, Inc., 268–69
Home computers, 234–40, 245–
    52
  competitive analysis, 240–43
Home study method of training,
    419–20
Home video market, 54–55
Hopkins, David S., 403 n, 404 n,
    406 n, 407 n, 411 n, 414 n,
    415 n, 416 n, 418 n, 419 n,
    420 n, 421 n
Horizontal marketing audit,
    562–63
Horizontal sales organization,
    103, 106–17
Horngren, Charles R., 601 n
House, Robert J., 311 n, 448 n
Howells, G. W., 342–43
Huak, James G., 203 n
Hughes, G. David, 585 n, 645 n
Hulin, Charles L., 442 n
Hulswet, Frank T., 182
Hurwood, David L., 140 n

I

IBM (International Business
    Machines), 17, 56–57,
    111 n, 147, 183, 223–24,
    243, 347, 372, 423
Iceberg principle, in sales analy-
    sis, 578–79
I'm O.K.—You're O.K. (Harris),
    410
Incentive
  sales force, 16–17
  from sales quotas, 210–11
Incentive pay, 469–70
Incentive programs, 455–61,
    477–82; *see also* Compensa-
    tion programs

bonuses, 528, 712–14
  and company objectives, 457–
    60
  and motivation, 449–50
  nonfinancial rewards, 480–82
  procedures for designing, 457
  promotion and career paths,
    480–81
  recognition programs, 481–82
  sales contests, 477–80, 535–
    36
  variety of rewards, 460–61
Incremental method of sales
    force size determination,
    184–87
Independent agents, 106–9
  transaction costs, 109 n
Indirect cost, 593
Industrial goods, territory de-
    mand estimate, 164–66
Industrial selling
  characteristics, 5
  missionary selling, 6–7
  new business selling, 7
  product characteristics, 70–
    71
  product information, 6–7
  versus retail selling, 5–6
  role inaccuracy of sales per-
    sonnel, 299
  technical selling, 7
  trade selling, 6
  types of jobs, 6–7
Industry orientation, in sales
    training, 408
Influencers, role in buying deci-
    sions, 76
Inland Steel, 347
Innovative roles, of sales person-
    nel, 313–14
Input measures, of performance,
    628–31
Inside sales force, 115–17
Instrumentalities
  accuracy of, 320–30
  magnitude of, 330
  of motivation, 299
  sales personnel's, 437–38
Intelligence tests, 382–83
Interviews
  equal opportunity require-
    ments, 386
  of job applicants, 378–79
Intrinsic rewards, 303

Isolate-and-explode principle, in
    sales analysis, 580–82
Ivancevich, John M., 321 n,
    640 n, 641 n, 642 n, 643 n
Ives, Norman, 290

J

Jackson, Donald W., Jr., 599 n,
    616 n, 627 n
Jackson Personality Profile, 344
Jaedicke, Robert H., 596 n,
    597 n
J. C. Penney Company, 35, 119,
    563
Jeans West stores, 90
Jenkins, G. M., 153 n
Job descriptions, 363–64, 491–
    93
  contents, 365–66
Job discrimination, 346
Job experience
  and motivation, 444
  sales personnel's, 444
Job performance, factors in-
    volved in, 297; *see also* Per-
    formance appraisal
Job role, 23–24
Job satisfaction, 487–89, 533–
    36
  of sales personnel, 303–4
  theories, 442–43
Johansson, Johnny K., 153 n
John, Christopher, 253–54
Johnson, Lynwood A., 150 n
Johnston, Jeffrey L., 147 n,
    158 n
Johnston, Wesley J., 75 n
Jolson, Marvin A., 96 n, 145 n,
    146 n, 226 n, 375 n, 410 n,
    481 n
Joy, Maurice O., 163 n
Jury of executive opinion
    method of forecasting, 144–
    45

K

Kahn, George N., 114 n
Kahn, Robert L., 311 n, 313 n,
    321 n
Kanuck, Leslie, 347 n, 348 n,
    350 n
Kenn, Roger, 231 n
Kennedy, Allan A., 56 n

Kennedy, Anita M., 80 n
Kerr, Willard A., 343
Kettelle, John D., 182 n
Key accounts, 117–21
    division, 119
    multilevel selling, 120–21
    sales executives, 118–19
    sales force, 119–20
    team selling, 120
Kickbacks, to customers, 50
King, William R., 55 n, 286–92
Kirchner, Wayne K., 343, 642 n
Kirkpatrick, Donald L., 426 n
Kirpalani, Vishnu H., 612 n
Kitchenware Company, 573–78,
    580, 583, 586
Klebba, Joanne M., 75 n
Klein, Calvin, 35
Klein Institute for Aptitude Test-
    ing, 367
Kniffen, Fred W., 186 n
Kodak, 78
Kohl, Jerry M., 423
Korman, Abraham K., 301 n,
    329 n, 445 n
Kotler, Philip, 78 n, 91 n, 133 n,
    580 n
Kraar, Louis, 35 n
Kraut, A. I., 397 n
Krepelka, Ernest J., 644 n
Kronholm, Brett, 523 n

L

Laczniak, Gene R., 567 n
La Forge, Raymond, 197 n,
    199 n
Lambert, Zarrell, 186 n, 187 n
Lamont, Lawrence M., 83–85,
    300 n, 314, 342–43, 640 n
Lanier Business Products, Inc.,
    14–19, 22, 25–26, 49, 70
Large role set, 312–13
Lauren, Ralph, 35
Laurence, Paul R., 106 n
Lawler, Edward E., III, 301 n,
    329 n, 330 n, 418 n, 439 n,
    442 n, 444 n
Leadership theory, and motiva-
    tion, 448
Learned proficiency, 301
Lecture method, of training, 418
Legal environment, 52
Lehman, Donald R., 81 n

Levin, Richard I., 221 n
L'Herisson, Laura L., 396 n
Likert scale, 488
Limited reimbursement plans,
    475–77
Linkage role inaccuracy, 324–30
    accuracy of expectancies, 327–
    29
    accuracy of instrumentalities,
    329–30
    causes and consequences,
    326–30
    magnitude of expectancies,
    329
Lirtzman, Sidney I., 311 n
Little, John D. C., 583 n
Locander, William, 327 n
Lodish, Leonard M., 179 n,
    200 n, 201 n, 203 n
Loen, Raymond O., 371 n
Longman, D. R., 596 n
Lorsch, Jay W., 106 n
Los Angeles County, Cal., 190
Lost account ratio, 631
Loving, Rush, 14 n
Lowell, Edgar L., 444 n
Lucas, Henry C., Jr., 57 n, 186,
    187 n, 202 n
Lundberg, Nancy, 275–82
Lundstrom, William J., 83–85,
    300 n, 314 n, 342–43,
    640 n
Lyskanycz, Myron R., 491 n,
    550 n

M

McCarry, Edmund D., 600
McCarthy, E. Jerome, 566 n,
    579 n
McClelland, David C., 444 n
McEachern, Alexander W.,
    311 n
McElwain, Carolyn S., 343 n
McGraw-Hill Laboratory of Ad-
    vertising Performance,
    178 n
McGraw-Hill Publications Re-
    search Department, 179 n
McMurry, Robert N., 370 n
Mahajan, Jayashree, 109 n
Major account management
    approach, 90–92

Makridakis, Spyros, 139 n,
    150 n, 151 n, 152 n, 155 n,
    163 n
Management by objectives, 449
Management information sys-
    tems, 582
Mannington Mills, Inc., 564
*Manual of Excellent Manage-
    ment* (American Institute of
    Management), 567
Manufacturer's representative,
    107
Manz, Charles C., 396 n
Margin information, 219
Market analysis
    Pure Drug Company, 656–78
    Twin City Electric Motor
        Company, 735–37
    Wentworth Industrial Clean-
        ing Supplies, 717–34
Market coverage, in a sales ter-
    ritory, 177–78
Market Development Depart-
    ment, 102
Market factor
    definition, 164
    in territory demand estimates,
        163–68
Market forecasting
    buying power index, 167–68
    Delphi technique, 145–47
    estimation of demand, 136–38
    jury of executive opinion
        method, 144–45
    market testing, 147–49
    motivation of customers, 138
    sales force composite method,
        141–44
    sales forecasts, 138–39
    for sales territories, 184–87,
        195
    selecting a method, 158–63
    time series analysis, 149–56
    statistical demand analysis,
        156–58
    terminology of, 133–36
    territory demand estimates,
        163–68
    usage estimate, 137
    users' expectations method,
        139–41
Market Identifiers, Dun's, 193,
    195
Market index, 164

Market motivation, 138
Market opportunity analysis, 44
Market orientation, 408
Market position, 58
Market potential, 133
Market target, 37
Market testing, 147–49
Market type sales force, 112–14
Marketing activities, 244–45
Marketing audit, 562–65
  methods and procedures, 565
  objectives, 563
  organization of company, 564
  personnel, 565
  policies, 563–64
  vertical and horizontal types, 562–63
Marketing budgets, 11–14
Marketing costs, 592–93
Marketing cost analysis; *see* Cost analysis
Marketing efforts, 58
Marketing failures, 54–55
Marketing functions, 41
Marketing manager, 48; *see also* Sales managers *and* Sales management
Marketing mix, 47
  role of personal selling, 65–66
Marketing planning
  audit and adjust, 47–48
  company mission and goals, 42–43
  and competition, 59–60
  and corporate culture, 56
  effects of external environment, 48–57
  environment, 38–39
  failures, 54–55
  hierarchy of plans, 41
  importance, 40–41
  marketing mix, 47
  market opportunity analysis, 44
  process, 41–48
  review and revision, 47
  selecting strategies, 47
  strategy generation, 44–47
  and territorial variations, 60
Marketing problems, 17–18
Marketing strategy
  advertising, 15
  aspects of, 22–23

  in a changing environment, 17–18
  company resources and objectives, 69
  customer oriented, 14–15
  definition, 40
  distribution processes, 71–72
  Evan-Picone, 35–38
  generating, 44–47
  integrating sales programs, 22
  Lanier Business Products, 14–19
  new, 36–38
  pricing policies, 72
  product and marketing problems, 17–18
  product characteristics, 70–71
  promotional tools, 66–72
  proper role of personal selling, 14–19, 68–72
  role of sales force, 15–17
  sales management problems, 18
  selection of, 47
  target market, 69–70
Markets, expanding, 57
Marshall, Judith, 326 n
Martin, Warren S., 349 n
Maslow, Abraham, 442
Mason, Ward S., 311 n
Mathews, H. Lee, 351 n
Mausner, Bernard, 442 n
Mayer, David, 343
Mental abilities, and sales aptitude, 340
Mental states approach to selling, 97
Meranda, Peter F., 342, 343 n
Mercedes Benz Company, 57
Merchandising representatives, 31
Metropolitan Statistical Area (MSA), 190
Meyers, Robert H., 438
Michael, George C., 160 n
Microcomputers, 644–45
Middlemen
  manufacturer's representative, 107
  selling agent, 107
Mid-State Coal Company, 512–19
Midwest Medical Equipment Corporation, 283–85

Miller, Arthur, 3
Miller, Mary Lynn, 455 n, 456 n, 457 n
Milner, Gene W., 14–15
Miner, John B., 342–43
Miner, R. B., 596 n
Minnesota Mining and Manufacturing (3M) Company, 54
Minorities, sales aptitude, 345–50
MIS; *see* Management information systems
Mission, in planning, 42–43
Missionary selling
  industrial, 6–7
  and sales aptitude, 354–55
Model system, in decision support systems, 583
Modified rebuy, 83
Monoky, John F., Jr., 351 n
Monsanto Company, 573
Montgomery, Douglas C., 150 n
Morale, 401–2
Moriarity, Rowland T., 75 n, 118 n
Morris, Don, 148 n
Morris, Malcolm L., 478 n
Morrison, Donald, 141 n
Mosinee Paper Company, 567
Moss, Stan, 337
Mossman, Frank H., 592 n
Motivation
  compensation programs, 455–77
  complexity of, 434
  component of sales personnel, 299–300
  and demography, 443
  expectancies, 299, 435–37
  failure of, 433–34
  impact of
    environmental conditions on, 445–47
    organizational variables on, 447–50
    sales personnel's characteristics, 441–45
  incentive programs, 449–50, 455–61, 477–82
  instrumentalities, 437–38
  and job experience, 444
  and job satisfaction, 442–43
  leadership theory, 448–49

model prediction of effort and
performance, 440–41
psychological process, 434–40,
444–45
of sales force, 433–50
of senior sales representatives,
537–41
sets of perceptions, 435
theories, 442–43
valences for performance,
299, 438–40
Moving averages method of
forecasting, 150–52
Moyer, Reed, 187 n
Mullick, Satinder R., 160 n
Multilevel selling, 78
to key accounts, 120–21
Multiple Personal Inventory,
383
Murdick, Robert G., 138 n
Murphy, Kevin, 504–9
Murphy, Liz, 423 n
Murphy, Matthew J., 459 n,
460 n, 462 n, 468 n,
470 n
Music Man, 3
Musselwhite, Ed, 410 n
Mutual of New York, 177
My Years With General Motors
(Sloan), 616

N

Narayanan, Vadake K., 55 n
National accounts, 117–21
National Lead, 140
National Manufacturing Com-
pany, 275–82
Natural accounts, 600
Natural environment, 52–55
Need anticipation, 79
Need-satisfaction approach to
selling, 97–98
Net profit approach; *see* Full-
cost approach, in cost anal-
ysis
Net profit quotas, 219–20
New business selling
industrial sales, 7
sales aptitude, 356
New customers, 7
New products, 520–22
development, 54
market testing, 147–49

New recruits, sales training for,
403–10, 510–11
Newton, Derek A., 6 n, 122 n,
353 n, 367 n
Nichols, Donald R., 163 n
Nonselling activities, 630–31
Nord, Walter R., 400 n
North, Harper Q., 146 n
Nowland Organization, Inc., 244

O

Objectives, organizational, 56
O'Connor, P. J., 6 n
Office of Federal Contract Com-
pliance, 346
Office of Management and
Budget, 190 n
Office computer systems, 17–18
OJT; *see* On-the-job training
Olsen, Jon, 261–67
Olsen, Joseph, 262, 264
Olsen Seed Farms, 261–67
Omega Medical Products, Inc.,
253–60
On-the-job training, 414–17
O'Neill, Paul J., 343 n
O'Neill, William J., 139 n
Opportunity analysis, 44
Opportunity rate, for promotion,
449
Order-cancellation ratio, 632
Order routine, 82
Orders-per-call ratio, 632
Organ, Dennis W., 311 n
Organizational buying
center, 76–78
modified rebuy, 83
need anticipation, 79
participants in decision making, 76
performance evaluation and
feedback, 82
process, 75
process stages, 79–83
proposals or bids, 80
quantity of needed items, 79–
80
repeat purchase behavior, 82–
83
sales planning implications,
78
search for potential suppliers,
80

selection of
order routine, 82
suppliers, 80–81
straight rebuy, 82–83
Organizational component of
sales personnel, 302
Organizational environment
effect on sales productivity,
58–59
financial resources, 56–57
goals, objectives, and culture,
56
marketing planning, 55–57
personnel, 56
production capabilities, 57
research and development, 57
Organizational variables, impact
on motivation, 447–50
Oschrin, Elsie, 338 n
O'Shaughnessy, John, 81 n
Ostrom, Lonnie L., 5989, 616 n,
627 n
Output measures of performance, 627–28
Outside sales force, 115–17
Owens, Barbara, 290
Owens Corning Company, 140 n

P

Palm Beach clothing, 37–39
Palmer, Arnold, 15
Pan, Judy, 163 n
Parasuraman, A., 197 n, 199 n,
203 n
Parker Brothers Company, 54–
55
Parker Pen Company, 148
Parkinson, Gerald, 202 n
Parsons, Leonard J., 134
Paul, Gordon W., 3 n, 46 n
Pearson, Andrall E., 120 n
Peck, Charles A., 10 n, 469 n
Pederson, Carlton A., 628 n
Penney (J. C.) Company; *see*
J. C. Penney Company
Perceived role
ambiguity, 299, 310
conflict, 298–99, 310
inaccuracy, 310–11
Performance account, 631–32
Performance appraisal
Anderson Distributors, Inc.,
708–16

Performance appraisal—*Cont.*
  behaviorally anchored rating
    scales, 641–43
  call activity ratio, 632
  central tendency, 641
  Christopher Industries, 695–
    707
  corrective action, 645–46
  critical success factors, 642
  decision support systems,
    644–45
  definition, 623–24
  and effectiveness, 624
  expense ratios, 631
  expenses, 630
  halo effect, 640
  ill-defined personality traits,
    640
  input measures, 628–31
  interpersonal bias, 641
  lack of outcome focus, 640
  leniency or harshness, 640–
    41
  nonselling activities, 630–31
  number of
    accounts, 628
    calls, 629
    orders secured, 627–28
  objective measures, 626–33
  organizational influence, 641
  output measures, 627–28
  problems with, 640–41
  productivity ratio, 632
  sales force, 725–27
  by sales quotas, 211
  Sierra Chemical Company,
    679–88
  subjective measures, 633–43
  Supersonic Stereo Company,
    689–94
  time utilization, 629–30
Perreault, William D., Jr., 73 n,
  75 n, 197 n, 623 n, 640 n
Personal component in sales
  personnel, 302
Personal computers, 245–52
  in comparative analysis, 240–
    43
  industry, 234–40
Personal interviews, 378–81
Personal selling
  advantages, 7–14
  advantages as a promotional
    tool, 67–68

costs for a company, 69
  disadvantages, 68
  distribution policies, 71–72
  division of labor, 104–5
  face-to-face contact, 67–68
  industrial sales, 70–71
  and marketing audit policies,
    563–64
  and marketing budgets, 11–
    14
  in overall market strategy, 68–
    72
  and pricing policies, 72
  process stages, 86–90
  reasons for success, 65–66
  role in
    marketing mix, 65–66
    marketing strategy, 14–19
  in a sales territory, 177–78
  use of decision support sys-
    tems, 583–85
Personality characteristics, 340–
  41, 383
Personnel, organizational, 56;
  see also Sales personnel
Persuasion, AIDA theory of, 96
Peter, J. Paul, 400 n
Peters, Thomas J., 56 n
Peterson, Robert A., 343 n
Philips, Lynn, 505
Physical examinations, 382
Physical volume quotas, 216
Picone, Joseph, 35–37
Pillsbury Company, 112
Planning; *see* Marketing plan-
  ning
PLATO computer system, 410
Plunkett, H. Doug, 101 n
Point quotas, 216–17
PoKempner, Stanley J., 138 n,
  160 n, 161 n
Political environment, 52
Pope, Jeffrey, 115 n
Porter-Cable Machine Company,
  217
Potential suppliers, 80
Powers (Elaine) salons; *see*
  Elaine Powers salons
Pritchard, Robert D., 299 n,
  434 n, 440 n
Problem-solution approach to
  selling, 98–99
Procter and Gamble, 347
Product knowledge, 407–8

Product line sales force, 111–12
Production capabilities, 57
Production information, industrial sales, 6–7
Productivity
  increase in sales, 401
  ratio, 632
Products
  characteristics, 70–71
  development, 54
  market testing, 147–49
  marketing problems, 17
  usage estimate, 137
Profit, 219–20
Profit margin information, 219
Profitability analysis, 598–611;
  see also Cost analysis
Profitable Distribution Management Program, 101
Program marketing mix, 47
Promotion
  by incentive plans, 480–81
  opportunity rate, 449
  from sales to management,
    537–41
Promotional tools, 66–72
  advantages of personal selling,
    67–68
  distribution policies, 71–72
  in personal selling, 65–66
  pricing policies, 72
  product characteristics, 70–
    71
  target market, 69–70
  types, 66–67
Prospects
  finding new customers, 86–
    87
  initial approach, 87–88
  qualifying, 88
Pruden, Henry O., 311 n, 321 n,
  322 n, 343 n
Psychological traits, and motivation, 444–45
Purchase
  modified rebuy, 83
  repeat, 82–83
  straight rebuy, 82
Purchase evaluation and feedback, 82
Purchasing agent, 75
Purchasing department, 79–83
Pure Drug Company, 656–78
Pyke, Donald L., 146 n

Q–R

Queram, Bonnie J., 253 n
Race and sales aptitude; *see* Equal employment opportunity
Rachmaciej, Wally, 275 n
Rand Corporation, 145 n
Rand McNally, 189
Random factor, in time series analysis, 154
Rao, Vithala R., 160 n
Rayburn, L. Gayle, 591 n, 595 n, 596 n, 598 n, 607 n, 616 n
Recognition programs, 481–82
Recruitment, 491–96
    from advertisements, 373–75
    costs, 335–36
    from educational institutions, 373
    from employment agencies, 375–76
    of job applicants, 367–76
    new applicants, 510–11
    from other firms, 372
    and selection process, 497–502
    from within the company, 371–72
Recruits, sales training for new, 403–10
Reese, Richard M., 311 n, 321 n, 322 n
Reference checks, 379–82
Regan, Martin, 515
Regression analysis, 167
Reimbursement plans
    absence of, 477
    compensation, 471–77
    direct, 475
    limited, 475–77
Reinke, Tom, 259–60
Reliable Meter Company, 497–502
Repeat purchase behavior, 82–83
Research and development capabilities, 57
Research Institute of America, 350, 409 n
Research Institute for Sales Executives, 176 n
Retail selling, 5–6
Retail Trading Area Map, 189

Return on assets managed, 612–16
Revlon, 36–38, 56
Rewards
    extrinsic and intrinsic, 303
    valence for, 438–40
Reynolds (R. J.) Company; *see* R. J. Reynolds Company
Ricci, Claudia, 563 n
Rich, Leslie, 209 n, 383 n
Richards, Dick, 290
Riegel, Carl D., 392 n, 399 n
Rink, David R., 349 n
Rippe, Richard, 141 n
Rizzo, John R., 311 n
R. J. Reynolds Company, 417
Roach, George, 545
Robertson, David E., 385 n
Robertson, Don H., 347 n, 631 n
Robinson, Patrick J., 79 n, 82 n
Robson, Bob, 523–32
Rockart, John F., 642 n
Roering, K., 75 n
Rokus, Josef W., 187 n, 612 n
Role
    innovative, 313–14
    sales personnel, 309–11
Role accuracy, 298
    nature of, 324–26
Role ambiguity, 299, 314–23
    behavioral consequences, 320–22
    causes, 322–23
    occurrence, 310
    psychological consequences, 320–22
Role conflict, 298–99, 314–23
    behavioral consequences, 322
    causes, 322–23
    consequences, 320–22
    occurrence, 310
Role expectations, 315–17
Role inaccuracy
    general or specific, 324–26
    occurrence, 310–11
Role perceptions, 298–99, 309–31
Role playing method of training, 319
Role set
    large, 312–13
    sales personnel's, 309
Roman, Murray, 116 n

Rosenbaum, Bernard L., 392 n, 422
Rossow, Gerald, 145 n, 146 n
Rothfeld, Michael B., 54 n
Rotter, Julian B., 301 n, 330 n, 444 n
Rubenstein, Albert H., 312 n
Rudelius, William, 49 n, 51 n, 52 n
Russell, Frederick A., 8 n, 86 n, 640 n
Russler, Joan, 717 n
Ryans, Adrian B., 57 n, 59 n, 60 n

S

Sackman, Harold, 147 n
St. Regis Paper Company, 224 n
Salary; *see also* Compensation programs
    definition, 464
    straight, 464–65
Sales
    closing, 89
    variety of activities, 83–90
Sales analysis, 27, 561–88
    bases for comparison, 569
    benefits, 566–67
    buying power index, 573–75, 579
    and cost analysis, 591
    decision support systems, 582–87
    definition, 565–67
    desired breakdowns, 571–73
    hierarchical, 573–82
    iceberg principle, 578–79
    isolate-and-explode principle, 580–82
    key decisions, 568–73
    marketing audit, 562–65
    nature of control, 561–62
    and sales quotas, 575–78
    simple versus comparative, 579–80
    sources and processing of information, 570–71
    type of evaluation system, 568–70
    types of reporting system, 569–70
    uses, 566

Sales aptitude, 335–57
  definition, 336
  formal education, 340
  mental abilities, 340
  missionary selling, 354–55
  new business selling, 356
  performance and personal
    characteristics, 338–50
  research on, 341–45
  sex and race, 339–40, 345–50
  skill levels, 340
  task-specific determinants,
    353–56
  technical selling, 355
  trade selling, 353–54
  view of sales managers, 337–
    38
Sales contests, 210–11, 477–80,
  535–36
  criticisms of, 480
  objectives, 478
  probability of winning, 478–
    79
  promotion and follow-through,
    479–80
  themes, 478
  types of rewards, 479
Sales Executive Club of New
  York, 345
Sales executives, key accounts,
  118–19
Sales-expense ratios, 631
Sales force; see also Sales personnel
  assignment to territories, 203–
    4
  behavior and performance
    analysis, 623–47
  CALLPLAN program, 200–
    202
  company, 106–9
  compensation and incentive
    programs, 16–17, 455–82
  customer or market type, 112–
    14
  decreasing returns principle,
    184
  determination of selection cri-
    teria, 364–69
  environmental constraints on
    performance, 57–58
  equal employment opportunity
    requirements, 385–87

  geographical organization,
    109–11
  horizontal structure, 106–17
  impact of new technologies, 54
  incremental method of size
    determination, 184–87
  independent agents, 106–9
  inside or outside, 115–17
  job analysis description, 363–
    64
  job qualifications, 364–69
  for major accounts, 119–20
  manufacturer's representa-
    tives, 107
  morale, 176–77
  motivation, 433–50
  for national and key accounts,
    117–21
  new products, 520–22
  Olsen Seed Farms, 263
  organization, 16
  performance appraisal, 679–
    88, 708–16, 735–37
  product line, 111–12
  Pure Drug Company, 658–61
  recruiting applicants, 369–76
  recruitment and selection pro-
    cedures, 362, 497–502
  responsibility for recruiting,
    361
  role in distribution channel,
    71–72
  role in marketing strategy, 15–
    17
  sales related functions, 125
  selection procedures, 376–85
  selling agents, 107
  selling function organization,
    114
  separate, 91–92
  size, 179–87
  staff support, 125–26
  telemarketing, 115–17
  training, 17, 391–428
  unit method breakdown, 180–
    81
  workload analysis, 196–201
  workload method of size de-
    termination, 181–83
Sales force composite method of
  forecasting, 141–44
Sales forecast, 133–34; see also
  Market forecasting

  importance, 138–39
  uses, 139, 209
Sales jobs; see also Personal selling and Selling
  advancement opportunities, 9
  attractive characteristics, 7–
    14
  diversity, 5–7
  freedom of action, 8
  perceptions of, 3
  stereotypes, 4–5
  types of industrial, 6–7
  variety and challenge, 8–9
  working conditions, 10–11
Sales management
  compensation and incentive
    programs, 455–82
  components, 19–28
  cost analysis, 591–617
  evaluation and control of sales
    programs, 26–28, 561–62
  implementing a sales pro-
    gram, 23–26
  implications of sales aptitude
    information, 356–57
  importance of sales personnel
    model, 304–5
  marketing planning, 38–48
  number of levels, 121–23
  overview, 20
  problems, 18
  policy guidelines, 50–52
  promotion of sales personnel
    to, 537–41
  promotion opportunity rate,
    449
  Pure Drug Company, 661–67
  roles and staff support, 123–
    26
  sales analysis, 561–88
  span of control, 121–23
  strategic sales program, 19–23
  successful marketing strategy,
    14–19
  supervisory policies, 25, 448–
    49
Sales Management, 162, 335,
  346
Sales management audit, 562–
  63
  methods and procedures, 565
  objectives, 563
  organization focus, 564

personnel, 565
Sales managers
   alternative selling techniques,
      95–99
   characteristics, 715–16
   compensation, 714
   evaluation and control of sales
      territories, 178
   implications of regional varia-
      tions, 60–61
   job description, 684
   job functions, 551–53
   motivation of sales personnel,
      297
   and personal traits of sales
      personnel, 445
   recruitment, 491–96
   role component, 330
   and sales personnel, 9
   selling responsibilities, 124
   span of control, 58–59
   training for, 421–22
   view of sales aptitude, 337–
      50
Sales and Marketing Manage-
   ment, 167, 411 n, 423,
   425 n, 573
Sales organization
   Ansul Company, 101–3
   coordination and integration,
      105–6
   by customers or markets, 112–
      14
   division of labor, 104–5
   geographic, 109–11
   horizontal, 103, 106–17
   management levels, 121–23
   management roles, 123–26
   national and key accounts,
      117–21
   product line, 111–12
   purposes, 103–6
   by selling function, 114
   span of control, 121–23
   stability and continuity of per-
      formance, 105
   staff support, 123–26
   telemarketing, 115–17
   vertical, 103–5, 121–26
Sales-per-account ratio, 632
Sales personnel; *see also* Sales
   force *and* Sales jobs
   advancement opportunities, 9

advantages of women in, 348–
   49
aptitude, 24, 300–301
assignment to territories, 203–4
behavioral analysis, 28, 623–
   47
boundary position, 311–12
CALLPLAN program, 200–
   202
close supervision of, 323
compensation and incentive
   programs, 455–82, 533–
   36
concept of sales ability, 300
and customer characteristics,
   350–53
demographic characteristics,
   443
development, 114
earnings opportunity ratio,
   449
environmental variables, 23
evaluation of performance,
   26–28, 623–41, 708–16
personal characteristics, 339–
   40, 350–53, 441–45
personal component, 302
personal histories, 367
policy guidelines, 50–52
predicting effort and performance, 440–41
promotion to management,
   537–41
psychological traits, 444–45
quota incentives, 210–11
reasons for failure, 367–68
recruitment and training
   costs, 335–36
responsibility for recruiting,
   361
rewards, 303
role, 209–11
role accuracy, 324–30
role ambiguity, 310, 314–23
role component of sales manager, 331
role conflict, 310, 314–23
role expectations, 315–17
role inaccuracy, 310–11
role perception determinant,
   298–99
role perceptions, 23–24, 309–
   31

sales contests, 210–11
sales aptitude, 335–57
skill levels, 25, 301–2
social and ethical dilemmas,
   49–52
stages in selling, 83–90
stereotypes, 4–5
successful, 391
supervisory policies, 25
susceptibility of role, 311–14
time apportionment, 183
time available, 182
training programs, 12–13, 25
travel requirements, 10–11
valence for rewards, 438–40
varying efforts, 74
view of job, 7–14
Sales potentials, 580 n
   definition, 133
   of sales territories, 184–87
   and territory variations, 60
Sales presentation, 88–89
   canned, 95–96
Sales productivity
   effect of organizational factors,
      58–59
   effects of external environ-
      ment, 59–60
Sales program
   account management policies,
      72–75
   alternative types of selling,
      95–99
   behavioral analysis, 28
   cost analysis, 28
   design, 21–23
   environmental factors, 22, 48–
      57
   evaluation and control, 19–28;
      see also Performance ap-
      praisal
   firm's internal environment,
      22
   implementation, 19, 23–26
   market forecasting, 133–69
   marketing planning, 38–48
   new marketing strategy, 36–
      38
   organizational buying, 78
   organizational environment,
      55–57
   promotional tools, 66–72
   sales analysis, 27

Sales program—*Cont.*
  sales organization, 101–6
  stages in selling process, 83–90
  strategic, 19–23
  target market, 69–70
  use of sales quotas, 209–28
Sales quota, 136, 215–17, 543
  Acme Machine Corporation, 547–49
  activity, 217–18, 226
  and bonuses, 467
  characteristics of a plan, 212–14
  commissions and bonuses, 211
  as control effort, 211–12
  dollar volume, 216
  expense quotas, 219
  financial, 218–20, 226–27
  gross margin, 219
  incentives for sales personnel, 210–11
  levels of each type, 222–27
  need for, 209–10
  net profit, 219–20
  performance evaluation, 211
  physical volume, 216
  point quotas, 216–17
  in practice, 222–25
  problems with, 212
  purposes, 210–12
  quota-setting process, 215–27
  relative importance of each type, 220–22
  in sales analysis, 573–78
  and sales contests, 210–11
  sales volume, 215–17, 222–25
  types, 215–20
Sales recruitment
  application blanks, 377–78
  equal employment opportunity requirements, 385–87
  personal interviews, 378–79
  physical examinations, 382
  reference checks, 379–82
  selection procedures, 376–85
  tests for applicants, 382–85
Sales-related knowledge, 340
Sales teams, 78
Sales territory, 513–15; *see also* Territory demand estimates adjustment, 201–3

assignment of sales force, 203–4
basic control unit, 187–95
CALLPLAN program, 200–202
cities, 190–93
clearly defined, 176–77
counties, 189–90
cost-control advantages, 178–79
customer classification, 181–82
definition, 175
design of, 187–204
effective design, 178
estimating market potential, 195
evaluation and control, 178–79
frequency of calls on accounts, 182
market coverage, 177–78
Metropolitan Statistical Areas, 190–93
need for, 175–79
Olsen Seed Farms, 262–63
poor design, 176
Pure Drug Company, 667–72
and sales force morale, 176–77
and sales force size, 179–87
sales potential, 184–87
states, 188–89
tentative, 196
trading areas, 189
variations in characteristics, 60
workload analysis, 196–201
ZIP code areas, 193–95
Sales training programs, 12–13, 17, 25, 391–428, 503–9
  back-to-basics approach, 396–400
  behavior modeling, 396–400
  centralized versus decentralized, 414–15
  company orientation, 408–9
  costs, 335–36, 424–25
  costs and benefits, 424–27
  creating credibility, 393–95
  for experienced personnel, 420–21
  home study method, 419–20

importance of methods, 415–16
improving customer relations, 402
improving morale, 401–2
improving quality of, 393–400
to increase productivity, 401
location of programs, 410–15
for lower turnover, 402
market/industry orientation, 408
measuring broad benefits, 426–27
measuring criteria, 425–26
methods, 416–20
for new recruits, 403–10, 510–11
objectives, 400–403, 427
on-the-job, 414–17
product knowledge, 407–8
problems with, 392–93
recent developments, 423–24
for sales managers, 421–22
transactional analysis in, 409–10
time and territory management, 403, 409
timing of, 403
Sales transportation expense, 631
Salsbury, Gregory B., 370 n
Samuels, Stuart A., 203 n
Saporito, Bill, 55 n
Satisfaction theories, 442–43
Scanlon, S., 101 n, 347 n, 348 n, 350 n, 417 n, 479 n
Schaefer. Arthur E., 138 n
Scheibelhut, John H., 342, 343 n
Schendel, Dan, 42 n
Schiff, J. S., 612 n
Schiff, Michael, 596 n, 612 n
Schroeder, Roger C., 147 n
Schuery, Eleanor, 346 n
Schwab, Donald P., 322 n, 401 n, 642 n
Schwartz, G., 203 n
Sealright-Oswego Falls Corporation, 144
Sears, 119
Seasonal factor, of time series analysis, 154
Selection procedures, for hiring sales personnel, 376–85

Selling
   activities, 83–90
   alternative techniques, 95–99
   closing the sale, 89
   cost analysis, 28
   direct; *see* Direct selling
   initial approach to customers, 87–88
   major accounts management approach, 90–92
   mental-states approach, 96
   multilevel; *see* Multilevel selling
   need-satisfaction approach, 97–98
   presenting a sales message, 88–89
   problem-solution approach, 98–99
   prospecting for customers, 86–87
   qualifying prospects, 88
   responsibility of managers, 124
   retail versus industrial, 5–6
   servicing accounts, 89–90
   steps in the process, 85–90
   stimulus-response approach, 95–97
   systems; *see* Systems selling
   team; *see* Team selling
   telemarketing, 86–87
"Selling: The Psychological Approach," 410
Selling agents, 107
Selling costs, in marketing budgets, 11–14
Selling expenses, 471–77
Selling function sales force, 114
Selling strategies, 399–400
Semlow, Walter J., 184, 186
Senior Marketing Executive Panel, of Conference Board, 160
Servicing accounts, 89–80
Sevin, Charles H., 567 n, 603 n, 604 n
Sex, and sales aptitude, 340, 345–50
Shapiro, Benson P., 72 n, 87 n, 91 n, 102 n, 118 n, 370 n, 433, 479 n
Shapiro, S. J., 370 n
Shapiro, Stanley S., 612 n

Sharp, Warren, 290
Shaw, Malcolm E., 396 n, 397, 399
Sheekon, E. P., 213
Shelley, Susan M., 487
Shepps, R. Ronald, 343 n
Shiskin, Julius, 155 n
Shuchman, Abraham, 114 n, 562 n
SIC; *see* Standard Industrial Classification codes
Sidex Corporation, 234–40
Sierra Chemical Company, 679–88
Similarity hypothesis, 350–53
Simon, Sanford R., 580 n, 593 n, 596 n, 599 n, 601 n
Sims, Henry P., Jr., 396 n
Skill level
   component of sales personnel, 301–2
   and sales aptitude, 340
Skills
   behavioral, 398–400
   sales, 25
Sloan, Alfred P., 616
Smackey, B. M., 612 n
Smith, Adam, 104
Smith, Donald D., 160 n
Smith, Steve, 545
Smyth, Richard C., 438 n, 459 n, 460 n, 462 n, 468 n, 469 n, 470 n
Snader, Jack R., 393 n, 400 n
Snyderman, Barbara, 492 n
Social dilemmas, 49–52
Social environment, 49
Sony business products, 14, 16
Sorenson, Ralph, 656 n
Spain, Daphne, 346 n
Specialization of labor, 104–5
Specific expense, 594
Spencer, Ruth, 492, 495
Spiro, Rosann L., 197 n
Spitalnick, Irving, 35–37
Sportswear, 35–38
Sprague, Ralph H., Jr., 583 n
Staelin, Richard, 143 n
Staff executives, 125–26
Stamper, Joe C., 57 n, 187 n
Standard Industrial Classification codes (SIC), 164–66
Standard Metropolitan Statistical Area, 190

Stanton, William J., 137 n, 187 n, 210 n, 322 n, 414 n, 566 n, 593 n
States, as sales territories, 188–89
Statistical demand analysis, 156–58
Steinbrink, John P., 477 n
Steiner, George A., 42 n
Stephenson, P. Ronald, 219 n, 329 n
Stern, Louis W., 107 n
Stern, Mark E., 40 n, 43 n, 47 n
Stevenson, Thomas H., 117 n
Still, Richard R., 71 n, 134 n, 181 n, 183 n, 204 n, 217 n
Stiller and Meara comedy team, 15
Stimulus-response approach to selling, 95–97
Stipp, Mervin, 283–85
Straight commission, 466–67
Straight rebuy, 82
Straight salary compensation, 464–65
Strander, Gregg O., 272
Strang, William A., 347 n, 352 n
Strategic business unit plans, 41
Strategic business units, 564
Strategic sales program, 19–23
Strategy
   behavioral, 398–400
   definition, 40
   generation, 44–47
Stroh, Thomas F., 40 n
Strong Vocational Interest Blank, 383
Structured interviews, 378–79
Students, perceptions of sales jobs, 3
Subjective measures of performance, 633–43
SUPERCALC, 585
Supervision, and motivation, 448–49
Suppliers
   approved or out, 82–83
   evaluation of, 80–81
   potential, 80
Suttle, J. Lloyd, 442 n
Swan, John E., 7 n, 347 n, 349 n
Sweitzer, Robert W., 351 n
Systems selling, 91

T

Tactics, behavioral, 398–400
Talley, Walter J., Jr., 181 n
Target market, 37
  characteristics, 69–70
Target sales quota, 543
Taylor, Thayer C., 68 n, 107 n,
  471 n, 473 n, 644 n
Team selling, 120
Technical environment, 54
Technical selling
  industrial sales, 7
  sales aptitude, 355
Technology, 54
Telemarketing, 86–87, 115–17
Telephone sales people, 115–17
Territory demand estimates
  consumer goods, 167–68
  industrial goods, 164–66
  market factor, 164
  market index, 164
  of sales, 163–68
  Standard Industrial Classifica-
    tion codes, 164–66
Territory management
  training to improve, 403
  training new recruits, 409
Test marketing, 147–49
Testor Corporation, 639
Tests
  aptitude, 383
  concern over use of, 383–84
  equal opportunity require-
    ments, 385
  guidelines for, 384–85
  intelligence, 382–83
  for job applicants, 382–85
  personality, 383
Texas Instruments, 241, 563
3M Company (Minnesota
  Mining and Manufactur-
  ing), 54
Thurlow, Michael L., 143 n,
  223 n
Time management
  training to improve, 403
  training new recruits, 409
Time series analysis, 149–56
  Box-Jenkins methods, 153 n
  decomposition method, 153–
    56
  exponential smoothing, 152–
    53

moving averages method,
  150–53
time factors, 154
trend factor, 154
Time utilization, 629–30
Timex, 242, 563
Tobolski, Frances P., 343
Todd, John T., 7 n, 347 n
Trade selling
  industrial, 6
  and sales aptitude, 353–54
Trading areas, 189
Training and Development Jour-
  nal, 392
Training programs; see Sales
  training programs
Transaction costs, 109 n
Transactional analysis, 409–10
Transcendental meditation, 410
Travel requirements, 10–11
Trend factor, in time series
  analysis, 154
Tripp, Richard, 544–45
Tronics Sales Corporation, 241–
  42
TRW, 146
Turner, Ronald E., 143 n
Turnover, training to lower, 402
Twin City Electric Motor Com-
  pany, 735–37

U

Udell, Jon G., 567 n
Umble, M. Michael, 157
Union Carbide, 147
United States Bureau of the
  Census, 164, 166, 189
United States Department of
  Commerce, 189
Unstructured interviews, 378–
  79
Users
  expectations methods of fore-
    casting, 139–41
  role in buying decisions, 76

V

Valence
  for performance, 299
  for rewards, 299, 438–40
Vandenberg, Jackie, 270, 272,
  274

Vertical marketing audit, 562–
  63
Vertical sales organization, 103–
  5, 121–26
Video game market, 54–55
VISICALC, 585, 655
Vizza, Robert F., 181 n, 183 n,
  201 n, 630 n
Volkswagen, 42
Voyance, Clair, 272

W

Wahlbin, Clas, 138 n
Walker, Orville C., Jr., 7 n, 8 n,
  9 n, 109 n, 297 n, 302 n,
  303 n, 309 n, 311 n, 314 n,
  321 n, 323 n, 327 n, 338 n,
  402 n, 439 n, 440 n, 443 n,
  448 n, 480 n, 623 n, 624 n,
  640 n
Walt Disney Productions, 42
Walton, Richard E., 312 n
Wang word processors, 17
Ward, Clark, 182 n
Ward, Elmer, Jr., 37
Ward, Nick, 422
Wards, 119
Warner Communications, Inc.,
  242
Warren, Walt, 506–9
Waterman, Robert H., Jr., 56 n
Watson, Thomas J., Jr., 56
Ways, Thomas C., 423 n
Weaver, Charles N., 342, 343 n
Weaver, H. B., 343
Webster, Frederick E., 76 n
Wecker, Jeffrey H., 181 n, 612 n
Weeks, David A., 124 n
Weick, Karl E., Jr., 418 n
Weinberg, Charles B., 57 n,
  59 n, 60 n, 186, 187 n,
  202 n
Weingarten, J., 148 n
Weinrauch, J. Donald, 312 n,
  313 n
Weitz, Barton A., 109 n, 336 n,
  339 n, 343 n, 352 n, 353 n,
  356 n, 628 n
Welch Foods, 147
Wentworth Industrial Cleaning
  Supplies, 717–34
Werneth, Richard, 492, 496
West, Paul, 258–60

Western Beef Breeders Association, 523
Western Business Forms, Inc., 533–36
Wexley, Kenneth N., 394 n
Wheatley, John J., 593 n, 598 n
Wheelwright, Steven C., 139 n, 150 n, 151 n, 152 n, 155 n, 162 n
Wide Area Telecommunications Service (WATS), 86
Wilkinson, Maurice, 141 n
Williams, Glenn B., 342, 343 n
Williams, J. Allen, 321 n
Williamson, Oliver E., 109 n
Wilson, David T., 351 n
Wilson, Scott, 272

Wind, Yoram, 76 n, 79 n, 80 n, 82 n
Windfalls in compensation, 470
Winer, Leon, 210 n
Wolfe, Harry D., 567 n
Wolk, Harry I., 595 n, 604 n
Women
    advantages in sales force, 348–49
    sales aptitude, 346–50
Wood, Douglas, 139 n
Woodruff, Robert B., 57 n, 187 n
Woodside, Arch G., 351 n
Wonderlic Personnel Test, 383
Working conditions, 10–11
Workload analysis, 196–201
Workload method of sales force size determination, 181–83

Wormald International, Ltd., 102
Worthing, Parker, 3 n
Wotruba, Thomas R., 143 n, 210 n, 214 n, 219 n, 223 n, 562 n, 566 n, 633 n
Wright, Milburn D., 628 n

X–Z

Xerox, 564
Zarnstorff, Patricia, 516 n
Zdep, S. M., 343
Zeithaml, Carl P., 448 n
Zeithaml, Valerie A., 448 n
ZIP code areas, as sales territories, 193–95

This book has been set Linotron 202, in 9 and 8 point Primer, leaded 3 points. Part and chapter numbers are 14 and 40 point Memphis Bold; part and chapter titles are 36 point Memphis Bold. The size of the type page is 33 by 46 picas, 9 points.